Reason and Insight

Western and Eastern Perspectives
on the Pursuit of Moral Wisdom

Reason and Insight

*Western and Eastern Perspectives
on the Pursuit of Moral Wisdom*

SECOND EDITION

Timothy Shanahan
Loyola Marymount University

Robin Wang
Loyola Marymount University

WADSWORTH
CENGAGE Learning™

Australia • Brazil • Japan • Korea • Mexico • Singapore • Spain • United Kingdom • United States

Reason and Insight: Western and Eastern Perspectives on the Pursuit of Moral Wisdom, Second Edition
Timothy Shanahan, Robin Wang

Publisher: Holly J. Allen

Philosophy Editor: Steve Wainwright

Assistant Editor: Lee McCracken

Editorial Assistant: Anna Lustig

Technology Project Manager: Susan DeVanna

Marketing Manager: Worth Hawes

Marketing Assistant: Justine Ferguson

Advertising Project Manager: Bryan Vann

Print/Media Buyer: Barbara Britton

Permissions Editor: Charles Hodgkins

Production Service: Scratchgravel Publising Services

Copy Editor: Toni Ackley

Cover Designer: Ross Carron

Compositor: Scratchgravel Publishing Services

For product information and technology assistance, contact us at
Cengage Learning Customer & Sales Support, 1-800-354-9706

For permission to use material from this text or product, submit all requests online at **www.cengage.com/permissions**
Further permissions questions can be emailed to
permissionrequest@cengage.com

Library of Congress Control Number: 2002104238

ISBN-13: 978-0-534-50599-8

ISBN-10: 0-534-50599-6

Wadsworth
10 Davis Drive
Belmont, CA 94002
USA

Cengage Learning is a leading provider of customized learning solutions with office locations around the globe, including Singapore, the United Kingdom, Australia, Mexico, Brazil, and Japan. Locate your local office at **www.cengage.com/global**

Cengage Learning products are represented in Canada by Nelson Education, Ltd.

To learn more about Wadsworth, visit **www.cengage.com/wadsworth**

Purchase any of our products at your local college store or at our preferred online store **www.ichapters.com**

Printed in the United States of America
4 5 6 7 8   24 23 22 21 20

for our parents

Brief Contents

PART IV

Contents

PART III
Eastern Ethical Perspectives   129

Preface

Each of us makes uncountably many choices every day, some momentous, many apparently inconsequential, yet together they shape the direction and determine the overall quality of our lives. Many of our choices impact the lives of others as well. Making such choices wisely is often difficult. The more perspectives one can effectively command in considering alternative courses of action, the wider one's reflections become and the greater one's chances of choosing wisely. The word *effectively* above is important. It does a person little good to achieve a superficial acquaintance with a huge array of perspectives if none of them are understood deeply enough to be applied effectively. Striking a balance between breadth and depth is critical. The central aim of this book is to help the college student enrolled in a course on ethics or moral philosophy to achieve such a balance through a study of some of the world's most important ethical perspectives.

This text is premised on the conviction that there are distinctively Western and Eastern ethical perspectives and that understanding each can contribute to the pursuit of moral wisdom. What differentiates these two perspectives? Although the differences are easier to recognize than to describe, some differences are fairly evident. Western ethical writers typically assume that they need to convince the reader to adopt their point of view by using logical reasoning, argumentation, and consideration of purported counterexamples. They speak to us as intellectual equals and attempt to convince us of the truth of their views by appealing to considerations with which they expect any similarly rational person to agree. Eastern ethical writers frequently speak with the voice of authority, basing their views on personal (sometimes mystical) experience, intuition, or insight into ancient wisdom. They speak as those who have had special insights and attempt through the imperfect medium of language to help us *see* what it is that they have seen. The difference between the two perspectives is, to put the matter in oversimplified terms, the difference between the "philosopher" and the "sage."

Of course, no such global distinction will be entirely free of counterexamples. Although they certainly use argumentation in their treatises, the perspectives of Augustine and Aquinas (discussed in Chapter 2) obviously depend a great deal on their faith in the truth of the Christian religion. They are therefore somewhat closer to the model of the Eastern sage than are the other Western thinkers represented. On the other side, the Buddhist philosopher Nagarjuna (who is profiled in Chapter 8) was an excellent logician whose writings are filled with highly sophisticated argumentation. So no hard-and-fast distinction between West and East can be rigidly maintained. Yet one might say that such thinkers are the exceptions that prove the rule. Although Western approaches might seem to make heavier use of reason, whereas Eastern approaches rely more heavily on insight, perhaps the safest statement is that both traditions rely on a combination of reason and insight, the proportions varying with each thinker and tradition, with broad contours discernible when we step back to compare Western and Eastern perspectives.

Nothing of importance hangs crucially on the identification of the West with reason and the East with insight. What is important is that these two sources of ethical reflection be brought to bear in the context of one's ethical reflections. The "reason and insight" in the title of this book refer to the interplay of faculties each of us must use in order to gain moral wisdom. Using the Daoist concept of the harmony of opposites (discussed in Chapter 6), we can see reason and insight as complementary, rather than opposing, approaches to ethical understanding. Knowing that understanding itself can take place in different ways is a crucial step in attaining a balanced perspective. By becoming familiar with the central ethical traditions of both East and West, a person acquires a much broader set of resources for ethical reflection and consequently is in a much better position to select guidelines for charting his or her life wisely.

A Note on the Organization of the Text

This book is divided into four parts. Part I discusses a number of fundamental metaethical issues concerning the foundations of ethical inquiry. Topics discussed in Part I include the relationship between law and morality, the relationship between religion and morality, moral relativism, the problem of determinism, and ethical egoism. For each of these metaethical issues we have tried to make clear the nature of the challenge and to argue that none of them obviates the need for ethical reflection. This material is largely critical in nature, raising and arguing against various objections to studying ethics. The last section in Part I takes a more positive approach by providing a sketch of the nature of moral wisdom and explaining how to use the material in the remainder of the book for acquiring such wisdom.

The next two parts of the text concern normative ethics, which includes (among other things) principles for living well, criteria of right and wrong, and the scope and limits of obligations and duties. Part II introduces some of the most influential Western ethical perspectives: Greek virtue ethics, Christian natural law ethics, Kantian duty ethics, and utilitarianism. Part III introduces the most influential Eastern ethical traditions: Confucianism, Daoism, Hinduism, and Buddhism. The chapters in Parts II and III include substantial material from each of these perspectives or traditions and have been selected both for the continuing importance of the ideas expressed and for their relative accessibility to students embarking on a study of ethics for the first time. No attempt has been made to do justice to the entire spectrum of cultural traditions found throughout the world, or indeed even to those found within the categories "West" and "East." Including a greater representation of traditions would necessitate abbreviating the presentation of each. This is something we have strongly resisted. We have thought it better to include more substantial reading selections for each of the moral traditions represented, and thus allow students to gain a more thorough understanding of each, than to cover more ground in a necessarily more superficial fashion.

Parts II and III provide a balanced treatment of Western and Eastern ethical traditions. Ultimately, however, such perspectives must be applied if they are to help us resolve the ethical problems we face. Consequently, Part IV contains contemporary articles that apply the different ethical perspectives to a range of concrete moral issues: sex, abortion, suicide and euthanasia, the family, technology, the media, business, and the environment. Each chapter includes two articles representing Western approaches and two articles representing Eastern approaches. Often each section includes contrasting positions, although sometimes the contrast is between Western and Eastern perspectives and sometimes between two different Western or two different Eastern perspectives.

Other features of the text are designed to further assist the student in comprehending the material. Introductions to the reading selections put each into context by supplying enough background information to allow students with little or no previous exposure to the traditions discussed to read the selections with greater understanding. Reading Questions preceding each reading selection alert the student to pay particular attention to important themes. Discussion and Reflection Questions following each reading selection encourage students to reflect more deeply on the ideas just encountered and to relate these ideas both to other ideas presented in the text and to their own experience. Suggestions for Further Reading at the end of each chapter provide additional guidance for students who wish to explore further the ideas presented.

An important feature designed to assist students in comprehending each moral tradition is the inclusion of "Profile" sections for each chapter in Parts II and III. These sections introduce thinkers or movements and place the main thinkers or movements in context by relating them to their progenitors (in Part II) or later expositors (in Part III) and highlighting the similarities and differences between them.

Changes in the Second Edition

We have been very pleased with the reception of the first edition of *Reason and Insight* and greatly encouraged by feedback from instructors who found it useful for their classes. Since the publication of the first edition, the importance of understanding and appreciating the rich moral traditions of both Western and Eastern ethical perspectives has only increased. *Globalization* is a term much thrown around at present, and it is now even clearer that a global perspective is needed to resolve, and even to ask the right questions about, the moral issues facing all of us. While maintaining its central aim of presenting substantial selections from Western and Eastern ethical perspectives, this second edition includes a number of significant changes in response to instructor feedback:

- A new translation of the *Analects* is included, as well as an updated translation of the *Dao De Jing*.

- Three new sections have been added to Part IV (Technology, Ethics in the Media, and Ethics in Business), consisting of twelve new essays. Many of these essays were commissioned and written expressly for this edition.
- Twenty new essays appear in those sections of Part IV preserved from the first edition. Many of these essays were also commissioned and written expressly for this edition.
- Suggestions for Further Reading for each chapter have been updated and expanded.
- InfoTrac terms have been added for each chapter.

We hope that as instructors and as students you find this edition of *Reason and Insight* useful in your pursuit of moral wisdom. We look forward to hearing from you concerning aspects of the text that you find especially useful, as well as ways in which the text might be further improved.

Acknowledgments

Our thanks go to the reviewers whose comments helped make this a better book: Rev. Leonard Alvey, Brescia University; Dr. Stafford Betty, California State University at Bakersfield; Erick R. Egerston, Midland Lutheran College; Patricia Hanna, University of Utah; Joe Frank Jones, III, Barton College; Gary Kessler, California State University at Bakersfield; Maire Liberace, Rockland Community College; Steven Luper-Foy, Trinity University; John Medslchiedler, College of DuPage; Chris Meyers, California State University at Bakersfield; Walter O'Briant, University of Georgia at Athens; Louis Pojman, United States Military Academy; Donald Porter, College of San Mateo; Justus Richards, Pasadena City College; Judy D. Saltzman, California Polytechnic University at San Luis Obispo; Katherine Shamey, Santa Monica College; Susan Stone, California State University at Bakersfield; Barbara Tucker, Trident Technical College; Sandra A. Wawrytko, San Diego State University; Lawrence Wenner, Loyola Marymount University; and Thomas I. White, Loyola Marymount University.

In addition, we gratefully acknowledge the following individuals for their assistance in preparing the text: Christopher Chapple, James Fredericks, Yajneshwar S. Shastri, Jisho Cary Warner, Anne Draus, David Jones, and Daryl Dunigan.

Timothy Shanahan
Robin Wang

PART I

Metaethical Issues

We are discussing no small matter, but how we ought to live.

—SOCRATES, AS REPORTED BY PLATO IN THE *REPUBLIC*, CA. 390 B.C.E.

How Ethical Issues Arise: An Example

Suppose for a moment that you have always wanted to learn how to play the guitar. From the first moment that you heard the opening chords of a guitar riff emanating from a radio, you knew that you wanted to be able to produce sounds like that, too. Unfortunately, other important activities (school, sports, work, watching television, and so on) have so far left little time for learning to play the guitar. Besides, learning to play any musical instrument well requires formal instruction, and that costs *money*. Since you do not yet have sufficient income to support such instruction, learning to play the guitar has thus far been nothing more than a deeply cherished, but unfulfilled, dream.

Realizing that you are not getting any younger and that you will never achieve your musical dream at this pace, you decide to take action. You take on an additional part-time job to earn money for lessons. After six months the Big Day has arrived. You have managed to save just enough money to pay for guitar lessons.

Feeling almost giddy with self-satisfaction at having mustered the self-discipline to work two jobs and to squirrel away enough money for lessons, you head to the music studio for your first lesson. As you walk along, alternative images parade through your mind: First you see yourself playing acoustic guitar to a small, intimate, appreciative coffeehouse crowd. Then the image switches: You are being aggressively pursued by record executives offering you six-figure recording contracts. The image changes once again: This time you are giving a virtuoso performance in front of a packed sports arena filled with fans screaming *your* name.

1

As you allow yourself to be entertained by such fantasies, you remember that your mother's birthday is next week and that you have not yet bought her a card or a present. You reflect upon all that she has done for you, remember that she seemed genuinely hurt that you completely forgot about her birthday *last* year. You realize that you really should do something special for her. Perhaps you could help her finance that expensive trip to Paris she has always wanted to take. You make a mental note of this and resolve not to forget her birthday *this* year. As you walk along, you resume your musical fantasizing but are soon interrupted again, this time by a poster in a store window. The doleful eyes of a grossly mal-nourished child from some distant Third World country stare back at you. Be-neath the picture of the child is a plea for financial assistance to help supply food to the people of that country. At the thought of food you notice that you are hungry and decide to try that new fast-food place on the next block—*after* your first guitar lesson, of course.

Finally you arrive at the music studio. You walk past a homeless man asking for any "spare change" and begin walking up the stairs to the upper-floor studio. You get only halfway when you are assaulted by a number of thoughts at once: "How will I help Mom take that trip she has been dreaming of if I am spending the only extra cash I have on guitar lessons? I have enough money for guitar les-sons *or* to assist Mom in taking that trip, but not enough for *both*. Isn't it kind of *selfish* of me to be putting guitar lessons ahead of helping my mother take that long-desired trip?" This is truly a dilemma that you had not considered before.

Troubled by such disturbing thoughts, you decide that such a difficult issue is impossible to resolve on an empty stomach. You decide to postpone your first gui-tar lesson (leaving the teacher with an unkept appointment and hence no fee) until you have thought this issue through, and you walk over to that new fast-food res-taurant. As you carry your tray to an empty table, sit down, and prepare to sink your teeth into a Gigantoburger, the haunting image of that malnourished child on the poster reenters your consciousness. As you gaze down at the assortment of food items before you, you begin to feel a slight twinge of guilt. "Why should I be sitting here with more food for one meal than many people eat in a week," you ask yourself, "when so many people in this world are starving to death?" You pop a french fry into your mouth, hoping that the salty taste will banish such uncomfort-able thoughts from your head. It doesn't work. The thought remains and begins to breed others of a similar nature. "Why do some people end up with plenty of good things in life, and others with virtually nothing? If it is just the 'luck of the draw,' then it could be *me* rather than someone else who is starving to death instead of sit-ting here eating a Gigantoburger and french fries. But I *am* sitting here, this is *my* life, and why should *I* be expected to save the rest of the world? After all, I'm just one person. How much can one person be expected to do?"

Comforted by such thoughts, you pop another french fry into your mouth and reach for your soda. As you do, you remember that homeless man outside the music studio. Certainly, you reflect, here is a case in which one person *could* be ex-pected to make a difference. It need not be a "big" difference, but what of it? At least one can have the satisfaction of knowing that one has done what is *right*. But *is* it right to help that man? Some people surely are victims of forces beyond their control and are in no way to blame for the dire situations they find themselves in. The malnourished child on the poster is undoubtedly such a person—a victim of government corruption, official greed, unpredictable climatic conditions, and other uncontrollable factors. Such people are truly victims, and one ought to try to help them in some way. Other people, however, are simply reaping the harvests that they have sown. Some homeless persons are nothing more than professional beggars, who manage to make a decent hourly wage through handouts. Begging is in fact their profession, and there is no reason why one should feel compelled to purchase what they are selling: a superficial feeling of satisfaction from giving money to a "needy" person. Others who ask for money have simply failed to muster the self-discipline to end their self-destructive habits, and any money given to such people will go straight into a bottle of whiskey or drugs. Giving money to such people is simply perpetuating the kind of miserable life they have chosen for themselves. Surely there is no obligation to give money to this latter sort of person. So some people may deserve a handout, but not others. But how can one possibly tell which sort of person one is dealing with?

Now your mind is a virtual torrent of thoughts that threaten to overwhelm you with their collective force, not to mention ruin what *could* have been a very pleasant dining experience. Confused, you wonder what you should do. You set out a short time ago with the intention of beginning guitar lessons. That certainly seemed innocent enough. But now you realize that there are much larger issues at stake, issues that you had not thought about much while working your part-time jobs or daydreaming about musical stardom. Spending money on guitar lessons, you now realize, commits you to a course of action that excludes and conflicts with a number of alternative actions you could perform. To begin with, spending the money on guitar lessons conflicts quite directly with helping your mother take that trip to Paris. Surely you *owe* her something, you feel, not just because of all the sacrifices that she has made for you, but also simply because she is your mother. People, you think, have special obligations to their parents and close kin that they don't have to just anyone. You would never worry about whether you ought to help the restaurant owner's mother take a trip, because that's *his* responsibility, not yours. But, given the thought you had earlier about the "luck of the draw," you wonder why this is so. After all, where and when one is born is just a matter of chance, and one could just as well have been born in a different place and time to different parents, right? So why should one feel any special obligation toward those who just happen to be related by an "accident of nature"? Besides, shouldn't the person's genuine *needs* be taken into account in some way? How can one justify spending money on a trip to Paris (even if it is your mother who will be enjoying it) when that money could be used to relieve the unspeakable misery and suffering of many people instead? Isn't relieving genuine misery more important than pursuing frivolous pleasure? Instead of using the money saved for guitar lessons for sending your mother on a trip, you might give it to some relief agency for alleviating the massive suffering in Third World countries, one small part of which is depicted in the poster you saw earlier. The amount of good coming from that money would surely be greater in this case, given the number of people who could be helped and the little it would take to help each one, than would come from one person enjoying a pleasurable but strictly unnecessary trip.

So much for Mom's trip, you conclude. Pleasure, while important, is not the most important thing. You'll send her flowers instead. Now those guitar lessons, on the other hand, were not intended to provide mere pleasure, although they surely would have been fun. You had also hoped to use those lessons to develop your hitherto neglected musical abilities, something you sorely need to do if you are to become the "well-rounded" person that is your ideal. It is really a matter of *self-development*, you tell yourself. Besides, after you become a great guitar player, you can bring lots of pleasure to others through your playing, and can perhaps even use part of the proceeds from that six-figure recording contract you dreamed of earlier to send your mother on that trip. In this way a reward for self-discipline on your part coincides perfectly with the pursuit of self-development and the fulfillment of your obligations to your mother. A perfect solution!

Feeling somewhat comforted by this line of thought, a worry nonetheless arises. What if the guitar lessons turn out to be a waste? After all, you're not sure that you have any musical talent, and at your age, you can hardly expect to become more than a mediocre player at best. Still, learning to play the guitar is something you've always wanted to do, and you expect to derive at least some benefit from such effort. *Some* self-development is better than none, right? The alternative might be to give the money to a relief agency to help those distant unfortunate people. Those people, you think, are certainly in need of and perhaps deserving of your assistance. But are such facts sufficient to make sending the money to a relief agency the right thing to do? The money given to the relief agency might be wasted or skimmed off by some corrupt official. How can you be *sure* that the money will do the good you intend it to? In addition to doing what one feels is the right thing, doesn't one also need to take into account the likely *consequences* of one's actions? What good is it to act on good intentions when the effect that one intended never comes to pass? On the other hand, one can never be entirely sure of the consequences of any well-intentioned action, but this does not mean that one should do *nothing*. On the other hand . . .

Feeling completely unsettled by these thoughts, you pick up your tray, leave the restaurant, walk down the street, give the tray of uneaten food along with the change in your pocket to the homeless man you encountered earlier, and begin to walk home. You feel good about your action, in a vague sort of way, but still wonder what you should do about the guitar lessons (and whether the restaurant will miss that tray you just walked away with). You realize now, a bit more clearly than you did when you began heading for the music studio, that even seemingly routine decisions necessarily implicate a person in a much wider web of issues and implicitly commit the person to adopting certain values over others. Every decision is a choice between alternatives, each of which has ramifications that extend far beyond the initial considerations. Although acting on impulse, as you eventually did, will settle some issues for the moment, such a practice is no way to live a good life. You will still need to decide what to do the *next* time you encounter a homeless person, a plea for help from a relief agency, a pang of guilt at not assisting a close friend or relative, or the painful awareness that you have let your own potential talents and abilities languish and remain unrealized. Such issues will never go away. They are part of the human condition. The only thing that you can do is try to clarify such issues and develop a reasonable strategy for dealing with them. Such an undertaking will undoubtedly take some time and effort. In the meantime, you realize that you still have a difficult choice to make about what to do with the money you have saved. As you walk home, still hungry, the question remains unresolved.

What Is Ethics?

What should you (the person in the above situation) do? You have a number of immediate options. You could devote the money you have so laboriously earned to the development of one of your personal capacities and to personal enjoyment, as you originally planned to do; or you could use the money to discharge a felt obligation to a parent; or you could use it to start a shelter for the homeless people in your neighborhood; or you could give the money to a relief agency devoted to easing the misery of a number of unfortunate, but more distant people. Your concern can be extended to yourself, to a close relative, to proximate nonrelatives, or to a number of distant people. Your concern could even be extended to cover aspects of the nonhuman world, by giving the money to organizations dedicated to preventing cruelty to animals, to preserving endangered species, to preventing the depletion of the ozone layer, and so on. The list could be extended indefinitely, with any number of other possibilities inserted between those already mentioned. Each course of action arguably has *some* merit, so it is not immediately or obviously apparent *what* you should do. What should be apparent, however, is that without clear principles to assist you in clarifying and evaluating each of the alternatives you face, any decision you make will have an element of arbitrariness about it. You will thus be unable to defend your decision to others and, perhaps more importantly, you will be unable to justify your decisions to yourself. Instead of steering your way through life, you will simply drift along.

What you need to do is return to "basics." What courses of action are available, and what considerations can be given in support of each one? What are the basic principles that should inform one's decision making, and how should such principles be prioritized? What values and ideals should one choose to live by? Such questions have long occupied philosophers and other reflective individuals. The name for sustained reflection on such issues is *ethics*. Ethics may be thought of as the attempt to determine in some reasonable manner how one should answer the basic questions posed above, and thereby to develop an approach to difficult situations such as the one described in the previous section. Ethics is concerned with the issue of how we ought to live. The subject of ethics is *morality*—the practices, judgments, principles, and beliefs that guide people's actions. But it is more than this. It attempts to go beyond simply reporting how people do *in fact* live, to address the issue of how we *ought* to live. How people actually live, and how they conceive of the best lives for themselves, are not, of course, unrelated. Social sciences such as anthropology and sociology have an important role to play in the development of our understanding of different ways of life. But they constitute some of the starting points, rather than the conclusions, of ethical inquiry.

Because ethics is concerned with the question of how we ought to live, it is necessarily concerned with *values* and with the reasons that can be given in support of one set of values over others. The emphasis on *reasons* is important. Everyone has values that guide their actions, but some of these values are better supported than others. If someone tells you that you ought to do such-and-such in a particular situation, you are entirely within your rights to ask them *why* you ought to do this. Asking why is a request for reasons. Without reasons, the advice someone gives you might be arbitrary or unfounded. But even if others can give you reasons for their position, this is not enough. Ideally, the reasons offered in support of a course of action should be *good* ones. That is, they should themselves be grounded on considerations that are both true and relevant to the situation under consideration.

Determining whether the considerations supporting reasons are true and relevant is not usually an easy matter. It requires a certain familiarity both with the facts of the matter and with basic ethical principles. It also requires a certain *insight* into morality. Ethical principles, like all principles, can be justified only so far. Eventually one has to rely on one's insights (or "intuition") about right and wrong, good and evil. Intuitions, however, are not simply given. One's ethical intuitions typically change in subtle ways as one reflects carefully on ethical matters. Reasons can often challenge our ethical intuitions, while our ethical intuitions may lead us to examine more closely the reasons for a given course of action someone proposes. Ethics is concerned with this interplay between reason and insight, logic and intuition. Ethics is, in the broadest sense, philosophical reflection on our values, moral principles, and rules of conduct, with the aim of determining how we ought to live.

The important point to take note of here is that ethics, in general, is concerned with elucidating the principles for living well, that is, for living a good life. Living a good life is everyone's concern. If everyone wants to live a good life and ethics is the formal study of what makes a life good, then it would seem that it is to everyone's advantage to study this subject. Consider an analogy. Who is more likely to excel at chess: the person who moves his pieces at random, hoping that he will make good moves and win the game, or the person who studies the rules of the game carefully, knows what the goal of the game is and the various strategies available to her, and plans and executes each move with a clear goal and strategy in mind? In life, as in chess, success is more likely to go to the person who has taken the time to think things through before acting and has considered both the aim of the activity and the various strategies that are available. Likewise, studying ethics may help a person live a better life than is attainable by those who have not taken the time to reflect carefully on the nature of, and means of attaining, such a life.

Why Simply Obeying the Law Is Not Sufficient

The main purpose of this book is to acquaint you with some of the most influential ethical perspectives from Western and Eastern philosophical and religious traditions. But before we embark on the study of these major ethical perspectives, it may prevent some unnecessary confusion if a few preliminary issues are dealt with at the outset. Before one begins a project, one ought to have some idea why one is doing so. You are about to embark on a course in ethics. Why? Why should you study ethics, anyway? Given what has been said about the example introduced earlier, it should be clear how important ethical reflection is. But we realize that not everyone will be convinced. In this and the following sections we will raise and respond to some familiar objections to studying ethics. Dealing (however briefly) with these objections in this part of the book will clear the way for a more fruitful examination of the perspectives introduced in Parts II, III, and IV.

Consider the following claim: "Being concerned with ethics is unnecessary. After all, we live in a country of *laws*. These laws have been designed to safeguard people's rights, and we have an army of lawyers standing ready to assist anyone who feels that his or her rights have been violated. Consequently, ethics is entirely superfluous." Or so one might argue. But notice two things.

First, there will be many cases, clearly of an ethical nature, that will call for a decision on your part that the law will not address. Recall, for instance, the example with which we began. You are faced with the difficult decision of whether to devote your hard-earned money to learning how to play the guitar or, say, to rendering somewhat less tragic the plight of a number of people leading miserable lives. Obviously in a case like this appealing to "the law" to resolve your dilemma will be of no help at all. There are no laws dictating how one must spend one's money in such cases. Appealing to the law is simply and utterly beside the point. What you need in a case like this are well-thought-out ethical principles to guide your decisions. Ethical reflection is, in cases like this, indispensable.

There is a second problem with thinking that the law can be a sufficient basis on which to ground decisions, one that reveals even more clearly the need for studying ethics. For any law we care to consider, we can always raise the question of whether that law itself is *right* (e.g., *just*) or not. If laws were the only standard by which to judge the goodness of anything, then there would be no way to judge the goodness of the laws themselves. One could never, for instance, justify resisting some law that one felt was unjust or evil, because there would be no higher standard to which one could appeal. Yet sometimes people feel, quite reasonably, that some laws ought not to be obeyed. Think of persons living in the American South in the early 1800s, in Nazi Germany in the 1930s, or, until recently, in racially segregated South Africa, who believed that it was right to resist the discriminatory laws of these societies. What this shows is that an appeal to standards besides those given in the laws is necessary. If we ask whether a given law *should* be obeyed or not, we are in essence asking whether the law in question reflects what is morally right. Hence the issue of moral rightness is (logically) prior to the issue of legality. Laws are "just," one might argue, to the extent that they reflect deeper, underlying moral principles. Hence the need for identifying, and evaluating, these moral principles. Laws are, of course, essential for governing life in society. But they are not sufficient to resolve the ethical problems individuals encounter. Appeal to some set of ethical principles is necessary. Ethics is the study and evaluation of ethical principles in order to decide which ones are worthy of acceptance.

There is one additional point that needs to be made regarding the idea that living in a country of laws makes ethics superfluous. It requires that one reflect for a moment on the nature and purpose of laws. If you consider most of the laws that govern our behavior in society, it is clear that most of them are *negative* in the sense that they forbid one from behaving in certain ways. Traffic laws forbid driving over a certain speed limit, driving the wrong way on a one-way street, driving on the median-strip, and so on. Laws concerning property forbid walking out of a store with an armful of goods that have not been paid for, damaging the belongings of other persons, and the like. Laws concerning other persons forbid assaulting, robbing, raping, and murdering people. All of these laws are necessary, and it would be a very different, and much less agreeable, society without such laws. But such laws merely forbid certain kinds of behaviors. They do not provide *positive* guidance for living a good human life. One could be a perfectly law-abiding citizen, never breaking any laws or having any run-ins with the authorities, yet also lead an utterly miserable and morally reprehensible life. Given most societal conditions, laws are *necessary* for lives to be good, but they are not *sufficient*. Sound ethical principles to guide one's life are also necessary. In fact, it could be argued that ethics is more fundamental than law: If everyone lived their lives by sound ethical principles, there would be no need of laws! (Such a view is very close to the ideal society as envisioned by many of the thinkers represented in this book—e.g., Confucius.) A concern with ethics is much more than a concern with staying out of trouble with the law. It is a concern with living well. Simply obeying the law is not enough.

Does Morality Depend on Religion?

Another reason that studying ethics may seem unnecessary stems from the widely held belief that morality depends on religion. Morality and religion are, in many people's minds, inseparably linked, so that morality is thought to be impossible apart from religion. This belief may be reflected in the fact that our society frequently considers religious leaders to be *the* experts on morality. Certainly they are among the most visible (and audible) spokespersons for *specific* moral perspectives. There are at least three different arguments that attempt to connect morality and religion. Each, however, loses much of its plausibility once it is carefully considered. It is worth devoting some time to this issue because the belief that morality depends on religion often proves to be a major obstacle to benefiting fully from serious ethical reflection.

The first argument tries to connect morality directly with God in the following way. If God did not exist, then the universe would be utterly barren of values. This is because God is the ultimate source of values. Without God, there are no objective values and hence no absolute right or wrong. (As Ivan in Fyodor Dostoyevsky's novel *The Brothers Karamazov* claims, "If God did not exist, everything would be permissible.") If the universe were like this, then morality wouldn't make any sense. Morality *does* make sense, and it does so precisely because there is a God who is the ultimate ground and source of morality. "Good" is defined in terms of God's will: Whatever God wills is, by definition, good and right. God provides the absolute standard of morality in the universe. Hence, without God morality is simply an illusion. This shows that morality depends on religion.

There is a serious objection to this view. It is a very old objection and was explicitly stated by the Greek philosopher Plato more than two thousand years ago in his dialogue entitled *Euthyphro*. Here we will simply paraphrase it. Suppose one claims that what is "right" and "good" is whatever God says is right and good. This raises an interesting question: Is an action right and good *because* God says it is, or does God say an action is right and good because it *is* right and good? That is, does God's saying that something is good *make* it good, or does God say that something is good because he recognizes that it really *is* good? Suppose that the former is the case, that something is right and good simply because God says it is. It would seem to follow that if God said that something *else* was right and good—say, the opposite of what he did say was right and good—then that other thing would be right and good. So, for example, suppose that one holds that murder is wrong because God says that it is. If God had said that murder was good, then it would be good. In this view God could change his mind every day, so murder would be wrong one day and right the next, alternating each day. This conclusion is disconcerting, to say the least, because it implies that good and evil are really quite arbitrary.

"But," someone might object, "God would never command something that was not right!" If so, then we are now considering the second alternative, namely, that God says something is right because it really is. Murder is wrong, for example, and caring for the poor is right, because these things really are wrong and right, respectively, and God has simply communicated these important moral facts to us. But notice that in this case what is right and wrong seem to be independent of God's will. God simply recognizes what is already right and wrong. If this is the case, then it is obvious that what is right and wrong does not depend on God at all, but rather is somehow a part of the structure of the universe (or of reality). If so, perhaps we can find out what it is. To summarize these considerations, if an action is claimed to be right simply because God considers it so, then morality is ultimately arbitrary, and we need not take it very seriously. If, on the other hand, God considers an action to be right because it really is right, then there is a standard for morality that is independent of God. In this case we would do well to try to find out what it is. Either way, the attempt to connect morality with God looks a good deal less promising than some have supposed.

This brings us to the second argument connecting morality and religion. Suppose we recognize that there is a serious problem in holding that something is good just because God says that it is, and we are thus driven to the second position, namely, that at most God recognizes what *is* good and communicates this important fact to us. This position might still seem to render the formal study of ethics unnecessary. Granted that God's will is not what *makes* something right or wrong, still, since he has infinitely better access to moral truths than we do, we should operate on the assumption that he would communicate these important truths to us and that he has done so through his prophets, the scriptures, the church, and occasionally through direct communication (i.e., through visions, auditions, and the promptings of conscience). Morality must be based on religion, therefore, because religion represents (among other things) God's communication of moral truths to his creatures. If religion embodies these moral truths, then studying ethics seems to be unnecessary. In studying ethics one would either arrive at the *same* moral truths as revealed in religion, in which case such study would be superfluous, or one would arrive at *different* moral "truths," in which case such study would be seen as resulting in error. Either way, studying ethics seems to be a rather bad idea, or at least a waste of time.

Several responses to this argument should be mentioned. First, in cases where you believe that God has communicated with you directly, how do you know that God has revealed to you what is right and wrong? Another way of putting this question is: How do you know that it is *God* who has revealed these truths to you? When Abraham was instructed to take his beloved son Isaac to the mountain and sacrifice him there (Gen. 22.1–18), how could Abraham be sure that it was God, and not the devil or some other being, telling him what to do? And what about the rest of us, to whom God speaks either very rarely or very softly? How will we know what to do? Even if we suspect that God has spoken to us, mustn't we still weigh the command against our most reasonable assessment of what is right and wrong? If we thought that God commanded us to kill our most beloved relative, friend, or even pet, wouldn't we at least stop to consider this command before carrying it out? Wouldn't we weigh it against our sense of what is right and wrong? Doesn't this imply that we are operating with a standard of morality that is independent of divine directives? We must also recognize the very real and dangerous possibility of self-deception, especially in cases where our own interests are at stake. When we conclude that God has spoken to us and told us what to do, how can we be sure that we have not simply attributed to God's will what we really wanted to do anyway? Depending on God to provide direct guidance in every case is quite problematic.

A second problem with making morality depend on religion is that there are, of course, many different religions, each with its own revealed set of moral precepts. Orthodox Jews and Muslims consider eating pork to be a great sin, whereas Christians do not even consider it a moral issue. Christians typically do not consider killing nonhuman animals for food to be morally problematic, whereas for a Jain (a disciple of one of the major religions of India) to kill any living thing is a serious act of moral degeneracy. Quakers are completely opposed to war, whereas the notion of a "holy war" is central to Islam. Christians are allowed to have only one spouse—at one time, at least—whereas Muslim men may have up to four wives at the same time. (Muslim women are not accorded the same opportunity for multiple spouses.) Additional examples could be multiplied ad infinitum from the world's many religions. The moral precepts embodied in one's religious tradition *might* be the ones actually revealed by God. But how can one be sure? Or, more to the point, how can one be confident that the ethical doctrines embodied in one's religious tradition are the correct ones, whereas those of every other religion—especially the ones that conflict with your own—are mistaken? What one would need, apparently, is some way to judge the moral precepts of the different religions to determine which ones are correct. Once one had done so, one could then determine which religion is the "true" one. But note: If you had in your possession such moral standards, what need would you have of the grounding in religion for such moral precepts? You could simply derive the right moral precepts directly from the standards without taking a "detour" through a particular religion. So it seems that if one is to judge a particular source (e.g., a particular religious tradition) to be a valid moral authority, one would have to be a moral authority oneself. Why not decide to become a moral authority directly by studying ethics, and save yourself the additional work (and problems)?

A third problem with basing morality on religion is that doing so leads to the same problem that basing morality on law does: Neither law nor religion is specific enough to assist us in many of the moral dilemmas we actually face. Recall the example introduced earlier about having to decide between taking guitar lessons or giving your money to help the distant poor. It might seem that a particular religion such as Christianity would solve this problem fairly easily. Clearly you should give the money to the poor instead of spending it on yourself, even if your motive for guitar lessons is the noble one of self-improvement. This is because Christianity teaches (at least in one of its more popular interpretations) that one should put others before oneself. This idea of "putting others before oneself" would not, of course, solve the problem of whether to use the money to help the distant poor or to use it to help your mother take that long-dreamed-of trip. Resolving this problem would require more extensive theological interpretation. But we can ignore this for the moment. Here is a more difficult problem. Suppose that the *reason* you want to take guitar lessons is that you want to play guitar as part of a religious service. By playing guitar, and doing so well, you will be in a position to help uplift the other members of the congregation and may even succeed in bringing people into the religion who would otherwise drift away. By bringing them into the religion, you might be assisting in their eternal salvation. Which is more important, from the religious perspective: to prolong the lives of human beings who may never be "saved" (in the religious sense) anyway, or to devote one's efforts to assisting in the eternal salvation a few well-fed but otherwise spiritually doomed neighbors? In this case it is not at all clear that religion will be able to determine for you what you should do, because either it is not specific enough or it tells you to do two mutually exclusive things—feed the poor *and* save souls. Of course, one might try to enlist religion to decide what to do in this case by asking which course of action is most conducive to *one's own* eternal salvation, but in so doing one has simply introduced yet another consideration that must be evaluated (see discussion below). It seems that you will just have to weigh your options and decide in the most reasonable manner you can. This may mean determining which of your possible courses of action will realize a higher value, or which course of action will result in greater overall happiness, or which course of action will fulfill your duties. Making such a decision on the most reasonable basis is, of course, just what ethics is concerned with. Ethics is, once again, unavoidable.

One last argument for linking morality with religion needs to be addressed, because it has proved to be persuasive to a great many people through the ages. It concerns the incentive for pursuing a moral life. The question is often raised, "Unless there is some reward or punishment after death for behaving morally or immorally in this life, what is the incentive to pursue a moral life? If God does not exist, then there is no afterlife. If there is no afterlife, then there is no final reckoning of good and evil. Good people will not be rewarded for their good lives, and evil people will not be punished for their evil lives. What, then, is the point in trying to act morally? Without God, religion, and an afterlife, morality loses its point, as well as its major incentive."

Although this argument has exerted a major influence on many people, it begs a number of important questions. Most glaringly, it assumes that the reality of an afterlife depends on God's existence, a claim that is neither obviously true nor accepted by large parts of the world's population, especially in Asia. More important, this argument assumes that the reason one acts in a certain way is irrelevant to God or to an administrator of divine justice. That is, it assumes that as long as one performs actions that appear, from the external perspective, to be good actions, it does not matter *why* one performed those actions. But this is highly questionable. God may consider performing "moral" actions for the sake of looking out for one's own long-term interests (i.e., for "fire insurance") to be no more worthy of reward than any other selfishly motivated action, because all such actions are performed for the wrong reasons. God may care as much, or more, about *why* one performs actions of a certain sort than he does about *what* one does—a suggestion that finds strong support in Christian scriptures (e.g., Matt. 5.21–30 and Mark 7.14–23). It is not even clear that one *can* act morally for utterly selfish reasons. (If a man saves a child from a burning house simply so that he might gain notoriety for his courage, with absolutely no concern for the child herself, has he acted morally?) So believing that the only reason for behaving "morally" is to ensure a place in the afterlife may well backfire and produce just the opposite of the results one had anticipated. Morality finds, and needs, no support from this quarter.

One final point needs to be mentioned here. If one insists that the only grounds for taking morality seriously must come from one's religious beliefs, then one has in effect claimed that persons recognizing no religious tradition have no reason to behave morally. Such a conclusion should at least give one pause, inasmuch as there are a great many nonreligious individuals who not only live morally exemplary lives but also believe that they have good reasons to do so. On the view that only religion can provide a basis for morality, such people must be considered deeply deluded, or worse. Yet these same people often seem to be quite rational and intelligent. The reasonable conclusions to draw from this are that perhaps morality has a basis independent of any specific religion and that there are good grounds for morality that are accessible through critical reflection.

It is important to note that the above considerations do not in any way constitute an argument against religion. They are merely intended to show how problematic it is to try to reduce ethics to religion without further ado. Indeed, perhaps the greatest Christian theologian of all time—St. Thomas Aquinas—felt the force of identifying morality with God's will and realized that ethics must have some other foundation. He realized that if good and evil are defined in terms of God's will, then whatever God wills is, by definition, good. If so, then it does not make any sense to praise or worship God for his goodness—whatever God wills is by definition good, so to say that God's commands are good is simply to say that God commands what God commands. This is hardly very enlightening! Aquinas concluded that ethics must be based on reason, albeit reason operating in a world that has been designed and created by God. (This emphasis on ethics drawing insights from, but not being reduced to, religious beliefs is common to many of the perspectives included in this book.)

In conclusion, then, religion may provide crucial insights into human nature and the nature of the world in which we live, and it indeed is a rich source of values and ideals that are eminently worthy of consideration. Religion may thus assist us in coming to know what is morally right, without thereby determining for us the basis of morality. In this sense it plays a role not unlike that attributed to various social sciences earlier. It may provide important information or perspectives that should be taken into account, without thereby obviating the need for sustained ethical reflection. It follows that if we want to become more enlightened moral beings, to have a better sense of how we ought to live, we shall have to exercise our critical faculties (our reason operating in coordination with reflective insight) to the utmost in pursuit of this goal. Religion may assist us in this, but it cannot do the work for us.

Are Moral Standards "Relative"?

"Ah," the skeptic will respond, "this talk of 'finding out how we ought to live' is all very well and good, but it presupposes that there are universal moral *truths* out there waiting to be discovered. But why should we think this? If there really were such moral truths, wouldn't one expect that we would have discovered them by now? If you look around the world, what you see is not moral unity but rather moral diversity. Each culture has its own peculiar (and sometimes *very* peculiar) moral perspective on the world, and these different moral perspectives frequently clash. One culture reveres its elderly and treats them with the utmost respect and honor, whereas another abandons its elderly to die in the elements. One culture practices pacifism and strict vegetarianism and reveres all life (even rats and cockroaches) as sacred, whereas another wages war on its neighbors and consumes the vanquished as part of the victory celebration. Even within a single culture there are a bewildering variety of different, and often mutually exclusive, ethical perspectives. Witness the highly publicized battles waged between the 'pro-life' (i.e., antiabortion) and 'pro-choice' (i.e., anti-antiabortion) forces in this country. In the face of the overwhelming fact of moral diversity, isn't it a bit far-fetched to think that there is some absolute moral standpoint from which to make moral judgments?"

There are in fact a number of different claims lumped together in the skeptic's position, claims that are often not distinguished by those who are impressed by the diversity of moral beliefs discernible in the world. If we are to assess these claims properly, it is important that they be sorted out and carefully evaluated. We may begin with the most basic element of the skeptic's position. The basis for the skeptic's argument is the claim that moral standards differ from one culture to the next. Call this claim *cultural relativism*. From the claim that moral codes differ from culture to culture, a number of *other* claims are supposed to follow, among them that there are no universal or general moral principles common to all (or most) cultures; there is no objective, culturally independent standard by which to judge the moral code of any culture; and the moral code of each culture determines what is right and wrong for the members of that culture (i.e., morality is "internal" to each culture or society). Some or all of these implications of the fact of moral diversity are what is meant by the term *moral relativism*. Whereas cultural relativism is a claim about the diversity of moral codes one discovers when one inspects different cultures, moral relativism is a set of claims about the implications of this apparent diversity.

Moral relativism grounded in cultural relativism has seemed attractive to a great many people, especially in Western societies. Part of its attraction is due to the fact that such a view has been thought to promote *tolerance*. If moral codes differ from culture to culture and there is no objective (culturally independent) standard by which to judge the moral code of any culture, then the moral code of one's own particular culture has no special status. It is merely one culturally specific moral code among many. No one, therefore, has the right to impose his or her moral views on anyone else, least of all on people in different cultures. The appropriate attitude is therefore one of respect and tolerance for other moral perspectives. This line of reasoning is often regarded as especially enlightened and sophisticated, and worthy of wholehearted assent.

The undeniable popularity of this view notwithstanding, there are a number of serious problems with it that should make one reflect carefully before rushing to embrace it. Suppose for the moment that cultural relativism is true (we will have occasion to question this shortly). From the assumed fact that moral codes differ from culture to culture, does it follow that there are no universal (or at least general) moral principles common to all (or most) cultures? That is, does the presence of a diversity of moral codes entail that there are no moral principles in common across cultures? Not really. The ethical diversity among cultures may be at a fairly high level and may be grounded on more basic moral principles that cultures have in common. In this case the "fact" of moral diversity may be more apparent than real.

Consider an analogy. Baseball, basketball, and football are obviously very different sports. Each has its own specific rules concerning hits and runs, dribbling and foul shots, touchdowns and field goals. After observing each of these sports for a while, one might be deeply impressed by the diversity of practices. One might suppose that these sports are completely different and that the rules that apply within a single sport do not apply within the others. One might then go on to conclude that there are no universal (or at least general) rules common to all or most sports. But upon closer analysis, we would realize that this is a superficial judgment, formed too hastily. "Beneath" the diversity of rules governing the different sports, there is a set of common underlying principles that are so basic to these activities that they are rarely made explicit. For instance, players on opposing teams are not allowed to hire assassins to dispatch members of opposing teams. Pitchers and quarterbacks are not allowed to place explosive devices in their respective projectiles. Players may not apply torque to an official's head if they are not pleased with the official's judgment concerning a particular play. This list could be extended indefinitely, but the basic point should be clear enough. Despite the manifest diversity of rules governing different sports, there is nonetheless a basic set of principles common to all these sports, which allow them to exist in the first place, and upon which the more specific rules of each are based. Such principles form the background against which the different rules stand out. The diversity is real, but so is the common underlying basis.

Leaving sports and returning to the sphere of morality, one could imagine how a similar state of affairs could obtain here as well. Despite the very real diversity of moral codes found in different cultures, there may nonetheless be a common underlying basis for all these different specific codes—a common basis that is overlooked or even obscured by overemphasizing diversity at the expense of communality. Describing a practice as "abandoning the elderly to die in the elements" may fail to reveal what is significant about this practice. When described in this way, the practice of some Inuit (formerly referred to as "Eskimo") peoples of dealing with the conflicting demands of survival in a harsh and unrelenting environment may strike many people as an inhumane way to dispose of society's elderly. But such a practice may, *within Inuit culture*, represent the highest reverence for the elderly *when understood in the context of that culture's beliefs*. They have one way of showing respect for their elderly (and of ensuring the continuing survival of the remainder of the group), while other cultures have other ways. The precise details of this example are not crucial to the point being made. The essential point here is that just because cultures differ in their practices (or higher-level moral codes) does not mean that they differ in their basic ethical principles. Similar ethical principles may give rise to different practices in different circumstances. (Another way this can happen, and give the illusion of deep moral disagreement, is when different groups disagree about the facts of the case under consideration. Both pro-life and pro-choice groups, for example, think that human life is valuable but typically differ on whether they consider a fetus to *be* a human life. In this case ethical disagreement may be just an artifact of a disagreement about nonethical facts and may not be indicative of a deeper disagreement about moral principles.)

Consider next the claim that if moral codes differ from culture to culture, then there is no objective standard by which to judge the moral code of any culture. The major flaw in this argument is simply that the fact of ethical diversity is perfectly consistent with the claim that there are objective moral standards. More generally, the fact that people disagree about a given issue is no evidence whatsoever for concluding that there is no truth of that matter. Consider a familiar example. A few hundred years ago there was widespread disagreement about whether the sun revolved around the earth or the earth revolved around the sun. If one had concluded from this manifest disagreement that there is no fact of the matter about the earth and the sun, or that "for one culture the sun goes around the earth, but for another the earth revolves around the sun," one would have been utterly mistaken. The earth goes around the sun in a precisely determined elliptical orbit, and not vice versa. This is so even though most people in human history have held (and some people even now hold) the opposite belief. During a time in the Renaissance and early modern period, there were a number of different views on this matter, with no one view enjoying universal assent. As it turned out, some of the beliefs held were true, others were false. Widespread disagreement is consistent with objective truth, because what people *believe* and what is the case need not coincide. Returning to the matter of moral relativism, from the fact that people disagree about ethical matters, it does not follow that there are no facts of the matter, no objective moral principles. Of course, there may not be any objective moral principles, but the argument from cultural relativism does nothing to establish such a claim. Moral relativists will have to find another argument to justify their view.

It is important to note that there is something a bit misleading about the ethical relativist's assumed dichotomy between "objective moral truths," on the one hand, and complete moral relativity, on the other. It may be the case that there are no moral values "outside of humanity," or that morality is essentially linked with human value judgments, and hence that there are no objective moral truths of the sort that could exist totally apart from any human beings. But this is perfectly consistent with the search for moral wisdom. What we *may* be after is not some set of moral truths that are true everywhere in the universe, but rather an understanding of what kinds of ethical principles are most appropriate for guiding human conduct, given the kinds of creatures we are. That is, it *may* be the case that being the kinds of creatures we are—namely, human beings—some things are generally good for us, whereas other things are generally bad for us. Ethics could then be concerned with trying to discover which things are good and which are not, and with introducing order into the difficult task of weighing competing goods. For instance, it might really be the case that truth-telling and promise-keeping are conducive to human welfare, regardless of the different customs that different societies display with regard to these practices. This is something that ethics would be concerned to clarify, understand, and explain.

Finally, consider the inference from the claim that moral codes differ from culture to culture to the conclusion that the moral code of each culture determines what is right and wrong for the members of that culture (i.e., morality is "internal" to each culture or society), and thence to the claim that moral relativism should be accepted because it fosters the admirable attitude of tolerance toward other cultures. There are a number of problems with these inferences. For brevity only three will be mentioned here.

First, it is important to be very clear about what acceptance of moral relativism commits one to. If this doctrine is true, what is morally right and wrong is a matter entirely internal to each culture. Since there are no objective (culturally independent) standards by which to judge the moral codes of any culture, one cannot criticize another culture's practices "from the outside." Apparently we must respect and *accept* whatever values a given society embraces. A corollary of this is that one must accept whatever moral values are predominant in the culture in which one happens to live. Both of these conclusions should give one pause. Although these conclusions seem harmless enough if one is considering issues such as the age at which sexual activity is condoned, whether the use of hallucinogenic drugs is tolerated, whether the dead are buried or cremated, whether women may appear in public with their breasts exposed, and so on, matters are quite different when one considers some of the more oppressive practices that human beings have invented. For the moral relativist, there can be no objective basis for saying that the institution of slavery in this country and elsewhere in the world two hundred years ago was a morally reprehensible practice, that the Nazis were wrong in persecuting and killing more than six million Jews and others during World War II, or that the policy of apartheid in South Africa, which defined that society's attitude toward race relations until fairly recently, is a morally repugnant policy.

To take another, especially disturbing example, consider the practice of clitorectomy (or "female circumcision"). Various groups in Africa still engage in the practice of removing the clitoris of young girls and then sewing their vagina almost shut. (The stitches are later forcefully ripped out by the girl's husband on their wedding night—a husband whom the girl may or may not have chosen or even met before.) This is not done in a sterile hospital environment, but is rather performed by an older woman of the tribe, often with crude glass, stone, or rusty metal instruments, without the benefit of anesthesia. The young girls wait in an adjoining room, listening to the cries of pain coming from the "operating room," and then watch as each waiting girl is dragged into the room, only to be carried out a few minutes later, sobbing, bleeding, and unable to walk. It is important to note that this is not a criminal act within the cultures in which it occurs, but is rather an accepted cultural practice. According to the doctrine of moral relativism, the appropriate attitude to adopt toward such a practice is one of tolerance. In lieu of any objective moral standards to which one could appeal, no criticism of such a practice is possible.

Just as moral relativism precludes criticizing the practices of other cultures, it also precludes criticism of one's own culture. If the values of a given culture define right and wrong for the members of that society at that time, then such members could not be right in claiming that the ideals of their society need to be reformed. (For instance, Gandhi, whose life will be described in Part III, could not have been justified in attempting to reform the social and political system in his native India. The same is true of Martin Luther King, Jr., and every other reformer one can think of.) Whatever one's society considers to be right, is right. In other words, an internal critique of one's own society becomes impossible on this view. The problems with accepting such a view are similar to those mentioned above regarding other cultures. In neither case is serious criticism possible. This is the "dark side" of moral relativism. So long as these practices are sanctioned in the cultures in which they occur, the consistent moral relativist will have to say that such practices are just. At some point many people will want to claim that surely it *is* possible, even *necessary*, to criticize both one's own culture *and* the practices of other cultures. If moral relativism is correct, neither is really possible. Moral relativism, although initially attractive, turns out to be a dead end that either inhibits critical evaluation or leads one to accept morally questionable practices without questioning them.

Finally, there is a major presupposition of both cultural and moral relativism that should at least be identified, even though it cannot be adequately addressed here. Once this presupposition is identified, it can be seen that the major premise of moral relativism threatens to render it incoherent. Here is the problem. In order for moral codes to be relative to specific cultures, it must be the case that each culture have an identifiable moral code. In small, homogeneous cultural groups, like a particular African tribe or an Inuit settlement, one might expect to find a high degree of consensus. But what about a "culture" like "Western culture," or even "American culture"? Given the heterogeneity of these groups, is it likely that a single moral code will emerge that represents these cultures as a whole? Given the heated debates that continue to surround controversial moral issues, the prospects look bleak. Perhaps there is no such thing as "Western culture," but only Western *cultures.* Perhaps the Irish form one culture, Norwegians another, and so on. Likewise, perhaps Irish-Americans in Boston form one culture, Norwegian-Americans in Minnesota form another, and so on. But presumably each of these groups could be further subdivided. Where should the division into groups end? At the limit one is left with individual human beings. The conceptual problem with cultural and moral relativism should now be apparent. Both wish to emphasize *diversity* over *commonality.* But diversity exists at many levels, and it is not clear precisely where one should stop, or how one should select the entities within which moral codes exist and between which they differ. The more the diversity of moral codes is emphasized, the less hope there is of finding the correct units in terms of which to make morality relative. This is not to say that no generalizations can be made. Indeed, this book is premised on the claim that, although not *completely* different, Western and Eastern cultures have developed recognizably different approaches to morality, and within each of these broad cultural designations exist a variety of identifiable moral traditions. The intent here is merely to point out that cultural and moral relativism rely on a claim of much greater distinctness of cultures than may in fact exist.

As we have seen, the doctrine of moral relativism, while attractive to a great many people, has a number of *very* serious problems associated with it. None of the interesting and controversial claims thought to follow from cultural relativism do in fact follow from it. From the mere fact that cultures (or individuals) *believe* different things about what is morally right or wrong, nothing whatsoever follows about what *is* morally right or wrong. As we know only too well from many other cases, people can be utterly mistaken in what they believe, even though they hold their beliefs with the utmost conviction and sincerity. What we need to determine, in pursuing moral wisdom, is not just *what* people believe, but whether there are *good reasons* for believing as they do.

The failure of moral relativism does not, however, mean that there is nothing of value to learn from the fact that a great deal of ethical diversity does exist in our world. Here is a lesson that one might validly infer from the fact of ethical diversity. We should realize that many of the moral practices we take for granted do not necessarily represent some universal, objective moral principle, but are rather the peculiar products of our particular society. It is important to be able to distinguish one kind of ethical norm from the other.

Here is another lesson from cultural relativism. Although the fact that moral codes often differ from one culture to the next does not imply moral relativism, it does suggest that there may be many different ways of conceiving of morality, and many different ways of applying basic ethical principles. Some of these applications may be appropriate in one kind of situation but not in another (recall the comment on the Inuit practices described earlier), whereas other applications might be "exportable" to different situations. What this line of thinking leads to is *not* the idea that all ethical perspectives are equally good (just in virtue of the fact that they exist and people believe in them), but rather that all ethical perspectives (and especially those that have enjoyed a very long existence) are worthy of our attention and consideration for the additional insights they might provide. That is, there is a *via media* (a "middle way") between the extremes of moral dogmatism (assuming that one's present moral perspective is sufficient unto itself and incapable of improvement), and moral relativism (where one makes the opposite mistake of uncritically assuming that all moral perspectives are equally valid). This *via media* would be to start from where one finds oneself, morally speaking, and then to approach different moral perspectives, especially those associated with major ethical traditions, with an open mind and a view to carefully considering which aspects of these perspectives could enrich your own understanding of morality. In this way different ethical perspectives become an invaluable resource for refining your own thinking. Moral relativism, its pretensions to enlightenment and multicultural sophistication notwithstanding, dishonors the spectrum of ethical perspectives by failing to take each perspective seriously enough to assess its merits and demerits. It settles for the intellectually slothful option of declaring them all equally valid or invalid, and in so doing denigrates the distinctive contributions each perspective might make to our understanding of morality. The approach recommended here, on the other hand, commits one to understanding and assessing each of these perspectives, in order to identify the strengths and weaknesses of each. To approach different moral perspectives in this way is to truly honor and respect them.

Is Ethics Possible, Given the Facts of Human Nature?

So far it has been assumed that ethical reflection can have an impact on how one actually lives. That is, it has been assumed that coming to know or understand something is sufficient to permit one to act upon that understanding. A person who arrives at a well-informed judgment about what to do in a particular situation can simply go ahead and follow that course of action. This seems simple enough. But is this really so? Are we really free to direct our own actions and thereby to direct our own lives in the ways that we choose? Unless we are free to direct our own actions, reflection on the best way to live seems to be quite beside the point.

Freedom and Determinism

The question of whether or not we choose our actions "freely" has long fascinated philosophers and has generated some long-standing and often extremely technical debates. But the basic issue at stake can be stated rather simply. On one side of this debate are classical "determinists," who believe that every event in the universe is governed by inexorable natural laws and hence that whatever happens is inevitable and completely explainable (at least in principle) in terms of antecedent causes. This is the simplest version of the thesis of determinism. Since human actions are clearly events in the universe, they too have their antecedent causes. Here determinists divide, with some emphasizing psychological factors, some emphasizing environmental (e.g., social or economic) factors, and still others emphasizing biological (e.g., genetic) factors. Frequently all such factors are taken into consideration as pointing to the same conclusion: All human actions can, at least in principle, be explained as the necessary, law-like effects of the multiple causes that preceded them. Given the operation of these causes, no other actions besides those that *do* occur *could* have occurred. Determinists hence deny that people are ever "free" in the strong sense of having genuine choices or that people are morally responsible for their actions.

On the other side of this debate are "indeterminists" or "libertarians" (not to be confused with the political party of the same name), who maintain that human beings possess "free will" and that in virtue of this free will people are able to consider alternatives and to choose between them. Libertarians admit that many, and indeed most, events taking place in the universe, including many human actions, are the results of antecedent causes and the laws of nature but insist that there remains a class of actions—free human actions—that are not so determined. Whereas determinists will point to the successes of various scientific explanations of human behavior in terms of specific causes, libertarians will typically appeal to the sense of freedom each of us experiences as we are confronted with a decision to be made. During such times we feel ourselves to be genuinely free with respect to the course of action we pursue. We may feel inclined toward one course of action over another, yet we also know that either course is a genuine option for us. Such free human actions make possible the moral assessment of actions and the ascription of moral responsibility to persons.

As noted above, there is a strong connection between the issue of freedom and determinism, and ethics. The connecting link is the notion of moral responsibility. If determinism is true and individuals are not free, then no actions are performed freely and individuals cannot be held morally responsible for their actions. If you were kidnapped against your will and subjected to "brainwashing" that led you to become an assassin of political leaders—as in the movie *The Manchurian Candidate*—you could not be held morally responsible for your actions after the brainwashing. If determinism is correct, then the same would be true for all human actions. On the other hand, if at least some human actions are free, then individuals may be held morally responsible for such actions. Freedom seems to be a necessary prerequisite for assigning moral responsibility to individuals.

Although philosophers have devised subtle alternatives to both determinism and libertarianism, each alternative seems, upon closer inspection, to collapse into one of these two original theories. Like many other philosophical debates, this one is still far from settled. This is certainly not the place to try to settle it. Perhaps it is sufficient to note here that each of us, whether we have determinist or libertarian leanings, acts *as if* we are free every time we make a decision. That is, when faced with a situation that calls for a decision to be made, we behave as if it is genuinely up to us what we shall do. We identify the alternatives, carefully weigh the pros and cons of each possible course of action, make a decision, and then attempt to act upon it. Often we feel regret or remorse later at having made decisions that did not turn out as well as we had hoped—a response that seems to make sense only if we accept the claim that we could have chosen differently. Indeed, it is difficult to imagine how we could approach the situations we encounter in any other way. Even if determinism is true, we would still feel the need to make decisions on a moment-to-moment basis and hence to act *as if* we have genuine freedom. Having such a feeling, of course, does nothing to settle the issue. Feelings, after all, are a notoriously unreliable guide to reality. Nonetheless, this apparently unavoidable feature of our experience is perhaps enough to justify the effort to understand the grounds and structure of morality more fully and to search for principles that will assist us in making wise decisions. The notion of human freedom may thus be taken as a "working hypothesis" whose adoption will allow us to explore the nature of good lives more fully without giving up prematurely.

Psychological Egoism

Given the purpose of this book, we cannot explore the issue of freedom and determinism in this context to the extent that it deserves. What we can do in this context, however, is consider one particular version of determinism that is especially relevant with regard to ethics. It is a version that, if correct, would have dire consequences for our attempts to freely construct lives for ourselves that satisfy commonly accepted norms of behavior.

Psychological egoism, in its strongest form, states that all human actions, no matter how altruistically motivated they may *appear* to be, are in reality selfish, in the sense that they are performed to enhance the well-being of the actor. On this view, people always act in their own self-interest and, given the facts of human nature, cannot do otherwise. Psychological egoism is a descriptive claim: It purports to tell us what human beings are like, whether we like it or not.

It is easy to see how such a doctrine, if true, would have serious repercussions for ethics. If one can act only to enhance one's own welfare, then what becomes of injunctions to assist others when doing so might require some sacrifice on one's part? Such recommendations are completely pointless, because one is being asked to do something that is psychologically impossible. It would be like being told that one should form an exact image in one's mind of a three-dimensional object having precisely 12,846 sides. No matter how well intentioned such advice might be, we cannot do what is psychologically impossible, given the kinds of creatures that we are. Ethical reflection, on this view, is just so much idle chatter, at least so far as altruism is concerned.

Psychological egoism is, to many, a plausible and appealing doctrine. (It is so appealing that it is taken for granted in many economic models of human behavior.) For any action anyone performs, it always seems possible to devise an explanation of that action in terms of the agent's self-interest. Consider the seemingly altruistic (other-regarding) action of giving one's lunch and spare change to a homeless person (perhaps as described at the beginning of this chapter). This action would seem to be the opposite of selfishness, right? The psychological egoist will insist, however, that we inquire more deeply into the *motives* for performing this action. One hands over the food and money and immediately feels somewhat "better." This assuages any guilt and provides temporary relief. The real reason the apparently altruistic action was performed, therefore, was to make one feel better or to help ease the discomfort produced by guilt. These are all in the agent's self-interest. A similar kind of story can be told about *any* apparently altruistic action. Once a person's real motives are revealed, any supposedly altruistic action can be understood to be basically selfish at bottom.

Although it appears to be a simple doctrine and almost invulnerable to criticism, psychological egoism is full of ambiguities that need to be sorted out if we are to properly assess its claims. For instance, what precisely does the claim that "persons act out of self-interest" mean? Is it merely the claim that persons *usually* act out of self-interest, or is it the much stronger claim that they *always* do? The former (weaker) claim would require some sort of empirical support (i.e., psychological or sociological evidence) to make it worthy of belief, and so far no one has found a way to establish its claim to truth. It is not even clear how it *could* be established empirically. How could we ever determine the real motives of every action performed and then the precise percentage of those that are altruistically motivated and those that are selfishly motivated? Asking people why they act as they do is of little help, because people may be reluctant to reveal the real motives behind their actions, and many people may simply hold mistaken beliefs about why they act as they do. But even if it were possible to determine the motives for performing actions and it turned out that people *usually* act out of self-interest (e.g., on average, 87 percent of the actions people perform are selfishly motivated), the fact that persons *usually* act out of self-interest is perfectly compatible with persons *sometimes* performing altruistic actions. Even if true, its implications for ethics are not very momentous. Perhaps its truth implies that it is rather difficult to act altruistically and that selfishness is hard to resist. These "insights" would hardly be earth-shattering news to anyone who has ever struggled to overcome self-centeredness (almost everyone at some time or another). So, this form of psychological egoism is not a very interesting doctrine.

The claim that persons *always* act out of self-interest is a much stronger claim, has greater ramifications for ethics, and hence is more interesting to consider. According to this doctrine, all human actions are, without exception, motivated by self-interest. But here again, we can ask precisely what this means. Is the claim that persons always act in ways that do *in fact* serve their self-interests, or is the claim that persons always act in ways that they *believe* serve their self-interests? Consider the former claim for a moment. Is it true that persons always act in ways that do in fact serve their self-interests? Although there is probably no case that could not be twisted in some way to make it seem as if an action that is harmful to the agent is in fact beneficial for the agent, there are plenty of cases that certainly seem to refute this version of psychological egoism. Consider the person who consumes a bowl of his favorite cereal (Chocolate-Covered Sugar Bombs with chocolate milk) for breakfast, several nitrate-laden hotdogs for lunch, and charcoal-blackened barbecued pork rinds for dinner. He washes down these meals with a six-pack of beer, a quart of vodka, and a cup of scotch whiskey, respectively. He chain-smokes unfiltered cigarettes throughout the day as he proudly works at his profession: removing asbestos from the ceilings and walls of condemned buildings—without the benefit of protective equipment. Weekends are spent watching cartoons and MTV and enjoying his favorite hobby: assembling small explosive devices while nibbling on greasy fried chicken skin.

In such an admittedly extreme case as this, it seems a bit implausible to claim that each and every one of this person's actions contribute to his self-interest. At the very least, it is very difficult to see how any of the above-described actions could be considered conducive to this person's physical or mental health. The fact that people sometimes (and perhaps often) perform actions that are *not* in their own self-interest seems to be as certain as anything could be and certainly more certain than anything anyone could use to challenge this claim. The version of psychological egoism that claims that people always act in their own self-interest is therefore quite implausible.

The claim that people always act in ways that they *believe* serve their self-interests is a bit harder to refute. Granted that the actions of the above-described person do not *really* serve that person's self-interests, might it not be that he sincerely *believes* that they do? Perhaps he was left alone by his parents for long periods of time and acquired his (rather peculiar) beliefs about what is good for human beings from watching too many television commercials and bad late-night movies as a child. But this would be grossly inadequate to establish the claim in question. The issue is not whether anyone ever acts in ways that they mistakenly believe are in their self-interest, but rather whether anyone ever performs actions that they know or believe to be contrary to their self-interest. A moment's reflection reveals that persons often *do* perform actions that they know to be contrary to their self-interest. Consider the common response smokers give to the advice to quit smoking: "I know that smoking is detrimental to my health, but I just can't help it. It's a habit." In such cases, which are very common, a person admits that something is not in their self-interest but continues to perform those actions anyway. If you are like most people, it is very likely that you can think of at least several such examples from your own life.

If there are cases in which people act in ways contrary to their self-interest and cases where people *know* themselves to be acting in ways contrary to their self-interest, then what are we to make of the psychological egoist's doctrine? Isn't it falsified by such cases? The psychological egoist might save the view by shifting his position once again. He might answer that what his doctrine states, properly understood, is that people always act for the sake of their own *immediate* self-interest, where "immediate self-interest" is identified with *pleasure* (or the avoidance of pain). In the cases described above, persons are acting in ways contrary to their *long-term* interests, but are nonetheless behaving as they do because their actions bring them some immediate sense of pleasure. Human beings, on this view, are always driven by desire for immediate gratification. Furthermore, persons are often not even *aware* that this is what they are doing. The person who continues to smoke even though she knows that it is dangerous to her health may convince herself that smoking is beneficial because it helps her avoid snacking and hence getting fat, helps her socialize with her friends, and so on. Hence, although smoking is not in fact in the person's long-term interests, the person continues to smoke because she derives immediate pleasure from smoking and has convinced herself that it is not contrary to her long-term interests. In this way the psychological egoist can attempt to preserve his doctrine in the face of apparently refuting evidence.

This move is not, however, without its difficulties, some of which may have occurred to you already. Is it really true that people *always* act solely to increase their immediate pleasure without regard for the long-term consequences of their actions? Consider the person who diets to lose weight, or the person who begins a fitness program to get in shape, or an athlete training for a competition, or a musician practicing a musical piece over and over, or someone drilling on verbs in learning a new language, or those of us who at least on occasion get up in the morning when the alarm clock rings instead of rolling over and going back to sleep. The list could be extended indefinitely. What all these examples have in common is that people frequently forego immediate pleasure for the sake of achieving some possibly distant goal that they deem important. The problem with the psychological egoist's revised claim that persons always act for their immediate self-interest, understood as pleasure, is that it seems to be refuted by a large number of familiar facts.

In response to this criticism, the psychological egoist could revise his doctrine once again to take account of these facts. He could maintain that what psychological egoism claims is not that every human action is performed for immediate gratification, but rather that human beings always act as they do because they believe that their actions will promote their own long-term interests (or "projects").

There are several problems with this move. First, it seems to be refuted by the example of the junkfood-eating, alcohol-imbibing, demolitions-tinkering individual described above. Such a person might continue to pursue these activities while fully realizing that they are *not* in his long-term interests.

Second, and more important, the notions of "long-term interest" and "projects" are too broad to serve the psychological egoist's purposes. Conceivably a person might have as a long-term project the goal of always acting according to duty, or helping others in need, or helping young people to develop their unique talents, or any of a variety of other actions intended to help other people achieve good lives. All of these actions might be performed as part of a person's project, and hence would satisfy the psychological egoist's criterion of "selfishness." But they are also precisely the kinds of actions that people are praised for, inasmuch as they are usually considered to be admirable altruistic actions. On this view, Mother Theresa's life devoted to caring for the poor and sick of Calcutta is a paradigm example of selfishness. Clearly, something has gone wrong with the psychological egoist's claim! If this is what the claim that "everyone always acts selfishly" amounts to, then psychological egoism is a trivial and hence uninteresting doctrine.

One final issue concerning psychological egoism needs to be addressed here. There is an important ambiguity in the way this doctrine is usually stated. The basic claim is that persons always act selfishly. But what is the force of the word "always" in this claim? There is both a stronger and a weaker form to consider. On the one hand, the claim might be that persons *necessarily* act selfishly. This claim can itself be resolved into two versions. It might be claimed that it is *causally* necessary that persons always act selfishly. This would mean that given the various psychological, environmental, and genetic factors operating on each individual, persons find it impossible to act altruistically. Although this might be true, there is little evidence that can be assembled to show that it is true, and, given at least the *appearance* of altruistic actions, it seems rather implausible.

On the other hand, it might be claimed that it is *logically* necessary that persons always act selfishly. Consider the case of Mother Theresa mentioned above, where it was implied that if ever there was an example of an altruistic, unselfish life, her life surely provides such an example. But couldn't the psychological egoist claim that even here the motivation is essentially selfish? Question: Why has Mother

Theresa devoted her life to helping the poor and sick of Calcutta? Answer: Because, given her unique psychological makeup, she gains satisfaction from doing so. Perhaps she finds herself with a strong desire to assist the most unfortunate members of our species and also feels a profound sense of personal satisfaction in helping such people. No matter how "noble" her life might seem, it too is ultimately motivated by selfishness, albeit a peculiar sort of selfishness.

Clearly, on this version of psychological egoism, no action, no matter how altruistically motivated it may *appear* to be, can ever actually be so. For any example of a supposedly altruistic action, the psychological egoist can always respond by claiming that the action in question is performed because it gives the agent satisfaction. Indeed, one can claim this without needing to examine the details of any particular action. The claim is made on purely logical grounds. Whatever actions an agent performs are performed for the sake of that agent's interests, suitably understood. There can thus be no escape from the psychological egoist's claim that all human actions are ultimately selfish.

In response, one should notice a very important shift that has taken place. Recall that psychological egoism was originally proposed as an *empirical* claim about human motivation. That is, it was put forward as a description of how human beings do, as a matter of fact, behave. What is interesting about empirical, factual claims is that they are falsifiable, at least in principle. What this means is that they are capable of being refuted by experience. Take an empirical claim like water freezes at zero degrees Celsius at one atmosphere of pressure. This claim is true, and no counterinstances have ever been found. Yet what makes the claim empirical (and hence scientific) is that it is entirely possible to conceive of an exception to this claim. Suppose that it was discovered that in a strong magnetic field water freezes at five degrees Celsius. This finding would force us to revise our claim about the freezing point of water. We would have to say that water freezes at zero degrees Celsius at one atmosphere of pressure only in the absence of strong magnetic forces. Note that this discovery need never be made in order for the claim about water to be a genuinely empirical claim. It is sufficient that it *could* happen.

This example contrasts markedly with the case of psychological egoism in the version we are considering. It seems that nothing could, *even in principle,* count against the claim that all human actions are ultimately selfish in character. For any case one could imagine, the psychological egoist could claim that, properly understood, it is really a confirmation of his doctrine. What this means is that the psychological egoist's claim is not really an empirical, descriptive claim after all. It is a bit like the claim that "all bachelors are unmarried males." One would not expect to encounter a bachelor who is married no matter how many bachelors one examined, because the terms *bachelor* and *unmarried* are related in such a way that any instance of the former will *necessarily* (i.e., *logically*) be an instance of the latter. This linguistic stipulation tells us nothing about whether there *are* any bachelors in the world, of course, but merely about what we will mean by the term *bachelor.* It is, in the terminology of logicians, merely an empty tautology. Returning now to the issue of psychological egoism, if the claim that all human actions are selfish is understood to mean merely that whatever is an "action" is by definition "selfish," then what began as an interesting and important empirical claim about human nature ends up as a trivial and unilluminating redefinition of our basic terminology.

We have been considering the psychological egoist's claim that persons always act selfishly, where "always" is understood to imply causal or logical necessity.

On the other hand, the "always" in the claim that "persons always act selfishly" might mean that although persons can choose to act altruistically, they never in fact make this choice. Interpreting psychological egoism in this weaker form, which says that people always *choose* to act in their own self-interest, allows the claim to avoid the problems facing determinism but leads to other equally serious problems. One of these problems is that it requires us to believe the conjunction of two rather implausible claims, namely, that (1) appearances to the contrary, no one ever acts against their own self-interest for the sake of others, and (2) although any person may freely choose to act out of a concern for others, no one ever in fact makes this choice and acts upon it. This will no doubt strike many readers as extremely implausible. This would be like saying that although it is entirely *possible* that a person falls in love with another person, and it often seems (to others) that a particular person has fallen in love with another person, and it even seems to that person that he or she has fallen in love with another person, in fact no one in the history of humanity has ever fallen in love with another person. Although it is perfectly possible and appears to happen all the time, this possibility has never been realized. Given the lack of evidence for this view and the overwhelming testimony of common sense to the contrary, it is difficult to see why anyone would be attracted to such a view. Similar considerations bear against the version of psychological egoism we are considering. If all persons always act in a certain way, one should probably conclude that there is something necessary (in some sense of "necessary") about this behavior. This "weaker" version of psychological egoism, therefore, collapses into the stronger version, and inherits all of its deficiencies.

Ethical Egoism

As we have seen, psychological egoism is the doctrine that persons always, and perhaps can only, act from selfish motives. As such, it is a *descriptive* claim that purports to describe how people do (or perhaps, given certain definitions, can only) act. Because this claim has appealed to many people, but the grounds for this claim are so weak, we have devoted a considerable amount of discussion to it. If the arguments given above are sound, then the claims of psychological egoism need not deter us from undertaking a serious exploration of ethics.

A related but importantly different doctrine called *ethical egoism* concerns how one *ought* to act (hence the adjective *ethical* in its name). According to ethical egoism, one's own welfare is the principle upon which one *should* base one's actions. One should always act for the sake of self-interest. Because ethical egoism tells us how one ought to act, it is a normative (or action-guiding) claim. Unlike psychological egoism, ethical egoism does not undermine ethics per se. It does not make reflecting on ethical issues irrelevant or impossible. Rather, it is a normative ethical doctrine that attempts to settle, as simply as possible, the issue of how one ought to act (for instance when there is a conflict between one's own interests and those of other people). The solution on this view is simple: In every situation, one should act for one's own benefit.

Although ethical egoism as just described is not inconsistent with the study of ethics per se, it does conflict with an aspect of nearly every ethical perspective one cares to think about. It conflicts with the claim that sometimes, and perhaps often, we should put another person's concerns ahead of our own. And it raises a number of questions that need to be addressed. Why should one ever act in ways not designed to enhance one's own welfare? Why should one ever act to enhance someone else's welfare at the expense of one's own? In other words, why shouldn't one be as selfish as possible? Why should one be concerned about the well-being of other persons at all?

Recall the example with which we began. You are faced with a difficult decision: how to spend your hard-earned cash. Among your options are the following: You could spend it on guitar lessons for yourself, a gift for your mother, or relief supplies for starving Third World people. What should you do? One suggestion would be that you should spend the money on guitar lessons, because self-interest takes priority over promoting the interests of others. Assuming for the sake of simplicity that taking guitar lessons serves your self-interest better than do either of the other two alternatives, then you should take the guitar lessons. Generalizing this approach, one can claim that in any situation, each individual should act for the sake of self-interest. This is the doctrine of ethical egoism.

Before we evaluate this view, it is important to clear away a potential misconception. It might be tempting to conclude from this description of ethical egoism that one should never perform actions that will benefit others. But this would be too simple an understanding of the notion of "acting for the sake of self-interest." On this view one may act for the benefit of others, but such actions must treat the welfare of others as a *means* (or just a side-effect) of activities designed to enhance one's own welfare. Sometimes self-interested actions will benefit others, sometimes they will not. Either way, what is important is that they be done for the sake of promoting one's own interests.

With this understanding of ethical egoism in mind, we can go on to ask why we should accept this view. What reasons can be given in support of the claim that people should always act for the sake of self-interest? It is sometimes thought that the doctrine of psychological egoism provides support for ethical egoism. A moment's reflection, however, will reveal how confused this thought is. Begin by noticing that the relationship between psychological egoism and ethical egoism is *not* the same sort of relationship as that between cultural relativism and moral relativism. Recall that the truth of moral relativism (the claim that morality is always relative to particular cultures) was supposed to follow from the truth of cultural relativism (the claim that moral codes differ from one culture to another). That is, cultural relativism was supposed to provide support for moral relativism. Psychological egoism and ethical egoism have practically the opposite relationship to one another. Psychological egoism claims that persons always (in some sense of "always") act selfishly (in some sense of "selfishly"). Ethical egoism claims that persons *should* always act selfishly. But what possible point could there be in telling people how they *should* act if they cannot, as a matter of fact, act in any other way?

To see this point, consider a fanciful analogy. "Physical gravitationism" claims that all bodies, including all human bodies, are subject to gravitational forces. "Ethical gravitationism" claims that one's body *should* be subject to gravitational forces. Obviously, if physical gravitationism is true, then ethical gravitationism is utterly superfluous. There is no point in telling someone that they ought to do something that they could not possibly avoid doing under any circumstances. Likewise, if psychological egoism (and determinism more generally) are true, then ethical egoism becomes empty advice. If people cannot but act in their own self-interest, then there can be no point in telling them that they ought to act in this way. Rather than providing support for ethical egoism, therefore, psychological egoism (if true) robs it of any point.

In addition to undermining the point of ethical egoism, there is another reason that psychological egoism could not provide any support for ethical egoism. This reason concerns an insight expressed some 250 years ago by the Scottish philosopher David Hume (a profile of Hume appears in Chapter 3). According to Hume, when he read the works of moral philosophers he invariably encountered a number of factual, descriptive statements, along with evidence in support of them, and then at some point the author would begin making normative ("ought" or "should" type) statements, apparently attempting to justify such statements by appealing to the descriptive claims previously made. This move, Hume claimed, is invalid. One cannot derive normative statements from purely descriptive statements, no matter how closely the latter seem to bear on the former. This principle has come down to us as the "is-ought thesis," which states that one cannot logically derive an "ought" (i.e., a normative) statement from an "is" (i.e., a descriptive) statement. Although some philosophers have challenged this principle, it has been enormously persuasive in moral philosophy in the two centuries since Hume enunciated it. Any claim that violates it will have to provide a strong argument for the cogency of doing so. Such arguments are clearly not available in any inference from psychological egoism to ethical egoism. This means that if a case is to be made for ethical egoism, it will have to made independently of psychological egoism.

Are there any other reasons in support of ethical egoism? Some people have argued that each person should only be concerned with his or her own welfare because this is, as a matter of fact, the best means for bringing about the greatest amount of good for others. The basic idea behind this argument is that each person is the best authority on what he or she as an individual needs for well-being. It follows that if we interfere in the lives of other persons, for example, by trying to help them in some way, we stand a greater chance of harming than of helping them. So, acting solely for the sake of one's own self-interest is justified because it is the best policy for bringing about the greatest good for others.

This is an exceedingly weak argument. To begin with, it is far from clear that all actions performed for the sake of others are more likely to harm than to help them. Consider the case of giving money to relief agencies to supply desperately needed food to starving people. Is it really plausible to think that this is an unjustified "interference" in their lives and that they would be better off without our meddling? In this and many other cases one can think of this seems simply incredible. Second, and more important, in emphasizing the good that will come to others through the undiluted pursuit of self-interest, the author of this argument has abandoned her basic premise, namely, that one should be concerned only with promoting self-interest. If the aim of the argument is to show why exclusive concern with self-interest is justified, then one cannot appeal to the promotion of the well-being of others as an argument in its support. This argument, in other words, is mired in inconsistency.

This brings us to the last point to be made in criticism of ethical egoism. Ethical egoism, in the form we have been discussing, asserts that each person should be concerned only about his or her own welfare and self-interest. The hidden assumption seems to be that by acting selfishly, a person is more likely to have his or her well-being enhanced. But this assumption depends on even more fundamental assumptions about the kinds of beings we are. Here is a point at which a consideration of human nature becomes extremely relevant to understanding ethics. As psychological egoists emphasize, people are naturally concerned with their own welfare. It could hardly be otherwise: Those who display no concern whatsoever for their own welfare do not stay around long, especially in a world filled with innumerable dangers! But it is easy to overemphasize this fact to the exclusion of the equally important fact that most people naturally find themselves concerned with the welfare of others as well. The existence of a few sociopaths who seem to display no regard at all for other persons does not change this fact. Such people are, luckily, the exception rather than the rule. Most people naturally feel concern for the welfare of others, often in direct proportion to their degree of intimacy with these other people (immediate family, extended family, friends, acquaintances, local strangers, and distant strangers). Given this fact of human nature, it could be suggested that we are the kinds of beings who cannot be fully satisfied, who cannot be happy, and who cannot fulfill our nature, without being concerned with others. What this suggests is that the psychological egoist has overlooked an important aspect of human nature—that our well-being depends on the quality of our lives as social creatures—and that the ethical egoist counsels us to do something that is very unlikely to increase the chances of our living good lives.

In sum, perhaps the best answer to psychological egoism and ethical egoism is that (contrary to the former doctrine) we *are* capable of acting out of concern for the welfare of other persons, and that (contrary to the latter doctrine) doing so is far more likely to contribute to our genuine happiness and sense of well-being than is the single-minded pursuit of selfishly construed self-interest. To return to the question posed some time ago ("Is ethics possible, given the facts of human nature?"), we might well ask instead: "Given the kinds of beings that we are—reflective, social, and concerned with living good lives—how could the study of ethics be considered optional or avoidable?"

The Pursuit of Moral Wisdom

In the previous sections of this part of the book we have been examining various objections to taking the study of ethics seriously. From the considerations raised above, it would seem that each of these challenges to ethics faces some serious difficulties. But if so, then this leaves us free to explore ethics to see for ourselves whether there is something of value there. That is what the rest of this book is about. In this section we will try to provide you with a few suggestions that will make your exploration of alternative ethical perspectives more rewarding.

This text has been designed to facilitate the appearance of moral wisdom in the lives of its readers or at least to help them to begin the pursuit of moral wisdom. Your pursuit of moral wisdom should be considered as a kind of journey. Before embarking on any journey it is important to know something about your intended destination, as well as some of the things (including obstacles) that you are likely to encounter along the way. There is no such thing as the definitive road map for acquiring moral wisdom, but the serious traveler like yourself may benefit from a brief description of what awaits you as you make your way through the remainder of this book.

The major theme of this book is that there are distinctive "moral traditions" associated with the West and the East, that these moral traditions contain an invaluable source of moral wisdom, and that only by becoming aware of perspectives from *both* of these sources can one fully develop one's own potential for moral wisdom. Each of the parts of the major theme requires some comment.

By a viable moral tradition we mean a set of ideals and principles to guide conduct that have informed the lives of a significant number of people over a significant period of time and that continue to attract adherents today. The word *viable* comes from the Latin *vita*, or *life*. These moral traditions are paths that may be followed in guiding your actions and, through your actions, in forming your life. A number of such traditions prominent in the West (Europe and America) and the East (Asia) are represented in this text. As even a momentary inspection of the material in Parts II and III of this book indicates, moral traditions can be of very different sorts. They may be ancient, having originated thousands of years ago, or of fairly recent origin, having come into existence only in the last century or so. They may be associated with particular religions or be completely independent of any religious concerns whatsoever. What is important, however, is that a moral tradition provide basic principles or perspectives that may serve to guide one's actions in accordance with specified ideals.

This brings us to the second element of the main theme of this book. Each of these moral traditions contains valuable moral wisdom. Although individual philosophers have sometimes gone astray, in general it is safe to say that philosophers have always desired one thing more than anything else: wisdom. It is what distinguishes the philosopher from all other inquirers. It is even part of the very definition of the word *philosophy*. The word *philosophy* comes from two Greek words: *philos*, meaning love, and *sophia*, meaning wisdom. Philosophy is literally the love of wisdom, and philosophers are lovers of wisdom. Because one naturally pursues what one loves, philosophers are constantly in pursuit of wisdom, seeking it wherever it may be found.

So philosophy is essentially concerned with wisdom. Wisdom may be understood as a kind of interpretive knowledge, an understanding that includes awareness of the significant implications of what is known. Moral wisdom is wisdom concerning questions of action. The morally wise person knows how he or she should act, both in particular situations and in life in general. One reason for talking of moral wisdom, instead of moral "truth" (or "correctness"), is that the very notion of "wisdom" suggests an understanding or comprehension that includes, but is not restricted to, knowledge that can be formulated in any finite set of sentences. In other words, wisdom includes knowledge but also contains an elusive affective or interpretive component as well. Wisdom denotes not just correct understanding but also a deep insight into the significance and implications of that understanding. This point is especially important to keep in mind while considering the perspectives represented in Part III of this text. Eastern writers rarely present their views as the conclusions of clearly articulated logical arguments. More often, their views are presented metaphorically, through the use of stories or analogies that are designed to assist the seeker after wisdom in "seeing" something new, or in seeing something familiar in a new light. This requires not merely understanding in the sense of acquiring information, but rather putting oneself in a state of mind such that the value and significance of what is being said becomes evident. This is why substantial selections from a range of different perspectives are included. Because these perspectives may be unfamiliar to you, it may take some time and effort to acquire such an appreciative state of mind.

This brings us to the final aspect of the theme of this book—developing one's own potential for moral wisdom. One does not become morally wise simply by reading material that (one has been assured) contains moral wisdom. This is because every person exists in a particular context, in a particular society, at a particular juncture in history. Each of us is equipped with both shared social categories of understanding as well as unique psychological characteristics. What is comprehensible and genuinely enlightening for one person, given his or her constellation of circumstantial factors, may not be for another. Wisdom is not something that can be prepackaged and dispensed on demand. Its appearance requires both suitably presented material and a suitably receptive mind. One of these without the other fails to produce the desired experience.

The importance of attending to the efforts of earlier seekers after wisdom in one's own pursuit needs to be emphasized. One would hardly expect to walk into a chemistry lab, begin mixing chemicals at random, and expect to arrive at a significant chemical discovery. One would be far better off first learning about basic chemical principles and then applying one's knowledge in the laboratory. The same is true of moral wisdom. It would be foolish not to take advantage of the accumulated wisdom of important moral traditions in the pursuit of your own apprehension of moral wisdom. One of the most effective ways to do this is to read and reflect upon a substantial body of material expressing the core ideas of these traditions. The understanding gained can then form the basis for your own further discoveries.

It should be clear that acquiring moral wisdom is no simple matter. It requires a subtle interplay of reason and insight. Ethical principles, in order to be worthy of assent, need to be supported with relevant reasons. Yet such reasons are never sufficient to decisively place one principle or perspective over another. Ethical principles, and values, are always underdetermined by reasons. At some point one is forced to select values on insufficient grounds. This is because, in addition to being convinced by reasons in support of a given view, if one is to truly adopt this view as a guide to living well, one has to find central elements of the view deeply attractive. As the philosopher David Hume pointed out in another context, reason by itself is insufficient to move us to action. To be motivated to act, some kind of attractiveness of the principle one is acting on must be present as well.

Ideas that seem alien, strange, and "obviously wrong" are difficult to find attractive. Keeping an open mind about the ideas you encounter is therefore essential. But you should also try to evaluate the various views you encounter in this book. It may not be possible to determine in some definitive way whether a given perspective is absolutely true or not. This probably should not be your aim in working through the readings that follow. Instead, you might think of the reading selections as providing you with perspectives from which to view and understand your own life. Some of these perspectives will undoubtedly seem quite familiar to you, although the formal names by which philosophers refer to them may be entirely new to you. Other perspectives will strike you as new, different, or even bizarre. It is important to pay careful attention to both kinds of experience, because each can teach you something important. As you read each selection, you should ask yourself not only "Is this right?" but also: "Does this perspective help me make sense of my life?" "Can I make use of the insights here to lead a better life?"

"How can I apply the ideas here to make life better, both for myself and for others?" Not all the perspectives presented below will appeal to you. But some will. It is important in developing your own view to find out why some do not appeal to you and why others do.

To summarize these points, ethics, construed broadly, is the study of the "best life" for human beings. It is concerned with the proper ideals of human life, the nature of goodness, the criteria of right and wrong, the scope and limits of duties and obligations, and many other things besides. The goal of ethical inquiry and reflection is moral wisdom. Wisdom may be thought of as a kind of interpretive knowledge of the nature of things and their significance. Moral wisdom would then be interpretive knowledge concerning the proper conduct of life. Moral wisdom cannot be acquired simply by reading a text but rather requires sustained reflection on the nature of human existence and the principles that others before have found valuable.

The Broader Context of Moral Wisdom

One final point about the pursuit of moral wisdom must be mentioned. Sometimes philosophers approach important topics like the best life for human beings as if they could be studied quite apart from any other beliefs or considerations that human beings have. As at least some of the readings that follow demonstrate, this is often not possible. Ethical beliefs are not always, or even usually, isolated from larger conceptual frameworks that people use. This is true not just of the Eastern views represented in Part III (although it might seem more evident there), but also of some of the readings in Part II. St. Thomas Aquinas's moral theory, for example, presupposes an entire worldview based on his understanding of Christian doctrine. Evaluating an ethical theory therefore also requires, to some extent, evaluating an entire worldview. This should not be thought of as a negative. Intellectual coherence is a good thing. We want ethical views that cohere with the rest of our beliefs (otherwise they become impractical and irrelevant). So, our suggestion is this: As you consider the moral traditions that follow, consider also the larger worldviews presupposed by them. You may end up not just with new insights into morality but with an entirely new way of looking at, and interacting with, the world.

Suggestions for Further Reading

There is extensive literature on the topics discussed in this part of the book. Much of the recent discussion of the relationship between religion and morality is due to the work of Robert Merihew Adams. See his "A Modified Divine Command Theory of Ethical Wrongness," in *Religion and Morality: A Collection of Essays*, edited by G. Outka and J. P. Reeder, Jr. (New York: Doubleday and Co., 1973), pp. 318–334, and his more recent "Divine Command Metaethics Modified Again," *Journal of Religious Ethics*, vol. 7, no. 1 (Spring 1979), pp. 71–79. For a collection of articles on this topic (including the first Adams article cited above), see *Divine Commands and Morality*, edited by Paul Helm (Oxford: Oxford University Press, 1981). Philip Quinn, *Divine Commands and Moral Requirements* (Oxford: Oxford University Press, 1978), presents a view sympathetic to the relationship between morality and religion. For a brief overview of the issues, see Jonathan Berg, "How Could Ethics Depend on

Religion?" in *A Companion to Ethics*, edited by Peter Singer (Oxford: Blackwell, 1991), pp. 525–533. Probably the classic argument for the implications of cultural relativism for moral relativism is Ruth Benedict's "A Defense of Moral Relativism," *Journal of General Psychology*, vol. 10 (1934), pp. 59–82. See also her *Patterns of Culture* (New York: Penguin, 1934). For a defense of moral relativism, see Gilbert Harmon, "Moral Relativism Defended," *Philosophical Review*, vol. 84 (1975), pp. 3–22. The pros and cons of moral relativism are discussed in the second part of *Relativism: Cognitive and Moral*, edited by Michael Krausz and Jack W. Meiland (Notre Dame, Ind.: University of Notre Dame Press, 1982). For a survey of work on moral relativism, see Robert M. Stewart and Lynn L. Thomas's "Recent Work on Ethical Relativism," *American Philosophical Quarterly*, vol. 28 (1991), pp. 85–100. For a defense of a moderate form of moral relativism, see David Wong, "Relativism," in *A Companion to Ethics*, pp. 442–450. See also his book *Moral Relativity* (Berkeley: University of California Press, 1984). An excellent introductory ethics text that takes an explicitly pluralistic, but not relativistic, approach to moral theory is Lawrence M. Hinman's *Ethics: A Pluralistic Approach to Moral Theory* (Fort Worth, Tex.: Harcourt, Brace, Jovanovich, 1994). A good, brief introduction to the bearing of determinism on ethics is Robert Young, "The Implications of Determinism," in *A Companion to Ethics*, pp. 534–542. K. N. Jayatilleke, *Ethics in Buddhist Perspective* (Kandy, Sri Lanka: Buddhist Publication Society, 1972), discusses the issue of freedom and determinism and its bearing on ethics from a Buddhist perspective. The two major kinds of egoism are discussed in Kurt Baier, "Egoism," in *A Companion to Ethics*, pp. 197–204. The classic arguments against ethical egoism are in Joseph Butler's *Fifteen Sermons Upon Human Nature* (London: Macmillan, 1900). Thomas Nagel's *The Possibility of Altruism* (New York: Oxford University Press, 1970) is a more recent, and technical, treatment.

InfoTrac

metaethics, moral relativism, freedom, determinism, egoism, moral wisdom

PART II

Western Ethical Perspectives

That which is proper to each thing is by nature best and most pleasant for each thing; for man, therefore, the life according to reason is best and pleasantest, since reason more than anything else is man.

—ARISTOTLE, *NICOMACHEAN ETHICS*

THE PURSUIT OF MORAL WISDOM has been a constant in Western intellectual history. From the ancient Greeks to the present day (a period spanning some twenty-five hundred years) philosophers have been concerned with the nature of the good life for human beings, the ultimate criterion of right and wrong, and the fundamental principles of morality. Along this continuous path, certain thinkers and their visions of moral wisdom stand out as landmarks in the history of moral theorizing in the West. These thinkers represent not just particular, individual viewpoints, but rather more encompassing moral perspectives and ongoing moral traditions. Some of the most important of these thinkers and their traditions are represented in this part of the text.

Chapter 1 is devoted to ancient Greek virtue ethics. The major thinkers of concern here are Socrates, Plato, and Aristotle. All three were intensely concerned with the kind of character that one ought to strive to develop and with the nature and acquisition of *virtue*. Together they provide the basis for virtually all subsequent ethical theorizing in the West.

In the years following the collapse of the Roman Empire, the world of the ancient Greeks gave way to medieval Christendom. Two of the greatest thinkers of this long period of Western history known as the Middle Ages are Augustine and Thomas Aquinas, both devout Christians and saints of the Church. Both developed ethical perspectives that attempt to situate human actions in a world designed by God and governed by divinely instituted natural laws. Their distinctive views are discussed in Chapter 2.

The European Enlightenment of the eighteenth century represents a continuation of the dramatic break with the religiously oriented culture of the Middle Ages that began in the Renaissance of the sixteenth and seventeenth centuries. Individuals—and the distinctive features of human nature they exemplify—replace institutions as sources of authority. Chapter 3 discusses the ethical views of two of the most profound Enlightenment thinkers: David Hume, who emphasized the power of sentiment in the moral life, and Immanuel Kant, who emphasized the authority of reason.

The nineteenth century spawned a moral theory that was in many ways quite in step with larger developments taking place in society. Utilitarianism, as developed by Jeremy Bentham and John Stuart Mill, adopts an economic approach to assessing the consequences of actions for the production of happiness, where happiness is understood as pleasure. Bentham's formulation and Mill's modifications of utilitarianism are discussed in Chapter 4.

We have been emphasizing the historical context of each of the major traditions included in this part of the text. But because each of the perspectives arose in a particular historical context, it should not be concluded that these perspectives are only historical curiosities that are of no interest to us now. On the contrary, each of these perspectives embodies insights that can serve to enlighten our own moral reflection. Historical circumstances change, but the kinds of situations that humans find themselves in—situations that require ethical reflection—remain remarkably constant. These perspectives should therefore be thought of as valuable *resources* to draw upon in attempting to develop one's own mature ethical perspective.

Chapter 1

Greek Virtue Ethics

Introduction: Knowledge, Virtue, and Happiness

Serious ethical reflection of a distinctively philosophical nature began in the West with the Greeks of the fifth century B.C.E. Easily the three most important Greek philosophers to concern themselves with ethical matters were Socrates (470?–399 B.C.E.), Plato (427–347 B.C.E.), and Aristotle (384–322 B.C.E.). It is Socrates, in particular, who is often credited with turning our attention to ourselves, to inquiring into the questions of how one ought to live and to the nature of the best life for human beings. Socrates, more than any other person, introduced into Western philosophy the concern with things human, especially the concern with questions of goodness and justice. Socrates' inquiries were continued by his pupil, Plato. Plato explored the nature of central moral concepts more thoroughly than anyone before him (and more thoroughly than most philosophers since), and sought to ground moral judgments in objective standards of goodness. Plato's most famous student was Aristotle. Aristotle was more of a systematizer, who sought to lay out the structure of the good life for human beings and the means for attaining happiness.

Together these three philosophers represent a distinctive approach to moral wisdom. To oversimplify somewhat, what all these thinkers have in common that distinguishes their approach to ethics from many later ones is their emphasis on the nature and attainment of moral *virtue*. All three emphasize the importance of acquiring virtue for leading a life that is fully human. For the Greeks, the most important element of morality concerns a person's *character*, for it is from one's character that all of one's actions naturally flow. The goal of the moral life is to cultivate the very best character one can. Such a character displays a variety of virtues, or excellent qualities. Virtuous activity is a prerequisite for happiness. Although each of the three philosophers mentioned emphasized some of these concepts more than others, it is nonetheless true that knowledge, virtue, and happiness are three of the central concepts in Greek ethics. The connection between knowledge and virtuous action is especially strong in Socrates and Plato—as explained in the Profile that follows. The connection between the cultivation of virtue and the attainment of happiness reaches its fullest expression in Aristotle's *Nicomachean Ethics*, selections from which are included below.

Socrates and Plato: The Reality of the Good, the Identity of Knowledge and Virtue

There were, of course, Greek philosophers before Socrates, but their concern was primarily with understanding nature and the cosmos, rather than the good life for human beings. Socrates turned the spotlight on humanity, and doggedly pursued answers to questions about goodness, justice, piety, and wisdom. Socrates' method was interrogation: He strove for wisdom by questioning anyone who claimed to have it. Philosophy, for him, was best pursued through the give-and-take of conversation. He wrote nothing, preferring conversation to writing treatises.

Fortunately for us, however, one of the young men who followed Socrates around Athens as he questioned the "wise" later recorded much of his master's thinking. Plato's dialogues feature Socrates as the hero as he interrogates (and more often than not, publicly embarrasses) some of Athens' leading citizens. In the process of recording and dramatizing the words of his teacher, Plato also added many ideas of his own. His dialogues therefore contain the thought of Socrates as well as his own unique contributions to philosophy. (Deciding which ideas are Socrates' and which are Plato's is a difficult matter that has kept scholars busy for years. It need not detain us here.)

Plato's contributions to philosophy are far too extensive to try to adequately cover here, but one idea is so important for understanding his view of ethics and the good life for human beings that it must be mentioned. Like his teacher, Plato was deeply disturbed by the activities of a group of itinerant teachers known as sophists. Sophists claimed to be experts in teaching anyone (who was willing to pay for it) how to become eloquent and to give pleasing speeches. Such skills were highly valued in Athenian society, inasmuch as they could be put to good use in the service of one's political ambitions. Plato's objection to the activity of the sophists is that they seemed to him to care insufficiently about the *truth* of the claims they would teach young men to make. Some notable sophists even claimed that truth and morality are entirely relative. In the famous words of Protagoras, "Man is the measure of what is." Plato realized that if this was correct, then morality would be without any objective basis, and the pursuit of a good human life something of a sham. This was a very disturbing implication, and one that Plato believed was utterly mistaken.

Plato's solution to the challenge posed by the sophists was to postulate a realm of unchanging, eternal principles (the "Forms") that could serve as the objective basis for claims about truth and morality. A particular shape might truly be called a "circle," for instance if it "participated" in the Form of Circularity. Likewise a particular action might truly be called "good" because it participated in the Form of the Good. Plato's theory of forms was an attempt to provide a secure, objective foundation for claims of truth and goodness that was not dependent on the ever-changing world of nature or of human beings.

Plato's identification of good actions with the Form of the Good had an interesting consequence. It meant that insofar as forms could be known (and Plato believed that they could be known), then goodness is a matter of knowledge. He therefore has Socrates in his dialogues uphold a doctrine that is at first sight somewhat surprising, given what we think we know about human nature. According to Socrates (or Plato speaking through the figure of Socrates), knowledge and virtue are *one*, in the sense that if one *knows* what is right, then one will *do* what is right. Virtue is a kind of knowledge—knowledge of the Form of the Good. When a person chooses what is evil, she chooses it with the (mistaken) belief that it is *good*. The corollary to this doctrine is that no one ever knowingly does what is wrong. If one does what is wrong, then it must be because one *thought* that what one was doing was right. Evil actions, on this view, are the result of ignorance. If one truly knows the Good, one will perform good actions.

How is this surprising doctrine to be reconciled with cases from everyday life, far from uncommon, when a person apparently does precisely what they know to be wrong? It is not easy to see how the Socratic-Platonic view could be true, but scholars have made a number of spirited attempts. Suppose, as Plato apparently believed, that good actions promote one's genuine happiness (which Plato conceived as a kind of harmony between the parts of the soul: reason, spirit, appetites). Everyone naturally seeks his or her own happiness, so everyone acts according to what they believe to be the right course of action. As Socrates states in the dialogue *Protagoras*, "No one who either knows or believes that there is another possible course of action, better than the one he is following, will ever continue on his present course when he might choose the latter." No one, that is, would deliberately choose what they knew would harm them, and no one would deliberately reject something they knew to be beneficial. So when a person appears to act in a way that they know is wrong, we have to ask in what *sense* they know this action to be wrong. Is it a kind of theoretical belief that they might assent to if pressed, or is it a deep personal conviction that they believe in, heart and soul? In the first case a person might fail to attend to the wrongness of the action they are performing, and not really believe that it is wrong. In the second case, however, it would be harder to see how a person could perform actions that they knew in this strong sense were wrong.

Another suggestion made to account for Socrates' "virtue is knowledge" doctrine is that because Socrates governed himself by rational thought, for *him* it was true that virtue was identical with knowledge of the right thing to do. If only all of us could attain the rationality of Socrates, and bring our desires and passions under rational control, we too would always do what we know to be right. This is, of course, little comfort to those of us not blessed with the consistent rationality of a Socrates. For us, knowing what is right and acting in accordance with this knowledge are, all too often, two quite different things. This fact of human nature was appreciated by Aristotle. His theory of moral virtue is designed, at least in part, to overcome the problems of the strict identification of virtue with knowledge found in the thought of his predecessors, Socrates and Plato.

Aristotle: Virtue and Human Flourishing

The nature of a human being is not what he is born as, but what he is born for.

—ARISTOTLE

Socrates had found a remarkable student in Plato. Plato, likewise, found an equally remarkable student in Aristotle. What is known about Aristotle's life is easily summarized. He was born in Stagira, a region just to the north of Greece in present-day

Macedonia, in 384 B.C.E. His father, Nicomachus, was a physician with connections at the Macedonian court. At the age of seventeen Aristotle went to Athens to study in Plato's Academy (probably the world's first university), and spent the next twenty years there, where he earned the nickname "the brains of the school." After Plato's death in 347 B.C.E., the Academy passed into the hands of Speusippus, Plato's nephew, and Aristotle decided to start his own school, first at Assos, and then at Mytilene on the island of Lesbos. After two years he was invited by Philip of Macedonia to be the tutor of the then thirteen-year-old Alexander (later to be known as Alexander the Great). After serving as a tutor for three years, Aristotle moved, first to his native Stagira, and then to Athens, where he opened his school, the Lyceum. There he spent the next twelve years teaching and writing. Alexander was not a popular figure in Athens, so when news of his death reached Athens in 323, Aristotle, because of his connections with the conqueror, was faced with trumped-up charges of impiety. He left the city, he is supposed to have said, lest Athens "sin twice against philosophy" (the first time, of course, was when the Athenian citizens had executed Socrates on similarly trumped-up charges of impiety). With his family he fled to Chalcis, the birthplace of his mother. He died there soon after, in 322, at the age of sixty-two. He left behind a treasure trove of writings that have continued to exert a profound influence on Western civilization.

Like Plato, Aristotle wrote both dialogues and more systematic treatises, but whereas the systematic treatises of Plato have been lost and his dialogues preserved, with Aristotle just the opposite is the case. The systematic treatises we have from Aristotle were apparently originally written as lecture notes delivered on various subjects at the Lyceum. These notes, like Aristotle's interests, were encyclopedic. He wrote on virtually every subject then known, and he invented many more subjects that are familiar to us today. Among the treatises we have from him are ones on physics, biology, psychology, meteorology, poetry, politics, logic, metaphysics, and rhetoric. On each of these topics he had original and, more often than not, brilliant things to say. Because he frequently begins a treatise by skillfully reviewing what has previously been said on the topic before going on to present his own views, and because he set such a high standard for intellectual inquiry for everyone following him, he has been called "the master of those who know." In the Middle Ages, so great was his stature that he was known simply as "The Philosopher."

Aristotle's moral theory is summarized in the *Nicomachean Ethics* (so named because the work was edited by Nicomachus, Aristotle's son, after his father's death). This book contains Aristotle's mature thinking on the nature and attainment of the best life for human beings. Ethics is for Aristotle a practical science, one aimed not at theoretical knowledge, but rather at action. The goal is to lead the very best life it is possible for humans to lead. The *Ethics* attempts to describe such a life in detail.

In the first book of the *Ethics* (most of which is included below), Aristotle makes it clear that for him ethics is the science of human teleology. The word *teleology* refers to the purposefulness or goal-directedness of things. Things act according to their nature and for their distinctive good. Acorns develop into oak trees, for example, because the mature oak tree is in some sense the realization of the nature of the acorn. The same principle applies to human beings. We act so as to realize our true natures. According to Aristotle, this realization consists in achieving happiness. Happiness is realized when a human being is living a life that is suitable for human beings. Happiness is what we all want most of all. It is, according to Aristotle, the final and self-sufficient good for human beings. The notion of happiness therefore occupies an important role in Aristotle's ethical theory.

How do human beings attain happiness, and what is it? The word Aristotle uses for happiness is *eudaimonia*. Unlike the meaning of the word *happiness* in English, by *eudaimonia* Aristotle means something that is not a feeling, but rather the activity of living well. It is not far from the notion of proper functioning. The proper function of a knife is to cut cleanly. The proper function of a key is to fit the mechanism of a lock precisely. Likewise, the proper function of human beings, for Aristotle, is to cultivate virtue in accordance with reason. Happiness, thus understood, is not a momentary sense of well-being, but the attainment of a lifetime. Such an achievement does not happen automatically, just in virtue of being alive. How then do we acquire it? Aristotle's answer is that we have to develop and exercise the appropriate virtues if we want to attain happiness.

Unfortunately, the word *virtue* has, since Victorian times, taken on a constricted meaning, suggesting to some people that it refers only (or primarily) to sexual restraint. But for Aristotle, as for Plato and their contemporaries, virtue (*arete*) had a quite different meaning. For them it meant *excellence*, or that set of properties that would permit a person to fulfill his function well. Virtues are deeply ingrained habits that guide one's actions. Aristotle defines virtue in the following terms: "Virtue, then, is a state of character concerned with choice, lying in a mean, i.e., the mean relative to us, this being determined by a rational principle, and by that principle by which the man of practical wisdom would determine it." (*Nicomachean Ethics*, Book II, Chapter 6). Taken together, the set of one's virtues makes up one's character. Recall that the proper goal of human life is happiness. So virtues would be qualities that permit a person to become happy. Who wouldn't want such virtues? The nature and acquisition of virtue is the subject of the second set of reading selections that follow.

The central concern of Aristotle's *Ethics* is happiness and how to attain it. Some people mistakenly identify happiness with pleasure, an identification Aristotle explicitly rejects. Pleasure is obviously a good thing. But what sort of a good thing is it, and what is its relationship to happiness? Aristotle discusses the nature of pleasure in the last reading selection included below. He notes that for each activity there is a distinctive pleasure associated with it. Although pleasure is good, it is not the chief good. This place is reserved for happiness. According to Aristotle, genuine happiness does not consist in amusement, but rather in contemplation. This is the exercise of our best part—reason—and this makes us akin to the gods and almost divine ourselves. It is on this note that Aristotle ends the *Ethics*, having established the life of the philosopher as above all blessed and happy and dear to the gods.

If there is a fundamental theme in Aristotle's moral theory, it is that a good life for human beings has a structure to it, and does not happen haphazardly. It is the result of appropriate activities designed to make oneself a certain kind of person, a person possessing virtue (excellence), and aiming at genuine happiness as one's goal. Aristotle's *Ethics* has provided an invaluable source of moral wisdom for innumerable people in the two millennia since it was written. It still merits careful reading today.

Reading Questions

1. *On the good for human beings:* How does Aristotle define "happiness"? According to Aristotle, what are the chief characteristics of happiness? How does he arrive at this definition? According to Aristotle, what is the distinctive "function" of human beings, and how does this relate to his understanding of happiness? Is happiness attainable without some measure of prosperity?

2. *On the nature of virtue:* According to Aristotle, how is virtue related to the attainment of happiness? How does Aristotle define "moral virtue"? How are such virtues acquired? What sort of "rule" does Aristotle provide to determine the nature of virtuous actions? What are some prominent examples of following this rule that Aristotle discusses?

3. *On pleasure and happiness:* How does Aristotle define "pleasure"? In what sense does pleasure "complete" an activity? What makes some pleasures superior to others? What is the ultimate standard of pleasure? What does Aristotle consider to be the best activity for human beings to engage in? Why? What, ultimately, is the role of philosophy in achieving happiness?

The Good for Human Beings

ARISTOTLE

Subject of Our Inquiry

ALL HUMAN ACTIVITIES AIM AT SOME GOOD: SOME GOODS SUBORDINATE TO OTHERS

1. Every art and every inquiry, and similarly every action and pursuit, is thought to aim at some good; and for this reason the good has rightly been declared to be that at which all things aim. But a certain difference is found among ends; some are activities, others are products apart from the activities that produce them. Where there are ends apart from the actions, it is the nature of the products to be better than the activities. Now, as there are many actions, arts, and sciences, their ends also are many; the end of the medical art is health, that of shipbuilding a vessel, that of strategy victory, that of economics wealth. But where such arts fall under a single capacity—as bridle-making and the other arts concerned with the equipment of horses fall under the art of riding, and this and every military action under strategy, in the same way other arts fall under yet others—in all of these the ends of the master arts are to be preferred to all the subordinate ends; for it is for the sake of the former that the latter are pursued. It makes no difference whether the activities themselves are the ends of the actions, or something else apart from the activities, as in the case of the sciences just mentioned.

THE SCIENCE OF THE GOOD FOR MAN . . .

2. If, then, there is some end of the things we do, which we desire for its own sake (everything else being desired for the sake of this), and if we do not choose everything for the sake of something else (for at that rate the process would go on to infinity, so that our desire would be empty and vain), clearly this must be the good and the chief good. Will not the knowledge of it, then, have a great influence on life? Shall we not, like archers who have a mark to aim at, be more likely to hit upon what is right? If so, we must try, in outline at least, to determine what it is, and of which of the sciences or capacities it is the object. . . .

From Aristotle, Nicomachean Ethics, *Book I, sections 1, 2, 7, 8, translated by W. D. Ross (1925). Reprinted by permission of Oxford University Press.*

THE GOOD MUST BE SOMETHING FINAL AND SELF-SUFFICIENT. DEFINITION OF HAPPINESS REACHED BY CONSIDERING THE CHARACTERISTIC FUNCTION OF MAN

7. Let us again return to the good we are seeking, and ask what it can be. It seems different in actions and arts; it is different in medicine, in strategy, and in the other arts likewise. What then is the good of each? Surely that for whose sake everything else is done. In medicine this is health, in strategy victory, in architecture a house, in any other sphere something else, and in every action and pursuit the end; for it is for the sake of this that all men do whatever else they do. Therefore, if there is an end for all that we do, this will be the good achievable by action, and if there are more than one, these will be the goods achievable by action.

So the argument has by a different course reached the same point; but we must try to state this even more clearly. Since there are evidently more than one end, and we choose some of these (e.g., wealth, flutes, and in general instruments) for the sake of something else, clearly not all ends are final ends; but the chief good is evidently something final. Therefore, if there is only one final end, this will be what we are seeking, and if there are more than one, the most final of these will be what we are seeking. Now we call that which is in itself worthy of pursuit more final than that which is worthy of pursuit for the sake of something else, and that which is never desirable for the sake of something else more final than the things that are desirable both in themselves and for the sake of that other thing, and therefore we call final without qualification that which is always desirable in itself and never for the sake of something else.

Now such a thing happiness, above all else, is held to be; for this we choose always for itself and never for the sake of something else, but honor, pleasure, reason, and every virtue we choose indeed for themselves (for if nothing resulted from them we should still choose each of them), but we choose them also for the sake of happiness, judging that through them we shall be happy. Happiness, on the other hand, no one chooses for the sake of these, nor, in general, for anything other than itself.

From the point of view of self-sufficiency the same result seems to follow; for the final good is thought to be self-sufficient. Now by self-sufficient we do not mean that which is sufficient for a man by himself, for one who lives a solitary life, but also for parents, children, wife, and in general for his friends and fellow citizens, since man is born for citizenship. But some limit must be set to this; for if we extend our requirement to ancestors and descendants and friends' friends we are in for an infinite series. Let us examine this question, however, on another occasion; the self-sufficient we now define as that which when isolated makes life desirable and lacking in nothing; and such we think happiness to be; and further we think it most desirable of all things, not a thing counted as one good thing among others—if it were so counted it would clearly be made more desirable by the addition of even the least of goods; for that which is added becomes an excess of goods, and of goods that greater is always more desirable. Happiness, then, is something final and self-sufficient, and is the end of action.

Presumably, however, to say that happiness is the chief good seems a platitude, and a clearer account of what it is is still desired. This might perhaps be given, if we could first ascertain the function of man. For just as for a flute-player, a sculptor, or any artist, and, in general, for all things that have a function or activity, the good and the "well" is thought to reside in the function, so would it seem to be for man, if he has a function. Have the carpenter, then, and the tanner certain functions or activities, and has man none? Is he born without a function? Or as eye, hand, foot, and in general each of the parts evidently has a function, may one lay it down that man similarly has a function apart from all these? What then can this be? Life seems to belong even to plants, but we are seeking what is peculiar to man. Let us exclude, therefore, the life of nutrition and growth. Next there would be a life of perception, but *it* also seems to be shared even by the horse, the ox, and every animal. There remains, then, an active life of the elements that has a rational principle; of this, one part has such a principle in the sense of being obedient to one, the other in the sense of possessing one and exercising thought. And, as "life of the rational element" also has two meanings, we must state that life in the sense of activity is what we mean; for this seems to be the more proper sense of the term. Now if the function of man is an activity of soul which follows or implies a rational principle, and if we say "a so-and-so" and "a good so-and-so" have a function which is the same in kind, e.g., a lyre-player and a good lyre-player, and so without qualification in all cases, eminence in respect of goodness being added to the name of the function (for the function of a lyre-player is to play the lyre, and that of a good lyre-player is to do so well): if this is the case (and we state the function of man to be a certain kind of life, and this to be an activity or actions of the soul implying a rational principle, and the function of a good man to be the good and noble performance of these, and if any action is well performed when it is performed in accordance with the appropriate excellence: if this is the case), human good turns out to be activity of soul exhibiting excellence, and if there are more than one excellence, in accordance with the best and most complete.

But we must add "in a complete life." For one swallow does not make a summer, nor does one day; and so too one day, or a short time, does not make a man blessed and happy. . . .

OUR DEFINITION IS CONFIRMED BY CURRENT BELIEFS ABOUT HAPPINESS

8. But we must consider happiness in the light not only of our conclusion and our premises, but also of what is commonly said about it; for with a true view all the data harmonize, but with a false one the facts soon clash. Now goods have been divided into three classes, and some are described as external, others as relating to soul or body; we call those that relate to soul most properly and truly goods, and psychical actions and activities we call as relating to soul. Therefore our account must be sound, at least according to this view, which is an old one and agreed on by philosophers. It is correct also in that we identify the end with certain actions and activities; for thus it falls among goods of the soul and not among external goods. Another belief which harmonizes with our account is that the happy man lives well and fares well; for we have practically defined happiness as a sort of living and faring well. The characteristics that are looked for in happiness seem also, all of them, to belong to what we have defined happiness as being. For some identify happiness with virtue, some with practical wisdom, others with a kind of philosophic wisdom, others with these, or one of these, accompanied by pleasure or not without pleasure; while others include also external prosperity. Now some of these views have been held by many men and men of old, others by a few eminent persons; and it is not probable that either of these should be entirely mistaken, but rather that they should be right in at least some one respect, or even in most respects.

With those who identify happiness with virtue or some one virtue our account is in harmony; for to virtue belongs virtuous activity. But it makes perhaps no small difference whether we place the chief good in possession or in use, in state of mind or in activity. For the state of mind may exist without producing any good result, as in a man who is asleep or in some other way quite inactive, but the activity cannot; for one who has the activity will of necessity be acting,

and acting well. And as in the Olympic Games it is not the most beautiful and the strongest that are crowned but those who compete (for it is some of these that are victorious), so those who act win, and rightly win, the noble and good things in life.

Their life is also in itself pleasant. For pleasure is a state of *soul*, and to each man that which he is said to be a lover of is pleasant; e.g., not only is a horse pleasant to the lover of horses, and a spectacle to the lover of sights, but also in the same way just acts are pleasant to the lover of justice and in general virtuous acts to the lover of virtue. Now for most men their pleasures are in conflict with one another because these are not by nature pleasant, but the lovers of what is noble find pleasant the things that are by nature pleasant; and virtuous actions are such, so that these are pleasant for such men as well as in their own nature. Their life, therefore, has no further need of pleasure as a sort of adventitious charm, but has its pleasure in itself. For, besides what we have said, the man who does not rejoice in noble actions is not even good; since no one would call a man just who did not enjoy acting justly, nor any man liberal who did not enjoy liberal actions; and similarly in all other cases. If this is so, virtuous actions must be in themselves pleasant. But they are also *good* and *noble*, and have each of these attributes in the highest degree, since the good man judges well about these attributes; his judgment is such as we have described. Happiness then is the best, noblest, and most pleasant thing in the world, and these attributes are not severed as in the inscription at Delos—

Most noble is that which is justest, and best is
    health;
But most pleasant it is to win what we love.

For all these properties belong to the best activities; and these, or one—the best—of these, we identify with happiness.

Yet evidently, as we said, it needs the external goods as well; for it is impossible, or not easy, to do noble acts without the proper equipment. In many actions we use friends and riches and political power as instruments; and there are some things the lack of which takes the luster from happiness—good birth, goodly children, beauty; for the man who is very ugly in appearance or ill-born or solitary and childless is not very likely to be happy, and perhaps a man would be still less likely if he had thoroughly bad children or friends or had lost good children or friends by death. As we said, then, happiness seems to need this sort of prosperity in addition; for which reason some identify happiness with good fortune, though others identify it with virtue. . . .

Moral Virtue

ARISTOTLE

Kinds of Virtue

DIVISION OF THE FACULTIES, AND
RESULTANT DIVISION OF VIRTUE
INTO INTELLECTUAL AND MORAL

13. Since happiness is an activity of soul in accordance with perfect virtue, we must consider the nature of virtue; for perhaps we shall thus see better the nature of happiness. . . . But clearly the virtue we must study is human virtue; for the good we were seeking was human good and the happiness human happiness. By human virtue we mean not that of the body but that of the soul; and happiness also we call an activity of soul. . . .

Virtue is distinguished into kinds . . . ; for we say that some of the virtues are intellectual and others moral, philosophic wisdom and understanding and practical wisdom being intellectual, liberality and temperance moral. For in speaking about a man's character we do not say that he is wise or has understanding, but that he is good-tempered or temperate; yet we praise the wise man also with respect to his state of mind; and of states of mind we call those which merit praise virtues.

Moral Virtue, How Produced, in What Medium and in What Manner Exhibited

MORAL VIRTUE, LIKE THE ARTS,
IS ACQUIRED BY REPETITION OF
THE CORRESPONDING ACTS

1. Virtue, then, being of two kinds, intellectual and moral, intellectual virtue in the main owes both its birth and its growth to teaching (for which reason it requires experience and time), while moral virtue comes about as a result of habit. . . . From this it is also plain that none of the moral virtues arises in us by nature; for nothing that exists by nature can form a habit contrary to its nature. For instance the stone which by nature moves downward cannot be habituated to move upward, not even if one tries to train it by throwing it up ten thousand times; nor can fire be

habituated to move downward, nor can anything else that by nature behaves in one way be trained to behave in another. Neither by nature, then, nor contrary to nature do the virtues arise in us; rather we are adapted by nature to receive them, and are made perfect by habit.

Again, of all the things that come to us by nature we first acquire the potentiality and later exhibit the activity (this is plain in the case of the senses; for it was not by often seeing or often hearing that we got these senses, but on the contrary we had them before we used them, and did not come to have them by using them); but the virtues we get by first exercising them, as also happens in the case of the arts as well. For the things we have to learn before we can do them, we learn by doing them, e.g., men become builders by building and lyre-players by playing the lyre; so too we become just by doing just acts, temperate by doing temperate acts, brave by doing brave acts. . . .

Again, it is from the same causes and by the same means that every virtue is both produced and destroyed, and similarly every art; for it is from playing the lyre that both good and bad lyre-players are produced. And the corresponding statement is true of builders and of all the rest; men will be good or bad builders as a result of building well or badly. For if this were not so, there would have been no need of a teacher, but all men would have been born good or bad at their craft. This, then, is the case with the virtues also; by doing the acts that we do in our transactions with other men we become just or unjust, and by doing the acts that we do in the presence of danger, and by being habituated to feel fear or confidence, we become brave or cowardly. The same is true of appetites and feelings of anger; some men become temperate and good-tempered, others self-indulgent and irascible, by behaving in one way or the other in the appropriate circumstances. Thus, in one word, states of character arise out of like activities. This is why the activities we exhibit must be of a certain kind; it is because the states of character correspond to the differences between these. It makes no

From Aristotle, Nicomachean Ethics, *Book I, section 13; Book II, sections 1–3, 5–7, 9, translated by* W. D. Ross *(1925). Reprinted by permission of Oxford University Press.*

small difference, then, whether we form habits of one kind or of another from our very youth; it makes a very great difference, or rather *all* the difference.

THESE ACTS CANNOT BE PRESCRIBED EXACTLY, BUT MUST AVOID EXCESS AND DEFECT

2. Since, then, the present inquiry does not aim at theoretical knowledge like the others (for we are inquiring not in order to know what virtue is, but in order to become good, since otherwise our inquiry would have been of no use), we must examine the nature of actions, namely how we ought to do them; for these determine also the nature of the states of character that are produced, as we have said. . . .

. . . First, then, let us consider this, that it is the nature of such things to be destroyed by defect and excess, as we see in the case of strength and of health (for to gain light on things imperceptible we must use the evidence of sensible things); exercise either excessive or defective destroys the strength, and similarly drink or food which is above or below a certain amount destroys the health, while that which is proportionate both produces and increases and preserves it. So too is it, then, in the case of temperance and courage and the other virtues. For the man who flies from and fears everything and does not stand his ground against anything becomes a coward, and the man who fears nothing at all but goes to meet every danger becomes rash; and similarly the man who indulges in every pleasure and abstains from none becomes self-indulgent, while the man who shuns every pleasure, as boors do, becomes in a way insensible; temperance and courage, then, are destroyed by excess and defect, and preserved by the mean.

But not only are the sources and causes of the origination and growth the same as those of their destruction, but also the sphere of their actualization will be the same; for this is also true of the things which are more evident to sense, e.g. of strength; it is produced by taking much food and undergoing much exertion, and it is the strong man that will be most able to do these things. So too is it with the virtues; by abstaining from pleasures we become temperate, and it is when we have become so that we are most able to abstain from them; and similarly too in the case of courage; for by being habituated to despise things that are fearful and to stand our ground against them we become brave, and it is when we have become so that we shall be most able to stand our ground against them.

PLEASURE IN DOING VIRTUOUS ACTS IS A SIGN THAT THE VIRTUOUS DISPOSITION HAS BEEN ACQUIRED: A VARIETY OF CONSIDERATIONS SHOW THE ESSENTIAL CONNECTION OF MORAL VIRTUE WITH PLEASURE AND PAIN

3. We must take as a sign of states of character the pleasure or pain that supervenes upon acts; for the man who abstains from bodily pleasures and delights in this very fact is temperate, while the man who is annoyed at it is self-indulgent, and he who stands his ground against things that are terrible and delights in this or at least is not pained is brave, while the man who is pained is a coward. For moral excellence is concerned with pleasures and pains; it is on account of the pleasure that we do bad things, and on account of the pain that we abstain from noble ones. Hence we ought to have been brought up in a particular way from our very youth, as Plato says, so as both to delight in and to be pained by the things that we ought; this is the right education.

Again, if the virtues are concerned with actions and passions, and every passion and every action is accompanied by pleasure and pain, for this reason also virtue will be concerned with pleasures and pains. This is indicated also by the fact that punishment is inflicted by these means; for it is a kind of cure, and it is the nature of cures to be effected by contraries.

Again, as we said but lately, every state of soul has a nature relative to and concerned with the kind of things by which it tends to be made worse or better; but it is by reason of pleasures and pains that men become bad, by pursuing and avoiding these—either the pleasures and pains they ought not or when they ought not or as they ought not, or by going wrong in one of the other similar ways that may be distinguished. Hence men even define the virtues as certain states of impassivity and rest; not well, however, because they speak absolutely, and do not say "as one ought" and "as one ought not" and "when one ought or ought not," and the other things that may be added. We assume, then, that this kind of excellence tends to do what is best with regard to pleasures and pains, and vice does the contrary.

The following facts also may show us that virtue and vice are concerned with these same things. There being three objects of choice and three of avoidance, the noble, the advantageous, the pleasant, and their contraries, the base, the injurious, the painful, about all of these the good man tends to go right and the bad man to go wrong, and especially about pleasure;

for this is common to the animals, and also it accompanies all objects of choice; for even the noble and the advantageous appear pleasant.

Again, it has grown up with us all from our infancy; this is why it is difficult to rub off this passion, engrained as it is in our life. And we measure even our actions, some of us more and other less, by the rule of pleasure and pain. For this reason, then, our whole inquiry must be about these; for to feel delight and pain rightly or wrongly has no small effect on our actions.

Again, it is harder to fight with pleasure than with anger, to use Heraclitus' phrase, but both art and virtue are always concerned with what is harder; for even the good is better when it is harder. Therefore for this reason also the whole concern both of virtue and of political science is with pleasures and pains; for the man who uses these well will be good, he who uses them badly bad.

That virtue, then, is concerned with pleasures and pains, and that by the acts from which it arises it is both increased and, if they are done differently, destroyed, and that the acts from which it arose are those in which it actualizes itself—let this be taken as said. . . .

Definition of Moral Virtue

THE GENUS OF MORAL VIRTUE: IT IS A STATE OF CHARACTER, NOT A PASSION, NOR A FACULTY

5. Next we must consider what virtue is. Since things that are found in the soul are of three kinds—passion, faculties, states of character—virtue must be one of these. By passions I mean appetite, anger, fear, confidence, envy, joy, friendly feeling, hatred, longing, emulation, pity, and in general the feelings that are accompanied by pleasure or pain; by faculties the things in virtue of which we are said to be capable of feeling these, e.g., of becoming angry or being pained or feeling pity; by states of character the things in virtue of which we stand well or badly with reference to the passions, e.g., with reference to anger we stand badly if we feel it violently or too weakly, and well if we feel it moderately; and similarly with reference to the other passions.

Now neither the virtues nor the vices are *passions*, because we are not called good or bad on the ground of our passions, but are so called on the ground of our virtues and our vices, and because we are neither praised nor blamed for our passions (for the man who feels fear or anger is not praised, nor is the man who simply feels anger blamed, but the man who feels it in a certain way), but for our virtues and our vices we *are* praised or blamed.

Again, we feel anger and fear without choice, but the virtues are modes of choice or involve choice. Further, in respect to the passions we are said to be moved, but in respect of the virtues and the vices we are said not to be moved but to be disposed in a particular way.

For these reasons also they are not *faculties*; for we are neither called good or bad, nor praised or blamed, for the simple capacity of feeling the passions; again, we have the faculties by nature, but we are not made good or bad by nature; we have spoken of this before.

If, then, the virtues are neither passions nor faculties, all that remains is that they should be *states of character*.

Thus we have stated what virtue is in respect of its genus.

THE DIFFERENTIA OF MORAL VIRTUE: IT IS A DISPOSITION TO CHOOSE THE MEAN

6. We must, however, not only describe virtue as a state of character, but also say what sort of state it is. We may remark, then, that every virtue or excellence both brings into good condition the thing of which it is the excellence and makes the work of that thing be done well; e.g., the excellence of the eye makes both the eye and its work good; for it is by the excellence of the eye that we see well. Similarly the excellence of the horse makes a horse both good in itself and good at running and at carrying its rider and at awaiting the attack of the enemy. Therefore, if this is true in every case, the virtue of man also will be the state of character which makes a man good and which makes him do his own work well.

How this is to happen we have stated already, but it will be made plain also by the following consideration of the specific nature of virtue. In everything that is continuous and divisible it is possible to take more, less, or an equal amount, and that either in terms of the thing itself or relatively to us; and the equal is an intermediate between excess and defect. By the intermediate in the object I mean that which is equidistant from each of the extremes, which is one and the same for all men; by the intermediate relatively to us that which is neither too much nor too little—and this is not one, nor the same for all. For instance, if ten is many and two is few, six is the intermediate, taken in terms of the object; for it exceeds and is exceeded by an equal amount; this is intermediate according to arithmetical proportion. But the intermediate relatively to us is not to be taken so; if ten pounds are too much for a particular person to eat and two too little, it does not follow that the trainer will order six pounds; for this also is perhaps too much for the person who is to take it, or too little—too little for Milo, too much for the beginner in athletic exercises. The same is true of running and wrestling. Thus a master of any art avoids excess and defect, but seeks the intermediate and chooses this—the intermediate not in the object but relatively to us.

If it is thus, then, that every art does its work well—by looking to the intermediate and judging its works by this standard (so that we often say of good works of art that it is not possible either to take away or to add anything, implying that excess and effect destroy the goodness of works of art, while the mean preserves it; and good artists, as we say, look to this in their work), and if, further, virtue is more exact and better than any art, as nature also is, then virtue must have the quality of aiming at the intermediate. I mean moral virtue; for it is this that is concerned with passions and actions, and in these there is excess, defect, and the intermediate. For instance, both fear and confidence and appetite and anger and pity and in general pleasure and pain may be felt both too much and too little, and in both cases not well; but to feel them at the right times, with reference to the right objects, toward the right people, with the right motive, and in the right way, is what is both intermediate and best, and this is characteristic of virtue. Similarly with regard to actions also there is excess, defect, and the intermediate. Now virtue is concerned with passions and actions, in which excess is a form of failure, and so is defect, while the intermediate is praised and is a form of success; and being praised and being successful are both characteristics of virtue. Therefore virtue is a kind of mean, since, as we have seen, it aims at what is intermediate.

Again, it is possible to fail in many ways (for evil belongs to the class of the unlimited, as the Pythagoreans conjectured, and good to that of the limited), while to succeed is possible only in one way (for which reason also one is easy and the other difficult—to miss the mark easy, to hit it difficult); for these reasons also, then, excess and defect are characteristic of vice, and the mean of virtue.

For men are good in but one way, but bad in many.

Virtue, then, is a state of character concerned with choice, lying in a mean, i.e., the mean relative to us, this being determined by a rational principle, and by that principle by which the man of practical wisdom would determine it. Now it is a mean between two vices, that which depends on excess and that which depends on defect; and again it is a mean because the vices respectively fall short of or exceed what is right in both passions and actions, while virtue both finds and chooses that which is intermediate. Hence in respect of what it is, i.e., the definition which states its essence, virtue is a mean, with regard to what is best and right an extreme.

But not every action nor every passion admits of a mean; for some have names that already imply badness, e.g., spite, shamelessness, envy, and in the case of actions adultery, theft, murder; for all of these and suchlike things imply by their names that they are themselves bad, and not the excesses or deficiencies of them. It is not possible, then, ever to be right with regard to them; one must always be wrong. Nor does goodness or badness with regard to such things depend on committing adultery with the right woman, at the right time, and in the right way, but simply to do any of them is to go wrong. It would be equally absurd, then, to expect that in unjust, cowardly, and voluptuous action there should be a mean, an excess, and a deficiency; for at that rate there would be a mean of excess and of deficiency, an excess of excess, and a deficiency of deficiency. But as there is no excess and deficiency of temperance and courage because what is intermediate is in a sense an extreme, so too of the actions we have mentioned there is no mean nor any excess and deficiency, but however they are done they are wrong; for in general there is neither a mean of excess and deficiency, nor excess and deficiency of a mean.

THE ABOVE PROPOSITION ILLUSTRATED BY REFERENCE TO PARTICULAR VIRTUES

7. We must, however, not only make this general statement, but also apply it to the individual facts. For among statements about conduct those which are general apply more widely, but those which are particular are more true, since conduct has to do with individual cases, and our statements must harmonize with the facts in these cases. We may take these cases from our table. With regard to feelings of fear and confidence courage is the mean; of the people who exceed, he who exceeds in fearlessness has no name (many of the states have no name), while the man who exceeds in confidence is rash, and he who exceeds in fear and falls short in confidence is a coward. With regard to pleasures and pains—not all of them, and not so much with regard to the pains—the mean is temperance, the excess self-indulgence. Persons deficient with regard to the pleasures are not often found; hence such persons also have received no name. But let us call them "insensible."

With regard to giving and taking of money the mean is liberality, the excess and the defect prodigality and meanness. In these actions people exceed and fall short in contrary ways; the prodigal exceeds in spending and falls short in taking, while the mean man exceeds in taking and falls short in spending. (At present we are giving a mere outline or summary, and are satisfied with this; later these states will be more exactly determined.) With regard to money there are also other dispositions—a mean, magnificence (for the magnificent man differs from the liberal man; the former deals with large sums, the latter with small ones), an excess, tastelessness and vulgarity, and a deficiency, niggardliness; these differ from the states opposed to liberality, and the mode of their difference will be stated later.

With regard to honor and dishonor the mean is proper pride, the excess is known as a sort of "empty vanity," and the deficiency is undue humility; and as we said liberality was related to magnificence, differing from it by dealing with small sums, so there is a state similarly related to proper pride, being concerned with small honors while that is concerned with great. For it is possible to desire honor as one ought, and more than one ought, and less, and the man who exceeds in his desires is called ambitious, the man who falls short unambitious, while the intermediate person has no name. The dispositions also are nameless, except that that of the ambitious man is called ambition. Hence the people who are at the extremes lay claim to the middle place; and we ourselves sometimes call the intermediate person ambitious and sometimes unambitious, and sometimes praise the ambitious man and sometimes the unambitious. The reason of our doing this will be stated in what follows; but now let us speak of the remaining states according to the method which has been indicated.

With regard to anger also there is an excess, a deficiency, and a mean. Although they can scarcely be said to have names, yet since we call the intermediate person good-tempered let us call the mean good temper; of the persons at the extremes let the one who exceeds be called irascible, and his vice irascibility, and the man who falls short an unirascible sort of person, and the deficiency unirascibility.

There are also three other means, which have a certain likeness to one another, but differ from one another: for they are all concerned with intercourse in words and actions, but differ in that one is concerned with truth in this sphere, the other two with pleasantness; and of this one kind is exhibited in giving amusement, the other in all the circumstances of life. We must therefore speak of these two, that we may the better see that in all things the mean is praiseworthy, and the extremes neither praiseworthy nor right, but worthy of blame. Now most of these states also have no names, but we must try, as in the other cases, to invent names ourselves so that we may be clear and easy to follow. With regard to truth, then, the intermediate is a truthful sort of person and the mean may be called truthfulness, while the pretense which exaggerates is boastfulness and the person characterized by it a boaster, and that which understates is mock modesty and the person characterized by it mock-modest. With regard to pleasantness in the giving of amusement the intermediate person is ready-witted and the disposition ready wit, the excess is buffoonery and the person characterized by it a buffoon, while the man who falls short is a sort of boor and his state is boorishness. With regard to the remaining kind of pleasantness, that which is exhibited in life in general, the man who is pleasant in the right way is friendly and the mean is friendliness, while the man who exceeds is an obsequious person if he has no end in view, a flatterer if he is aiming at his own advantage, and the man who falls short and is unpleasant in all circumstances is a quarrelsome and surly sort of person.

There are also means in the passions and concerned with the passions; since shame is not a virtue, and yet praise is extended to the modest man. For even in these matters one man is said to be intermediate, and another to exceed, as for instance the bashful man who is ashamed of everything; while he who falls short or is not ashamed of anything at all is shameless, and the intermediate person is modest. Righteous indignation is a mean between envy and spite, and these states are concerned with the pain and pleasure that are felt at the fortunes of our neighbors; the man who is characterized by righteous indignation is pained at undeserved good fortune, the envious man, going beyond him, is pained at all good fortune, and the spiteful man falls so far short of being pained that he even rejoices. . . .

THE MEAN IS HARD TO ATTAIN, AND IS GRASPED BY PERCEPTION, NOT BY REASONING

9. That moral virtue is a mean, then, and in what sense it is so, and that it is a mean between two vices, the one involving excess, the other deficiency, and that it is such because its character is to aim at what is intermediate in passions and in actions, has been sufficiently stated. Hence also it is no easy task to be good. For in everything it is no easy task to find the middle, e.g., to find the middle of a circle is not for everyone but for him who knows; so, too, anyone can get angry—that is easy—or give or spend money; but to do this to the right person, to the right extent, at the right time, with the right motive, and in the right way, *that* is not for everyone, nor is it easy; wherefore goodness is both rare and laudable and noble.

Hence he who aims at the intermediate must first depart from what is the more contrary to it, as Calypso advises—

Hold the ship out beyond that surf and spray.

For of the extremes one is more erroneous, one less so; therefore, since to hit the mean is hard in the extreme, we must as a second best, as people say, take the least of the evils; and this will be done best in the way we describe.

But we must consider the things toward which we ourselves also are easily carried away; for some of us tend to one thing, some to another; and this will be recognizable from the pleasure and the pain we feel. We must drag ourselves away to the contrary extreme; for we shall get into the intermediate state by drawing well away from error, as people do in straightening sticks that are bent.

Now in everything the pleasant or pleasure is most to be guarded against; for we do not judge it impartially. We ought, then, to feel toward pleasure as the elders of the people felt toward Helen, and in all circumstances repeat their saying; for if we dismiss pleasure thus we are less likely to go astray. It is by doing this, then (to sum the matter up), that we shall best be able to hit the mean.

But this is no doubt difficult, and especially in individual cases; for it is not easy to determine both how and with whom and on what provocation and how long one should be angry; for we too sometimes praise those who fall short and call them good-tempered, but sometimes we praise those who get angry and call them manly. The man, however, who deviates little from goodness is not blamed, whether he do so in the direction of the more or of the less, but only the man who deviates more widely; for he does not fail to be noticed. But up to what point and to what extent a man must deviate before he becomes blameworthy it is not easy to determine by reasoning, any more than anything else that is perceived by the senses; such things depend on particular facts, and the decision rests with perception. So much, then, is plain, that the intermediate state is in all things to be praised, but that we must incline sometimes toward the excess, sometimes toward the deficiency; for so shall we most easily hit the mean and what is right.

Pleasure and Happiness

ARISTOTLE

Pleasure

TWO OPPOSED VIEWS ABOUT PLEASURE

1. After these matters we ought perhaps next to discuss pleasure. For it is thought to be most intimately connected with our human nature, which is the reason why in educating the young we steer them by the rudders of pleasure and pain; it is thought, too, that to enjoy the things we ought and to hate the things we ought has the greatest bearing on virtue of character.

For these things extend right through life, with a weight and power of their own in respect both to virtue and to the happy life, since men choose what is pleasant and avoid what is painful; and such things, it will be thought, we should least of all omit to discuss, especially since they admit of much dispute. For some say pleasure is the good, while others, on the contrary, say it is thoroughly bad—some no doubt being persuaded that the facts are so, and others thinking it has a better effect on our life to exhibit pleasure as a bad

From Aristotle, Nicomachean Ethics, *Book X, sections 1–2, 5–8, translated by W. D. Ross (1925). Reprinted by permission of Oxford University Press.*

thing even if it is not; for most people (they think) incline toward it and are the slaves of their pleasures, for which reason they ought to lead them in the opposite direction, since thus they will reach the middle state. But surely this is not correct. For arguments about matters concerned with feelings and actions are less reliable than facts: and so when they clash with the facts of perception they are despised, and discredit the truth as well; if a man who runs down pleasure is once seen to be aiming at it, his inclining toward it is thought to imply that it is all worthy of being aimed at; for most people are not good at drawing distinctions. True arguments seem, then, most useful, not only with a view to knowledge but with a view to life also; for since they harmonize with the facts they are believed, and so they stimulate those who understand them to live according to them. Enough of such questions; let us proceed to review the opinions that have been expressed about pleasure.

DISCUSSION OF THE VIEW THAT PLEASURE IS THE GOOD

2. Eudoxus thought pleasure was the good because he saw all things, both rational and irrational, aiming at it, and because in all things that which is the object of choice is what is excellent, and that which is most the object of choice the greatest good; thus the fact that all things moved toward the same object indicated that this was for all things the chief good (for each thing, he argued, finds its own good, as it finds its own nourishment); and that which is good for all things and at which all aim was *the* good. His arguments were credited more because of the excellence of his character than for their own sake; he was thought to be remarkably temperate, and therefore it was thought that he was not saying what he did say as a friend of pleasure, but that the facts really were so. He believed that the same conclusion followed no less plainly from a study of the contrary of pleasure: pain was in itself an object of aversion to all things, and therefore its contrary must be similarly an object of choice. And again, that is most an object of choice which we choose not because or for the sake of something else, and pleasure is admittedly of this nature; for no one asks to what end he is pleased, thus implying that pleasure is in itself an object of choice. Further, he argued that pleasure when added to any good, e.g., to just or temperate action, makes it more worthy of choice, and that it is only by itself that the good can be increased.

This argument seems to show it to be one of the goods, and no more a good than any other; for every

good is more worthy of choice along with another good than taken alone. And so it is by an argument of this kind that Plato proves the good *not* to be pleasure; he argues that the pleasant life is more desirable with wisdom than without, and that if the mixture is better, pleasure is not the good; for the good cannot become more desirable by the addition of anything to it. Now it is clear that nothing else, any more than pleasure, can be the good if it is made more desirable by the addition of any of the things that are good in themselves. What, then, is there that satisfies this criterion, which at the same time we can participate in? It is something of this sort that we are looking for. . . .

One might think that all men desire pleasure because they all aim at life; life is an activity, and each man is active about those things and with those faculties that he loves most; e.g., the musician is active with his hearing in reference to tunes, the student with his mind in reference to theoretical questions, and so on in each case; now pleasure completes the activities, and therefore life, which they desire. It is with good reason, then, that they aim at pleasure too, since for every one it completes life, which is desirable. But whether we choose life for the sake of pleasure or pleasure for the sake of life is a question we may dismiss for the present. For they seem to be bound up together and not to admit of separation, since without activity pleasure does not arise, and every activity is completed by the attendant pleasure.

PLEASURES DIFFER WITH THE ACTIVITIES WHICH THEY ACCOMPANY AND COMPLETE: CRITERION OF THE VALUE OF PLEASURES

5. For this reason pleasures seem, too, to differ in kind. For things different in kind are, we think, completed by different things (we see this to be true both of natural objects and of things produced by art, e.g., animals, trees, a painting, a sculpture, a house, an implement); and similarly, we think that activities differing in kind are completed by things differing in kind. Now the activities of thought differ from those of the senses, and both differ among themselves, in kind; so, therefore, do the pleasures that complete them.

This may be seen, too, from the fact that each of the pleasures is bound up with the activity it completes. For an activity is intensified by its proper pleasure, since each class of things is better judged of and brought to precision by those who engage in the activity with pleasure; e.g., it is those who enjoy geometrical thinking that become geometers and grasp the various propositions better, and similarly, those who are fond of music or of building, and so on, make progress in their proper function by enjoying it; so the pleasures intensify the activities; and what intensifies a thing is proper to it, but things different in kind have properties different in kind. . . .

Now since activities differ in respect of goodness and badness, and some are worthy to be chosen, others to be avoided, and others neutral, so, too, are the pleasures; for to each activity there is a proper pleasure. The pleasure proper to a worthy activity is good and that proper to an unworthy activity bad; just as the appetites for noble objects are laudable, those for base objects culpable. . . .

Each animal is thought to have a proper pleasure, as it has a proper function; viz. that which corresponds to its activity. If we survey then species by species, too, this will be evident; horse, dog, and man have different pleasures, as Heraclitus says, "asses would prefer sweepings to gold"; for food is pleasanter than gold to asses. So the pleasures of creatures different in kind differ in kind, and it is plausible to suppose that those of a single species do not differ. But they vary to no small extent, in the case of men at least; the same things delight some people and pain others, and are painful and odious to some, and pleasant to and liked by others. This happens, too, in the case of sweet things; the same things do not seem sweet to a man in a fever and a healthy man—nor hot to a weak man and one in good condition. The same happens in other cases. But in all such matters that which appears to the good man is thought to be really so. If this is correct, as it seems to be, and virtue and the good man as such are the measure of each thing, those also will be pleasures which appear so to him, and those things pleasant which he enjoys. If the things he finds tiresome seem pleasant to someone, that is nothing surprising; for men may be ruined and spoilt in many ways; but the things are not pleasant, but only pleasant to these people and to people in this condition. Those which are admittedly disgraceful plainly should not be said to be pleasures, except to a perverted taste; but of those that are thought to be good what kind of pleasure or what pleasure should be said to be that proper to man? Is it not plain from the corresponding activities? The pleasures follow these. Whether, then, the perfect and supremely happy man has one or more activities, the pleasures that perfect these will be said in the strict sense to be pleasures proper to man, and the rest will be so in a secondary and fractional way, as are the activities.

Happiness

HAPPINESS IS GOOD ACTIVITY, NOT AMUSEMENT

6. Now that we have spoken of the virtues, and the varieties of pleasure, what remains is to discuss in outline the nature of happiness, since this is what we state the end of human affairs to be. Our discussion will be the more concise if we first sum up what we have said already. We said, then, that it is not a state; for if it were it might belong to someone who was asleep throughout his life, living the life of a plant, or, again, to someone who was suffering the greatest misfortunes. If these implications are unacceptable, and we must rather class happiness as an activity, as we have said before, and if some activities are necessary, and desirable for the sake of something else, while others are so in themselves, evidently happiness must be placed among those desirable in themselves, not among those desirable for the sake of something else; for happiness does not lack anything, but is self-sufficient. Now those activities are desirable in themselves from which nothing is sought beyond the activity. And of this nature virtuous actions are thought to be; for to do noble and good deeds is a thing desirable to its own sake.

Pleasant amusements also are thought to be of this nature: we choose them not for the sake of other things; for we are injured rather than benefited by them, since we are led to neglect our bodies and our property. But most of the people who are deemed happy take refuge in such pastimes, which is the reason why those who are ready-witted at them are highly esteemed at the courts of tyrants; they make themselves pleasant companions in the tyrants' favorite pursuits, and that is the sort of man they want. Now these things are thought to be of the nature of happiness because people in despotic positions spend their leisure in them, but perhaps such people prove nothing; for virtue and reason, from which good activities flow, do not depend on despotic position; nor, if these people, who have never tasted pure and generous pleasure, take refuge in the bodily pleasures, should these for that reason be thought more desirable; for boys, too, think the things that are valued among themselves are the best. It is to be expected, then, that, as different things seem valuable to boys and to men, so they should to bad men and to good. Now, as we have often maintained, those things are both valuable and pleasant which are such to the good man; and to each man the activity in accordance with his own state is most desirable, and therefore to the good man that which is in accordance with virtue. Happiness, therefore, does not lie in amusement; it would, indeed, be strange if the end were amusement; and one were to take trouble and suffer hardship all one's life in order to amuse oneself. For, in a word, everything that we choose we choose for the sake of something else—except happiness, which is an end. Now to exert oneself and work for the sake of amusement seems silly and utterly childish. But to amuse oneself in order that one may exert oneself, as Anacharsis puts it, seems right; for amusement is a sort of relaxation, and we need relaxation because we cannot work continuously. Relaxation, then, is not an end; for it is taken for the sake of activity.

The happy life is thought to be virtuous; now a virtuous life requires exertion, and does not consist in amusement. And we say that serious things are better than laughable things and those connected with amusement, and that the activity of the better of any two things—whether it be two elements of our being or two men—is the more serious; but the activity of the better is *ipso facto* superior and more of the nature of happiness. And any chance person—even a slave—can enjoy the bodily pleasures no less than the best man; but no one assigns to a slave a share in happiness—unless he assigns to him also a share in human life. For happiness does not lie in such occupations, but, as we have said before, in virtuous activities.

HAPPINESS IN THE HIGHEST SENSE IS THE CONTEMPLATIVE LIFE

7. If happiness is activity in accordance with virtue, it is reasonable that it should be in accordance with the highest virtue; and this will be that of the best thing in us. Whether it be reason or something else that is this element which is thought to be our natural ruler and guide and to take thought of things noble and divine, whether it be itself also divine or only the most divine element in us, the activity of this in accordance with its proper virtue will be perfect happiness. That this activity is contemplative we have already said.

Now this would seem to be in agreement both with what we said before and with the truth. For, firstly, this activity is the best (since not only is reason the best thing in us, but the objects of reason are the best of knowable objects); and, secondly, it is the most continuous, since we can contemplate truth more continuously than we can *do* anything. And we think happiness ought to have pleasure mingled with it,

but the activity of philosophic wisdom is admittedly the pleasantest of virtuous activities; at all events the pursuit of it is thought to offer pleasures marvelous for their purity and their enduringness, and it is to be expected that those who know will pass their time more pleasantly than those who inquire. And the self-sufficiency that is spoken of must belong most to the contemplative activity. For while a philosopher, as well as a just man or one possessing any other virtue, needs the necessaries of life, when they are sufficiently equipped with things of that sort the just man needs people toward whom and with whom he shall act justly, and the temperate man, the brave man, and each of the others is in the same case, but the philosopher, even when by himself, can contemplate truth, and the better the wiser he is; he can perhaps do so better if he has fellow workers, but still he is the most self-sufficient. And this activity alone would seem to be loved for its own sake; for nothing arises from it apart from the contemplating, while from practical activities we gain more or less apart from the action. And happiness is thought to depend on leisure; for we are busy that we may have leisure, and make war that we may live in peace. Now the activity of the practical virtues is exhibited in political or military affairs, but the actions concerned with these seem to be unleisurely. Warlike actions are completely so (for no one chooses to be at war, or provokes war, for the sake of being at war; anyone would seem absolutely murderous if he were to make enemies of his friends in order to bring about battle and slaughter); but the action of the statesman also is unleisurely, and aims—beyond the political action itself—at despotic power and honors, or at all events happiness, for him and his fellow citizens, a happiness different from political action, and evidently sought as being different. So if among virtuous actions political and military actions are distinguished by nobility and greatness, and these are unleisurely and aim at an end and are not desirable for their own sake, but the activity of reason, which is contemplative, seems both to be superior in serious worth and to aim at no end beyond itself (and this augments the activity), and the self-sufficiency, leisureliness, unweariedness (so far as this is possible for man), and all the other attributes ascribed to the supremely happy man are evidently those connected with this activity, it follows that this will be the complete happiness of man, if it be allowed a complete term of life (for none of the attributes of happiness is *in*complete).

But such a life would be too high for man; for it is not in so far as he is man that he will live so, but in so far as something divine is present in him; and by so much as this is superior to our composite nature is its activity superior to that which is the exercise of the other kind of virtue. If reason is divine, then, in comparison with man, the life according to it is divine in comparison with human life. But we must not follow those who advise us, being men, to think of human things, and, being mortal, of mortal things, but must, so far as we can, make ourselves immortal, and strain every nerve to live in accordance with the best thing in us; for even if it be small in bulk, much more does it in power and worth surpass everything. And this would seem actually to *be* each man, since it is the authoritative and better part of him. It would be strange, then, if he were to choose not the life of himself but that of something else. And what we said before will apply now: that which is proper to each thing is by nature best and most pleasant for each thing; for man, therefore, the life according to reason is best and pleasantest, since reason more than anything else *is* man. This life therefore is also the happiest.

SUPERIORITY OF THE CONTEMPLATIVE LIFE FURTHER CONSIDERED

8. But in a secondary degree the life in accordance with the other kind of virtue is happy; for the activities in accordance with this befit our human estate. Just and brave acts, and other virtuous acts, we do in relation to each other, observing our respective duties with regard to contracts and services and all manner of actions and with regard to passions; and all of these seem to be typically human. Some of them seem even to arise from the body, and virtue of character to be in many ways bound up with the passions. Practical wisdom, too, is linked to virtue of character, and this to practical wisdom, since the principles of practical wisdom are in accordance with the moral virtues and rightness in morals is in accordance with practical wisdom. Being connected with the passions also, the moral virtues must belong to our composite nature; and the virtues of our composite nature are human; so, therefore, are the life and the happiness which correspond to these. The excellence of the reason is a thing apart: we must be content to say this much about it, for to describe it precisely is a task greater than our purpose requires. It would seem, however, also to need external equipment but little, or less than moral virtue does. Grant that both need the necessaries, and do so equally, even if the statesman's work is the more concerned with the body and things of that sort; for there will be little difference there; but in what they need for the exercise of their activities there

will be much difference. The liberal man will need money for the doing of his liberal deeds, and the just man too will need it for the returning of services (for wishes are hard to discern, and even people who are not just *pretend* to wish to act justly); and the brave man will need power if he is to accomplish any of the acts that correspond to his virtue, and the temperate man will need opportunity; for how else is either he or any of the others to be recognized? It is debated, too, whether the will or the deed is more essential to virtue, which is assumed to involve both; it is surely clear that its perfection involves both; but for deeds many things are needed, and more, the greater and nobler the needs are. But the man who is contemplating the truth needs no such thing, at least with a view to the exercise of his activity; indeed they are, one may say, even hindrances, at all events to his contemplation; but in so far as he is a man and lives with a number of people, he chooses to do virtuous acts; he will therefore need such aids to living a human life. . . .

. . . Happiness extends, then, just so far as contemplation does, and those to whom contemplation more fully belongs are more truly happy, not as a mere concomitant but in virtue of the contemplation; for this is in itself precious. Happiness, therefore, must be some form of contemplation.

But, being a man, one will also need external prosperity; for our nature is not self-sufficient for the purpose of contemplation, but our body also must be healthy and must have food and other attention. Still, we must not think that the man who is to be happy will need many things or great things, merely because he cannot be supremely happy without external goods; for self-sufficiency and action do not involve excess, and we can do noble acts without ruling earth and sea; for even with moderate advantages one can act virtuously (this is manifest enough; for private persons are thought to do worthy acts no less than despots—indeed even more); and it is enough that we should have so much as that; for the life of the man who is active in accordance with virtue will be happy. Solon, too, was perhaps sketching well the happy man when he described him as moderately furnished with externals but as having done (as Solon thought) the noblest acts, and lived temperately; for one can with but moderate possessions do what one ought. Anaxagoras also seems to have supposed the happy man not to be rich nor a despot, when he said that he would not be surprised if the happy man were to seem to most people a strange person; for they judge by externals, since these are all they perceive. The opinions of the wise seem, then, to harmonize with our arguments. But while even such things carry some conviction, the truth in practical matters is discerned from the facts of life; for these are the decisive factor. We must therefore survey what we have already said, bringing it to the test of the facts of life, and if it harmonizes with the facts we must accept it, but if it clashes with them we must suppose it to be mere theory. Now he who exercises his reason and cultivates it seems to be both in the best state of mind and most dear to the gods. For if the gods have any care for human affairs, as they are thought to have, it would be reasonable both that

they should delight in that which was best and most akin to them (i.e., reason) and that they should reward those who love and honor this most, as caring for the things that are dear to them and acting both rightly and nobly. And that all these attributes belong most of all to the philosopher is manifest. He, therefore, is the dearest to the gods. And he who is that will presumably be also the happiest; so that in this way too the philosopher will more than any other be happy. . . .

Discussion and Reflection Questions

1. *On the good for human beings:* Aristotle states at the very beginning of the *Ethics*, "Every art and every inquiry, and similarly every action and pursuit, is thought to aim at some good. . . ." Is this true? What about your reading these words right now? What good are you aiming at? What is the ultimate good that you aim to achieve by answering these questions? Is Aristotle right about the chief good for human beings?

2. *On the nature of virtue:* Aristotle explains that one becomes virtuous by performing virtuous actions. But how is this possible? How can you act virtuously if you are not already virtuous? Have you ever tried to overcome some bad habit? Did you succeed? Does Aristotle's analysis ring true? He also says that virtue lies in the mean between two extremes. Are there cases in which acting in an extreme manner is actually better than aiming at the mean? Would Aristotle consider this to be an objection to his view?

3. *On pleasure and happiness:* How important is pleasure in your life? What sorts of things give you the most pleasure? Is it true, as Aristotle suggests, that pleasure accompanies activities done well? Many people live as if exertion (e.g., work) was for the sake of amusement, but Aristotle suggests that the opposite is true (i.e., that amusement is for the sake of exertion). Which view seems right to you? How important is contemplation (e.g., reflection, thinking) in your life? Did Aristotle succeed in convincing you that the philosophic life is, above all, a happy life? Explain!

Suggestions for Further Reading

For some historical context regarding the perspectives on ethics discussed in this section, see K. J. Dover, *Greek Popular Morality in the Time of Plato and Aristotle* (Oxford: Blackwell, 1974). For a general introduction to Greek ethics, see William J. Prior, *Virtue and Knowledge: An Introduction to Ancient Greek Ethics* (New York: Routledge, 1991). N. Gulley, *The Philosophy of Socrates* (New York: St. Martin's Press, 1968), provides a detailed analysis of Socrates' approach to wisdom. For essays on all aspects of Socratic thought, see *Essays on the Philosophy of Socrates*, edited by Hugh H. Benson (New York: Oxford University Press, 1992). Plato's ethical theory is analyzed in Terence Irwin, *Plato's Moral Theory: The Early and Middle Dialogues* (New York: Oxford University Press, 1979). G. E. R. Lloyd, *Aristotle: The Growth and Structure of His Thought* (Cambridge: Cambridge University Press, 1968), gives an excellent account of the development of Aristotle's philosophy. His ethical views are discussed in Chapter 10. A number of books are worth consulting for further discussion of Aristotle's approach to ethics. See especially John Cooper, *Reason and Human Good in Aristotle* (Cambridge, Mass.: Harvard University Press, 1975); Roger Sullivan, *Morality and the Good Life*

(Memphis: Memphis State University, 1977); W. F. R. Hardie, *Aristotle's Ethical Theory*, 2nd ed. (Oxford: Oxford University Press, 1980); J. O. Urmson, *Aristotle's Ethics* (Oxford: Blackwell, 1988); Richard Kraut's *Aristotle on the Human Good* (Princeton, N.J.: Princeton University Press, 1989); Nancy Sherman, *The Fabric of Character: Aristotle's Theory of Virtue* (Oxford: Clarendon Press, 1989); and Gerard J. Hughes, *Aristotle on Ethics* (New York: Routledge Press, 2001). Two essays that take up specific issues in Aristotle's ethics are Dominic Scott, "Aristotle on Well-Being and Intellectual Contemplation: Primary and Secondary 'Eudaimonia,' " *Proceedings of the Aristotelian Society* 73 (Summer 2000): 225–243, and Lesley Brown, "What Is 'the Mean Relative to Us' in Aristotle's Ethics?" *Phronesis* 42 (1997): 77–93. A good collection of essays on nearly every aspect of Aristotle's ethical theory, written by leading Aristotle scholars, can be found in *Essays on Aristotle's Ethics*, edited by Amelie Oksenberg Rorty (Berkeley and Los Angeles: University of California Press, 1980). Much of the current revival of interest in virtue ethics is due to Alasdair MacIntyre's *After Virtue* (Notre Dame, Ind.: University of Notre Dame Press, 1981; 2nd ed., 1984). A critical evaluation of contemporary virtue theory is Greg Pence, "Virtue Theory," in *A Companion to Ethics*, edited by Peter Singer (Oxford: Blackwell, 1991), pp. 249–258. For more work on virtues, see *The Virtues: Contemporary Essays on Moral Character*, edited by R. Kruschwitz and R. Roberts (Belmont, Cal.: Wadsworth, 1987).

InfoTrac

Socrates, Plato, Aristotle, virtue, happiness, pleasure, contemplation

Chapter 2

Christian Natural Law Ethics

Introduction: Faith and Reason in Medieval Philosophy

The figures of Socrates, Plato, and Aristotle dominate the intellectual landscape of Greek philosophy. Although each occasionally acknowledged "the gods," none of them, so far as we know, were devoted to an organized religion. The end of the "ancient world" and the beginning of the Middle Ages is often associated with what is arguably the most historically significant event in Western history: the triumph of Christianity as the dominant religion of Europe. Next to Greek philosophy, perhaps no other force has had so great an impact on Western culture as Christianity. What began as a small "Jesus movement" in the areas around the Mediterranean Sea in the first century spread rapidly, until in the fourth century it had become the official state religion.

The so-called Dark Ages that followed for the next thousand years were "dark" only from the point of view of acquiring new scientific knowledge of the world. Theology and philosophy flourished. Two brilliant lights illuminated this period, one near the beginning, the other closer to the end. St. Augustine in the fourth century and St. Thomas Aquinas in the thirteenth represent the clearest articulations of moral wisdom that the medieval world produced. Both were primarily theologians concerned with elucidating and defending the Christian faith. For both, morality is intimately connected with human nature, which in turn is understood to exist in a world designed by an all-knowing, all-powerful, and good God. In such a world, good actions must be understood in their relationship to the purposes for which God has created the various aspects of human nature.

Besides their commitments to a Christian interpretation of reality, both men were also deeply indebted to the philosophical traditions founded by Plato and Aristotle, respectively. Augustine immersed himself in Plato's philosophy as it was known to him through various later writers. Like Plato, Augustine made a sharp distinction between the imperfect world we now inhabit and the perfect world that reflects divine wisdom, and that (for Augustine at least) awaits us in the hereafter. Aquinas knew of Plato, but he was much more impressed by the work of Aristotle. Aquinas attempted to take the insights from the pagan philosopher and adapt them to the truths of the Christian faith. Whereas with Augustine the emphasis is on love and will, with Aquinas the emphasis is on reason and in-tellect. The two greatest philosophers of the ancient world thus have counterparts in the medieval world. Together Augustine and Aquinas constitute "the Plato and Aristotle of the Middle Ages." Their concern with upholding and elucidating the truths of the Christian faith, however, gives their moral philosophies a distinctive character. Augustine's central ethical concerns are discussed in the profile below. Aquinas's moral theory is represented in the discussion and the reading selections that follow it.

<table>
<tr><td>PROFILE</td><td></td></tr>
</table>

Augustine: Human Sinfulness and the Love of God

Augustine lived at an exciting, not to mention dangerous, time. Born in 354 C.E. in Thagaste, in northern Africa, he lived during what has come to be known as the fall of the Roman Empire. Born of a pagan father and a Christian mother, his youth was spent, as he later recounted in his autobiographical *Confessions*, "caring for nothing but to love and be loved." Lest we think that Augustine was just an incurable romantic, he goes on to tell his readers what sort of "love" he cared about:

> My love went beyond the affection of one mind for another, beyond the arc of the bright beam of friendship. Bodily desire, like a morass, and adolescent sex welling up within me, exuded mists which clouded over and obscured my heart, so that I could not distinguish the clear light of true love from the murk of lust. Love and lust together seethed within me. In my tender youth they swept me away over the precipice of my body's appetites and plunged me in the whirlpool of sin. . . . I tossed and spilled, floun-dering in the broiling sea of my fornication, . . . restless in fatigue, sowing more and more seeds whose only crop was grief.

Augustine continues in more passion-soaked detail, but the course that his life was taking is clear enough. All this came to an end in 386 when he finally relented (much to his mother's relief) and became a Christian convert. He spent the rest of his long life engaged in the articulation and defense of the Christian faith. So per-suasive were his interpretations of Christian doctrines that they dominated phi-losophy and theology in medieval Europe for the next nine centuries. He was the greatest of the church fathers, and an unrivaled authority on Christian doctrine until Aquinas, in the thirteenth century, came to share that honor with him.

Like the Greek philosophers before him, Augustine's moral theory is eudai-monistic; that is, it treats happiness as the proper end for human beings. But Au-gustine was a Christian, whereas the Greek philosophers who preceded him were pagans. Hence Augustine insists that genuine happiness is to be found only in a proper relationship with God. The attainment of this relationship with God is happiness itself. But such happiness is not to be had by merely understanding or knowing God. Rather, it consists in the supernatural union with God in love. To live well is nothing else than to love God with all one's heart, with all one's soul, and with all one's mind. Augustine's moral theory, therefore, is primarily an ethic of love, first for God, and then for one's neighbor. "A good and honest life," he says, "is not formed otherwise than by loving as they should be loved those things which we ought to love, namely, God and our neighbor." Love of God leads to love of things, persons, and self in the right way. Such a life is not easy to attain. Fortunately, God has left his mark on human minds in the form of natural laws, so that human beings are, by nature, oriented toward the love of God and, ultimately, eternal happiness.

But if we are naturally oriented toward God, then from whence comes evil? Loving is an act of the will, so Augustine's ethics emphasizes as well freedom of the will and man's moral responsibility. The possession of free will, however, poses certain dangers, the most serious of which is that one may choose to love something other than God and one's neighbor, or to love self, persons, and things in the wrong way. This is the source of evil. But does not God, then, who created human beings with free will, become ultimately responsible for the evil in the world? Not exactly, according to Augustine. Evil is not a *thing*, in the sense of being a positive reality, for if it were then it would have to be ascribed to God, which is impossible. On Augustine's view (based on a philosophical school called Neoplatonism), evil is a privation, that is, something that is missing. What is missing is the right ordering of the will toward the love of God. Moral evil, therefore, is a privation of right order in the created will. For Augustine the essence of morality is the right ordering of the will toward the love of God. With this conclusion, he had finally found the proper object for the passionate longings that had so dominated his youth. "Our hearts are restless," Augustine said, "until they find their rest in God."

St. Thomas Aquinas:
Reason, Happiness, and Divine Law

We do not offend God except by doing something contrary to our own good.
—ST. THOMAS AQUINAS, *SUMMA CONTRA GENTILES*

Thomas Aquinas led a life devoted to studying, writing, teaching, and traveling. It was, by general agreement, one of the most philosophically productive lives anyone has ever lived. (Perhaps only Aristotle, who might be called Aquinas's philosophical hero, was a more prolific writer.) He was born at Roccasecca, Italy, around 1225. At about the age of five he began his elementary studies at the Benedictine monastery at nearby Monte Cassino, and later went on to study liberal arts at the newly established University of Naples. In 1244 he entered the Dominican order, and in 1248 began his studies under Albert the Great at Cologne. In 1256 he was awarded the doctorate in theology at the University of Paris, and he continued to teach at a Dominican convent in Paris until 1259. For the next decade he traveled and lectured on theology and philosophy at various Dominican monasteries in the vicinity of Rome. In 1268 he returned to the University of Paris to teach, and stayed until he was called back to Italy in 1272, at which time he began teaching at his old alma mater, the University of Naples. Toward the end of 1273 illness forced him to discontinue his writing and teaching, and in 1274 he died at Fossanova, not far from his birthplace. He was canonized in 1323. In 1567 Pope Pius V bestowed on him the title Angelic Doctor. His was a life devoted single-mindedly to the pursuit of truth, with the Christian faith as his ultimate foundation and Aristotle as his philosophical guide.

Aquinas wrote an enormous number of works, in the form of commentaries, summaries of Christian doctrine, sermons, and short treatises. Aquinas's works show mastery of a wide diversity of philosophical traditions, including Stoicism, Neoplatonism (two philosophies that flourished during the Roman Empire), and Augustinianism. But by far the greatest philosophical influence on Aquinas was Aristotle. It is sometimes said that Aquinas "baptized" Aristotle, meaning that he adapted Aristotle's naturalistic philosophy to the supernaturalistic, revealed religion of Christianity. There is some truth in this. Aquinas's philosophy is a kind of Christianized Aristotelianism, but the elements Aquinas added to Aristotle's thought clearly show the marks of an original and brilliant thinker. In all of his works he shows a tendency to seek the middle position between extreme views that have been put forth by others. Like Aristotle, he tried to find the elements of truth in opposing positions and to incorporate these into his own, original point of view. Above all, Aquinas displays confidence in the power of reason to separate the true from the false. His guiding principle was that all that was rational in the ancient philosophers, especially Aristotle, could be made more so in the light of Christian revelation.

The two longest treatises Aquinas wrote are the two *Summa*s, or summaries of Christian doctrine. The *Summa Theologiae* is a massive work that fills a couple of library shelves. (That Aquinas considered it to be a mere "summary" tells you something about the depth and breadth of his mind.) It was designed to be a kind of textbook for seminarians. The other *Summa* is the *Summa Contra Gentiles*, intended as a compact manual of Christian doctrine for missionaries in Spain. More generally, it represents the sustained effort of a Christian scholar to confront the learning and science of the non-Christian world and to defend the Christian worldview against intellectual threats from without. It is one of the most accessible of Aquinas's works, as well as the only summary of Christian doctrine that he completed, and provides many of the ideas central to his philosophical worldview, including his moral philosophy. The selections included below are all taken from this work (hereafter referred to as the *SCG*).

In order to better understand the reading selections included below, something should be said about the context in which they appear. The *SCG* is divided into four books. In Book I Aquinas considers God, his existence and perfections, knowledge, will, and love. Book II is devoted to creation, especially God's freedom in creation and human nature, including the unity of soul and body in human beings. Book III, from which the selections below are taken, discusses the order of creation, including human beings' relation to God, and divine providence. In Book IV Aquinas investigates the trinity, the incarnation, and the end of the universe.

According to Aquinas, divine truth has a twofold nature. Some truths about God, for example his existence and unity, can be established by reason. Other truths about God (e.g., the trinity—the doctrine that God is three persons in one godhead) exceed human reason. Human reason, by its own unaided powers, would never be able to demonstrate the truth of such doctrines. Such divinely revealed truths are not contrary to natural reason but rather transcend natural reason. Truth cannot contradict itself, because God is the author of all truths and God cannot contradict himself. God has disclosed both kinds of truth to human beings, because most people are not capable of attaining either kind of truth without divine assistance. Aquinas's task in the first three books of the *SCG*, in keeping with its intended purpose, is to convince readers of the truths about God (and derivatively, about human beings) that can be established by natural reason. The last book of the *SCG* argues for the reasonableness of truths that surpass human reason and thus can be known only by divine revelation.

Book III, as alluded to above, is devoted to an exposition of God as the end and ruler of created things. In the first set of selections below, Aquinas begins by showing that every agent acts for an end, that the end is a good, and that this good is ultimately God himself. This is true of all creatures. But creatures with intellects are a special case. They are capable of understanding God in a way that nonintelligent creatures are not. Hence the end for intelligent creatures is to understand God. Aquinas insists, however, that such understanding is not attainable by human beings through their own unaided intellectual powers. Divine grace is also needed. The attainment of man's end is, following Aristotle, that which is called happiness.

As Aristotle had already noted, all persons desire happiness, but there is a wide diversity of opinion on what happiness consists in and what other goods conduce to the attainment of happiness. Aquinas argues at length that many of the things that are often taken to be constitutive of happiness really are not. One might expect a Christian theologian to argue that happiness does not consist in the pleasures of the flesh or in riches, and Aquinas does not disappoint us. Surprisingly, he also argues that happiness does not consist either in loving God or in acts of moral virtue. What it does consist in is the contemplation of God. This, however, is only possible in the next life. Hence genuine happiness, although its pursuit is begun in this life, is not attainable in this life. This life points beyond itself to another life following it.

The central project of being human, then, is to attain to an intellectual understanding of God, which is only fully attainable in the next life. But various factors in this life can either assist us or deflect us from attaining this goal. Fortunately, however, God has provided us with assistance in the form of laws. As Aquinas states in the final set of readings below, unintelligent creatures are directed to God by their specific natures. That is, they automatically do what comes "naturally" to them. Rational creatures, on the other hand, have the ability to direct their actions not only in accordance with their specific natures but also in accordance with their own understanding. It is as individuals that we direct our own activities in accordance with laws. Divine law principally directs us toward the love of God and our neighbors. Aquinas applies these ideas to the issues of sexual intercourse outside of marriage, to marriage itself, and to homosexuality. Ultimately, Aquinas wants to show that some things are right, not merely because they are prescribed by divine law, but because they are in accord with nature. Likewise, some things are considered wrong because they are "against nature" (e.g., homosexuality, sexual intercourse outside of marriage, marriage between relatives). These ideas have had an enormous influence on subsequent thinking both within and outside of Christian circles. You will have to judge for yourself whether you find his arguments persuasive or not.

Reading Questions

1. *The proper end for human beings:* What, according to Aquinas, is the proper end for human beings? How does he arrive at this conclusion? How is Aquinas's discussion of the

end for human beings similar to that developed by Aristotle in Book I of his *Nicomachean Ethics*? How does Aquinas's account of the attainment of one's end differ from that of Aristotle?

2. *Human happiness*: Why, according to Aquinas, can't human beings attain happiness in this life? What sorts of obstacles to attaining happiness do we face? In what, according to Aquinas, does ultimate human happiness consist?

3. *On divine and natural law*: How does Aquinas define the term "law"? In what ways are intelligent creatures governed by God both in virtue of their specific natures (e.g., as human beings) and as individuals? How do the laws God gives to human beings differ from the natural laws discovered in physics or other natural sciences? What is the basis for Aquinas's argument that some things are right, and other things are wrong, by nature?

The Proper End for Human Beings

ST. THOMAS AQUINAS

Foreword

. . . There is one First Being, possessing the full perfection of all being, whom we call God, and who of the abundance of His perfection, bestows being on all that exists, so that He is proved to be not only the first of beings, but also the beginning of all. Moreover He bestows being on others, not through natural necessity, but according to the decree of His will, as we have shown above. Hence it follows that He is the Lord of the things made by Him: since we dominate over those things that are subject to our will. And this is a perfect dominion that He exercises over things made by Him, forasmuch as in their making He needs neither the help of an extrinsic agent, nor matter as the foundation of His work: since He is the universal efficient cause of all being.

Now everything that is produced through the will of an agent is directed to an end by that agent: because the good and the end are the proper object of the will, wherefore whatever proceeds from a will must needs be directed to an end. And each thing attains its end by its own action, which action needs to be directed by him who endowed things with the principles whereby they act.

Consequently God, who in Himself is perfect in every way, and by His power endows all things with being, must needs be the Ruler of all, Himself ruled by none: nor is any thing to be excepted from His ruling, as neither is there any thing that does not owe its being to Him. Therefore as He is perfect in being and causing, so is He perfect in ruling.

The effect of this ruling is seen to differ in different things, according to the difference of natures. For some things are so produced by God that, being intelligent, they bear a resemblance to Him and reflect His image: wherefore not only are they directed, but they direct themselves to their appointed end by their own actions. And if in thus directing themselves they be subject to the divine ruling, they are admitted by that divine ruling to the attainment of their last end; but are excluded therefrom if they direct themselves otherwise.

Others there are, bereft of intelligence, which do not direct themselves to their end, but are directed by another. Of these some being incorruptible, even as they are not patient of defect in their natural being, so neither do they wander, in their own action, from the direction to their appointed end, but are subject, without fail, to the ruling of the supreme ruler; such are the heavenly bodies, whose movements are invariable. Others, however, being corruptible, are patient of defects in their natural being; yet this defect is supplied to the advantage of another: since when one thing is corrupted, another is generated. Likewise,

From St. Thomas Aquinas, Summa Contra Gentiles, *Book III, Chapters 1–3, 16–17, 25, translated by the English Dominican Fathers (London: Burns, Oates, & Washbourne, Ltd., 1924). Reprinted by permission of the English Dominican Fathers.*

they fail from their natural direction in their own actions, yet this failing is compensated by some resultant good. Whence it is clear that not even those things which are seen to wander from the direction of the supreme ruling, escape from the power of the supreme ruler: because also these corruptible bodies, even as they are created by God, so too are they perfectly subject to Him. . . .

That Every Agent Acts for an End

Accordingly we must first show that every agent, by its action, intends an end.

For in those things which clearly act for an end, we declare the end to be that toward which the movement of the agent tends: for when this is reached, the end is said to be reached, and to fail in this is to fail in the end intended; as may be seen in the physician who aims at health, and in a man who runs toward an appointed goal. Nor does it matter, as to this, whether that which tends to an end be cognitive or not: for just as the target is the end of the archer, so is it the end of the arrow's flight. Now the movement of every agent tends to something determinate: since it is not from any force that any action proceeds, but heating proceeds from heat, and cooling from cold; wherefore actions are differentiated by their active principles. Action sometimes terminates in something made, for instance building terminates in a house, healing ends in health: while sometimes it does not so terminate, for instance, understanding and sensation. And if action terminates in something made, the movement of the agent tends by that action toward that thing made: while if it does not terminate in something made, the movement of the agent tends to the action itself. It follows therefore that every agent intends an end while acting, which end is sometimes the action itself, sometimes a thing made by the action.

Again. In all things that act for an end, that is said to be the last end, beyond which the agent seeks nothing further: thus the physician's action goes as far as health, and this being attained, his efforts cease. But in the action of every agent, a point can be reached beyond which the agent does not desire to go; else actions would tend to infinity, which is impossible, for since *it is not possible to pass through an infinite medium*, the agent would never begin to act, because nothing moves towards what it cannot reach. Therefore every agent acts for an end. . . .

Again. Every agent acts either by nature or by intelligence. Now there can be no doubt that those which act by intelligence act for an end; since they act

with an intellectual preconception of what they attain by their action, and act through such preconception, for this is to act by intelligence. Now just as in the preconceiving intellect there exists the entire likeness of the effect that is attained by the action of the intellectual being, so in the natural agent there pre-exists the similitude of the natural effect, by virtue of which similitude its action is determined to the appointed effect: for fire begets fire, and an olive produces an olive. Wherefore even as that which acts by intelligence tends by its action to a definite end, so also does that which acts by nature. Therefore every agent acts for an end. . . .

Moreover. Fault is not found save in those things which are for an end: for we do not find fault with one who fails in that to which he is not appointed; thus we find fault with a physician if he fails to heal, but not with a builder or a grammarian. But we find fault in things done according to art, as when a grammarian fails to speak correctly; and in things that are ruled by nature, as in the case of monstrosities. Therefore every agent, whether according to nature, or according to art, or acting of set purpose, acts for an end.

There are, however, certain actions which would seem not to be for an end, such as playful and contemplative actions, and those which are done without attention, such as scratching one's beard, and the like: whence some might be led to think that there is an agent that acts not for an end. But we must observe that contemplative actions are not for another end, but are themselves an end. Playful actions are sometimes an end, when one plays for the mere pleasure of play; and sometimes they are for an end, as when we play that afterward we may study better. Actions done without attention do not proceed from the intellect, but from some sudden act of the imagination, or some natural principle: thus a disordered humor produces an itching sensation and is the cause of a man scratching his beard, which he does without his mind attending to it. Such actions do tend to an end, although outside the order of the intellect. Hereby is excluded the error of certain natural philosophers of old, who maintained that all things happen by natural necessity, thus utterly banishing the final cause from things.

That Every Agent Acts for a Good

Hence we must go on to prove that every agent acts for a good.

For that every agent acts for an end clearly follows from the fact that every agent tends to something definite. Now that to which an agent tends definitely must needs be befitting to that agent: since the latter would not tend to it save on account of some fittingness thereto. But that which is befitting to a thing is good for it. Therefore every agent acts for a good.

Further. The end is that wherein the appetite of the agent or mover is at rest, as also the appetite of that which is moved. Now it is the very notion of good to be the term of appetite, since *good is the object of every appetite*. Therefore all action and movement is for a good.

Again. All action and movement would seem to be directed in some way to being: either for the preservation of being in the species or in the individual; or for the acquisition of being. Now this itself, being to wit, is a good: and for this reason all things desire being. Therefore all action and movement is for a good. . . .

Moreover. The intellectual agent acts for an end, as determining on its end: whereas the natural agent, though it acts for an end, as proved above, does not determine its end for itself, since it knows not the nature of end, but is moved to the end determined for it by another. Now an intellectual agent does not determine the end for itself except under the aspect of good; for the intelligible object does not move except it be considered as a good, which is the object of the will. Therefore also the natural agent is not moved, nor does it act for an end, except in so far as this end is a good: since the end is determined for the natural agent by an appetite. Therefore every agent acts for a good.

Again. To shun evil and to seek good are in the same ratio: even as movement from below and upward movement are in the same ratio. Now we observe that all things shun evil: for intellectual agents shun a thing for the reason that they apprehend it as an evil: and all natural agents, in proportion to their strength, resist corruption which is the evil of everything. Therefore all things act for a good.

Again. That which results from the agent's action beside his intention, is said to happen by chance or luck. Now we observe in the works of nature that either always or more often that happens which is best: thus in plants the leaves are so placed as to protect the fruit; and the parts of an animal are so disposed as to conduce to the animal's safety. Wherefore, if this happens beside the intention of the natural agent, it will be the result of chance or luck. But that is impossible: because things that happen always or frequently, are not casual or fortuitous, but those which occur seldom. Therefore the natural agent tends to that which is best: and much more evidently is this so with the intellectual agent. Therefore every agent intends a good in acting. . . .

Hence the philosophers in defining the good said: *The good is the object of every appetite;* and Dionysius . . . says that *all things desire the good and the best. . . .*

That the End of Everything Is a Good

Accordingly if every agent acts for some good, as we have shown above, it follows that good is the end of each thing. For everything is directed by its action to some end; since either the action itself is an end; or the end of the action is also the end of the agent: and this is its good.

Again. The end of a thing is the term of its appetite. Now the appetite of a thing terminates in a good: for the Philosopher [Aristotle] defines good as *the object of all appetite*. Therefore the end of everything is a good. . . .

Further. Things that know the end, and things that do not know the end, are equally directed to the end: although those which know the end are moved thereto *per se;* whereas those which do not know it, tend thereto as directed by another, as may be seen in the archer and the arrow. Now those that know the end, are always directed to a good as their end; because the will which is the appetite of a previously known end, does not tend toward a thing except under the aspect of good, which is its object. Therefore also those things that do not know the end, are directed to a good as their end. Therefore the end of all is a good.

That All Things Are Directed to One End, Which Is God

From the foregoing it is clear that all things are directed to one good as their last end.

For if nothing tends to something as its end, except in so far as this is good, it follows that good, as such, is an end. Consequently that which is the supreme good is supremely the end of all. Now there is but one Supreme good, namely God. Therefore all things are directed to the Supreme good, namely God, as their end.

Again. *That which is supreme in any genus, is the cause of everything in that genus:* thus fire which is supremely hot is the cause of heat in other bodies. Therefore the Supreme good, namely God, is the cause of goodness in all things good. Therefore He is the cause of every end being an end: since whatever is an end, is such, in so far as it is good. Now *the cause of a thing being such, is yet more so.* Therefore God is supremely the end of all things.

Further. In every series of causes, the first cause is more a cause than the second cause: since the second cause is not a cause save through the first. Therefore that which is the first cause in the series of final causes, must needs be more the final cause of each thing, than the proximate final cause. Now God is the first cause in the series of final causes: for He is supreme in the order of good things. Therefore He is the end of each thing more even than any proximate end.

Moreover. In all mutually subordinate ends the last must needs be the end of each preceding end: thus if a potion be mixed to be given to a sick man, and is given to him that he may be purged, and he be purged that he may be lowered, and lowered that he may be healed, it follows that health is the end of the lowering, and of the purging, and of those that precede. Now all things are subordinate in various degrees of goodness to the one supreme good, that is the cause of all goodness: and so, since good has the aspect of an end, all things are subordinate to God as preceding ends under the last end. Therefore God must be the end of all. . . .

That to Know God Is the End of Every Intelligent Substance

Now, seeing that all creatures, even those that are devoid of reason, are directed to God as their last end: and that all reach this end in so far as they have some share of a likeness to him: the intellectual creature attains to him in a special way, namely through its proper operation, by understanding him. Consequently this must be the end of the intelligent creature, namely to understand God.

For, as we have shown above, God is the end of each thing: wherefore as far as it is possible each thing intends to be united to God as its last end. Now a thing is more closely united to God by reaching in a way to the very substance of God; which happens when it knows something of the divine substance, than when it reaches to a divine likeness. Therefore the intellectual substance tends to the knowledge of God as its last end.

Again. The operation proper to a thing is the end thereof: for it is its second perfection; so that when a thing is well conditioned for its proper operation it is said to be efficient and good. Now understanding is the proper operation of the intellectual substance: and consequently it is its end. Therefore whatever is most perfect in this operation, is its last end; especially in those operations which are not directed to some product, such as understanding and sensation.

And since operations of this kind take their species from their objects, by which also they are known, it follows that the more perfect the object of any such operation, the more perfect is the operation. Consequently to understand the most perfect intelligible, namely God, is the most perfect in the genus of this operation which is to understand. Therefore to know God by an act of intelligence is the last end of every intellectual substance.

Someone, however, might say that the last end of an intellectual substance consists indeed in understanding the best intelligible: but that what is the best intelligible for this or that intellectual substance, is not simply the best intelligible; and that the higher the intellectual substance, the higher is its best intelligible. So that possibly the supreme intellectual substance has for its best intelligible that which is best simply, and its happiness will consist in understanding God: whereas the happiness of any lower intellectual substance will consist in understanding some lower intelligible, which however will be the highest thing understood by that substance. Especially would it seem not to be in the power of the human intellect to understand that which is simply the best intelligible, on account of its weakness: for it is as much adapted for knowing the supreme intelligible, *as the owl's eye for seeing the sun.*

Nevertheless it is evident that the end of any intellectual substance, even the lowest, is to understand God. For it has been shown above that God is the last end toward which all things tend. And the human intellect, although the lowest in the order of intelligent substances, is superior to all that are devoid of understanding. Since then a more exalted substance has not a less exalted end, God will be the end also of the human intelligence. Now every intelligent being attains to its last end by understanding it, as we have proved. Therefore the human intellect attains to God as its end, by understanding Him. . . .

Moreover. Man has a natural desire to know the causes of whatever he sees: wherefore through wondering at what they saw, and ignoring its cause, men first began to philosophize, and when they had discovered the cause they were at rest. Nor do they cease inquiring until they come to the first cause; and *then do we deem ourselves to know perfectly when we know the first cause.* Therefore man naturally desires, as his last end, to know the first cause. But God is the first cause of all. Therefore man's last end is to know God. . . .

. . . Aristotle agrees with this statement when he says that man's ultimate happiness is *contemplative, in regard to his contemplating the highest object of contemplation.*

Human Happiness

ST. THOMAS AQUINAS

That Man's Ultimate Happiness Is Not in This Life

Seeing then that man's ultimate happiness does not consist in that knowledge of God whereby he is known by all or many in a vague kind of opinion, nor again in that knowledge of God whereby he is known in science through demonstration; nor in that knowledge whereby he is known through faith, . . . and seeing that it is not possible in this life to arrive at a higher knowledge of God in His essence, or at least so that we understand other separate substances, and thus know God through that which is nearest to Him, so to say, . . . and since we must place our ultimate happiness in some kind of knowledge of God, . . . it is impossible for man's happiness to be in this life.

Again. Man's last end is the term of his natural appetite, so that when he has obtained it, he desires nothing more: because if he still has movement toward something, he has not yet reached an end wherein to be at rest. Now, this cannot happen in this life: since the more man understands, the more is the desire to understand increased in him, this being natural to man, unless perhaps someone there be who understands all things: and in this life this never did nor can happen to anyone that was a mere man; seeing that in this life we are unable to know separate substances which in themselves are most intelligible, as we have proved. Therefore man's ultimate happiness cannot possibly be in this life.

Besides. Whatever is in motion toward an end, has a natural desire to be established and at rest therein: hence a body does not move away from the place toward which it has a natural movement, except by a violent movement which is contrary to that appetite. Now happiness is the last end which man desires naturally. Therefore it is his natural desire to be established in happiness. Consequently unless together with happiness he acquires a state of immobility, he is not yet happy, since his natural desire is not yet at

rest. When therefore a man acquires happiness, he also acquires stability and rest; so that all agree in conceiving stability as a necessary condition of happiness: hence the Philosopher says: *We do not look upon the happy man as a kind of chameleon.* Now, in this life there is no sure stability; since, however happy a man may be, sickness and misfortune may come upon him, so that he is hindered in the operation, whatever it be, in which his happiness consists. Therefore man's ultimate happiness cannot be in this life. . . .

Further. All admit that happiness is a perfect good: else it would not bring rest to the appetite. Now perfect good is that which is wholly free from any admixture of evil: just as that which is perfectly white is that which is entirely free from any admixture of black. But man cannot be wholly free from evils in this state of life; not only from evils of the body, such as hunger, thirst, heat, cold and the like, but also from evils of the soul. For no one is there who at times is not disturbed by inordinate passions; who sometimes does not go beyond the mean, wherein virtue consists, either in excess or in deficiency; who is not deceived in some thing or another; or at least ignores what he would wish to know; or feels doubtful about an opinion of which he would like to be certain. Therefore no man is happy in this life.

Again. Man naturally shuns death, and is sad about it: not only shunning it now when he feels its presence, but also when he thinks about it. But man, in this life, cannot obtain not to die. Therefore it is not possible for man to be happy in this life. . . .

Further. The more a thing is desired and loved, the more does its loss bring sorrow and pain. Now happiness is most desired and loved. Therefore its loss brings the greatest sorrow. But if there be ultimate happiness in this life, it will certainly be lost, at least by death. Nor is it certain that it will last till death: since it is possible for every man in this life to

From St. Thomas Aquinas, Summa Contra Gentiles, *Book III, Chapters 48, 63, 147, translated by the English Dominican Fathers (London: Burns, Oates, & Washbourne, Ltd., 1924). Reprinted by permission of the English Dominican Fathers.*

encounter sickness, whereby he is wholly hindered from the operation of virtue; such as madness and the like which hinder the use of reason. Such happiness therefore always has sorrow naturally connected with it: and consequently it will not be perfect happiness.

But someone might say that, since happiness is a good of the intellectual nature, perfect and true happiness is for those in whom the intellectual nature is perfect, namely in separate substances: and that it is imperfect in man, by way of a kind of participation. Because he can arrive at a full understanding of the truth, only by a sort of movement of inquiry; and fails entirely to understand things that are by nature most intelligible, as we have proved. Wherefore neither is happiness, in its perfect form, possible to man: yet he has a certain participation thereof, even in this life. This seems to have been Aristotle's opinion about happiness. Wherefore . . . inquiring whether misfortunes destroy happiness, he shows that happiness seems especially to consist in deeds of virtue, which seem to be most stable in this life, and concludes that those who in this life attain to this perfection, are happy *as men*, as though not attaining to happiness simply, but in a human way.

We must now show that this explanation does not avoid the foregoing arguments. For although man is below the separate substances in the natural order, he is above irrational creatures: wherefore he attains his ultimate end in a more perfect way than they. Now these attain their last end so perfectly that they seek nothing further: thus a heavy body rests when it is in its own proper place; and when an animal enjoys sensible pleasure, its natural desire is at rest. Much more therefore when man has obtained his last end, must his natural desire be at rest. But this cannot happen in this life. Therefore in this life man does not obtain happiness considered as his proper end, as we have proved. Therefore he must obtain it after this life.

Again. The natural desire cannot be void; since *nature does nothing in vain*. But nature's desire would be void if it could never be fulfilled. Therefore man's natural desire can be fulfilled. But not in this life, as we have shown. Therefore it must be fulfilled after this life. Therefore man's ultimate happiness is after this life.

Besides. As long as a thing is in motion toward perfection it has not reached its last end. Now in the knowledge of truth all men are ever in motion and tending toward perfection: because those who follow, make discoveries in addition to those made by their predecessors. . . . Therefore in the knowledge of truth

man is not situated as though he had arrived at his last end. Since then as Aristotle himself shows . . . man's ultimate happiness in this life consists apparently in speculation, whereby he seeks the knowledge of truth, we cannot possibly allow that man obtain his last end in this life. . . .

Therefore man's ultimate happiness will consist in that knowledge of God which he possesses after this life; a knowledge similar to that by which separate substances know him. . . .

How in That Ultimate Happiness Man's Every Desire Is Fulfilled

It is evident from what has been said, that in this happy state which results from the divine vision, man's every desire is fulfilled, according to Ps. 102.5, *Who satisfieth thy desire with good things*, and his every end achieved. This is clear to anyone who considers man's various desires in kind.

There is a desire in man, as an intellectual being, to *know the truth*: and men pursue this desire by the study of the contemplative life. And this will be most clearly fulfilled in that vision, when the intellect by gazing on the First Truth will know all that it naturally desires to know, as we have proved above. . . .

In this life there is nothing so like this ultimate and perfect happiness as the life of those who contemplate the truth, as far as possible here below. Hence the philosophers who were unable to obtain full knowledge of that final beatitude, placed man's ultimate happiness in that contemplation which is possible during this life. For this reason too, Holy Writ commends the contemplative rather than other forms of life, when our Lord said (Luke 10.42): *Mary hath chosen the better part*, namely the contemplation of truth, *which shall not be taken from her*. For contemplation of truth begins in this life, but will be consummated in the life to come: while the active and civic life does not transcend the limits of this life. . . .

That Man Needs the Divine Assistance in Order to Obtain Beatitude

Whereas it is clear from the foregoing, that divine providence governs rational creatures otherwise than other things, inasmuch as they differ from others in natural condition, it remains to be proved that also on account of the excellence of their end, a more exalted mode of government is applied to them by divine providence.

It is evident that in keeping with their nature, they attain to a higher participation of the end. For, since they are of an intellectual nature, they are able by their operation to be in touch with intelligible truth: which is impossible for other things, since they lack intelligence. And, forasmuch as they attain to intelligible truth by their natural operation, it is clear that God provides for them otherwise than for other things: in that to man is given intelligence and reason, that thereby he may be able both to discern and to discover the truth: also to him are given the sensitive powers, both interior and exterior, that by them he may be assisted to discover the truth: also to him is given the use of speech, so that by making use of it, one who has conceived the truth in his mind, may be able to impart it to another: so that men may thus assist one another in the knowledge of truth, even as in other necessaries of life, since man is *by nature a social animal*.

Furthermore, the knowledge of truth that is appointed as man's last end is one which surpasses his natural faculty: for it consists in his seeing the First Truth itself in itself, as we have proved above. Now this is not competent to lower creatures, namely that they be able to reach an end surpassing their natural faculty. Consequently, there arises from this end an additional reason why a different manner of government should be accorded to men, and to other creatures of a lower nature. Because the means should be proportional to the end. So that, if man be directed to an end surpassing his natural faculty, he stands in need of a supernatural assistance from God, to enable him to tend to that end.

Moreover. A thing of inferior nature cannot attain to what is proper to a higher nature except by virtue of that higher nature: thus the moon, that shines not of itself, is made to shine by the power and action of the sun: and water that is not hot of itself, becomes hot by the power and action of fire. Now, to see the First Truth itself in itself, so far surpasses the faculty of human nature, that it belongs to God alone, as we have shown above. Therefore man needs the divine assistance in order to reach that end.

Again. Everything obtains its last end by its own operation. Now, an operation derives its efficacy from the operating principle: wherefore by the action of the seed something is produced in a definite species, through the efficacy pre-existing in the seed. Therefore man cannot, by his own operation, attain to his last end, which surpasses the faculty of his natural powers, unless his operation be enabled by the divine power to bring him thereto.

Besides. No instrument can achieve ultimate perfection by virtue of its own form, but only by virtue of the principal agent: although by virtue of its own form it can cause some disposition to the ultimate perfection. Thus a saw, by reason of its own form, causes the cutting of the wood, but the form of the bench is produced by the art that employs the instrument: likewise in the body of an animal, resolution and consumption is the result of the animal heat, but the formation of flesh, and regulation of increase and other such things, come from the vegetative soul, which uses heat as its instrument. Now, to God the first agent by intellect and will, all intellects and wills are subordinate, as instruments under the principal agent. Consequently their operations have no efficacy in respect of their ultimate perfection, which is the attainment of final beatitude, except by the power of God. Therefore the rational nature needs the divine assistance in order to obtain its last end.

Further. Many obstacles prevent man from reaching his end. For he is hindered by the weakness of his reason, which is easily drawn into error which bars him from the straight road that leads to his end. He is also hindered by the passions of the sensitive faculty, and by the affections whereby he is drawn to sensible and inferior things, since the more he adheres to them, further is he removed from his last end: for such things are below man, whereas his end is above him. Again he is often hindered by weakness of the body from doing acts of virtue, whereby he tends to beatitude. Therefore he needs the help of God, lest by such obstacles he turn away utterly from his last end. . . .

On Divine and Natural Law

ST. THOMAS AQUINAS

That the Rational Creature Is Directed to Its Action by God Not Only in Its Relation to the Species, but Also in Its Relation to the Individual

Hence it is clear that the rational creature alone is directed to its actions by God, with due regard not only to the species, but also to the individual. For, seemingly, everything is on account of its operation: since operation is the ultimate perfection of a thing. Wherefore each thing is directed to its action by God, according as it stands under divine providence. Now, the rational creature stands under divine providence as being governed and cared for, on its own account, and not, as other corruptible creatures, on account of the species only: because the individual that is governed only for the sake of the species, is not governed for its own sake; whereas the rational creature is governed for its own sake, as we have made clear. Accordingly, rational creatures alone are directed by God to their actions for the sake, not only of the species, but also of the individual.

Besides. Things that are directed in their actions only so far as these refer to the species, have not the power to act or not to act: since whatever results from the species, is common and natural to all the individuals contained in the species; and we have no choice about natural things. Hence if man were directed in his actions in reference only to the demands of the species, he would not have the power to act, or not to act, and he would have to follow the natural inclination common to the whole species, as in the case with all irrational creatures. It is therefore clear that rational creatures are directed in their actions, with regard not only to the species, but also to the individual. . . .

Again. God provides for every nature according to its capacity: for He made each creature such that He knew it to be adapted to obtain its end through being governed by Him. Now, the rational creature alone is capable of being directed to its actions, in respect not only of the species but also of the individual: because it has intellect and reason, so as to be able to perceive the different ways in which a certain thing is good or evil in relation to various persons, times, and places. Therefore the rational creature alone is directed by God to its actions, in respect not only of the species but also of the individual.

Besides. The rational creature is subject to divine providence in such a way, that not only is it governed thereby, but is able to know something of the nature of providence: so that it is capable of providence and government in respect of others. This is not the case with other creatures, for they only participate in providence by being subject to it. Now, through being capable of providence, a man can direct and govern his own actions also. Therefore the rational creature participates in divine providence not only in being governed, but also in governing: for it governs itself in its own actions, and other things too. Now, every lower providence is subject to divine providence as supreme. Therefore the government of a rational creature's acts, as personal acts, belongs to divine providence.

Again. The personal acts of a rational creature are properly those that proceed from the rational soul. Now, the rational soul is capable of perpetuity, not only in respect of the species, like other creatures, but also in respect of the individual. Therefore the actions of a rational creature are directed by divine providence, not only in the point of their belonging to the species, but also inasmuch as they are personal.

Hence it is that, though all things are subject to divine providence, yet Holy Writ ascribes the care of men to it in a special manner; according to Ps. 8.5: *What is man that thou art mindful of him?* and 1 Cor. 9.9: *Doth God take care of oxen?* These things are said because God watches over man's actions not only as belonging to the species, but also as personal acts.

That Laws Are Given by God to Man

It is evident from this that it was necessary for man to receive laws from God. For, as we have shown, just as the acts of irrational creatures are directed by God,

From St. Thomas Aquinas, Summa Contra Gentiles, *Book III, Chapters 113–117, 121–126, 129, translated by the English Dominican Fathers (London: Burns, Oates, & Washbourne, Ltd., 1924). Reprinted by permission of the English Dominican Fathers.*

inasmuch as they belong to the species, so are man's actions directed by God, inasmuch as they belong to the individual. Now, in so far as they are actions belonging to the species, actions of irrational creatures are directed by God by a certain natural inclination, which is consequent to the specific nature. Therefore in addition to this something must be given to man whereby he is directed in his personal actions. And this is what we call law.

Again. The rational creature, as stated above, is subject to divine providence, in such a way as to participate in a certain likeness of divine providence, inasmuch as it is able to govern itself in its own actions, and other things also. Now, that by which the actions of people are governed is a law. Therefore it was reasonable that a law should be given to man by God.

Besides. Since a law is nothing else than a reason and rule of action, it is reasonable that to those alone a law be given, who know the reason of their action. Now, this applies only to the rational creature. Therefore it was fitting that a law should be given to the rational creature alone.

Further. A law should be given to those in whom is the power to act or not to act. But this belongs to the rational creature alone. Therefore only the rational creature is adapted to receive a law.

Moreover. Since a law is nothing else than a reason of action: and the reason for everyone's action is his end: everyone who is capable of receiving a law must receive the law from the one who guides him to his end: even as the inferior craftsman is guided by the master-craftsman, and soldier by the commander-in-chief. Now, the rational creature obtains his last end in God and from God, as we have already shown. Therefore it was reasonable that a law should be given to men by God. . . .

That the Divine Law Directs Man Chiefly to God

From this we may gather what is the principal intention of the divine law.

For it is evident that every lawgiver intends by his law to direct men to his own end: as the commander-in-chief leads to victory, and the governor of a state, to peace. Now the end intended by God, is God Himself. Therefore the chief intention of the divine law is to lead men to God.

Again. Law, as stated above, is a rule which God's governing providence sets before the rational creature. Now the government of God's providence leads each thing to its proper end. Consequently the law given by God directs man chiefly to his end. But the

end of the human creature is to adhere to God: since in this does his happiness consist, as we have proved above. Therefore the divine law directs man chiefly to union with God.

Also. The intention of every lawgiver is to make those good for whom he legislates: hence precepts of law should be about acts of virtue. Therefore the divine law aims at those acts that are best. Now, of all human acts the best are those whereby man adheres to God, as being most akin to His end. Therefore the divine law directs man to these acts before all others.

Besides. That which gives a law its force should hold the chief place in the law. But the law given by God derives its force with men from men being subject to God; for no one is bound by the law of a king whose subject he is not. Therefore the union of man's mind with God should be the chief thing in the divine law. . . .

That the End of God's Law Is the Love of God

Since the chief intention of God's law is that man adhere to God; and since man adheres most firmly to God by love: it follows of necessity that the principal purpose of law is directed to love.

It is evident that man adheres to God principally by love. In man there are two things whereby he can adhere to God, his intellect and his will: for by the inferior faculties of his soul he cannot adhere to God, but to lower beings. But the adhesion of the intellect is completed by the adhesion of the will, because by his will man, as it were, rests in that which the intellect apprehends. Now, the will adheres to a thing either by love or by fear, but not in the same way. For when it adheres to a thing through fear, it adheres on account of something else, namely in order to avoid an evil that threatens unless it adhere to that thing. But when it adheres to a thing through love, it adheres for its own sake. Now, that which is for its own sake is of more account than that which is for another's sake. Therefore to adhere to God by love is to adhere to Him in the closest way possible: and consequently this is the chief intention of the divine law.

Again. The end of every, and especially the divine, law is to make men good. Now, man is said to be good because he has a good will, whereby he brings into act whatever good is in him. Also, a will is good through willing the good, and above all the greatest good, which is the end. Therefore the more his will wills this good, so much the better is the man. Now a man wills more that which he wills on account of love, than that which he wills on account of fear alone: for when he wills a thing only through fear, he is partly unwilling: as when a man, through fear, wills to cast his cargo overboard. Therefore above all the love of the Sovereign Good, namely God, makes men good, and is intended by the divine law above all else.

Further. Man's goodness results from virtue: since *it is virtue that makes its possessor good.* Hence the law intends to make men virtuous; and the precepts of the law are about acts of virtue. But a condition of virtue is that the virtuous act *with both firmness and pleasure.* Now, this is especially the effect of love: because through love we do a thing steadfastly and pleasurably. Therefore love of the good is the ultimate aim of the divine law. . . .

That We Are Directed by the Divine Law to the Love of Our Neighbor

From this it follows that the divine law aims at the love of our neighbor.

For there should be union of affection between those who have one common end. Now, men have one common last end, namely happiness, to which they are directed by God. Therefore men should be united together by mutual love.

Again. Whosoever loves a man, loves those whom he loves, and those who are his kindred. Now, men are loved by God, since He prepared for them a last end consisting in the enjoyment of Himself. Therefore as a man is a lover of God, so must he be a lover of his neighbor.

Moreover. Since man by nature is a *social animal,* he needs assistance from other men in order to obtain his own end. Now this is most suitably done if men love one another mutually. Hence the law of God, which directs men to their last end, commands us to love one another.

Again. In order to apply himself to divine things, man needs calm and peace. Now mutual love, more than aught else, removes the obstacles to peace. Seeing then that the divine law directs men to apply themselves to divine things, we must conclude that this same law leads men to love one another.

Further. The divine law is offered to man in aid of the natural law. Now it is natural to all men to love one another: a proof of which is that a man, by a kind of natural instinct, comes to the assistance of anyone even unknown that is in need, for instance by warning him, should he have taken the wrong road, by helping him to rise, should he have fallen, and so forth: *as though everyman were intimate and friendly with his fellow-man.* Therefore mutual love is prescribed to man by the divine law. . . .

That the Divine Law Directs Man According to Reason as Regards Things Corporeal and Sensible

Just as the human mind can be raised to God by corporeal and sensible things, provided one make right use of them for God's honor, even so their abuse either wholly withdraws the mind from God, if the will places its end in lower things; or distracts the mind's intention from God, when we are too attached to those things. Now, the divine law was given chiefly that man might adhere to God. Therefore it belongs to the divine law to direct man in his love and use of corporeal and sensible things.

Again. Just as the mind of man is subordinate to God, so is the body subordinate to the soul, and the lower powers to reason. Now, it belongs to divine providence, which God sets before man under the form of the divine law, that everything should retain its order. Therefore man should be directed by the divine law, in such wise that the lower powers be subject to reason; the body to the soul; and external things be employed for man's needs.

Further. Every law that is framed aright, is conducive to virtue. Now, virtue is the reason's rule applied to both interior affections and the use of corporeal things. Therefore this should be prescribed by the divine law.

Moreover. Every lawgiver should legislate for those things that are necessary for the observance of the law. Since, then, the law is proposed to the reason, man would not obey the law, unless all that is in man be subject to reason. Therefore it is for the divine law to command that all that is in man be subject to reason. . . .

Hereby we refute the error of those who assert that there is no sin unless our neighbor be injured or scandalized.

How, According to the Divine Law, Simple Fornication Is a Sin: And That Matrimony Is Natural

Hence it is clear how futile is the reasoning of those who say that simple fornication is no sin. For they say: Take, for instance, a woman who is not bound by the marriage tie, or under any authority, paternal or otherwise. If with her consent, a man have intercourse with her, he does her no wrong: since she pleases herself, and has the disposal of her own body. He does not wrong a third party: because, in the supposition, she is under no one's authority. Therefore there is no sin.

Nor, seemingly, is it enough to reply that he does a wrong to God. Because we do not wrong God unless we wrong our own good as stated above. But this would not seem to be contrary to man's good. Consequently no wrong, seemingly, is done to God thereby.

Likewise, it would not seem to meet the case if one reply that the man wrongs his neighbor by scandalizing him. For one may be scandalized at something that is not a sin in itself, so that it becomes a sin accidentally. But the point at issue is whether simple fornication be a sin, not accidentally, but in itself.

Accordingly we must seek the solution from what has been said above. For it has been stated that God cares for everything in respect of what is good for it. Now, it is good for everything that it obtain its end: and its evil that it turn from its end. This applies to the parts as well as to the whole: so that man's every part, even as his every act, should attain to its due end. Now, though the seed be superfluous for the preservation of the individual, it is necessary for the propagation of the species. Other superfluities such as excretions, urine, sweat and the like are not necessary for anything, and so it is only their discharge that is good for man. Seed, however, has another end in view, since it is emitted for the purpose of generation, which is the object of coition. Moreover generation would be in vain, if due nourishment were not to follow: because the offspring would not survive if deprived of its due nourishment. Hence the emission of seed should be ordered in such wise, that befitting generation, and rearing of the offspring may follow.

It is therefore clearly contrary to man's good that the seed be emitted in such a way that generation cannot ensue: and if this be done deliberately it must needs be a sin. I mean, if it be done in a way that is *directly* opposed to generation, such as every emission of seed without the natural union of male and female: hence sins of this kind are said to be *against nature*. If, however, it be accidental that generation cannot ensue, it is not on this account contrary to nature, or sinful: for instance if the woman be sterile.

In like manner it must be contrary to man's good, if, though seed be emitted so that generation can ensue, the proper upbringing of the offspring is hindered. For it must be observed that in those animals in which the female alone suffices for the rearing of the offspring—dogs for instance—the male and female do not remain together after coition. On the other hand, in all cases in which the female does not suffice to rear the offspring, the male and female remain together after coition, as long as may be necessary for the rearing and development of the young. We have an instance of this in certain birds, whose young are unable to seek food as soon as they are hatched. For since the bird does not feed its young on milk—which is ready at hand through being prepared by nature, as in the case of quadrupeds—and needs to go in search of food for them, and besides this fosters them by incubation; the female alone would not suffice for all this. Wherefore divine providence has given the male of such animals the natural instinct to remain with the female for the rearing of the offspring. Now it is clear that in the human species the female is far from sufficing alone for the rearing of the children, since the needs of human life require many things that one person alone cannot provide. It is therefore in keeping with human nature that the man remain with the woman after coition, and not leave her at once, indulging in promiscuous intercourse, as those do who have the habit of fornication.

Nor is this argument weakened because some woman has sufficient means to rear her offspring by herself. Because natural rectitude in human acts depends, not on what is accidentally in one individual but on that which is proper to the whole species. Again, we must observe that, in the human species, the offspring needs not only nourishment for its body, as with other animals, but also instruction for its soul. For other animals have their natural forethought which enables them to provide for themselves: whereas man lives by reason, which can attain to forethought only after long experience: so that children need to be instructed by their parents who are experienced.

Moreover children are not capable of this instruction as soon as they are born, but only after a long time, and especially when they reach the age of discretion. Besides, this instruction requires a long time. And even then, on account of the assaults of the passions whereby the judgment of prudence is perverted, they need not only instruction but correction. Now a woman is insufficient for these things, in fact there is more need for a man for such things, for his reason is more perfect for instruction, and his arm is stronger for punishment. Consequently a short space of time such as suffices for birds is not sufficient for the education of the offspring in the human species, and a great part of life is required for the purpose. So that, as in all animals it behooves the male to remain with the female as long as the father is needed by the offspring, it is natural in the human race that the man should have not a short-lived but a lasting fellowship with a definite woman: and this fellowship is called *matrimony*. Therefore matrimony is natural to man: and the intercourse of fornication, which is apart from matrimony, is contrary to man's good. For this reason it must needs be a sin.

Moreover, the emission of seed without the requisite intention of procreation and education, must not be thought a slight sin, for that it is a small sin, or none at all, to use some part of one's body for some other purpose than that for which nature intended it: for instance if one walk on one's hands, or use one's feet to do what the hands should do. Because by suchlike actions man's good is not prejudiced very much; whereas the inordinate discharge of semen is perversive of a natural good, which is the preservation of the species. Wherefore, after the sin of murder, whereby human nature is deprived of actual existence, this kind of sin, whereby the generation of human nature is hindered, holds, seemingly, the second place.

The foregoing conclusions are confirmed by divine authority. That the discharge of semen in such wise that no offspring can ensue, is unlawful, is clear from the words of Lev. 6.23: *Thou shalt not lie with mankind as with womankind . . . thou shalt not copulate with any beast;* and of 1 Cor. 6.10: *Nor the effeminate, nor liers with mankind . . . shall possess the kingdom of God.*

Again, that fornication and all intercourse with other than one's own wife, is unlawful, is evident from the words of Deut. 23.17: *There shall be no whore among the daughters of Israel, nor whoremonger among the sons of Israel;* and of Job 4.13: *Take heed to keep thyself . . . from all fornication, and beside thy wife never endure to know a crime:* and of 1 Cor. 6.18: *Fly fornication.*

Hereby we exclude the error of those who denied that there was a greater sin in the emission of seed than in the discharge of other superfluities: and of those who said that fornication is no sin.

That Matrimony Should Be Indissoluble

If one consider the matter rightly, it will be seen that the foregoing arguments not only show that the fellowship of male and female in human nature, which we call matrimony, should be lasting, but also that it should endure throughout life.

For possessions are directed to the preservation of the natural life: and since the natural life which cannot be preserved in the person of an undying father, is preserved, by a kind of succession, in the person of the son, it is naturally befitting that the son succeed in things belonging to the father. Therefore it is natural that the father's care for his son should endure to the end of his life. If, then, the father's care for his son causes, even among birds, the continued fellowship of male and female, the natural order demands that in the human species father and mother should remain together to the end of life.

It would seem also contrary to equity for the aforesaid fellowship to be dissolved. For the female requires the male, not only for procreation, as in other animals, but also for governance: because the male excels both in intelligence and in strength. Now, the woman is taken into partnership with the man for the purpose of procreation. Consequently when the woman ceases to be fruitful and fair, this is an obstacle against her being taken by another man. Hence, if a man after taking a wife in her youth, while she is yet fair and fruitful, can put her away when she has aged, he does her an injury, contrary to natural equity.

Again. It is clearly unfitting that the woman be allowed to put away the man: since she is naturally subject to the man's authority: and one who is subject to another is not free to withdraw himself from his authority. Hence it would be contrary to the natural order if a wife could leave her husband. Consequently, if the husband could leave his wife, there would not be just fellowship between husband and wife, but a kind of slavery on the part of the latter.

Also. There is in man a certain natural anxiety to be assured of his offspring: and this is necessary, because the child needs the father's authority for a long time. Hence whatever prevents him from being assured of having children, is contrary to the natural instinct of the human species. Now, if the husband may put away his wife, or the wife leave her husband, and take another man, thus being copulated first to one, and afterward to another, the certainty of offspring would be hindered. Therefore it is contrary to the natural instinct of the human species that husband and wife be separated: and in consequence the union of male and female in the human race must be not only long lasting but indissoluble.

Moreover. The greater the friendship the more stable and lasting is it. Now, seemingly between husband and wife there is the greatest friendship: for they are made one not only in the act of carnal intercourse, which even among dumb animals causes an agreeable fellowship, but also as partners in the whole intercourse of daily life: so that, to indicate this, man must *leave father and mother* (Gen. 2.24) for his wife's sake. Therefore it is right that matrimony should be altogether indissoluble. It must also be observed that among natural acts generation alone is directed to the common good: since eating, and the discharge of other superfluities, regards the individual: whereas procreation regards the preservation of the species. Hence, as the law is made for the common good, whatever regards procreation should be regulated, before other things, by laws both divine and human. Now positive laws should be based on natural instinct, if they be human: even as in demonstrative sciences, all human discoveries must needs be founded on principles naturally known. And if they be divine, not only do they express the instinct of nature, but they also supply the defect of natural instinct: even as the things that God reveals, are beyond the grasp of natural reason. Since, then, the natural instinct of the human species is that the union of male and female be indissoluble, and that one man be united to one woman, it behooved this to be ordered by human law. Moreover, the divine law adds a kind of supernatural reason taken from the representation of the indissoluble union of Christ and the Church, which is union of one with one. Wherefore inordinateness in the act of generation not only is contrary to the natural instinct, but it also transgresses laws both divine and human. Hence, this kind of disorder is more sinful than that which may occur in taking food, or in similar things.

And since in man all other things should be subordinate to what is best in him, the union of male and female is ordered by law not only in the point of its relation to the procreation of children, as in other animals, but also in its relation to good morals, which right reason regulates, both as regards man in himself, and considered as a member either of a private family, or of the civil community. Now, the indissolubility of the union of male and female belongs to good morals. Because their mutual love will be the more constant if they know that they are indissolubly united. They will also be more carefully provident in the conduct of the household, when they realize that they are always to remain together in possession of the same things. Again, this precludes the origin of quarrels which must needs arise between the husband and his wife's relatives, if he were to put his wife away: and those who are connected through affinity have a greater regard for one another. Moreover it removes the occasions of adultery which would occur, were the husband free to put away his wife, or vice versa: for this would encourage the seeking of further marriage. . . .

That Matrimony Should Be the Union of One Man with One Woman

It is also to be observed, seemingly, that all animals that are used to copulate, have a natural instinct to resist another's intercourse with their consort: wherefore, animals fight on account of copulation. And as regards all animals there is one common reason for this, because every animal desires to indulge at will in the pleasure of copulation, even as in the pleasure of eating: and this freedom ceases if many males have access to one female, or vice versa: just as an animal is deprived of the free enjoyment of its food, if another animal despoil it of the food it desires to consume. Hence animals fight both for food and for copulation. But with regard to men there is a special reason: because as already stated, man naturally desires to be assured of his offspring: and this assurance would be altogether nullified in the case of promiscuous copulation. Therefore the union of one man with one woman comes from a natural instinct.

A difference, however, is to be noted here. For as regards one woman not being united to several men, both the foregoing arguments avail. But as regards one man not being joined to several women, the second argument is of no use: since the certainty of having offspring is not removed if one man be joined to several women. The first argument, however, avails against this: for just as freedom of access to the woman is denied, if she have another man, so too the same freedom is denied the woman, if the man have several women. Hence, as certainty of having offspring is the chief good sought from marriage, no human law or custom has permitted polyandry. This was considered to be wrong even among the ancient Romans, of whom Maximum Valerius relates that they deemed that not even on account of barrenness should the marriage bond be severed.

Again. In every animal species where the father has a certain care for his offspring, the one male has but one female, as may be seen in birds, where both unite in feeding their young: for one male would not suffice to rear the progeny of several females. On the other hand where the male animal has not the care of the offspring, we find indifferently union of one male with several females, or of one female with several males: such is the case with dogs, hens, and so forth. Since then of all animals the male of the human species is preeminent in the care of his offspring, it is clearly natural to man that one man should have one wife and vise versa.

Besides. Equality is a condition of friendship. Hence a woman may not have several husbands, because this removes the certainty of offspring; were it lawful for a man to have several wives, the friendship of a wife for her husband would not be freely bestowed, but servile as it were. And this argument is confirmed by experience: since where men have several wives, the wives are treated as servants.

Further. In perfect friendship it is impossible to be friends with many, according to the Philosopher. . . . Hence if the wife has but one husband, while the husband has several wives, the friendship will not be equal on either side: and consequently it will be not a freely bestowed but a servile friendship as it were.

Moreover. As we have already stated matrimony among men should be so ordered as to be consistent with good morals. Now it is contrary to good morals that one man have several wives, for this leads to discord in the family, as shown by experience. Therefore it is not right for one man to have several wives. . . .

Hereby polygamy stands condemned, as also the opinion of Plato who said that wives should be possessed in common. . . .

That Marriage Should Not Be Contracted Between Relatives

For these reasonable motives the laws have decreed that certain persons belonging to a common stock should be debarred from marriage.

Because, as marriage is the union of different persons, those who should consider themselves as one through having a common ancestor, are rightly debarred from marriage, that they may have a greater regard for each other, through realizing that for that reason they are one.

Again. Since in the relations between husband and wife there is a certain natural shame, relations should be forbidden between those who through being united in blood should revere each other. This motive seems to be indicated in the law, where it is said: *Thou shalt not uncover the nakedness of thy sister*, and so on.

Further. That men be too much given to the pleasure of copulation is corruptive of good morals: because, since, more than any other, this pleasure absorbs the mind, the reason would be hindered in things pertaining to rectitude. Now there would result an abuse of pleasure if man were allowed to be united in copulation with those, in whose society he must needs live, such as sisters and other relatives: for it would be impossible to remove the occasion of intercourse with such persons. It was therefore in keeping with good morals that the laws should forbid such unions.

Moreover. *The pleasure of copulation corrupts entirely the judgment of prudence.* Therefore frequency of that pleasure is contrary to good morals. Now, this pleasure is increased by the mutual love of those who are thus united. Hence it would be contrary to good morals for relatives to marry: for then there would be in them the love arising from community of blood and nourishment in addition to the love of desire; and, in consequence, through multiplicity of loves the soul would be all the more a slave to pleasures.

Besides. It is most necessary in human society that friendship be among many. Now friendships among men are multiplied if marriage be contracted between persons of different stock. Therefore it was becoming for the laws to direct that marriage be contracted with those of different stock, and not between relatives.

Also. It is unsuitable that a person be united socially with those to whom he should naturally be subject. Now, it is natural for a man to be subject to his parents. Therefore it is unfitting for one to marry one's parent, since marriage is a social union.

Hence it is said (Lev. 18.6): *No man shall approach to her that is near of kin to him.*

Hereby stands condemned the custom of those who contract bonds of the flesh with persons of their kindred. . . .

That Not All Carnal Intercourse Is Sinful

Just as it is contrary to reason to indulge in carnal intercourse so as to frustrate the begetting and rearing of children, so is it in keeping with reason to make use of it in a manner consistent with procreation and upbringing. Now, the divine law forbids only those things that are contrary to reason, as we have shown above. Therefore, it is unreasonable to say that all carnal intercourse is sinful.

Again. Since the members of the body are instruments of the soul, the end of each member, as of any other instrument, is its use. Now, the use of certain members of the body is carnal intercourse. Therefore carnal intercourse is the end of certain members of the body. But that which is the end of any natural thing, cannot be evil in itself: since that which is according to nature, is directed to an end by divine providence, as stated above. Therefore carnal intercourse cannot possibly be evil in itself.

Further. Natural inclinations are implanted in things by God, who moves all things. Therefore the natural inclination of a species cannot be to that which is evil in itself. Now, in all perfect animals there is a natural inclination to carnal intercourse. Therefore carnal intercourse cannot be evil in itself.

Moreover. That which is a necessary condition for something good and very good, is not evil in itself. But the preservation of the animal species cannot be enduring except by means of generation by carnal intercourse. Therefore carnal intercourse cannot be evil in itself. . . .

Hereby we refute the error of those who say that all carnal intercourse is unlawful: wherefore they utterly condemn matrimony and nuptials. Some of them are led to this assertion because they believe that bodies were made not by a good but by an evil principle. . . .

That Some Human Acts Are Right by Nature, and Not Because They Are Prescribed by Law

From what has been said it may be seen that the things prescribed by the divine law are right not only because they are prescribed by law, but also by their very nature.

For the divine law subjects the human mind to God, and all the rest of man, to reason. Now, the natural order demands that the inferior be subject to the superior. Therefore the precepts of the divine law are in themselves right by nature.

Further. Divine providence has endowed man with the natural tribunal of reason, as the principle of his own acts. Now, natural principles are directed to things that are naturally. Hence there are certain actions naturally becoming to man, and in themselves right by nature, and not merely because they are prescribed by law.

Moreover. Whatsoever has a determinate nature must have determinate actions, becoming to that nature: since the proper operation of a thing is consequent to its nature. Now, it is clear that man has a determinate nature. Therefore there must needs be certain actions that are in themselves becoming to man.

Besides. If a thing is natural to a man, that also must be natural to him, without which he cannot have that thing: for *nature is not wanting in necessaries*. Now, it is natural to man to be a *social animal*, and this is proved by the fact that one man alone does not suffice to procure all the necessities of human life. Con-

sequently whatever is necessary for the maintenance of human society, is naturally becoming to man: such are to observe the rights of others, and to refrain from doing them any harm. Therefore in human acts some things are naturally right.

Also. It has been shown above that it is natural for man to use things beneath him for the needs of his life. Now, there is a certain measure according to which the use of the aforesaid things is expedient for human life, and if that measure be ignored, a wrong is done to man, as in the inordinate consumption of food. Therefore certain human acts are naturally right, and some naturally wrong.

Again. According to the natural order, the body is on account of the soul, and the lower powers of the soul are on account of the reason: even as in other things, matter is for the form, and instruments for the sake of the principal agent. Now, if a thing be ordered to another, it should be a help to it and not a hindrance. Therefore it is naturally right that man should so care for his body and the lower powers of the soul, that they be not a hindrance but a help to the act of reason and to his own good; if it happens otherwise, it will be evil by nature. Therefore winebibbing and feasting; inordinate use of venery which hinders the use of reason; and submission to the passions which thwart the free judgment of reason, are all evil by nature.

Moreover. Those things are natural to every man, whereby he tends to his natural end: while those which are of a contrary nature, are naturally unbecoming to him. Now we have proved above that man is by nature directed to God as his end. Consequently those things whereby man is brought to the knowledge and love of God, are naturally right: and whatever things have a contrary result, are naturally bad for man.

It is therefore clear that good and evil in human acts result not only from the prescription of the law, but also from the order of nature. . . .

Hereby we refute the statement of those who assert that the just and the right are prescribed by law only. . . .

Discussion and Reflection Questions

1. *On the proper end for human beings*: Aquinas believes that there is a single end for all human beings, in virtue of being the kind of creatures we are. Is this true? How can intellectually average people (i.e., almost all of us!) expect to attain to a genuine under-

standing of God, when we cannot even understand how our automobiles work? Do you think that Aquinas overintellectualizes the goal of human life?

2. *On human happiness*: Obviously, Aquinas was, and wrote as, a devout Christian, and his view of human happiness presupposes the acceptance of many Christian doctrines. Do you think that one has to be a Christian to find value in what he says? What insights does Aquinas present that could be utilized apart from his theological presuppositions? Does one have to be a Christian to attain happiness?

3. *On divine and natural law*: In what sense is it true in Aquinas's view that "we do not offend God except by doing something contrary to our own good"? What does this suggest about God's concern for human beings? How does this view relate to Aquinas's claims regarding extramarital sexual intercourse? In what sense, if any, is such activity "contrary to our own good"? How would gays and lesbians respond to Aquinas's suggestion that homosexuality is "unnatural" and therefore something to be prohibited? What are some of the potential problems in arguing from what is "natural" to what is right? What is "natural," anyway?

Suggestions for Further Reading

Vernon J. Bourke, ed., *The Essential Augustine* (Indianapolis: Hackett Publishing Co., 1974), contains a selection of central writings by Augustine. For essays on Augustinian moral philosophy, see *The Ethics of St. Augustine*, edited by William S. Babcock (Atlanta, Ga.: Scholars Press, 1991). Gillian Rosemary Evans, *Augustine on Evil* (New York: Cambridge University Press, 1990) provides a more specialized study of Augustine's moral thought. To get a better feel for Aquinas's thinking on a wide variety of topics, a good place to start is with *An Aquinas Reader: Selections from the Writings of Thomas Aquinas*, edited by Mary T. Clark (New York: Fordham University Press, 1988). A good, brief introduction to the basic ideas of Aquinas's moral theory by a well-known Thomist (i.e., an admirer of St. Thomas) is Ralph McInerny's *Ethica Thomistica: The Moral Philosophy of Thomas Aquinas* (Washington, D.C.: Catholic University of America Press, 1982). See also McInerny's longer introduction to Aquinas's philosophy, *St. Thomas Aquinas* (Notre Dame, Ind.: University of Notre Dame Press, 1982). Other books on Aquinas's moral philosophy include: Peter A. Redpath, *The Moral Wisdom of St. Thomas: An Introduction* (Lanham, Md.: University Press of America, 1983); James F. Keenan, *Goodness and Rightness in Thomas Aquinas's Summa Theologiae* (Washington, D.C.: Georgetown University Press, 1992); and Daniel Mark Nelson, *The Priority of Prudence: Virtue and Natural Law in Thomas Aquinas and the Implications for Modern Ethics* (University Park, Pa.: Pennsylvania State University Press, 1992). For an interesting cross-cultural comparison of the moral theories of an early Confucian and a medieval Christian theologian, see Lee H. Yearle's *Mencius and Aquinas: Theories of Virtue and Conceptions of Courage* (Albany: State University of New York Press, 1990). The natural law tradition in ethics is discussed in Stephen Bucke, "Natural Law," in *A Companion to Ethics*, edited by Peter Singer (Oxford: Blackwell, 1991), pp. 161–174, as well as in L. Weintraub, *Natural Law and Justice* (Cambridge, Mass.: Harvard University Press, 1987). For a contemporary defense of a natural law approach to ethics, see John Finnis, *Natural Law and Natural Rights* (Oxford: Oxford University Press, 1980). For criticisms, see R. Hittinger, *A Critique of the New Natural Law Theory* (Notre Dame, Ind.: University of Notre Dame Press, 1984). Following Aristotle, much of Aquinas's moral theory centers on the nature and acquisition of virtues, albeit understood in a theological context. For some detailed studies of Thomistic virtue ethics, see: Robert C. Miner, "Non-Aristotelian Prudence in the 'Prima Secundae,'" *Thomist* 64 (July 2000): 401–422; *Aquinas' Moral Theory*, edited by Scott MacDonald and Eleonore Stump (Ithaca, N.Y.: Cornell University Press, 1998); John Peterson, "Natural Law, End, and Virtue in Aquinas," *Journal of Philosophical Research* 24 (1999): 397–413; Carlos

Steel, "Rational by Participation: Aquinas and Ockham on the Subject of the Moral Virtues," *Franciscan Studies* 56 (1998): 359–382; and Maria Carl, "Law, Virtue, and Happiness in Aquinas' Moral Theory," *Thomist* 61 (1997): 425–447.

InfoTrac

divine law, natural law, Christian ethics, Augustine, "Thomas Aquinas, Saint"

Chapter 3

The Ethics of Duty

Introduction: Ethics in the European Enlightenment

The ethical theories of Augustine and Aquinas start with the basic assumption of divinely revealed truth about human nature and the world. By the eighteenth century, the age of the European Enlightenment, that starting point could no longer be taken for granted. Europe was still a part of "Christendom," to be sure, but the authority of the church had eroded badly since the Protestant Reformation. People increasingly turned outward to science for their understanding of the world, and inward to their own reason and conscience for guidance in life. When Aquinas talks about the "laws" by which human behavior is to be judged, he is referring to the laws established by the Creator. When that paradigmatic Enlightenment thinker Immanuel Kant speaks of such "laws," he is referring to the rules of conduct that rational beings lay down for themselves in the light of reason. The source of moral authority has shifted from a divinely revealed source external to human beings to their own inner nature. In the Enlightenment, morality becomes something to be worked out by humans for humans.

Ideas of which part of one's own inner nature is the benchmark for morality differed, however, from one philosopher to another. The Scottish philosopher David Hume argued that morality is a matter of sentiment and feeling. Other philosophers were more likely to emphasize the importance of reason over both faith and sentiment, and to stress the autonomy of rationally operating individual judgment over adherence to institutionalized rules of conduct. The ethical writings of Immanuel Kant embody this newfound optimism regarding human capabilities in its fullest form. For Kant genuine morality must be based on reason. Despite their common rejection of religion as the ultimate source of morality, the positions of Hume and Kant could hardly be more different. In his writings (especially the *Treatise of Human Nature*, published in 1739–1740) Hume unflinchingly compares animals to humans and, by parity of reasoning, humans to animals, although he is also careful to note some important differences. Kant, on the other hand, is at pains to distinguish humans from animals, and frequently argues that a particular action is morally unacceptable precisely because it lowers humans to the level of mere animals. Here we have what might be called the Enlightenment dilemma: how to acknowledge the animal nature of human beings while giving due weight to the fact that human beings are also endowed with something almost divine—reason.

In Kant's writings we encounter the outpouring of a mind devoted to the discovery of truth through the rigorous application of rational thinking. Principles of morality become analogous to inviolable laws of nature, equally binding on each rational being. Instead of basing ethics on feelings, ethics must be based on an understanding of what *duty* requires of us. Kant's ethics are often described as deontological ethics, from the Greek word *deon*, meaning duty or obligation. Hume's view is described in the profile that follows. Kant's view is discussed in more detail below, the contrast revealing nicely the differences between them.

PROFILE

David Hume: Reason, the Slave of the Passions

According to the influential philosopher David Hume (1711–1776), morality is more a matter of "sentiment" than of reason. Hume believed that human beings are endowed with certain natural dispositions that make some events immediately agreeable to us, and others immediately disagreeable to us. Our moral judgments are ultimately based on these natural dispositions. To consider a certain character trait or action good or bad is essentially to have a certain feeling of approval or disapproval toward it. This makes moral judgments different from "factual" judgments. Judgments of fact, such as the statement that the sun is larger than the earth, are either true or false, and reason plays a central role in determining the fact of the matter. Judgments of morality, however, cannot be true *or* false, any more than any feeling can be. As Hume summarizes this point, "Morality, therefore, is more properly felt than judged of."

To clarify this claim further, Hume suggests that we consider a particular instance of "wrongness," and that we examine it carefully:

> Take any action allowed to be vicious. Willful murder, for instance. Examine it in all lights, and see if you can find that matter of fact, or real existence, which you call vice. In whichever way you take it, you find only certain passions, motives, volitions, and thoughts. There is no other matter of fact in the case. The vice entirely escapes you, so long as you consider the object. You never can find it, till you turn your reflection into your own breast, and find a sentiment of disapprobation, which arises in you, toward this action. Here is a matter of fact; but it is the object of feeling, not of reason. It lies in yourself, not in the object. So that when you pronounce any action or character to be vicious, you mean nothing, but that from the constitution of your nature you have a feeling or sentiment of blame from the contemplation of it.

"Murder is morally wrong," then, amounts to the claim that when we contemplate murder, we feel intense disapproval. The basis for our common moral judgment about the wrongness of murder is the common moral sentiments we share as human beings. Reason has little or nothing to do with it. Reason does play a small role in morality. It can tell us about the best way to achieve a given end that we have selected. But reason cannot tell us what end we ought to pursue. The choosing of ends is ultimately a matter of sentiment and feeling, or, in the terminology that Hume prefers, our "passions." In a famous phrase, Hume declares that, "Reason is, and ought only to be, the slave of the passions, and can never pretend to any other office than to serve and obey them." This is a view that Kant would shortly attempt to turn on its head. Whether Kant was successful is still a hotly debated issue. Nevertheless, Hume's view of morality has continued to exercise a profound influence on philosophy through the twentieth and twenty-first centuries, and still attracts enthusiastic supporters.

Immanuel Kant:
Reason and Universal Ethical Principles

Nothing can possibly be conceived in the world, or even out of it, which can be called good, without qualification, except a Good Will.

—IMMANUEL KANT, *FUNDAMENTAL PRINCIPLES OF THE METAPHYSIC OF MORALS*

Immanuel Kant's life was as simple as his thought was profound. Some writers have joked that a "Life of Kant" could not be written, because he had no life. While humorous, this remark fails to appreciate the kind of life Kant lived. Some people lead lives of external activity. Kant's life was in his mind, and judging from the depth and breadth of his thinking, his life must be judged to have been quite remarkable. He was born in Königsberg, East Prussia (in what is now Russia), in 1724. His family were Pietists, a Lutheran sect known for their deeply ethical orientation and lack of theological dogmatism. These were characteristics that the young Kant absorbed and that deeply informed his later thinking. After attending the University of Königsberg, he worked as a tutor for several years before becoming a *Privatdozent* (instructor) at the university. During the fifteen years that he held this position he lectured and wrote on philosophy, mathematics, and natural science. Kant lived at a time when one could still make significant contributions in more than one field. Besides his groundbreaking work in philosophy, he invented the nebular hypothesis of the origin of planetary systems that is still accepted, in outline, today. In 1770 he was appointed professor at the University of Königsberg, and he taught there for nearly three decades. Kant never married, but he made it a point to enjoy the company of friends during meals. Conversation, he believed, aided the digestion. He died in Königsberg, where he had spent his entire life, in 1804.

Kant's magnum opus appeared in 1781. In the *Critique of Pure Reason* he sought to stage his own "Copernican Revolution" with regard to the mind and its knowledge of the world. Its philosophical importance was not immediately appreciated, like Hume's *Treatise* before it. The trouble, it seems, was not that the readers of the critique disagreed with the book, but that they were unable to discover what the book as a whole was *about*. Kant had inherited from his philosophical predecessors an overly formalistic style that made his main points anything but clear. Kant continued to work on clarifying and elaborating his philosophy, and in the years thereafter produced a steady stream of books and received a great deal of well-deserved fame. Among these books were several on moral philosophy, including the *Critique of Practical Reason* (1788). One of the best, and clearest, of his ethical works is the gloriously titled *Fundamental Principles of the Metaphysic of Morals* (1785). The selections below are taken from this latter work, in which Kant meticulously lays out his view of the structure of morality.

The title of the *Fundamental Principles of the Metaphysic of Morals* needs to be taken seriously if we are to understand the work. It is a study of the foundations of morality, not a complete system of ethics with applications to various specific moral problems. It is concerned with the most basic principles to be used in constructing a general system of morality. "Metaphysic" in the title refers to basic concepts established by reason, in this case the basic concepts concerning morality. Kant's purpose in this work is, he says, nothing less than "the search for and establishment of the supreme principle of morality." By this he means that he wishes to identify the factor that uniquely makes moral action possible, and by which any action can be judged as to its moral worth. Hume had argued that reason is the slave of the passions, from which it seems to follow that the "decisions" that lead to actions are a product of passion as well. But Kant was convinced that although many of our actions are undertaken to satisfy some desire or another, not all of them are. Moral actions are undertaken, not to accomplish some end, but rather simply because of the principle they embody or are grounded on. The moral worth of an action, he insists, lies "not with the purpose to be attained by it, but in the maxim in accordance with which it is decided upon." Principles, not purposes, are the stuff of morally worthy actions.

As Kant points out, natural philosophy (i.e., science) is in the business of determining the laws according to which everything in the natural world happens. Moral philosophy is in the business of recognizing the laws according to which everything *ought* to happen. "Is it not," he asks, "of the utmost necessity to construct a pure moral philosophy which is completely freed from everything which may be only empirical and thus belong to anthropology?" Kant's project is to construct such a pure moral philosophy based solely on reason and not on particular facts about human beings. Only in this way, he believes, can the moral principles arrived at be valid for all rational beings. Notice how different all of this is from Aristotle's procedure, which is firmly based on the common opinions and practices of human beings, and is more like an inductive science of human nature. Kant's approach is more akin to formal logic or mathematics.

The first section of the *Fundamental Principles of the Metaphysic of Morals* begins with the famous statement of Kant's that is quoted above: "Nothing can possibly be conceived in the world, or even out of it, which can be called good, without qualification, except a Good Will." Notice how different this conclusion is from that reached by Aristotle and Aquinas, both of whom considered happiness (whether achieved naturally or supernaturally) to be the chief good. Kant's concern is not with happiness, but rather with *worthiness* for happiness. The distinction is crucial. Happiness, along with other good and desirable things like power, courage, intelligence, and so on, can be used for evil if not controlled by a good will. One can be happy without a good will, but one cannot be *deserving* (i.e., worthy) of happiness without a good will. It follows that a good will alone can be called good without qualification. Besides, on Kant's view, happiness is subjective and subject to change over time. What makes a person happy at one time may not make her happy at some later time, and happiness differs from person to person. Hence to take happiness as a moral standard is to adopt a shifting, ever-changing gauge. Kant wanted to discover the grounds for a universal, objectively grounded ethics and thought that the notion of a "good will," rather than happiness, was central to such ethics.

The notion of a good will is directly connected with the concept of duty. "Duty," Kant informs us, "is the necessity to do an action from respect for law," quite apart from any expected results from so acting. An action done from respect for law completely excludes inclination as one of its motivating factors. Kant thought that maxims, or subjective principles of volition or willing, were especially important for morality: For example, always treat persons as ends in themselves, never merely as means. What this maxim essentially directs us to do is to treat persons (ourselves included) as beings with dignity and worth, not as mere instruments for our own pursuits. This maxim is to be acted upon quite irrespective of our inclination to do so. It is a principle that, if followed in a lawlike (i.e., consistent) manner, will satisfy the demands of morality.

Kant was especially insistent on the importance of establishing inviolable principles for morality. He thought that people should always act in ways that could serve as rules for anyone to act on in similar circumstances. This is the foundation for his various articulations of what he called the categorical imperative, one version of which states: "Act only according to that maxim by which you can at the same time will that it should become a universal law of nature." What this means, roughly, is that you should not act on any principle or policy that, were it to become the rule for how everyone acts, would destroy or undermine a vitally important societal practice. For example, you should not act on the maxim that you should lie whenever it suits you, because such a maxim would undermine the social practice of truth-telling. If this were to happen, the maxim about lying would in a sense self-destruct: How can you lie when truth-telling is no longer the norm? Lying is only possible against a background of truth-telling. Once you understand this, according to Kant, you realize that you do not need any special moral insight to know what to do in particular situations and need only ask: "Can I will that my maxim become a universal law?" If the answer is no, then the action is prohibited; if yes, it is permitted. Kant had found, he believed, the supreme principle of morality that he sought. You will need to decide for yourself, using your own reasoning powers, whether you find Kant's positions to be plausible or not. Kant himself would demand nothing less from his readers.

Reading Questions

1. *The good will and duty:* Why, according to Kant, is the good will alone worthy of being called good without qualification? What prevents other good things from being good in this way? Why does Kant make a distinction between happiness and worthiness of happiness as the goal of the moral life? How does his account differ from that of Aristotle and Aquinas in this respect? What is the distinction between actions done in accord with duty and actions done for the sake of duty? Which kind of action has moral worth? Why is this distinction important for Kant's moral theory?

2. *The categorical imperative:* What does Kant mean by "imperatives"? How do hypothetical and categorical imperatives differ from one another? Why are hypothetical imperatives an insufficient basis for genuine morality? Kant says that there is only one categorical imperative for morality. What is it? How are duties derived from this imperative? What are some of the specific duties that Kant derives from the categorical imperative of morality?

3. *The autonomy of the will:* What does Kant mean by the terms *autonomy, realm of ends, dignity,* and *respect*? In what way does Kant think that autonomy of the will can be the

supreme principle of morality? What does Kant mean by "heteronomy of the will"? Why are moral principles based on heteronomy said to be spurious? What conclusion does Kant draw from this claim?

The Good Will and Duty

IMMANUEL KANT

Transition from the Common Rational Knowledge of Morality to the Philosophical

Nothing can possibly be conceived in the world, or even out of it, which can be called good, without qualification, except a Good Will. Intelligence, wit, judgment, and the other *talents* of the mind, however they may be named, or courage, resolution, perseverance, as qualities of temperament, are undoubtedly good and desirable in many respects; but these gifts of nature may also become extremely bad and mischievous if the will which is to make use of them, and which, therefore, constitutes what is called *character*, is not good. It is the same with the *gifts of fortune*. Power, riches, honor, even health, and the general well-being and contentment with one's condition which is called *happiness*, inspire pride, and often presumption, if there is not a good will to correct the influence of these on the mind, and with this also to rectify the whole principle of acting, and adapt it to its end. The sight of a being who is not adorned with a single feature of a pure and good will, enjoying unbroken prosperity, can never give pleasure to an impartial rational spectator. Thus a good will appears to constitute the indispensable condition even of being worthy of happiness.

There are even some qualities which are of service to this good will itself, and may facilitate its action, yet which have no intrinsic unconditional value, but always presuppose a good will, and this qualifies the esteem that we justly have for them, and does not permit us to regard them as absolutely good. Moderation in the affections and passions, self-control, and calm deliberation are not only good in many respects, but even seem to constitute part of the intrinsic worth of the person; but they are far from deserving to be called good without qualification, although they have been so unconditionally praised by the ancients. For without the principles of a good will, they may become extremely bad; and the coolness of a villain not only makes him far more dangerous, but also directly makes him more abominable in our eyes than he would have been without it.

A good will is good not because of what it performs or effects, not by its aptness for the attainment of some proposed end, but simply by virtue of the volition, that is, it is good in itself, and considered by itself is to be esteemed much higher than all that can be brought about by it in favor of any inclination, nay, even of the sum-total of all inclinations. Even if it should happen that, owing to special disfavor of fortune, or the niggardly provision of a step-motherly nature, this will should wholly lack power to accomplish its purpose, if with its greatest efforts it should yet achieve nothing, and there should remain only the good will (not, to be sure, a mere wish, but the summoning of all means in our power), then, like a jewel, it would still shine by its own light, as a thing which has its whole value in itself. Its usefulness or fruitlessness can neither add of nor take away anything from this value. It would be, as it were, only the setting to enable us to handle it the more conveniently in common commerce, or to attract to it the attention of those who are not yet connoisseurs, but not to recommend it to true connoisseurs, or to determine its value.

There is, however, something so strange in this idea of the absolute value of the mere will, in which no account is taken of its utility, that notwithstanding

Immanuel Kant, *"Fundamental Principles of the Metaphysic of Morals,"* pp. 9–22 *in* Kant's Critique of Practical Reason and Other Works on the Theory of Ethics, *6th ed., translated by Thomas Kingsmill Abbott (London: Longmans, Green and Co., 1909).*

the thorough assent of even common reason to the idea, yet a suspicion must arise that it may perhaps really be the product of mere high-flown fancy, and that we may have misunderstood the purpose of nature in assigning reason as the governor of our will. Therefore we will examine this idea from this point of view.

In the physical constitution of an organized being, that is, a being adapted suitably to the purposes of life, we assume it as a fundamental principle that no organ for any purpose will be found but what is also the fittest and best adapted for that purpose. Now in a being which has reason and a will, if the proper object of nature were its *conservation*, its *welfare*, in a word, its *happiness*, then nature would have hit upon a very bad arrangement in selecting the reason of the creature to carry out this purpose. For all the actions which the creature has to perform with a view to this purpose, and the whole rule of its conduct, would be far more surely prescribed to it by instinct, and that end would have been attained thereby much more certainly than it ever can be by reason. Should reason have been communicated to this favored creature over and above, it must only have served it to contemplate the happy constitution of its nature, to admire it, to congratulate itself thereon, and to feel thankful for it to the beneficent cause, but not that it should subject its desires to that weak and delusive guidance, and meddle bunglingly with the purpose of nature. In a word, nature would have taken care that reason should not break forth into *practical exercise*, nor have the presumption, with its weak insight, to think out for itself the plan of happiness, and of the means of attaining it. Nature would not only have taken on herself the choice of the ends, but also of the means, and with wise foresight would have entrusted both to instinct.

And, in fact, we find that the more a cultivated reason applies itself with deliberate purpose to the enjoyment of life and happiness, so much the more does the man fail of true satisfaction. And from this circumstance there arises in many, if they are candid enough to confess it, a certain degree of *misology*, that is, hatred of reason, especially in the case of those who are most experienced in the use of it, because after calculating all the advantages they derive, I do not say from the invention of all the arts of common luxury, but even from the sciences (which seem to them to be after all only a luxury of the understanding), they find that they have, in fact, only brought more trouble on their shoulders, rather than gained in happiness; and they end by envying, rather than despising, the more common stamp of men who keep closer to the guidance of mere instinct, and do not allow their reason much influence on their conduct. And this we must admit, that the judgment of those who would very much lower the lofty eulogies of the advantages which reason gives us in regard to the happiness and satisfaction of life, or who would even reduce them below zero, is by no means morose or ungrateful to the goodness with which the world is governed, but that there lies at the root of these judgments the idea that our existence has a different and far nobler end, for which, and not for happiness, reason is properly intended, and which must, therefore, be regarded as the supreme condition to which the private ends of man must, for the most part, be postponed.

For as reason is not competent to guide the will with certainty in regard to its objects and the satisfaction of all our wants (which it to some extent even multiplies), this being an end to which an implanted instinct would have led with much greater certainty; and since, nevertheless, reason is imparted to us as a practical faculty, i.e., as one which is to have influence on the *will*, therefore, admitting that nature generally in the distribution of her capacities has adapted the means to the end, its true destination must be to produce a *will*, not merely good as a *means* to something else, but *good in itself*, for which reason was absolutely necessary. This will then, though not indeed the sole and complete good, must be the supreme good and the condition of every other, even of the desire of happiness. Under these circumstances, there is nothing inconsistent with the wisdom of nature in the fact that the cultivation of the reason, which is requisite for the first and unconditional purpose, does in many ways interfere, at least in this life, with the attainment of the second, which is always conditional, namely, happiness. Nay, it may even reduce it to nothing, without nature thereby failing of her purpose. For reason recognized the establishment of a good will as its highest practical destination, and in attaining this purpose is capable only of a satisfaction of its own proper kind, namely, that from the attainment of an end, which end again is determined by reason only, notwithstanding that this may involve many a disappointment to the ends of inclination.

We have then to develop the notion of a will which deserves to be highly esteemed for itself, and is good without a view to anything further, a notion which exists already in the sound natural understanding, requiring rather to be cleared up than to be taught, and which in estimating the value of our actions always takes the first place, and constitutes the condition of all the rest. In order to do this, we will take the notion of duty, which includes that of a good will, although implying certain subjective restrictions and hindrances. These, however, far from concealing it, or rendering it unrecognizable, rather bring it out by contrast, and make it shine forth so much the brighter.

I omit here all actions which are already recognized as inconsistent with duty, although they may be useful for this or that purpose, for with these the question whether they are done *from duty* cannot arise at all, since they even conflict with it. I also set aside those actions which really conform to duty, but to which men have *no* direct *inclination*, performing them because they are impelled thereto by some other inclination. For in this case we can readily distinguish whether the action which agrees with duty is done *from duty*, or from a selfish view. It is much harder to make this distinction when the action accords with duty, and the subject has besides a *direct* inclination to it. For example, it is always a matter of duty that a dealer should not overcharge an inexperienced purchaser; and whenever there is much commerce the prudent tradesman does not overcharge, but keeps a fixed price for everyone, so that a child buys of him as well as any other. Men are thus *honestly* served; but this is not enough to make us believe that the tradesman has so acted from duty and from principles of honesty: his own advantage required it; it is out of the question in this case to suppose that he might besides have a direct inclination in favor of the buyers, so that, as it were, from love he should give no advantage to one over another. Accordingly the action was done neither from duty nor from direct inclination, but merely with a selfish view.

On the other hand, it is a duty to maintain one's life; and, in addition, everyone has also a direct inclination to do so. But on this account the often anxious care which most men take for it has no intrinsic worth, and their maxim has no moral import. They preserve their life *as duty requires* no doubt, but not *because duty requires*. On the other hand, if adversity and hopeless sorrow have completely taken away the relish for life; if the unfortunate one, strong in mind, indignant at his fate rather than desponding or dejected, wishes for death, and yet preserves his life without loving it—not from inclination or fear, but from duty—then his maxim has a moral worth.

To be beneficent when we can is a duty; and besides this, there are many minds so sympathetically constituted that, without any other motive of vanity or self-interest, they find a pleasure in spreading joy around them, and can take delight in the satisfaction of others so far as it is their own work. But I maintain that in such a case an action of this kind, however proper, however amiable it may be, has nevertheless no true moral worth, but is on a level with other inclinations, e.g., the inclination to honor, which, if it is happily directed to that which is in fact of public utility and accordant with duty, and consequently honorable, deserves praise and encouragement, but not esteem. For the maxim lacks the moral import, namely, that such actions be done *from duty*, not from inclination. Put the case that the mind of that philanthropist was clouded by sorrow of his own, extinguishing all sympathy with the lot of others, and that while he still has the power to benefit others in distress, he is not touched by their trouble because he is absorbed with his own; and now suppose that he tears himself out of this dead insensibility, and performs the action without any inclination to it, but simply from duty, then first has his action its genuine moral worth. Further still; if nature has put little sympathy in the heart of this or that man; if he, supposed to be an upright man, is by temperament cold and indifferent to the sufferings of others, perhaps because in respect of his own he is provided with the special gift of patience and fortitude, and supposes, or even requires, that others should have the same—and such a man would certainly not be the meanest product of nature—but if nature had not specially framed him for a philanthropist, would he not still find in himself a source from whence to give himself a far higher worth than that of a good-natured temperament could be? Unquestionably. It is just in this that the moral worth of the character is brought out which is incomparable the highest of all, namely, that he is beneficent, not from inclination, but from duty.

To secure one's own happiness is a duty, at least indirectly; for discontent with one's condition, under a pressure of many anxieties and amidst unsatisfied wants, might easily become a great *temptation to transgression of duty*. But here again, without looking to duty, all men have already the strongest and most intimate inclination to happiness, because it is just in this idea that all inclinations are combined in one total. But the precept of happiness is often of such a sort that it greatly interferes with some inclinations, and yet a man cannot form any definite and certain conception of the sum of satisfaction of all of them which is called happiness. It is not then to be wondered at that a single inclination, definite both as to what it promises and as to the time within which it can be gratified, is often able to overcome such a fluctuating idea, and that a gouty patient, for instance, can choose to enjoy what he likes, and to suffer what he may, since, according to his calculation, on this occasion at least, he has [only] not sacrificed the enjoyment of the present moment to a possible mistaken expectation of a happiness which is supposed to be found in health. But even in this case, if the general desire for happiness did not influence his will, and supposing that in his particular case health was not a necessary element in this calculation, there yet remains in this, as in all other cases, this law, namely, that he would promote his happiness not from inclination but from duty, and by this would his conduct first acquire true moral worth.

It is in this manner, undoubtedly, that we are to understand those passages of Scripture also in which we are commanded to love our neighbor, even our enemy. For love, as an affection, cannot be commanded, but beneficence for duty's sake may; even though we are not impelled to it by any inclination—nay, are even repelled by a natural and unconquerable aversion. This is *practical* love, and not *pathological*—a love which is seated in the will, and not in the propensions of sense—in principles of action and not of tender sympathy; and it is this love alone which can be commanded.

The second[1] proposition is: That an action done from duty derives its moral worth, *not from the purpose* which is to be attained by it, but from the maxim by which it is determined, and therefore does not depend on the realization of the object of the action, but merely on the *principle of volition* by which the action has taken place, without regard to any object of desire. It is clear from what precedes that the purposes which we may have in view in our actions, or their effects regarded as ends and springs of the will, cannot give to actions any unconditional or moral worth. In what, then, can their worth lie, if it is not to consist in the will and in reference to its expected effect? It cannot lie anywhere but in the *principle of the will* without regard to the ends which can be attained by the action. For the will stands between its a priori principle, which is formal. And its a posteriori spring, which is material, as between two roads, and as it must be determined by something, it follows that it must be determined by the formal principle of volition when an action is done from duty, in which case every material principle has been withdrawn from it.

The third proposition, which is a consequence of the two preceding, I would express thus: *Duty is the necessity of acting from respect for the law.* I may have *inclination* for an object as the effect of my proposed action, but I cannot have *respect* for it, just for this reason, that it is an effect and not an energy of will. Similarly, I cannot have respect for inclination, whether my own or another's; I can at most, if my own, approve it; if another's, sometimes even love it; i.e., look on it as favorable to my own interest. It is only what is connected with my will as a principle, by no means as an effect—what does not subserve my inclination, but overpowers it, or at least in case of choice excludes it from its calculation—in other words, simply the law of itself, which can be an object of respect, and hence a command. Now an action done from duty must wholly exclude the influence of inclination, and with it every object of the will, so that nothing remains which can determine the will except objectively the *law*, and subjectively *pure respect* for this practical law, and consequently the maxim[2] that I should follow this law even to the thwarting of all my inclinations.

Thus the moral worth of an action does not lie in the effect expected from it, nor in any principle of action which requires to borrow its motive from this expected effect. For all these effects—agreeableness of one's condition, and even the promotion of the happiness of others—could have been also brought about by other causes, so that for this there would have been no need of the will of a rational being; whereas it is in this alone that the supreme and unconditional good can be found. The preeminent good which we call moral can therefore consist in nothing else than *the conception of law* in itself, *which certainly is only possible in a rational being,* so far as this conception, and not the expected effect, determines the will. This is a good which is already present in the person who acts accordingly, and we have not to wait for it to appear first in the result.[3]

[2]A *maxim* is the subjective principle of volition. The objective principle (i.e., that which would also serve subjectively as a practical principle to all rational beings if reason had full power over the faculty of desire) is the practical *law*.

[3]It might be here objected to me that I take refuge behind the word *respect* in an obscure feeling, instead of giving a distinct solution of the question by a concept of the reason. But although respect is a feeling, it is not a feeling *received* through influence, but is *self-wrought* by a rational concept, and, therefore, is specifically distinct from all feelings of the former kind, which may be referred either to inclination or fear. What I recognize immediately as a law for me, I recognize with respect. This merely signifies the consciousness that my will is *subordinate* to a law, without the intervention of other influences on my sense. The immediate determination of the will by the law, and the consciousness of this, is called *respect*, so that this is regarded as an *effect* of the law on the subject, and not as the *cause* of it. Respect is properly the conception of a worth which thwarts my self-love. Accordingly it is something which is considered neither as an object of inclination nor of fear, although it has something

[1][The first proposition was that to have moral worth an action must be done from duty.]

But what sort of law can that be, the conception of which must determine the will, even without paying any regard to the effect expected from it, in order that this will may be called good absolutely and without qualification? As I have deprived the will of every impulse which could arise to it from obedience to any law, there remains nothing but the universal conformity of its actions to law in general, which alone is to serve the will as a principle, i.e., I am never to act otherwise than so *that I could also will that my maxim should become a universal law.* Here, now, it is the simple conformity to law in general, without assuming any particular law applicable to certain actions, that serves the will as its principle, and must so serve it, if duty is not to be a vain delusion and a chimerical notion. The common reason of men in its practical judgments perfectly coincides with this, and always has in view the principle here suggested. Let the question be, for example: May I when in distress make a promise with the intention not to keep it? I readily distinguish here between the two significations which the question may have: Whether it is prudent, or whether it is right, to make a false promise? The former may undoubtedly often be the case. I see clearly indeed that it is not enough to extricate myself from a present difficulty by means of this subterfuge, but it must be well considered whether there may not hereafter spring from this lie much greater inconvenience than that from which I now free myself, and as, with all my supposed *cunning*, the consequences cannot be so easily foreseen but that credit once lost may be much more injurious to me than any mischief which I seek to avoid at present, it should be considered whether it would not be more *prudent* to act herein according to a universal maxim, and to make it a habit to promise nothing except with the intention of keeping it. But it is soon clear to me that

such a maxim will still only be based on the fear of consequences. Now it is a wholly different thing to be truthful from duty, and to be so from apprehension of injurious consequences. In the first case, the very notion of the action already implies a law for me; in the second case, I must first look about elsewhere to see what results may be combined with it which would affect myself. For to deviate from the principle of duty is beyond all doubt wicked; but to be unfaithful to my maxim of prudence may often be very advantageous to me, although to abide by it is certainly safer. The shortest way, however, and an unerring one, to discover the answer to this question whether a lying promise is consistent with duty, is to ask myself, Should I be content that my maxim (to extricate myself from difficulty by a false promise) should hold good as a universal law, for myself as well as for others? And should I be able to say to myself, "Every one may make a deceitful promise when he finds himself in a difficulty from which he cannot otherwise extricate himself"? Then I presently become aware that while I can will the lie, I can by no means will that lying should be a universal law. For with such a law there would be no promises at all, since it would be in vain to allege my intention in regard to my future actions to those who would not believe this allegation, or if they over-hastily did so, would pay me back in my own coin. Hence my maxim, as soon as it should be made a universal law, would necessarily destroy itself.

I do not, therefore, need any far-reaching penetration to discern what I have to do in order that my will may be morally good. Inexperienced in the course of the world, incapable of being prepared for all its contingencies, I only ask myself: Canst thou also will that thy maxim should be a universal law? If not, then it must be rejected, and that not because of a disadvantage accruing from it to myself or even to others but because it cannot enter as a principle into a possible universal legislation, and reason extorts from me immediate respect for such legislation. I do not indeed as yet *discern* on what this respect is based (this the philosopher may inquire), but at least I understand this, that it is an estimation of the worth which far outweighs all worth of what is recommended by inclination, and that the necessity of acting from *pure* respect for the practical law is what constitutes duty, to which every other motive must give place, because it is the condition of a will being good *in itself*, and the worth of such a will is above everything. . . .

---

analogous to both. The *object* of respect is the *law* only, and that, the law which we impose on *ourselves*, and yet recognize as necessary in itself. As a law, we are subjected to it without consulting self-love; as imposed by us on ourselves, it is a result of our will. In the former aspect it has an analogy to fear, in the latter to inclination. Respect for a person is properly only respect for the law (of honesty, etc.) of which he gives us an example. Since we also look on the improvement of our talents as a duty, we consider that we see in a person of talents, as it were, the *example of a law* (viz. to become like him in this by exercise), and this constitutes our respect. All so-called moral *interest* consists simply in *respect* for the law.

The Categorical Imperative

IMMANUEL KANT

Transition from Popular Moral Philosophy to the Metaphysic of Morals

... Everything in nature works according to laws. Rational beings alone have the faculty of acting according *to the conception* of laws, that is according to principles, i.e., have a *will*. Since the deduction of actions from principles requires *reason*, the will is nothing but practical reason. If reason infallibly determines the will, then the actions of such a being which are recognized as objectively necessary are subjectively necessary also, i.e., the will is a faculty to choose *that only* which reason independent on inclination recognizes as practically necessary, i.e., as good. But if reason of itself does not sufficiently determine the will, if the latter is subject also to subjective conditions (particular impulses) which do not always coincide with the objective conditions; in a word, if the will does not *in itself* completely accord with reason (which is actually the case with men), then the actions which objectively are recognized as necessary are subjectively contingent, and the determination of such a will according to objective laws is *obligation*, that is to say, the relation of the objective laws to a will that is not thoroughly good is conceived as the determination of the will of a rational being by principles of reason, but which the will from its nature does not of necessity follow.

The conception of an objective principle, in so far as it is obligatory for a will, is called a command (of reason), and the formula of the command is called an Imperative.

All imperatives are expressed by the word *ought* [or *shall*], and thereby indicate the relation of an objective law of reason to a will, which from its subjective constitution is not necessarily determined by it (an obligation). They say that something would be good to do or to forbear, but they say it to a will which does not always do a thing because it is conceived to be good to do it. That is practically *good*, however, which determines the will by means of the conceptions of reason, and consequently not from

subjective causes, but objectively, that is on principles which are valid for every rational being as such. It is distinguished from the *pleasant*, as that which influences the will only by means of sensation from merely subjective causes, valid only for the sense of this or that one, and not as a principle of reason, which holds for every one.[1]

A perfectly good will would therefore be equally subject to objective laws (viz. laws of good), but could not be conceived as *obliged* thereby to act lawfully, because of itself from its subjective constitution it can only be determined by the conception of good. Therefore no imperatives hold for the Divine will, or in general for a *holy* will; *ought* is here out of place, because the volition is already of itself necessarily in unison with the law. Therefore imperatives are only formulæ to express the relation of objective laws of all volition to the subjective imperfection of the will of this or that rational being, e.g., the human will.

Now all *imperatives* command either *hypothetically* or *categorically*. The former represent the practical necessity of a possible action as means to something

---

[1]The dependence of the desires on sensations is called inclination, and this accordingly always indicates a *want*. The dependence of a contingently determinable will on principles of reason is called an *interest*. This, therefore, is found only in the case of a dependent will which does not always of itself conform to reason; in the Divine will we cannot conceive any interest. But the human will can also *take an interest* in a thing without therefore acting *from interest*. The former signifies the *practical* interest in the action, the latter the *pathological* in the object of the action. The former indicates only dependence of the will on principles of reason in themselves; the second, dependence on principles of reason for the sake of inclination, reason supplying only the practical rules how the requirement of the inclination may be satisfied. In the first case the action interests me; in the second the object of the action (because it is pleasant to me). We have seen in the first section that in an action done from duty we must look not to the interest in the object, but only to that in the action itself, and in its rational principle (viz. the law).

Immanuel Kant, "Fundamental Principles of the Metaphysics of Morals," pp. 29–59 in Kant's Critique of Practical Reason and Other Works on the Theory of Ethics, *6th ed., translated by Thomas Kingsmill Abbott (London: Longmans, Green and Co., 1909).*

else that is willed (or at least which one might possibly will). The categorical imperative would be that which represented an action as necessary of itself without reference to another end, i.e., as objectively necessary.

Since every practical law represents a possible action as good, and on this account, for a subject who is practically determinable by reason, necessary, all imperatives are formulæ determining an action which is necessary according to the principle of a will good in some respects. If now the action is good only as a means *to something else*, then the imperative is *hypothetical*; if it is conceived as good *in itself* and consequently as being necessarily the principle of a will which of itself conforms to reason, then it is *categorical*.

Thus the imperative declares what action possible by me would be good, and presents the practical rule in relation to a will which does not forthwith perform an action simply because it is good, whether because the subject does not always know that it is good, or because, even if it know this, yet its maxims might be opposed to the objective principles of practical reason.

Accordingly the hypothetical imperative only says that the action is good for some purpose, *possible* or *actual*. In the first case it is a Problematical, in the second an Assertorial practical principle. The categorical imperative which declares an action to be objectively necessary in itself without reference to any purpose, i.e., without any other end, is valid as an Apodictic (practical) principle.

Whatever is possible only by the power of some rational being may also be conceived as a possible purpose of some will; and therefore the principles of action as regards the means necessary to attain some possible purpose are in fact infinitely numerous. All sciences have a practical part, consisting of problems expressing that some end is possible for us, and of imperatives directing how it may be attained. These may, therefore, be called in general imperatives of Skill. Here there is no question whether the end is rational and good, but only what one must do in order to attain it. The precepts for the physician to make his patient thoroughly healthy, and for a poisoner to ensure certain death, are of equal value in this respect, that each serves to effect its purpose perfectly. Since in early youth it cannot be known what ends are likely to occur to us in the course of life, parents seek to have their children taught a *great many things*, and provide for their *skill* in the use of means for all sorts of arbitrary ends, of none of which can they determine whether it may not perhaps hereafter be an object to their pupil, but which it is at all events *possible* that he might aim at; and this anxiety is so great that

they commonly neglect to form and correct their judgment on the value of the things which may be chosen as ends.

There is *one* end, however, which may be assumed to be actually such to all rational beings (so far as imperatives apply to them, viz. as dependent beings), and, therefore, one purpose which they not merely *may* have, but which we may with certainty assume that they all actually *have by* a natural necessity, and this is *happiness*. The hypothetical imperative which expresses the practical necessity of an action as means to the advancement of happiness is Assertorial. We are not to present it as necessary for an uncertain and merely possible purpose, but for a purpose which we may presuppose with certainty and a priori in every man, because it belongs to his being. Now skill in the choice of means to his own greatest well-being may be called *prudence*[2] in the narrowest sense. And thus the imperative which refers to the choice of means to one's own happiness, i.e., the precept of prudence, is still always *hypothetical*; the action is not commanded absolutely, but only as means to another purpose.

Finally, there is an imperative which commands a certain conduct immediately, without having as its condition any other purpose to be attained by it. This imperative is Categorical. It concerns not the matter of the action, or its intended result, but its form and the principle of which it is itself a result; and what is essentially good in it consists in the mental disposition, let the consequence be what it may. This imperative may be called that of Morality.

There is a marked distinction also between the volitions on these three sorts of principles in the *dissimilarity* of the obligation of the will. In order to mark this difference more clearly, I think they would be most suitably named in their order if we said they are either *rules* of skill, or *counsels* of prudence, or *commands* (*laws*) of morality. For it is *law* only that involves the conception of an *unconditional* and objective necessity, which is consequently universally valid; and commands are laws which must be

---

[2] The word *prudence* is taken in two senses: in the one it may bear the name of knowledge of the world, in the other that of private prudence. The former is a man's ability to influence others so as to use them for his own purposes. The latter is the sagacity to combine all these purposes for his own lasting benefit. This latter is properly that to which the value even of the former is reduced, and when a man is prudent in the former sense, but not in the latter, we might better say of him that he is clever and cunning, but, on the whole, imprudent.

obeyed, that is, must be followed, even in opposition to inclination. *Counsels*, indeed, involve necessity, but one which can only hold under a contingent subjective condition, viz. they depend on whether this or that man reckons this or that as part of his happiness; the categorical imperative, on the contrary, is not limited by any condition, and as being absolutely, although practically, necessary, may be quite properly called a command. We might also call the first kind of imperatives *technical* (belonging to art), the second *pragmatic*[3] (to welfare), the third *moral* (belonging to free conduct generally, that is, to morals).

Now arises the question, how are all these imperatives possible? This question does not seek to know how we can conceive the accomplishment of the action which the imperative ordains, but merely how we can conceive the obligation of the will which the imperative expresses. No special explanation is needed to show how an imperative of skill is possible. Whoever wills the end, wills also (so far as reason decides his conduct) the means in his power which are indispensably necessary thereto. This proposition is, as regards the volition, analytical; for, in willing an object as my effect, there is already thought the causality of myself as an acting cause, that is to say, the use of the means; and the imperative educes from the conception of volition of an end the conception of actions necessary to this end. Synthetical propositions must no doubt be employed in defining the means to a proposed end; but they do not concern the principle, the act of the will, but the object and its realization. E.g., that in order to bisect a line on an unerring principle I must draw from its extremities two intersecting arcs; this no doubt is taught by mathematics only in synthetical propositions; but if I know that it is only by this process that the intended operation can be performed, then to say that if I fully will the operation, I also will the action required for it, is an analytical proposition; for it is one and the same thing to conceive something as an effect which I can produce in a certain way, and to conceive myself as acting in this way.

If it were only equally easy to give a definite conception of happiness, the imperatives of prudence would correspond exactly with those of skill, and would likewise be analytical. For in this case as in that, it could be said, whoever wills the end, wills also (according to the dictate of reason necessarily) the indispensable means thereto which are in his power. But, unfortunately, the notion of happiness is so indefinite that although every man wishes to attain it, yet he never can say definitely and consistently what it is that he really wishes and wills. The reason of this is that all the elements which belong to the notion of happiness are altogether empirical, i.e., they must be borrowed from experience, and nevertheless the idea of happiness requires an absolute whole, a maximum of welfare in my present and all future circumstances. Now it is impossible that the most clear-sighted and at the same time most powerful being (supposed finite) should frame to himself a definite conception of what he really wills in this. Does he will riches, how much anxiety, envy, and snares might he not thereby draw upon his shoulders? Does he will knowledge and discernment, perhaps it might prove to be only an eye so much the sharper to show him so much the more fearfully the evils that are now concealed from him, and that cannot be avoided, or to impose more wants on his desires, which already give him concern enough. Would he have long life? Who guarantees to him that it would not be a long misery? Would he at least have health? How often has uneasiness of the body restrained from excesses into which perfect health would have allowed one to fall? And so on. In short, he is unable, on any principle, to determine with certainty what would make him truly happy; because to do so he would need to be omniscient. We cannot therefore act on any definite principles to secure happiness, but only on empirical counsels, e.g., of regimen, frugality, courtesy, reserve, etc., which experience teaches do, on the average, most promote well-being. Hence it follows that the imperatives of prudence do not, strictly speaking, command at all, that is, they cannot present actions objectively as practically *necessary*; that they are rather to be regarded as counsels (*consilia*) than precepts (*præcepta*) of reason, that the problem to determine certainly and universally what action would promote the happiness of a rational being is completely insoluble, and consequently no imperative respecting it is possible which should, in the strict sense, command to do what makes happy; because happiness is not an ideal of reason but of imagination, resting solely on empirical grounds, and it is vain to expect that these should define an action by which one could attain the totality of a series of consequences which is really

---

[3] It seems to me that the proper signification of the word *pragmatic* may be most accurately defined in this way. For *sanctions* are called pragmatic which flow properly, not from the law of the states as necessary enactments, but from *precaution* for the general welfare. A history is composed pragmatically when it teaches *prudence*, i.e., instructs the world how it can provide for its interests better, or at least as well as the men of former time.

endless. This imperative of prudence would, however, be an analytical proposition if we assume that the means to happiness could be certainly assigned; for it is distinguished from the imperative of skill only by this, that in the latter the end is merely possible, in the former it is given; as, however, both only ordain the means to that which we suppose to be willed as an end, it follows that the imperative which ordains the willing of the means to him who wills the end is in both cases analytical. Thus there is no difficulty in regard to the possibility of an imperative of this kind either.

On the other hand, the question, how the imperative of *morality* is possible, is undoubtedly one, the only one, demanding a solution, as this is not at all hypothetical, and the objective necessity which it presents cannot rest on any hypothesis, as is the case with the hypothetical imperatives. Only here we must never leave out of consideration that we *cannot* make out *by any example*, in other words empirically, whether there is such an imperative at all; but it is rather to be feared that all those which seem to be categorical may yet be at bottom hypothetical. For instance, when the precept is: Thou shalt not promise deceitfully; and it is assumed that the necessity of this is not a mere counsel to avoid some other evil, so that it should mean: Thou shalt not make a lying promise, lest if it become known thou shouldst destroy thy credit, but that an action of this kind must be regarded as evil in itself, so that the imperative of the prohibition is categorical; then we cannot show with certainty in any example that the will was determined merely by the law, without any other spring of action, although it may appear to be so. For it is always possible that fear of disgrace, perhaps also obscure dread of other dangers, may have a secret influence on the will. Who can prove by experience the nonexistence of a cause when all that experience tells us is that we do not perceive it? But in such a case the so-called moral imperative, which as such appears to be categorical and unconditional, would in reality be only a pragmatic precept, drawing our attention to our own interests, and merely teaching us to take these into consideration.

We shall therefore have to investigate a priori the possibility of a categorical imperative, as we have not in this case the advantage of its reality being given in experience, so that [the elucidation of] its possibility should be requisite only for its explanation, not for its establishment. In the meantime it may be discerned beforehand that the categorical imperative alone has the purport of a practical law: all the rest may indeed be called *principles* of the will but not laws, since

whatever is only necessary for the attainment of some arbitrary purpose may be considered as in itself contingent, and we can at any time be free from the precept if we give up the purpose: on the contrary, the unconditional command leaves the will no liberty to choose the opposite; consequently it alone carries with it that necessity which we require in a law.

Secondly, in the case of this categorical imperative or law of morality, the difficulty (of discerning its possibility) is a very profound one. It is an a priori synthetical practical proposition;[4] and as there is so much difficulty in discerning the possibility of speculative propositions of this kind, it may readily be supposed that the difficulty will be no less with the practical.

In this problem we will first inquire whether the mere conception of a categorical imperative may not perhaps supply us also with the formula of it, containing the proposition which alone can be a categorical imperative; for even if we know the tenor of such an absolute command, yet how it is possible will require further special and laborious study, which we postpone to the last section.

When I conceive a hypothetical imperative, in general I do not know beforehand what it will contain until I am given the condition. But when I conceive a categorical imperative, I know at once what it contains. For as the imperative contains besides the law only the necessity that the maxims[5] shall conform to this law, while the law contains no conditions restricting it, there remains nothing but the general statement that the maxim of the action should conform to a universal law, and it is this conformity alone that the imperative properly represents as necessary.

---

[4] I connect the act with the will without presupposing any condition resulting from any inclination, but a priori, and therefore necessarily (though only objectively, i.e., assuming the idea of a reason possessing full power over all subjective motives). This is accordingly a practical proposition which does not deduce the willing of an action by mere analysis from another already presupposed (for we have not such a perfect will), but connects it immediately with the conception of the will of a rational being, as something not contained in it.

[5] A maxim is a subjective principle of action, and must be distinguished from the *objective principle*, namely, practical law. The former contains the practical rule set by reason according to the conditions of the subject (often its ignorance or its inclinations), so that it is the principle on which the subject *acts*; but the law is the objective principle valid for every rational being, and is the principle on which it *ought to act* that is an imperative.

There is therefore but one categorical imperative, namely, this: *Act only on that maxim whereby thou canst at the same time will that it should become a universal law.*

Now if all imperatives of duty can be deduced from this one imperative as from their principle, then, although it should remain undecided whether what is called duty is not merely a vain notion, yet at least we shall be able to show what we understand by it and what this notion means.

Since the universality of the law according to which effects are produced constitutes what is properly called *nature* in the most general sense (as to form), that is the existence of things so far as it is determined by general laws, the imperative of duty may be expressed thus: *Act as if the maxim of thy action were to become by thy will a universal law of nature.*

We will now enumerate a few duties, adopting the usual division of them into duties to ourselves and to others, and into perfect and imperfect duties.[6]

1. A man reduced to despair by a series of misfortunes feels wearied of life, but is still so far in possession of his reason that he can ask himself whether it would not be contrary to his duty to himself to take his own life. Now he inquires whether the maxim of his actions could become a universal law of nature. His maxim is: From self-love I adopt it as a principle to shorten my life when its longer duration is likely to bring more evil than satisfaction. It is asked then simply whether this principle founded on self-love can become a universal law of nature. Now we see at once that a system of nature of which it should be a law to destroy life by means of the very feeling whose special nature it is to impel to the improvement of life would contradict itself, and therefore could not exist as a system of nature; hence that maxim cannot possibly exist as a universal law of nature, and consequently would be wholly inconsistent with the supreme principle of all duty.

[6]It must be noted here that I reserve the division of duties for a future *metaphysic of morals*; so that I give it here only as an arbitrary one (in order to arrange my examples). For the rest, I understand by a perfect duty one that admits no exception in favor of inclination, and then I have not merely external but also internal perfect duties. This is contrary to the use of the word adopted in the schools; but I do not intend to justify it here, as it is all one for my purpose whether it is admitted or not. [*Perfect* duties are usually understood to be those which can be enforced by external law; *imperfect*, those which cannot be enforced. They are also called respectively *determinate* and *indeterminate*, *officio juris* and *officio virtutis*.]

2. Another finds himself forced by necessity to borrow money. He knows that he will not be able to repay it, but sees also that nothing will be lent to him, unless he promises stoutly to repay it in a definite time. He desires to make this promise, but he has still so much conscience as to ask himself: Is it not unlawful and inconsistent with duty to get out of a difficulty in this way? Suppose, however, that he resolves to do so, then the maxim of his action would be expressed thus: When I think myself in want of money, I will borrow money and promise to repay it, although I know that I never can do so. Now this principle of self-love or of one's own advantage may perhaps be consistent with my whole future welfare; but the question now is, Is it right? I change then the suggestion of self-love into a universal law, and state the question thus: How would it be if my maxim were a universal law? Then I see at once that it could never hold as a universal law of nature, but would necessarily contradict itself. For supposing it to be a universal law that everyone when he thinks himself in a difficulty should be able to promise whatever he pleases, with the purpose of not keeping his promise, the promise itself would become impossible, as well as the end that one might have in view of it, since no one would consider that anything was promised to him, but would ridicule all such statements as vain pretenses.

3. A third finds in himself a talent which with the help of some culture might make him a useful man in many respects. But he finds himself in comfortable circumstances, and prefers to indulge in pleasure rather than to take pains in enlarging and improving his happy natural capacities. He asks, however, whether his maxim of neglect of his natural gifts, besides agreeing with his inclination to indulgence, agrees also with what is called duty. He sees then that a system of nature could indeed subsist with such a universal law although men (like the South Sea islanders) should let their talents rest, and resolve to devote their lives merely to idleness, amusement, and propagation of their species—in a word, to enjoyment; but he cannot possibly *will* that this should be a universal law of nature, or be implanted in us as such by a natural instinct. For, as a rational being, he necessarily wills that his faculties be developed, since they serve him, and have been given him, for all sorts of possible purposes.

4. A fourth, who is in prosperity, while he sees that others have to contend with great wretchedness and that he could help them, thinks: What concern is it of mine? Let everyone be as happy as Heaven pleases, or as he can make himself; I will take nothing from him nor even envy him, only I do not wish to contribute anything to his welfare or to his assistance in distress! Now no doubt if such a mode of thinking were a universal law, the human race might very well subsist, and doubtless even better than in a state in which everyone talks of sympathy and goodwill, or even takes care occasionally to put it into practice, but, on the other side, also cheats when he can, betrays the rights of men, or otherwise violates them. But although it is possible that a universal law of nature might exist in accordance with that maxim, it is impossible to *will* that such a principle should have the universal validity of a law of nature. For a will which resolved this would contradict itself, inasmuch as many cases might occur in which one would have need of the love and sympathy of others, and in which, by such a law of nature, sprung from his own will, he would deprive himself of all hope of the aid he desires.

These are a few of the many actual duties, or at least what we regard as such, which obviously fall into two classes on the one principle that we have laid down. We must be *able to will* that a maxim of our action should be a universal law. This is the canon of the moral appreciation of the action generally. Some actions are of such a character that their maxim cannot without contradiction be even *conceived* as a universal law of nature, far from it being possible that we should *will* that it *should* be so. In others this intrinsic impossibility is not found, but still it is impossible to *will* that their maxim should be raised to the universality of a law of nature, since such a will would contradict itself. It is easily seen that the former violates strict or rigorous (inflexible) duty; the latter only laxer (meritorious) duty. Thus it has been completely shown by these examples how all duties depend as regards the nature of the obligation (not the object of the action) on the same principle.

If now we attend to ourselves on occasion of any transgression of duty, we shall find that we in fact do not will that our maxim should be a universal law, for that is impossible for us; on the contrary, we will that the opposite should remain a universal law, only we assume the liberty of making an *exception* in our own

favor or (just for this time only) in favor of our inclination. Consequently if we considered all cases from one and the same point of view, namely, that of reason, we should find a contradiction in our own will, namely, that a certain principle should be objectively necessary as a universal law, and yet subjectively should not be universal, but admit of exceptions. As, however, we at one moment regard our action from the point of view of a will wholly conformed to reason, and then again look at the same action from the point of view of a will affected by inclination, there is not really any contradiction, but an antagonism of inclination to the precept of reason, whereby the universality of the principle is changed into a mere generality, so that the practical principle of reason shall meet the maxim half way. Now, although this cannot be justified in our own impartial judgment, yet it proves that we do really recognize the validity of the categorical imperative and (with all respect for it) only allow ourselves a few exceptions, which we think unimportant and forced from us.

We have thus established at least this much, that if duty is a conception which is to have any import and real legislative authority for our actions, it can only be expressed in categorical, and not at all in hypothetical imperatives. We have also, which is of great importance, exhibited clearly and definitely for every practical application the content of the categorical imperative, which must contain the principle of all duty if there is such a thing at all. We have not yet, however, advanced so far as to prove a priori that there actually is such an imperative, that there is a practical law which commands absolutely of itself, and without any other impulse, and that the following of this law is duty.

With the view of attaining to this it is of extreme importance to remember that we must not allow ourselves to think of deducing the reality of this principle from the *particular attributes of human nature*. For duty is to be a practical, unconditional necessity of action; it must therefore hold for all rational beings (to whom an imperative can apply at all), and *for this reason only* be also a law for all human wills. On the contrary, whatever is deduced from the particular natural characteristics of humanity, from certain feelings and propensions, nay, even, if possible, from any particular tendency proper to human reason, and which need not necessarily hold for the will of every rational being; this may indeed supply us with a maxim, but not with a law; with a subjective principle on which we may have a propension and inclination to act, but not with an objective principle on which we should be *enjoined* to act, even though all

our propensions, inclinations, and natural dispositions were opposed to it. In fact, the sublimity and intrinsic dignity of the command in duty are so much
the more evident, the less the subjective impulses favor it and the more they oppose it, without being
able in the slightest degree to weaken the obligation
of the law or to diminish its validity.

Here then we see philosophy brought to a critical
position, since it has to be firmly fixed, notwithstanding that it has nothing to support it in heaven or
earth. Here it must show its purity as absolute director of its own laws, not the herald of those which are
whispered to it by an implanted sense or who knows
what tutelary nature. Although these may be better
than nothing, yet they can never afford principles
dictated by reason, which must have their source
wholly a priori and thence their commanding authority, expecting everything from the supremacy of the
law and the due respect for it nothing from inclination, or else condemning the man to self-contempt
and inward abhorrence.

Thus every empirical element is not only quite incapable of being an aid to the principle of morality,
but is even highly prejudicial to the purity of morals;
for the proper and inestimable worth of an absolutely
good will consists just in this, that the principle of action is free from all influence of contingent grounds,
which alone experience can furnish. We cannot too
much or too often repeat our warning against this lax
and even mean habit of thought which seeks for its
principle amongst empirical motives and laws; for
human reason in its weariness is glad to rest on this
pillow, and in a dream of sweet illusions (in which,
instead of Juno, it embraces a cloud) it substitutes for
morality a bastard patched up from limbs of various
derivation, which looks like anything one chooses to
see in it; only not like virtue to one who has once beheld her in her true form.[7]

The question then is this: Is it a necessary law *for all
rational beings* that they should always judge of their
actions by maxims of which they can themselves will
that they should serve as universal laws? If it is so,
then it must be connected (altogether a priori) with
the very conception of the will of a rational being generally. But in order to discover this connection we

must, however reluctantly, take a step into
metaphysic, although into a domain of it which is distinct from speculative philosophy, namely, the
metaphysic of morals. In a practical philosophy,
where it is not the reasons of what *happens* that we
have to ascertain, but the laws of what *ought to happen*,
even though it never does, i.e., objective practical
laws, there it is not necessary to inquire into the reasons why anything pleases or displeases, how the
pleasure of mere sensation differs from taste, and
whether the latter is distinct from a general satisfaction of reason; on what the feeling of pleasure or pain
rests, and how from it desires and inclinations arise,
and from these again maxims by the cooperation of
reason: for all this belongs to an empirical psychology,
which would constitute the second part of physics, if
we regard physics as the *philosophy* of nature, so far as
it is based on *empirical laws*. But here we are concerned
with objective practical laws, and consequently with
the relation of the will to itself so far as it is determined by reason alone, in which case whatever has
reference to anything empirical is necessarily excluded; since if *reason of itself alone* determines the conduct (and it is the possibility of this that we are now
investigating), it must necessarily do so a priori.

The will is conceived as a faculty of determining
oneself to action *in accordance with the conception of certain laws*. And such a faculty can be found only in rational beings. Now that which serves the will as the
objective ground of its self-determination is the *end*,
and if this is assigned by reason alone, it must hold for
all rational beings. On the other hand, that which
merely contains the ground of possibility of the action
of which the effect is the end, this is called the *means*.
The subjective ground of the desire is the *spring*, the
objective ground of the volition is the *motive*; hence
the distinction between subjective ends which rest on
springs, and objective ends which depend on motives
valid for every rational being. Practical principles are
formal when they abstract from all subjective ends;
they are *material* when they assume these, and therefore particular springs of action. The ends which a rational being proposes to himself at pleasure as *effects*
of his actions (material ends) are all only relative, for it
is only their relation to the particular desires of the
subject that gives them their worth, which therefore
cannot furnish principles universal and necessary for
all rational beings and for every volition, that is to say
practical laws. Hence all these relative ends can give
rise only to hypothetical imperatives.

Supposing, however, that there were something
whose existence has *in itself* an absolute worth, something which, being *an end in itself*, could be a source of

---

[7] To behold virtue in her proper form is nothing else but to
contemplate morality stripped of all admixture of sensible
things and of every spurious ornament of reward or self-
love. How much she then eclipses everything else that appears charming to the affections, every one may readily perceive with the least exertion of his reason, if it be not wholly
spoiled for abstraction.

definite laws, then in this and this alone would lie the source of a possible categorical imperative, i.e., a practical law.

Now I say: man and generally any rational being *exists* as an end in himself, *not merely as a means* to be arbitrarily used by this or that will, but in all his actions, whether they concern himself or other rational beings, must be always regarded at the same time as an end. All objects of the inclinations have only a conditional worth; for if the inclinations and the wants founded on them did not exist, then their object would be without value. But the inclinations themselves being sources of want are so far from having an absolute worth for which they should be desired, that, on the contrary, it must be the universal wish of every rational being to be wholly free from them. Thus the worth of any object which is *to be acquired* by our action is always conditional. Beings whose existence depends not on our will but on nature's, have nevertheless, if they are rational beings, only a relative value as means, and are therefore called *things*; rational beings, on the contrary, are called *persons*, because their very nature points them out as ends in themselves, that is as something which must not be used merely as means, and so far therefore restricts freedom of action (and is an object of respect). These, therefore, are not merely subjective ends whose existence has a worth *for us* as an effect of our action, but *objective ends*, that is things whose existence is an end in itself: an end moreover for which no other can be substituted, which they should subserve *merely* as means, for otherwise nothing whatever would possess *absolute worth*; but if all worth were conditioned and therefore contingent, then there would be no supreme practical principle of reason whatever.

If then there is a supreme practical principle or, in respect of the human will, a categorical imperative, it must be one which, being drawn from the conception of that which is necessarily an end for everyone because it is *an end in itself*, constitutes an *objective* principle of will, and can therefore serve as a universal practical law. The foundation of this principle is: *rational nature exists as an end in itself*. Man necessarily conceives his own existence as being so: so far then this is a *subjective* principle of human actions. But every other rational being regards its existence similarly, just on the same rational principle that holds for me: so that it is at the same time an objective principle, from which as a supreme practical law all laws of the will must be capable of being deduced. Accordingly the practical imperative will be as follows: *So act as to treat humanity, whether in thine own person or in that of any other, in every case as an end withal,*

never as means only. We will now inquire whether this can be practically carried out.

To abide by the previous examples:

Firstly, under the head of necessary duty to oneself: He who contemplates suicide should ask himself whether his action can be consistent with the idea of humanity *as an end in itself*. If he destroys himself in order to escape from painful circumstances, he uses a person merely as *a mean* to maintain a tolerable condition up to the end of life. But a man is not a thing, that is to say, something which can be used merely as means, but must in all his actions be always considered as an end in himself. I cannot, therefore, dispose in any way of a man in my own person so as to mutilate, to damage or kill him. (It belongs to ethics proper to define this principle more precisely, so as to avoid all misunderstanding, e.g., as to the amputation of the limbs in order to preserve myself; as to exposing my life to danger with a view to preserve it, etc. This question is therefore omitted here.)

Secondly, as regards necessary duties, or those of strict obligation, toward others; he who is thinking of making a lying promise to others will see at once that he would be using another man *merely as a mean*, without the latter containing at the same time the end in himself. For he whom I propose by such a promise to use for my own purposes cannot possibly assent to my mode of acting toward him, and therefore cannot himself contain the end of this action. This violation of the principle of humanity in other men is more obvious if we take in examples of attacks on the freedom and property of others. For then it is clear that he who transgresses the rights of men intends to use the person of others merely as means, without considering that as rational beings they ought always to be esteemed also as ends, that is, as beings who must be capable of containing in themselves the end of the very same action.

Thirdly, as regards contingent (meritorious) duties to oneself; it is not enough that the action does not violate humanity in our own person as an end in itself, it must also *harmonize with* it. Now there are in humanity capacities of greater perfection which belong to the end that nature has in view in regard to humanity in ourselves as the subject: to neglect these might perhaps be consistent with the *maintenance* of humanity as an end in itself, but not with the *advancement* of this end.

Fourthly, as regards meritorious duties toward others: the natural end which all men have is their own happiness. Now humanity might indeed subsist, although no one should contribute anything to the happiness of others, provided he did not intentionally withdraw anything from it; but after all, this would only harmonize negatively, not positively, with *humanity as an end in itself*, if everyone does not also endeavor, as far as in him lies, to forward the ends of others. For the ends of any subject which is an end in himself, ought as far as possible to be *my* ends also, if that conception is to have its *full* effect with me.

This principle, that humanity and generally every rational nature is *an end in itself* (which is the supreme limiting condition of every man's freedom of action), is not borrowed from experience, *firstly*, because it is universal, applying as it does to all rational beings whatever, and experience is not capable of determining anything about them; *secondly*, because it does not present humanity as an end to men (subjectively), that is as an object which men do of themselves actually adopt as an end; but as an objective end, which must as a law constitute the supreme limiting condition of all our subjective ends, let them be what we will; it must therefore spring from pure reason. In fact the objective principle of all practical legislation lies (according to the first principle) in *the rule* and its form of universality which makes it capable of being a law (say, e.g., a law of nature); but the *subjective* principle is in the *end*; now by the second principle the subject of all ends is each rational being inasmuch as it is an end in itself. Hence follows the third practical principle of the will, which is the ultimate condition of its harmony with the universal practical reason, viz.: the idea of *the will of every rational being as a universally legislative will.*

On this principle all maxims are rejected which are inconsistent with the will being itself universal legislator. Thus the will is not subject simply to the law, but so subject that it must be regarded *as itself giving the law*, and on this ground only, subject to the law (of which it can regard itself as the author).

In the previous imperatives, namely, that based on the conception of the conformity of actions to general laws, as in a *physical system of nature*, and that based on the universal *prerogative* of rational beings as *ends* in themselves—these imperatives just because they were conceived as categorical, excluded from any share in their authority all admixture of any interest as a spring of action; they were, however, only *assumed* to be categorical, because such an assumption was necessary to explain the conception of duty. But we could not prove independently that there are practical propositions which command categorically, nor can it be proved in this section; one thing, however, could be done, namely, to indicate in the imperative itself by some determinate expression, that

in the case of volition from duty all interest is renounced, which is the specific criterion of categorical as distinguished from hypothetical imperatives. This is done in the present (third) formula of the principle, namely, in the idea of the will of every rational being as a *universally legislating will.*

For although a will *which is subject to laws* may be attached to this law by means of an interest, yet a will which is itself a supreme lawgiver so far as it is such cannot possibly depend on any interest, since a will so dependent would itself still need another law restricting the interest of its self-love by the condition that it should be valid as universal law.

Thus the *principle* that every human will is a *will which in all its maxims gives universal laws*, provided it be otherwise justified, would be very *well adapted* to be the categorical imperative, in this respect, namely, that just because of the idea of universal legislation it is *not based on any interest*, and therefore it alone among all possible imperatives can be *unconditional*. Or still better, converting the proposition, if there is a categorical imperative (i.e., a law for the will of every rational being), it can only command that everything be done from maxims of one's will regarded as a will which could at the same time will that it should itself give universal laws, for in that case only the practical principle and the imperative which it obeys are unconditional, since they cannot be based on any interest.

Looking back now on all previous attempts to discover the principle of morality, we need not wonder why they all failed. It was seen that man was bound to laws by duty, but it was not observed that the laws to which he is subject are *only those of his own giving*, though at the same time they are *universal*. And that he is only bound to act in conformity with his own will; a will, however, which is designed by nature to give universal laws. For when one has conceived man only as subject to a law (no matter what), then this law required some interest, either by way of attraction or constraint, since it did not originate as a law from *his own* will, but this will was according to a law obliged by *something else* to act in a certain manner. Now by this necessary consequence all the labor spent in finding a supreme principle of *duty* was irrevocably lost. For men never elicited duty, but only a necessity of acting from a certain interest. Whether this interest was private or otherwise, in any case the imperative must be conditional, and could not by any means be capable of being a moral command. I will therefore call this the principle of *Autonomy* of the will, in contrast with every other which I accordingly reckon as *Heteronomy*.

The conception of every rational being as one which must consider itself as giving in all the maxims of its will universal laws, so as to judge itself and its actions from this point of view—this conception leads to another which depends on it and is very fruitful, namely, that of a *kingdom of ends*.

By a *kingdom* I understand the union of different rational beings in a system by common laws. Now since it is by laws that ends are determined as regards their universal validity, hence, if we abstract from the personal differences of rational beings, and likewise from all the content of their private ends, we shall be able to conceive all ends combined in a systematic whole (including both rational beings as ends in themselves, and also the special ends which each may propose to himself), that is to say, we can conceive a kingdom of ends, which on the preceding principles is possible.

For all rational beings come under the *law* that each of them must treat itself and all others *never merely as means*, but in every case *at the same time as ends in themselves*. Hence results a systematic union of rational beings by common objective laws, i.e., a kingdom which may be called a kingdom of ends, since what these laws have in view is just the relation of these beings to one another as ends and means. It is certainly only an ideal.

A rational being belongs as a *member* to the kingdom of ends when, although giving universal laws in it, he is also himself subject to these laws. He belongs to it *as sovereign* when, while giving laws, he is not subject to the will of any other.

A rational being must always regard himself as giving laws either as member or as sovereign in a kingdom of ends which is rendered possible by the freedom of will. He cannot, however, maintain the latter position merely by the maxims of his will, but only in case he is a completely independent being without wants and with unrestricted power adequate to his will.

Morality consists then in the reference of all action to the legislation which alone can render a kingdom of ends possible. This legislation must be capable of existing in every rational being, and of emanating from his will, so that the principle of this will is, never to act on any maxim which could not without contradiction be also a universal law, and accordingly always so to act *that the will could at the same time regard itself as giving in its maxims universal laws.* If now the maxims of rational beings are not by their own nature coincident with this objective principle, then the necessity of acting on it is called practical necessitation, i.e., *duty.* Duty does not apply to the sov-

ereign in the kingdom of ends, but it does to every member of it and to all in the same degree.

The practical necessity of acting on this principle, i.e., duty, does not rest at all on feelings, impulses, or inclinations, but solely on the relation of rational beings to one another, a relation in which the will of a rational being must always be regarded as *legislative*, since otherwise it could not be conceived as *an end in itself*. Reason then refers every maxim of the will, regarding it as legislating universally, to every other will and also to every action toward oneself; and this not on account of any other practical motive or any future advantage, but from the idea of the *dignity* of a rational being, obeying no law but that which he himself also gives.

In the kingdom of ends everything has either Value or Dignity. Whatever has a value can be replaced by something else which is *equivalent*; whatever, on the other hand, is above all value, and therefore admits of no equivalent, has a dignity.

Whatever has reference to the general inclinations and wants of mankind has a *market value*; whatever, without supposing a want, corresponds to a certain taste, that is to a satisfaction in the mere purposeless play of our faculties, has a *fancy value*; but that which constitutes the condition under which alone anything can be an end in itself, this has not merely a relative worth, i.e., value, but an intrinsic worth, that is *dignity*.

Now morality is the condition under which alone a rational being can be an end in himself, since by this alone it is possible that he should be a legislating member in the kingdom of ends. Thus morality, and humanity as capable of it, is that which alone has dignity. Skill and diligence in labor have a market value; wit, lively imagination, and humor, have fancy value; on the other hand, fidelity to promises, benevolence from principle (not from instinct), have an intrinsic worth. Neither nature nor art contains anything which in default of these it could put in their place, for their worth consists not in the effects which spring from them, not in the use and advantage which they secure, but in the disposition of mind, that is, the maxims of the will which are ready to manifest themselves in such actions, even though they should not have the desired effect. These actions also need no recommendation from any subjective taste or sentiment, that they may be looked on the immediate favor and satisfaction: they need no immediate propension or feeling for them; they exhibit the will that performs them as an object of an immediate respect, and nothing but reason is required to *impose* them on the will; not to *flatter* it into them, which, in the case of duties, would be a contradiction.

This estimation therefore shows that the worth of such a disposition is dignity, and places it infinitely above all value, with which it cannot for a moment be brought into comparison or competition without as it were violating its sanctity.

What then is it which justifies virtue or the morally good disposition, in making such lofty claims? It is nothing less than the privilege it secures to the rational being of participating in the giving of universal laws, by which it qualifies him to be a member of a possible kingdom of ends, a privilege to which he was already destined by his own nature as being an end in himself, and on that account legislating in the kingdom of ends; free as regards all laws of physical nature, and obeying those only which he himself gives and by which his maxims can belong to a system of universal law, to which at the same time be submits himself. For nothing has any worth except what the law assigns it. Now the legislation itself which assigns the worth of everything must for that very reason possess dignity, that is an unconditional incomparable worth; and the word *respect* alone supplies a becoming expression for the esteem which a rational being must have for it. *Autonomy* then is the basis of the dignity of human and of every rational nature.

The three modes of presenting the principle of morality that have been adduced are at bottom only so many formulæ of the very same law, and each of itself involves the other two. There is, however, a difference in them, but it is rather subjectively than objectively practical, intended namely to bring an idea of the reason nearer to intuition (by means of a certain analogy), and thereby nearer to feeling. All maxims, in fact, have—

1. A *form*, consisting in universality; and in this view the formula of the moral imperative is expressed thus, that the maxims must be so chosen as if they were to serve as universal laws of nature.
2. A *matter*, namely, an end, and here the formula says that the rational being, as it is an end by its own nature and therefore an end in itself, must in every maxim serve as the condition limiting all merely relative and arbitrary ends.
3. A *complete characterization* of all maxims by means of that formula, namely, that all maxims ought by their own legislation to harmonize with a possible kingdom of ends as with a kingdom of nature.[8]

There is a progress here in the order of the categories of *unity* of the form of the will (its universality), *plurality* of the matter (objects, i.e., the ends), and *totality* of the system of these. In forming our moral *judgment* of actions it is better to proceed always on the strict method, and start from the general formula of the categorical imperative: *Act according to a maxim which can at the same time make itself a universal law.* If, however, we wish to gain an *entrance* for the moral law, it is very useful to bring one and the same action under the three specified conceptions, and thereby as far as possible to bring it nearer to intuition.

We can now end where we started at the beginning, namely, with the conception of a will unconditionally good. *That will* is *absolutely good* which cannot be evil—in other words, whose maxim, if made a universal law, could never contradict itself. This principle, then, is its supreme law: Act always on such a maxim as thou canst at the same time will to be a universal law; this is the sole condition under which a will can never contradict itself; and such an imperative is categorical. Since the validity of the will as a universal law for possible actions is analogous to the universal connection of the existence of things by general laws, which is the formal notion of nature in general, the categorical imperative can also be expressed thus: *Act on maxims which can at the same time have for their object themselves as universal laws of nature.* Such then is the formula of an absolutely good will.

Rational nature is distinguished from the rest of nature by this, that it sets before itself an end. This end would be the matter of every good will. But since in the idea of a will that is absolutely good without being limited by any condition (of attaining this or that end) we must abstract wholly from every end *to be effected* (since this would make every will only relatively good), it follows that in this case the end must be conceived, not as an end to be effected, but as an *independently* existing end. Consequently it is conceived only negatively, i.e., as that which we must never act against, and which, therefore, must never be regarded merely as means, but must in every volition be esteemed as an end likewise. Now this end can be nothing but the subject of all possible ends, since this is also the subject of a possible absolutely

[8]Teleology considers nature as a kingdom of ends; ethics regards a possible kingdom of ends as a kingdom of nature. In the first case, the kingdom of ends is a theoretical idea, adopted to explain what actually is. In the latter it is a practical idea, adopted to bring about that which is not yet, but which can be realized by our conduct, namely, if it conforms to this idea.

good will; for such a will cannot without contradiction be postponed to any other object. This principle: So act in regard to every rational being (thyself and others), that he may always have place in thy maxim as an end in himself, is accordingly essentially identical with this other: Act upon a maxim which, at the same time, involves its own universal validity for every rational being. For that in using means for every end I should limit my maxim by the condition of its holding good as a law for every subject, this comes to the same thing as that the fundamental principle of all maxims of action must be that the subject of all ends, i.e., the rational being himself, be never employed merely as means, but as the supreme condition restricting the use of all means, that is in every case as an end likewise.

It follows incontestably that, to whatever laws any rational being may be subject, he being an end in himself must be able to regard himself as also legislating universally in respect of these same laws, since it is just this fitness of his maxims for universal legislation that distinguishes him as an end in himself; also it follows that this implies his dignity (prerogative) above all mere physical beings, that he must always take his maxims from the point of view which regards himself, and likewise every other rational being, as lawgiving beings (on which account they are called persons). In this way a world of rational beings (*mundus intelligibilis*) is possible as a kingdom of ends, and this by virtue of the legislation proper to all persons as members. Therefore every rational being must so act as if he were by his maxims in every case a legislating member in the universal kingdom of ends. The formal principle of these maxims is: So act as if thy maxim were to serve likewise as the universal law (of all rational beings). A kingdom of ends is thus only possible on the analogy of a kingdom of nature, the former, however, only by maxims, that is self-imposed rules, the latter only by the laws of efficient causes acting under necessitation from without. Nevertheless, although the system of nature is looked upon as a machine, yet so far as it has reference to rational beings as its ends, it is given on this account the name of a kingdom of nature. Now such a kingdom of ends would be actually realized by means of maxims conforming to the canon which the categorical imperative prescribes to all rational beings, *if they were universally followed*. But although a rational being, even if he punctually follows this maxim himself, cannot reckon upon all others being therefore true to the same, nor expect that the kingdom of nature and its orderly arrangements shall be in harmony with him as a fitting member, so as to form a

kingdom of ends to which he himself contributes, that is to say, that it shall favor his expectation of happiness, still that law: Act according to the maxims of a member of a merely possible kingdom of ends legislating in it universally, remains in its full force, inasmuch as it commands categorically. And it is just in this that the paradox lies; that the mere dignity of man as a rational creature, without any other end or advantage to be attained thereby, in other words, respect for a mere idea, should yet serve as an inflexible precept of the will, and that it is precisely in this independence of the maxim on all such springs of action that its sublimity consists; and it is this that makes every rational subject worthy to be a legislative member in the kingdom of ends: for otherwise he would have to be conceived only as subject to the physical law of his wants. And although we should suppose the kingdom of nature and the kingdom of ends to be united under one sovereign, so that the latter kingdom thereby ceased to be a mere idea and acquired true reality, then it would no doubt gain the accession of a strong spring, but by no means any increase of its intrinsic worth. For this sole absolute lawgiver must, notwithstanding this, be always conceived as estimating the worth of rational beings only by their disinterested behavior, as prescribed to themselves from that idea [the dignity of man] alone. The essence of things is not altered by their external relations, and that which, abstracting from these, alone constitutes the absolute worth of man, is also that by which he must be judged, whoever the judge may be, and even by the Supreme Being. *Morality*, then, is the relation of actions to the autonomy of the will, that is, to the potential universal legislation by its maxims. An action that is consistent with the autonomy of the will is *permitted*; one that does not agree therewith is *forbidden*. A will whose maxims necessarily coincide with the laws of autonomy is a *holy* will, good absolutely. The dependence of a will not absolutely good on the principle of autonomy (moral necessitation) is obligation. This, then, cannot be applied to a holy being. The objective necessity of actions from obligation is called *duty*.

From what has just been said, it is easy to see how it happens that although the conception of duty implies subjection to the law, we yet ascribe a certain *dignity* and sublimity to the person who fulfills all his duties. There is not, indeed, any sublimity in him, so far as he is *subject* to the moral law; but inasmuch as in regard to that very law he is likewise a *legislator*, and on that account alone subject to it, he has sublimity. We have also shown above that neither fear nor inclination, but simply respect for the law, is the spring which can give actions a moral worth. Our own will, so far as we suppose it to act only under the condition that its maxims are potentially universal laws, this ideal will which is possible to us is the proper object of respect; and the dignity of humanity consists just in this capacity of being universally legislative, though with the condition that it is itself subject to this same legislation.

The Autonomy of the Will

IMMANUEL KANT

THE AUTONOMY OF THE WILL AS THE SUPREME PRINCIPLE OF MORALITY

Autonomy of the will is that property of it by which it is a law to itself (independently of any property of the objects of volition). The principle of autonomy then is: Always so to choose that the same volition shall comprehend the maxims of our choice as a universal law. We cannot prove that this practical rule is an imperative, i.e., that the will of every rational being is necessarily bound to it as a condition, by a mere analysis of the conceptions which occur in it, since it is a synthetical proposition; we must advance beyond the cognition of the objects to a critical examination of the subject, that is of the pure practical reason, for this synthetic proposition which commands apodictically must be capable of being cognized wholly a priori. This matter, however, does not belong to the present section. But that the principle of autonomy in question is the sole principle of morals can be readily shown by mere analysis of the conceptions of morality. For by this analysis we find that its principle must be a categorical imperative, and that what this commands is neither more nor less than this very autonomy.

HETERONOMY OF THE WILL AS THE SOURCE OF ALL SPURIOUS PRINCIPLES OF MORALITY

If the will seeks the law which is to determine it *anywhere else* than in the fitness of its maxims to be universal laws of its own dictation, consequently if it goes out of itself and seeks this law in the character of any of its objects, there always results *heteronomy*. The will in that case does not give itself the law, but it is given by the object through its relation to the will. This relation, whether it rests on inclination or on conceptions of reason, only admits of hypothetical imperatives: I ought to do something *because I wish for something else*. On the contrary, the moral, and therefore categorical, imperative says: I ought to do so and so, even though I should not wish for anything else. E.g., the former says: I ought not to lie if I would retain my reputation; the latter says: I ought not to lie although it should not bring me the least discredit. The latter therefore must so far abstract from all objects that they shall have no *influence* on the will, in order that practical reason (will) may not be restricted to administering an interest not belonging to it but may simply show its own commanding authority as the supreme legislation. Thus, e.g., I ought to endeavor to promote the happiness of others, not as if its realization involved any concern of mine (whether by immediate inclination or by any satisfaction indirectly gained through reason), but simply because a maxim which excludes it cannot be comprehended as a universal law in one and the same volition.

Classification

OF ALL PRINCIPLES OF MORALITY WHICH CAN BE FOUNDED ON THE CONCEPTION OF HETERONOMY

Here as elsewhere human reason in its pure use, so long as it was not critically examined, has first tried all possible wrong ways before it succeeded in finding the one true way.

Immanuel Kant, "Fundamental Principles of the Metaphysic of Morals," pp. 59–63 in Kant's Critique of Practical Reason and Other Works on the Theory of Ethics, *6th ed., translated by Thomas Kingsmill Abbott (London: Longmans, Green and Co., 1909).*

All principles which can be taken from this point of view are either *empirical* or *rational*. The *former*, drawn from the principle of *happiness*, are built on physical or moral feelings; the *latter*, drawn from the principle of *perfection*, are built either on the rational conception of perfection as a possible effect, or on that of an independent perfection (the will of God) as the determining cause of our will.

Empirical principles are wholly incapable of serving as a foundation for moral laws. For the universality with which these should hold for all rational beings without distinction, the unconditional practical necessity which is thereby imposed on them is lost when their foundation is taken from the *particular constitution of human nature*, or the accidental circumstances in which it is placed. The principle of *private happiness*, however, is the most objectionable, not merely because it is false, and experience contradicts the supposition that prosperity is always proportioned to good conduct, nor yet merely because it contributes nothing to the establishment of morality—since it is quite a different thing to make a prosperous man and a good man, or to make one prudent and sharp-sighted for his own interests, and to make him virtuous—but because the springs it provides for morality are such as rather undermine it and destroy its sublimity, since they put the motives to virtue and to vice in the same class, and only teach us to make a better calculation, the specific difference between virtue and vice being entirely extinguished. On the other hand, as to moral feeling, this supposed special sense,[1] the appeal to it is indeed superficial when those who cannot *think* believe that *feeling* will help them out, even in what concerns general laws; and besides, feelings which naturally differ infinitely in degree cannot furnish a uniform standard of good and evil, nor has anyone a right to form judgments for others by his own feelings: nevertheless this moral feeling is nearer to morality and its dignity in this respect, that it pays virtue the honor of ascribing to her *immediately* the satisfaction and esteem we have for her, and does not, as it were, tell her to her face that we are not attached to her by her beauty but by profit.

Amongst the *rational* principles of morality, the ontological conception of *perfection*, notwithstanding its defects, is better than the theological conception which derives morality from a Divine absolutely perfect will. The former is, no doubt, empty and indefinite, and consequently useless for finding in the boundless field of possible reality the greatest amount suitable for us; moreover, in attempting to distinguish specifically the reality of which we are now speaking from every other, it inevitably tends to turn in a circle, and cannot avoid tacitly presupposing the morality which it is to explain; it is nevertheless preferable to the theological view, first, because we have no intuition of the Divine perfection, and can only deduce it from our own conceptions, the most important of which is that of morality, and our explanation would thus be involved in a gross circle; and, in the next place, if we avoid this, the only notion of the Divine will remaining to us is a conception made up of the attributes of desire of glory and dominion, combined with the awful conceptions of might and vengeance, and any system of morals erected on this foundation would be directly opposed to morality.

However, if I had to choose between the notion of the moral sense and that of perfection in general (two systems which at least do not weaken morality, although they are totally incapable of serving as its foundation), then I should decide for the latter, because it at least withdraws the decision of the question from the sensibility and brings it to the court of pure reason; and although even here it decides nothing, it at all events preserves the indefinite idea (of a will good in itself) free from corruption, until it shall be more precisely defined.

For the rest I think I may be excused here from a detailed refutation of all these doctrines; that would only be superfluous labor, since it is so easy, and is probably so well seen even by those whose office requires them to decide for one of those theories (because their hearers would not tolerate suspension of judgment). But what interests us more here is to know that the prime foundation of morality laid down by all these principles is nothing but heteronomy of the will, and for this reason they must necessarily miss their aim.

In every case where an object of the will has to be supposed, in order that the rule may be prescribed which is to determine the will, there the rule is simple heteronomy; the imperative is conditional, namely, *if* or *because* one wishes for this object, one should act so and so: hence it can never command morally, that is categorically. Whether the object determines the will by means of inclination, as in the principle of private happiness, or by means of reason directed to objects

---

[1] I class the principle of moral feeling under that of happiness, because every empirical interest promises to contribute to our well-being by the agreeableness that a thing affords, whether it be immediately and without a view to profit, or whether profit be regarded. We must likewise, with Hutcheson, class the principle of sympathy with the happiness of others under his assumed moral sense.

of our possible volition generally, as in the principle of perfection, in either case the will never determines itself *immediately* by the conception of the action, but only by the influence which the foreseen effect of the action has on the will; *I ought to do something, on this account, because I wish for something else:* and here there must be yet another law assumed in me as its subject, by which I necessarily will this other thing, and this law again requires an imperative to restrict this maxim. For the influence which the conception of an object within the reach of our faculties can exercise on the will of the subject in consequence of its natural properties, depends on the nature of the subject, either the sensibility (inclination and taste), or the understanding and reason, the employment of which is by the peculiar constitution of their nature attended with satisfaction. It follows that the law would be, properly speaking, given by nature, and as such, it must be known and proved by experience, and would consequently be contingent, and therefore incapable of being an apodictic practical rule, such as the moral rule must be. Not only so, but it is *inevitably only heteronomy*; the will does not give itself the law, but it is given by a foreign impulse by means of a particular natural constitution of the subject adapted to receive it. An absolutely good will, then, the principle of which must be a categorical imperative, will be indeterminate as regards all objects, and will contain merely the *form of volition* generally, and that as autonomy, that is to say, the capability of the maxims of every good will to make themselves a universal law, is itself the only law which the will of every rational being imposes on itself, without needing to assume any spring or interest as a foundation. . . .

Discussion and Reflection Questions

1. *The good will and duty:* Kant states that the actions performed by a person who finds tremendous inner satisfaction in helping others and making them happy has no moral worth. Why does he say this? Is Kant saying that one's actions can only have moral worth if they are contrary to one's inclinations? What do we mean when we say that "someone did the right thing but for the wrong reasons"? How does this saying reflect a Kantian view of morality? Think about your own actions. Which ones do you think would have moral worth in Kant's eyes? Why? Do you agree with him? Why or why not?

2. *The categorical imperative:* Does anyone ever act from a pure motive of duty, without at the same time acting because of one's perceptions of the good consequences of acting in this way? Have you ever had such an experience? How would Kant respond to the objection that, as far as experience teaches us, no person ever acts from a pure motive of duty? Would he believe that this undermines his view? At one point Kant formulates the categorical imperative as the principle that one should always treat others as "ends in themselves, not merely as means." What does this mean? Have you ever been treated by someone else purely as a means to their own ends, and not as an end in yourself? Did that person treat you with respect and dignity? How did it make you feel? Angry? Why?

3. *The autonomy of the will:* Kant criticizes very strongly the idea that morality could be based on feelings, rather than on pure reason. Do you find his arguments to be plausible? Is there some role for feelings in morality? Is there some way to use both reason and feelings in moral decision-making? How?

Suggestions for Further Reading

Hume's moral theory is developed in Book III of his *Treatise of Human Nature* (Oxford: Oxford University Press, 1978) [originally published in 1739 and 1740] and in his *Enquiry Concerning the Principles of Morals*, edited by J. B. Schneewind (Indianapolis: Hackett, 1983) [originally published in 1751]. For recent essays on all aspects of Hume's philosophy by leading Hume scholars, see *The Cambridge Companion to Hume*, edited by David Fate Norton (New York: Cambridge University Press, 1993). Included in this volume are essays on "Hume's Moral Psychology," by Terence Penelhum, and "Hume, Human Nature, and the Foundations of Morality," by David Fate Norton. Richard Bosley, "Do Mencius and Hume Make the Same Ethical Mistake?" *Philosophy East and West,* vol. 38 (1988), pp. 3–18, compares and criticizes the ethical views of Hume and Mencius (one of the Eastern thinkers considered in Part III of this book). The selections from Kant above are taken from his *Fundamental Principles of the Metaphysic of Morals.* In this work, Kant the professional philosopher sets out the supreme principle of morality in a rigorous manner. In the *Lectures on Ethics,* translated by Louis Infield (New York: Harper & Row, 1963), he is concerned more broadly with the good life for man, which includes morality, of course, but includes much else as well, just as being human includes more than pure reason. From the *Lectures* we can form a more concrete idea of Kant's conception of the good life. Kant connects his views on morality with his larger philosophical projects in his *Critique of Practical Reason,* translated by Lewis Beck White (Indianapolis: Bobbs-Merrill, 1956). An excellent introduction to Kant's ethics is Onora O'Neill's essay, "Kantian Ethics," in *A Companion to Ethics,* edited by Peter Singer (Oxford: Blackwell, 1991), pp. 175–185. See also her *Constructions of Reason: Explorations in Kant's Practical Philosophy* (Cambridge: Cambridge University Press, 1989). Two books treating Kant's moral philosophy in some detail are: Roger J. Sullivan, *Immanuel Kant's Moral Theory* (New York: Cambridge University Press, 1989), and Barbara Herman, *Morality as Rationality: A Study of Kant's Ethics* (New York: Garland Publishing, 1990). Other works devoted primarily to explicating the themes in Kant's *Fundamental Principles of the Metaphysic of Morals* include: Robert Paul Wolff, *The Autonomy of Reason* (New York: Harper Torchbooks, 1973); Bruce Aune, *Kant's Theory of Morals* (Princeton: Princeton University Press, 1979); and Thomas E. Hill, *Dignity and Practical Reason in Kant's Moral Theory* (Ithaca, N.Y.: Cornell University Press, 1992). Kant's moral theory is also a regular subject of scholarly journal articles. See, for example: Walter E. Schaller, "Kant on Rights and Moral Rights," *Southern Journal of Philosophy* 38 (Summer 2000): 321–342; Anthony Cunningham, "Kantian Ethics and Intimate Attachments," *American Philosophical Quarterly* 36 (October 1999): 279–294; Peter J. Steinberger, "The Standard View of the Categorical Imperative," *Kant Studien* 90 (1999): 91–99; Allen Wood, "The Final Form of Kant's Practical Philosophy," *Southern Journal of Philosophy* 36 (1997): 1–20; and Lara Denis, "Kant's Ethics and Duties to Oneself," *Pacific Philosophical Quarterly* 78 (1997): 321–348. Taking a broader perspective, Sandra A. Wawrytko, "Confucius and Kant: The Ethics of Respect," *Philosophy East and West,* vol. 32 (1982), pp. 237–257, draws many insightful comparisons between the ethical views of Confucius and Kant. As noted, Kant's moral theory is a kind of deontological moral theory. For a look at contemporary deontological theories, see Nancy (Ann) Davis, "Contemporary Deontology," in *A Companion to Ethics,* edited by Peter Singer (Oxford: Blackwell, 1991), pp. 205–218.

InfoTrac

"Hume, David", "Kant, Immanuel", categorical imperative, truthfulness and falsehood, duty, respect, good will, autonomy

Chapter 4

Utilitarianism

Introduction: Pleasure, Pain, and Utility

The nineteenth century is often identified with the Industrial Revolution, when means of mass production became commonplace and machines took over many of the tasks formerly performed by people. Economics, with its cost-benefit style of analysis and quantification of "goods" (defined as what people are willing to pay for), began to look like a viable science. The notion of progress as an almost inevitable development toward ever better states of affairs had widespread appeal, and the conviction that the possibility of such progress lies squarely in the hands of hardworking and far-seeing individuals became common.

It was in this social and cultural environment that the ethical theory known as *utilitarianism* came into being and found a receptive home. First propounded by Jeremy Bentham, and then later popularized and extended by John Stuart Mill, utilitarianism, or the "doctrine of utility," seemed to fit the age perfectly. Utilitarian ethics concerns the problem of how to produce the greatest amount of good for the greatest number of people. As such, it can be considered an essentially "economic" problem, subject to quantification and certain laws of production. Since one measure of the "good" is *pleasure*, the question is how to maximize the total quantity of pleasure in existence.

The idea that pleasure is the highest good for human beings can be traced at least as far back as Epicurus (a Greek contemporary of Aristotle) and his followers. But it was really Jeremy Bentham and his disciple John Stuart Mill who, in the eighteenth and nineteenth centuries, articulated and defended this view with the most success. Pleasure, they held, is a consequence of performing certain kinds of actions. If pleasure is the highest good, then the right thing to do is to perform those actions that are likely to produce the greatest amount of pleasure. This is the essence of the utilitarian approach to ethics.

Utilitarian principles and considerations have continued to exert a powerful influence to the present and are still one of the main Western approaches to morality. Despite the simplicity and attractiveness of this view, however, it has turned out to be a good deal more complicated than some utilitarians had anticipated.

Some of these problems are described in the Profile describing Bentham's unique contribution to hedonism (the view that pleasure is the sole good), while others are identified in the discussion of Mill's version of utilitarianism.

Jeremy Bentham:
Quantifying Pleasure and Pain

Jeremy Bentham (1748–1832) was a radical reformer. His central project in life was to reform law, government, and economics to make them serve the principle of utility, or the greatest happiness principle. This is the view, quite simply, that the rightness or wrongness of an action is to be judged entirely on the basis of the goodness or badness of the consequences that follow from that action. Bentham's view is a kind of hedonism: Goodness and badness are identical to pleasure and pain, respectively. In a famous quote Bentham says, "Nature has placed mankind under the governance of two sovereign masters, pain and pleasure."

Hedonism was not invented by Bentham. The identification of good with pleasure was already asserted by the Epicureans and was assumed by many of Bentham's contemporaries. What Bentham contributed to this "hedonistic utilitarianism" was the idea that pleasure, and hence utility, could be quantified and hence made the basis for social policy. This is his famous "hedonistic calculus." The way to judge between alternative courses of action is to weigh the consequences of each alternative in terms of the amount of pleasure and pain resulting for all the people affected by them and then to choose the action that produces the greatest balance of pleasure over pain, that is, the greatest *utility*.

Bentham's idea can be illustrated with a simple example. Suppose that one course of action would produce 10 units of pleasure for oneself, but 6 units of pain for someone else, whereas a second course of action would produce 8 units of pain for oneself but 14 units of pleasure for someone else. Suppose that we call units of pleasure "hedons," units of pain "dolors," and measure the resultant utility in "utiles." Which course of action should one pursue? The calculation in this case is straightforward: 10 hedons + 6 dolors = 4 utiles, whereas 8 dolors + 14 hedons = 6 utiles. (You can think of hedons as positive and dolors as negative.) The second course of action produces more net utility than the first one, and hence is to be pursued. In principle, any number of different courses of action could be decided upon in this manner. What is important to notice about this example, besides the fact that pleasure and pain are assumed to be quantities capable of being measured, is that what matters ultimately is the total quantity of utility produced, regardless of who happens to be enjoying the pleasure or suffering the pain. Utilitarianism is anything but an egoistical ("me-first") moral theory.

Bentham himself did not think that pleasure could always be quantified in exact terms, as in the simple example just given, but he apparently did believe that some such weighing of alternatives in terms of pleasure and pain does, and should, go on in the process of deciding what to do. Notice also that only quantity and not quality of pleasure is at issue. On Bentham's view, so long as they were alike in terms of duration, intensity, and other quantifiable dimensions, all pleasures are to be weighed alike. So, the pleasure of making a monumental scientific discovery might be worth no more, in terms of pleasure, than scratching an itch.

As Bentham himself put it, "Quantity of pleasure being equal, pushpin is as good as poetry." This is a view that his most famous disciple, John Stuart Mill, would reject in favor of a more nuanced version of utilitarianism.

John Stuart Mill:
The Doctrine of Utility Defended

According to the greatest happiness principle . . . the ultimate end with reference to which and for the sake of which all other things are desirable . . . is an existence exempt as far as possible from pain, and as rich as possible in enjoyments, both in point of quantity and quality.

—JOHN STUART MILL, *UTILITARIANISM*

John Stuart Mill was born in London in 1806. He never went to school, but was instead educated by his father, who had him begin the study of Greek at the age of three, and Latin and arithmetic at eight. He began logic at twelve, and political economy at thirteen. By the time he was fourteen he had studied most of the major Greek and Latin classics, as well as world history, and he had done intensive work in logic and mathematics. At fifteen he read a summary of Bentham's philosophy, which provided the aim for his life: to reform the world along Benthamite lines. In 1826 he suffered a mental breakdown, after which he re-evaluated the views upon which he had been raised. He came to believe that the rigorous training his father had provided for him had stunted the emotional side of his nature, to the point where he could think clearly about everything but feel strongly about nothing. Reading the poetry of Wordsworth began to effect something of a cure, the completion of which was accomplished by his meeting with Harriet Taylor in 1831. Mrs. Taylor, the wife of London merchant John Taylor, was then twenty-two years old and nearly Mill's equal in intellectual training, having read philosophy at the age of eleven and studied logic at fourteen. They began a friendship that would last more than twenty years. In 1849 John Taylor died, and three years later Mrs. Taylor married Mill. Mill was later to say (in his *Autobiography*) that his various works could not have been written, or at least could not have been as successful as they were, without her: "What was abstract and purely scientific was generally mine; the properly human element came from her."

Mill wrote a number of books and essays on government, legislation, political economy, logic, scientific method, and ethics. The selections below are from his work entitled *Utilitarianism*, which first appeared as a series of essays in *Fraser's Magazine* in 1861. In this work Mill sets out to explain and defend utilitarianism as a test of right and wrong. Like Kant, he is looking for "some one fundamental principle or law at the root of all morality." His solution, however, could not be more different from Kant's.

In Chapter 1 Mill sets the stage for the chapters that follow. His aim, he says, is to uncover the roots of morality, the fundamental principles that lie beneath the surface of everyday moral discourse and that provide the ultimate support for the moral distinctions we make. He makes it clear that such questions are not susceptible of absolute proof. Rather, what we are after are sound reasons for acceptance.

He explains that the chief obstacle to the acceptance of the doctrine of utility are the various misconceptions people have about this doctrine.

His first task, therefore, in Chapter 2, is to clarify the meaning of the doctrine with reference to specific examples. "Utility" means pleasure, or pleasure and the absence of pain, pure and simple. Utilitarianism, Mill tells us, "holds that actions are right in proportion as they tend to promote happiness; wrong as they tend to produce the reverse of happiness. By happiness is meant pleasure and the absence of pain; by unhappiness, pain and the privation of pleasure." This theory of morality is grounded in the view that "pleasure and freedom from pain are the only things desirable as ends; and that all desirable things . . . are desirable either for pleasure inherent in themselves or as means to the promotion of pleasure and the prevention of pain." Mill was sensitive to the objection that in the utilitarian view, which makes the good identical with pleasure, the best life for human beings is nothing more than a life "worthy of swine"—that is, a life devoted to the "lowest" aspect of human nature. To respond to this "doctrine of swine objection," Mill distinguishes between "higher" and "lower" pleasures. Like Bentham, Mill believes that pleasures differ in quantity. But unlike Bentham, Mill also believes that pleasures differ in quality: Some pleasures are "higher" than others. He thus adds a qualitative element to the purely quantitative analysis of pleasure introduced by Bentham. Having distinguished between higher and lower pleasures, Mill then faces the challenge of explaining how one is to judge between higher and lower pleasures. He claims that "it is better to be a human being dissatisfied than a pig satisfied; better to be Socrates dissatisfied than a fool satisfied." His explanation of why this is so continues to be one of the most controversial features of his theory.

Utilitarianism makes the consequences of an action for the production of happiness the ultimate criterion of morality. But the happiness in question is not just the happiness of the person performing the action. It is the happiness of society. But why, one might ask, should one do what is conducive to the happiness of everyone in society and not just act for the sake of one's own happiness? What is the motive for doing so? In Chapter 3 Mill addresses such questions. His strategy is to show that while there may indeed be problems with motivation for acting in accordance with the greatest happiness principle, these problems are certainly no greater than they are for any other system of morality. Mill then explores the various sanctions that may compel someone to act morally.

Recall that Mill wants to persuade his readers that utility, or the greatest happiness principle, is the ultimate principle of morality. "The utilitarian doctrine is that happiness is desirable, and the only thing desirable, as an end; all other things being only desirable as means to that end." He asks, "What ought to be required of this doctrine, what conditions is it requisite that the doctrine should fulfill, to make good its claim to be believed?" Chapter 4 is devoted to answering this question. All human beings do, as a matter of fact, desire happiness, and desire nothing which is not either a part of happiness or a means to the attainment of happiness. Since happiness is universally desired, it follows that happiness is desirable. "If so," Mill writes, "happiness is the sole end of human action, and the promotion of it the test by which to judge of all human conduct; from whence it necessarily follows that it must be the criterion of morality, since a part is included in the whole." Yes, but why must the general happiness be the ultimate criterion of morality? Because, Mill suggests, if each person's happiness is a good to that person, then the general happiness is a good to the aggregate of all persons. In this way Mill tries to establish the general happiness as the criterion of morality. You will have to decide for yourself whether you find Mill's argument convincing or not.

Reading Questions

1. *Utilitarianism: general remarks:* How does Mill's moral theory differ from that of Kant? What aspects of Kant's moral theory does Mill find unacceptable? Why?

2. *What utilitarianism is:* What, precisely, does the doctrine of utility state is the criterion for moral rightness? Why do opponents of the doctrine of utility liken its proponents to swine? Why is this a criticism of utilitarianism? How does Mill respond to this criticism? How does Mill distinguish between different kinds of pleasures in terms of quality? What is the basis for this distinction? Who is qualified to judge which of two pleasures is "higher"?

3. *Of the ultimate sanction of the principle of utility:* According to Mill, why is the problem of the motive for acting morally not a special problem for utilitarianism? What is his solution for overcoming this problem? What is a "sanction," and how does Mill distinguish between external and internal sanctions? How does Mill respond to the objection that the doctrine of utility does not have any binding force because it is not grounded in some "transcendental fact" but rather has its origin in human consciousness? What, according to Mill, is the immediate source of all actions?

4. *Of what sort of proof the principle of utility is susceptible:* How, exactly, does Mill attempt to "prove" the greatest happiness principle? What sort of proof is possible for such a principle? From the fact that people actually desire something, does it follow that it is desirable? What does it mean to say that something is "desirable"? How does Mill deal with the objection that not everyone desires happiness above all else?

Utilitarianism: General Remarks

JOHN STUART MILL

THERE ARE FEW CIRCUMSTANCES among those which make up the present condition of human knowledge more unlike what might have been expected, or more significant of the backward state in which speculation on the most important subjects still lingers, than the little progress which has been made in the decision of the controversy respecting the criterion of right and wrong. From the dawn of philosophy, the question concerning the *summum bonum*, or, what is the same thing, concerning the foundation of morality, has been accounted the main problem in speculative thought, has occupied the most gifted intellects and divided them into sects and schools carrying on a vigorous warfare against one another. And after more than two thousand years the same discussions continue, philosophers are still ranged under the same contending banners, and neither thinkers nor mankind at large seem nearer to being unanimous on the subject that when the youth Socrates listened to the old Protagoras and asserted (if Plato's dialogue be grounded on a real conversation) the theory of utilitarianism against the popular morality of the so-called sophist.

It is true that similar confusion and uncertainty and, in some cases, similar discordance exist respecting the first principles of all the sciences, not

John Stuart Mill, Utilitarianism, *7th ed. (London: Longmans, Green, 1879), pp. 1–7.*

excepting that which is deemed the most certain of them—mathematics, without much impairing, generally indeed without impairing at all, the trustworthiness of the conclusions of those sciences. An apparent anomaly, the explanation of which is that the detailed doctrines of a science are not usually deduced from, nor depend for their evidence upon, what are called its first principles. Were it not so, there would be no science more precarious, or whose conclusions were more insufficiently made out, than algebra, which derives none of its certainty from what are commonly taught to learners as its elements, since these, as laid down by some of its most eminent teachers, are as full of fictions as English law, and of mysteries as theology. The truths which are ultimately accepted as the first principles of a science are really the last results of metaphysical analysis practiced on the elementary notions with which the science is conversant; and their relation to the science is not that of foundations to an edifice, but of roots to a tree, which may perform their office equally well though they be never dug down to and exposed to light. But though in science the particular truths precede the general theory, the contrary might be expected to be the case with a practical art, such as morals or legislation. All action is for the sake of some end, and rules of action, it seems natural to suppose, must take their whole character and color from the end to which they are subservient. When we engage in a pursuit, a clear and precise conception of what we are pursuing would seem to be the first thing we need, instead of the last we are to look forward to. A test of right and wrong must be the means, one would think, of ascertaining what is right or wrong, and not a consequence of having already ascertained it.

The difficulty is not avoided by having recourse to the popular theory of a natural faculty, a sense or instinct, informing us of right and wrong. For—besides that the existence of such a moral instinct is itself one of the matters in dispute—those believers in it who have any pretensions to philosophy have been obliged to abandon the idea that it discerns what is right or wrong in the particular case in hand, as our other senses discern the sight or sound actually present. Our moral faculty, according to all those of its interpreters who are entitled to the name of thinkers, supplies us only with the general principles of moral judgments; it is a branch of our reason, not of our sensitive faculty, and must be looked to for the abstract doctrines of morality, not for perception of it in the concrete. The intuitive, no less than what may be termed the inductive, school of ethics insists on the necessity of general laws. They both agree that the morality of an individual action is not a question of direct perception, but of the application of a law to an individual case. They recognize also, to a great extent, the same moral laws, but differ as to their evidence and the source from which they derive their authority. According to the one option, the principles of morals are evident a priori, requiring nothing to command assent except that the meaning of the terms be understood. According to the other doctrine, right and wrong, as well as truth and falsehood, are questions of observation and experience. But both hold equally that morality must be deduced from principles; and the intuitive school affirm as strongly as the inductive that there is a science of morals. Yet they seldom attempt to make out a list of the a priori principles which are to serve as the premises of the science; still more rarely do they make any effort to reduce those various principles to one first principle or common ground of obligation. They either assume the ordinary precepts of morals as of a priori authority, or they lay down as the common groundwork of those maxims some generality much less obviously authoritative than the maxims themselves, and which has never succeeded in gaining popular acceptance. Yet to support their pretensions there ought either to be some one fundamental principle or law at the root of all morality, or, if there be several, there should be a determinate order of precedence among them; and the one principle, or the rule for deciding between the various principles when they conflict, ought to be self-evident.

To inquire how far the bad effects of this deficiency have been mitigated in practice, or to what extent the moral beliefs of mankind have been vitiated or made uncertain by the absence of any distinct recognition of an ultimate standard, would imply a complete survey and criticism of past and present ethical doctrine. It would, however, be easy to show that whatever steadiness or consistency these moral beliefs have attained has been mainly due to the tacit influence of a standard not recognized. Although the nonexistence of an acknowledged first principle has made ethics not so much a guide as a consecration of men's actual sentiments, still, as men's sentiments, both of favor and of aversion, are greatly influenced by what they suppose to be the effects of things upon their happiness, the principle of utility, or, as Bentham latterly called it, the greatest happiness principle, has had a large share in forming the moral doctrines even of those who most scornfully reject its authority. Nor is there any school of thought which refuses to admit that the influence of actions on happiness is a most material and even predominant consideration in many of the details of morals, however unwilling to acknowledge it as the fundamental principle of morality and the source of moral obligation. I might go much further and say that to all those a priori moralists who deem it necessary to argue at all, utilitarian arguments are indispensable. It is not my present purpose to criticize these thinkers; but I cannot help referring, for illustration, to a systematic treatise by one of the most illustrious of them, the *Metaphysics of Ethics* by Kant. This remarkable man, whose system of thought will long remain one of the landmarks in the history of philosophical speculation, does, in the treatise in question, lay down a universal first principle as the origin and ground of moral obligation; it is this: "So act that the rule on which thou actest would admit of being adopted as a law by all rational beings." But when he begins to deduce from this precept any of the actual duties of morality, he fails, almost grotesquely, to show that there would be any contradiction, any logical (not to say physical) impossibility, in the adoption by all rational beings of the most outrageously immoral rules of conduct. All he shows is that the *consequences* of their universal adoption would be such as no one would choose to incur.

On the present occasion, I shall, without further discussion of the other theories, attempt to contribute something toward the understanding and appreciation of the Utilitarian or Happiness theory, and toward such proof as it is susceptible of. It is evident that this cannot be proof in the ordinary and popular meaning of the term. Questions of ultimate ends are not amenable to direct proof. Whatever can be proved to be good must be so by being shown to be a means to something admitted to be good without proof. The medical art is proved to be good by its conducing to health; but how is it possible to prove that health is good? The art of music is good, for the reason, among others, that it produces pleasure; but what proof is it possible to give that pleasure is good? If, then, it is asserted that there is a comprehensive formula, including all things which are in themselves good, and that whatever else is good is not so as an end but as a means, the formula may be accepted or rejected, but is not a subject of what is commonly understood by proof. We are not, however, to infer that its acceptance or rejection must depend on blind impulse or arbitrary choice. There is a larger meaning of the word "proof," in which this question is as amenable to it as any other of the disputed questions of philosophy. The subject is within the cognizance of the rational faculty; and neither does that faculty deal with it solely in the way of intuition. Considerations may be presented capable of determining the intellect either to give or withhold its assent to the doctrine; and this is equivalent to proof.

We shall examine presently of what nature are these considerations; in what manner they apply to the case, and what rational grounds, therefore, can be given for accepting or rejecting the utilitarian formula. But it is a preliminary condition of rational acceptance or rejection that the formula should be correctly understood. I believe that the very imperfect notion ordinarily formed of its meaning is the chief obstacle which impedes its reception, and that, could it be cleared even from only the grosser misconceptions, the question would be greatly simplified and a large proportion of its difficulties removed. Before, therefore, I attempt to enter into the philosophical grounds which can be given for assenting to the utilitarian standard, I shall offer some illustrations of the doctrine itself, with the view of showing more clearly what it is, distinguishing it from what it is not, and disposing of such of the practical objections to it as either originate in, or are closely connected with, mistaken interpretations of its meaning. Having thus prepared the ground, I shall afterwards endeavor to throw such light as I can call upon the question considered as one of philosophical theory.

What Utilitarianism Is

JOHN STUART MILL

A PASSING REMARK is all that need be given to the ignorant blunder of supposing that those who stand up for utility as the test of right and wrong use the term in that restricted and merely colloquial sense in which utility is opposed to pleasure. An apology is due to the philosophical opponents of utilitarianism

John Stuart Mill, Utilitarianism, *7th ed. (London: Longmans, Green, 1879), pp. 8–38.*

for even the momentary appearance of confounding them with anyone capable of so absurd a misconception; which is the more extraordinary, inasmuch as the contrary accusation, of referring everything to pleasure, and that, too, in its grossest form, is another of the common charges against utilitarianism: and, as has been pointedly remarked by an able writer, the same sort of persons, and often the very same persons, denounce the theory "as impracticably dry when the word 'utility' precedes the word 'pleasure,' and as too practically voluptuous when the word 'pleasure' precedes the word 'utility.'" Those who know anything about the matter are aware that every writer, from Epicurus to Bentham, who maintained the theory of utility meant by it, not something to be contradistinguished from pleasure, but pleasure itself, together with exemption from pain; and instead of opposing the useful to the agreeable or the ornamental, have always declared that the useful means these, among other things. Yet the common herd, including the herd of writers, not only in newspapers and periodicals, but in books of weight and pretension, are perpetually falling into this shallow mistake. Having caught up the word "utilitarian," while knowing nothing whatever about it but its sound, they habitually express by it the rejection or the neglect of pleasure in some of its forms: of beauty, of ornament, or of amusement. Nor is the term thus ignorantly misapplied solely in disparagement, but occasionally in compliment, as though it implied superiority to frivolity and the mere pleasures of the moment. And this perverted use is the only one in which the word is popularly known, and the one from which the new generation are acquiring their sole notion of its meaning. Those who introduced the word, but who had for many years discontinued it as a distinctive appellation, may well feel themselves called upon to resume it if by doing so they can hope to contribute anything toward rescuing it from this utter degradation.

The creed which accepts as the foundation of morals, Utility, or the Greatest Happiness Principle, holds that actions are right in proportion as they tend to promote happiness, wrong as they tend to produce the reverse of happiness. By happiness is intended pleasure and the absence of pain; by unhappiness, pain and the privation of pleasure. To give a clear view of the moral standard set up by the theory, much more requires to be said; in particular, what things it includes in the ideas of pain and pleasure, and to what extent this is left an open question. But these supplementary explanations do not affect the theory of life on which this theory of morality is grounded—namely, that pleasure and freedom from pain are the only things desirable as ends; and that all desirable things (which are as numerous in the utilitarian as in any other scheme) are desirable either for pleasure inherent in themselves or as means to the promotion of pleasure and the prevention of pain.

Now such a theory of life excites in many minds, and among them in some of the most estimable in feeling and purpose, inveterate dislike. To suppose that life has (as they express it) no higher end than pleasure—no better and nobler object of desire and pursuit—they designate as utterly mean and groveling, as a doctrine worthy only of swine, to whom the followers of Epicurus were, at a very early period, contemptuously likened; and modern holders of the doctrine are occasionally made the subject of equally polite comparisons by its German, French, and English assailants.

When thus attacked, the Epicureans have always answered that it is not they, but their accusers, who represent human nature in a degrading light, since the accusation supposes human beings to be capable of no pleasures except those of which swine are capable. If this supposition were true, the charge could not be gainsaid, but would then be no longer an imputation; for if the sources of pleasure were precisely the same to human beings and to swine, the rule of life which is good enough for the one would be good enough for the other. The comparison of the Epicurean life to that of beasts is felt as degrading, precisely because a beast's pleasures do not satisfy a human being's conceptions of happiness. Human beings have faculties more elevated than the animal appetites and, when once made conscious of them, do not regard anything as happiness which does not include their gratification. I do not, indeed, consider the Epicureans to have been by any means faultless in drawing out their scheme of consequences from the utilitarian principle. To do this in any sufficient manner, many Stoic, as well as Christian, elements require to be included. But there is no known Epicurean theory of life which does not assign to the pleasures of the intellect, of the feelings and imagination, and of the moral sentiments a much higher value as pleasures than to those of mere sensation. It must be admitted, however, that utilitarian writers in general have placed the superiority of mental over bodily pleasures chiefly in the greater permanency, safety, uncostliness, etc., of the former—that is, in their circumstantial advantages rather than in their intrinsic nature. And on all these points utilitarians have fully proved their case; but they might have taken the other and, as it may be called, higher ground with entire consistency. It is quite compatible with the principle of utility to recognize the fact that some kinds of pleasure are more desirable and more valuable than others. It would be absurd that, while in estimating all other things quality is considered as well as quantity, the estimation of pleasure should be supposed to depend on quantity alone.

If I am asked what I mean by difference of quality in pleasures, or what makes one pleasure more valuable than another, merely as a pleasure, except it being greater in amount, there is but one possible answer. Of two pleasures, if there be one to which all or almost all who have experience of both give a decided preference, irrespective of any feeling of moral obligation to prefer it, that is the more desirable pleasure. If one of the two is, by those who are competently acquainted with both, placed so far above the other that they prefer it, even though knowing it to be attended with a greater amount of discontent, and would not resign it for any quantity of the other pleasure which their nature is capable of, we are justified in ascribing to the preferred enjoyment a superiority in quality so far outweighing quantity as to render it, in comparison, of small account.

Now it is an unquestionable fact that those who are equally acquainted with and equally capable of appreciating and enjoying both do give a most marked preference to the manner of existence which employs their higher faculties. Few human creatures would consent to be changed into any of the lower animals for a promise of the fullest allowance of a beast's pleasures; no intelligent human being would consent to be a fool, no instructed person would be an ignoramus, no person of feeling and conscience would be selfish and base, even though they should be persuaded that the fool, the dunce, or the rascal is better satisfied with his lot than they are with theirs. They would not resign what they possess more than he for the most complete satisfaction of all the desires which they have in common with him. If they ever fancy they would, it is only in cases of unhappiness so extreme that to escape from it they would exchange their lot for almost any other, however undesirable in their own eyes. A being of higher faculties requires more to make him happy, is capable probably of more acute suffering, and certainly accessible to it at more points, than one of an inferior type; but in spite of these liabilities, he can never really wish to sink into what he feels to be a lower grade of existence. We may give what explanation we please of this unwillingness; we may attribute it to pride, a name which is given indiscriminately to some of the most and to some of the least estimable feelings of

which mankind are capable; we may refer it to the love of liberty and personal independence, an appeal to which was with the Stoics one of the most effective means for the inculcation of it; to the love of power or to the love of excitement, both of which do really enter into and contribute to it; but its most appropriate appellation is a sense of dignity, which all human beings possess in one form or other, and in some, though by no means in exact, proportion to their higher faculties, and which is so essential a part of the happiness of those in whom it is strong that nothing which conflicts with it could be otherwise than momentarily an object of desire to them. Whoever supposes that this preference takes place at a sacrifice of happiness—that the superior being, in anything like equal circumstances, is not happier than the inferior—confounds the two very different ideas of happiness and content. It is indisputable that the being whose capacities of enjoyment are low has the greatest chance of having them fully satisfied; and a highly endowed being will always feel that any happiness which he can look for, as the world is constituted, is imperfect. But he can learn to bear its imperfections, if they are at all bearable; and they will not make him envy the being who is indeed unconscious of the imperfections, but only because he feels not at all the good which those imperfections qualify. It is better to be a human being dissatisfied than a pig satisfied; better to be Socrates dissatisfied than a fool satisfied. And if the fool, or the pig, are of a different opinion, it is because they only know their own side of the question. The other party to the comparison knows both sides.

It may be objected that many who are capable of the higher pleasures occasionally, under the influence of temptation, postpone them to the lower. But this is quite compatible with a full appreciation of the intrinsic superiority of the higher. Men often, from infirmity of character, make their election for the nearer good, though they know it to be the less valuable; and this no less when the choice is between two bodily pleasures than when it is between bodily and mental. They pursue sensual indulgences to the injury of health, though perfectly aware that health is the greater good. It may be further objected that many who begin with youthful enthusiasm for everything noble, as they advance in years, sink into indolence and selfishness. But I do not believe that those who undergo this very common change voluntarily choose the lower description of pleasures in preference to the higher. I believe that, before they devote themselves exclusively to the one, they have already become incapable of the other. Capacity for the nobler feelings is in most natures a very tender plant, easily killed, not only by hostile influences, but by mere want of sustenance; and in the majority of young persons it speedily dies away if the occupations to which their position in life has devoted them, and the society into which it has thrown them, are not favorable to keeping that higher capacity in exercise. Men lose their high aspirations as they lose their intellectual tastes, because they have not time or opportunity for indulging them; and they addict themselves to inferior pleasures, not because they deliberately prefer them, but because they are either the only ones to which they have access or the only ones which they are any longer capable of enjoying. It may be questioned whether anyone who has remained equally susceptible to both classes of pleasures ever knowingly and calmly preferred the lower, though many, in all ages, have broken down in an ineffectual attempt to combine both.

From this verdict of the only competent judges, I apprehend there can be no appeal. On a question which is the best worth having of two pleasures, or which of two modes of existence is the most grateful to the feelings, apart from its moral attributes and from its consequences, the judgment of those who are qualified by knowledge of both, or, if they differ, that of the majority among them, must be admitted as final. And there needs be the less hesitation to accept this judgment respecting the quality of pleasures, since there is no other tribunal to be referred to even on the question of quantity. What means are there of determining which is the acutest of two pains, or the intensest of two pleasurable sensations, except the general suffrage of those who are familiar with both? Neither pains nor pleasures are homogeneous, and pain is always heterogeneous with pleasure. What is there to decide whether a particular pleasure is worth purchasing at the cost of a particular pain, except the feelings and judgment of the experienced? When, therefore, those feelings and judgment declare the pleasures derived from the higher faculties to be preferable *in kind*, apart from the question of intensity, to those of which the animal nature, disjoined from the higher faculties, is susceptible, they are entitled on this subject to the same regard.

I have dwelt on this point as being part of a perfectly just conception of Utility or Happiness considered as the directive rule of human conduct. But it is by no means an indispensable condition to the acceptance of the utilitarian standard; for that standard is not the agent's own greatest happiness, but the greatest amount of happiness altogether; and if it may possibly be doubted whether a noble character is al-ways the happier for its nobleness, there can be no doubt that it makes other people happier, and that the world in general is immensely a gainer by it. Utilitarianism, therefore, could only attain its end by the general cultivation of nobleness of character, even if each individual were only benefited by the nobleness of others, and his own, so far as happiness is concerned, were a sheer deduction from the benefit. But the bare enunciation of such an absurdity as this last renders refutation superfluous.

According to the Greatest Happiness Principle, as above explained, the ultimate end, with reference to and for the sake of which all other things are desirable (whether we are considering our own good or that of other people), is an existence exempt as far as possible from pain, and as rich as possible in enjoyments, both in point of quantity and quality; the test of quality and the rule for measuring it against quantity being the preference felt by those who, in their opportunities of experience, to which must be added their habits of self-consciousness and self-observation, are best furnished with the means of comparison. This, being according to the utilitarian opinion the end of human action, is necessarily also the standard of morality, which may accordingly be defined the rules and precepts for human conduct, by the observance of which an existence such as has been described might be, to the greatest extent possible, secured to all mankind; and not to them only, but, so far as the nature of things admits, to the whole sentient creation.

Against this doctrine, however, arises another class of objectors who say that happiness, in any form, cannot be the rational purpose of human life and action; because, in the first place, it is unattainable; and they contemptuously ask, What right hast thou to be happy?—a question which Mr. Carlyle clinches by the addition, What right, a short time ago, hadst thou even *to be*? Next they say that men can do *without* happiness; that all noble human beings have felt this, and could not have become noble but by learning the lesson of *Entsagen*, or renunciation; which lesson, thoroughly learned and submitted to, they affirm to be the beginning and necessary condition of all virtue.

The first of these objections would go to the root of the matter were it well founded; for if no happiness is to be had at all by human beings, the attainment of it cannot be the end of morality or of any rational conduct. Though, even in that case, something might still be said for the utilitarian theory, since utility includes not solely the pursuit of happiness, but the prevention or mitigation of unhappiness; and if the former aim be chimerical, there will be all the greater scope and more imperative need for the latter, so long at least as mankind think fit to live and do not take refuge in the simultaneous act of suicide recommended under certain conditions by Novalis. When, however, it is thus positively asserted to be impossible that human life should be happy, the assertion, if not something like a verbal quibble, is at least an exaggeration. If by happiness be meant a continuity of highly pleasurable excitement, it is evident enough that this is impossible. A state of exalted pleasure lasts only moments or in some cases, and with some intermissions, hours or days, and is the occasional brilliant flash of enjoyment, not its permanent and steady flame. Of this the philosophers who have taught that happiness is the end of life were as fully aware as those who taunt them. The happiness which they meant was not a life of rapture, but moments of such, in an existence made up of few and transitory pains, many and various pleasures, with a decided predominance of the active over the passive, and having as the foundation of the whole not to expect more from life than it is capable of bestowing. A life thus composed, to those who have been fortunate enough to obtain it, has always appeared worthy of the name of happiness. And such an existence is even now the lot of many during some considerable portion of their lives. The present wretched education and wretched social arrangements are the only real hindrance to its being attainable by almost all.

The objectors perhaps may doubt whether human beings, if taught to consider happiness as the end of life, would be satisfied with such a moderate share of it. But great numbers of mankind have been satisfied with much less. The main constituents of a satisfied life appear to be two, either of which by itself is often found sufficient for the purpose: tranquillity and excitement. With much tranquillity, many find that they can be content with very little pleasure; with much excitement, many can reconcile themselves to a considerable quantity of pain. There is assuredly no inherent impossibility of enabling even the mass of mankind to unite both, since the two are so far from being incompatible that they are in natural alliance, the prolongation of either being a preparation for, and exciting a wish for, the other. It is only those in whom indolence amounts to a vice that do not desire excitement after an interval of respose; it is only those in whom the need of excitement is a disease that feel the tranquillity which follows excitement dull and insipid, instead of pleasurable in direct proportion to the excitement which preceded it. When people who are tolerably fortunate in their outward lot do not

find in life sufficient enjoyment to make it valuable to them, the cause generally is caring for nobody but themselves. To those who have neither public nor private affections, the excitements of life are much curtailed, and in any case dwindle in value as the time approaches when all selfish interests must be terminated by death; while those who leave after them objects of personal affection, and especially those who have also cultivated a fellow-feeling with the collective interests of mankind, retain as lively an interest in life on the eve of death as in the vigor of youth and health. Next to selfishness, the principal cause which makes life unsatisfactory is want of mental cultivation. A cultivated mind—I do not mean that of a philosopher, but any mind to which the fountains of knowledge have been opened, and which has been taught, in any tolerable degree, to exercise its faculties—finds sources of inexhaustible interest in all that surrounds it: in the objects of nature, the achievements of art, the imaginations of poetry, the incidents of history, the ways of mankind, past and present, and their prospects in the future. It is possible, indeed, to become indifferent to all this, and that too without having exhausted a thousandth part of it, but only when one has had from the beginning no moral or human interest in these things and has sought in them only the gratification of curiosity.

Now there is absolutely no reason in the nature of things why an amount of mental culture sufficient to give an intelligent interest in these objects of contemplation should not be the inheritance of everyone born in a civilized country. As little is there an inherent necessity that any human being should be a selfish egotist, devoid of every feeling or care but those which center in his own miserable individuality. Something far superior to this is sufficiently common even now, to give ample earnest of what the human species may be made. Genuine private affections and a sincere interest in the public good are possible, though in unequal degrees, to every rightly brought up human being. In a world in which there is so much to interest, so much to enjoy, and so much also to correct and improve, everyone who has this moderate amount of moral and intellectual requisites is capable of an existence which may be called enviable; and unless such a person, through bad laws or subjection to the will of others, is denied the liberty to use the sources of happiness within his reach, he will not fail to find this enviable existence, if he escapes the positive evils of life, the great sources of physical and mental suffering—such as indigence, disease, and the unkindness, worthlessness, or premature loss of objects of affection. The main stress of the problem lies, therefore, in the contest with these calamities from which it is a rare good fortune entirely to escape; which, as things now are, cannot be obviated, and often cannot be in any material degree mitigated. Yet no one whose opinion deserves a moment's consideration can doubt that most of the great positive evils of the world are in themselves removable, and will, if human affairs continue to improve, be in the end reduced within narrow limits. Poverty, in any sense implying suffering, may be completely extinguished by the wisdom of society combined with the good sense and providence of individuals. Even that most intractable of enemies, disease, may be indefinitely reduced in dimensions by good physical and moral education and proper control of noxious influences, while the progress of science holds out a promise for the future of still more direct conquests over this detestable foe. And every advance in that direction relieves us from some, not only of the chances which cut short our own lives, but, what concerns us still more, which deprive us of those in whom our happiness is wrapt up. As for vicissitudes of fortune and other disappointments connected with worldly circumstances, these are principally the effect either of gross imprudence, of ill-regulated desires, or of bad or imperfect social institutions. All the grand sources, in short, of human suffering are in a great degree, many of them almost entirely, conquerable by human care and effort; and though their removal is grievously slow—though a long succession of generations will perish in the breach before the conquest is completed, and this world becomes all that, if will and knowledge were not wanting, it might easily be made—yet every mind sufficiently intelligent and generous to bear a part, however small and inconspicuous, in the endeavor will draw a noble enjoyment from the contest itself, which he would not for any bribe in the form of selfish indulgence consent to be without.

And this leads to the true estimation of what is said by the objectors concerning the possibility and the obligation of learning to do without happiness. Unquestionably it is possible to do without happiness; it is done involuntarily by nineteen-twentieths of mankind, even in those parts of our present world which are least deep in barbarism; and it often has to be done voluntarily by the hero or the martyr, for the sake of something which he prizes more than his individual happiness. But this something, what is it, unless the happiness of others or some of the requisites of happiness? It is noble to be capable of resigning entirely one's own portion of happiness, or chances of it; but, after all, this self-sacrifice must be for some end; it is not its own end; and if we are told

that its end is not happiness but virtue, which is better than happiness, I ask, would the sacrifice be made if the hero or martyr did not believe that it would earn for others immunity from similar sacrifices? Would it be made if he thought that his renunciation of happiness for himself would produce no fruit for any of his fellow creatures, but to make their lot like his and place them also in the condition of persons who have renounced happiness? All honor to those who can abnegate for themselves the personal enjoyment of life when by such renunciation they contribute worthily to increase the amount of happiness in the world; but he who does it or professes to do it for any other purpose is no more deserving of admiration than the ascetic mounted on his pillar. He may be an inspiriting proof of what men *can* do, but assuredly not an example of what they *should*.

Though it is only in a very imperfect state of the world's arrangements that anyone can best serve the happiness of others by the absolute sacrifice of his own, yet, so long as the world is in that imperfect state, I fully acknowledge that the readiness to make such a sacrifice is the highest virtue which can be found in man. I will add that in this condition of the world, paradoxical as the assertion may be, the conscious ability to do without happiness gives the best prospect of realizing such happiness as is attainable. For nothing except that consciousness can raise a person above the chances of life by making him feel that, let fate and fortune do their worst, they have not power to subdue him; which, once felt, frees him from excess of anxiety concerning the evils of life and enables him, like many a Stoic in the worst times of the Roman Empire, to cultivate in tranquillity the sources of satisfaction accessible to him, without concerning himself about the uncertainty of their duration any more than about their inevitable end.

Meanwhile, let utilitarians never cease to claim the morality of self-devotion as a possession which belongs by as good a right to them as either to the Stoic or to the Transcendentalist. The utilitarian morality does recognize in human beings the power of sacrificing their own greatest good for the good of others. It only refuses to admit that the sacrifice is itself a good. A sacrifice which does not increase or tend to increase the sum total of happiness, it considers as wasted. The only self-renunciation which it applauds is devotion to the happiness, or to some of the means of happiness, of others, either of mankind collectively or of individuals within the limits imposed by the collective interests of mankind.

I must again repeat what the assailants of utilitarianism seldom have the justice to acknowledge, that the happiness which forms the utilitarian standard of what is right in conduct is not the agent's own happiness but that of all concerned. As between his own happiness and that of others, utilitarianism requires him to be as strictly impartial as a disinterested and benevolent spectator. In the golden rule of Jesus of Nazareth, we read the complete spirit of the ethics of utility. "To do as you would be done by," and "to love your neighbor as yourself," constitute the ideal perfection of utilitarian morality. As the means of making the nearest approach to this ideal, utility would enjoin, first, that laws and social arrangements should place the happiness or (as, speaking practically, it may be called) the interest of every individual as nearly as possible in harmony with the interest of the whole; and, secondly, that education and opinion, which have so vast a power over human character, should so use that power as to establish in the mind of every individual an indissoluble association between his own happiness and the good of the whole, especially between his own happiness and the practice of such modes of conduct, negative and positive, as regard for the universal happiness prescribes; so that not only he may be unable to conceive the possibility of happiness to himself, consistently with conduct opposed to the general good, but also that a direct impulse to promote the general good may be in every individual one of the habitual motives of action, and the sentiments connected therewith may fill a large and prominent place in every human being's sentient existence. If the impugners of the utilitarian morality represented it to their own minds in this its true character, I know not what recommendation possessed by any other morality they could possible affirm to be wanting to it; what more beautiful or more exalted developments of human nature any other ethical system can be supposed to foster, or what springs of action, not accessible to the utilitarian, such systems rely on for giving effect to their mandates.

The objectors to utilitarianism cannot always be charged with representing it in a discreditable light. On the contrary, those among them who entertain anything like a just idea of its disinterested character sometimes find fault with its standard as being too high for humanity. They say it is exacting too much to require that people shall always act from the inducement of promoting the general interest of society. But this is to mistake the very meaning of a standard of morals and confound the rule of action with the motive of it. It is the business of ethics to tell us what are our duties, or by what test we may know them; but no system of ethics requires that the sole motive of all we do shall be a feeling of duty; on the contrary, ninety-nine hundredths of all our actions are done from other motives, and rightly so done if the rule of duty does not condemn them. It is the more unjust to utilitarianism that this particular misapprehension should be made a ground of objection to it, inasmuch as utilitarian moralists have gone beyond almost all others in affirming that the motive has nothing to do with the morality of the action, though much with the worth of the agent. He who saves a fellow creature from drowning does what is morally right, whether his motive be duty or the hope of being paid for his trouble; he who betrays the friend that trusts him is guilty of a crime, even if his object be to serve another friend to whom he is under greater obligations.[1] But to speak only of actions done from the motive of duty, and in direct obedience

[1]An opponent, whose intellectual and moral fairness it is a pleasure to acknowledge (the Rev. J. Llewellyn Davies), has objected to this passage, saying, "Surely the rightness or wrongness of saving a man from drowning does depend very much upon the motive with which it is done. Suppose that a tyrant, when his enemy jumped into the sea to escape from him, saved him from drowning simply in order that he might inflict upon him more exquisite tortures, would it tend to clearness to speak of that rescue as 'a morally right action'? Or suppose again, according to one of the stock illustrations of ethical inquiries, that a man betrayed a trust received from a friend, because the discharge of it would fatally injure that friend himself or someone belonging to him, would utilitarianism compel one to call the betrayal 'a crime' as much as if it had been done from the meanest motive?"

I submit that he who saves another from drowning in order to kill him by torture afterward does not differ only in motive from him who does the same thing from duty or benevolence; the act itself is different. The rescue of the man is, in the case supposed, only the necessary first step of an act far more atrocious than leaving him to drown would have been. Had Mr. Davies said, "The rightness or wrongness of saving a man from drowning does depend very much"— not upon the motive, but—"upon the *intention*," no utilitarian would have differed from him. Mr. Davies, by an oversight too common not to be quite venial, has in this case confounded the very different ideas of Motive and Intention. There is no point which utilitarian thinkers (and Bentham preeminently) have taken more pains to illustrate than this. The morality of the action depends entirely upon the intention—that is, upon what the agent *wills to do*. But the motive, that is, the feeling which makes him will so to do, if it makes no difference in the act, makes none in the morality; though it makes a great difference in our moral estimation of the agent, especially it if indicates a good or bad habitual *disposition*—a bent of character from which useful, or from which hurtful actions are likely to arise.

to principle: it is a misapprehension of the utilitarian mode of thought to conceive it as implying that people should fix their minds upon so wide a generality as the world, or society at large. The great majority of good actions are intended not for the benefit of the world, but for that of individuals, of which the good of the world is made up; and the thoughts of the most virtuous man need not on these occasions travel beyond the particular persons concerned, except so far as is necessary to assure himself that in benefiting them he is not violating the rights, that is, the legitimate and authorized expectations, of anyone else. The multiplication of happiness is, according to the utilitarian ethics, the object of virtue: the occasions on which any person (except one in a thousand) has it in his power to do this on an extended scale—in other words, to be a public benefactor—are but exceptional; and on these occasions alone is he called on to consider public utility; in every other case, private utility, the interest or happiness of some few persons, is all he has to attend to. Those alone the influence of whose actions extends to society in general need concern themselves habitually about so large an object. In the case of abstinences indeed—of things which people forbear to do from moral considerations, though the consequences in the particular case might be beneficial—it would be unworthy of an intelligent agent not to be consciously aware that the action is of a class which, if practiced generally, would be generally injurious, and that this is the ground of the obligation to abstain from it. The amount of regard for the public interest implied in this recognition is no greater than is demanded by every system of morals, for they all enjoin to abstain from whatever is manifestly pernicious to society.

The same considerations dispose of another reproach against the doctrine of utility, founded on a still grosser misconception of the purpose of a standard of morality and of the very meaning of the words "right" or "wrong." It is often affirmed that utilitarianism renders men cold and unsympathizing; that it chills their moral feelings toward individuals; that it makes them regard only the dry and hard considerations of the consequences of actions, not taking into their moral estimate the qualities from which those actions emanate. If the assertion means that they do not allow their judgment respecting the rightness or wrongness of an action to be influenced by their opinion of the qualities of the person who does it, this is a complaint not against utilitarianism, but against any standard or morality at all; for certainly no known ethical standard decides an action to be good or bad because it is done by a good or bad

man, still less because done by an amiable, a brave, or a benevolent man, or the contrary. These considerations are relevant, not to the estimation of actions, but of persons; and there is nothing in the utilitarian theory inconsistent with the fact that there are other things which interest us in persons besides the rightness and wrongness of their actions. The Stoics, indeed, with the paradoxical misuse of language which was part of their system, and by which they strove to raise themselves above all concern about anything but virtue, were fond of saying that he who has that has everything; that he, and only he, is rich, is beautiful, is a king. But no claim of this description is made for the virtuous man by the utilitarian doctrine. Utilitarians are quite aware that there are other desirable possessions and qualities besides virtue, and are perfectly willing to allow to all of them their full worth. They are also aware that a right action does not necessarily indicate a virtuous character, and that actions which are blamable often proceed from qualities entitled to praise. When this is apparent in any particular case, it modifies their estimation, not certainly of the act, but of the agent. I grant that they are, notwithstanding, of opinion that in the long run the best proof of a good character is good actions; and resolutely refuse to consider any mental disposition as good of which the predominant tendency is to produce bad conduct. This makes them unpopular with many people, but it is an unpopularity which they must share with everyone who regards the distinction between right and wrong in a serious light; and the reproach is not one which a conscientious utilitarian need be anxious to repel.

If no more be meant by the objection than that many utilitarians look on the morality of actions, as measured by the utilitarian standards, with too exclusive a regard, and do not lay sufficient stress upon the other beauties of character which go toward making a human being lovable or admirable, this may be admitted. Utilitarians who have cultivated their moral feelings, but not their sympathies, nor their artistic perceptions, do fall into this mistake; and so do all other moralists under the same conditions. What can be said in excuse for other moralists is equally available for them, namely, that, if there is to be any error, it is better that it should be on that side. As a matter of fact, we may affirm that among utilitarians, as among adherents of other systems, there is every imaginable degree of rigidity and of laxity in the application of their standard; some are even puritanically rigorous, while others are as indulgent as can possibly be desired by sinner or by sentimentalist. But on the whole, a doctrine which brings prominently forward the interest that mankind have in the repression and prevention of conduct which violates the moral law is likely to be inferior to no other in turning the sanctions of opinion against such violations. It is true, the question "What does violate the moral law?" is one on which those who recognize different standards of morality are likely now and then to differ. But difference of opinion on moral questions was not first introduced into the world by utilitarianism, while that doctrine does supply, if not always an easy, at all events a tangible and intelligible, mode of deciding such differences.

It may not be superfluous to notice a few more of the common misapprehensions of utilitarian ethics, even those which are so obvious and gross that it might appear impossible for any person of candor and intelligence to fall into them; since persons, even of considerable mental endowment, often give themselves so little trouble to understand the bearings of any opinion against which they entertain a prejudice, and men are in general so little conscious of this voluntary ignorance as a defect that the vulgarest misunderstandings of ethics doctrines are continually met with in the deliberate writings of persons of the greatest pretensions both to high principle and to philosophy. We not uncommonly hear the doctrine of utility inveighed against a *godless* doctrine. If it be necessary to say anything at all against so mere an assumption, we may say that the question depends upon what idea we have formed of the moral character of the Deity. If it be a true belief that God desires, above all things, the happiness of his creatures, and that this was his purpose in their creation, utility is not only not a godless doctrine, but more profoundly religious than any other. If it be meant that utilitarianism does not recognize the revealed will of God as the supreme law of morals, I answer that a utilitarian who believes in the perfect goodness and wisdom of *God* necessarily believes that whatever God has thought fit to reveal on the subject of morals must fulfill the requirements of utility in a supreme degree. But others besides utilitarians have been of opinion that the Christian revelation was intended, and is fitted, to inform the hearts and minds of mankind with a spirit which should enable them to find for themselves what is right, and incline them to do it when found, rather than to tell them, except in a very general way, what it is; and that we need a doctrine of ethics, carefully followed out, to *interpret* to us the will of God. Whether this opinion is correct or not, it is superfluous here to discuss; since whatever aid religion, either natural or revealed, can afford to ethical investigation is as open to the utilitarian moralist as

to any other. He can use it as the testimony of God to the usefulness or hurtfulness of any given course of action by as good a right as others can use it for the indication of a transcendental law having no connection with usefulness or with happiness.

Again, utility is often summarily stigmatized as an immoral doctrine by giving it the name of Expediency, and taking advantage of the popular use of that term to contrast it with Principle. But the expedient, in the sense in which it is opposed to the Right, generally means that which is expedient for the particular interest of the agent himself; as when a minister sacrifices the interests of his country to keep himself in place. When it means anything better than this, it means that which is expedient for some immediate object, some temporary purpose, but which violates a rule whose observance is expedient in a much higher degree. The Expedient, in this sense, instead of being the same thing with the useful, is a branch of the hurtful. Thus it would often be expedient, for the purpose of getting over some momentary embarrassment, or attaining some object immediately useful to ourselves or others, to tell a lie. But inasmuch as the cultivation in ourselves of a sensitive feeling on the subject of veracity is one of the most useful, and the enfeeblement of that feeling one of the most hurtful, things to which our conduct can be instrumental; and inasmuch as any, even unintentional, deviation from truth does that much toward weakening the trustworthiness of human assertion, which is not only the principal support of all present social well-being, but the insufficiency of which does more than any one thing that can be named to keep back civilization, virtue, everything on which human happiness on the largest scale depends—we feel that the violation, for a present advantage, of a rule of such transcendent expediency is not expedient, and that he who, for the sake of convenience to himself or to some other individual, does what depends on him to deprive mankind of the good, and inflict upon them the evil, involved in the greater or less reliance which they can place in each other's words, acts the part of one of their worst enemies. Yet that even this rule, sacred as it is, admits of possible exceptions is acknowledged by all moralists; the chief of which is when the withholding of some fact (as of information from a malefactor, or of bad news from a person dangerously ill) would save an individual (especially an individual other than oneself) from great and unmerited evil, and when the withholding can only be effected by denial. But in order that the exception may not extend itself beyond the need, and may have the least possible effect in weakening reliance on veracity, it ought to be recognized and, if possible, its limits defined; and, if the principle of utility is good for anything, it must be good for weighing these conflicting utilities against one another and marking out the region within which one or the other preponderates.

Again, defenders of utility often find themselves called upon to reply to such objections as this—that there is not time, previous to action, for calculating and weighing the effects of any line of conduct on the general happiness. This is exactly as if anyone were to say that it is impossible to guide our conduct by Christianity because there is not time, on every occasion on which anything has to be done, to read through the Old and New Testaments. The answer to the objection is that there has been ample time, namely, the whole past duration of the human species. During all that time mankind have been learning by experience the tendencies of actions; on which experience all the prudence as well as all the morality of life are dependent. People talk as if the commencement of this course of experience had hitherto been put off, and as if, at the moment when some man feels tempted to meddle with the property or life of another, he had to begin considering for the first time whether murder and theft are injurious to human happiness. Even then I do not think that he would find the question very puzzling; but, at all events, the matter is now done to his hand. It is truly a whimsical supposition that, if mankind were agreed in considering utility to be the test of morality, they would remain without any agreement as to what *is* useful, and would take no measures for having their notions on the subject taught to the young and enforced by law and opinion. There is no difficulty in proving any ethical standard whatever to work ill if we suppose universal idiocy to be conjoined with it; but on any hypothesis short of that, mankind must by this time have acquired positive beliefs as to the effects of some actions on their happiness; and the beliefs which have thus come down are the rules of morality for the multitude, and for the philosopher until he has succeeded in finding better. That philosophers might easily do this, even now, on many subjects; that the received code of ethics is by no means of divine right; and that mankind have still much to learn as to the effects of actions on the general happiness, I admit or rather earnestly maintain. The corollaries from the principle of utility, like the precepts of every practical art, admit of indefinite improvement, and, in a progressive state of the human mind, their improvement is perpetually going on. But to consider the rules of morality as improvable is one thing; to pass over the intermediate generalization entirely

and endeavor to test each individual action directly by the first principle is another. It is a strange notion that the acknowledgment of a first principle is inconsistent with the admission of secondary ones. To inform a traveler respecting the place of his ultimate destination is not to forbid the use of landmarks and direction-posts on the way. The proposition that happiness is the end and aim of morality does not mean that no road ought to be laid down to that goal, or that persons going thither should not be advised to take one direction rather than another. Men really ought to leave off talking a kind of nonsense on this subject, which they would neither talk nor listen to on other matters of practical concernment. Nobody argues that the art of navigation is not founded on astronomy because sailors cannot wait to calculate the Nautical Almanac. Being rational creatures, they go to sea with it ready calculated; and all rational creatures go out upon the sea of life with their minds made up on the common questions of right and wrong, as well as on many of the far more difficult questions of wise and foolish. And this, as long as foresight is a human quality, it is to be presumed they will continue to do. Whatever we adopt as the fundamental principle of morality, we require subordinate principles to apply it by; the impossibility of doing without them, being common to all systems, can afford no argument against any one in particular; but gravely to argue as if no such secondary principles could be had, and as if mankind had remained till now, and always must remain, without drawing any general conclusions from the experience of human life is as high a pitch, I think, as absurdity has ever reached in philosophical controversy.

The remainder of the stock arguments against utilitarianism mostly consist in laying to its charge the common infirmities of human nature, and the general difficulties which embarrass conscientious persons in shaping their course through life. We are told that a utilitarian will be apt to make his own particular case an exception to moral rules, and, when under temptation, will see a utility in the breach of a rule, greater than he will see in its observance. But is utility the only creed which is able to furnish us with excuses for evil-doing and means of cheating our own conscience? They are afforded in abundance by all doctrines which recognize as a fact in morals the existence of conflicting considerations, which all doctrines do that have been believed by sane persons. It is not the fault of any creed, but of the complicated nature of human affairs, that rules of conduct cannot be so framed as to require no exceptions, and that hardly any kind of action can safely be laid down as either always obligatory or always condemnable. There is no ethical creed which does not temper the rigidity of its laws by giving a certain latitude, under the moral responsibility of the agent, for accommodation to peculiarities of circumstances; and under every creed, at the opening thus made, self-deception and dishonest casuistry get in. There exists no moral system under which there do not arise unequivocal cases of conflicting obligation. These are the real difficulties, the knotty points both in the theory of ethics and in the conscientious guidance of personal conduct. They are overcome practically, with greater or with less success, according to the intellect and virtue of the individual; but it can hardly be pretended that anyone will be the less qualified for dealing with them, from possessing an ultimate standard to which conflicting rights and duties can be referred. If utility is the ultimate source of moral obligations, utility may be invoked to decide between them when their demands are incompatible. Though the application of the standard may be difficult, it is better than none at all; while in other systems, the moral laws all claiming independent authority, there is no common umpire entitled to interfere between them; their claims to precedence one over another rest on little better than sophistry, and, unless determined, as they generally are, by the unacknowledged influence of consideration of utility, afford a free scope for the action of personal desires and partialities. We must remember that only in these cases of conflict between secondary principles is it requisite that first principles should be appealed to. There is no case of moral obligation in which some secondary principle is not involved; and if only one, there can seldom be any real doubt which one it is, in the mind of any person by whom the principle itself is recognized.

Of the Ultimate Sanction of the Principle of Utility

JOHN STUART MILL

THE QUESTION IS OFTEN ASKED, and properly so, in regard to any supposed moral standard—What is its sanction? what are the motives to obey? or, more specifically, what is the source of its obligation? whence does it derive its binding force? It is a necessary part of moral philosophy to provide the answer to this question, which, though frequently assuming the shape of an objection to the utilitarian morality, as if it had some special applicability to that above others, really arises in regard to all standards. It arises, in fact, whenever a person is called on to *adopt* a standard, or refer morality to any basis on which he has not been accustomed to rest it. For the customary morality, that which education and opinion have consecrated, is the only one which presents itself to the mind with the feeling of being *in itself* obligatory; and when a person is asked to believe that this morality *derives* its obligation from some general principle round which custom has not thrown the same halo, the assertion is to him a paradox; the supposed corollaries seem to have a more binding force than the original theorem; the superstructure seems to stand better without than with what is represented as its foundation. He says to himself, I feel that I am bound not to rob or murder, betray or deceive; but why am I bound to promote the general happiness? If my own happiness lies in something else, why may I not give that the preference?

If the view adopted by the utilitarian philosophy of the nature of the moral sense be correct, this difficulty will always present itself until the influences which form moral character have taken the same hold of the principle which they have taken of some of the consequences—until, by the improvement of education, the feeling of unity with our fellow creatures shall be (what it cannot be denied that Christ intended it to be) as deeply rooted in our character, and to our own consciousness as completely a part of our nature, as the horror of crime is in an ordinarily well brought up young person. In the meantime, however, the difficulty has no peculiar application to the doctrine of utility, but is inherent in every attempt to analyze morality and reduce it to principles; which, unless the principle is already in men's minds invested

John Stuart Mill, Utilitarianism, *7th ed. (London: Longmans, Green, 1879), pp. 39–51.*

with as much sacredness as any of its applications, always seems to divest them of a part of their sanctity.

The principle of utility either has, or there is no reason why it might not have, all the sanctions which belong to any other system of morals. Those sanctions are either external or internal. Of the external sanctions it is not necessary to speak at any length. They are the hope of favor and the fear of displeasure from our fellow creatures or the Ruler of the Universe, along with whatever we may have of sympathy or affection for them, or of love and awe of Him, inclining us to do His will independently of selfish consequences. There is evidently no reason why all these motives for observance should not attach themselves to the utilitarian morality as completely and as powerfully as to any other. Indeed, those of them which refer to our fellow creatures are sure to do so, in proportion to the amount of general intelligence; for whether there be any other ground of moral obligation than the general happiness or not, men do desire happiness; and however imperfect may be their own practice, they desire and commend all conduct in others toward themselves by which they think their happiness is promoted. With regard to the religious motive, if men believe, as most profess to do, in the goodness of God, those who think that conduciveness to the general happiness is the essence or even only the criterion of good must necessarily believe that it is also that which God approves. The whole force therefore of external reward and punishment, whether physical or moral, whether proceeding from God or from our fellow men, together with all that the capacities of human nature admit of disinterested devotion to either, become available to enforce the utilitarian morality, in proportion as that morality is recognized; and the more powerfully, the more the appliances of education and general cultivation are bent to the purpose.

So far as to external sanctions. The internal sanction of duty, whatever our standard of duty may be, is one and the same—a feeling in our own mind; a pain, more or less intense, attendant on violation of duty, which in properly cultivated moral natures rises, in the more serious cases, into shrinking from it as an impossibility. This feeling, when disinterested and connecting itself with the pure idea of duty, and not with some particular form of it, or with any of the merely accessory circumstances, is the essence of Conscience; though in that complex phenomenon as it actually exists, the simple fact is in general all encrusted over with collateral associations derived from sympathy, from love, and still more from fear; from all the forms of religious feeling; from the recollections of childhood and of all our past life; from self-esteem, desire of the esteem of others, and occasionally even self-abasement. This extreme complication is, I apprehend, the origin of the sort of mystical character which, by a tendency of the human mind of which there are many other examples, is apt to be attributed to the idea of moral obligation, and which leads people to believe that the idea cannot possibly attach itself to any other objects than those which, by a supposed mysterious law, are found in our present experience to excite it. Its binding force, however, consists in the existence of a mass of feeling which must be broken through in order to do what violates our standard of right, and which, if we do nevertheless violate that standard, will probably have to be encountered afterward in the form of remorse. Whatever theory we have of the nature or origin of conscience, this is what essentially constitutes it.

The ultimate sanction, therefore, of all morality (external motives apart) being a subjective feeling in our own minds, I see nothing embarrassing to those whose standard is utility in the question, What is the sanction of that particular standard? We may answer, the same as of all other moral standards—the conscientious feelings of mankind. Undoubtedly this sanction has no binding efficacy on those who do not possess the feelings it appeals to; but neither will these persons be more obedient to any other moral principle than to the utilitarian one. On them morality of any kind has no hold but through the external sanctions. Meanwhile the feelings exist, a fact in human nature, the reality of which, and the great power with which they are capable of acting on those in whom they have been duly cultivated, are proved by experience. No reason has ever been shown why they may not be cultivated to as great intensity in connection with the utilitarian as with any other rule of morals.

There is, I am aware, a disposition to believe that a person who sees in moral obligation a transcendental fact, an objective reality belonging to the province of "Things in themselves," is likely to be more obedient to it than one who believes it to be entirely subjective, having its seat in human consciousness only. But whatever a person's opinion may be on this point of ontology, the force he is really urged by is his own subjective feeling, and is exactly measured by its strength. No one's belief that Duty is an objective reality is stronger than the belief that God is so; yet the belief in God, apart from the expectation of actual reward and punishment, only operates on conduct through, and in proportion to, the subjective religious feeling. The sanction, so far as it is disinterested, is always in the mind itself; and the notion, therefore, of the transcendental moralists must be that this sanction will not exist *in* the mind unless it is believed to have its root out of the mind; and that if a person is able to say to himself, "That which is restraining me and which is called my conscience is only a feeling in my own mind," he may possibly draw the conclusion that when the feeling ceases the obligation ceases, and that if he find the feeling inconvenient, he may disregard it and endeavor to get rid of it. But is this danger confined to the utilitarian morality? Does the belief that moral obligation has its seat outside the mind make the feeling of it too strong to get rid of? The fact is so far otherwise that all moralists admit and lament the ease with which, in generality of minds, conscience can be silenced or stifled. The question, "Need I obey my conscience?" is quite as often put to themselves by persons who never heard of the principle of utility as by its adherents. Those whose conscientious feelings are so weak as to allow of their asking this question, if they answer it affirmatively, will not do so because they believe in the transcendental theory, but because of the external sanctions.

It is not necessary, for the present purpose, to decide whether the feeling of duty is innate or implanted. Assuming it to be innate, it is an open question to what objects it naturally attaches itself; for the philosophic supporters of that theory are now agreed that the intuitive perception is of principles of morality and not of the details. If there be anything innate in the matter, I see no reason why the feeling which is innate would not be that of regard to the pleasures and pains of others. If there is any principle of morals which is intuitively obligatory, I should say it must be that. If so, the intuitive ethics would coincide with the utilitarian, and there would be no further quarrel between them. Even as it is, the intuitive moralists, though they believe that there are other intuitive moral obligations, do already believe this to be one; for they unanimously hold that a large *portion* of morality turns upon the consideration due to the interests of our fellow creatures. Therefore, if the belief in the transcendental origin of moral obligation gives any additional efficacy to the internal sanction, it appears to me that the utilitarian principle has already the benefit of it.

On the other hand, if, as is my own belief, the moral feelings are not innate but acquired, they are not for that reason the less natural. It is natural to man to speak, to reason, to build cities, to cultivate the ground, though these are acquired faculties. The moral feelings are not indeed a part of our nature in the sense of being in any perceptible degree present in all of us; but this, unhappily, is a fact admitted by those who believe the most strenuously in their transcendental origin. Like the other acquired capacities above referred to, the moral faculty, if not a part of our nature, is a natural outgrowth from it; capable, like them, in a certain small degree, of springing up spontaneously; and susceptible of being brought by cultivation to a high degree of development. Unhappily it is also susceptible, by a sufficient use of the external sanctions and of the force of early impressions, of being cultivated in almost any direction, so that there is hardly anything so absurd or so mischievous that it may not, by means of these influences, be made to act on the human mind with all the authority of conscience. To doubt that the same potency might be given by the same means to the principle of utility, even if it had no foundation in human nature, would be flying in the face of all experience.

But moral associations which are wholly of artificial creation, when the intellectual culture goes on, yield by degrees to the dissolving force of analysis; and if the feeling of duty, when associated with utility, would appear equally arbitrary; if there were no leading department of our nature, no powerful class of sentiments, with which that association would harmonize, which would make us feel congenial and incline us not only to foster it in others (for which we have abundant interested motives), but also to cherish it in ourselves—if there were not, in short, a natural basis of sentiment for utilitarian morality, it might well happen that this association also, even after it had been implanted by education, might be analyzed away.

But there *is* this basis of powerful natural sentiment; and that it is which, when once the general happiness is recognized as the ethical standard, will constitute the strength of the utilitarian morality. This firm foundation is that of the social feelings of mankind—the desire to be in unity with our fellow creatures, which is already a powerful principle in human nature, and happily one of those which tend to become stronger, even without express inculcation, from the influences of advancing civilization. The social state is at once so natural, so necessary, and so habitual to man, that, except in some unusual circumstances or by an effort of voluntary abstraction, he never conceives himself otherwise than as a member of a body; and this association is riveted more and more, as mankind are further removed from the state of savage independence. Any condition, therefore, which is essential to a state of society becomes more and more an inseparable part of every person's conception of the state of things which he is born into, and which is the destiny of a human being. Now society between human beings, except in the relation of master and slave, is manifestly impossible on any other footing than that the interests of all are to be consulted. Society between equals can only exist on the understanding that the interests of all are to be regarded equally. And since in all states of civilization, every person, except an absolute monarch, has equals, everyone is obliged to live on these terms with somebody; and in every age some advance is made toward a state in which it will be impossible to live permanently on other terms with anybody. In this way people grow up unable to conceive as possible to them a state of total disregard of other people's interests. They are under a necessity of conceiving themselves as at least abstaining from all the grosser injuries, and (if only for their own protection) living in a state of constant protest against them. They are also familiar with the fact of cooperating with others and proposing to themselves a collective, not an individual, interest as the aim (at least for the time being) of their actions. So long as they are cooperating, their ends are identified with those of others; there is at least a temporary feeling that the interests of others are their own interests. Not only does all strengthening of social ties, and all healthy growth of society, give to each individual a stronger personal interest in practically consulting the welfare of others, it also leads him to identify his *feelings* more and more with their good, or at least with an even greater degree of practical consideration for it. He comes, as though instinctively, to be conscious of himself as a being who *of course* pays regard to others. The good of others becomes to him a thing naturally and necessarily to be attended to, like any of the physical conditions of our existence. Now, whatever amount of this feeling a person has, he is urged by the strongest motives both of interest and of sympathy to demonstrate it, and to the utmost of his power encourage it in others; and even if he has none of it himself, he is as greatly interested as anyone else that others should have it. Consequently, the smallest germs of the feeling are laid hold of and nourished by the contagion of sympathy and the influences of education; and a complete web of corroborative association is woven round it by the powerful agency of the external sanctions. This mode of conceiving ourselves and human life, as civilization goes on, is felt to be more and more natural. Every step in political improvement renders it more so, by removing the sources of opposition of interest and leveling those inequalities of legal privilege between individuals or classes, owing to which there are large portions of mankind whose happiness it is still practicable to disregard. In

an improving state of the human mind, the influences are constantly on the increase which tend to generate in each individual a feeling of unity with all the rest; which, if perfect, would make him never think of, or desire, any beneficial condition for himself in the benefits of which they are not included. If we now suppose this feeling of unity to be taught as a religion, and the whole force of education, of institutions, and of opinion directed, as it once was in the case of religion, to make every person grow up from infancy surrounded on all sides both by the profession and the practice of it, I think that no one who can realize this conception will feel any misgiving about the sufficiency of the ultimate sanction for the Happiness morality. To any ethical student who finds the realization difficult, I recommend, as a means of facilitating it, the second of M. Comte's two principal works, the *Traité de Politique Positive*. I entertain the strongest objections to the system of politics and morals set forth in that treatise, but I think it has superabundantly shown the possibility of giving to the service of humanity, even without the aid of belief in a Providence, both the psychological power and the social efficacy of a religion, making it take hold of human life, and color all thought, feeling, and action in a manner of which the greatest ascendancy ever exercised by any religion may be but a type and foretaste; and of which the danger is, not that it should be insufficient, but that it should be so excessive as to interfere unduly with human freedom and individuality.

Neither is it necessary to the feeling which constitutes the binding force of the utilitarian morality on those who recognize it to wait for those social influences which would make its obligation felt by mankind at large. In the comparatively early state of human advancement in which we now live, a person cannot, indeed, feel that entireness of sympathy with all others which would make any real discordance in the general direction of their conduct in life impossible, but already a person in whom the social feeling is at all developed cannot bring himself to think of the rest of his fellow creatures as struggling rivals with him for the means of happiness, whom he must desire to see defeated in their object in order that he may succeed in his. The deeply rooted conception which every individual even now has of himself as a social being tends to make him feel it one of his natural wants that there should be harmony between his feelings and aims and those of his fellow creatures. If differences of opinion and of mental culture make it impossible for him to share many of their actual feelings—perhaps make him denounce and defy those feelings—he still needs to be conscious that his real aim and theirs do not conflict; that he is not opposing himself to what they really wish for, namely their own good, but is, on the contrary, promoting it. This feeling in most individuals is much inferior in strength to their selfish feelings, and is often wanting altogether. But to those who have it, it possesses all the characters of a natural feeling. It does not present itself to their minds as a superstition of education or a law despotically imposed by the power of society, but as an attribute which it would not be well for them to be without. This conviction is the ultimate sanction of the greatest happiness morality. This it is which makes any mind of well-developed feelings work with, and not against, the outward motives to care for others, afforded by what I have called the external sanctions; and, when those sanctions are wanting or act in an opposite direction, constitutes in itself a powerful internal binding force, in proportion to the sensitiveness and thoughtfulness of the character, since few but those whose mind is a moral blank could bear to lay out their course of life on the plan of paying no regard to others except so far as their own private interest compels.

Of What Sort of Proof the Principle of Utility Is Susceptible

JOHN STUART MILL

IT HAS ALREADY BEEN REMARKED that questions of ultimate ends do not admit of proof, in the ordinary acceptation of the term. To be incapable of proof by reasoning is common to all first principles, to the first premises of our knowledge, as well as to those of our conduct. But the former, being matters of fact, may be the subject of a direct appeal to the faculties which judge of fact—namely, our senses and our internal consciousness. Can an appeal be made to the same faculties on questions of practical ends? Or by what other faculty is cognizance taken of them?

Questions about ends are, in other words, questions about what things are desirable. The utilitarian doctrine is that happiness is desirable, and the only thing desirable, as an end; all other things being only desirable as means to that end. What ought to be required of this doctrine, what conditions is it requisite that the doctrine should fulfill—to make good its claim to be believed?

The only proof capable of being given that an object is visible is that people actually see it. The only proof that a sound is audible is that people hear it; and so of the other sources of our experience. In like manner, I apprehend, the sole evidence it is possible to produce that anything is desirable is that people do actually desire it. If the end which the utilitarian doctrine proposes to itself were not, in theory and in practice, acknowledged to be an end, nothing could ever convince any person that it was so. No reason can be given why the general happiness is desirable, except that each person, so far as he believes it to be attainable, desires his own happiness. This, however, being a fact, we have not only all the proof which the case admits of, but all which it is possible to require, that happiness is a good, that each person's happiness is a good to that person, and the general happiness, therefore, a good to the aggregate of all persons. Happiness has made out its title as *one* of the ends of conduct and, consequently, one of the criteria of morality.

But it has not, by this alone, proved itself to be the sole criterion. To do that, it would seem, by the same rule, necessary to show, not only that people desire happiness, but that they never desire anything else. Now it is palpable that they do desire things which, in common language, are decidedly distinguished from happiness. They desire, for example, virtue and the absence of vice no less really than pleasure and the absence of pain. The desire of virtue is not as universal, but it is as authentic a fact as the desire of happiness. And hence the opponents of the utilitarian standard deem that they have a right to infer that there are other ends of human action besides happiness, and that happiness is not the standard of approbation and disapprobation.

But does the utilitarian doctrine deny that people desire virtue, or maintain that virtue is not a thing to

John Stuart Mill, Utilitarianism, *7th ed. (London: Longmans, Green, 1879), pp. 52–61.*

be desired? The very reverse. It maintains not only that virtue is to be desired, but that it is to be desired disinterestedly, for itself. Whatever may be the opinion of utilitarian moralists as to the original conditions by which virtue is made virtue, however they may believe (as they do) that actions and dispositions are only virtuous because they promote another end than virtue, yet this being granted, and it having been decided, from considerations of this description, what *is* virtuous, they not only place virtue at the very head of the things which are good as means to the ultimate end, but they also recognize as a psychological fact the possibility of its being, to the individual, a good in itself, without looking to any end beyond it; and hold that the mind is not in a right state, not in a state conformable to Utility, not in the state most conducive to the general happiness, unless it does love virtue in this manner—as a thing desirable in itself, even although, in the individual instance, it should not produce those other desirable consequences which it tends to produce, and on account of which it is held to be virtue. This opinion is not, in the smallest degree, a departure from the Happiness principle. The ingredients of happiness are very various, and each of them is desirable in itself, and not merely when considered as swelling an aggregate. The principle of utility does not mean that any given pleasure, as music, for instance, or any given exemption from pain, as for example health, is to be looked upon as means to a collective something termed happiness, and to be desired on that account. They are desired and desirable in and for themselves; besides being means, they are a part of the end. Virtue, according to the utilitarian doctrine, is not naturally and originally part of the end, but it is capable of becoming so; and in those who live it disinterestedly it has become so, and is desired and cherished, not as a means to happiness, but as a part of their happiness.

To illustrate this further, we may remember that virtue is not the only thing originally a means, and which if it were not a means to anything else would be and remain indifferent, but which by association with what it is a means to comes to be desired for itself, and that too with the utmost intensity. What, for example, shall we say of the love of money? There is nothing originally more desirable about money than about any heap of glittering pebbles. Its worth is solely that of the things which it will buy; the desires for other things than itself, which it is a means of gratifying. Yet the love of money is not only one of the strongest moving forces of human life, but money is, in many cases, desired in and for itself; the desire

to possess it is often stronger than the desire to use it, and goes on increasing when all the desires which point to ends beyond it, to be compassed by it, are falling off. It may, then, be said truly that money is desired not for the sake of an end, but as part of the end. From being a means to happiness, it has come to be itself a principal ingredient of the individual's conception of happiness. The same may be said of the majority of the great objects of human life: power, for example, or fame, except that to each of these there is a certain amount of immediate pleasure annexed, which has at least the semblance of being naturally inherent in them—a thing which cannot be said of money. Still, however, the strongest natural attraction, both of power and of fame, is the immense aid they give to the attainment of our other wishes; and it is the strong association thus generated between them and all our objects of desire which gives to the direct desire of them the intensity it often assumes, so as in some characters to surpass in strength all other desires. In these cases the means have become a part of the end, and a more important part of it than any of the things which they are means to. What was once desired as an instrument for the attainment of happiness has come to be desired for its own sake. In being desired for its own sake it is, however, desired as *part* of happiness. The person is made, or thinks he would be made, happy by its mere possession; and is made unhappy by failure to obtain it. The desire of it is not a different thing from the desire of happiness any more than the love of music or the desire of health. They are included in happiness. They are some of the elements of which the desire of happiness is made up. Happiness is not an abstract idea but a concrete whole; and these are some of its parts. And the utilitarian standard sanctions and approves their being so. Life would be a poor thing, very ill provided with sources of happiness, if there were not this provision of nature by which things originally indifferent, but conducive to, or otherwise associated with, the satisfaction of our primitive desires, become in themselves sources of pleasure more valuable than the primitive pleasures, both in permanency, in the space of human existence that they are capable of covering, and even in intensity.

Virtue, according to the utilitarian conception, is a good of this description. There was no original desire of it, or motive to it, save its conduciveness to pleasure, and especially to protection from pain. But through the association thus formed it may be felt a good in itself, and desired as such with as great intensity as any other good; and with this difference between it and the love of money, of power, or of fame—that all of these may, and often do, render the individual noxious to the other members of the society to which he belongs, whereas there is nothing which makes him so much a blessing to them as the cultivation of the disinterested love of virtue. And consequently, the utilitarian standard, while it tolerates and approves those other acquired desires, up to the point beyond which they would be more injurious to the general happiness than promotive of it, enjoins and requires the cultivation of the love of virtue up to the greatest strength possible, as being above all things important to the general happiness.

It results from the preceding considerations that there is in reality nothing desired except happiness. Whatever is desired otherwise than as a means to some end beyond itself, and ultimately to happiness, is desired as itself a part of happiness, and is not desired for itself until it has become so. Those who desire virtue for its own sake desire it either because the consciousness of it is a pleasure, or because the consciousness of being without it is a pain, or for both reasons united; as in truth the pleasure and pain seldom exist separately, but almost always together— the same person feeling pleasure in the degree of virtue attained, and pain in not having attained more. If one of these gave him no pleasure, and the other no pain, he would not love or desire virtue, or would desire it only for the other benefits which it might produce to himself or to persons whom he cared for.

We have now, then, an answer to the question, of what sort of proof the principle of utility is susceptible. If the opinion which I have now stated is psychologically true—if human nature is so constituted as to desire nothing which is not either a part of happiness or a means of happiness—we can have no other proof, and we require no other, that these are the only things desirable. If so, happiness is the sole end of human action, and the promotion of it the test by which to judge of all human conduct; from whence it necessarily follows that it must be the criterion of morality, since a part is included in the whole.

And now to decide whether this is really so, whether mankind do desire nothing for itself but that which is a pleasure to them, or of which the absence is a pain, we have evidently arrived at question of fact and experience, dependent, like all similar questions, upon evidence. It can only be determined by practiced self-consciousness and self-observation, assisted by observation of others. I believe that these sources of evidence, impartially consulted, will declare that desiring a thing and finding it pleasant, aversion to it and thinking of it as painful, are phenomena entirely inseparable or, rather, two parts of the same phenomenon—in strictness of language, two different modes of naming the same psychological fact; that to think of an object as desirable (unless for the sake of its consequences) and to think of it as pleasant are one and the same thing; and that to desire anything except in proportion as the idea of it is pleasant is a physical and metaphysical impossibility.

So obvious does this appear to me that I expect it will hardly be disputed; and the objection made will be, not that desire can possibly be directed to anything ultimately except pleasure and exemption from pain, but that the will is a different thing from desire; that a person of confirmed virtue or any other person whose purposes are fixed carries out his purposes without any thought of the pleasure he has in contemplating them or expects to derive from their fulfillment, and persists in acting on them, even though these pleasures are much diminished by changes in his character or decay of his passive sensibilities, or are outweighed by the pains which the pursuit of the purposes may bring upon him. All this I fully admit and have stated it elsewhere as positively and emphatically as anyone. Will, the active phenomenon, is a different thing from desire, the state of passive sensibility, and, though originally an offshoot from it, may in time take root and detach itself from the parent stock, so much so that in the case of a habitual purpose, instead of willing the thing because we desire it, we often desire it only because we will it. This, however, is but an instance of that familiar fact, the power of habit, and is nowise confined to the case of virtuous actions. Many indifferent things which men originally did from a motive of some sort they continue to do from habit. Sometimes this is done unconsciously, the consciousness coming only after the action; at other times with conscious volition, but volition which has become habitual and is put in operation by the force of habit, in opposition perhaps to the deliberate preference, as often happens with those who have contracted habits of vicious or hurtful indulgence. Third and last comes the case in which the habitual act of will in the individual instance is not in contradiction to the general intention prevailing at other times, but in fulfillment of it, as in the case of the person of confirmed virtue and of all who pursue deliberately and consistently any determinate end. The distinction between will and desire thus understood is an authentic and highly important psychological fact; but the fact consists solely in this—that will, like all other parts of our constitution, is amenable to habit, and that we may will from habit what we no longer desire for itself, or desire only because we will it. It is not the less true that will, in the beginning, is entirely produced by desire, including in that term the repelling influence of pain as well as the attractive one of pleasure. Let us take into consideration no longer the person who has a confirmed will to do right, but him in whom that virtuous will is still feeble, conquerable by temptation, and not to be fully relied on; by what means can it be strengthened? How can the will to be virtuous, where it does not exist in sufficient force, be implanted or awakened? Only by making the person *desire* virtue—by making him think of it in a pleasurable light, or of its absence in a painful one. It is by associating the doing right with pleasure, or the wrong with pain, or by eliciting and impressing and bringing home to the person's experience the pleasure naturally involved in the one or the pain in the other, that it is possible to call forth that will to be virtuous which, when confirmed, acts without any thought of either pleasure or pain. Will is the child of desire, and passes out of the dominion of its parent only to come under that of habit. That which is the result of habit affords no pre-

sumption of being intrinsically good; and there would be no reason for wishing that the purpose of virtue should become independent of pleasure and pain were it not that the influence of the pleasurable and painful associations which prompt to virtue is not sufficiently to be depended on for unerring constancy of action until it has acquired the support of habit. Both in feeling and in conduct, habit is the only thing which imparts certainty; and it is because of the importance to others of being able to rely absolutely on one's feelings and conduct, and to oneself of being able to rely on one's own, that the will to do right ought to be cultivated into this habitual independence. In other words, this state of the will is a means to good, not intrinsically a good; and does not contradict the doctrine that nothing is a good to human beings but in so far as it is either itself pleasurable or a means of attaining pleasure or averting pain.

But if this doctrine be true, the principle of utility is proved. Whether it is so or not must now be left to the consideration of the thoughtful reader.

Discussion and Reflection Questions

1. *Utilitarianism, general remarks:* Why might Mill's theory be called a *consequentialist* moral theory? When Mill talks of the consequences of an action, how far do these consequences extend? Is there any way, in principle, of saying which consequences of an action should count toward the evaluation of that action and which ones do not matter? Why is this an important issue? How would it affect Mill's theory to consider, not the consequences of *individual actions*, but rather the consequences of following certain *rules*? Would some form of "rule utilitarianism" provide a better interpretation of Mill's theory?

2. *What utilitarianism is:* Mill wants to be able to distinguish between different qualities of pleasure. According to Mill, there is a simple way to judge which of two pleasures is of a higher quality: "Of two pleasures, if there be one to which all or almost all who have experience of both give a decided preference, irrespective of any feeling of moral obligation to prefer it, that is the more desirable pleasure." Is this an adequate way of distinguishing between higher and lower pleasures? Is it really better, as he says, "to be a human being dissatisfied, than a pig satisfied"? Is it better to be a genius dissatisfied than a person of ordinary intellectual talents completely satisfied?

3. *Of the ultimate sanction of the principle of utility:* How could Mill try to convince a person unconvinced of the value of the doctrine of utility to act in accordance with it? Would Mill even try? How important is having the proper kind of education for having a motive to act on the principle of utility? Think about your own moral principles. What is your motive for acting in accordance with them (that is, when you do act in accordance with them)? How would you convince someone else to act morally when they were not especially inclined to do so?

4. *Of what sort of proof the principle of utility is susceptible:* Think of some of the things that people do, as a matter of fact, desire. Presumably all of these things are "desirable" in the sense that they *can* be desired. Are all of these things also "desirable" in the sense that they *ought* to be desired? Is Mill guilty of an equivocation in his argument for the greatest

happiness principle? From the fact that each person does as a matter of fact desire his or her own happiness, would it follow that all people desire the happiness of everyone? Does this seem like a good argument to you? Explain your reasoning.

Suggestions for Further Reading

Bentham's defense of utilitarianism is most fully presented in his *An Introduction to the Principles of Morals and Legislation* (New York: Hafner Publishing Co., 1948; originally published 1789). For introductions to Bentham's moral and political thought, see Ross Harrison, *Bentham* (London: Routledge and Kegan Paul, 1984), and John Dinwiddly, *Bentham* (Oxford: Oxford University Press, 1989). Mill's *Utilitarianism* is available in an inexpensive edition (Indianapolis: Hackett Publishing Co., 1979), as well as part of the multivolume *Collected Works* (Toronto: University of Toronto Press, 1963). For essays on various aspects of Mill's philosophy, see J. B. Schneewind, ed., *Mill: A Collection of Critical Essays* (Notre Dame, Ind.: University of Notre Dame Press, 1969). Alan Ryan's *The Philosophy of John Stuart Mill* (Atlantic Highlands, N.J.: Humanities Press International, 1990) is a treatment of Mill's philosophy as a whole. Books on Mill's moral philosophy include Fred R. Berger, *Happiness, Justice, and Freedom: The Moral and Political Philosophy of John Stuart Mill* (Berkeley: University of California Press, 1984), and Wendy Donner, *The Liberal Self: John Stuart Mill's Moral and Political Philosophy* (Ithaca, N.Y.: Cornell University Press, 1991). Essays on specific aspects of Mill's utilitarianism include: Tom Warke, "Multi-Dimensional Utility and the Index Number Problem: Jeremy Bentham, J. S. Mill, and Qualitative Hedonism," *Utilitas* 12 (July 2000): 175–203; Elijah Millgram, "Mill's Proof of the Principle of Utility," *Ethics* 110 (January 2000): 393–310; and Geoffrey Scarre, "Happiness in the Millian," *British Journal for the History of Philosophy* 7 (October 1999): 491–502. Vijitha Rajapakse, "Early Buddhism and John Stuart Mill's Thinking in the Fields of Philosophy and Religion: Some Notes Toward a Comparative Study," *Philosophy East and West*, vol. 37 (1987), pp. 260–285, finds many parallels and convergences between Buddhism and Mill's thought. For a critical examination of utilitarianism, see Alan O. Ebenstein, *The Greatest Happiness Principle: An Examination of Utilitarianism* (New York: Garland Publishers, 1991). Collections of essays on utilitarianism include: *The Limits of Utilitarianism*, edited by Harlan B. Miller and William H. Williams (Minneapolis: University of Minnesota Press, 1982); *Consequentialism and Its Critics*, edited by Samuel Scheffler (Oxford: Oxford University Press, 1988); *Utilitarianism and Its Critics*, edited by Jonathan Glover (New York: Macmillan Publishing Co., 1990); *Utilitarianism and Beyond*, edited by Bernard Williams and Amartya Sen (Cambridge: Cambridge University Press, 1982); and *Mill's "Utilitarianism": Critical Essays*, edited by David Lyons (Lanham, Md.: Rowman and Littlefield, 1997). As noted above, utilitarianism is a kind of consequentialist moral theory. For a look at contemporary consequentialism, of both a utilitarian and nonutilitarian sort, see Philip Petit, "Consequentialism," in *A Companion to Ethics*, edited by Peter Singer (Oxford: Blackwell, 1991), pp. 230–240.

InfoTrac

utilitarianism, "Bentham, Jeremy", "Mill, John Stuart", hedonism, utility, majority rule, utility theory, pleasure

PART III

Eastern Ethical Perspectives

The supreme ideal of Greece is to save the ego from anarchy and chaos. The supreme ideal of the Orient is to dissolve the ego into the infinite and to become one with it.

—KIMON FRIAR

PHILOSOPHICAL REFLECTION DEVELOPED in the East simultaneously with, and largely independently from, Western philosophical thinking. Although there are some remarkable similarities between certain elements of Western and Eastern moral traditions, it is the differences that are most striking. The Western moral perspectives presented in Part II are typically developed on the basis of argumentation and appeals to reason (this is even true, to some extent, of the theological ethics of Aquinas), whereas the perspectives in this part of the book may be seen as united in their reliance on gaining insights from some authoritative source. The source taken as authoritative, however, differs from one tradition to another.

To consider just one example, reflect for a moment on the philosophical approaches of the earliest philosophers considered in this book: Socrates in the West and Confucius in the East. In Plato's dialogue the *Meno,* Socrates declares: "[There is] one thing I am ready to fight for as long as I can, in word and act—that is, that we shall be better, braver, and more active men if we believe it is right to look for what we do not know than if we believe there is no point in looking because what we do not know we can never discover" (*Meno,* 86). Socrates is passionately interested in pushing inquiry to the limit in order discover hitherto unknown truths. Confucius, on the other hand, says of himself: "I am a transmitter, not a creator. I believe in and have a passion for ancient studies" (*Analects* 7:1). Confucius sees himself as an informant, passing on to his contemporaries the rites that were practiced by the ancients and encouraging them to follow the path of virtue set out in these rites. Socrates emphasizes the discovery of new truths, whereas Confucius stresses the recovery of ancient principles. This basic difference in philosophical orientation, seen in some of the earliest reflections on ethics, foretells much of the later development of ethics in the West and the East. The West tends to emphasize reason and the intellectual search for moral truth, and the East leans more heavily toward intuition and the development of insights gleaned from ancient sources.

In this respect Eastern moral perspectives may be said to resemble religious rather than philosophical approaches to the good life for human beings. There is a good deal of plausibility to this view. All the perspectives represented in this part of the book have organized religions associated with them, whereas this is not true for all those represented in Part II. However, the religion-philosophy distinction is far less clear, and consequently less useful, for Eastern ways of thought than for Western ones, inasmuch as the Eastern perspectives presented here blend both religious and philosophical concerns in the same works. In any case, we will be focusing on the ethical aspects of these Eastern traditions. What makes the perspectives in this part of the book recognizable moral traditions is their overriding concern for guiding conduct with respect to ideals and goals deemed worthy of pursuit. Each expresses an influential view of the nature and goal of human life.

Although the moral traditions discussed in this part of the book may be related historically, such historical relations are often less helpful than was the case with the Western perspectives discussed in Part II. This is partly because their development often spans centuries, with different traditions developing simultaneously and sometimes in interaction with one another. A historical approach is also less helpful here because these perspectives have a kind of timeless quality to them. They are meant to be living ways for all ages.

Chapters 5 and 6 include selections from the two most important moral traditions originating in China: Confucianism and Daoism (Taoism). Despite the fact that these two traditions differ in significant respects, they are bound together not just geographically, but also by their common devotion to the ideal of harmony. This emphasis on harmony leads to a corresponding emphasis on the interrelations between people, between people and communities, and between people and nature. Confucianism is grounded in respect for rituals and tradition and emphasizes harmony between the parts of society, whereas Daoism takes its insights from a reflective observation of nature and emphasizes harmony within individuals and between individuals and nature. Chinese ethical thought tends to be holistic and integrative, and the goal of life in both traditions might be said to be the establishment, maintenance, and enjoyment of harmony in the world.

Like China, India gave birth to two major ethical traditions that continue to attract millions of adherents: Hinduism and Buddhism. The precise origins of Hinduism are shrouded in the mists of antiquity. What is clear is that Hindu ethical beliefs form a rich tapestry that must be understood in the context of the specific doctrines of Hindu religion, especially beliefs about an afterlife and the determinants of reincarnation. Chapter 7 includes selections from basic Hindu scriptures that are the starting points for appreciating the Hindu moral tradition.

The origins of Buddhism are somewhat better known. In much the same way that Christianity eventually spread far beyond its origin in the Middle East, so too Buddhism spread far beyond its birthplace in northern India. In both cases the original doctrines changed as followers encountered different cultures and situations. Buddhism divided into two major branches—Theravada and Mahayana, each with numerous sects—and grew in popularity and spread across Asia. Theravada Buddhism is the primary form in Southeast Asia, and Mahayana Buddhism is the main tradition in China, Korea, and Japan. Mahayana Buddhism developed further in China and continued to evolve as Buddhism took root in Japan, where it became known as Zen Buddhism. All Buddhists, however, trace their doctrines back to the teachings of the Buddha. Chapter 8 is devoted to Buddhism in its original form, as taught by the Buddha and his immediate followers.

Chapter 5

Confucianism

Introduction: Benevolence and Humanity

Confucianism is one of the main schools of philosophy in China and the rest of Asia. After Confucius introduced it, many other thinkers—some of whose names are now completely unknown to us—developed and elaborated its doctrines. Confucianism embodies a worldview, a social ethic, a political ideology, a scholarly tradition, and a way of life. It has exerted a profound influence on every aspect of East Asian culture. For over two thousand years Confucian ethical values have served as a foundation for individual, familial, communal, and national behaviors. It would be quite impossible to understand the ways of life of more than a quarter of the world's population without an appreciation of the main doctrines of Confucianism. Introducing these doctrines is the aim of this chapter.

Confucian ethics, like those of the Greeks, is an ethics of virtue. The goal of the moral life is to cultivate a certain kind of character (the character of the gentleman, as explained below). Confucian ethics also emphasizes a number of obligations for individuals, especially as relating to a person's role within his family. It thus contains duties of the sort that Kant also clearly thought to be crucial to morality. However, rather than focusing on axioms of conduct (like Kantian categorical imperatives), Confucianism emphasizes socially determined roles and the proper activities associated with them. The family and society are considered natural entities, and so the role of the person as a group member is also naturally determined. Another difference between the Confucian and the Kantian approaches to duties should be noted. Kant treats all persons as individuals to whom we have equal obligations, whereas Confucianism explicitly locates the individual in a nested set of relationships extending through the immediate and extended family to teachers, neighbors, and society at large. A person's obligations are determined by the relationship she has to people in each of these different naturally and socially determined categories.

Confucian ethics, as developed by Confucius himself, is based on an acceptance of *li*, or ancient rituals. These were conventional codes of conduct that instructed individuals on how to conduct themselves, especially in public. Becoming a morally virtuous person requires learning and observing these rituals. Hence study and education are essential for morality. The most important and influential later Confucian, Mencius, radically revised Confucius's original teaching, while retaining much of what was most central to it. Like Confucius, Mencius believed that observance of the rituals is central to morality. Although Confucius appears to have thought that the rituals ultimately are grounded in nature in some way, Mencius laid greater stress on the naturalness of rituals. The rituals are, in a sense, the natural human response to inevitable events that people face. Morality is not conventional, but rather natural, organic, genetic. Our inclination for morality comes from nature, not from training. One can no more force the growth of one's natural moral concern by education than one can force the growth of a stalk of rice by pulling on it.

As this brief overview suggests, Confucianism embodies a number of different themes and perspectives. What is common to its various forms is an insistence on the importance of observing the rituals for the cultivation of virtue, and on the family as the center of the moral life. These two themes give it a distinctive character that is quite unlike any of the moral traditions examined in Part II of this book. The remainder of this chapter delves into these emphases in more detail.

Confucius: The Ritualization of Life

The gentleman has morality as his basic stuff, and by observing the rites puts it into practice.

—CONFUCIUS, THE *ANALECTS*

Confucius (ca. 551–ca. 479 B.C.E.), the "Grand Master of All Ages," remains the most influential and revered person in Chinese history. According to legend, a unicorn foretold his birth. In its mouth it held a jade tablet bearing the following prophecy: "A child as pure as crystal will be born for the continuation of the declining Chou, to become a king without a kingdom." In fact, the restoration of the previous glory of the Chou dynasty (ca. 1122–225 B.C.E.) was to become Confucius's lifelong mission.

Legends aside, what we know about Confucius is that he was born to a poor but formerly aristocratic family in the feudal state of Lu, in what is now the eastern Chinese province of Shandong. His family name was Kong, and he later became known as Kong Fu-zi, meaning Master Kong. ("Confucius" is a Latinization of his name that is used in this book because of its familiarity.) His father died when he was just three, and he was raised by his mother. He decided, probably by the age of fifteen, to devote his life to learning for the sake of reforming his society, which had become corrupt. But in order to help support his family, the man who would eventually be revered as China's greatest philosopher had a series of jobs as a shepherd, cowherder, clerk, and bookkeeper, and eventually obtained a government appointment. After working in a number of minor posts, he left the government bureaucracy and became an itinerant teacher, traveling throughout China. His reputation for knowledge spread, and as it did he attracted a large number of students. At one point, according to some accounts, he had three thousand pupils. His personal presence, no less than the nobility of his ideas, proved a powerful attractive force.

Some of those ideas form the basis for Confucian ethics. The fundamental concept in Confucian ethics is *ren*, which stands for the ideal relationship among human beings. (The Chinese character for *ren* is made of the symbols for "human being" and "two," suggesting relationship between two persons.) *Ren* is often translated as benevolence but also suggests the virtues of gentility, magnanimity, humanity, compassion, love, altruism, kindness, and goodness of character. It has been suggested that for Confucius the notion of *ren* functions as the notion of respect for persons does for Kant. In this sense both Confucius and Kant developed ethics of respect for persons as members of the community of beings to whom moral obligations are due. Perhaps the notion of "human-heartedness," or genuine concern for one's fellow human beings, captures the concept of *ren* best. It is the perfect virtue of human beings, an ideal to be sought after even if it is never fully realized by anyone. It is the highest goal of moral cultivation.

Confucius draws a sharp contrast between the superior person (*jun zi*), who has a thorough understanding of *ren* and who constantly practices it, and thus whose action is based on moral principle, and the inferior person (*xiao ren*), whose action is based simply on profit. The superior person (or gentleman) is the one who practices *ren* in accordance with *li*, the rites, or rules of propriety. Such a person treasures and seeks the *dao*, the right Way. The rites were a body of rules governing every aspect of life, and included ceremonies, rituals, manners, etiquette, and customs. Unlike his contemporary in the West, Socrates, Confucius did not question the authority of the conventional norms he has been taught. Confucius devoted a great deal of his time in later life to editing and promoting the ancient rites. Confucius saw himself not as a philosopher but as a historical scholar, transmitting ancient wisdom as embodied in the rites. The importance of the rites for morality is that they represent the repository of past insights into proper conduct. Everyone should observe them unless there are compelling reasons not to. Confucius laid great stress on observing these rites, as they provide fundamental guidance for the right way to live. It is not enough to have the right inclinations; one must also know how to implement them.

This emphasis on observing the ancient rites is a distinctive feature of Confucius's view, and is intimately connected with the concept of benevolence. As he says in the *Analects*, "To return to the observance of the rites through overcoming the self constitutes benevolence. If for a single day a man could return to the observance of the rites through overcoming himself, then the whole Empire would consider benevolence to be his." He makes clear, however, that "the practice of benevolence depends on oneself alone, and not on others." Each person must take responsibility for his own behavior.

The ideal that the rites assist us in achieving is the attainment of harmony between the perfect individual and the well-ordered society. This harmony is based on the mutual moral obligations of the five human relationships: between ruler and subject, father and son, elder and younger brother, husband and wife, and friends. Practicing the fundamental virtue of filial piety is the first step toward moral perfection. Cultivating genuine feelings for your parents enhances your personal dignity and identity. It does not demand unconditional submissiveness to your parents, but rather the recognition that a special kind of reverence is due them.

Confucius assumed that most human beings are teachable, improvable, and perfectible through the coordination of communal and personal effort. It has been said that Confucius was responsible for the "democratization of self-cultivation" in China. Anyone can cultivate virtue, so individuals are responsible for their moral well-being. Education plays a crucial role in this process. The purpose of education is to become a superior person, not for the sake of self-realization, but to contribute to the harmony of society. In Confucian societies, as in most other non-Western societies, "individualism" does not have the same value that it does in our society. The individual self is realized not through its independence but rather through its appropriate relations with the society or group it is associated with. When asked by someone why he himself did not take part in government, Confucius replied, "Simply by being a good son and friendly to his brothers a man can exert an influence upon government." Confucius's model of the moral life is the properly organized family, in which the different members contribute to the common welfare by fulfilling their role-specific obligations. These obligations are determined by a person's position within the traditional family structure. The cultivation of one's self and immediate relationships, and the fulfillment of personal responsibilities constitute the basis for the social order, which in turn is the basis for political stability and universal peace. Confucius emphasizes right order in the family in part because the natural bonds within the family are the earliest and strongest bonds human beings form, and in part because harmony within the family is the source and precondition for achieving right order in society.

Confucius advocated morality as the foundation of life in an ideal world where courtesy, filial piety, and the virtues of benevolence, righteousness, loyalty, and trustworthiness would prevail. His vision of the ideal world is well expressed in the following passage (probably written by one of his followers):

> When the perfect order prevails, the world is like a home shared by all. Virtuous and worthy men are elected to public office, and capable men hold posts of gainful employment in society; peace and trust among all men are the maxims of living. All men love and respect their own parents and children, as well as the parents and children of others. There is caring for the old; there are jobs for the adults; there are nourishment and education for the children. There is a means of support for the widows, and the widowers; for all who find themselves alone in the world; and for the disabled. Every man and woman has an appropriate role to play in the family and society. A sense of sharing displaces the effects of selfishness and materialism. A devotion to public duty leaves no room for idleness. Intrigues and conniving for ill gain are unknown. Villains such as thieves and robbers do not exist. The door to every home need never be locked and bolted by day or night. These are the characteristics of an ideal world, the commonwealth state. (*The Record of Rites*, Book IX)

As noted earlier, Confucius stands at the beginning of a long tradition of Confucianism. Many scholars took up and developed Confucius's ideas further. The central Confucian doctrines are contained in what is known as the Four Books. These are the *Analects*, the *Doctrine of the Mean*, *The Great Learning*, and the *Book of Mencius*. The first is the one attributed most closely to Confucius himself; the others are works by later Confucian scholars. These four books formed the basis for Chinese civil service examinations for some six hundred years.

The *Analects* (*Lun Yu*) is a collection of Confucius's sayings recorded by his disciples and their students. It was probably compiled during the early years of the Warring States Period (475–221 B.C.E.). It is more a book *about* Confucius and his teaching than a book *by* him. Rather than presenting a systematic account of Confucian principles, it reads more like a series of observations and conversations designed to stimulate thought and reflection on the part of the reader. It is the closest thing we have to hearing the Master's voice directly.

Scholars generally consider *The Great Learning* to be a work by Confucianists in the Qin dynasty (221–207 B.C.E.) and the Han dynasty (206 B.C.E.–220 C.E.). The central theme of this work is that self-cultivation is essential to the good ordering of the family, and well-ordered families are essential for the realization of the ideal society. Therefore, self-cultivation has society's benefit as its aim, not personal improvement for its own sake.

The *Doctrine of the Mean* dates from the same period as *The Great Learning*, and its authorship is likewise uncertain. The work attempts to provide a metaphysical justification for Confucian ideals by connecting the Way of Heaven with the Way of Humanity. The Way of Heaven is sincerity. Hence people should strive for sincerity in their actions. The book also concerns moderation in feelings, with correct emotions achieving a mean between extremes. The sincere pursuit of moderation conforms a person's feelings to nature and thus contributes to the universal harmony of the world. Once again, it is the emphasis on the good of society, and indeed of the whole world, rather than simply the narrow preoccupation with one's own welfare, that is the distinctive mark of Confucian moral theory.

Finally, the *Book of Mencius* was written by Confucius's most famous follower, who according to legend was a student of Confucius's grandson. The book explains, among other things, Mencius's view that human nature is fundamentally good and that people need simply to cultivate the goodness that is already within them. Selections from the *Analects*, *The Great Learning*, and the *Doctrine of the Mean* are included below. Mencius's ideas are explained in more detail in the profile section that follows.

PROFILE

Mencius: Cultivating the *Ren*-Mind

Meng zi (371–289 B.C.E.), or Mencius as he is known in the West, sought to promote Confucian philosophy by articulating more clearly the foundations in human nature for Confucian moral idealism. Like Confucius, Mencius insists that most human beings are improvable through persistent self-effort. Human nature is essentially oriented toward goodness, and we become good by willing to be so. Each human being is endowed with four basic feelings: commiseration, shame, modesty, and a sense of right and wrong. These four feelings are the basis for cultivating the four cardinal virtues: humanity, righteousness, ritual, and wisdom.

We become good, Mencius believes, not because we are told that we *must* be good, but because our deepest nature spontaneously expresses itself as goodness. In one of his striking analogies, he suggests that goodness naturally flows from a human heart as trees grow upon a mountain, or as water flows downhill. Left unimpeded by unnecessarily restrictive social conventions, for example, it goes where it ought to—naturally. Expressing one's natural goodness spontaneously is having a *ren*-mind: a mind that is oriented toward embracing humanity. Still, despite this native orientation, goodness is something that needs to be cultivated lest it wither and die. People may fail to fully develop their natural goodness either because of circumstances such as war or poverty, or because of a lack of self-resolve. The rewards of success in this endeavor, however, are great. Mencius writes that "he who cultivates his *ren*-mind to the utmost knows his essential nature. He who knows his essential nature knows Heaven. To attend to one's mind and to nourish one's nature, is the way to serve Heaven."

Mencius displays a tremendous faith in the human capacity for self-knowledge and understanding. Fully realizing your potential as a human being requires the cultivation of your sensitivity to the whole universe as part of your lived experience. One of his sayings, which also embodies his version of the Golden Rule, captures his thought beautifully and expresses his positive view of human nature: "All the ten thousand things are there in me. There is no greater joy for me than to find, on self-examination, that I am true to myself. Try your best to treat others as you would wish to be treated yourself, and you will find that this is the shortest way to humanity."

Reading Questions

1. *Filial piety:* In the *Analects* Confucius returns again and again to the topic of the proper relationships between members of a family. According to Confucius, what sort of relationship should there be between parents and children? What examples does he give of appropriate behavior of children toward their parents? Why, according to him, are such relationships so important?

2. *The gentleman and benevolence:* Confucius never tired of speaking of the Gentleman (i.e., the superior man) and of benevolence. What are the defining characteristics of the gentleman? What is benevolence? In what ways does the gentleman cultivate the virtue of benevolence? What makes displaying benevolence, and being a superior person, so difficult? If one is to become virtuous, what obstacles must one overcome?

3. *The ideal society:* Confucius was as concerned with securing the public good as he was with guiding individual behavior. How are the two related? What sort of connection does Confucius see between relationships within the family and within society? In what sense can family harmony contribute to the harmony of society?

4. *Sincerity:* The issue of sincerity is discussed a great deal in the *Doctrine of the Mean.* The text even goes so far as to state that the attainment of sincerity is the most excellent thing for humanity. How is sincerity described? How is it connected with knowing what is right and acting on this knowledge?

Selections from the *Analects*

CONFUCIUS

Book One

1.1 The Master said, "To study, and then in a timely fashion to practice what you have learned—is this not satisfying? To have companions arrive from afar—is this not a joy? To remain unrecognized by others and yet remain free of resentment—is this not the mark of the gentleman?"

1.2 Youzi said, "It is unlikely that one who has grown up as a filial son and respectful younger brother will then be inclined to defy his superiors, and there has never been a case of one who is disinclined to defy his superiors stirring up rebellion.

"The gentleman applies himself to the roots. Once the roots are firmly planted, the Way will grow

Confucius, "Selections from the Analects." *Translated by Edward Gilman Slingerland, in* Readings in Classical Chinese Philosophy, *edited by Philip J. Ivanhoe and Bryan Van Norden (New York: Seven Bridges Press, 2001). Reprinted by permission of Seven Bridges Press.*

therefrom. Might we thus say that filiality and brotherly respect represent the root of *ren*?"

1.9 Zengzi said, "Be meticulous in observing the passing of those close to you and do not fail to continue the sacrifices to your distant ancestors. This will be enough to cause the Virtue of the people to return to fullness."

1.10 Ziqin said to Zigong, "When our Master arrives in a state, he invariably finds out about its government. Does he actively seek out this information? Surely it is not simply offered to him!"

Zigong answered, "Our Master acquires it through being cordial, good, respectful, frugal, and deferential. The Master's way of seeking it is rather different from other people's way of seeking it, is it not?"

1.12 Youzi said, "In the application of ritual, it is harmonious ease that is to be valued. It is precisely such harmony that makes the Way of the Former Kings so beautiful. If you merely stick rigidly to ritual in all matters, great and small, there will remain that which you cannot accomplish. Yet if you know enough to value harmonious ease but try to attain it without being regulated by the rites, this will not work either."

1.15 Zigong said, "Poor and yet not obsequious, rich and yet not arrogant—what would you say about someone like that?"

The Master answered, "That is acceptable, but it is not as good as being poor and yet full of joy, rich and yet fond of ritual."

Zigong said, "In the *Odes* we read,

As if cut, as if polished;
As if carved, as if ground.

Is this not what you have in mind?"

The Master said, "Zigong, you are precisely the kind of person with whom one can begin to discuss the *Odes*. Informed as to what has gone before, you know what is to come."

1.16 The Master said, "Do not be concerned about whether or not others know you; be concerned about whether or not you know others."

Book Two

2.1 The Master said, "One who rules through the power of Virtue might be compared to the Pole Star, which simply remains in its place while receiving the homage of the myriad lesser stars."

2.3 The Master said, "If you try to lead the common people with governmental regulations and keep them in line with punishments, the laws will simply be evaded and the people will have no sense of shame. If, however, you guide them with Virtue, and keep them in line by means of ritual, the people will have a sense of shame and will moreover reform themselves. "

2.4 The Master said, "At age fifteen I set my heart upon learning; at thirty I took my stand; at forty I became free of doubts; at fifty I understood the Heavenly Mandate; at sixty my ear was attuned; and at seventy I could follow my heart's desire without overstepping the bounds of propriety."

2.7 Ziyou asked about filial piety. The Master said, "Nowadays, 'filial' is used to refer to anyone who is merely able to provide their parents with nourishment. But even dogs and horses are provided with nourishment. If you do not treat your parents with reverence, wherein lies the difference?"

2.10 The Master said, "Pay attention to the means a man employs, observe the path he follows, and discover where it is he feels at home. How can his character remain hidden? How can his character remain hidden?"

2.11 The Master said, "A true teacher is one who, keeping the past alive, is also able to understand the present."

2.12 The Master said, "The gentleman does not serve as a vessel."

2.15 The Master said, "To learn without *si*, 'thinking,' will lead to confusion. To think without learning, however, will lead to fruitless exhaustion."

2.17 The Master said, "Zilu, remember well what I am about to tell you! This is wisdom: When you know something, to know that you know it; and when you do not know something, to know that you do not know it."

Book Three

3.3 The Master said, "A man who is not *ren*—what has he to do with ritual? A man who is not *ren*—what has he to do with music?"

Book Four

4.1 The Master said, "With regard to neighborhoods, it is the presence of those who are *ren* that makes them desirable. Given a choice, then, how could someone who does not choose to dwell in *ren* be considered wise?"

4.2 The Master said, "Those who are not *ren* cannot remain constant in adversity and cannot enjoy enduring happiness. Those who are *ren* find their repose in *ren*; those who are wise follow *ren* because they know that they will *li*, 'profit,' from it."

4.4 The Master said, "Having merely set your heart sincerely upon *ren*, you can be sure of remaining free of odium."

4.5 The Master said, "Wealth and honor are things that all people desire, and yet unless they are acquired in the proper way I will not abide them. Poverty and disgrace are things that all people hate, and yet unless they are avoided in the proper way I will not despise them.

"If the gentleman abandons *ren*, how can he be worthy of that name? The gentleman does not violate *ren* even for the amount of time required to eat a meal. Even in times of urgency or distress, he does not depart from it."

4.6 The Master said, "I have yet to meet a person who truly loved *ren* or hated a lack of *ren*. One who loved *ren* could not be surpassed, while one who hated a lack of *ren* would at least be able to act in a *ren* fashion, insofar as he would not tolerate that which is not *ren* being associated with his person.

"Is there a person who can, for the space of a single day, simply devote his efforts to *ren*? I have never seen one whose strength is insufficient for this task. Perhaps such a person exists, but I have yet to meet him."

4.8 The Master said, "Having in the morning learned the Way, one could die that evening without regret."

4.9 The Master said, "A true *shi*, 'scholar,' is one who has set his heart upon the Way. A fellow who is ashamed merely of shabby clothing or meager rations is not even worth conversing with."

4.10 The Master said, "Acting in the world, the gentleman has no predispositions for or against anything. He merely seeks to be on the side of what is *yi*, 'right.' "

4.12 The Master said, "If your conduct is determined solely by considerations of profit you will arouse great resentment."

4.14 The Master said, "Do not be concerned that you lack an official position, but rather concern yourself with the means by which you might take your stand. Do not be concerned that no one has heard of you, but rather strive to become a person worthy of being known."

4.15 The Master said, "Zengzi! All that I teach is unified by one guiding principle."

Zengzi answered, "Yes."

After the Master left, the other disciples asked, "What did he mean by that?"

Zengzi said, "All of what the Master teaches amounts to nothing more than *zhong*, 'loyalty,' tempered by *shu*, 'sympathetic understanding.' "

4.16 The Master said, "The gentleman understands what is right, whereas the petty man understands profit."

4.18 The Master said, "In serving your parents you may gently remonstrate with them. However, once it becomes apparent that they have not taken your criticism to heart you should be respectful and not oppose them, and follow their lead diligently without resentment."

4.19 The Master said, "When your parents are alive, you should not travel far, and when you do travel you must keep to a fixed itinerary."

4.20 The Master said, "One who makes no changes to the ways of his father for three years after his father has passed away may be called a filial son."

4.21 The Master said, "You must always be aware of your parents' age. On the one hand, it is a cause for rejoicing, on the other, a source of anxiety."

4.24 The Master said, "The gentleman wishes to be slow of speech and cautious with regard to his actions."

4.25 The Master said, "Virtue is never alone; it always has neighbors."

Book Five

5.8 Meng Wubo asked, "Is Zilu *ren*?"

The Master said, "I do not know."

The question was repeated.

The Master said, "In a state that can field one thousand chariots, Zilu could be employed to organize the collection of military taxes, but I do not know whether or not he is *ren*."

"What about Ranyou?"

"In a town of one thousand households, or an aristocratic family that can field one hundred chariots, Ranyou could be employed as a steward, but I do not know whether he is *ren*."

"What about Zihua?"

"With his sash tied, standing in his proper place at court, Zihua could be employed to converse with guests and visitors, but I do not know whether or not he is *ren*."

5.10 Zaiyu was in the habit of sleeping during the daytime. The Master said, "Rotten wood cannot be carved, and a wall of dung cannot be beautified. As for Zaiyu, what would be the use of reprimanding him?"

The Master added, "At first, when evaluating people, I would listen to their words and then simply trust that the corresponding conduct would follow. Now when I evaluate people I listen to their words but then closely observe their conduct. It is my experience with Zaiyu that has motivated this change."

5.12 Zigong said, "What I do not wish others to do unto me, I also wish not to do unto others."

5.26 Yan Hui and Zilu were in attendance. The Master said to them, "Why don't each of you speak to me of your aspirations?"

Zilu said, "I would like to be able to share my carts and horses, clothing and fur with my friends, and not become resentful if they are returned damaged."

Yan Hui said, "I would like to avoid being boastful about my own abilities or exaggerating my accomplishments."

Zilu said, "I would like to hear of the Master's aspirations."

The Master said, "To bring contentment to the aged, to have trust in my friends, and to cherish the young."

5.27 The Master said, "I should just give up! I have yet to meet the man who is able to perceive his own faults and then take himself to task inwardly."

5.28 The Master said, "In any town of ten households you will be certain to find someone who is as *zhong*, 'loyal,' or *xin*, 'trustworthy,' as I am, but you will not find anyone who matches my love for learning."

Book Six

6.3 Duke Ai asked, "Who among your disciples might be said to love learning?"

Kongzi answered, "There was one named Yan Hui who loved learning. He never misdirected his anger, and never repeated a mistake twice. Unfortunately he was fated to live a short life, and has since passed away."

6.11 The Master said, "What a worthy man was Yan Hui! Living in a narrow alley, subsisting on meager bits of rice and water—other people could not have borne such hardship, and yet it never spoiled Hui's joy. What a worthy man was Hui!"

6.18 The Master said, "When *zhi*, 'native substance,' overwhelms *wen*, 'cultural refinement,' the result is a crude rustic. When cultural refinement overwhelms native substance, the result is a foppish pedant. Only when culture and native substance are perfectly mixed and balanced do you have a gentleman."

6.20 The Master said, "One who knows it is not the equal of one who loves it, and one who loves it is not the equal of one who takes joy in it."

6.22 Fan Chi asked about wisdom.

The Master said, "Devoting yourself to transforming the values of the common people, to serving the ghosts and spirits with reverence and yet keeping them at a distance—this might be called wisdom."

He then asked about *ren*.

The Master said, "One who is *ren* sees as his first priority the hardship of self-cultivation, and does not think about attaining any results or rewards. Yes, this is what we might call ren."

6.23 The Master said, "One who is wise takes joy in the rivers, while one who is *ren* takes joy in the mountains. The wise are active, while the *ren* are still. The wise are joyful, while the *ren* are long-lived."

6.27 The Master said, "A gentleman who is broadly learned with regard to culture and whose comportment has been disciplined by the rites can, I think, rely upon this training and so avoid straying from the Way."

6.29 The Master said, "Acquiring virtue through the use of *zhong*, 'the mean'—is this not best? And yet for some time now such virtue has been quite hard to find among people."

6.30 Zigong said, "If there were one able to universally extend his benevolence to the people and bring succor to the multitudes, what would you make of him? Could such a person be called *ren*?"

The Master said, "Why stop at *ren*? Such a person should surely be called a sage! Even someone like Yao or Shun would find such a task daunting.

"Desiring to take his stand, one who is *ren* helps others to take their stand; wanting to realize himself, he helps others to realize themselves. Being able to take what is near at hand as an example could perhaps be called the method of *ren*."

Book Seven

7.6 The Master said, "Set your heart upon the Way, rely upon Virtue, lean upon *ren*, and explore widely in your cultivation of the arts."

7.8 The Master said, "I will not enlighten a heart that is not already struggling to understand, nor will I provide the proper words to a tongue that is not already struggling to speak. If I hold up one corner of a problem and the student cannot come back to me with the other three, I will not attempt to instruct him again."

7.12 The Master said, "If wealth could be pursued in a proper manner, I would pursue it, even if that meant serving as an officer holding a whip at the entrance to the marketplace. If there is no proper manner in which to pursue it, however, then I would prefer to follow that which I love."

7.16 The Master said, "Eating plain rice and drinking water, having only your bent arm as a pillow—there is certainly joy to be found in this! Wealth and fame attained improperly concern me no more than the floating clouds."

7.20 The Master said, "I am not the kind of person who is born with knowledge. Rather, I am the kind of person who loves antiquity, and who diligently looks there for knowledge."

7.22 The Master said, "When walking with two other people, I will always find a teacher among them. Those who are good I seek to emulate, and those who are bad provide me with reminders of what needs to be changed in myself."

7.30 The Master said, "Is *ren* really so far away? If I merely desire *ren*, I will find that *ren* is already here."

7.37 The Master said, "The gentleman is relaxed and at ease, while the petty man is anxious and full of worry."

7.38 The Master was tolerant while still remaining strict, impressive without being overly imposing, and respectful while still remaining at ease.

Book Eight

8.7 Zengzi said, "The *shi*, 'scholar,' cannot but be strong and resolute, for his burden is heavy and his Way is long. To take up *ren* as your own personal task—is this not a heavy burden? To strive without respite until death overtakes you—is this Way not long?"

8.8 The Master said, "Find inspiration in the *Odes*, take your stand through ritual, and be perfected by music."

8.12 The Master said, "It is not easy to find someone who is able to study for even the space of three years without the inducement of an official salary."

8.13 The Master said, "If you are strong, trustworthy, and fond of learning, you can remain firm in your love of the Way even in the face of death. Do not take up residence in a state that is troubled, and leave the state that is disordered. If the Way is being realized in the world then show yourself; if it is not, then retire to reclusion. In a state that has the Way, to be poor and of low status is a cause for shame; in a state that is without the Way, to be wealthy and honored is equally a cause for shame."

Book Nine

9.18 The Master said, "I have yet to meet a man who is as fond of Virtue as he is of sex."

9.19 The Master said, "[The task of self-cultivation] might be compared to the task of building up a mountain: if I stop even one basketful of earth short of completion, then I have stopped completely. It might also be compared to the task of leveling ground: even if I have only dumped one basketful of earth, at least I am moving forward."

9.29 The Master said, "One who understands the Way is free of confusion, one who possesses *ren* is free of worries, and one who is courageous is free of fear."

Book Eleven

11.12 Zilu asked about serving the ghosts and spirits. The Master said, "You are not yet able to serve people—how could you be able to serve the ghosts and spirits?"

"May I inquire about death?"

"You do not yet understand life—how could you possibly understand death?"

Book Twelve

12.1 Yan Hui asked about *ren*.

The Master said, "Restraining yourself and returning to the rites constitutes *ren*. If for one day you manage to restrain yourself and return to the rites, in this way you could lead the entire world back to *ren*. The key to achieving *ren* lies within yourself—how could it come from others?"

Yan Hui asked, "May I inquire as to the specifics?"

The Master said, "Do not look unless it is in accordance with the rites; do not listen unless it is in accordance with the rites; do not move unless it is in accordance with the rites."

Yan Hui replied, "Although I am not quick to understand, I ask permission to devote myself to this teaching."

12.2 Zhong Gong asked about *ren*.

The Master said, "When in public, comport yourself as if you were receiving an important guest; in your management of the people, behave as if you were overseeing a great sacrifice. Do not impose upon others what you yourself do not desire. In this way, you will encounter no resentment in your state or in your family."

Zhong Gong replied, "Although I am not quick to understand, I ask permission to devote myself to this teaching."

12.11 Duke Jing of Qi asked Kongzi about governing.

Kongzi responded, "Let the ruler be a true ruler, the ministers true ministers, the fathers true fathers, and the sons true sons."

The Duke replied, "Well put! Certainly if the ruler is not a true ruler, the ministers not true ministers, the fathers not true fathers, and the sons not true sons, even if there is sufficient grain, will I ever get to eat it?"

12.17 Jikangzi asked Kongzi about governing.

Kongzi responded, "To *zheng*, 'govern,' means to *zheng*, 'correct.' If you set an example by being correct, who will dare to be incorrect?"

12.19 Jikangzi, questioning Kongzi about governing, asked, "If I were to execute those who lacked the Way in order to advance those who possessed the Way, what would you think of that?"

Kongzi responded, "In your governing what need is there for executions? If you desire good, then the people will also desire good. The Virtue of the gentleman is like the wind, and the Virtue of the petty person is like the grass—when the wind blows over the grass, the grass must bend."

12.22 Fan Chi asked about *ren*. The Master replied, "Care for others." He asked about wisdom. The Master replied, "Know others." Fan Chi still did not understand, so the Master added, "By raising up the straight and applying it to the crooked, the crooked can be made straight."

12.24 Zengzi said, "The gentleman acquires friends by means of his cultivation, and then relies upon his friends for support in becoming *ren*."

Book Thirteen

13.3 Zilu asked, "If the Lord of Wei were to employ you to serve in the government of his state, what would be your first priority?"

The Master answered, "It would be of course, to assure that *ming*, 'names,' were being applied *zheng*, 'correctly!' "

Zilu said, "Is this really a matter of concern? It would seem that the Master's suggestion is rather wide of the mark. Why worry about correcting names?"

The Master replied, "How boorish you are, Zilu! When it comes to matters that he does not understand, the gentleman should refrain from flaunting his ignorance. If names are not correct, speech will not be in accordance with actuality; when speech is not in accordance with actuality, things will not be successfully accomplished. When things are not successfully accomplished, ritual practice and music will fail to flourish; when ritual and music fail to flourish, punishments and penalties will miss the mark. And when punishments and penalties miss the mark, the people will be at a loss as to what to do with themselves. This is why the gentleman only applies names that can be properly spoken, and assures that what he says can be properly put into action. The gentleman simply guards against arbitrariness in his speech. That is all there is to it."

13.6 The Master said, "When the ruler's person is *zheng*, 'correct,' his will is put into effect without the need for official orders. When the ruler's person is not correct, he will not be obeyed no matter how many orders he issues."

13.18 The Lord of She said to Kongzi, "Among my people there is one we call 'Upright Gong.' When his father stole a sheep, he reported him to the authorities."

Kongzi replied, "Among my people, those we consider 'upright' are different from this: fathers cover up for their sons, and sons cover up for their fathers. This is what it means to be 'upright.' "

13.20 Zigong asked, "What does a person have to be like before he could be called a true *shi*, 'scholar'?"

The Master said, "Conducting himself with a sense of shame, and not doing dishonor to his ruler's mandate when sent abroad as a diplomat—such a person could be called a scholar."

"May I ask what the next best type of person is like?"

"His lineage and clan consider him filial, and his fellow villagers consider him deferential to his elders."

"And the next best?"

"His speech is invariably trustworthy, and his actions invariably bear fruit. What a narrow, rigid little man he is! And yet he might still be considered the next best."

"How about those who today are involved in government?"

The Master exclaimed, "Oh! Those petty functionaries are not even worth considering."

Book Fourteen

14.12 Zilu asked about the complete person.

The Master said, "Take a person as wise as Zang Wuzhong, as free of desire as Gongzhuo, as courageous as Zhuangzi of Bian, and as accomplished in the arts as Ranyou, and then acculturate them by means of ritual and music—such a man might be called a complete person."

He then continued: "But must a complete person today be exactly like this? When seeing a chance for profit he thinks of what is right; when confronting danger he is ready to take his life into his own hands; when enduring an extended period of hardship, he does not forget what he had professed in more fortunate times—such a man might also be called a complete person."

14.24 The Master said, "In ancient times scholars worked for their own improvement; nowadays they seek only to win the approval of others."

14.27 The Master said, "The gentleman is ashamed to have his words exceed his actions."

14.30 The Master said, "Do not worry that you are not known to others; worry rather that you yourself lack ability."

14.44 Zilu asked about the gentleman.

The Master said, "He cultivates himself in order to achieve reverence."

"Is that all?"

"He cultivates himself in order to bring peace to others."

"Is that all?"

"He cultivates himself in order to bring peace to the people. Cultivating oneself and thereby bringing peace to the people is an accomplishment that even a Yao or a Shun would not disdain."

Book Fifteen

15.5 The Master said, "Was not Shun one who ruled by means of *wuwei* [nonaction]? What did he do? He made himself reverent and took his [ritual] position facing south, that is all."

15.9 The Master said, "The scholar with great aspirations and the person of *ren* will not pursue life at the expense of *ren*, and they may be called upon to give up their lives in order to assure *ren*'s completion."

15.18 The Master said, "The gentleman takes *yi*, 'rightness,' as his *zhi*, 'substance,' and then puts this substance into practice by means of ritual, gives it expression through modesty, and perfects it by being *xin*, 'trustworthy.' Now that is a gentleman."

15.24 Zigong asked, "Is there one teaching that can serve as a guide for one's entire life?"

The Master answered, "Is it not *shu*, 'sympathetic understanding'? Do not impose upon others what you yourself do not desire."

Book Sixteen

16.5 Kongzi said, "Beneficial types of joy are three, as are harmful types of joy. Taking joy in regulating yourself through the rites and music, in speaking well of others, and in possessing many worthy friends—these are the beneficial types of joy. Taking joy in arrogant gratification, dissolute pleasure-seeking, or decadent licentiousness—these are the harmful types of joy."

16.8 The Master said, "The gentleman stands in awe of three things: *tianming*, 'the Heavenly Mandate,' great men, and the teachings of the sages. The petty person does not understand the Mandate of Heaven and thus does not regard it with awe; he shows disrespect to great men and ridicules the teachings of the sages."

16.9 Kongzi said, "Those who are born understanding it are the best; those who understand it through learning are second. Those who find it difficult and yet persist in their studies are still lower. The worst are the people who find it difficult but do not even try to learn."

Book Seventeen

17.2 The Master said, "By *xing*, 'nature,' people are similar; they diverge as the result of *xi*, 'practice.'"

17.8 The Master said, "Zilu! Have you heard about the six virtuous teachings and the six corresponding vices?"

Zilu replied, "I have not."

"Sit! I will tell you about them. Loving *ren* without balancing it with a love for learning will result in the vice of foolishness. Loving knowledge without balancing it with a love for learning will result in the vice of deviant thought. Loving trustworthiness without balancing it with a love for learning will result in the vice of harmful rigidity. Loving uprightness without balancing it with a love for learning will result in the vice of intolerance. Loving courage without balancing it with a love for learning will result in the vice of unruliness. Loving resoluteness without balancing it with a love for learning will result in the vice of willfulness."

17.19 The Master sighed, "Would that I did not have to speak!"

Zigong said, "If the Master did not speak, then how would we little ones receive guidance?"

The Master replied, "What does Heaven ever say? Yet the four seasons go round and find their impetus there, and the myriad creatures are born from it. What does Heaven ever say?"

17.23 Zilu asked, "Does the gentleman admire courage?"

The Master said, "The gentleman admires what is right most of all. A gentleman who possessed courage but lacked a sense of rightness would create great disorder, while a petty person who possessed cour-age but lacked a sense of rightness would become a thief or robber."

Book Nineteen

19.6 Zixia said, "Being broadly learned and resolute of *zhi*, 'purpose,' incisive in one's questioning, and able to *si*, 'reflect upon,' what is near at hand—this is where *ren* is to be found."

Book Twenty

20.3 Kongzi said, "One who does not understand the Heavenly Mandate lacks the means to become a gentleman. One who does not understand the rites lacks the means to take his stand. One who does not understand how to evaluate the words of others lacks the means to understand people."

Selections from *The Great Learning*

CONFUCIUS

1. WHAT *THE GREAT LEARNING* teaches, is—to illustrate illustrious virtue; to renovate the people; and to rest in the highest excellence.

2. The point where to rest being known, the object of pursuit is then determined; and, that being determined, a calm unperturbedness may be attained to. To that calmness there will succeed a tranquil repose. In that repose there may be careful deliberation, and that deliberation will be followed by the attainment of the desired end.

3. Things have their root and their branches. Affairs have their end and their beginning. To know what is first and what is last will lead near to what is taught in *The Great Learning*.

4. The ancients who wished to illustrate illustrious virtue throughout the kingdom, first ordered well their own States. Wishing to order well their States, they first regulated their families. Wishing to regulate their families, they first cultivated their persons. Wishing to cultivate their persons, they first rectified their hearts. Wishing to rectify their hearts, they first sought to be sincere in their thoughts. Wishing to be sincere in their thoughts, they first extended to the utmost their knowledge. Such extension of knowledge lay in the investigation of things.

5. Things being investigated, knowledge became complete. Their knowledge being complete, their thoughts were sincere. Their thoughts being sincere, their hearts were then rectified. Their hearts being rectified, their persons were cultivated. Their persons being cultivated, their families were regulated. Their families being regulated, their States were rightly governed. Their States being rightly governed, the whole kingdom was made tranquil and happy.

6. From the Son of Heaven down to the mass of the people, all must consider the cultivation of the person the root of everything besides.

7. It cannot be, when the root is neglected, that what should spring from it will be well ordered. It never has been the case that what was of great importance has been slightly cared for, and, at the same time, that what was of slight importance has been greatly cared for.

Confucius, "Selections from The Great Learning." *Translated by James Legge.*

Selections from the *Doctrine of the Mean*

CONFUCIUS

Chapter I

1. What Heaven has conferred is called THE NA-TURE; an accordance with this nature is called THE PATH of duty; the regulation of this path is called IN-STRUCTION.

2. The path may not be left for an instant. If it could be left, it would not be the path. On this account, the superior man does not wait till he sees things, to be cautious, nor till he hears things, to be apprehensive.

4. While there are no stirrings of pleasure, anger, sorrow, or joy, the mind may be said to be in the state of EQUILIBRIUM. When those feelings have been stirred, and they act in their due degree, there ensues what may be called the state of HARMONY. This EQUILIBRIUM is the great root from which grow all the human actions in the world, and this HARMONY is the universal path which they all should pursue.

5. Let the states of equilibrium and harmony exist in perfection, and a happy order will prevail throughout heaven and earth, and all things will be nourished and flourish.

Chapter II

2. "The superior man's embodying the course of the Mean is because he is a superior man, and so always maintains the Mean. The mean man's acting contrary to the course of the Mean is because he is a mean man, and has no caution."

Chapter III

The Master said, "Perfect is the virtue which is according to the Mean! Rare have they long been among the people, who could practice it!"

Chapter XII

1. The way which the superior man pursues, reaches wide and far, and yet is secret.

2. Common men and women, however ignorant, may intermeddle with the knowledge of it; yet in its utmost reaches, there is that which even the sage does not know. Common men and women, however much below the ordinary standard of character, can carry it into practice; yet in its utmost reaches, there is that which even the sage is not able to carry into practice. Great as heaven and earth are, men still find some things in them with which to be dissatisfied. Thus it is that, were the superior man to speak of his way in all its greatness, nothing in the world would be found able to embrace it, and were he to speak of it in its minuteness, nothing in the world would be found able to split it.

4. The way of the superior man may be found, in its simple elements, in the intercourse of common men and women; but in its utmost reaches, it shines brightly through heaven and earth.

Chapter XIII

1. The Master said, "The path is not far from man. When men try to pursue a course, which is far from the common indications of consciousness, this course cannot be considered THE PATH.

3. "When one cultivates to the utmost the principles of his nature, and exercises them on the principle of reciprocity, he is not far from the path. What you do not like when done to yourself, do not do to others.

4. "In the way of the superior man there are four things, to not one of which have I as yet attained.—To serve my father, as I would require my son to serve me: to this I have not attained; to serve my prince, as I would require my minister to serve me: to this I have not attained; to serve my elder brother, as I would require my younger brother to serve me: to this I have not attained; to set the example in behaving to a friend, as I would require him to behave to me: to this I have not attained. Earnest in practicing the ordinary virtues, and careful in speaking about them, if, in his practice, he has anything defective, the superior man dares not but exert himself; and if, in his words, he has any excess, he dares not allow himself such license. Thus his words have respect to his actions, and his actions have respect to his words; is it not just an entire sincerity which marks the superior man?"

Confucius, "Selections from the Doctrine of the Mean." Translated by James Legge.

Chapter XIV

1. The superior man does what is proper to the station in which he is; he does not desire to go beyond this.

2. In a position of wealth and honor, he does what is proper to a position of wealth and honor. In a poor and low position, he does what is proper to a poor and low position. Situated among barbarous tribes, he does what is proper to a situation among barbarous tribes. In a position of sorrow and difficulty, he does what is proper to a position of sorrow and difficulty. The superior man can find himself in no situation in which he is not himself.

4. Thus it is that the superior man is quiet and calm, waiting for the appointments of Heaven, while the mean man walks in dangerous paths, looking for lucky occurrences.

5. The Master said, "In archery we have something like the way of the superior man. When the archer misses the center of the target, he turns round and seeks for the cause of his failure in himself."

Chapter XV

1. The way of the superior man may be compared to what takes place in traveling, when to go to a distance we must first traverse the space that is near, and in ascending a height, when we must begin from the lower ground.

2. It is said in the Book of Poetry, "Happy union with wife and children is like the music of lutes and harps. When there is concord among brethren, the harmony is delightful and enduring. Thus may you regulate your family, and enjoy the pleasure of your wife and children."

Chapter XX

5. "Benevolence is the characteristic element of humanity, and the great exercise of it is in loving relatives. Righteousness is the accordance of actions with what is right, and the great exercise of it is in honoring the worthy. The decreasing measures of the love due to relatives, and the steps in the honor due to the worthy, are produced by the principle of propriety.

8. "The duties of universal obligation are five, and the virtues wherewith they are practiced are three. The duties are those between sovereign and minister, between father and son, between husband and wife, between elder brother and younger, and those belonging to the intercourse of friends. Those five are the duties of universal obligation. Knowledge, magnanimity, and energy, these three, are the virtues universally binding. And the means by which they carry the duties into practice is singleness.

9. "Some are born with the knowledge of those duties; some know them by study; and some acquire the knowledge after a painful feeling of their ignorance. But the knowledge being possessed, it comes to the same thing. Some practice them with a natural ease; some from a desire for their advantages; and some by strenuous effort. But the achievement being made, it comes to the same thing."

10. The Master said, "To be fond of learning is to be near to knowledge. To practice with vigor is to be near to magnanimity. To possess the feeling of shame is to be near to energy.

11. "He who knows these three things knows how to cultivate his own character. Knowing how to cultivate his own character, he knows how to govern other men. Knowing how to govern other men, he knows how to govern the kingdom with all its states and families."

Chapter XXIII

The way of man;—the development of perfect sincerity in those not naturally possessed of it.

Next to the above is he who cultivates to the utmost the shoots of goodness in him. From those he can attain to the possession of sincerity. This sincerity becomes apparent. From being apparent, it becomes manifest. From being manifest, it becomes brilliant. Brilliant, it affects others. Affecting others, they are changed by it. Changed by it, they are transformed. It is only he who is possessed of the most complete sincerity that can exist under heaven, who can transform.

Chapter XXXIII

4. It is said in the Book of Poetry, "In silence is the offering presented, and the spirit approached to; there is not the slightest contention." Therefore the superior man does not use rewards, and the people are stimulated to virtue. He does not show anger, and the people are awed more than by hatchets and battle-axes.

5. It is said in the Book of Poetry, "What needs no display is virtue. All the princes imitate it." Therefore, the superior man being sincere and reverential, the whole world is conducted to a state of happy tranquility.

Discussion and Reflection Questions

1. *Filial piety:* Confucius thought children have special duties toward their parents. What sorts of obligations do you think children have toward their parents? Should children always obey their parents, even if they think the parents are wrong? Do grown children have a moral obligation to care for their parents when the latter are old and incapable of caring for themselves? Why?

2. *The gentleman and benevolence:* Confucius obviously thought that some people are superior to others, and evaluated a person's status in terms of his or her moral attributes. How are persons judged in our society? Is having an impressive moral character—displaying benevolence, for instance—considered as worthy of emulation as having a successful career? Who is the most "benevolent" person you know?

3. *The ideal society:* Confucius presents his vision of the ideal society. Would you add or subtract anything from his picture? What would be the ideal society in your view? What would it be like? Would it be different from the ideal that Confucius presents in some way? How? Is there anything you could do that would make a contribution to bringing about your ideal society? What is it?

4. *Sincerity:* How important is sincerity to you? Why is sincerity considered a valuable thing? Why would one value sincerity in one's friends? Is sincerity the same thing as honesty, or is there some difference? Is there some sense in which one should strive to be sincere with *oneself*? Explain.

Suggestions for Further Reading

An excellent source for exploring the many facets of Asian thought is *A Sourcebook in Asian Philosophy,* edited by John M. and Patricia Koller (New York: Macmillan, 1991). For an extensive list of additional sources, see the bibliographical essays by Christopher Cleary, "Ancient Chinese Ethics," and Thomas W. Selover, "Neo-Confucian Religious Ethics," in *A Bibliographic Guide to the Comparative Study of Ethics,* edited by John Carmen, et al. (New York: Cambridge University Press, 1991). A brief and very accessible introduction to Confucian ethics is provided in the article "Classical Chinese Ethics," by Chad Hansen, in *A Companion to Ethics,* edited by Peter Singer (Oxford: Blackwell, 1991), pp. 69–81. Chung M. Tse, "Confucianism and Contemporary Ethical Issues," in *World Religions and Global Ethics,* edited by S. Cromwell Crawford (New York: Paragon House, 1989), pp. 91–125, provides a good introduction to Confucian ethical principles and shows how these principles might be applied to various contemporary ethical issues, such as sexual morality, racism and sexism, economic fairness, and punishment and justice. Tu Wei-ming provides an excellent overview of the Confucian tradition and its basic principles, from which the introductory material above has greatly benefited, in his essay, "The Confucian Tradition in Chinese History," in *Heritage of China: Contemporary Perspectives on Chinese Civilization,* edited by Paul R. Ropp (Berkeley: University of California Press, 1990), pp. 112–137. For an interesting cross-cultural comparison of the moral theories of an early Confucian and a medieval Christian theologian, see Lee Yearle's *Mencius and Aquinas: Theories of Virtue and Conceptions of Courage* (Albany: State University of New York Press, 1990). Richard Bosley, "Do Mencius and Hume Make the Same Ethical Mistake?" *Philosophy East and West,* vol. 38 (1988), pp. 3–18, compares and criticizes the ethical views of Hume and Mencius. Sandra A. Wawrytko, "Confucius and Kant: The Ethics of Respect," *Philosophy East and West,* vol. 32 (1982), pp. 237–257, draws many insightful comparisons between the ethical views of Confucius and Kant. There are, of course, many other scholarly sources on Confucian ethics, including: *The Confucian Creation of Heaven: Philosophy and the Defense of Ritual Mastery,* edited by Robert Eno (New York: State University of New York Press, 1990); *Thinking Through Confucius,* edited by David L. Hall and Roger T. Ames (New York: State University of New York Press, 1987); *The Ways of Confucianism: Investigations in Chinese Philosophy,* edited by David S.

Nivison and Bryan Van Norden (Chicago and La Salle, Ill.: Open Court Press, 1998); *Confucian Ethics of the Axial Age*, edited by Heiner Roetz (New York: State University of New York Press, 1993); Shun Kwong-loi, "*Jen* and *Li* in the *Analects*," *Philosophy East and West* 43 (1993): 457–479; *Confucius and the Analects: New Essays*, edited by Bryan Van Norden (New York: Oxford University Press, 2000); Angus C. Graham, "The Background of the Mencian Theory of Human Nature," in his *Studies in Chinese Philosophy and Philosophical Literature*, pp. 7–66 (New York: State University of New York Press, 1990); Kim Chong Chong, "Confucius's Virtue Ethics: 'Li, Yi, Wen' and 'Chih' in the 'Analects,'" *Journal of Chinese Philosophy* 25 (1998): 101–130; Hsei Yung Hsu, "Confucius and Act-Centered Morality," *Journal of Chinese Philosophy* 27 (September 2000): 331–344; Roger T. Ames and Henry Rosemont, Jr., *The Analects of Confucius: A Philosophical Translation* (New York: Ballantine Books, 1998); and Kwong-loi Shun, *Mencius and Early Chinese Thought* (Stanford, Calif.: Stanford University Press, 1997).

InfoTrac

Confucianism, Confucian ethics, self-cultivation, benevolence, humanity

Chapter 6

Daoism (Taoism)

Introduction: Finding the Way

Daoism (Taoism) represents one of the two most important schools of thought indigenous to China (the other, of course, is Confucianism). The contrast between Confucianism and Daoism is striking. Confucians believe that human beings should be fully involved in society, striving to bring peace and harmony to the world through the strict observance of traditional rites. According to Daoists, however, beliefs like those held by the Confucians—that the world somehow needs the interference of human beings to make it harmonious—are precisely the root of the problem. While Confucians believe that humans introduced order into the world, Daoists believe that the world was originally well ordered and that humans, following Confucian principles, have disrupted the natural order. Confucians stress the need for education in the rites to fully develop character, and Daoists stress the need to *unlearn* the beliefs imposed by society to return to the stage of natural instinctive response.

Early Daoist sages took the farmer and his life as their ideal. The farmer is by nature a practical person who knows what is to be done and goes about doing it without being concerned with the small-minded concerns that often occupy more urban folk. Farmers of necessity live close to the land and are acutely aware of their complete dependence on it. They realize that they are quite powerless against its forces, and that the only strategy to pursue is to accommodate to nature as fully as possible—work with, rather than fight against, nature. They adjust their own schedules to the rhythms of nature, both the daily cycle of day and night, and the seasonal rhythms determining when to plant, when to cultivate, and when to harvest. At some point the farmer's life and the rhythms of nature become indistinguishable: The farmer has submerged himself so deeply in nature that he has become an integral *part* of nature. He has returned to the source. Such a model of human existence captures perfectly the Daoist attitude toward life. This and other distinctive features of Daoist thought will be explored more fully as we consider the thought of the founder of Daoism—Lao Zi—and the major doctrines found in the most famous text of Daoism, the *Dao De Jing*.

Lao Zi: Nature and the Harmony of Opposites

In the pursuit of learning one knows more every day; in the pursuit of the Way one does less every day. One does less and less until one does nothing at all, and when one does nothing at all there is nothing left undone.

—LAO ZI, *DAO DE JING*, 48

The *Dao De Jing* (or, *The Classic of the Way and Its Power*) is the central text of Daoism. More than a thousand commentaries have been written on this slim book (it contains about five thousand Chinese characters) in China and Japan, and it is second only to the Bible in the number of translations available in English. It has exercised an inestimable influence on Chinese thought and culture. Although its authorship remains obscure, the *Dao De Jing* has traditionally been attributed to Lao Zi, about whom reliable biographical information is scarce. The traditional view is that he was an older contemporary of Confucius and a native of Ku Xian in the state of Chu. He is said to have worked as a historian in charge of the archives in Chu.

The traditional story of how the *Dao De Jing* came to be written is as follows. Lao Zi lived in the state of Chu for a long time (160 years, according to some accounts), and, becoming disturbed at its moral decline, he decided to leave. As he was leaving his native state to live in the wilderness, far away from other people, the keeper of the pass at Han-ku said to him, "As you are about to leave the world behind, could you write a book for my sake?" As a result of this request, Lao Zi wrote a book of about five thousand characters, setting out the meaning of the Way, and then went on his way. He was never seen or heard from again.

This story is, of course, impossible to confirm, but we will continue the tradition of assuming that Lao Zi is the author of the *Dao De Jing*. This book, as it has come down to us, is not a systematic treatise and cannot be read as such. It is, rather, a kind of anthology consisting of a number of short passages whose connection with other passages is often difficult to determine. It is best read as a series of insights that, taken together, express the Daoist perspective on reality. It was probably originally written as a series of rhyming verses meant to be memorized and passed on orally.

Several concepts or themes may be identified as central to Daoist thought: Dao, yin-yang, the harmony of opposites and relativity, cyclicity and reversal, and non-action. Because these concepts arise in a number of forms in the readings that follow, and because of their importance for understanding Daoism, we will discuss each of them.

Dao

The central concept of Daoism is, not surprisingly, *Dao*. In its origin the word means "road" or "path," as in the celestial paths of the stars in the night sky and, by extension, the whole orderly procession of the heavenly bodies. In Daoism the word acquires a more elusive meaning. Making categorical statements about the Dao is difficult, inasmuch as the opening lines of the *Dao De Jing* tell us that "the Dao that is the subject of discussion is not the true Dao." That is, the Dao is not the sort of thing that can be given a definite description. Our language is hopelessly inadequate for expressing the Dao. It must forever remain "nameless." Obviously this presents a problem if one wishes to communicate something of the Dao to others. The solution is to admit that the Dao is in fact unknowable, but capable of being alluded to through analogies and metaphors.

According to Lao Zi, the Way (Dao) that can be spoken of is not the Way. Hence the Dao cannot be defined. How, then, can we study and learn about the Way? It seems to be impossible! The answer is that we can only do so indirectly. Words provide reminders of experiences, of things dimly glimpsed, of fleeting insights and spontaneous understanding. To use an illustration borrowed from Zen (which was heavily influenced by Daoism), words are like a finger pointing at the moon. The finger is not the moon, it is only an imperfect means of drawing our attention to the moon. So, too, words may point us toward the Way, but they can never fully express or capture the meaning of the Way. The Way must be experienced to be understood. Still, we can get a glimmer of the Dao by recognizing its various aspects, the most important of which are described below.

Yin-yang

Although it does not feature prominently in the *Dao De Jing* and probably antedates considerably the rise of Daoism, the concept of yin-yang is crucial to an understanding of Daoism. Perhaps the best known and most influential doctrine of Daoism, yin-yang is the idea that nature consists of the continual interplay of two opposite but complementary forces that appear in a number of different guises. These basic principles underlie the dynamism of nature. Yin and yang operate together to bring about all the phenomena of nature. Yin is the receptive element in things: it is weak, negative, dark, and destructive, and it is identified with the female. Yang is the active element in things: it is strong, positive, light, and constructive, and it is identified with the male. Neither is to be understood as good or evil in itself. Rather, goodness is the proper balance between yin and yang; evil is an excess of one of these over the other.

Harmony of Opposites and Relativity

As the concept of yin-yang implies, each thing makes sense only in terms of its opposite. The beautiful appears as such only when contrasted with the ugly. Without the ugly there could be no such thing as beauty. Without valleys there could be no mountains. Night and day replace each other in a constant cycle. Things in nature exist in complementary pairs of opposites.

An alternative reading of such ideas focuses on the relativity of all things. According to this interpretation, terms such as good and evil, right and wrong, beauty and ugliness, strength and weakness, high and low are not terms of absolute appraisal but rather are always used relative to a particular person or situation. What is cold to a person from Los Angeles might seem warm to a person from Anchorage. Water is precious to someone dying of thirst in the desert, but is a life-threatening hazard to someone caught in a flood. Thus whether something is considered hot or cold, good or evil, useful or useless, depends on the particular circumstances. Viewed from the perspective of the Dao, there are no absolutes, moral or otherwise.

Reversal and Cyclicity

As the concept of yin-yang implies, many of the terms that we use to describe things have opposites: strong and weak, high and low, tall and short, and so on. These opposites are not, however, equal in all respects. Contrary to usual logic, according to the *Dao De Jing* the receptive and the weak overcome the hard and the strong. This reversal is best seen in the relation between water and stone. Water is weak and stone is hard, yet water eventually overcomes stones through erosion. This overcoming takes on a cyclical feature: The weak overcomes the strong, and in so doing becomes the strong, which is then overcome by the weak, and so on in an endless cycle of transformation. Change, not stability, is characteristic of nature.

Nonaction

The notion of opposites described above suggests that for Daoism there are no absolutes, or at least none that can be known by us. If there are no absolutes, then how should one act? Does Daoism provide any guide for action? This is where another central Daoist concept becomes relevant. This is the concept of *wu wei*, which literally means "without action." It can best be understood by returning to the concept of Dao. To say that the Dao acts is to limit it, because doing something implies that something else is left undone. The Dao, however, leaves nothing undone. By acting naturally and without effort, nature changes. By doing nothing, by not striving for some result, everything gets done. As part of nature, we should pattern our lives after the Dao.

The doctrine of *wu wei* does not, however, counsel people to do absolutely nothing, but only to refrain from acting in ways contrary to nature. In other words, you should let nature take its course and participate in that course. Instead of acting, you allow the Dao to act through you. The result will be naturalness. The correct course is thus the one that is natural, simple, spontaneous, and harmonious. Daoism thus counsels people to free themselves from desires for things that go beyond what is necessary. Food is eaten to satisfy hunger, clothes are worn to protect the body from cold. This does not mean that one cannot enjoy one's food or clothing; Daoism does not counsel asceticism. But delicacies and fancy clothing are superfluous and to be avoided. Ideally, people should be lacking in both knowledge and desires. Knowledge informs people of what there is, and desires lead them to want such things. Instead, we should take the "uncarved block" as our model. The uncarved block is a symbol of simplicity and of the original state of humanity before desires are induced by unnatural means. A tree whose shape has been determined by the wind and climate is natural; a figure carved in the wood taken from a tree is not. In all things we should model ourselves on the Dao, on nature. This means acting spontaneously, without premeditation or planning. To act in such a way is to be in harmony with the Dao.

The one who truly understands such things is the sage. The sage is, first and foremost, the person who understands the Dao. From this understanding flows a comprehension of all other things.

Zhuang Zi (Chuang Tzu): The Equality of Things

The effect of life in society is to complicate and confuse our existence, making us forget who we really are by causing us to become obsessed with what we are not.

—ZHUANG ZI

Zhuang Zi (ca. 399–295 B.C.E.) is the second great Daoist sage. Like Lao Zi, very little reliable information is known about him. He is said to have served as a minor government official. When offered the position of prime minister he refused, explaining that it would detract from his personal freedom. His major work, appropriately called the *Zhuang Zi*, is a series of essays and commentaries on various aspects of Daoist philosophy. Where Lao Zi writes as a mystical poet who delights in ambiguity and hidden meanings, Zhuang Zi writes as a philosopher concerned with showing the paradoxical nature of human attempts to grasp reality. In a famous passage he wrote:

> Once Chuang Chou [i.e., Zhuang Zi] dreamt he was a butterfly, a butterfly flitting and fluttering around, happy with himself and doing as he pleased. He didn't know he was Chuang Chou. Suddenly he woke up and there he was, solid and unmistakable Chuang Chou. But he didn't know if he was Chuang Chou who had dreamt he was a butterfly, or a butterfly dreaming he was Chuang Chou. Between Chuang Chou and a butterfly there must be *some* distinction! This is called the Transformation of Things. (Chuang Tzu, "Discussion on Making All Things Equal")*

Zhuang Zi was especially critical of the Confucians, who he thought were well versed in playing the artificial games of social custom, but who through their allegiance to the rites had lost the capacity for authentic, spontaneous behavior. They were "virtuous gentlemen" on the outside who were nonetheless empty inside.

If there is a central theme of Zhuang Zi's thought, it is *freedom*. To be free, a person must rid himself of the conventional values that society imposes. Things appear good or bad because of using society's standards for labeling things. If a person stops labeling things good or bad, they will cease to be good or bad. If a person views events not as good or bad but rather as part of the natural course of things, he becomes free from conventional values and the bondage they impose. The person who has thus freed himself from society's conventions can no longer be made to suffer, because he refuses to recognize the usual kinds of suffering as any less desirable than their opposites. He remains neutral, as it were, and practices *wu wei*, nonaction or harmony with the nature of things. He thus realizes genuine freedom.

Reading Questions

1. *Dao:* What images or metaphors do Lao Zi and Zhuang Zi use to describe the Dao? What role does this concept play in their sayings and stories?

---

*Chuang Tzu: Basic Writings, translated by Burton Watson (London and New York: Columbia University Press, 1964), p. 45.

2. *Yin-yang—harmony of opposites:* What are some examples of pairs of opposites that can be understood as manifestations of yin and yang? In what ways are the items in these pairs actually complementary to each other?

3. *Relativity:* How do Lao Zi and Zhuang Zi illustrate the relativity of human values? What sorts of examples do they use? What sorts of lessons for life do they draw from these examples?

4. *Natural way—nonaction:* How does Daoism counsel following the natural course of things? What examples does Zhuang Zi give of the benefits of letting nature take its course? How does following the doctrine of *wu wei* (nonaction) lead to a more harmonious life?

Dao De Jing

LAO ZI

I
Marking Out the Path

The Dao that is the subject of discussion is not the true Dao.

The quality which can be named is not its true attribute.

That which was before Heaven and Earth is called the Nonexistent.

The Existent is the mother of all things.

Therefore doth the wise man seek after the first mystery of the Nonexistent, while seeing in that which exists the Ultimates thereof.

The Nonexistent and Existent are identical in all but name.

This identity of apparent opposites I call the profound, the great deep, the open door of bewilderment.

II
Self-Perfection

When the world speaks of beauty as being beautiful, ugliness is at once defined.

When goodness is seen to be good, evil is at once apparent.

So do existence and nonexistence mutually give rise to one another, as that which is difficult and that which is easy, distant and near, high and low, shrill and bass, preceding and following.

The Sage therefore is occupied only with that which is without prejudice.

He teaches without verbosity; he acts without effort; he produces without possessing; he acts without regard to the fruit of action; he brings his work to perfection without assuming credit; and claiming nothing as his own, he cannot at any time be said to lose.

III
Resting the People

Avoiding distinctions of merit among the people prevents jealousy.

Not setting a value on rare things prevents theft.

Not seeking the things of sense keeps the mind in peace.

Thus the Sage governs by ridding the heart of its desires, giving the stomach due satisfaction, by resting the muscles and strengthening the bones, by preserving the world from a knowledge of evil and hence from its desire, and by making those who have such knowledge afraid to use it.

He acts by nonaction, and by this he governs all.

IV
The Causeless

Dao is without limitation; its depth is the source of whatsoever is.

Lao Zi, Dao De Jing, *translated by Walter Gorn Old as* The Simple Way of Laotzu *(Philadelphia: David McKay Co., 1913), pp. 25–179. Sections VI, VII, VIII, X, XII, XIII, XXXVI, XXXVII, XL, LVI, LX, and LXXIV from* The Wisdom of China and India *by Lin Yutang, copyright © 1942 and renewed 1970 by Random House, Inc. Used by permission of Random House, Inc.*

It makes sharp things round, it brings order out of chaos, it obscures the brilliant, it is wholly without attachment.

I know not who gave it birth; it is more ancient than God.

V
The Value of Nothing

Neither Heaven nor Earth has any predilections; they regard all persons and things as sacrificial images.

The wise man knows no distinctions; he beholds all men as things made for holy uses.

The celestial space is like unto bellows—though containing nothing that is solid, it does not at any time collapse; and the more it is set in motion, the more does it produce.

The inflated man, however, is soon exhausted.

Than self-restraint there is nothing better.

VI
The Spirit of Valley

The spirit of the valley never dies. It is called the mystic female,

Is the root of Heaven and Earth. Continuously, continuously,

It seems to remain. Draw upon it and it serves you with ease.

VII
Living for Others

The universe is everlasting.

The reason the universe is everlasting, is that it does not live for Self.

Therefore it can long endure.

Therefore the Sage puts himself last, and finds himself in the foremost place,

Regards his body as accidental, and his body thereby preserved.

Is not because he does not live for Self, that his Self is realized.

VIII
Water

The greatest virtue is like water; water benefits all things.

And does not compete with them.

It dwells in (the lowly) places that all disdain, wherein it comes near to the Dao.

In his dwelling, Sage loves the (lowly) earth,

In his heart, he loves what is profound,

In his relations with others, he loves kindness,

In his words, he loves sincerity,

In government, he loves peace,

In business affairs, he loves ability,

In his actions, he loves choosing the right time.

It is because he does not contend, that he is without reproach.

IX
Making Things Equal

It is advisable to refrain from continual reaching after wealth.

Continual handling and sharpening wears away the most durable thing.

If the house be full of jewels, who shall protect it?

Wealth and glory bring care along with pride.

To stop when good work is done and honor advancing is the way of Heaven.

X
Embracing the One

In embracing the One with your soul, can you never forsake the Dao?

In controlling your vital force to achieve gentleness, can you become like the newborn child?

In cleansing and purifying your mystic vision, can you strive after perfection?

In loving the people and governing the kingdom, can you rule without interference?

In opening and shutting the Gate of Heaven, can you play the part of the Female?

In comprehending all knowledge, can you renounce the mind?

XI
The Use of Nothing

The thirty spokes of a carriage wheel uniting at the nave are made useful by the hole in the center, where nothing exists.

Vessels of molded earth are useful by reason of their hollowness.

Doors and windows are useful by being cut out.

A house is useful because of its emptiness.

Existence, therefore, is like unto gain, but Nonexistence to use.

XII
The Senses

The five colors blind the eyes of man, the five musical notes deafen the ears of man, the five flavors dull the taste of man, horse-racing, hunting and chasing madden the minds of man, rare, valuable goods keep their owners awake at night.

Therefore does the wise man provide for the soul and not for the senses.

He takes the one and rejects the other.

XIII
Preventing a Fall

Honor and shame are the same as fear.

Fortune and disaster are the same as the person.

What is said of honor and shame is this: shame is abasement, which is feared whether it be absent or present.

So dignity and shame are inseparable from the fear which both occasion.

What is said of fortune and disaster is this: fortune and disaster are things which befall the person.

So without personality how should I suffer disaster or the reverse?

Therefore by the accident of good fortune a man may rule the world for a time.

But by virtue of love he may rule the world forever.

XIV
Praising the Void

Plainness is that which cannot be seen by looking at it.

Stillness is that which cannot be heard by listening to it.

Rareness is that which cannot be felt by handling it.

These, being indiscernible, may be regarded as a unity—Dao.

It is not bright above nor dark beneath.

Infinite in operation, it is yet without name.

Issuing forth it enters into Itself.

This the appearance of the Nonapparent, the form of the Nonexistent.

This is the unfathomable mystery.

Going before, its face is not seen; following after, its back is not observed.

Yet to regulate one's life by the ancient knowledge of Dao is to have found the path.

XV
Exhibiting Virtue

The ancient wise men were skillful in their mysterious acquaintance with profundities.

They were fathomless in their depths; so profound, that I cannot bring them forth to my mind.

They were cautious, like one who crosses a swollen river.

They were reserved, like one who doubts his fellows.

They were watchful, like one who travels abroad.

They were retiring, like snow beneath the sun.

They were simple, like newly felled timber.

They were lowly, like the valley.

They were obscure, like muddy water.

May not a man take muddy water and make it clear by keeping still?

May not a man take a dead thing and make it alive by continuous motion?

Those who follow this Dao have no need of replenishing, and being devoid of all properties, they grow old without need of being filled.

XVI
Going Home

Having emptied yourself of everything, remain where you are.

All things spring forth into activity with one accord, and whither do we see them return?

After blossoming for a while, everything dies down to its root.

This going back to one's origin is called peace; it is the giving of oneself over to the inevitable.

This giving of oneself over to the inevitable is called preservation.

He who knows this preservation is called enlightened.

He who knows it not continues in misery.

He who knows this preservation is great of soul.

He who is great of soul is prevailing.

Prevailing, he is a king.

Being kingly, he is in accord with nature, being in accord with nature, he is in accord with Dao.

Being in accord with Dao, he is eternal, and his whole life is preserved from harm.

XVII
Being Natural

In the first age of mankind the people recognized their superiors.

In the second age they served and flattered them.

In the third age they feared them.

In the fourth age they despised them.

Where faith is lacking it does not inspire confidence.

How careful they were in their expressions!

When they had done a good thing they would say, "How very natural we are!"

XVIII
Patching Up

When the great Dao is lost men follow after charity and duty to one's neighbor.

When wisdom has met with honors the world is full of pretenders.

When family ties are severed then filial duty and parental indulgence take their place.

When a nation is filled with strife then do patriots flourish.

XIX
Reverting to Nature

By giving up their self-righteousness and abandoning their wisdom the people would be immensely improved.

Forsaking Charity and Duty to the neighbor, they might revert to their natural relations.

Abandoning excellence and foregoing gain, the people would have no more thieves.

The cultivation of these three things has been a failure, therefore should they go back whence they came.

As for you, do you come forth in your natural simplicity, lay hold on verities, restrain selfishness, and rid yourself of ambition.

XX
Holding Aloof

Dispense with your learning and save yourselves anxiety; the difference between certainly and perhaps is not much after all.

Do they help us to distinguish between good and evil? for one must always be careful of distinctions!

Alas! but the people will never be free from their folly.

They are filled with ambition, as the stallion ox is filled with lust.

I am singular in my bashfulness, I am devoid of ambition, I am undeveloped as a little child.

I am but a waif, a stray, a child without a home.

All others have an excess of good things, but I am as one abandoned.

How foolish and simple am I! I am bewildered.

Everyone sparkles with intelligence, I am alone in my obscurity.

The people are full of discernment; I alone am dull.

I am tossed about like the ocean; I roll and am never at rest.

Everyone has something to do; I alone am incapable and without merit.

I alone am estranged from the people, but I glory on the breast of my mother!

XXI
The Empty Source

The greatest virtue is in simply following Dao, the intangible, inscrutable.

Inscrutable, intangible, and yet containing forms.

Intangible, inscrutable, and yet containing things.

Profound and obscure, but having an essence, a veritable essence in which is consistence.

From eternity until now its nature has remained unchanged.

It inheres in all things from their beginnings.

How do I know of the origin of things?

I know by Dao.

XXII
Futility of Contention

To yield is to be preserved whole.

To be bent is to become straight.

To be hollow is to be filled.

To be tattered is to be renewed.

To be in want is to possess.

To have plenty is to be confused.

Therefore the sage embraces the One, and becomes the model of the world.

He does not reveal himself, and is therefore luminous.

He does not justify himself, and is therefore far-famed.

He does not boast of himself, and therefore people give him credit.

He does not pride himself, and is therefore the chief among men.

The ancient maxim, "Whosoever adapteth himself shall be preserved to the end," verily it is no idle saying.

Without doubt he shall go back to his Home in peace.

XXIII
Nonidentification

Moderate your speech, and preserve yourself.

A hurricane will not outlast the morning, a heavy rain will not outlast the day.

Who have the power to make these things but Heaven and Earth?

And if Heaven and Earth cannot continue them long, how shall a man do so?

If a man accords with Dao in all things, he is identified with Dao by that agreement.

A virtuous man is identified with virtue, a vicious man is identified with vice.

Whoever is identified with Dao, him do the Daoists receive with gladness.

Whoever is identified with virtue, him do the virtuous receive with gladness.

But whoever is identified with vice, him do the vicious gladly serve with vice.

For wherever confidence is lacking, it is not met with trust.

XXIV
Undesirable Honors

By standing on tiptoe one cannot keep still.

Astride of one's fellow one cannot progress. By displaying oneself one does not shine.

By self-approbation one is not esteemed.

In self-praise there is no merit.

He who exalts himself does not stand high.

Such things are to Dao what refuse and excreta are to the body.

They are everywhere detested.

Therefore the man of Dao will not abide with them.

XXV
Apprehending the Void

Before Heaven and Earth existed there was in Nature a primordial substance.

It was serene, it was fathomless.

It was self-existent, it was homogeneous.

It was omnipresent, nor suffered any limitation.

It is to be regarded as the universal mother.

I do not know its name, but I call it Dao.

If forced to qualify it, I call it the boundless.

Being boundless, I call it the inconceivable.

Being inscrutable, I call it the inaccessible.

Being inaccessible, I call it the omnipresent.

Dao is supreme, Heaven is supreme, Earth is supreme, the King is supreme.

There are in the universe four kinds of supremacy, and their rulership is one.

Man models himself after the Earth, the Earth models itself after Heaven, Heaven models itself after Dao, Dao models itself after nature.

XXVI
The Virtue of Gravity

Weight underlies lightness, quiescence underlies motion.

Therefore the Sage never loses his gravity and quiescence from day to day.

Though glorious palaces should belong to him, he would dwell in them peacefully, without attachment.

Alas that a king with many chariots should conduct himself with frivolity in the midst of his kingdom!

By levity he loses his ministers, and by inconstancy his throne.

XXVII
The Use of Skill

The good walker makes no dust after him.

The good speaker incurs no discussion.

The good reckoner needs no arithmetic.

The good keeper needs no bolts or bars, and none can open after him.

The good binder needs no rope, and none can loose after him.

The wise man is a constant and good helper of his fellows. He rejects none.

He is a continual good preserver of things. He disdains nothing.

His intelligence is all-embracing.

Good men instruct one another; and bad men are the materials they delve in.

Whoever, therefore, does not honor his teacher and cherish his material, though he be called wise, is yet in a state of delusion.

This is no less important than strange.

XXVIII
Becoming a Child

He who, being a man, remains a woman, will become a universal channel.

As a universal channel the eternal virtue will never forsake him. He will rebecome a child.

He who, being in the light, remains in obscurity, will become a universal model.

As a universal model the eternal virtue will not pass him by. He will go back to the all-perfect.

He who, being glorious, continues in humility, will become a universal valley.

As a universal valley the eternal virtue will fill him. He will revert to the first essence.

The first essence is that which, being differentiated, gives rise to innumerable vessels of life.

A wise man, by embracing it, becomes the wisest of governors.

A liberal government is that which neither disregards nor hurts anyone.

XXIX
Nonaction

When a man who wishes to reform the world takes it in hand, I perceive that there will be no end to it!

Spiritual vessels are not fashioned in the world.

Whoever makes destroys; whoever grasps loses.

For perforce if one advances another is left behind; if one blows hot another will blow cold; if one be strengthened another will be weakened; if one be supported another will be undermined.

Therefore the Sage gives up all enthusiasm, levity, and pomp.

XXX
Declining from Strife

The man who aids the King by the use of Dao forces the people into submission without resort to the use of arms. He will not regard the fruit of his actions.

Prickly briars and thorns flourish where battalions have quartered.

Bad years follow on the heels of armies in motion.

The good soldier is brave when occasion requires, but he does not risk himself for power.

Brave is he when occasion requires, but he does not oppress.

Brave is he when occasion requires, but he does not boast.

Brave is he when occasion requires, but he is not haughty.

Brave is he when occasion requires, but he is not mean.

Brave is he when occasion requires, but he does not rage.

Things become old through excess of vigor. This is called Non-Dao; and what is Non-Dao is soon wasted!

XXXI
Ceasing from War

Weapons, however ornamental, are not a source of happiness, but are dreaded by all.

Therefore the man of Dao will not abide where such things are.

A respectable man at home sets the place of honor at his left hand; but the warrior on going forth to battle gives honor to the right hand. For weapons are things of ill omen, and the man of enlightenment does not use them except when he cannot help it.

His great desire is peace, and he does not take joy in conquest.

To joy in conquest is to joy in the loss of human life.

He who joys in bloodshed is not fit to govern the country.

When affairs are prosperous the left side is preferred, but when things are adverse the right is esteemed.

The adjutant-general is therefore on the left side, while the general-in-chief is on the right.

This I perceive is the manner also observed at a funeral!

He who has occasion to kill many people has cause for deep sorrow and tears.

Therefore a victorious army observes the order of a funeral.

XXXII
Intelligent Virtue

Dao the absolute has no name.

But although insignificant in its original simplicity, the world does not presume to bemean it.

If a king could lay hold on it, the world would of itself submit to him.

Heaven and Earth would conspire to nourish him.

The people without pressure would peacefully fall into their own places.

If he should dispose them by titles and names, he would be making a name for himself.

Yet he would wisely stop short of the name, and thus avoid the evil of distinctions.

Dao is to the world what the streams and valleys are to the great rivers and seas.

XXXIII
Knowing Oneself

He is wise who knows others.

He who knows himself is enlightened.

He is strong who conquers others.

He who conquers himself is mighty.

He is rich who is well satisfied.

He walks fast who has an object.

He who fills his place remains secure.

He who dies without being corrupted enjoys a good old age.

XXXIV
The Perfect Condition

Mighty Dao is all-pervading.

It is simultaneously on this side and on that.

All living things subsist from it, and all are in its care.

It works, it finishes, and knows not the name of merit.

In love it nurtures all things, and claims no excellence therein.

It knows neither ambition nor desire.

It can be classed with the humblest of things.

All things finally revert to it, and it is not thereby increased.

It can be mentioned with the greatest of things.

Thus does the wise man continually refrain from self-distinction.

XXXV
The Virtue of Bounty

Attain to the Great Idea, and all the world will flock to you.

It will flock to you and will not be hurt therein, for it will rest in a wonderful peace.

Where there is a festival the wayfarer will stay.

To the palate the Dao is insipid and tasteless.

In regarding it the eye is not impressed.

In listening to it the ear is not filled.

But in its uses it is inexhaustible.

XXXVI
The Rhythm of Life

When Nature is about to withhold a thing it is first sure to increase it.

When about to weaken it is first sure to strengthen.

When about to debase it is certain first to exalt.

When about to deprive it is first sure to give.

This is what I call the covert agreement.

The soft and the weak overcome the hard and the strong.

As a fish out of water is in danger, so a nation is in peril when its armaments are revealed to the people.

XXXVII
The Art of Government

Dao remains quiescent, and yet leaves nothing undone.

If a ruler or a king could hold it, all things would of their own accord assume the desired shape.

If in the process of transformation desire should arise, I would check it by the ineffable simplicity.

The ineffable simplicity would bring about an absence of desire, and rest would come back again.

Thus the world would regenerate itself.

XXXVIII
Of Virtue

The superior virtue is not recognized as such, and it is therefore the very essence of virtue.

The inferior virtue has the distinction of virtue, and therefore it lacks the essence.

The superior virtue is spontaneous, and makes no claim to merit.

The inferior virtue is designing, and lays claim to recognition.

The higher benevolence acts without pretension to merit.

The inferior justice acts, and also makes pretensions.

The inferior expediency is designing, and therefore no one honors it.

Therefore does it bare its arm and assert itself by force.

Thus it transpires that when virtue is lost, benevolence takes its place.

When benevolence is lost, justice ensues.

When justice is lost, then expediency follows.

But expediency is the mere shadow of what is right and true, and is portentous of confusion.

Superficial virtue is the mere tinsel of Dao, and the fool makes use of it.

But the truly great man establishes himself on that which is solid, and will not lean upon a shadow.

He keeps to the real, and avoids display.

He rejects the one, and takes the other with both hands.

XXXIX
Tracing the Source

Certain things have, by unity, lasted from most ancient times, namely:

The transparency of Heaven;
The steadfastness of Earth;
The incorporeality of spirits;
The watery plenitude of valleys;
The life of all creations;
The government of kings and princes;
All these endure by unity.

But for the cause of its transparency Heaven would be in danger of obscuration.

But for the cause of its steadfastness the Earth would be in danger of disintegration.

But for the cause of their incorporeality spirits would be in danger of decease.

But for the cause of their plenitude the valleys would be in danger of sterility.

But for the cause of their vitality all creations would be in danger of destruction.

But for the cause of their honor and greatness princes and kings would be in danger of an overthrow.

Herein we see how honor is derived from that which is without distinction; and how greatness rests upon, and is sustained by, that which is insignificant.

Hence do princes and kings call themselves "orphans," "solitary men," and "chariots without wheels."

Do they not thereby acknowledge their authority to be vested in, and supported by, their superiors?

Who can deny it?

Surely "a chariot without wheels" is no chariot at all!

It is as hard for a man to be isolated like a single gem as to be lost in the crowd like a common pebble.

XL
The Principle of Reversion

Reversion is the action of Dao.

Gentleness is the function of Dao.

Everything in the universe comes from existence, and existence from nonexistence.

XLI
Like and Unlike

When a wise man hears the Dao, he follows it.

When one of average mind hears it, he holds to it a while and presently loses it.

When a foolish man hears it, he only laughs at it.

If it were not held in derision by such men, it could not rightly be called Dao.

Therefore, as the verse-makers would say:

Who shines with Dao is lost in shade;
His path in Dao is retrograde,
And all his actions are obscure.
The highest virtue has no name,
The greatest pureness seems but shame;
True wisdom seems the least secure.
Inherent goodness seems most strange;
What most endures is changeless Change;
And squareness doth no angles make.
The largest vessel none can gird;
The loudest voice was never heard;
The greatest thing no form doth take.

For Dao is hidden, and it has no name; but it is good at beginning and finishing.

XLII
The Changes of Dao

Dao [emanated] the One; the one [emanated] the Two; and the two [emanated] the Three.

From the Three all things have proceeded.

Everything embodies yin and embraces yang, through the union of the pervading principles it reaches harmony.

Orphanage, isolation, and a chariot without wheels are shunned by the people; but kings and great men appropriate these names to themselves.

For things are increased by being deprived; and being added to they are diminished.

That which people teach by their actions I make use of to instruct them.

Those who are violent and headstrong, for example, do not die a natural death.

They teach a good lesson, and so I make use of them.

XLIII
Unlimited Usefulness

The gentlest thing in the world will override the strongest.

The Nonexistent pervades everything, though there be no inlet.

By this I comprehend how effectual is nonaction.

To teach without words and to be useful without action, few among men are capable of this.

XLIV
Standing Still

Which is the nearer to you, your name or your person?

Which is the more precious, your person or your wealth?

Which is the greater evil, to gain or to lose?

Great devotion requires great sacrifice.

Great wealth implies great loss.

He who is content can never be ruined.

He who stands still will never meet danger.

These are the people who endure.

XLV
Indefinite Virtue

He who sees that his highest attainments are always incomplete may go on working indefinitely.

He who sees his greatest possessions to be inadequate may go on acquiring forever.

His highest rectitude is but crookedness.

His greatest wisdom is but foolishness.

His sweetest eloquence is but stammering.

Action overcomes cold; inaction overcomes heat.

With virtue and quietness one may conquer the world.

XLVI
Curbing Desire

When Dao is in the world, horses are used in the pasture land.

When Dao has left the world, chargers are reared in the wilderness.

There is no greater sin than indulging desire.

There is no greater pain than discontent.

There is nothing more disastrous than the greed of gain.

Hence the satisfaction of contentment is an everlasting competence.

XLVII
Looking Abroad

A man may know the world without leaving his own home.

Through his windows he can see the supreme Dao.

The further afield he goes the less likely is he to find it.

Therefore the wise man knows without traveling, names things without seeing them, and accomplishes everything without action.

XLVIII
The Distress of Knowledge

Bodily and mental distress is increased every day in the effort to get knowledge.

But this distress is daily diminished by the getting of Dao.

Do you continually curtail your effort till there be nothing of it left?

By nonaction there is nothing which cannot be effected.

A man might, without the least distress, undertake the government of the world.

But those who distress themselves about governing the world are not fit for it.

XLIX
The Virtue of Concession

The wise man has no fixed opinions to call his own.

He accommodates himself to the minds of others.

I would return good for good; I would also return good for evil.

Virtue is good.

I would meet trust with trust; I would likewise meet suspicion with confidence.

Virtue is trustful.

The wise man lives in the world with modest restraint, and his heart goes out in sympathy to all men.

The people give him their confidence, and he regards them all as his children.

L
The Value of Life

Men go forth from Life and enter into Death.

The Gates of Life are thirteen in number; and the same are the Gates of Death.

By as many ways does Life pass quickly in Death. And wherefore?

Because men strive only after the Sensuous Life.

It has been said that one who knows how to safeguard Life can go through the country without protection against the rhinoceros and tiger.

He may enter into battle without fear of the sword.

The rhinoceros finds no place wherein to drive his horn.

The tiger finds no place wherein to fix his claws.

The sword finds no place wherein to thrust itself.

Why is this?

It is because he has overcome Death.

LI
Cherishing Virtue

Dao brings forth, and De nourishes.[1]

All things take up their several forms, and natural forces bring them to perfection.

Therefore all things conspire to exalt Dao and to cherish virtue.

But this regard of Dao and De is not in deference to any mandate.

It is unconstrained, and therefore it endures forever.

For Dao produces all things, and De nourishes, increases, feeds, matures, protects, and watches over them.

To produce without possessing; to work without expecting; to enlarge without usurping; this is the sublime virtue!

LII
Going Back to the Cause

That from which the universe sprang may be looked upon as its Mother.

By knowing the Mother you have access to the child.

And if, knowing the child, you prefer the Mother, though your body perish, yet you will come to no harm.

Keep your mouth shut, and close up the doors of sight and sound, and as long as you live you will have no vexation.

But open your mouth, or become inquisitive, and you will be in trouble all your life long.

To perceive things in the germ is intelligence.

To remain gentle is to be invincible.

Follow the light that guides you homeward, and do not get lost in the darkness.

This I call using the eternal.

[1]Editor's note: *De* means "true virtue" or "vital power."

LIII
Increasing Evidence

Ah that I were wise enough to follow the great Dao!

Administration is a great undertaking.

The great Dao is extremely simple, but the people prefer the complex ways.

While the palace is extremely well appointed, the fields may be full of tares, and the granaries may be empty.

To dress grandly, to carry sharp swords, to eat and drink excessively, and to amass great wealth, this I call stylish theft.

That it is not Dao is certain.

LIV
The Root and Its Branches

He who plants rightly never uproots.

He who lays hold rightly never relinquishes.

His posterity will honor him continually.

Whoever develops the Dao in himself will be rooted in virtue.

Whoever develops the Dao in his family will cause his virtue to spread.

Whoever develops the Dao in his village will increase prosperity.

Whoever develops the Dao in the kingdom will make good fortune prevalent.

Whoever develops the Dao in the world will make virtue universal.

I observe myself, and so I come to know others.

I observe my family, and all others grow familiar.

I study this world, and others come within my knowledge.

How else should I come to know the laws which govern all things, save thus, that I observe them in myself?

LV
The Wonderful Harmony

The man who is saturated with Virtue is like a little child.

Scorpions will not sting him, wild beasts will not seize him, nor will birds of prey pluck at him.

His young bones are not hard, neither are his sinews strong, yet his grasp is firm and sure.

He is full of virility, though unconscious of his sex.

Though he should cry out all day, yet he is never hoarse.

Herein is shown his harmony with Nature.

The knowledge of this harmony is the eternal Dao.

The knowledge of the eternal Dao is illumination.

Habits of excess grow upon a man, and the mind, giving way to the passions, they increase day by day.

And when the passions have reached their climax, they also fail.

This is against the nature of Dao.

What is contrary to Dao soon comes to an end.

LVI
Beyond Honor and Disgrace

He who knows does not speak;

He who speaks does not know.

To keep the lips closed, to shut the doors of sight and sound, to smooth off the corners, to temper the glare, and to be on a level with the dust of the earth, this is the mysterious virtue.

Whoever observes this will regard alike both frankness and reserve, kindness and injury, honor and degradation.

For this reason he will be held in great esteem of all men.

LVII
The Genuine Government

The righteous man may rule the nation.

The strategic man may rule the army.

But the man who refrains from active measures should be the king.

How do I know how things should be?

I know by this:

When the actions of the people are controlled by prohibited laws, the country becomes more and more impoverished.

When the people are allowed the free use of arms, the Government is in danger.

The more crafty and dexterous the people become, the more do artificial things come into use.

And when these cunning arts are publicly esteemed, then do rogues prosper.

Therefore the wise man says:

I will design nothing; and the people will shape themselves.

I will keep quiet; and the people will find their rest.

I will not assert myself; and the people will come forth.

I will discountenance ambition; and the people will revert to their natural simplicity.

LVIII
Letting Others Reform Themselves

A free and generous government gives the people a chance to develop.

When the government is rigid and exacting the people are cramped and miserable.

Misery is but the shadow of happiness.

Happiness is but the cloak of misery.

When will there be an end to them?

If we dispense with rectitude, distortion will assert itself; and what was good in its way will give place to what is evil.

Verily the people have been under a cloud for a long time.

Therefore the wise man is full of rectitude, but he does not chip and carve at others.

He is just, but does not admonish others.

He is upright, but he does not straighten others.

He is enlightened, but he does not offend with his brightness.

LIX
Preserving the Dao

In ruling men and in serving Heaven there is nothing like moderation.

By means of it one attains to his first estate.

When this is attained a man is possessed of an indefinite store of virtue.

With such a store of virtue he will overcome everything.

And of this mastery there will be no limit.

Thus, without hindrance, he may possess the Kingdom.

Such a man has the mother-constitution, and will endure indefinitely.

He is like the plant whose roots are deep and whose stem is firm.

Thus may a man live long and see many days.

LX
Ruling a Big Country

The state should be governed as we cook small fish, without much business.

Bringing the Dao to the governing of the Kingdom will give rest to the shades of the dead.

Not that the Spirits will be inactive, but that they will cease to trouble the people.

But what is of more importance, the wise ruler of the people will not hurt them.

And in so far as they do not interfere with one another, their influences conspire to the general good!

LXI
The Virtue of Humility

The kingdom, like a river, becomes great by being lowly; it is thereby the center to which all the world tends.

It is similar in the case of woman:

She conquers man by continual quietness.

And quietness is the same as submission.

Therefore a great state, by condescension to those beneath it, may gain the government of them.

Likewise a small state, by submission to one that is greater, may secure its alliance.

Thus the one gains adherence, and the other obtains favors.

Although the great state desires to annex and to nourish others, yet the small state desires to be allied to and serve the greater.

Thus both will be satisfied, if only the greater will condescend.

LXII
Practical Dao

Dao is the secret guardian of all things.

It enriches the good man and forefends the evil-doer.

Its counsel is always in season; its benevolence is always in demand.

Even those who are not good it does not forsake.

Therefore, when the Emperor takes his throne and appoints his nobles, he who comes before him bearing the insignia of a prince and escorted by a mounted retinue is not to be compared with one who humbly presents this Dao.

For why did the ancients hold it in such esteem?

Was it not because it could be had without much seeking, and because by means of it man might escape from sin?

For this it was esteemed the greatest thing in the world!

LXIII
Forethought

Acting without design, occupying oneself without making a business of it, finding the great in what is small, and the many in the few, repaying injury with kindness, effecting difficult things while they are easy, and managing great things in their beginnings, is the method of Dao.

All difficult things have their origin in that which is easy, and great things in that which is small.

Therefore the wise man can accomplish great things without even attempting them.

He who lightly assents will seldom keep his word.

He who accounts all things easy will have many difficulties.

Therefore the Sage takes great account of small things, and so never has any difficulty.

LXIV
Guarding the Small

What is still is easily held.

What is expected is easily provided for.

What is brittle is easily broken.

What is small is soon dispersed.

Transact your business before it takes shape.

Regulate things before confusion begins.

The tree which fills the arms grew from a tender shoot.

The castle of nine stories was raised on a heap of earth.

The journey of a thousand miles begins with one step.

Whoever designs only destroys.

Whoever grasps, loses.

The Sage does not thus act, therefore he does no harm.

He does not grasp, and therefore he never loses.

But the common people, in their undertakings, fail on the eve of success.

If they were as prudent at the end as they are at the beginning, there would be no such failures.

Therefore the Sage is only ambitious of what others despise, and sets no value on things difficult to obtain.

He acquires no common learning, but returns to that which the people have passed by.

Thus he aims at simple development in all things, and acts without design.

LXV
Simple Virtue

The ancients who practiced the Dao did not make use of it to render the people brilliant, but to make them simple and natural.

The difficulty in governing the people is through overmuch policy.

He who tries to govern the kingdom by policy is only a scourge to it; while he who governs without it is a blessing.

To know these two things is the perfect knowledge of government, and to keep them continually in view is called the virtue of simplicity.

Deep and wide is this simple virtue; and though opposed to other methods it can bring about a perfect order.

LXVI
Going Behind

That by which the great rivers and seas receive the tribute of all the streams, is the fact of their being lowly; that is the cause of their superiority.

Thus the Sage, wishing to govern the people, speaks of himself as beneath them; and wishing to lead them, places himself behind them.

So, while he is yet above them, they do not feel his weight; and being before them, he yet causes no obstruction.

Therefore all men exalt him with acclamations, and none is offended.

And because he does not strive, no man is his enemy.

LXVII
Three Precious Things

All the world avows that while my Daoism is great, it is yet incompetent!

It is its greatness which makes it appear incompetent.

If it were like others, it would long ago have been recognized as incompetent.

But I hold fast to three precious things, which also I cherish.

The first is gentleness.

The second is economy.

The third is humility.

With such gentleness I can be daring.

With such economy I can be generous.

With such humility I can be great in service, as a vessel of honor.

But in these days men forsake gentleness and become only obtrusive.

They abandon economy and become only excessive.

They relinquish humility and strive for precedence, and thus for death.

Gentleness is ever victorious in attack and secure in defense.

Therefore when Heaven would preserve a man it enfolds him with gentleness.

LXVIII
Imitating Heaven

The good commander is not imperious.

The good fighter is not wrathful.

The greatest conqueror does not wage war.

The best master governs by condescension.

This is the virtue of not contending.

This is the virtue of persuasion.

This is the imitation of Heaven, and this was the highest aim of the ancients.

LXIX
The Use of Supreme Virtue

A great warrior has said, "I dare not be the host, I would rather be the guest; I dare not advance an inch, I would rather retire a foot."

Now this I call filing in without marshaling the ranks; baring the arms without preparing to fight; grasping the sword without unsheathing it; and advancing upon the enemy without coming into conflict.

There is nothing so unfortunate as entering lightly into battle.

For by so doing we are in danger of losing that which is most precious.

Thus it happens that when opposing forces meet in battle, he who feels the pity of it assuredly conquers.

LXX
The Difficult Recognition

Easy are my words to know, and also to practice.

Yet none is able to understand nor yet to practice them.

For there is a remote origin for my words, and a supreme law for my actions.

Not knowing these, men cannot know me.

Those who know me are few, and by them I am esteemed.

For the wise man is outwardly poor, but he carries his jewel in his bosom.

LXXI
The Disease of Knowing

To know one's ignorance is the best part of knowledge.

To be ignorant of such knowledge is a disease.

If one only regards it as a disease, he will soon be cured of it.

The wise man is exempt from this disease.

He knows it for what it is, and so is free from it.

LXXII
Loving Oneself

When men do not have a right fear of present dangers, they run into extremes of peril.

Let them beware of enlarging the house, being weary of present conditions.

If they do not despise it, no such weariness will arise.

This is why the Sage, while possessed of self-knowledge, does not parade himself.

He loves, but does not value himself highly.

Thus he puts away pride, and is content.

LXXIII
Freedom of Action

He whose courage is expressed in daring will soon meet death.

He whose courage is shown in self-restraint will be preserved.

There are, then, two kinds of courage; the one is injurious and the other of advantage.

But who is to say why one of them should incur the judgment of Heaven?

That is why the Sage finds it difficult to act.

The celestial Dao does not strive, and yet overcomes everything.

It does not speak, yet it is skillful in replying.

It does not call, yet things come to it readily.

It is quiet in its methods, yet its plans are thoroughly effective.

The net of Heaven has large meshes, and yet nothing escapes it!

LXXIV
On Punishment

The people are not afraid of death, why threaten them with death?

Supposing that the people are afraid of death, and we can seize and kill the unruly, who dare to do so?

Often it happens that the executioner is killed. And to take the place of the executioner is like handing the hatchet for the master carpenter.

He who handles the hatchet for the master carpenter seldom escapes injury to his hands.

LXXV
The Evil of Avarice

The people suffer from famine on account of the heavy taxation put upon them.

This is the cause of their need.

The people are difficult to govern because of the overbearing of their superiors.

This is the cause of their trouble.

The people make light of dying because of the great hardships of trying to live.

This is the reason of their indifference to death.

Therefore to keep living in obscurity is better than making overmuch of it.

LXXVI
The Danger of Strength

Man at his birth is supple and tender, but in death he is rigid and strong.

It is the same with everything.

Trees and plants in their early growth are pliant and soft, but at the end they are withered and tough.

Thus rigidity and strength are companions of death, but softness and gentleness are companions of life.

Therefore the warrior who relies on his strength cannot conquer death, while the powerful tree becomes a mere timber support.

For the place of the strong and the firm is below, while that of the gentle and yielding is above.

LXXVII
The Dao of Heaven

Like the bending of an archer's bow is the Dao of Heaven!

It brings down that which is high, and raises up that which is depressed.

It takes away where there is excess, and gives where there is deficiency.

The Dao of Heaven makes all things equal.

This Dao is not of man.

Man takes from the needy to add to his own excess.

Who is he that, having a superabundance, can bring it to the service of the world?

Only he who has the Dao.

This is why the wise man acts without expectation of reward, and completes his task without claiming merit.

For thus he hides his wealth.

LXXVIII
Accepting the Truth

Nothing on earth is so weak and yielding as water, but for breaking down the firm and strong it has no equal.

This admits of no alternative.

All the world knows that the soft can wear away the hard, and weak can conquer the strong; but none can carry it out in practice.

Therefore the Sage says: He who bears the reproach of his country is really the lord of the land. He who bears the woes of the people is in truth their king.

The words of truth are always paradoxical!

LXXIX
Keeping One's Bond

When a compromise is effected after a long dispute, one of the parties retains a grudge: how can this be called a good settlement?

Therefore the wise man takes his part of the bond, and does not insist upon having the other.

The virtuous man attends only to his engagements in the bond, while the man without virtue contrives for his own advantage.

The Dao of Heaven has no favorites; it always aids the good man.

LXXX
Standing Alone

If I had a small kingdom and but ten or a hundred men of ability, I would not administrate with them.

I would teach the people to look upon death as a grievous thing, and then they would not go abroad to meet it.

Though they had boats and carriages, yet they would not go away in them.

Though they had armor, yet they would never have occasion to wear it.

The people should return to the use of the quipu.[2]

They should find their coarse food sweet, think their plain clothes grand, regard their homes as places of rest, and take delight in their own simple pleasures.

Though the neighboring state could be seen by us, and the crowing of the cocks and the barking of the dogs could be heard,

Yet my people would grow old, and die before ever feeling the need of having intercourse with it.

LXXXI
The Evidence of Simplicity

Sincere words are not grand.

Grand words are not faithful.

The man of Dao does not dispute.

They who dispute are not skilled in Dao.

Those who know it are not learned.

The learned do not know it.

The wise man does not lay up treasure.

The more he expends on others, the more he gains for himself.

The more he gives to others, the more he has for his own.

This is the Dao of Heaven, which penetrates but does not injure.

This is the Dao of the wise man, who acts but does not strive.

[2]Editor's note: A *quipu* is a knotted cord used for simple reckoning or counting.

Basic Writings

CHUANG TZU

Discussion of Making All Things Equal

. . . Now I am going to make a statement here. I don't know whether it fits into the category of other people's statements or not. But whether it fits into their category or whether it doesn't, it obviously fits into some category. So in that respect it is no different

Chuang Tzu, selections from Chuang Tzu: Basic Writings, *translated by Burton Watson (New York: Columbia University Press, 1964). Reprinted with permission of Columbia University Press.*

from their statements. However, let me try making my statement.

There is a beginning. There is a not yet beginning to be a beginning. There is a not yet beginning to be a not yet beginning to be a beginning. There is being. There is nonbeing. There is a not yet beginning to be nonbeing. There is a not yet beginning to be a not yet beginning to be nonbeing. Suddenly there is being and nonbeing. But between this being and nonbeing, I don't really know which is being and which is nonbeing. Now I have just said something. But I don't know whether what I have said has really said something or whether it hasn't said something.

There is nothing in the world bigger than the tip of an autumn hair,[1] and Mount T'ai is little. No one has lived longer than a dead child, and P'eng-tsu died young. Heaven and earth were born at the same time I was, and the ten thousand things are one with me.

We have already become one, so how can I say anything? But I have just *said* that we are one, so how can I not be saying something? The one and what I said about it make two, and two and the original one make three. If we go on this way, then even the cleverest mathematician can't tell where we'll end, much less an ordinary man. If by moving from nonbeing to being we get to three, how far will we get if we move from being to being? Better not to move, but to let things be!

The Way has never known boundaries; speech has no constancy. But because of [the recognition of a] "this," there came to be boundaries. Let me tell you what the boundaries are. There is left, there is right, there are theories, there are debates, there are divisions, there are discriminations, there are emulations, and there are contentions. These are called the Eight Virtues.[2] Beyond the Six Realms,[3] the sage exists but does not theorize. Within the Six Realms, he theorizes but does not debate. In the case of the *Spring and Autumn*,[4] the record of the former kings of past ages, the sage debates but does not discriminate. So [I say,] those who divide fail to divide; those who discriminate fail to discriminate. What does this mean, you ask? The sage embraces things. Ordinary men discriminate among them and parade their discrimina-

tions before others. So I say, those who discriminate fail to see.

The Great Way is not named; Great Discriminations are not spoken; Great Benevolence is not benevolent; Great Modesty is not humble; Great Daring does not attack. If the Way is made clear, it is not the Way. If discriminations are put into words, they do not suffice. If benevolence has a constant object, it cannot be universal. If modesty is fastidious, it cannot be trusted. If daring attacks, it cannot be complete. These five are all round, but they tend toward the square.[5]

Therefore understanding stops when it has reached what it does not understand. Who can understand discriminations that are not spoken, the Way that is not a way? If he can understand this, he may be called the Reservoir of Heaven. Pour into it and it is never full, dip from it and it never runs dry, and yet it does not know where the supply comes from. This is called the Shaded Light.

So it is that long ago Yao said to Shun, "I want to attack the rulers of Tsung, K'uai, and Hsü-ao. Even as I sit on my throne, this thought nags at me. What is this?"

Shun replied, "These three rulers are only little dwellers in the weeds and brush. Why this nagging desire? Long ago, ten suns came out all at once and the ten thousand things were all lighted up. And how much greater is virtue than these suns!"[6]

Nieh Ch'üeh asked Wang Ni, "Do you know what all things agree in calling right?"

"How would I know that?" said Wang Ni.

"Do you know that you don't know it?"

"How would I know that?"

"Then do things know nothing?"

"How would I know that? However, suppose I try saying something. What way do I have of knowing that if I say I know something I don't really not know it? Or what way do I have knowing that if I say I don't know something I don't really in fact know it? Now let me ask *you* some questions. If a man sleeps in a damp place, his back aches and he ends up half paralyzed, but is this true of a loach? If he lives in a tree, he is terrified and shakes with fright, but is this true of a monkey? Of these three creatures, then, which one knows the proper place to live? Men eat the flesh of grass-fed and grain-fed animals, deer eat

---

[1]The strands of animal fur were believed to grow particularly fine in autumn; hence "the tip of an autumn hair" is a cliché for something extremely tiny. . . .

[2]. . . Chuang Tzu is deliberately parodying the ethical categories of the Confucians and Mo-ists.

[3]Heaven, earth, and the four directions, i.e., the universe.

[4]Perhaps a reference to the *Spring and Autumn Annals*, a history of the state of Lu said to have been compiled by Confucius. . . .

[5]All are originally perfect, but may become "squared," i.e., impaired, by the misuses mentioned.

[6]Here virtue is to be understood in a good sense, as the power of the Way.

grass, centipedes find snakes tasty, and hawks and falcons relish mice. Of these four, which knows how food ought to taste? Monkeys pair with monkeys, deer go out with deer, and fish play around with fish. Men claim that Mao-ch'iang and Lady Li were beautiful, but if fish saw them they would dive to the bottom of the stream, if birds saw them they would fly away, and if deer saw them they would break into a run. Of these four, which knows how to fix the standard of beauty for the world? The way I see it, the rules of benevolence and righteousness and the paths of right and wrong are all hopelessly snarled and jumbled. How could I know anything about such discriminations?"

Nieh Ch'üeh said, "If you don't know what is profitable or harmful, then does the Perfect Man likewise know nothing of such things?"

Wang Ni replied, "The Perfect Man is godlike. Though the great swamps blaze, they cannot burn him; though the great rivers freeze, they cannot chill him; though swift lightning splits the hills and howling gales shake the sea, they cannot frighten him. A man like this rides the clouds and mist, straddles the sun and moon, and wanders beyond the four seas. Even life and death have no effect on him, much less the rules of profit and loss!"

Chü Ch'üeh-tzu said to Chang Wu-tzu, "I have heard Confucius say that the sage does not work at anything, does not pursue profit, does not dodge harm, does not enjoy being sought after, does not follow the Way, says nothing yet says something, says something yet says nothing, and wanders beyond the dust and grime. Confucius himself regarded these as wild and flippant words, though I believe they describe the working of the mysterious Way. What do you think of them?"

Chang Wu-tzu said, "Even the Yellow Emperor would be confused if he heard such words, so how could you expect Confucius to understand them? What's more, you're too hasty in your own appraisal. You see an egg and demand a crowing cock, see a crossbow pellet and demand a roast dove. I'm going to try speaking some reckless words and I want you to listen to them recklessly. How will that be? The sage leans on the sun and moon, tucks the universe under his arm, merges himself with things, leaves the confusion and muddle as it is, and looks on slaves as exalted. Ordinary men strain and struggle; the sage is stupid and blockish. He takes part in ten thousand ages and achieves simplicity in oneness. For him, all the ten thousand things are what they are, and thus they enfold each other.

"How do I know that loving life is not a delusion? How do I know that in hating death I am not like a man who, having left home in his youth, has forgotten the way back?

"Lady Li was the daughter of the border guard of Ai. When she was first taken captive and brought to the state of Chin, she wept until her tears drenched the collar of her robe. But later, when she went to live in the palace of the ruler, shared his couch with him, and ate the delicious meats of his table, she wondered why she had ever wept. How do I know that the dead do not wonder why they ever longed for life?

"He who dreams of drinking wine may weep when morning comes; he who dreams of weeping may in the morning go off to hunt. While he is dreaming he does not know it is a dream, and in his dream he may even try to interpret a dream. Only after he wakes does he know it was a dream. And someday there will be a great awakening when we know that this is all a great dream. Yet the stupid believe they are awake, busily and brightly assuming they understand things, calling this man ruler, that one herdsman—how dense! Confucius and you are both dreaming! And when I say you are dreaming, I am dreaming, too. Words like these will be labeled the Supreme Swindle. Yet, after ten thousand generations, a great sage may appear who will know their meaning, and it will still be as though he appeared with astonishing speed.

"Suppose you and I have had an argument. If you have beaten me instead of my beating you, then are you necessarily right and am I necessarily wrong? If I have beaten you instead of your beating me, then am I necessarily right and are you necessarily wrong? Is one of us right and the other wrong? Are both of us right or are both of us wrong? If you and I don't know the answer, then other people are bound to be even more in the dark. Whom shall we get to decide what is right? Shall we get someone who agrees with you to decide? But if he already agrees with you, how can he decide fairly? Shall we get someone who agrees with me? But if he already agrees with me, how can he decide? Shall we get someone who disagrees with both of us? But if he already disagrees with both of us, how can he decide? Shall we get someone who agrees with both of us? But if he already agrees with both of us, how can he decide? Obviously, then, neither you nor I nor anyone else can know the answer. Shall we wait for still another person?

"But waiting for one shifting voice [to pass judgment on another] is the same as waiting for none of them. Harmonize them all with the Heavenly

Equality, leave them to their endless changes, and so live out your years. What do I mean by harmonizing them with the Heavenly Equality? Right is not right; so is not so. If right were really right, it would differ so clearly from not right that there would be no need for argument. If so were really so, it would differ so clearly from not so that there would be no need for argument. Forget the years; forget distinctions. Leap into the boundless and make it your home!"

Penumbra said to Shadow, "A little while ago you were walking and now you're standing still; a little while ago you were sitting and now you're standing up. Why this lack of independent action?"

Shadow said, "Do I have to wait for something before I can be like this? Does what I wait for also have to wait for something before it can be like this? Am I waiting for the scales of a snake or the wings of a cicada? How do I know why it is so? How do I know why it isn't so?"[7]

Once Chuang Chou dreamt he was a butterfly, a butterfly flitting and fluttering around, happy with himself and doing as he pleased. He didn't know he was Chuang Chou. Suddenly he woke up and there he was, solid and unmistakable Chuang Chou. But he didn't know if he was Chuang Chou who had dreamt he was a butterfly, or a butterfly dreaming he was Chuang Chou. Between Chuang Chou and a butterfly there must be *some* distinction! This is called the Transformation of Things.

The Secret of Caring for Life

Your life has a limit but knowledge has none. If you use what is limited to pursue what has no limit, you will be in danger. If you understand this and still strive for knowledge, you will be in danger for certain! If you do good, stay away from fame. If you do evil, stay away from punishments. Follow the middle; go by what is constant, and you can stay in one piece, keep yourself alive, look after your parents, and live out your years.

Cook Ting was cutting up an ox for Lord Wen-hui. At every touch of his hand, every heave of his shoulder, every move of his feet, every thrust of his knee—zip! zoop! He slithered the knife along with a zing, and all was in perfect rhythm, as though he were per-

forming the dance of the Mulberry Grove or keeping time to the Ching-shou music.

"Ah, this is marvelous!" said Lord Wen-hui. "Imagine skill reaching such heights!"

Cook Ting laid down his knife and replied, "What I care about is the Way, which goes beyond skill. When I first began cutting up oxen, all I could see was the ox itself. After three years I no longer saw the whole ox. And now—now I go at it by spirit and don't look with my eyes. Perception and understanding have come to a stop and spirit moves where it wants. I go along with the natural makeup, strike in the big hollows, guide the knife through the big openings, and follow things as they are. So I never touch the smallest ligament or tendon, much less a main joint.

"A good cook changes his knife once a year—because he cuts. A mediocre cook changes his knife once a month—because he hacks. I've had this knife of mine for nineteen years and I've cut up thousands of oxen with it, and yet the blade is as good as though it had just come from the grindstone. There are spaces between the joints, and the blade of the knife has really no thickness. If you insert what has no thickness into such spaces, then there's plenty of room—more than enough for the blade to play about in. That's why after nineteen years the blade of my knife is still as good as when it first came from the grindstone.

"However, whenever I come to a complicated place, I size up the difficulties, tell myself to watch out and be careful, keep my eyes on what I'm doing, work very slowly, and move the knife with the greatest subtlety, until—flop! the whole thing comes apart like a clod of earth crumbling to the ground. I stand there holding the knife and look all around me, completely satisfied and reluctant to move on, and then I wipe off the knife and put it away."

"Excellent!" said Lord Wen-hui. "I have heard the words of Cook Ting and learned how to care for life!" . . .

Fit for Emperors and Kings

. . . T'ien Ken was wandering on the sunny side of Yin Mountain. When he reached the banks of the Liao River, he happened to meet a Nameless Man. He questioned the man, saying, "Please may I ask how to rule the world?"

The Nameless Man said, "Get away from me, you peasant! What kind of a dreary question is that! I'm just about to set off with the Creator. And if I get bored with that, then I'll ride on the Light-and-Lissome Bird out beyond the six directions, wandering in the

---

[7]That is, to ordinary men the shadow appears to depend upon something else for its movement, just as the snake depends on its scales (according to Chinese belief) and the cicada on its wings. But do such causal views of action really have any meaning?

village of Not-Even-Anything and living in the Broad-and-Borderless field. What business do you have coming with this talk of governing the world and disturbing my mind?"

But T'ien Ken repeated his question. The Nameless Man said, "Let your mind wander in simplicity, blend your spirit with the vastness, follow along with things the way they are, and make no room for personal views—then the world will be governed." . . .

Do not be an embodier of fame; do not be a storehouse of schemes; do not be an undertaker of projects; do not be a proprietor of wisdom. Embody to the fullest what has no end and wander where there is no trail. Hold on to all that you have received from Heaven but do not think you have gotten anything. Be empty, that is all. The Perfect Man uses his mind like a mirror—going after nothing, welcoming nothing, responding but not storing. Therefore he can win out over things and not hurt himself. . . .

Autumn Floods

. . . Chuang Tzu and Hui Tzu were strolling along the dam of the Hao River when Chuang Tzu said, "See how the minnows come out and dart around where they please! That's what fish really enjoy!"

Hui Tzu said, "You're not a fish—how do you know what fish enjoy?"

Chuang Tzu said, "You're not I, so how do you know I don't know what fish enjoy?"

Hui Tzu said, "I'm not you, so I certainly don't know what you know. On the other hand, you're certainly not a fish—so that still proves you don't know what fish enjoy!"

Chuang Tzu said, "Let's go back to your original question, please. You asked me *how* I know what fish enjoy—so you already knew I knew it when you asked the question. I know it by standing here beside the Hao."

Supreme Happiness

Is there such a thing as supreme happiness in the world or isn't there? Is there some way to keep yourself alive or isn't there? What to do, what to rely on, what to avoid, what to stick by, what to follow, what to leave alone, what to find happiness in, what to hate?

This is what the world honors: wealth, eminence, long life, a good name. This is what the world finds happiness in: a life of ease, rich food, fine clothes, beautiful sights, sweet sounds. This is what it looks

down on: poverty, meanness, early death, a bad name. This is what is finds bitter: a life that knows no rest, a mouth that gets no rich food, no fine clothes for the body, no beautiful sights for the eye, no sweet sounds for the ear.

People who can't get these things fret a great deal and are afraid—this is a stupid way to treat the body. People who are rich wear themselves out rushing around on business, piling up more wealth than they could ever use—this is a superficial way to treat the body. People who are eminent spend night and day scheming and wondering if they are doing right—this is a shoddy way to treat the body. Man lives his life in company with worry, and if he lives a long while, till he's dull and doddering, then he has spent that much time worrying instead of dying, a bitter lot indeed! This is a callous way to treat the body.

Men of ardor are regarded by the world as good, but their goodness doesn't succeed in keeping them alive. So I don't know whether their goodness is really good or not. Perhaps I think it's good—but not good enough to save their lives. Perhaps I think it's no good—but still good enough to save the lives of others. So I say, if your loyal advice isn't heeded, give way and do not wrangle. Tzu-hsü wrangled and lost his body. But if he hadn't wrangled, he wouldn't have made a name. Is there really such a thing as goodness or isn't there?

What ordinary people do and what they find happiness in—I don't know whether such happiness is in the end really happiness or not. I look at what ordinary people find happiness in, what they all make a mad dash for, racing around as though they couldn't stop—they all say they're happy with it. I'm not happy with it and I'm not unhappy with it. In the end is there really happiness or isn't there?

I take inaction to be true happiness, but ordinary people think it is a bitter thing. I say: the highest happiness has no happiness, the highest praise has no praise. The world can't decide what is right and what is wrong. And yet inaction can decide this. The highest happiness, keeping alive—only inaction gets you close to this!

Let me try putting it this way. The inaction of Heaven is its purity, the inaction of earth is its peace. So the two inactions combine and all things are transformed and brought to birth. Wonderfully, mysteriously, there is no place they come out of. Mysteriously, wonderfully, they have no sign. Each thing minds its business and all grow up out of inaction. So I say, Heaven and earth do nothing and there is nothing that is not done. Among men, who can get hold of this inaction? . . .

Mastering Life

He who has mastered the true nature of life does not labor over what life cannot do. He who has mastered the true nature of fate does not labor over what knowledge cannot change. He who wants to nourish his body must first of all turn to things. And yet it is possible to have more than enough things and for the body still to go unnourished. He who has life must first of all see to it that it does not leave the body. And yet it is possible for life never to leave the body and still fail to be preserved. The coming of life cannot be fended off, its departure cannot be stopped. How pitiful the men of the world, who think that simply nourishing the body is enough to preserve life! Then why is what the world does worth doing? It may not be worth doing, and yet it cannot be left undone—this is unavoidable.

He who wants to avoid doing anything for his body had best abandon the world. By abandoning the world, he can be without entanglements. Being without entanglements, he can be upright and calm. Being upright and calm, he can be born again with others. Being born again, he can come close [to the Way].

But why is abandoning the affairs of the world worthwhile, and why is forgetting life worthwhile? If you abandon the affairs of the world, your body will be without toil. If you forget life, your vitality will be unimpaired. With your body complete and your vitality made whole again, you may become one with Heaven. Heaven and earth are the father and mother of the ten thousand things. They join to become a body; they part to become a beginning. When the body and vitality are without flaw, this is called being able to shift. Vitality added to vitality, you return to become the Helper of Heaven.

Master Lieh Tzu said to the Barrier Keeper Yin, "The Perfect Man can walk under water without choking, can tread on fire without being burned, and can travel above the ten thousand things without being frightened. May I ask how he manages this?"

The Barrier Keeper Yin replied, "This is because he guards the pure breath—it has nothing to do with wisdom, skill, determination, or courage. Sit down and I will tell you about it. All that have faces, forms, voices, colors—these are all mere things. How could one thing and another thing be far removed from each other? And how could any of them be capable of leading you to what preceded them? They are forms, colors—nothing more. But that which creates things has no form, and it rests where there is no change. If a man can get hold of *this* and exhaust it fully, then

how can things stand in his way? He may rest within the bounds that know no excess, hide within the borders that know no source, wander where the ten thousand things have their end and beginning, unify his nature, nourish his breath, unite his virtue, and thereby communicate with that which creates all things. A man like this guards what belongs to Heaven and keeps it whole. His spirit has no flaw, so how can things enter in and get at him?

"When a drunken man falls from a carriage, though the carriage may be going very fast, he won't be killed. He has bones and joints the same as other men, and yet he is not injured as they would be, because his spirit is whole. He didn't know he was riding, and he doesn't know he has fallen out. Life and death, alarm and terror do not enter his breast, and so he can bang against things without fear of injury. If he can keep himself whole like this by means of wine, how much more can he keep himself whole by means of Heaven! The sage hides himself in Heaven—hence there is nothing that can do him harm.

"A man seeking revenge does not go so far as to smash the sword of his enemy; a man, no matter how hot-tempered, does not rail at the tile that happens to fall on him. To know that all things in the world are equal and the same—this is the only way to eliminate the chaos of attack and battle and the harshness of punishment and execution!

"Do not try to develop what is natural to man; develop what is natural to Heaven. He who develops Heaven benefits life; he who develops man injures life. Do not reject what is of Heaven, do not neglect what is of man, and the people will be close to the attainment of Truth." . . .

Confucius was seeing the sights at Lü-liang, where the water falls from a height of thirty fathoms and races and boils along for forty li, so swift that no fish or other water creature can swim in it. He saw a man dive into the water and, supposing that the man was in some kind of trouble and intended to end his life, he ordered his disciples to line up on the bank and pull the man out. But after the man had gone a couple of hundred paces, he came out of the water and began strolling along the base of the embankment, his hair streaming down, singing a song. Confucius ran after him and said, "At first I thought you were a ghost, but now I see you're a man. May I ask if you have some special way of staying afloat in the water?"

"I have no way. I began with what I was used to, grew up with my nature, and let things come to completion with fate. I go under with the swirls and come out with the eddies, following along the way the water goes and never thinking about myself. That's how I can stay afloat."

Confucius said, "What do you mean by saying that you began with what you were used to, grew up with your nature, and let things come to completion with fate?"

"I was born on the dry land and felt safe on the dry land—that was what I was used to. I grew up with the water and felt safe in the water—that was my nature. I don't know why I do what I do—that's fate."

Woodworker Ch'ing carved a piece of wood and made a bell stand, and when it was finished, everyone who saw it marveled, for it seemed to be the work of gods or spirits. When the marquis of Lu saw it, he asked, "What art is it you have?"

Ch'ing replied, "I am only a craftsman—how would I have any art? There is one thing, however. When I am going to make a bell stand, I never let it wear out my energy. I always fast in order to still my mind. When I have fasted for three days, I no longer have any thought of congratulations or rewards, of titles or stipends. When I have fasted for five days, I no longer have any thought of praise or blame, of skill or clumsiness. And when I have fasted for seven days, I am so still that I forget I have four limbs and a form and body. By that time, the ruler and his court no longer exist for me. My skill is concentrated and all outside distractions fade away. After that, I go into the mountain forest and examine the Heavenly nature of the trees. If I find one of superlative form, and I can see a bell stand there, I put my hand to the job of carving; if not, I let it go. This way I am simply matching up 'Heaven' with 'Heaven.'[8] That's probably the reason that people wonder if the results were not made by spirits." . . .

[8] That is, matching up his own innate nature with that of the tree.
[9] A Daoist term for the mind.

Artisan Ch'ui could draw as true as a compass or a T square because his fingers changed along with things and he didn't let his mind get in the way. Therefore his Spirit Tower[9] remained unified and unobstructed.

You forget your feet when the shoes are comfortable. You forget your waist when the belt is comfortable. Understanding forgets right and wrong when the mind is comfortable. There is no change in what is inside, no following what is outside, when the adjustment to events is comfortable. You begin with what is comfortable and never experience what is uncomfortable when you know the comfort of forgetting what is comfortable. . . .

External Things

. . . Hui Tzu said to Chuang Tzu, "Your words are useless!"

Chuang Tzu said, "A man has to understand the useless before you can talk to him about the useful. The earth is certainly vast and broad, though a man uses no more of it than the area he puts his feet on. If, however, you were to dig away all the earth from around his feet until you reached the Yellow Springs,[10] then would the man still be able to make use of it?"

"No, it would be useless," said Hui Tzu.

"It is obvious, then," said Chuang Tzu, "that the useless has its use." . . .

"The fish trap exists because of the fish; once you've gotten the fish, you can forget the trap. The rabbit snare exists because of the rabbit; once you've gotten the rabbit, you can forget the snare. Words exist because of the meaning; once you've gotten the meaning, you can forget the words. Where can I find a man who has forgotten words so I can have a word with him?"

[10] The underworld.

Discussion and Reflection Questions

1. *Dao:* Describe the Dao. If you cannot give an adequate description of it, does this mean that there is no such thing, or that the concept of Dao is not useful? The Dao often sounds like a mystical concept, yet many recent books have made a connection between Dao and what at first appears to be a most unlikely ally: modern science. Why might some find a comfortable home for the concept of Dao in the context of modern science (e.g., cosmology)?

2. *Yin-yang—harmony of opposites:* How are the principles of yin and yang manifested in your life? What aspects of your life (or of *you*) have a yin nature? Which ones have a yang nature? How might emphasizing the contrary principle make your life more harmonious?

3. *Relativity:* Daoism seems to suggest that all values are relative to specific situations. For example, obviously something is "useful" only if someone has a use for it in a particular situation. Are all values relative in this way? What might be an objection to this view? What are the benefits of being aware of the relativity of many values?

4. *Natural way—nonaction:* Daoism counsels *wu wei* (nonaction) as the appropriate response to the challenges and difficulties of life. Suppose that you were approached by someone brandishing a gun and demanding that you hand over your wallet or purse. What would the doctrine of *wu wei* suggest that you do in this situation? Are there situations in which adopting the doctrine of *wu wei* would be a wise thing to do? Does this doctrine recommend a "passive" approach to life? What are the strengths and weaknesses of this doctrine?

Suggestions for Further Reading

Wing-tsit Chan, ed., *A Sourcebook in Chinese Philosophy* (Princeton: Princeton University Press, 1963), is an invaluable resource for Chinese philosophical traditions. Robert E. Allison, ed., *Understanding the Chinese Mind: The Philosophical Roots* (New York: Oxford University Press, 1989), discusses both Confucianism and Daoism. D. C. Lau provides valuable historical information on the *Dao De Ching* in the introduction to his translation of that work (New York: Penguin Books, 1963). *What is Taoism? And Other Studies in Chinese Cultural History*, edited by Herrlee G. Creel (Chicago, Ill.: The University of Chicago Press, 1970) provides some of the cultural context of Daoism. Kuang-ming Wu, *Chuang Tzu: World Philosopher at Play* (New York: Crossroad Publishing Co., 1982), is a book-length exploration of the thought of Chuang Tzu. Additional essays may be found in *Studies in Chinese Philosophy and Philosophical Literature*, edited by Angus Charles Graham (Albany: State University of New York Press, 1990), and in *Lao-tzu and the Tao-te-ching*, edited by Livia Kohn and Michael LaFargue (Albany: State University of New York Press, 1998). Alan Fox, "Reflex and Reflectivity: *Wuwei* in the *Zhuangzi*," *Asian Philosophy* 6 (1996): 59–73, is a study of a central concept in Daoism. The identification and discussion of the five central concepts of Daoism above are indebted to the discussion in S. A. Nigosian, *World Faiths*, 2nd ed. (New York: St. Martin's Press, 1994). This book provides a good overview of the other Eastern traditions discussed as well. A brief and very readable introduction to Daoist ethics is provided in the article "Classical Chinese Ethics," by Chad Hansen, in *A Companion to Ethics*, edited by Peter Singer (Oxford: Blackwell, 1991), pp. 69–81. See also his book, *A Daoist Theory of Chinese Thought: A Philosophical Interpretation* (New York: Oxford University Press, 1992). Christopher Cleary, "Ancient Chinese Ethics," and Terry F. Kleeman, "Taoist Ethics," both in *A Bibliographic Guide to the Comparative Study of Ethics*, edited by John Carmen (New York: Cambridge University Press, 1991), provide useful references for further study. A scholarly treatment of the various schools of philosophy in ancient China, including Confucianism and Daoism, is Angus Charles Graham, *Disputers of the Tao: Philosophical Argument in Ancient China* (LaSalle, Ill.: Open Court, 1989). Lisa Ann Raphals, *Knowing Words: Wisdom and Cunning in the Classical Traditions of China and Greece* (Ithaca, N.Y.: Cornell University Press, 1992), provides a fascinating cross-cultural comparison of two of the traditions discussed in this text.

InfoTrac

Daoism, yin-yang, wu-wei, nonaction, "harmony and life", holism, mind-body

Chapter 7

Hinduism

Introduction: Spirituality, Freedom, and the Conduct of Life

Hinduism may well be the oldest continuous philosophical tradition in the world, with roots extending back to about 2500 B.C.E. It would be difficult to exaggerate the importance of Hinduism for the development and present state of Indian culture. Yet Hinduism is not a monolithic religion. What may be most striking (and perplexing) to non-Hindus is the diversity of beliefs it includes. This is only to be expected given the length of time it has been developing. Yet despite the diversity of philosophical perspectives developed in India's long history, four central themes may be identified.

Foremost among these is the emphasis on the spiritual aspect of life. Human beings, and indeed the universe as a whole, are essentially spiritual in nature, and philosophy, no less than religion, is concerned with understanding and directing us to our spiritual destinies. In this sense philosophy and religion are intimately related. Second, in Indian thought, philosophy is seen as directly relevant to the conduct of life, focusing on the tragic problems of life and seeking the truth in order to solve them. The goal is not simply to know the truth, but rather to become one with it and thereby to achieve release (*moksa*, liberation or freedom), the supreme goal of human life. Third, Indian philosophy is characterized by an introspective approach to truth and reality, and emphasis is placed on the subjective inner life of human beings, rather than on the nature of the external world. Accordingly, psychology and ethics are given greater attention than natural science. Finally, and related to what has been said above, Indian philosophical thought accepts intuition as the favored method through which the ultimate nature of reality can be known. Reason, on this view, is not irrelevant, but rather is viewed as insufficient. To simply know reality is not enough. One must *realize* it as well. To realize truth is to have a direct intuitive experience of it that affects one's life in a profound way.

Realizing truth is achieved primarily through the practice of nonattachment. A person who becomes committed to achieving spiritual liberation continues to live her life but refuses to become entangled in or emotionally disturbed by events or the consequences of her own actions. Such a person refuses to be enslaved by worldly values, but rather keeps her eye on the achievement of the goal of life: spiritual perfection and the liberation (and genuine happiness) it entails.

The Sacred Scriptures of Hinduism: Wisdom through the Ages

He who is satisfied with whatever comes by chance, who has passed beyond the dualities of pleasure and suffering, who is free from jealousy, who remains the same in success and failure—even when he acts, he is not bound.

—BHAGAVAD GITA

The selections included below are taken from some of the most important and influential sacred texts of India: the *Rg Veda*, the *Upanishads*, the *Bhagavad Gita*, the *Mahabharata*, and the *Laws of Manu*. The authors of these works are not emphasized; in most cases authorship is unknown. In India the philosophical texts and timeless ideas they embody have always been considered more important than the philosophers who developed or transmitted them. Because of the difficulty of some of the ideas expressed in these texts, some additional historical background information may be useful.

The earliest period of Indian thought, dating from around 2500 B.C.E. to 600 B.C.E., is called the Vedic period and represents the emergence of philosophical thinking in the context of religious concerns and themes. The *Rg Veda*, which consists of hymns on various topics, dates from this period and hence constitutes the actual beginning of Indian philosophy. The hymns included below contain some of the earliest known writings expressing the human awareness of the immensity of the universe and the inexhaustible mystery of life. (The word *veda* means "wisdom.") The cosmological hymns in the *Rg Veda* serve a purpose analogous to the discussion of the Dao in the *Dao De Jing*. Both set moral wisdom in the context of a universe that is unfathomably ancient and mysterious. The "Hymn of Creation" expresses the ultimate mystery of the universe. The "Hymn of Eternal Law" tells of the order underlying reality. The "Hymn of Right Conduct" directs people to perform their duties in accordance with the order of the universe. Correct human conduct is therefore seen as required by the very order of the universe. Although we may concentrate on morality more than metaphysics, the former is always dependent on the latter. Together these early hymns provide the foundations for the philosophical developments within Hinduism that follow.

The *Upanishads* belong to the Vedic period as well and may be considered a continuation of Vedic religious thought. The *Upanishads* are an important part of Hindu revealed literature. The word *upanishad* comes from words meaning "near," "down," and "sit." The *Upanishads* are the teachings of sages who spoke from their own enlightenment to groups of students who would sit near them to listen. They express the typical Indian tendency toward spiritualistic monism (the idea that the universe ultimately consists of just one thing, spirit) and the conviction that intuition rather than reason is the true guide to ultimate truth. The aim of the *Upanishads* is to provide knowledge as a means to achieving spiritual freedom. Of particular interest are the doctrines of Brahman and Atman—the Absolute discovered outside of us and the Absolute discovered within each of us. Enlightenment consists of realizing that the Absolute we seek is within us and *is* us.

The second period of philosophical development in India extends from about 600 B.C.E. to 200 C.E. and is known as the Epic period. This was a fertile period, during which philosophy was beginning to flourish in the West and in China as well, and during which Buddhism originated. This period is distinguished by the indirect presentation of philosophical doctrines through great epic poems. The *Bhagavad Gita* is the most famous of these epics. The *Bhagavad Gita* (or "Song of God") is a central religious classic of India. It takes its main inspiration from the *Upanishads* and develops further some of the themes introduced there. Although this is a work of both metaphysics and ethics, it is its latter role that is of primary concern to us here. Union with the Absolute is the goal of human life, to be obtained through knowledge, devotion, and work. The selections included below explain some of the means for integrating these factors and begin and end with descriptions of the perfect sage, the one who has succeeded in doing so.

The *Mahabharata* is one of the two great Indian epics (the other being the *Ramayana*) dating from the sixth century B.C.E. The *Bhagavad Gita* is actually a part of this larger work, but it is usually distinguished from it. It contains the orthodox social codes that governed life in ancient India. Parts of it can be read as a compendium of practical wisdom, providing a guide to correct living. It extols the virtues of concern to all living creatures (not just for fellow humans): truth, knowledge, righteousness, forgiveness, nonattachment, and renunciation. When acquired, these virtues lead to the attainment of lasting happiness.

The *Laws of Manu* dates from the Epic period as well. It is a treatise of religion, law, custom, and politics. According to it, there are four great aims of human life: righteousness, wealth, enjoyment, and spiritual freedom. There is a strong emphasis in this work on the importance of following society's conventions, because doing so is the most reliable means of maintaining a stable society and thereby bringing about the most good for everyone. This work is also important for clearly distinguishing the four stages of life, each with its respective duties, and the four castes of societies, each with its own appropriate modes of conduct. The selections included below end on what is by now a familiar theme: the means necessary for attaining supreme bliss.

PROFILE

Mahatma Gandhi:
The Way of Nonviolence and Truth

Mahatma Gandhi (1869–1948) was a pivotal figure in India's struggle for national independence, but his significance extends far beyond the role he played in that country's political history. In his life and thought we can see vividly displayed the practical expression of some of the highest ideals of Hindu moral thought.

"Mahatma," a name given to Gandhi by his devoted followers, literally means the "Great-Souled One." A brief sketch of his life makes clear why this title is apt. He was born in Gujarat, in western India, into a family of the merchant class, and grew up in Kathiawar. At the age of nineteen he began law studies in England. After completing his legal studies, he returned to India and began practicing law in Bombay—quite unsuccessfully. (He told of standing before a courtroom packed with people waiting to hear his case, having absolutely nothing to say, and having to tell his client that he had better find another attorney.) Upon being offered a case in Durban, Natal, South Africa, he gladly moved his law practice to that country in 1893, hoping to be more successful there. He was, and he continued to practice law there for twenty-one years. Throughout this time he was deeply concerned about the plight of Indians in South Africa. The treatment of Indian workers there especially appalled him, and he subsequently led a movement to have laws established to protect their rights. It was during this time that he worked out the methods of political resistance that he would later use to good effect in his fight for Indian independence from the British. Because of his success in South Africa he was famous in his native country by the time he returned there in 1915. In 1920 he became a leader of the Indian National Congress. He continued to work on behalf of independence, leading marches, conducting fasts, and employing other nonviolent means to make the authorities respond. Largely as a result of his efforts, India gained its independence in 1947. The victory was, unfortunately, marred by civil unrest: The country was in danger of being torn apart by Hindu-Muslim conflicts. Going against the stream of so many around him, Gandhi advocated respect for religious diversity. While leading a prayer meeting in New Delhi in 1948, he was assassinated by a fanatical Hindu nationalist who resented Gandhi's kindness toward Muslims.

In his autobiography, entitled *The Story of My Experiments with Truth,* Gandhi says that his entire life consisted of nothing but a series of "experiments with truth." Early in life, he tells us, while still a teen, "one thing took deep root in me—the conviction that morality is the basis of things and that truth is the substance of morality. Truth became my sole objective. . . . A Gujarati stanza likewise gripped my mind and heart. Its precept—return good for evil—became my guiding principle." He states that all of his actions after that were devoted toward one end: to see the Truth, and thereby to achieve salvation, self-realization, liberation. But to do so requires practicing love toward all things. "To see the universal and all-pervading Spirit of Truth face to face one must be able to love the meanest of creation as oneself."

To understand how to do this, Gandhi turned to that part of Hindu scripture that most fascinated him: the *Bhagavad Gita.* "To me the *Gita* became an infallible guide of conduct. . . . Just as I turned to the English dictionary for the meanings of English words that I did not understand, I turned to this dictionary of conduct for a ready solution of all my troubles and trials." One of the doctrines that struck him most forcefully was that of nonattachment or nonpossession. "I understood the *Gita* teaching of non-possession to mean that those who desired Salvation should act like the trustee who, though having control over great possessions, regards not an iota of them as his own." He then details his struggle to overcome the lure of possessions. "It was painful in the beginning. But as days went by I saw I had to throw overboard many other things which I used to consider as mine, and a time came when it became a matter of positive joy to give up those things. . . . One after another, then by almost geometric progression, things slipped away from me." In virtue of this effort he was rewarded with a sense of release and freedom. "A great burden fell off my shoulders, and I felt I could now walk with ease and do my work also in the service of my fellow men with great comfort and still greater joy. The possession of anything then became a troublesome thing and a burden." This personal freedom then became a freedom to serve others. "We thus arrive at the idea of total renunciation and learn to use the body for the purposes of service so long as it exists, so much so that service, and not bread, becomes with us the staff of life. We eat and drink, sleep and awake, for service alone. Such an attitude of mind brings us real happiness."

Although committed to the ideals of nonattachment, Gandhi was no hermit or recluse. His life of service took a political form through his efforts to gain independence for India. He believed that the most powerful weapon against oppression was the Hindu notion of *ahimsa*. *Ahimsa* means more than nonviolence. Its literal meaning is "not to injure or harm in any way." This extends not just to actions but also to attitudes, including the attitude of nonhatred. So in practicing nonviolence, a person's motives must be pure: You cannot use nonviolence against oppression if in your heart you hate your oppressors. Genuine love for one's enemies, Gandhi believed, effects a moral change in the enemies' hearts, such that they voluntarily do what is morally right. A person who engages in nonviolence "seeks to convert his opponent by sheer force of character and suffering. The purer he is and the more he suffers, the quicker the progress." Genuine *ahimsa* extends to all people, and indeed to all creatures. Although rooted in traditional Hindu texts, it is not bound by conventional distinctions. It is flexible and must be adapted to each unique situation. In this way the traditional Hindu ideas and ideals become a living force for good. In Gandhi's life and work we see how powerful such ideals can be.

Reading Questions

1. *Upanishads:* How do the *Upanishads* distinguish between what is *better* and what is more *pleasant*? Which one does the wise person choose, and why? How is true enlightenment to be realized? Is intelligence (in the sense of logical reasoning) important for this? How is the highest state of consciousness described? According to the *Upanishads*, what would realizing such a state be like? What sort of character is being encouraged in the "Practical Precepts to a Student"? How should a serious student behave?

2. *Bhagavad Gita:* How is the perfect sage described? What are his most important characteristics? How should one approach work? Is work to be avoided or actively pursued? What sort of attitude should a person have toward work, and toward the fruits of one's work? How is inner peace to be achieved? How does work contribute to the attainment of this state? In what way is inner peace a function of one's attitude toward pleasure and suffering?

3. *Mahabharata:* Are the principles of conduct expressed in the *Mahabharata* given as divine commandments, rigid and admitting of no exceptions, or as flexible guides to living well that need to be adjusted to particular circumstances? In what ways are the consequences of actions to be taken into account in determining the value of those actions? According to this text, if truth and positive benefits come into conflict, which should take precedence?

4. *Laws of Manu:* According to the *Laws of Manu*, which is considered more important in judging the morality of an action: the disposition of the person who produced the action or the consequences of the action itself? Why? What examples are given of actions that are to be avoided? What sort of reward (or punishment) is described as resulting from the character of a person's life? How is "supreme bliss" to be achieved?

Creation, Eternal Law, and Right Conduct

FROM THE *RG VEDA*

Hymn of Creation[1]

Nonbeing then existed not nor being:
There was no air, nor sky that is beyond it.
What was concealed? Wherein? In whose protection?
And was there deep unfathomable water?

Death then existed not nor life immortal;
Of neither night nor day was any token.
By its inherent force the One breathed windless:
No other thing than that beyond existed.

Darkness there was at first by darkness hidden;
Without distinctive marks, this all was water.
That which, becoming, by the void was covered,
That One by force of heat came into being.

Desire entered the One in the beginning:
It was the earliest seed, of thought the product.
The sages searching in their hearts with wisdom,
Found out the bond of being in nonbeing.

Their ray extended light across the darkness:
But was the One above or was it under?
Creative force was there, and fertile power:
Below was energy, above was impulse.

Who knows for certain? Who shall here declare it?
Whence was it born, and whence came this creation?
The gods were born after this world's creation:
Then who can know from whence it has arisen?

None knoweth whence creation has arisen;
And whether he has or has not produced it:
He who surveys it in the highest heaven,
He only knows, or haply he may know not.

Hymn of Eternal Law[2]

Eternal Law [Rta] hath varied food that strengthens;
    thought of eternal law removes transgressions.
The praise-hymn of eternal law, arousing, glowing,
    hath oped the deaf ears of the living.

Firm-seated are eternal law's foundations; in its fair
    form are many splendid beauties.
By holy law long lasting food they bring us; by holy
    law have cows come to our worship.

Fixing eternal law he [Indra], too, upholds it: swift
    moves the might of law and wins the booty.
To law belong the vast deep earth and heaven:
    milch-kine supreme, to law their milk they
    render.

From fervor kindled to its height Eternal Law and
    Truth were born:
Thence was the night produced, and thence the
    billowy flood of sea arose.

From that same billowy flood of sea the year was
    afterward produced,
Ordainer of the days, nights, Lord over all who close
    the eye.

Dhātar, the great creator, then formed in due order
    sun and moon.
He formed in order heaven and earth, the regions of
    the air, and light.

Mitra and Varuna, through Law, lovers and
    cherishers of Law,
Have ye obtained your mighty power.

Firm is this new-wrought hymn of praise, and meet
    to be told forth, O gods.
The flowing of the floods is Law, Truth is the sun's
    extended light. Mark this my woe, ye earth and
    heaven.

That pathway of the sun in heaven, made to be
    highly glorified,
Is not to be transgressed, O gods. O mortals, ye
    behold it not. Mark this my woe, ye earth and
    heaven. . . .

. . . The far-refulgent mornings make apparent the
    lovely treasures which the darkness covered.

The one departeth and the other cometh; unlike in
    hue, day's halves march on successive.
One hides the gloom of the surrounding parents.
    Dawn on her shining chariot is resplendent.

The same in form today, the same tomorrow, they
    still keep Varuna's eternal statute. . . .

[1]"The Hymn of Creation," in *Hymns from the Rigveda*, translated by A. A. Macdonell (London: Oxford University Press, 1922), pp. 19–20.
[2]"The Hymn of Eternal Law," in *The Hymn of the Rigveda*, 2 vols., 3rd ed., translated by R. T. H. Griffith (Benares: E. J. Lazarus and Co., 1920–1926), pp. 25–27.

. . . The maiden breaketh not the law of Order, day by day coming to the place appointed.

Obedient to the reign of Law Eternal give us each thought that more and more shall bless us. . . .

Hymn of Right Conduct[3]

The gods inflict not hunger as a means to kill:
Death frequently befalls even satiated men.
The charitable giver's wealth melts not away;
The niggard never finds a man to pity him.

Who, of abundant food possessed, makes hard his heart
Toward a needy and decrepit suppliant
Whom once he courted, come to pray to him for bread:
A man like this as well finds none to pity him.

[3]"The Hymn of Right Conduct," in *Hymns from the Rigveda*, translated by A. A. Macdonell (London: Oxford University Press, 1922) pp. 92–93.

He is the liberal man who helps the beggar
That, craving food, emaciated wanders,
And coming to his aid, when asked to succour,
Immediately makes him a friend hereafter.

He is no friend who gives not of his substance
To his devoted, intimate companion:
This friend should turn from him—here is no haven—
And seek a stranger elsewhere as a helper.

The wealthier man should give unto the needy,
Considering the course of life hereafter;
For riches are like chariot wheels revolving:
Now to one man they come, now to another.

The foolish man from food has no advantage;
In truth I say: it is but his undoing;
No friend he ever fosters, no companion:
He eats alone, and he alone is guilty.

The plow that cleaves the soil produces nurture;
He that bestirs his feet completes his journey.
The speaking *brāhmin* earns more than the silent;
A friend who gives is better than the niggard. . . .

The Nature of the Self and the Way to Brahman

FROM THE *UPANISHADS*

The Failure of Pleasure and of Ignorance; the Wisdom of the Better Knowledge

The better is one thing, and the pleasanter quite another.
Both these, of different aim, bind a person.
Of these two, well it is for him who takes the better;
He fails of his aim who chooses the pleasanter.

Both the better and the pleasanter come to a man.
Going all around the two, the wise man discriminates.
The wise man chooses the better, indeed, rather than the pleasanter.
The stupid man, from getting-and-keeping, chooses the pleasanter.

Thou indeed, upon the pleasant and pleasantly appearing desires
Meditating, has let them go, O Naciketas.

Thou are not one who has taken that garland of wealth
In which many men sink down.

Widely opposite and asunder are these two:
Ignorance and what is known as "knowledge."
I think Naciketas desirous of obtaining knowledge!
Many desires rend thee not.

Those abiding in the midst of ignorance,
Self-wise, thinking themselves learned,
Running hither and thither, go around deluded,
Like blind men led by one who is himself blind.

The Eternal Indestructible Self

The wise one [i.e., the *Ātman*, the Self] is not born, nor dies.
This one has not come from anywhere, has not become anyone.

The Thirteen Principal Upanishads, translated by R. E. Hume (London: Oxford University Press, 1921).

Unborn, constant, eternal, primeval, this one
Is not slain when the body is slain.

If the slayer think to slay,
If the slain think himself slain,
Both these understand not.
This one slays not, nor is slain.

More minute than the minute, greater than the great,
Is the Self that is set in the heart of a creature here.
One who is without the active will beholds Him, and
    becomes freed from sorrow—
When through the grace of the Creator he beholds
    the greatness of the Self.

Him who is the bodiless among bodies,
Stable among the unstable,
The great, all-pervading Self—
On recognizing Him, the wise man sorrows not.

This Self is not to be obtained by instruction,
Nor by intellect, nor by much learning.
He is to be obtained only by the one whom he
    chooses;
To such a one that Self reveals his own person.

Not he who has not ceased from bad conduct,
Not he who is not tranquil, not he who is not
    composed,
Not he who is not of peaceful mind
Can obtain Him by intelligence.

He for whom the priesthood and the nobility
Both are as food,
And death is as a sauce—
Who really knows where He is?

Higher than the senses are the objects of sense.
Higher than the objects of sense is the mind;
And higher than the mind is the intellect.
Higher than the intellect is the Great Self (*Ātman*).

Higher than the Great is the Unmanifest.
Higher than the Unmanifest is the Person.
Higher than the Person there is nothing at all.
That is the goal. That is the highest course.

Though He is hidden in all things,
That Self shines not forth.
But He is seen by subtle seers
With superior, subtle intellect.

An intelligent man should suppress his speech and
    his mind.
The latter he should suppress in the Understanding-
    Self (*jñana ātman*).
The understanding he should suppress in the Great
    Self.
That he should suppress in the Tranquil Self. . . .

Arise ye! Awake ye!
Obtain your boons and understand them!
A sharpened edge of a razor, hard to traverse,
A difficult path is this—poets declare!

What is soundless, touchless, formless,
    imperishable,
Likewise tasteless, constant, odorless,
Without beginning, without end, higher than the
    great, stable—
By discerning That, one is liberated from the mouth
    of death.

The Universal and the Individual Self

Know thou the self (*ātman*) as riding in a chariot,
The body as the chariot.
Know thou the intellect (*buddhi*) as the chariot-driver,
And the mind as the reins.

The senses, they say, are the horses;
The objects of sense, what they range over.
The self combined with senses and mind
Wise men call "the enjoyer."

He, however, who has not understanding,
Who is unmindful and ever impure,
Reaches not the goal,
But goes on to transmigration [rebirth].

He, however, who has understanding,
Who is mindful and ever pure,
Reaches the goal
From which he is born no more. . . .

The Immortal Self Not to Be Sought by Outward Knowledge

The Self-existent pierced the openings [of the senses]
    outward;
Therefore one looks outward, not within himself.
A certain wise man, while seeking immortality,
Introspectively beheld the Self face to face.

The childish go after outward pleasures;
They walk into the net of widespread death.
But the wise, knowing immortality,
Seek not the stable among things which are unstable
    here.

That by which [one discerns] form, taste, smell,
Sound, and mutual touches—
It is with That indeed that one discerns.
What is there left over here!
This, verily, is That!

By recognizing as the great pervading Self
That whereby one perceives both
The sleeping state and the waking state,
The wise man sorrows not.

Whatever is here, that is there.
What is there, that again is here.
He obtains death after death
Who seems to see a difference here.

By the mind, indeed, is this [realization] to be
   attained:
There is no difference here at all!
He goes from death to death
Who seems to see a difference here.

One's Real Person (Self), the Same as the World-Ground

He who is awake in those that sleep,
The Person who fashions desire after desire—
   That indeed is the Pure. That is *Brahman.*
   That indeed is called the Immortal.
   On it all the worlds do rest;
   And no one soever goes beyond it.
This, verily, is That!

As the one fire has entered the world
And becomes corresponding in form to every form,
So the one Inner Self of all things
Is corresponding in form to every form, and yet is
   outside.

As the one wind has entered the world
And becomes corresponding in form to every form,
So the one Inner Self of all things
Is corresponding in form to every form, and yet is
   outside.

As the sun, the eye of the whole world,
Is not sullied by the external faults of the eyes,
So the one Inner Self of all things
Is not sullied by the evil in the world, being external
   to it.

The Inner Self of all things, the One Controller,
Who makes His one form manifold—
The wise who perceive Him as standing in oneself,
They, and no others, have eternal happiness!

The World-Tree Rooted in Brahman [Ways to Brahman]

Its root is above, its branches below—
This eternal fig-tree!
That (root) indeed is the Pure. That is *Brahman.*

That indeed is called the Immortal.
On it all the worlds do rest,
And no one soever goes beyond it.
This, verily, is That!

This whole world, whatever there is,
Was created from and moves in Life.
The great fear, the upraised thunderbolt—
They who know That, become immortal.

From fear of Him fire doth burn.
From fear the sun gives forth heat.
From fear both Indra and Wind,
And Death as fifth, do speed along. . . .

The separate nature of the senses,
And that their arising and setting
Is of things that come into being apart [from
   himself],
The wise man recognizes, and sorrows not.

His form is not to be beheld.
No one soever sees Him with the eye.
He is framed by the heart, by the thought, by the
   mind.
They who know That become immortal.

When cease the five
[Sense-] knowledges, together with the mind,
And the intellect stirs not—
That, they say, is the highest course.

This they consider as *yoga*—
The firm holding back of the senses.
Then one becomes undistracted.
Yoga, truly, is the origin and the end.

Not by speech, not by mind,
Not by sight can He be apprehended.
How can He be comprehended
Otherwise than by one's saying "He is"?. . .

He can indeed be comprehended by the thought
   "He is"
And by [admitting] the real nature of both [his
   comprehensibility and his incomprehensibility].
When He has been comprehended by the thought
   "He is"
His real nature manifests itself.

When are liberated all
The desires that lodge in one's heart,
Then a mortal becomes immortal!
Therein he reaches *Brahman!*

When are cut all
The knots of the heart here on earth,
Then a mortal becomes immortal!
—Thus far is the instruction.

The Doctrine of Brahman-Ātman

This is the truth:
As, from a well-blazing fire, sparks
By the thousand issue forth of like form,
So from the Imperishable, my friend, beings mani-
    fold
Are produced, and thither also go.

Heavenly, formless is the Person.
He is without and within, unborn,
Breathless, mindless, pure,
Higher than the high Imperishable.

From Him is produced breath,
Mind, and all the senses,
Space, wind, light, water,
And earth, the supporter of all.

Fire is His head; His eyes, the moon and sun;
The regions of space, His ears; His voice, the
    revealed Vedas;
Wind, His breath; His heart, the whole world. Out of
    His feet,
The earth. Truly, He is the Inner Self *(Ātman)* of all.

From him [proceeds] fire, whose fuel is the sun;
From the moon, rain; herbs, on the earth.
The male pours seed in the female.
Many creatures are produced from the Person.

From Him, too, gods are manifoldly produced,
The celestials, men, cattle, birds,
The in-breath and the out-breath, rice and barley,
    austerity,
Faith, truth, chastity, and the law.

The Person himself is everything here;
Work and austerity and *Brahman*, beyond death.
He who knows That, set in the secret place [of the
    heart]—
He here on earth, my friend, rends asunder the knot
    of ignorance.

The All-Inclusive Brahman

Manifest, [yet] hidden; called "Moving-in-secret";
The great abode! Therein is placed that
    Which moves and breathes and winks.
    What that is, know as Being and Nonbeing,
As the object of desire, higher than understanding,
As what is the best of creatures!

That which is flaming, which is subtler than the
    subtle,
On which the worlds are set, and their inhabitants,
    That is the imperishable *Brahman*.

It is life, and It is speech and mind.
That is the real. It is immortal.
It is [a mark] to be penetrated. Penetrate It, my
    friend!

Taking as a bow the great weapon of the *Upanishad*,
One should put upon it an arrow sharpened by
    meditation.
Stretching it with a thought directed to the essence
    of That,
Penetrate that Imperishable as the mark, my friend.

The mystic syllable *Om* is the bow. The arrow is the
    Self *(Ātman)*.
Brahman is said to be the mark.
By the undistracted man is It to be penetrated.
One should come to be in It, as the arrow [in the
    mark].

In the highest golden sheath
Is *Brahman*, without stain, without parts.
Brilliant is It, the light of lights—
That which knowers of the Self *(Ātman)* do know!

The Way to Brahman

Two birds, fast bound companions,
Clasp close the self-same tree.
Of these two, the one eats sweet fruit;
The other looks on without eating.

On the self-same tree a person, sunken,
Grieves for his impotence, deluded;
When he sees the other, the Lord, contented,
And his greatness, he becomes freed from sorrow.

When a seer sees the brilliant
Maker, Lord, Person, the *Brahman*-source,
Then, being a knower, shaking off good and evil,
Stainless, he attains supreme identity [with Him].

This Self *(Ātman)* is obtainable by truth, by austerity,
By proper knowledge, by the student's life of
    chastity constantly [practiced].
Within the body, consisting of light, pure is He
Whom the ascetics, with imperfections done away,
    behold.

Not by sight is It grasped, not even by speech,
Not by any other sense-organs, austerity, or work.
By the peace of knowledge, one's nature purified—
In that way, however, by meditating, one does
    behold Him who is without parts.

. . . They who, being without desire, worship the
    Person
And are wise, pass beyond the see [of rebirth] here.

He who in fancy forms desires,
Because of his desires is born [again] here and there.
But of him whose desire is satisfied, who is a
    perfected self,
All desires even here on earth vanish away.

This Self (*Ātman*) is not to be obtained by
    instruction,
Nor by intellect, nor by much learning.
He is to be obtained only by the one whom He
    chooses;
To such a one that Self reveals His own person.

This Self is not to be obtained by one destitute of
    fortitude,
Nor through heedlessness, nor through a false
    notion of austerity.
But he who strives by these means, provided he
    knows—
Into his *Brahman*-abode this Self enters.

Attaining Him, the seers who are satisfied with
    knowledge,
Who are perfected selves, from passion free,
    tranquil—
Attaining Him who is the universally omnipresent,
    those wise,
Devout selves into the All itself do enter.

Gone are the fifteen parts according to their station,
Even all the sense-organs in their corresponding
    divinities!
One's deeds and the self that consists of under-
    standing—
All become unified in the supreme Imperishable.

As the flowing rivers in the ocean
Disappear, quitting name and form,
So the knower, being liberated from name and form,
Goes unto the Heavenly Person, higher than the
    high.

He, verily, who knows that supreme *Brahman*,
    becomes very *Brahman*. . . .

Practical Precepts to a Student

Having taught the Veda, a teacher further instructs a
    pupil:—

Speak the truth.
Practice virtue (*dharma*).
Neglect not study of the Vedas.
Having brought an acceptable gift to the teacher, cut
    not off the line of progeny.
One should not be negligent of truth.
One should not be negligent of virtue.
One should not be negligent of welfare.
One should not be negligent of prosperity.
One should not be negligent of study and teaching.
One should not be negligent of duties to the gods
    and to the fathers.
Be one to whom a mother is as a god.
Be one to whom a father is as a god.
Be one to whom a teacher is as a god.
Be one to whom a guest is as a god.
Those acts which are irreproachable should be
    practiced, and no others.
Those things which among us are good deeds
    should be revered by you, and no others.
Whatever *brāhmins* there are who are superior to us,
    should be comforted [or refreshed] by you with a
    seat.
One should give with faith.
One should not give without faith.
One should give with plenty.
One should give with modesty.
One should give with fear.
One should give with sympathy.
Now, if you should have doubt concerning an act, or
    doubt concerning conduct, if there should be
    there *brāhmins* competent to judge, apt, devoted,
    not harsh, lovers of virtue—as they may behave
    themselves in such a case, so should you behave
    yourself in such a case.
Now, with regard to [people] spoken against, if there
    should be there *brāhmins* competent to judge, apt,
    devoted, not harsh, lovers of virtue—as they may
    behave themselves with regard to such, so should
    you behave yourself with regard to such.
This is the teaching. This is the admonition. This is
    the mystic doctrine of the Veda (*veda-upaniṣad*).
    This is the instruction. Thus should one worship.
    Thus, indeed, should one worship.

Work, Nonattachment, and Wisdom

FROM THE *BHAGAVAD GITA*

Work without Concern for the Results

To action alone hast thou a right and never at all to its fruit; let not the fruits of action be thy motive; neither let there be in thee any attachment to inaction.

Fixed in *yoga*, do thy work, O winner of wealth (Arjuna), abandoning attachment, with an even mind in success and failure, for evenness of mind is called *yoga*.

Far inferior indeed is mere action to the discipline of intelligence, O winner of wealth (Arjuna); seek refuge in intelligence. Pitiful are those who seek for the fruits of their action.

One who has yoked his intelligence [with the Divine] (or is established in his intelligence) casts away even here both good and evil. Therefore strive for *yoga*; *yoga* is skill in action.

The wise who have united their intelligence [with the Divine], renouncing the fruits which their action yields and freed from the bonds of birth, reach the sorrowless state.

When thine intelligence shall cross the whirl of delusion, then shalt thou become indifferent to what has been heard and what is yet to be heard.

When thine intelligence, which is bewildered by the Vedic texts, shall stand unshaken and stable in spirit (*samādhi*), then shalt thou attain to insight (*yoga*).

The Characteristics of the Perfect Sage

Arjuna said:

What is the description of the man who has this firmly founded wisdom, whose being is steadfast in spirit, O Keśava (Kṛṣṇa)? How does the man of settled intelligence speak; how does he sit; how does he walk?

The Blessed Lord said:

When a man puts away all the desires of his mind, O Pārtha (Arjuna), and when his spirit is content in itself, then is he called stable in intelligence.

He whose mind is untroubled in the midst of sorrows and is free from eager desire amid pleasures, he from whom passion, fear, and rage have passed away—he is called a sage of settled intelligence.

He who is without affection on any side, who does not rejoice or loathe as he obtains good or evil—his intelligence is firmly set [in wisdom].

He who draws away the senses from the objects of sense on every side as a tortoise draws in his limbs into the shell—his intelligence is firmly set [in wisdom].

The objects of sense turn away from the embodied soul who abstains from feeding on them, but the taste for them remains. Even the taste turns away when the Supreme is seen.

Even though a man may ever strive [for perfection] and be ever so discerning, O Son of Kunti (Arjuna), his impetuous senses will carry off his mind by force.

Having brought all the senses under control, he should remain firm in *yoga*, intent on Me; for he, whose senses are under control, his intelligence is firmly set.

When a man dwells in his mind on the objects of sense, attachment to them is produced. From attachment springs desire, and from desire comes anger.

From anger arises bewilderment, from bewilderment loss of memory, and from loss of memory the destruction of intelligence; and from the destruction of intelligence he perishes.

But a man of disciplined mind, who moves among the objects of sense, with the senses under control and free from attachment and aversion—he attains purity of spirit.

And in that purity of spirit, there is produced for him an end of all sorrow; the intelligence of such a man of pure spirit is soon established [in the peace of the self].

For the uncontrolled, there is no intelligence; nor for the uncontrolled is there the power of concentration; and for him without concentration, there is no peace; and for the unpeaceful, how can there be happiness?

When the mind runs after the roving senses, it carries away the understanding, even as a wind carries away a ship on the waters.

Therefore, O Mighty-armed (Arjuna), he whose senses are all withdrawn from their objects—his intelligence is firmly set.

The Bhagavadgita, *translated by S. Radhakrishnan (New York: Harper & Row, 1948), pp. 119–192.*

What is night for all beings is the time of waking for the disciplined soul; and what is the time of waking for all beings is night for the sage who sees (or the sage of vision).

He unto whom all desires enter as waters into the sea, which, though ever being filled, is ever motionless, attains to peace, and not he who hugs his desires.

He who abandons all the desires and acts free from longing, without any sense of mineness or egotism—he attains to peace.

This is the divine state, O Pārtha (Arjuna); having attained thereto, one is not again bewildered; fixed in that state at the end [at the hour of death] one can attain to the bliss of God.

Life Is Work; Unconcern for Results Is Needful

The Blessed Lord said:

O blameless One, in this world a twofold way of life has been taught of yore by Me, the path of knowledge for men of contemplation and that of works for men of action.

Not by abstention from work does a man attain freedom from action; nor by mere renunciation does he attain to his perfection.

For no one can remain even for a moment without doing work; everyone is made to act helplessly by the impulses born of nature.

He who restrains his organs of action but continues in his mind to brood over the objects of sense, whose nature is deluded, is said to be a hypocrite [a man of false conduct].

But he who controls the senses by the mind, O Arjuna, and without attachment engages to organs of action in the path of work, he is superior.

Be Satisfied in the Self

But the man whose delight is in the Self alone, who is content with the Self, who is satisfied with the Self—for him there exists no work that needs to be done.

Similarly, in this world he has no interest whatever to gain by the actions that he has done and none to be gained by the actions that he has not done. He does not depend on all these beings for any interest of his.

Therefore, without attachment, perform always the work that has to be done, for man attains to the highest by doing work without attachment.

Set an Example to Others

It was even by works that Janaka and others attained to perfection. Thou shouldst do works also with a view to the maintenance of the world.

Whatsoever a great man does, the same is done by others as well. Whatever standard he sets, the world follows.

There is not for me, O Pārtha (Arjuna), any work in the three worlds which has to be done or anything to be obtained which has not been obtained; yet I am engaged in work.

For, if ever I did not engage in work unwearied, O Pārtha (Arjuna), men would in every way follow my path.

If I should cease to work, these worlds would fall in ruin, and I should be the creator of disordered life and destroy these people.

As the unlearned act from attachment to their work, so should the learned also act, O Bhārata (Arjuna), but without any attachment, with the desire to maintain the world-order.

Let him not unsettle the minds of the ignorant who are attached to action. The enlightened man doing all works in a spirit of *yoga* should set others to act (as well).

The Self Is No Doer

While all kinds of work are done by the modes of nature (guṇas), he whose soul is bewildered by the self-sense thinks, "I am the doer."

But he who knows the true character of the distinction of the soul from the modes of nature and their works, O Mighty-armed (Arjuna), understanding that it is the modes which are acting on the modes themselves, does not get attached.

Those who are misled by the modes of nature get attached to the works produced by them. But let no one who knows the whole unsettle the minds of the ignorant who know only a part.

Resigning all thy works to Me, with thy consciousness fixed in the Self, being free from desire and egoism, fight, delivered, from thy fever.

Those men, too, who, full of faith and free from cavil, constantly follow this teaching of Mine are released from the bondage of works.

But those who slight My teaching and do not follow it, know them to be blind to all wisdom, lost and senseless.

Nature and Duty

Even the man of knowledge acts in accordance with his own nature. Beings follow their nature. What can repression accomplish?

For every sense-attachment and [every] aversion are fixed in regard to the objects of that sense. Let no one come under their sway, for they are his two enemies.

Better is one's own law though imperfectly carried out than the law of another carried out perfectly. Better is death in the fulfillment of one's own law, for to follow another's law is perilous.

Action and Inaction

What is action? What is inaction?—as to this even the wise are bewildered. I will declare to thee what action is, knowing which thou shalt be delivered from evil.

One has to understand what action is, and likewise one has to understand what is wrong action, and one has to understand about inaction. Hard to understand is the way of work.

He who in action sees inaction and action in inaction—he is wise among men, he is a *yogin*, and he has accomplished all his work.

He whose undertakings are all free from the will of desire, whose works are burned up in the fire of wisdom—him the wise call a man of learning.

Having abandoned attachment to the fruit of works, ever content, without any kind of dependence, he does nothing though he is ever engaged in work.

Having no desires, with his heart and self under control, giving up all possessions, performing action by the body alone, he commits no wrong.

He who is satisfied with whatever comes by chance, who has passed beyond the dualities (of pleasure and pain), who is free from jealousy, who remains the same in success and failure—even when he acts, he is not bound.

Wisdom and Work

Knowledge as a sacrifice is greater than any material sacrifice, O scourge of the foe (Arjuna), for all works without any exception culminate in wisdom.

Learn that by humble reverence, by inquiry, and by service. The men of wisdom who have seen the truth will instruct thee in knowledge.

In Praise of Wisdom

When thou hast known it, thou shalt not fall again into this confusion, O Pāṇḍava (Arjuna), for by this thou shalt see all existences without exception in the Self, then in Me.

Even if thou shouldst be the most sinful of all sinners, thou shalt cross over all evil by the boat of wisdom alone.

As the fire which is kindled turns its fuel to ashes, O Arjuna, even so does the fire of wisdom turn to ashes all work.

There is nothing on earth equal in purity to wisdom. He who becomes perfected by *yoga* finds this of himself, in his self *[ātman]* in course of time.

Faith Is Necessary for Wisdom

He who has faith, who is absorbed in it [i.e., wisdom], and who has subdued his senses, gains wisdom, and having gained wisdom he attains quickly the supreme peace.

But the man who is ignorant, who has no faith, who is of a doubting nature, perishes. For the doubting soul *[ātman]* there is neither this world nor the world beyond, nor any happiness.

Works do not bind him who has renounced all works by *yoga*, who has destroyed all doubt by wisdom, and who ever possesses his soul, O winner of wealth (Arjuna).

Therefore, having cut asunder with the sword of wisdom this doubt in thy heart that is born of ignorance, resort to *yoga* and stand up, O Bhārata (Arjuna).

The Enlightened Self

The embodied self who has controlled his nature, having renounced all actions by the mind [inwardly], dwells at ease in the city of nine gates,[1] neither working or causing work to be done.

The Sovereign Self does not create for the people agency, nor does He act. Nor does He connect works with their fruits. It is nature that works out these.

The All-pervading Spirit does not take on the sin or the merit of any. Wisdom is enveloped by ignorance; thereby creatures are bewildered.

But for those in whom ignorance is destroyed by wisdom—for them wisdom lights up the Supreme Self like the sun.

Thinking of That, directing one's whole conscious being to That, making That their whole aim, with That as the sole object of their devotion, they reach a state from which there is no return, their sins washed away by wisdom.

Sages see with an equal eye, a learned and humble *brāhmin*, a cow, an elephant, or even a dog, or an outcaste.

Even here on earth the created world is overcome by those whose mind is established in equality. God is flawless and the same in all. Therefore are these persons established in God.

---

[1]The nine gates are the two eyes, the two ears, the two nostrils, the mouth, and the two organs of excretion and generation.

One should not rejoice on obtaining what is pleasant or sorrow on obtaining what is unpleasant. He who is thus firm of understanding and unbewildered—such a knower of God is established in God.

When the self is no longer attached to external contacts [objects], one finds the happiness that is in the Self. Such a one who is in union with God enjoys undying bliss.

Whatever pleasures are born of contacts with objects are only sources of pain: they have a beginning and an end, O Son Kunti (Arjuna); no wise man delights in them.

He who is able to resist the rush of desire and anger—even here before he gives up his body, he is a *yogin*, he is the happy man.

Peace from Within

He who finds his happiness within, his joy within, and likewise his light only within, that *yogin* becomes divine and attains to the beatitude of God.

The holy men whose sins are destroyed, whose doubts [dualities] are cut asunder, whose minds are disciplined, and who rejoice in doing good to all creatures attain to the beatitude of God.

To those austere souls who are delivered from desire and anger and who have subdued their minds and have knowledge of the Self—near to them lies the beatitude of God.

Shutting out all external objects, fixing the vision between the eyebrows, making even the inward and the outward breaths moving within the nostrils, the sage who has controlled the senses, mind, and understanding, who is intent on liberation, who has cast away desire, fear, and anger—he is ever freed.

And having known Me as the Enjoyer of sacrifices and austerities, the Great Lord of all the worlds, the Friend of all beings, he [the sage] attains peace.

The Pathway and the Goal

Work is said to be the means of the sage who wishes to attain to *yoga*; when he has attained to *yoga*, serenity is said to be the means.

When one does not get attached to the objects of sense or to works, and has renounced all purposes, then he is said to have attained to *yoga*.

Let a man lift himself by himself; let him not degrade himself; for the Self alone is the friend of the self and the Self alone is the enemy of the self.

For him who has conquered his [lower] self by the [higher] Self his Self is a friend, but for him who has not possessed his [higher] Self, his very Self will act in enmity, like an enemy.

When one has conquered one's [lower] self and has attained to the calm of self-mastery, his Supreme Self abides ever concentrate: he is at peace in cold and heat, in pleasure and pain, in honor and dishonor.

The ascetic (*yogi*) whose soul is satisfied with wisdom and knowledge, who is unchanging and master of his senses, to whom a clod, a stone, and a piece of gold are the same, is said to be controlled [in *yoga*].

He who is equal-minded among friends, companions, and foes, among those who are neutral and impartial, among those who are hateful and related, among saints and sinners—he excels.

The Conduct of Life

FROM THE *MAHABHARATA*

1. General Rules of Conduct

. . . Abstention from injury, truthfulness of speech, justice, compassion, self-restraint.

Procreation (of offspring) [with] one's own wife, amiability, modesty, patience,—the practice of these is the best of all religions as said by . . . Manu himself. . . .

Refusal to appropriate what is not given, gift, study (of scriptures), penance, abstention from injury, truth, freedom from wrath, and worship of the gods in sacrifices,—these are the characteristics of virtue.

Abstention from injury, by act, thought, and word, in respect of all creatures, compassion, and gift [charity], constitute behavior that is worthy of praise.

The Mahabharata, *translated by Pratap Chandra Ray (Calcutta: Bharata Press, 1890).*

That act or exertion by which others are not benefited, or that act in consequence of which one has to feel shame, should never be done.

. . . It is difficult to say what righteousness is. It is not easy to indicate it. No one, in discoursing upon righteousness, can indicate it accurately.

Righteousness was declared (by Brahmā) for the advancement and growth of all creatures. Therefore, that which leads to advancement and growth is righteousness.

Righteousness was declared for restraining creatures from injuring one another. Therefore, that is righteousness which prevents injury to creatures.

. . . I know morality, which is eternal, with all its mysteries. It is nothing else than the ancient morality which is known to all, and which consists of universal friendliness, and is fraught with beneficence to all creatures.

That mode of living which is founded upon a total harmlessness toward all creatures or (in case of actual necessity) upon a minimum of such harm, is the highest morality.

There is no expiation for them that cast off the duties and practices of their order and class, country, and family, and those that abandon their very creed.

2. Expediency and Moderation

That again which is virtue may, according to time and place, be sin. Thus appropriation (of what belongs to others), untruth, and injury and killing, may, under special circumstances, become virtue.

Acts that are (apparently) evil, when undertaken from considerations connected with the gods, the scriptures, life itself, and the means by which life is sustained, produce consequences that are good.

Know, O child, these two truths with certainty, viz., that might is not always meritorious and forgiveness also is not always meritorious! He that forgiveth always suffereth many evils. Therefore it is that . . . the learned applaud not a constant habit of forgiveness.

Listen now . . . to the demerits of those that are never-forgiving! The man of wrath who, surrounded by darkness, always inflicteth, by help of his own energy, various kinds of punishments on persons whether they deserve them or not, is necessarily separated from his friends in consequence of that energy of his. Such a man is hated by both relatives and strangers. Such a man, because he insulteth others, suffereth loss of wealth and reapeth disregard and sorrow and hatred and confusion and enemies. . . . He . . . is an object of alarm to the world. People al-

ways do him an injury when they find a hole. Therefore, should men never exhibit might in excess or forgiveness on all occasions.

[It is said]: "To tell the truth is consistent with righteousness. There is nothing higher than truth." I shall now, O Bhārata, say unto thee that which is not generally known to men.

There where falsehood would assume the aspect of truth, truth should not be said. There, again, where truth would assume the aspect of falsehood, even falsehood should be said. . . .

It is always proper to speak the truth. It is better again to speak what is beneficial than to speak what is true. I hold that this is truth which is fraught with the greatest benefit to all creatures.

. . . In seasons of distress, a person by even speaking an untruth acquires the merit of speaking the truth, even as a person who accomplishes an unrighteous act acquires by that very means the merit of having done a righteous act. Conduct is the refuge of righteousness. Thou shouldst know what righteousness is, aided by conduct.

Know that the *kṣatriya* [warrior or king] is the protector and the destroyer of the people. Therefore, a *kṣatriya* in distress should take (by force) what he can, with a view to (ultimately) protect the people.

No person in this world . . . can support life without injuring other creatures. The very ascetic leading a solitary life in the depths of the forest is no exception.

The irresistible course of time affects all mortals. All earthly things, ripened by time, suffer destruction.

Some, O King, slay some men. The slayers, again, are slain by others. This is the language of the world. In reality, however, no one slays, and no one is slain.

Some one thinks men slay (their fellow men). Another thinks men do not slay. The truth is that the birth and destruction of all creatures have been ordained to happen in consequence of their very nature.

3. Destiny and Effort

All acts, good and bad, done in past lives come to the doer. Knowing that everything one enjoys or endures at present is the result of the acts of past lives, the self urges the understanding on different directions (so that it may act in such a way as to avoid all unpleasant fruits).

. . . And think also how thou hast been forced by the Supreme Ordainer to do such an act (as the slaughter of so many human beings)!

As a weapon made by a smith or carpenter is under the control of the person that is handling it, and moves as he moves it, similarly this universe, controlled by actions done in time, moves as those actions move it.

. . . Thou shouldst always exert with promptitude, . . . for without promptitude of exertion mere destiny never accomplishes the objects cherished by kings.

These two, viz., exertion and destiny, are equal (in their operation). Of them, I regard exertion to be superior, for destiny is ascertained from the results of what is begun with exertion.

Learning, penances, vast wealth, indeed, everything, can be earned by exertion. Exertion, as it occurs in embodied creatures, is governed by intelligence.

The king . . . should never depend upon destiny. . . .

4. Conventional Conduct

. . . Conduct [conventional practice] is the root of prosperity. Conduct is the enhancer of fame.

It is conduct that prolongs life. It is conduct that destroys all calamities and evils. Conduct has been said to be superior to all the branches of knowledge.

It is conduct that begets righteousness, and it is righteousness that prolongs life. Conduct is the most efficacious rite of propitiating the deities (for bringing about auspiciousness of every kind).

5. Nonattachment and Asceticism

A complete disregard for all (worldly) things, perfect contentment, abandonment of hope of every kind, and patience,—these constitute the highest good of one that has subjugated one's senses and acquired a knowledge of self.

No need of attaching thyself to things of this world. Attachment to worldly objects is productive of evil.

Relatives, sons, spouses, the body itself, and all one's possessions stored with care, are unsubstantial and prove of no service in the next world. Only acts, good and bad, that one does, follow one to the other world.

That man is said to be truly learned and truly possessed of wisdom who abandons every act, who never indulges in hope, who is completely dissociated from all worldly surroundings, and who has renounced everything that appertains to the world.

That person, who, without being attached thereto, enjoys all objects of sense with the aid of the senses that are completely under his control, who is pos-

sessed of a tranquil self, who is never moved by joy or sorrow, who is engaged in *yoga*-meditation, who lives in companionship with the deities presiding over his senses and dissociated also from them, and who, though endowed with a body, never regards himself as identifiable with it, becomes emancipated and very soon attains to that which is his highest good.

Whatever objects, amongst things that are desired, are cast off, become sources of happiness. The man that pursues objects of desire meets with destruction in the course of the pursuit.

Neither the happiness that is derived from a gratification of the senses nor that great felicity which one may enjoy in heaven, approaches to even a sixteenth part of the felicity which arises from the destruction of all desire.

. . . Freedom from attachment, emancipation from desire, contentment, tranquillity, truth, self-restraint, forgiveness, and universal compassion, are the qualities that have now come to me.

. . . Pure happiness has now come to me.

The understanding of the man unconversant with *yoga* can never be directed toward emancipation. One unconversant with *yoga* can never have happiness. Patience and the resolution to cast off sorrow, these two indicate the advent of happiness.

6. True Knowledge Versus Renunciation

. . . One becomes cleansed of all sins by means of knowledge alone, living the while in [the] Supreme Brahmā [deity].

The wearing of brown cloths, shaving of the head, bearing of the triple stick, and the *kamaṇḍalu* [the begging bowl]—these are the outward signs of one's mode of life. These have no value in aiding one to the attainment of emancipation.

When, notwithstanding the adoption of these emblems of a particular mode of life, knowledge alone becomes the cause of one's emancipation from sorrow, it would appear that the adoption of mere emblems is perfectly useless.

Or, if, beholding the mitigation of sorrow in it, thou has betaken thyself to these emblems of *sannyāsa* [asceticism], why then should not the mitigation of sorrow be beheld in the umbrella and the scepter to which I have betaken myself?

Emancipation does not exist in poverty; nor is bondage to be found in affluence. One attains to emancipation through knowledge alone, whether one is indigent or affluent.

For these reasons, know that I am living in a condition of freedom, though ostensibly engaged in the enjoyment of religion [*dharma*], wealth, pleasure, in the form of kingdom and spouses, which constitute a field of bondage (for the generality of men).

The bonds constituted by kingdom and affluence, and the bondage of attachments, I have cut off with the sword of renunciation whetted on the stone of the scriptures bearing upon emancipation.

7. Against Worldly Goods

The desire for wealth can never be fraught with happiness. If acquired, great is the anxiety that the acquirer feels. If lost after acquisition, that is felt as death. Lastly, respecting acquisition itself, it is very uncertain.

Wealth cannot be got by even the surrender of one's person. What can be more painful than this? When acquired, one is never gratified with its measure, but one continues to seek it.

Like the sweet water of the Ganges, wealth only increases one's hankering.

8. Happiness and Sorrow

In this respect it is said that they [who] are possessed of wisdom, beholding that the world of life is overwhelmed with sorrow both bodily and mental, and with happiness that is sure to end in misery, never suffer themselves to be stupefied.

He that is wise will strive to rescue himself from sorrow. The happiness of living creatures is unstable both here and hereafter.

Happiness is said to be of two kinds, viz., bodily and mental. Both in this and the other world, the visible and the invisible fruits (of action) are specified (in the Vedas) for the sake of happiness. There is nothing more important than happiness among the fruits or consequences of the triple aggregate.[1] Happiness is desirable. It is an attribute of the self. Both virtue and profit are sought for its sake. Virtue is its root. This, indeed, is its origin. All acts have for their end the attainment of happiness.

There is only sorrow in this world but no happiness. . . .

Sorrow comes after happiness, and happiness after sorrow. One does not always suffer sorrow or always enjoy happiness.

Happiness always ends in sorrow, and sometimes proceeds from sorrow itself. He, therefore, that desires eternal happiness must abandon both.

Be it happiness or sorrow, be it agreeable or disagreeable, whatever comes should be borne with an unaffected heart.

They that are highly stupid and they that are masters of their self enjoy happiness here. They, however, that occupy an intermediate place suffer misery.

. . . There is no end of grief, and grief arises from happiness itself.

Happiness and misery, prosperity and adversity, gain and loss, death and life, in their turn, wait upon all creatures. For this reason the wise man of tranquil self would neither be elated with joy nor be depressed with sorrow.

When one reflects properly (one's heart being purified by such reflection), one comes to know that the things of this world are as valueless as straw. Without doubt, one is then freed from attachment in respect of those things.

When the world, . . . which is full of defects, is so constituted, every man of intelligence should strive for the attainment of the emancipation of his self.

. . . Behold, all creatures,—the superior, the middling, and the inferior,—in consequence of their respective acts, are entangled in grief!

I do not regard even my own self to be mine. On the other hand, I regard the whole world to be mine. I again think that all this (which I see) is as much mine as it belongs to others! Grief cannot approach me in consequence of this thought.

Having acquired such an understanding, I do not yield either to joy or grief.

As two pieces of wood floating on the ocean come together at one time and are again separated, even such is the union of (living) creatures in this world.

Sons, grandsons, kinsmen, relatives, are all of this kind. One should never feel affection for them, for separation with them is certain.

Grief arises from the disease constituted by desire. Happiness again results from the disease of desire being cured. From joy springs sorrow, and sorrow arises repeatedly.

Sorrow comes after joy, and joy after sorrow. The joys and sorrows of human beings are revolving on a wheel.

After happiness sorrow has come to thee. Thou shalt again have happiness. No one suffers sorrow forever, and no one enjoys happiness forever.

---

[1]Virtue, wealth, and pleasure

The Means of Attaining the Chief Good

FROM THE *LAWS OF MANU*

1. One's Actions and Mental Attitude Determine One's Destiny . . .

. . . With whatever disposition of mind (a man) performs any act, he reaps its results in a (future) body endowed with the same quality.

Action, which springs from the mind, from speech, and from the body, produces either good or evil results; by action are caused the (various) conditions of men, the highest, the middling, and the lowest.

Know that the mind is the instigator here below, even to that (action) which is connected with the body, (and) which is of three kinds, has three locations, and falls under ten heads.

Coveting the property of others, thinking in one's heart of what is undesirable, and adherence to false (doctrines), are the three kinds of (sinful) mental action.

Abusing (others, speaking) untruth, detracting from the merits of all men, and talking idly, shall be the four kinds of (evil) verbal action.

Taking what has not been given, injuring (creatures) without the sanction of the law, and holding criminal intercourse with another man's wife, are declared to be the three kinds of (wicked) bodily action.

(A man) obtains (the result of) a good or evil mental (act) in his mind, (that of) a verbal (act) in his speech, (that of) a bodily (act) in his body.

In consequence of (many) sinful acts committed with his body, a man becomes (in the next birth) something inanimate, in consequence (of sins) committed by speech, a bird, or a beast, and in consequence of mental (sins he is reborn in) a low caste.

That man who keeps this threefold control (over himself) with respect to all created beings and wholly subdues desire and wrath, thereby assuredly gains complete success.

Austerity and sacred learning are the best means by which a *brāhmin* secures supreme bliss; by austerities he destroys guilt, by sacred learning he obtains the cessation of (births and) deaths.

All those traditions (*smṛti*) and all those despicable systems of philosophy, which are not based on the Veda, produce no reward after death; for they are declared to be founded on darkness.

Giving no pain to any creature, let him slowly accumulate spiritual merit, for the sake (of acquiring) a companion to the next world. . . .

For in the next world neither father, nor mother, nor wife, nor sons, nor relations stay to be his companions; spiritual merit alone remains (with him).

Single is each being born; single it dies; single it enjoys (the reward of its) virtue; single (it suffers the punishment of its) sin.

Let him, untired, follow the conduct of virtuous men, connected with his occupations, which has been fully declared in the revealed texts and in the sacred tradition (*smṛti*) and is the root of the sacred law.

Through virtuous conduct he obtains long life, through virtuous conduct desirable offspring, through virtuous conduct imperishable wealth; virtuous conduct destroys (the effect of) inauspicious marks.

For a man of bad conduct is blamed among people, constantly suffers misfortunes, is afflicted with diseases, and [is] short-lived.

A man who follows the conduct of the virtuous, has faith and is free from envy, lives a hundred years, though he be entirely destitute of auspicious marks.

Unrighteousness, practiced in this world, does not at once produce its fruit, like a cow; but, advancing slowly, it cuts off the roots of him who committed it.

If (the punishment falls) not on (the offender) himself, (it falls) on his sons, if not on the sons, (at least) on his grandsons; but an iniquity (once) committed, never fails to produce to him who wrought it.

He prospers for a while through unrighteousness, then he gains great good fortune, next he conquers his enemies, but (at last) he perishes (branch and) root.

Let him always delight in truthfulness, (obedience to) the sacred law, conduct worthy of an Āryan, and purity. . . .

Those endowed with Goodness reach the state of gods, those endowed with Activity the state of men, and those endowed with Darkness ever sink to the condition of beasts; that is the threefold course of transmigrations.

The Laws of Manu, *translated by G. Buhler,* The Sacred Books of the East, *vol. 25 (Oxford: Clarendon Press, 1886).*

The sages declare *Brahman*, the creators of the universe, the law, the Great One, and the Undiscernible One (to constitute) the highest order of beings produced by Goodness.

2. General Pattern of the Social Order

The student, the householder, the hermit, and the ascetic, these (constitute) four separate orders, which all spring from (the order of) householders. . . .

Contentment, forgiveness, self-control, abstention from unrighteously appropriating anything, (obedience to the rules of) purification, coercion of the organs [control of the senses], wisdom, knowledge (of the supreme Self), truthfulness, and abstention from anger (form) the tenfold law.

Abstention from injuring (creatures), veracity, abstention from unlawfully appropriating (the goods of others), purity, and control of the organs, Manu has declared to be the summary of the law for the four castes. . . .

3. The Gaining of Supreme Bliss

In whatever order (a man) who knows the true meaning of the Veda-science may dwell, he becomes even while abiding in this world, fit for the union with *Brahman*.

Studying the Veda, (practicing) austerities, the (acquisition of true) knowledge, the subjugation of the organs, abstention from doing injury, and serving the *Guru* [preceptor] are the best means for attaining supreme bliss.

(If you ask) whether among all these virtuous actions, (performed) here below, (there be) one which has been declared more efficacious (than the rest) for securing supreme happiness to man,

(The answer is that) the knowledge of the Self is stated to be the most excellent among all of them; for that is the first of all sciences, because immortality is gained through that.

He who sacrifices to the Self (alone), equally recognizing the Self in all created beings, and all created beings in the Self, becomes (independent like) an autocrat and self-luminous.

He who thus recognizes the Self through the Self in all created beings, becomes equal (-minded) toward all, and enters the highest state, *Brahman*.

A twice-born man who recites these Institutes, revealed by Manu, will be always virtuous in conduct, and will reach whatever condition he desires.

Discussion and Reflection Questions

1. *The nature of the self and the way to Brahman:* The *Upanishads*, with their emphasis on the Self as the ultimate reality, seem at first to be at odds with much Western thinking that locates ultimate reality outside personal selves. How would adopting the notion of the Self as the most real thing change your perspective on the world? Would it lead you to think of yourself, or of others, differently from the way you do now? Is enlightenment of the sort that the *Upanishads* speak of possible, in your view? Is it a suitable goal for human life? Explain your views on these issues.

2. *Work, nonattachment, and wisdom:* The *Bhagavad Gita* recognizes the necessity of work, but counsels that one take a particular attitude toward it: nonattachment. What does this mean? Is it possible to take such an attitude toward work and yet perform that work well? Give an example of performing some work or pursuing some project while adopting an attitude of nonattachment toward it. What are the benefits of doing this? What do you think is the most important insight expressed in the advice given?

3. *The conduct of life:* The *Mahabharata* presents principles of conduct as flexible rules requiring adjustment to particular circumstances, rather than as divine commandments which admit of no exceptions. In your view, is this feature a strength or a weakness of these principles? According to these principles, how does one go about deciding what to do in a particular situation? In what sense is this a form of "consequentialism," the doctrine that the goodness or badness of an action is determined by the goodness or badness of the consequences of that action? Are there any dangers to this view?

4. *The means of attaining the chief good:* The *Laws of Manu* emphasizes the motives behind actions, the nature of actions, and the consequences of actions for morality. How are these three related? In your view, is one of these elements more important than the other two? If so, which one, and why?

Suggestions for Further Reading

The introduction to *The Sourcebook in Indian Philosophy*, edited by Sarvepalli Radhakrishnan and Charles A. Moore (Princeton: Princeton University Press, 1957), provides an excellent overview of Indian philosophy. A brief and very readable introduction to Hindu ethics is provided in the article "Indian Ethics," by Purusottama Bilimoria, in *A Companion to Ethics*, edited by Peter Singer (Oxford: Blackwell, 1991), pp. 43–57. This article includes a section discussing Gandhian ethics as well. More detailed treatments include S. Thakur, *Christian and Hindu Ethics* (London: George Allen & Unwin, 1969), C. Crawford, *The Evolution of Hindu Ethical Ideals* (Honolulu: University of Hawaii Press, 1982), and Saral Jhingran, *Aspects of Hindu Morality* (Delhi: Motilal Banarsidass Publishers, 1989). Barbara H. Holdrege, "Hindu Ethics," in *A Bibliographic Guide to the Comparative Study of Ethics*, edited by John Carmen et al. (New York: Cambridge University Press, 1991), provides many references for further study. Scholarly journal articles dealing with aspects of Hindu ethics include: Saral Jhingran, "An Inquiry into Ethical Relativism in Hindu Thought," *Indian Philosophical Quarterly* 23 (1996): 363–378, and Jagat Pal, "Two Dogmas of the Bhagavadgita," *Journal of Indian Council of Philosophical Research* 15 (1997): 98–108. Selections of Gandhi's writings include Louis Fischer, ed., *The Essential Gandhi: An Anthology* (New York: Random House, 1962), and K. Swaminathan and C. N. Patel, eds., *A Gandhi Reader* (New York: APT Books, 1988). Scholarly studies of Gandhi's thought include E. H. Erikson, *Gandhi's Truth: On the Origins of Militant Nonviolence* (New York: W. W. Norton and Co., 1969), Raghavan Narasimhan Iyer, *The Moral and Political Thought of Mahatma Gandhi* (New York: Oxford University Press, 1973), and Glyn Richards, *The Philosophy of Gandhi: A Study of His Basic Ideas* (Totowa, N.J.: Barnes and Noble, 1982).

InfoTrac

Hinduism, Gandhi, "philosophy, Indian", conduct of life, karma, "fate and fatalism", rebirth

Chapter 8

Buddhism

Introduction: The Path to Enlightenment

Buddhism provides a unique perspective on reality and the best life for human beings. It seeks to transcend all cultures and traditions by teaching the *Dharma*—the eternal truth about reality. Unlike many Western religions, Buddhism recognizes no supreme God and has no theology of the sort that characterizes Christianity. Its initial orientation is human experience rather than divine revelation. Buddhism starts with a recognition of the human condition, a diagnosis of its essential nature (especially the fact of suffering), and a prescription for its transcendence.

In its twenty-five-hundred-year history Buddhism has undergone numerous developments and has divided into a number of branches emphasizing different doctrines, practices, or both. The two largest branches of Buddhism are the Theravada and Mahayana schools. The Theravada or Southern school is the older school and is currently represented more strongly in Sri Lanka, Thailand, and the rest of Southeast Asia. The collection of sacred literature for Theravada Buddhism is called the Southern Canon. The Mahayana or Northern school is dominant in Nepal, Tibet, China, Korea, and Japan. Although Mahayana Buddhism accepts much of the Southern Canon, it has a sacred literature of its own as well, developed centuries after the Southern Canon.

The initial readings and doctrines discussed in this chapter represent the earliest Theravada tradition in Buddhism, rather than the later Mahayana developments. We will focus especially on Buddhism's founder—the Buddha—and the primary elements of his teaching about human existence, morality, and the path to enlightenment. We will also examine the Buddhist teaching on karma, rebirth, and nirvana and take a look as well at the thought of the second-century Buddhist philosopher Nagarjuna. Together these writings provide an introduction to one of the world's greatest moral traditions.

The Buddha: Suffering and the Middle Way

What is the Middle Way, which gives sight? It is the noble Eightfold Path, namely, right understanding, right intention, right speech, right action, right livelihood, right effort, right mindfulness, right concentration. This is the Middle Way.

—BUDDHA, "SETTING IN MOTION THE WHEEL OF TRUTH"

The sixth century B.C.E. was a time of religious upheaval in India. Many Indians had become disenchanted with popular Hinduism's emphasis on ritualistic observances and were searching for a more practical expression of their faith. Siddhartha (later to become the Buddha) was one such seeker. Because stories of the life of Siddhartha circulated for over four centuries before being committed to writing, it is impossible to be sure of all of the details of his life. The following account is based on the earliest historical records we have.

Siddhartha Gautama (ca. 563–483 B.C.E.) was born in what is now Nepal to a family of the warrior caste. His father was a ruler in a northeast region of the Indian subcontinent. Legend has it that on the night before he was born his mother dreamed that a white elephant entered her womb through her side. Called in to interpret this strange dream, priests predicted the birth of a son who would become either a universal ruler or an enlightened sage. His mother died a week after his birth, and he was raised by his mother's sister. His father, fearing that Siddhartha would fulfill the prophecy and renounce his throne, kept his son ensconced in the lap of luxury, surrounded by beauty and comfort, and protected from all exposure to sickness, decay, and death. The boy was given the best possible education and was married to his beautiful cousin at the age of sixteen. Together they had a son. According to worldly standards, he lived a life of enviable opulence.

The decisive events that would set his life on a different path took place when he was twenty-nine. Restless and bored with his cloistered existence, Siddhartha wished to travel outside the family compound. His father, ever mindful of the prophecy, ordered all sick persons, old persons, monks, and funeral processions from the streets of the city as his son passed by. Nonetheless, his father's servants were not completely successful, and while riding in his carriage through the city Siddhartha spied an old white-haired man leaning on a staff. He asked his charioteer about this man, and his driver explained the process of aging to him—how this man had once been a baby, then a handsome young man, and finally a decrepit old man. Old age, the driver said, is the murderer of beauty, the ruin of vigor, the birthplace of sorrow, the grave of pleasure, the destroyer of memory, and the enemy of the senses. Upon learning that old age was the fate of everyone who is born, Siddhartha ordered the carriage to return to the palace immediately.

Although distressed by what he had seen, Siddhartha was also curious to learn more. On two subsequent excursions outside the palace, he saw a sick man lying by the side of the road, covered with filth, and a human corpse being carried to its place of cremation. He now realized the true nature of human existence and was close to despair. But on his fourth excursion he saw something that gave him hope: a wandering ascetic monk with a shaven head, wearing a yellow robe, his face peaceful and serene. This man radiated the sense that he had found the way to live amidst the suffering of the world.

The effect on Siddhartha was cataclysmic. He realized that suffering is the primary fact of human existence and decided that discovering the solution to this problem was to be his life's mission. What followed is what has become known as "the great renunciation." One night he left his wife and son while they were asleep, fled the palace and went into the forest. There he took off his jewelry, replaced his robes with simple clothing, and gave up his worldly life of luxury and comfort in order to become a wandering ascetic in search of an understanding of human suffering.

For the next six years Siddhartha struggled to understand the cause of suffering and the way to overcome it. His struggles took the form of what can only be described as a series of religious experiments. First, with the help of a sage, he tried meditating to achieve a state of "nothingness." This he accomplished, but he still had no answer to his problem concerning human suffering. He next consulted with another sage who taught him to attain the "realm of neither perception nor nonperception." This also failed to give him the answers he sought. He continued to travel and decided to abandon all teachers and seek the truth through himself. Arriving in Gaya (in India), he was joined by a group of five ascetics and together with them subjected himself to a regimen of severe self-mortification, which included sitting on a couch of thorns, eating all sorts of nauseous foods, and letting filth accumulate on his body. He became so emaciated that he could grasp his backbone through his abdomen. Not surprisingly, his health deteriorated to such an extent that his friends thought he was dead. He came to the conclusion that a regimen of severe self-mortification was no more likely to lead him to absolute truth than were the various meditation exercises he had tried, so he decided to restore his health by eating and caring for his body properly again. His five companions, outraged by what they viewed as his shameless self-indulgence, left him in disgust.

Gradually he regained his strength and set out once again in his quest for truth. Remembering a time as a child when he had sat beneath a tree and calmed his mind, he decided to try to repeat that experience again. Still in Gaya, he sat down cross-legged at the foot of a tree, determined not to rise until he had attained enlightenment. There he sat and spent the night in deep meditation. Moving into ever deeper states of consciousness, he suddenly understood the nature of human suffering and the way to overcome it. He was thirty-five. He had realized enlightenment and had become the Buddha (which means "the Enlightened One"). He spent the next several weeks meditating on the truth he had discovered and debating with himself whether he should attempt to communicate this truth to others. He decided that if there were even a few people likely to be able to comprehend the truth, he had to go forth and teach. He found his five former companions and, after overcoming some reluctance on their part, convinced them to listen to him. His first discourse, delivered to these companions, is known as "Setting in Motion the Wheel of Truth" or simply as the "First Sermon" (included in the first set of readings below). In it he enunciates the wisdom he has attained and in the process articulates what are perhaps the three best-known Buddhist doctrines: the Middle Way, the Four Noble Truths, and the Eightfold Path. Because these doctrines are so central to Buddhism, each will be explained briefly here.

The Middle Way

The Indian sage was a person who was able to completely renounce the things of this world. This often took the form of leading an extremely ascetic life, devoid of pleasure and physical satisfactions. As Siddhartha learned from his own efforts to attain truth, however, practicing self-mortification is no more conducive to enlightenment than is self-indulgence. Both are extremes that contribute nothing to self-realization. By avoiding these extremes, the seeker is in a position to have insight. The Middle Way is the way of the center. It is the understanding that extremes such as self-mortification and self-indulgence lead one away from the truth.

The Four Noble Truths

The Four Noble Truths concern suffering and the way to deal with it. To become enlightened one must, first of all, recognize the significance of suffering. Suffering is the central fact of human existence: birth, old age, sickness, and finally death all involve suffering. The word *suffering* here (which is a translation of the Pali word *dukkha*) should be taken more broadly to include dissatisfaction, anxiety, frustration, suffering, pain, misery, and in general any state that disturbs a person's sense of contentment. Recognizing the centrality of suffering to human existence is the first prerequisite for gaining enlightenment. Second, the seeker must understand the cause of suffering. Suffering is the direct result of craving, of having a desire for pleasure, for possessions, for relationships, for existence itself, all of which are by their very nature transitory and impermanent. To the extent that a person desires something, he must remain unsatisfied and in suffering. The solution to this problem is contained in the third Noble Truth: the way to end suffering is to relinquish desires. If suffering is the result of having desires, then eliminating desires eliminates suffering as well, so practicing abandonment and nonattachment is essential. But how should a person do this? Not by committing suicide, but rather by following the Middle Way. This is the life of the wise person who avoids the extremes of self-indulgence, on the one hand, and self-mortification, on the other. According to the fourth Noble Truth, the way to overcome desires is to follow the Eightfold Path.

The Eightfold Path

The Eightfold Path is a practical description of how to follow the Middle Way. Avoiding the extremes of self-indulgence and self-mortification consists in practicing right views, right intention, right speech, right action, right livelihood, right effort, right mindfulness, and right concentration. Right understanding is knowledge of the Four Noble Truths. Right intention is renouncing sensual pleasures, having malice toward no one. Right speech is not only abstaining from falsehood and speaking the truth, but also avoiding all frivolous talk. Right action is abstaining from taking life, stealing, and acting in an immoral manner. Right livelihood is earning a living from a noble profession. Right effort is exerting oneself to attain the perfection of the beneficial qualities already mentioned. Right mindfulness is ridding oneself of lust and grief. Right concentration is attaining a state of indifference to pleasure and suffering. Together these practices direct the individual along the Middle Way, and assist in the attainment of complete insight and serenity.

The goal of understanding the Four Noble Truths and following the Middle Way and Eightfold Path is to attain the state of nirvana. The term literally means "extinction," in the sense in which the flame of a candle might be extinguished. Life may be thought of as an endless stream of individuals going through an endless cycle of births, deaths, and rebirths. The nature of one's present life is determined by the moral quality of one's previous lives, that is, the good or evil deeds one has performed (i.e., life is governed by the principle of karma, or moral cause and effect). This cycle ends only when one overcomes delusion, especially false ideas of the self, and the self-centeredness we are naturally inclined to. The realization of nirvana—the state of total release from life, suffering, and death—is the supreme goal of Buddhism and must be undertaken by each individual for himself.

These were the doctrines the Buddha continued to preach for the forty-five years of his wandering ministry. In that time he attracted thousands of followers, and formed a monastic order to practice his teachings. Foremost among these teachings was the idea that the things of this world are temporary and that enlightenment requires avoiding attachment to them. The Buddha reminded his disciples of this truth at the moment of his own departure from this world. His last words, addressed to his disciples just before he died, were: "And now, O priests, I take my leave of you; all the constituents of the world are transitory; work out your salvation with diligence."

The reading selections included below fill out the picture sketched above in more detail. The first set of readings includes the Buddha's first sermon to his followers, in which he describes the Four Noble Truths and the Eightfold Path. "The Synopsis of Truth" and "Dependent Origination" elaborate on these doctrines. The second set of readings—"On Karma and Rebirth"—discuss the nature of human life according to Buddhism. One's present life is simply one episode in a longer ongoing cycle of birth, death, and rebirth. The practical precepts of Buddhism should be understood within this larger perspective. The third set of readings—"The Path to Nirvana"—is attributed to the fifth-century C.E. monk Buddha-ghosa. It sets out the goal of human life, nirvana, and the means for achieving this goal. Together these materials provide a fascinating introduction to the moral wisdom embodied in the earliest Buddhist writings.

Nagarjuna: Emptiness and the State of Perfect Wisdom

Nagarjuna is perhaps the most famous philosophical exponent of Buddhism. Of the man himself we know virtually nothing except that he probably lived in the first or second century C.E. in southern India, and belonged to the Shunyavadin sect of Buddhism. The adherents of this sect thought of themselves as drawing out the essence of the Buddha's message. We also know that he produced one of the most radical versions of Buddhism to date. The Buddha's fundamental attitude, the rejection of unanswerable questions about metaphysics in favor of enunciating the more practical truth requisite for attaining nirvana, is taken to its logical and most radical extreme by Nagarjuna.

According to Nagarjuna, the kinds of things that people are usually prone to consider real—physical objects, wealth, the self—are in fact a kind of illusion, yet powerful enough that most people cling to them. In truth things have only a momentary existence, without any kind of permanence. All is empty. Understanding this is the first step toward enlightenment. Nagarjuna gives the following summary of his view:

> Our view is that *nirvana* represents quiescence, i.e., the nonapplicability of all the variety of names and the nonexistence of particular objects. This very quiescence, so far as it is the natural quiescence of the world, is called bliss. The quiescence of plurality is also a bliss because of the cessation of speech or because of the cessation of thought. It is also a bliss because, by putting an end to all defiling agencies, all individual existences are stopped. It is also a bliss because, by quenching all defiling forces, all instinct and habits of thought have been extirpated without residue. It is also a bliss because, since all the objects of knowledge have died away, knowledge itself has also died.
> (Nagarjuna, *Treatise on the Middle Doctrine*)

So the goal of nonattachment is to break free from particulars, as well as from all habits of thought, and thereby to attain perfect wisdom. But if perfect wisdom is the result of being free from all inclinations and goals, then in what sense can a person pursue perfect wisdom as a goal? In other words, what does it mean to strive after perfect wisdom as a goal while eschewing all goals? Nagarjuna deals with this apparent inconsistency by taking the final, radical step suggested toward the end of the passage quoted above. Complete detachment requires detaching oneself from detachment itself. Attaining perfect wisdom requires that one cling to nothing. Since all knowledge signifies a kind of attachment, attaining perfect wisdom requires the shattering of all knowledge. Knowledge of the necessity of detachment is useful and indeed essential for attaining perfect wisdom, but once such wisdom is achieved, knowledge is relinquished, just as one might discard a boat after one has crossed a river, or a ladder after one has scaled a wall.

The state of perfect wisdom, or nirvana, is a state of freedom from conflict, where thoughts are made free and mastery over all thought is gained in the detached knowledge that masters itself. Desires and cravings bring about suffering. Once the emptiness of suffering is realized, it is overcome. In emptiness one attains a state of being untouched by birth, suffering, or death. Thus for Nagarjuna nirvana is a state that can be attained within this life. As he says, "What makes the limit of nirvana is also then the limit of samsara [the cycle of birth and death]. Between the two we cannot find the slightest shade of difference." Realizing nirvana, then, does not depend on finally escaping from the cycle of birth, suffering, and death, but rather in rejecting the idea that such a cycle represents a genuine reality.

A person who has realized perfect wisdom looks upon life from a distance. She is aware of momentary fulfillments but never becomes enslaved to them. Such a person refrains from absolutizing any representation, idea, or proposition. To look upon all things as without absolute being is the profoundest understanding of the world and the self. As the great German philosopher Karl Jaspers notes, "The Buddhist Sage goes through the world like a duck; he no longer gets wet. He has transcended the world by dropping it. He seeks fulfillment in an unthinkable unworld." Jaspers goes on to point out that the emptiness so valued by Nagarjuna and later Buddhists naturally encourages the greatest openness: Indifference to all worldly things leaves every possibility open. This accounts for the characteristic Buddhist tolerance toward other religions, modes of life, and views of the world. "The Buddhist lives with all these as expressions of a lower, worldly truth, each equally satisfactory as a point of departure toward higher things." It is perhaps not accidental that Buddhism has never instigated any religious wars and has never had an Inquisition. It is largely this spirit of openness that best accounts for Buddhism's continuing vitality.

Reading Questions

1. *Basic doctrines:* What is the Middle Way? What are the Four Noble Truths? What is the Eightfold Path? How are these doctrines related to one another? What examples are given of right views, right intention, right speech, right action, right livelihood, right effort, right mindfulness, and right concentration? What is the doctrine of dependent origination, and how does it relate to the Four Noble Truths?

2. *Karma and rebirth:* What is karma? How does this concept account for the manifest inequality in the world? Does the notion of karma presuppose the notion of rebirth (reincarnation), or vice versa? How does the notion of karma provide an incentive to live a morally good life? How does one eventually escape the cycle of birth, suffering, death, and rebirth?

3. *The path to nirvana:* What is nirvana? How is it described? How does it differ from the notion of heaven, and which, according to the Buddhist scriptures, is to be preferred? Is nirvana described as "full" or "empty"? Why? How is nirvana to be realized? What must one do to experience nirvana?

Basic Doctrines

BUDDHA

The First Sermon[1]

These two extremes, O monks , are not to be practiced by one who has gone forth from the world. What are the two? That conjoined with the passions, low, vulgar, common, ignoble, and useless, and that conjoined with self-torture, painful, ignoble, and useless. Avoiding these two extremes the Tathāgata has gained the knowledge of the Middle Way, which gives sight and knowledge, and tends to calm, to insight, enlightenment, Nirvāṇa.

What, O monks, is the Middle Way, which gives sight . . . ? It is the noble Eightfold Path, namely, right views, right intention, right speech, right action, right livelihood, right effort, right mindfulness, right concentration. This, O monks, is the Middle Way. . . .

(1) Now this, O monks, is the noble truth of suffering[2]: birth is painful, old age is painful, sickness is painful, death is painful, sorrow, lamentation, dejection, and despair are painful. Contact with unpleasant things is painful, not getting what one wishes is painful. . . .

(2) Now this, O monks, is the noble truth of the cause of suffering: that craving, which leads to rebirth, combined with pleasure and lust, finding pleasure here and there, namely the craving for passion, the craving for existence, the craving for nonexistence.

(3) Now this, O monks, is the noble truth of the cessation of suffering: the cessation without a remainder of the craving, abandonment, forsaking, release, nonattachment.

(4) Now this, O monks, is the noble truth of the way that leads to the cessation of suffering: this is the noble Eightfold Path, namely, right views, right intention, right speech, right action, right livelihood, right effort, right mindfulness, right concentration. "This is the noble truth of suffering." Thus, O monks, among

[1]Buddha, "Basic Doctrines," translated by Henry Clarke Warren. Reprinted by permission of the publisher from *Buddhism in Translations: Passages Selected from the Buddhist Sacred Books and Translated from the Original Pali into English* by Henry Clarke Warren, Student's Edition, Harvard Oriental Series, 3, Cambridge, Mass.: Harvard University Press. Copyright © 1953 by the President and Fellows of Harvard College.

[2]Editor's note: The term *pain* in this section has been replaced by *suffering,* for the sake of consistency.

doctrines unheard before, in me sight and knowledge arose, wisdom, knowledge, light arose. "This noble truth of suffering must be comprehended." Thus, O monks, among doctrines heard before, by me was this truth comprehended. And thus, O monks, among doctrines unheard before, in me sight and knowledge arose. . . .

As long as in these noble truths my threefold knowledge and insight . . . was not well purified, even so long, O monks, in the world with its gods, Māra, Brahmā, with ascetics, brahmins, gods and men, I had not attained the highest complete enlightenment. Thus I knew.

But when in these noble truths my threefold knowledge and insight duly with its twelve divisions was well purified, then, O monks, in the world . . . I had attained the highest complete enlightenment. Thus I knew. Knowledge arose in me, insight arose that the release of my mind is unshakeable; this is my last existence; now there is no rebirth. . . .

The Synopsis of Truth[3]

Thus have I heard. Once when the Lord was staying at Benares in the Isipatana deerpark, he addressed the Almsmen as follows: It was here in this very deerpark at Benares that the Truth-finder, Arahat all-enlightened, set a-rolling the supreme Wheel of the Doctrine—which shall not be turned back from its onward course by recluse or brahmin, god or Māra or Brahmā or by anyone in the universe,—the announcement of the Four Noble Truths, the teaching, declaration, and establishment of those Four Truths, with their unfolding, exposition and manifestation.

What are these four?—The announcement, teaching . . . and manifestation of the Noble Truth of Suffering—of the origin of Suffering[4]—of the cessation of Suffering—of the path that leads to the cessation of Suffering.

Follow Sāriputta and Moggallāna and be guided by them; they are wise helpers unto their fellows in the higher life. . . .

Having thus spoken, the Blessed One arose and went into his own cell.

The Lord had not been gone long when the reverend Sāriputta proceeded to the exposition of the Truth-finder's Four Noble Truths, as follows:

[3]*Further Dialogues of the Buddha*, translated by Lord Chalmers, *Sacred Books of the Buddhists*, vol. 6 (London: Oxford University Press, 1927), pp. 296–299.
[4]Editor's note: The term *Ill* in this section has been replaced by *Suffering*, for the sake of consistency.

What, reverend sirs, is the Noble Truth of Suffering?—Birth is Suffering; decay is Suffering; death is Suffering; grief and lamentation, pain, misery and tribulation are Sufferings; it is Suffering not to get what is desired;—in brief all the factors of the fivefold grip on existence are Sufferings.

Birth is, for living creatures of each several class, the being born or produced, the issue, the arising or the rearising, the appearance of the plastic forces, the growth of faculties.

Decay, for living creatures of each several class, is the decay decaying, loss of teeth, gray hair, wrinkles, a dwindling term of life, sere faculties.

Death, for living creatures of each several class, is the passage and passing hence, the dissolution, disappearance, dying, death, decease, the dissolution of the plastic forces, the discarding of the dead body.

Grief is the grief, grieving and grievousness, the inward grief and inward anguish of anyone who suffers under some misfortune or is in the grip of some type of Suffering.

Lamentation is the lament and lamentation the wailing and the lamenting of anyone who suffers under some misfortune or is in the grip of some type of Suffering.

Pain is any bodily Suffering or bodily evil, any Suffering bred of bodily contact, any evil feeling.

Misery is mental Suffering and evil, any evil feeling of the mind.

Tribulation is the tribulation of heart and mind, the state to which tribulation brings them, in anyone who suffers under some misfortune or is in the grip of some type of Suffering.

There remains not to get what is desired. In creatures subject to birth—or decay—or death—or grief and lamentation, pain, misery and tribulation—the desire arises not to be subject thereto but to escape them. But escape is not to be won merely by desiring it; and failure to win it is another suffering.

What are in brief all the factors of the fivefold grip on existence which are Sufferings?—They are: The factors of form, feeling, perception, plastic forces, and consciousness.

The foregoing, sirs, constitutes the Noble Truth of Suffering.

What now is the Noble Truth of the Origin of Suffering? It is any craving that makes for rebirth and is tied up with passion's delights and culls satisfaction now here now there;—such as the craving for sensual pleasure, the craving for continuing existence, and the craving for annihilation.

Next, what is the Noble Truth of the Cessation of Suffering?—It is the utter and passionless cessation of this same craving,—the abandonment and rejection of craving, Deliverance from craving, and aversion from craving.

Lastly, what is the Noble Truth of the Path that leads to the Cessation of Suffering?—It is just the Noble Eightfold Path, consisting of—right outlook, right resolves, right speech, right acts, right livelihood, right endeavor, right mindfulness and right rapture of concentration.

Right [views are] to know Suffering, the origin of Suffering, the cessation of Suffering, and the path that leads to the cessation of Suffering.

Right [intention is] the resolve to renounce the world and to do no hurt or harm.

Right speech is to abstain from lies and slander, from reviling, and from tattle.

Right acts are to abstain from taking life, from stealing and from lechery.

Right livelihood is that by which the disciple of the Noble One supports himself, to the exclusion of wrong modes of livelihood.

Right [effort] is when an Almsman brings his will to bear, puts forth endeavor and energy, struggles and strives with all his heart, to stop bad and wrong qualities which have not yet arisen from ever arising, to renounce those which have already arisen, to foster good qualities which have not yet arisen, and, finally, to establish, clarify, multiply, enlarge, develop, and perfect those good qualities which are there already.

Right mindfulness is when realizing what the body is,—what feelings are—what the heart is—and what the mental states are,—an Almsman dwells ardent, alert and mindful, in freedom from the wants and discontents attendant on any of these things.

Right . . . concentration is when, divested of lusts and divested of wrong dispositions, an Almsman develops, and dwells in, the First Ecstasy with all its zest and satisfaction, a state bred of aloofness and not divorced from observation and reflection. By laying to rest observation and reflection, he develops and dwells in inward serenity, in focusing of heart, in the zest and satisfaction of the Second Ecstasy, which is divorced from observation and reflection and is bred of concentration,—passing thence to the Third and Fourth Ecstasies.

This, sirs, constitutes the Noble Truth of the Path that leads to the Cessation of Suffering.

Such, reverend sirs, is the announcement . . . and manifestation of the Four Noble Truths,—the supreme Wheel of the Doctrine set a-rolling in the deerpark at Benares by the Truth-finder, Arahat all-enlightened, that Wheel which shall not be turned back from its onward course by recluse or brahmin, god, Māra or Brahmā, or by anyone in the whole universe.

Thus spoke the reverend Sāriputta. Glad at heart, those Almsmen rejoiced in what the reverend Sāriputta had said.

Dependent Origination[5]

That things have being, O Kaccāna, constitutes one extreme of doctrine; that things have no being is the other extreme. These extremes, O Kaccāna, have been avoided by the Tathāgata, and it is a middle doctrine he teaches:

On ignorance depends karma;
On karma depends consciousness;
On consciousness depend name and form;
On name and form depend the six organs of sense;
On the six organs of sense depends contact;
On contact depends sensation;
On sensation depends desire;
On desire depends attachment;
On attachment depends existence;
On existence depends birth;
On birth depend old age and death, sorrow, lamentation, misery, grief, and despair. Thus does this entire aggregation of misery arise.

But on the complete fading out and cessation of ignorance ceases karma;
On the cessation of karma ceases consciousness;
On the cessation of consciousness cease name and form;
On the cessation of name and form cease the six organs of sense;
On the cessation of the six organs of sense ceases contact;
On the cessation of contact ceases sensation;
On the cessation of sensation ceases desire;
On the cessation of desire ceases attachment;
On the cessation of attachment ceases existence;
On the cessation of existence ceases birth;
On the cessation of birth cease old age and death, sorrow, lamentation, misery, grief, and despair. Thus does this entire aggregation of misery cease. . . .

[5]Henry Clarke Warren, *Buddhism in Translations* (New York: Atheneum, 1976; originally published by Harvard University Press, 1896), p. 166. Reprinted by permission of Harvard University Press. © Harvard University Press.

On Karma and Rebirth

Be a Friend to Yourself

Thus have I heard.

On a certain occasion The Blessed One was dwelling at Sāvatthi, a Jetavana monastery in Anāthapiṇḍika's Park.

Then drew new king Pasenadi the Kosalan to where The Blessed One was; and having drawn near and greeted The Blessed One, he sat down respectfully at one side. And seated respectfully at one side, king Pasenadi the Kosalan spoke to The Blessed One as follows:

"Reverend Sir, it happened to me, as I was just now in seclusion and plunged in meditation, that a consideration presented itself to my mind, as follows: 'Who are those who love themselves? and who do not love themselves?' And, Reverend Sir, it occurred to me as follows: 'All they who do evil with their body, who do evil with their voice, who do evil with their mind, they do not love themselves.' And although they should say thus: 'We love ourselves,' nevertheless, they do not love themselves. And why do I say so? Because, whatever a man would do to one whom he did not love, that they do to themselves. Therefore, they do not love themselves.

"But all they who do good with their body, who do good with their voice, who do good with their mind, they love themselves. And although they should say thus: 'We do not love ourselves,' nevertheless, they do love themselves. And why do I say so? Because, whatever a man would do to one whom he loved, that they do to themselves. Therefore, they love themselves.

"Thus it is, great king! Thus it is! Certainly, great king, all they who do evil with their body, who do evil with their voice, who do evil with their mind, they do not love themselves. And although they should say thus: 'We love ourselves,' nevertheless, they do not love themselves. And why do I say so? Because, whatever a man would do to one whom he did not love, that they do to themselves. Therefore, they do not love themselves.

"But all they, great king, who do good with their body, who do good with their voice, who do good

with their mind, they love themselves. And although they should say thus: 'We do not love ourselves,' nevertheless, they do love themselves. And why do I say so? Because whatever a man would do to one he loved, that they do to themselves. Therefore, they love themselves."

Let any one who holds self dear,
That self keep free from wickedness;
For happiness can ne'er be found
By any one of evil deeds.

Assailed by death, in life's last throes,
At quitting of this human state,
What is it one can call his own?
What with him take as he goes hence?
What is it follows after him,
And like a shadow ne'er departs?

His good deeds and his wickedness,
Whate'er a mortal does while here;
'Tis this that he can call his own,
This with him take as he goes hence.
This is what follows after him,
And like a shadow ne'er departs.

Let all, then, noble deeds perform,
A treasure-store for future weal;
For merit gained this life within,
Will yield a blessing in the next.

The Cause of Inequality in the World

Said the king, "Bhante Nāgasena, what is the reason that men are not alike, but some long-lived and some short-lived, some healthy and some sickly, some handsome and some ugly, some powerful and some weak, some rich and some poor, some of high degree and some of low degree, some wise and some foolish?"

Said the elder, "Your majesty, why are not trees all alike, but some sour, some salt, some bitter, some pungent, some astringent, some sweet?"

"I suppose, bhante, because of a difference in the seed."

"In exactly the same way, your majesty, it is through a difference in their karma that men are not all alike, but some long-lived, some healthy and some sickly, some handsome and some ugly, some powerful and some weak, some rich and some poor, some of high degree and some of low degree, some wise and some foolish. Moreover, your majesty, The Blessed One has said as follows: 'All beings, O youth, have karma as their portion; they are heirs of their karma; they are sprung from their karma; their karma is their kinsman; their karma is their refuge; karma allots beings to meanness or greatness.'"

"You are an able man, bhante Nāgasena."

Good and Bad Karma

Thus have I heard.

On a certain occasion The Blessed One was dwelling at Sāvatthi, in Jetavana monastery in Anāthapiṇḍika's Park.

Then drew near king Pasenadi the Kosalan, at an unusual time of day, to where The Blessed One was; and having drawn near and greeted the Blessed One, he sat down respectfully at one side. And king Pasenadi the Kosalan being seated respectfully at one side, The Blessed One spoke to him as follows:

"Pray, whence have you come, great king, at this unusual time of day?"

"Reverend Sir, a householder who was treasurer in Sāvatthi has just died leaving no son, and I have come from transferring his property to my royal palace; and, Reverend Sir, he had ten million pieces of gold, and silver beyond all reckoning. But this householder, Reverend Sir, would eat sour gruel and kaṇājaka, and the clothes he wore were made of hemp, . . . and the conveyance in which he rode was a broken-down chariot with an umbrella of leaves."

"Even so, great king! Even so, great king! Formerly, great king, that householder and treasurer gave food in alms to a Private Buddha named Tagarasikkhi. But after he had given the order, saying, 'Give food to this monk,' and had risen from his seat and departed, he repented him of the gift and said to himself, 'It would have been better if my slaves or my servants had had this food.' And, moreover, he murdered his brother's only son for the sake of the inheritance. Now whereas, great king, that householder and treasurer gave food in alms to the Private Buddha Tagarasikkhi, as the fruit of this deed he was born seven times in a higher state of existence, into a heavenly world; and as a further result of this deed he has held the treasureship seven times here in Sāvatthi. And whereas, great king, that householder and treasurer repented him of the gift,

and said to himself, 'It would have been better if my slaves or my servants had had this food,' as the result of this sinful thought his mind has been averse to sumptuous food, to sumptuous clothing, to sumptuous equipages, to a sumptuous gratification of the five senses. And whereas, great king, the treasurer murdered his brother's only son for the sake of the inheritance, as a result of this deed he has suffered in hell for many years, for many hundreds of years, for many thousands of years, for many hundreds of thousands of years; and as a further result of this deed he has now for the seventh time died without leaving any son and forfeited his property into the royal treasury. But now, great king, the former merit of this treasurer has become exhausted, and no new merit has been accumulated, and at the present time, great king, the treasurer is suffering in the Mahā-Roruva hell."

"Reverend Sir, has the treasurer been reborn in the Mahā-Roruva hell?"

"Yes, great king. The treasurer has been reborn in the Mahā-Roruva hell."

Nor grain, nor wealth, nor store of gold and
  silver,
Not one amongst his women-folk and children,
Nor slave, domestic, hired man,
Nor any one that eats his bread,
Can follow him who leaves this life,
But all things must be left behind.

But every deed a man performs,
With body, or with voice, or mind,
'Tis this that he can call his own,
This with him take as he goes hence.
This is what follows after him,
And like a shadow ne'er departs.

Let all, then, noble deeds perform,
A treasure-store for future weal;
For merit gained this life within,
Will yield a blessing in the next.

How to Obtain Wealth, Beauty, and Social Position

On a certain occasion The Blessed One was dwelling at Sāvatthi, in Jetavana monastery in Anāthapiṇḍika's Park. Then drew near Mallikā the queen to where The Blessed One was; and having drawn near and greeted The Blessed One, she sat down respectfully at one side. And seated respectfully at one side, Mallikā the queen spoke to The Blessed One as follows:

"Reverend Sir, what is the reason, and what is the cause, when a woman is ugly, of a bad figure, and horrible to look at, and indigent, poor, needy, and low in the social scale?

"Reverend Sir, what is the reason, and what is the cause, when a woman is ugly, of a bad figure, and horrible to look at, and rich, wealthy, affluent, and high in the social scale?

"Reverend Sir, what is the reason, and what is the cause when a woman is beautiful, attractive, pleasing, and possessed of surpassing loveliness, and indigent, poor, needy, and low in the social scale?

"Reverend Sir, what is the reason, and what is the cause, when a woman is beautiful, attractive, pleasing, and possessed of surpassing loveliness, and rich, wealthy, affluent, and high in the social scale?"

"Mallikā, when a woman has been irascible and violent, and at every little thing said against her has felt spiteful, angry, enraged, and sulky, and manifested anger, hatred, and heart-burning; when she has given no alms to monk or Brahman, of food, drink, building-sites, carriages, garlands, scents, ointments, bedding, dwelling-houses, and lamps, but has been of an envious disposition, and felt envy at the gains, honor, reverence, respect, homage, and worship that came to others, and been furious and envious threeat; then, when she leaves that existence and comes to this one, wherever she may be born, she is ugly, of a bad figure, and horrible to look at, and indigent, poor, needy, and low in the social scale.

"And, again, Mallikā, when a woman has been irascible and violent, and at every little thing said against her has felt spiteful, angry, enraged, and sulky, and manifested anger, hatred, and heart-burning; but has given alms to monks and Brahmans, of food, drink, building-sites, carriages, garlands, scents, ointments, bedding, dwelling-houses, and lamps, and has not been of an envious disposition, nor felt envy at the gains, honor, reverence, respect, homage, and worship that came to others, nor been furious and envious threeat; then, when she leaves that existence and comes to this one, wherever she may be born, she is ugly, of a bad figure, and horrible to look at, and rich, wealthy, affluent, and high in the social scale.

"And, again, Mallikā, when a woman has not been irascible or violent, and though much had been said against her, has not felt spiteful, angry, enraged, or sulky, nor manifested anger, hatred, and heart-burning; when she has given no alms to monk or Brahman, of food, drink, building-sites, carriages, garlands, scents, ointments, bedding, dwelling-houses, and lamps, but has been of an envious disposition, and felt envy at the gains, honor, reverence, respect, homage, and worship that came to others, and

been furious and envious, threeat; then, when she leaves that existence and comes to this one wherever she may be born, she is beautiful, attractive, pleasing, and possessed of surpassing loveliness, and indigent, poor, needy, and low in the social scale.

"And, again, Mallikā, when a woman has not been irascible or violent, and though much had been said against her, has not felt spiteful, angry, enraged, or sulky, nor manifested anger, hatred, and heart-burning; when she has given alms to monks and Brahmans, of food, drink, building-sites, carriages, garlands, scents, ointments, bedding, dwelling-houses, and lamps, and has not been of an envious disposition, nor felt envy at the gains, honor, reverence, respect, homage, and worship that came to others, nor been furious and envious threeat; then, when she leaves that existence and comes to this one, wherever she may be born, she is beautiful, attractive, pleasing, and possessed of surpassing loveliness, and rich, wealthy, affluent, and high in the social scale.

"This, Mallikā, is the reason, this is the cause, when a woman is ugly, of a bad figure, and horrible to look at, and indigent, poor, needy, and low in the social scale.

"This, Mallikā, is the reason, this is the cause, when a woman is ugly, of a bad figure, and horrible to look at, and rich, wealthy, affluent, and high in the social scale.

"This, Mallikā, is the reason, this is the cause, when a woman is beautiful, attractive, pleasing, and possessed of surpassing loveliness, and indigent, poor, needy, and low in the social scale.

"This, Mallikā, is the reason, this is the cause, when a woman is beautiful, attractive, pleasing, and possessed of surpassing loveliness, and rich, wealthy, affluent, and high in the social scale."

When he had thus spoken, Mallikā the queen replied to The Blessed One as follows:

"Since, now, Reverend Sir, in a former existence I was irascible and violent, and at every little thing said against me felt spiteful, angry, enraged, and sulky, and manifested anger, hatred, and heart-burning, therefore am I now ugly, of a bad figure, and horrible to look at. Since, now, Reverend Sir, in a former existence I gave alms to monks and Brahmans, of food, drink, building-sites, carriages, garlands, scents, ointments, bedding, dwelling-houses, and lamps, therefore am I now rich, wealthy, and affluent. Since, now, Reverend sir, in a former existence I was not of an envious disposition, nor felt envy at the gains, honor, reverence, respect, homage, and worship that came to others, nor was furious and envious threeat, therefore am I now high in the social scale.

"Now, in this royal family, Reverend Sir, there are maidens of the warrior caste, maidens of the Brahman caste, and maidens of the householder caste, and I bear rule over them. From this day forth I will not be irascible nor violent, and though much be said against me, I will not feel spiteful, angry, enraged, or sulky, nor manifest anger, hatred, and heart-burning; I will give alms to monks and Brahmans, of food, drink, building-sites, carriages, garlands, scents, ointments, bedding, dwelling-houses, and lamps; and I will not be of an envious disposition, nor feel envy at the gains, honor, reverence, respect, homage, and worship that shall come to others, nor be furious and envious thereat.

"O wonderful is it, Reverend Sir! O wonderful is it, Reverend sir! It is as if, Reverend Sir, one were to set up that which was overturned; or were to disclose that which was hidden; or were to point out the way to a lost traveler; or were to carry a lamp into a dark place that they who had eyes might see forms. Even so has The Blessed One expounded the Doctrine in many different ways. I betake myself to The Blessed One for refuge, to the Doctrine, and to the Congregation of the priests. Let The Blessed One receive me, who have come to him for refuge, and accept me as a disciple from this day forth as long as life shall last."

The Round of Existence

"Bhante Nāgasena," said the king, "when you say 'round of existence,' what is that?"

"Your majesty, to be born here and die here, to die here and be born elsewhere, to be born there and die there, to die there and be born elsewhere,—this, your majesty, is the round of existence."

"Give an illustration."

"It is as if, your majesty, a man were to eat a ripe mango, and plant the seed; and from that a large mango-tree were to spring and bear fruit; and then the man were to eat a ripe mango from that tree also and plant the seed; and from that seed also a large mango-tree were to spring and bear fruit; thus of these trees there is no end discernible. In exactly the same way, your majesty, to be born here and die here, to die here and be born elsewhere, to be born there and die there, to die there and be born else-

where, this, your majesty, is the round of existence."

"You are an able man, bhante Nāgasena."

Cause of Rebirth

"Bhante Nāgasena," said the king, "are there any who die without being born into another existence?"

"Some are born into another existence," said the elder, "and some are not born into another existence."

"Who is born into another existence, and who is not born into another existence?"

"Your majesty, he that still has the corruptions is born into another existence; he that no longer has the corruptions is not born into another existence."

"But will you, bhante, be born into another existence?"

"Your majesty, if there shall be in me any attachment, I shall be born into another existence; if there shall be in me no attachment, I shall not be born into another existence."

"You are an able man, bhante Nāgasena."

Is This to Be My Last Existence?

"Bhante Nāgasena," said the king, "does a man know when he is not to be born into another existence?"

"Assuredly, your majesty, a man knows when he is not to be born into another existence."

"Bhante, how does he know it?"

"He knows it from the cessation of all cause or reason for being born into another existence."

"Give an illustration."

"It is as if, your majesty, a house-holding farmer were to plow and sow and fill his granary; and then were neither to plow nor sow, and were to use the grain previously stored up, or give it away, or do with it however else might suit him: your majesty, would this house-holder farmer know that his granary would not become filled up again?"

"Assuredly, bhante, would he know it."

"How would he know it?"

"He would know it from the cessation of all cause or reason for the filling up of the granary."

"In exactly the same way, your majesty, a man knows when he is not to be born into another existence, from the cessation of all cause or reason for being born into another existence."

"You are an able man, bhante Nāgasena."

The Path to Nirvana

The Way of Purity

Therefore has The Blessed One said:

> What man his conduct guardeth, and hath
> wisdom,
> And thoughts and wisdom traineth well,
> The strenuous and the able priest,
> He disentangles all this snarl.

When it is said *hath wisdom*, there is meant a wisdom for which he does not need to strive. For it comes to him through the power of his deeds in a former existence.

The strenuous and the able priest. Perseveringly by means of the above-mentioned heroism, and intelligently through the force of his wisdom, should he *guard* his *conduct*, and *train* himself in the quiescence and insight indicated by the words *thoughts* and *wisdom*.

Thus does The Blessed One reveal the Way of Purity under the heads of conduct, concentration, and wisdom. Thus does he indicate the three disciplines, a thrice noble religion, the advent of the threefold knowledge, etc., the avoidance of the two extremes and the adoption of the middle course of conduct, the means of escape from the lower and other states of existence, the threefold abandonment of the corruptions, the three hostilities, the purification from the three corruptions, and the attainment of conversion and of the other degrees of sanctification.

And how?

By conduct is indicated the discipline in elevated conduct, by concentration, the discipline in elevated thoughts; and by wisdom, the discipline in elevated wisdom.

By conduct, again, is indicated the nobleness of this religion in its beginning. The fact that conduct is the beginning of this religion appears from the passage, "What is the first of the meritorious qualities? Purity of conduct." And again from that other, which begins by saying, "It is the nonperformance of any wickedness." And it is noble because it entails no remorse or other like evils.

By concentration is indicated its nobleness in the middle. The fact that concentration is the middle of this religion appears from the passage which begins by saying, "It is richness in merit." It is noble because it brings one into the possession of the magical powers and other blessings.

By wisdom is indicated its nobleness at the end. The fact that wisdom is the end of this religion appears from the passage,

> To cleanse and purify the thoughts,
> 'Tis this the holy Buddhas teach,

and from the fact that there is nothing higher than wisdom. It is noble because it brings about imperturbability whether in respect of things pleasant or unpleasant. As it is said:

> Even as the dense and solid rock
> Cannot be stirred by wind and storm;
> Even so the wise cannot be moved
> By voice of blame or voice of praise.

By conduct, again, is indicated the advent of the threefold knowledge. For by virtuous conduct one acquires the threefold knowledge, but gets no further. By concentration is indicated the advent of the Six High Powers. For by concentration one acquires the Six High Powers, but gets no further. By wisdom is indicated the advent of the four analytical sciences. For by wisdom one acquires the four analytical sciences, and in no other way.

By conduct, again, is indicated the avoidance of the extreme called sensual gratification; by concentration, the avoidance of the extreme called self-torture. By wisdom is indicated the adoption of the middle course of conduct.

By conduct, again, is indicted the means of escape from the lower states of existence; by concentration, the means of escape from the realm of sensual pleasure; by wisdom, the means of escape from every form of existence.

By conduct, again, is indicated the abandonment of the corruptions through the cultivation of their opposing virtues; by concentration, the abandonment of the corruptions through their avoidance; by wisdom, the abandonment of the corruptions through their extirpation.

Buddha, "The Path to Nirvana," translated by Henry Clarke Warren. Reprinted by permission of the publisher from Buddhism in Translations: Passages Selected from the Buddhist Sacred Books and Translated from the Original Pali into English *by Henry Clarke Warren, Student's Edition, Harvard Oriental Series, 3, Cambridge, Mass.: Harvard University Press. Copyright © 1953 by the President and Fellows of Harvard College.*

By conduct, again, is indicated the hostility to corrupt acts; by concentration, the hostility to corrupt feelings; by wisdom, the hostility to corrupt propensities.

By conduct, again, is indicated the purification from the corruption of bad practices; by concentration, the purification from the corruption of desire; by wisdom, the purification from the corruption of heresy.

And by conduct, again, is indicated the attainment of conversion, and of once returning; by concentration, the attainment of never returning; by wisdom, the attainment of saintship. For the converted are described as "Perfect in the precepts," as likewise the once returning; but the never returning as "Perfect in concentration," and the saint as "Perfect in wisdom."

Thus are indicated the three disciplines, a thrice noble religion, the advent of the threefold knowledge etc., the avoidance of the two extremes and the adoption of the middle course of conduct, the means of escape from the lower and other states of existence, the threefold abandonment of the corruptions, the three hostilities, the purification from the three corruptions, and the attainment of conversion and of the other degrees of sanctification; and not only these nine triplets, but also other similar ones.

Now although this *Way of Purity* was thus taught under the heads of conduct, concentration, and wisdom, and of the many good qualities comprised in them, yet this with excessive conciseness; and as, consequently, many would fail to be benefited, we here give its exposition in detail.

Concentration

What is concentration? Concentration is manifold and various, and an answer which attempted to be exhaustive would both fail of its purpose and tend to still greater confusion. Therefore we will confine ourselves to the meaning here intended, and say—Concentration is an intentness of meritorious thoughts.

And what, O priests, is the discipline in elevated concentration?

Whenever, O priests, a priest having isolated himself from sensual pleasures, having isolated himself from demeritorious traits, and still exercising reasoning, still exercising reflection, enters upon the first trance, which is produced by isolation and characterized by joy and happiness; when, through the subsidence of reasoning and reflection, and still retaining joy and happiness, he enters upon the second trance, which is an interior tranquilization and intentness of thoughts, and is produced by concentration; when,

through the paling of joy, indifferent, contemplative, conscious, and in the experience of bodily happiness—that state which eminent men describe when they say, "Indifferent, contemplative, and living happily"—he enters upon the third trance; when, through the abandonment of happiness, through the abandonment of misery, through the disappearance of all antecedent gladness and grief, he enters upon the fourth trance, which has neither misery nor happiness, but is contemplation as refined by indifference, this, O priests, is called the discipline in elevated concentration.

What advantage, O priests, is gained by training in quiescence? The thoughts are trained. And what advantage is gained by the training of the thoughts? Passion is abandoned.

Wisdom

What is wisdom? Wisdom is manifold and various, and an answer that attempted to be exhaustive would both fail of its purpose and tend to still greater confusion. Therefore we will confine ourselves to the meaning here intended,—Wisdom is knowledge consisting in insight and conjoined with meritorious thoughts.

And what, O priests, is the discipline in elevated wisdom?

Whenever, O priests, a priest knows the truth concerning misery, knows the truth concerning the origin of misery, knows the truth concerning the cessation of misery, knows the truth concerning the path leading to the cessation of misery, this, O priests, is called the discipline in elevated wisdom.

What advantage, O priests, is gained by training in insight? Wisdom is developed. And what advantage is gained by the development of wisdom? Ignorance is abandoned.

The Fire-Sermon

Then The Blessed One, having dwelt in Uruvelā as long as he wished, proceeded on his wanderings in the direction of Gayā Head, accompanied by a great congregation of priests, a thousand in number, who had all of them aforetime been monks with matted hair. And there in Gayā, on Gayā Head, The Blessed One dwelt, together with the thousand priests.

And there The Blessed One addressed the priests:

"All things, O priests, are on fire. And what, O priests, are all these things which are on fire?

"The eye, O priests, is on fire; forms are on fire; eye-consciousness is on fire; impressions received by the eye are on fire; and whatever sensation, pleasant, unpleasant, or indifferent, originates in dependence on impressions received by the eye, that also is on fire.

"And with what are these on fire?"

"With the fire of passion, say I, with the fire of hatred, with the fire of infatuation; with birth, old age, death, sorrow, lamentation, misery, grief, and despair are they on fire.

"The ear is on fire; sounds are on fire; . . . the nose is on fire; odors are on fire; . . . the tongue is on fire; tastes are on fire; . . . the body is on fire; things tangible are on fire; . . . the mind is on fire; ideas are on fire; . . . mind-consciousness is on fire; impressions received by the mind are on fire; and whatever sensation, pleasant, unpleasant, or indifferent, originates in dependence on impressions received by the mind, that also is on fire.

"And with what are these on fire?"

"With the fire of passion, say I, with the fire of hatred, with the fire of infatuation; with birth, old age, death, sorrow, lamentation, misery, grief, and despair are they on fire.

"Perceiving this, O priests, the learned and noble disciple conceives an aversion for the eye, conceives an aversion for forms, conceives an aversion for eye-consciousness, conceives an aversion for the impressions received by the eye; and whatever sensation, pleasant, unpleasant, or indifferent, originates in dependence on impressions received by the eye, for that also he conceives an aversion. Conceives an aversion for the ear, conceives an aversion for sounds, . . . conceives an aversion for the nose, conceives an aversion for odors, . . . conceives an aversion for the tongue, conceives an aversion for tastes, . . . conceives an aversion for the body, conceives an aversion for things tangible, . . . conceives an aversion for the mind, conceives an aversion for ideas, conceives an aversion for mind-consciousness, conceives an aversion for the impression received by the mind; and whatever sensation, pleasant, unpleasant, or indifferent, originates in dependence on impressions received by the mind, for this also he conceives an aversion. And in conceiving an aversion, he becomes divested of passion, and by the absence of passion he becomes free, and when he is free he becomes aware that he is free; and he knows that rebirth is exhausted, that he has lived the holy life, that he has done what it behooved him to do, and that he is no more for this world."

Now while this exposition was being delivered, the minds of the thousand priests became free from attachment and delivered from the depravities.

The Nature of Suffering[1]

But again, O priests, a priest lives, as respects the elements of being, observant of the elements of being in the four noble truths.

And how, O priests, does a priest live, as respects the elements of being, observant of the elements of being in the four noble truths?

Whenever, O priests, a priest knows the truth concerning suffering, knows the truth concerning the origin of suffering, knows the truth concerning the cessation of suffering, knows the truth concerning the path leading to the cessation of suffering.

And what, O priests, is the noble truth of suffering?

Birth is suffering; old age is suffering; disease is suffering; death is suffering; sorrow, lamentation, misery, grief, and despair are suffering; to wish for what one cannot have is suffering; in short, all the five attachment-groups are suffering.

And what, O priests, is birth?

When of such and such a being, into such and such a class of beings, takes place the birth, the being born, the descent into the womb, the rebirth, the appearance of the groups, the obtaining of the organs of sense, this, O priests, is called birth.

And what, O priests, is old age?

When to such and such a being, in such and such a class of beings, there comes old age, decrepitude, toothlessness, hoariness, wrinkledness of the skin, subsidence of the vital powers, decay of the faculties, this, O priests, is called old age.

And what, O priests, is death?

When of such and such a being, from such and such a class of beings, takes place the passing, the passing away, the breaking up, the disappearance, the dying, the death, the meeting its end, the breaking up of the groups, the laying away of the corpse, this, O priests, is called death.

And what, O priests, is sorrow?

Whenever, O priests, in any one who has experienced some great loss, or is afflicted by some misfortune, there arises sorrow, sorrowing, sorrowfulness, heart-sorrow, heart-sorrowfulness, this, O priests, is called sorrow.

And what, O priests, is lamentation?

Whenever, O priests, any one who has experienced some great loss, or is afflicted by some misfortune, gives way to lamenting, lamentation, laments,

[1]Editor's note: The term *misery* in this section has been replaced by *suffering,* for the sake of consistency.

lamenting cries, lamentable cries, cries of lamentation, this, O priests, is called lamentation.

And what, O priests, is suffering?

Bodily suffering, O priests, bodily discomfort, suffering and sensations of discomfort experienced in the impressions received by the body, this, O priests, is called suffering.

And what, O priests, is grief?

Mental suffering, O priests, mental discomfort, suffering and sensations of discomfort experienced in the impressions received by the mind, this, O priests, is called grief.

And what, O priests, is despair?

Whenever, O priests, in any one who has experienced some great loss, or is afflicted by some misfortune, there arises desperation, despair, a state of desperation, a state of despair, this, O priests, is called despair.

And what, O priests, is meant by saying, "To wish for what one cannot have is suffering?"

In beings, O priests, subject to birth there arises the wish, "O that we were not subject to birth! O that birth might never come to us!" Nevertheless this cannot be obtained by wishing. This is what is meant by saying, "To wish for what one cannot have is suffering."

To beings, O priests, subject to old age . . . disease . . . death . . . sorrow . . . lamentation . . . suffering . . . grief . . . despair there arises the wish, "O that we were not subject to despair! O that despair might never come to us!" Nevertheless this cannot be obtained by wishing. This is what is meant by saying, "To wish for what one cannot have is suffering."

And what, O priests, are meant by saying, "In short, all the five attachment-groups are suffering?" The form-attachment-group, the sensation-attachment-group, the perception-attachment-group, the predisposition-attachment-group, the consciousness-attachment-group,—these, O priests, are what are meant by saying, "In short, all the five attachment-groups are suffering."

This, O priests, is called the noble truth of suffering.

The Origin of Suffering

And what, O priests, is the noble truth of the origin of suffering?

It is desire leading to rebirth, joining itself to pleasure and passion, and finding delight in every existence,—desire, namely, for sensual pleasure, desire for permanent existence, desire for transitory existence.

But where, O priests, does this desire spring up and grow? where does it settle and take root?

Where anything is delightful and agreeable to men, there desire springs up and grows, there it settles and takes root.

And what is delightful and agreeable to men, where desire springs up and grows, where it settles and takes root?

THE SIX ORGANS OF SENSE

The eye is delightful and agreeable to men; there desire springs up and grows, there it settles and takes root.

The ear . . . the nose . . . the tongue . . . the body . . . the mind is delightful and agreeable to men; there desire springs up and grows, there it settles and takes root.

THE SIX OBJECTS OF SENSE

Forms . . . sounds . . . odors . . . tastes . . . things tangible . . . ideas are delightful and agreeable to men; there desire springs up and grows, there it settles and takes root.

THE SIX CONSCIOUSNESSES

Eye-consciousness . . . ear-consciousness . . . nose-consciousness . . . tongue-consciousness . . . body-consciousness . . . mind-consciousness is delightful and agreeable to men; there desire springs up and grows, there it settles and takes root.

THE SIX CONTACTS

Contact of the eye . . . ear . . . nose . . . tongue . . . body . . . mind is delightful and agreeable to men; there desire springs up and grows, there it settles and takes root.

THE SIX SENSATIONS

Sensation produced by contact of the eye . . . ear . . . nose . . . tongue . . . body . . . mind is delightful and agreeable to men; there desire springs up and grows, there it settles and takes root.

THE SIX PERCEPTIONS

Perception of forms . . . sounds . . . odors . . . tastes . . . things tangible . . . ideas is delightful and agreeable to men; there desire springs up and grows, there it settles and takes root.

THE SIX THINKINGS

Thinking on forms . . . sounds . . . odors . . . tastes . . . things tangible . . . ideas is delightful and agreeable to men; there desire springs up and grows, there it settles and takes root.

THE SIX DESIRES

Desire for forms . . . sounds . . . odors . . . tastes . . . things tangible . . . ideas is delightful and agreeable to men; there desire springs up and grows, there it settles and takes root.

THE SIX REASONINGS

Reasoning on forms . . . sounds . . . odors . . . tastes . . . things tangible . . . ideas is delightful and agreeable to men; there desire springs up and grows, there it settles and takes root.

THE SIX REFLECTIONS

Reflection on forms . . . sounds . . . odors . . . tastes . . . things tangible . . . ideas is delightful and agreeable to men; there desire springs up and grows, there it settles and takes root.

This, O priests, is called the noble truth of the origin of suffering.

The Cessation of Suffering

And what, O priests, is the noble truth of the cessation of suffering?

It is the complete fading out and cessation of this desire, a giving up, a loosing hold, a relinquishment, and a nonadhesion.

But where, O priests, does this desire wane and disappear? Where is it broken up and destroyed?

Where anything is delightful and agreeable to men; there desire wanes and disappears, there it is broken up and destroyed.

And what is delightful and agreeable to men, where desire wanes and disappears, where it is broken up and destroyed?

The eye is delightful and agreeable to men; there desire wanes and disappears, there it is broken up and destroyed.

[Similarly respecting the other organs of sense, the six objects of sense, the six sense-consciousnesses, the six contacts, the six sensations, the six perceptions, the six thinkings, the six desires, the six reasonings, and the six reflections.]

This, O priests, is called the noble truth of the cessation of suffering.

The Path Leading to the Cessation of Suffering

And what, O priests, is the noble truth of the path leading to the cessation of suffering?

It is this noble eightfold path, to wit, right belief, right resolve, right speech, right behavior, right occupation, right effort, right contemplation, right concentration.

And what, O priests, is right belief?

The knowledge of suffering, O priests, the knowledge of the origin of suffering, the knowledge of the cessation of suffering, and the knowledge of the path leading to the cessation of suffering, this, O priests, is called "right belief."

And what, O priests, is right resolve?

The resolve to renounce sensual pleasures, the resolve to have malice toward none, and the resolve to harm no living creature, this, O priests, is "right resolve."

And what, O priests, is right speech?

To abstain from falsehood, to abstain from backbiting, to abstain from harsh language, and to abstain from frivolous talk, this, O priests, is called "right speech."

And what, O priests, is right behavior?

To abstain from destroying life, to abstain from taking that which is not given one, and to abstain from immorality, this, O priests, is called "right behavior."

And what, O priests, is right occupation?

Whenever, O priests, a noble disciple, quitting a wrong occupation, gets his livelihood by a right occupation, this, O priests, is called "right occupation."

And what, O priests, is right effort?

Whenever, O priests, a priest purposes, makes an effort, heroically endeavors, applies his mind, and exerts himself that evil and demeritorious qualities not yet arisen may not arise; purposes, makes an effort, heroically endeavors, applies his mind, and exerts himself that evil and demeritorious qualities already arisen may be abandoned; purposes, makes an effort, heroically endeavors, applies his mind, and exerts himself that meritorious qualities not yet arisen may arise; purposes, makes an effort, heroically endeavors, applies his mind, and exerts himself for the preservation, retention, growth, increase, development, and perfection of meritorious qualities already arisen, this, O priests, is called "right effort."

And what, O priests, is right contemplation?

Whenever, O priests, a priest lives, as respects the body, observant of the body, strenuous, conscious, contemplative, and has rid himself of lust and grief; as respects sensations, observant of sensations, strenuous, conscious, contemplative, and has rid himself of lust and grief; as respects the mind, observant of the mind, strenuous, conscious, contemplative, and has rid himself of lust and grief; as respects the elements of being, observant of the elements of being, strenuous, conscious, contemplative, and has rid himself of lust and grief, this, O priests, is called "right contemplation."

And what, O priests, is right concentration?

Whenever, O priests, a priest having isolated himself from sensual pleasures, having isolated himself from demeritorious traits, and still exercising reasoning, still exercising reflection, enters upon the first trance which is produced by isolation and characterized by joy and happiness; when, through the subsidence of reasoning and reflection, and still retaining joy and happiness, he enters upon the second trance, which is an interior tranquilization and intentness of the thoughts, and is produced by concentration; when, through the paling of joy, indifferent, contemplative, conscious, and in the experience of bodily happiness—that state which eminent men describe when they say, "Indifferent, contemplative, and living happily"—he enters upon the third trance; when, through the abandonment of happiness, through the abandonment of suffering, through the disappearance of all antecedent gladness and grief, he enters upon the fourth trance, which has neither suffering nor happiness, but is contemplation as refined by indifference, this, O priests, is called "right concentration."

This, O priests, is called the noble truth of the path leading to the cessation of suffering.

Sermon on the Four Intent Contemplations

Any one, O priests, who for seven years shall thus practice these Four Intent Contemplations, may expect one or the other of two rewards—either he will attain to perfect knowledge in his present life, or, if at death the groups still remain, to never returning.

But setting aside, O priests, all question of seven years, any one, O priests, who for six years shall thus practice the above Four Intent Contemplations, may expect one or the other of the two rewards—either he will attain to perfect knowledge in his present life, or, if at death the groups still remain, to never returning.

But setting aside, O priests, all question of six years, . . . five years, . . . four years, . . . three years, . . . two years, . . . one year, . . . seven months, . . . six months, . . . five months, . . . four months, . . . three months, . . . two months, . . . one month, . . . a half month, any one, O priests, who for seven days shall thus practice the above Four Intent Contemplations, may expect one or the other of two rewards—either he will attain to perfect knowledge in his present life, or, if at death the groups still remain, to never returning.

This, therefore, is the meaning of my opening words: "Priests, there is but one way open to mortals for the attainment of purity, for the overcoming of sorrow and lamentation, for abolition of suffering and grief, for the acquisition of the correct rule of conduct, for the realization of Nirvana, and that is the Four Intent Contemplations."

Thus spake The Blessed One, and the delighted priests applauded the speech of The Blessed One.

Discussion and Reflection Questions

1. *Basic doctrines*: Many people seek satisfaction (often unsuccessfully) by trying to satisfy their desires. The Buddha's prescription for dealing with suffering is quite different. Instead of trying to satisfy your desires, try to eliminate them. Do you think that this is possible? Think of a strong (but unsatisfied) desire you have, one that is causing you some degree of misery. Could you eliminate this desire? What would be the result? How could the Buddha's advice be fruitfully implemented in regard to other aspects of your life?

2. *On karma and rebirth*: People commonly wonder why some persons (perhaps themselves) have been born into unfortunate circumstances, while others have been born into quite fortunate circumstances. In a sense, the world seems unfair. How does the concept of karma help to alleviate this problem? Does viewing human existence as ruled by karma

make life seem more, or less, comprehensible? Do you think that believing in karma provides an incentive to leading a morally good life?

3. *The path to nirvana*: Nirvana is described as a state of "emptiness." Why might this be an attractive state to be in, given the Buddha's emphasis on the inevitable suffering of human existence? Would attaining such a state be more attractive to one who leads a life of intense suffering, or to one who feels that his life is more or less satisfactory? Does it seem to you like a worthwhile goal to strive for?

Suggestions for Further Reading

On the important notion of Dharma, see A. Creel, "*Dharma* as an Ethical Category Relating to Freedom and Responsibility," *Philosophy East and West,* vol. 22 (1972), pp. 155–168 and J. Koller, "*Dharma*: An Expression of Universal Order," *Philosophy East and West,* vol. 22 (1972), pp. 131–144. On the notion of samsara and its relation to ethics, see George Rupp, "The Relationship Between Nirvana and Samsara: An Essay on the Evolution of Buddhist Ethics," *Philosophy East and West,* vol. 21 (Jan. 1971), pp. 55–67. For more on the Buddha, see Bart K. Gruzalski, *On the Buddha* (Belmont, Calif.: Wadsworth, 2000).

For a good selection of Buddhist scriptures, see William Theodore de Bary, ed., *The Buddhist Tradition in India, China, and Japan* (New York: Modern Library, 1969), and Edward Conze, et al., eds., *Buddhist Texts Through the Ages* (New York: Harper Colophon, 1964). Ok Sun An, *Compassion and Benevolence: A Comparative Study of Early Buddhist and Classical Confucian Ethics* (New York: Lang, 1998), as the title suggests, compares Buddhist and Confucian ethics. For a discussion of Buddhist ethics as it relates to issues in Western ethics, see Padmasiri de Silva, "Buddhist Ethics," in *A Companion to Ethics,* edited by Peter Singer (Oxford: Blackwell, 1991), pp. 58–68. Other useful works include H. Saddhatissa, *Buddhist Ethics* (London: Allen and Unwin, 1970); K. N. Jayatilleke, *Ethics in Buddhist Perspective* (Kandy, Sri Lanka: Buddhist Publication Society, 1972); Shundo Tachibana, *The Ethics of Buddhism* (New York: Barnes and Noble, 1975); G. Dharmasiri, *Fundamentals of Buddhist Ethics* (Singapore: Buddhist Research Society, 1986); Russell F. Sizemore and Donald K. Swearer, eds., *Ethics, Wealth, and Salvation: A Study in Buddhist Social Ethics* (Columbia, S.C.: University of South Carolina Press, 1990); and Charles S. Prebish, *Buddhist Ethics: A Cross-Cultural Approach* (Dubuque, Ia.: Kendall Hunt Publishing Co., 1992). Douglas Renfrew Brooks, "Indian, Tibetan, and Southeast Asian Buddhist Ethics," and Kyoko Tokuno, "Chinese Buddhist Ethics," both in *A Bibliographic Guide to the Comparative Study of Ethics,* edited by John Carmen, et al. (New York: Cambridge University Press, 1991), provide additional references for study. Another good source is *A Companion to World Philosophies,* edited by Eliot Deutsch (Cambridge: Blackwell Publishers, 1997), which contains two interesting essays on Buddhist ethics: Knut A. Jacobsen, "Humankind and Nature in Buddhism," and P. D. Premasiri, "Ideas of the Good in Buddhist Philosophy." Karl Jaspers, *The Great Philosophers*, edited by Hannah Arendt and translated by Ralph Manheim (New York: Harcourt, Brace and World, 1966), devotes a chapter to the thought of Nagarjuna. Frederick J. Steng, *Emptiness: A Study in Religious Meaning* (Nashville: Abington Press, 1967), is a more extended discussion of Nagarjuna's philosophy.

InfoTrac

Buddhism, Buddhist, dharma, "ritual and ceremony", suffering, self (philosophy), Nagarjuna

PART IV

Some Contemporary Moral Issues

Quid vitae sectabor iter?
(What way of life shall I follow?)

—AUSONIUS

THE WESTERN AND EASTERN moral perspectives presented in Parts II and III of this book represent much of the accumulated moral wisdom of humanity. As such they might well be sufficient to set the serious seeker of moral wisdom well on her way. But serious ethical reflection has always occurred in the context of specific problems that individuals have felt to be pressing and in need of solution. One of the best ways to test the perspectives introduced in Parts II and III is to attempt to apply them to moral issues that affect nearly all people at some time in their life and that are practically unavoidable given the present context in which we live. Alternatively, one may regard the perspectives represented in previous parts of this book as providing resources for approaching the difficult moral issues introduced below. Ideally, major ethical perspectives and specific moral problems may illuminate each other, casting light in both directions.

One of the central areas in which our ability to choose wisely is tested is the realm of sexuality. Sex has a peculiar "pull" on most of us. Next to the will to live, the desire for sexual satisfaction may be the most intense drive people experience. As such it has the potential to affect the quality of our lives profoundly. It also raises a number of issues of a distinctively ethical nature. How should this drive be directed? Under what conditions is satisfaction of sexual urges morally permissible? What is the purpose (or what are the purposes) of sex, and under what conditions is this purpose best satisfied? These and related questions are discussed from both Western and Eastern perspectives in the readings in Chapter 9.

Obviously, one of the common consequences of sexual activity is pregnancy. When such a consequence is desired there are rarely any moral complications to interfere with the joy of parenthood. But when pregnancy is unwanted, a number of extremely difficult moral issues arise. Foremost among these is the problem of abortion. Besides its very public nature in this country, this is an intensely personal issue that reveals, or makes us determine, our fundamental values concerning life—our own and that of others. The reading selections below that discuss this issue treat it as one that is properly approached in a reflective manner, rather than as an occasion for advancing a political program. Nonreligious and religiously influenced Western and Eastern perspectives are included in Chapter 10.

The question of when it is morally permissible to take a fetus's life is a difficult one. Equally difficult is the question of whether it is morally permissible to end a person's life when that person has reached a point where life no longer seems to be worth continuing. Although we often fail to realize it, except in times of extreme hardship each of us possesses a power that is staggering in its implications: Each of us has the power of life and death over ourselves, and often over others as well. We can choose when to die. How this choice is to be exercised has been a matter of intense disagreement. When (if ever) is it right to take one's own life? When (if ever) is it right to take the life of another person? Is it permissible to end a person's life when that person is in pain and has very little prospect for a life that would be fulfilling? Chapter 11 discusses the related issues of suicide and euthanasia, again providing Western and Eastern perspectives on these difficult issues.

Most people who find themselves in the difficult situation of having to contemplate euthanasia do so in relation to a close family member. This situation raises additional moral issues of a special nature. For most of us, our first exposure to morality occurs within the family: Parents instill ideals of correct behavior in children. As children grow, they come to question the standards articulated by their parents. (This may be more common in the West than in the East.) At a certain age they are able to defy their parents' wishes and do as they see fit. But the parent-child relationship does not end at this point. Children will continue being the offspring of their parents regardless of other changes taking place in the relationship. Do grown children still have moral obligations toward their parents? If so, how far do such obligations extend? These questions are tackled in Chapter 12. Again, Western and Eastern perspectives are represented.

One of the aspects of modern culture that dramatically affects both the length and quality of our lives is technology. We live in a time of unprecedented advances in the ability to control and manipulate our world. Technology brings with it the potential for tremendous goods. The danger, however, is that our technology advances faster than our ability to adequately reflect on the moral implications of technology in its various guises. How should ethics be re-thought in light of our new capabilities? How is technology changing the ways in which people relate to one another? What are the cultural implications of technologies like the Internet? And what about the incredible advances being made in medically related fields, like genetic engineering? Chapter 13 examines these and other related issues.

One of the most salient ways in which many of us come into contact with the products of technology is through the various forms of media we employ: television, radio, films, the Internet, and the like. Much (or all) of this is driven by the goal of advertisers to make us notice their products, and then to redistribute some of our financial resources to them (i.e., buy what they are selling). It hardly needs pointing out that a variety of different strategies can be employed in order to get us to part with our hard-earned dollars, some of them more ethically benign than others. But why should ethical matters enter at all into an area such as advertising? Does truthfulness, for example, matter in the marketing of items? What about honesty? Should advertising be seen as communicating reliable information, or instead as a form of entertainment? In addition, how does exposure to advertising change the way we think about the world? How should such changes be morally assessed? Chapter 14 raises and examines such questions from a number of different perspectives.

The goal of advertising is to generate income for the advertisers. Advertising is a form of business. Business is often competitive with a focus on maximizing profits. But a single-minded focus on maximizing profits can easily blind one to the ethical issues at stake. How might one pursue business activity in a morally responsible manner? What sorts of values should be emphasized in business transactions? Is it even possible to articulate a coherent ethics for business? Is "business ethics" an oxymoron? How might a concern with profits and a concern with doing the right thing be harmonized? Finally, how might some of the great thinkers of the past help us to see how one might conduct business activity in a morally acceptable manner? Chapter 15 is devoted to exploring such issues.

The sections described above all focus, in one way or another, on interpersonal relationships. Perhaps this is not surprising, given the centrality of such relationships in our lives. But in recent years there has been a growing awareness that human beings constitute only part of the domain of beings worthy of moral consideration. We share this world with an astounding diversity of living beings as well as the environments they inhabit. For most of human history the most urgent concern was with overcoming nature for the sake of human survival. Now the roles have reversed. Nature, as we have known it, is now in imminent danger from the activities of human beings. What sort of considerations ought to be extended to nature? Upon what principles should we develop policies for our interactions with the natural world? These are difficult questions that continue to be debated. Chapter 16 contains Western and Eastern perspectives on these questions.

Each of the sections below contains two Western and two Eastern perspectives. However, Western views and Eastern views do not always align themselves on the same side for each of these issues. Sometimes the two Western views included agree with one another. Other times they do not. The same is true for the Eastern perspectives included. Given the complexity and richness of each of these traditions, this should hardly be cause for surprise. What is important is not such agreement, but rather the realizations that any moral issue may be approached from a number of different perspectives and that each of these perspectives may have something of genuine value to contribute to the resolution, or at least to the advancement, of that issue. This is where the active involvement of the reader becomes essential. As a serious seeker after moral wisdom, it is up to you to try to understand and critically evaluate each of these perspectives and to then develop your own perspective on the issue. Only through your own involvement with these issues will the value of the perspectives offered be realized.

Chapter 9

Sexual Morality

Introduction: The Ethics of Sex

It would be difficult to think of an issue that people find more fascinating than sex. Advertisers, songwriters, and movie executives can count on this interest whenever selecting topics or themes around which to create forms of entertainment. In our personal lives, concerns about sex dominate an unusually significant proportion of our time and attention. For most of us, sex is both a blessing and a problem, although not necessarily in that order. Sexuality becomes a philosophical, and especially moral, issue when we stop to reflect more carefully on this powerful force that affects us so profoundly. Under what conditions is engaging in sexual activity morally permissible? Is premarital sex immoral? Extramarital sex? Sex without love? What about homosexuality? Am I entitled to make moral judgments about other people's sexuality? What, after all, is the purpose and role of sexuality in human life? All these questions, and many others as well, are unavoidable once one begins reflecting seriously on sexuality.

The reading selections included below have been selected to help you begin answering such questions for yourself. The first two reading selections discuss the nature and purpose of sexual desire and activity from Western perspectives. Roger Scruton defends an Aristotelian perspective on sexual morality, in which human beings are treated as essentially "embodied" beings, and in which considerations of the good for "human nature" play especially important roles. Alan Goldman, on the other hand, defends what he calls a Kantian approach to sexual morality. He carefully distinguishes what properly belongs to sexual desire and activity from various extraneous elements that have been mistakenly associated with it. His view stands in stark contrast with that of Scruton.

The second two reading selections discuss the nature and role of sexual activity in human life from two different Eastern perspectives: Confucianism and Taoism. As an examination of these selections will make clear, it would be a mistake to think there is a single "Eastern view" of such matters. Asian philosophers differ as much among themselves as do Western philosophers, and for much the same reason. How sexual activity (or any substantial human activity) is viewed depends a great deal on one's larger conception of the purpose of human life and the role of that activity in regard to this purpose. The Confucian and Taoist perspectives represented below begin with very different views of these matters and hence end with quite different conclusions.

Roger Scruton, Sexual Morality

In the following reading selection, Roger Scruton presents an explicitly Aristotelian approach to sexual morality. Recall that central to Aristotle's moral theory is the concept of moral virtue. Moral virtue is a settled disposition to act in certain characteristic ways, for example, to select the "mean" between extremes of action. The point of the moral life is to achieve happiness by realizing the distinctive aspects of one's nature. Scruton applies these ideas to sexuality. He explicitly juxtaposes the "traditional," Aristotelian understanding of sexuality with Kantian and utilitarian approaches. His view contrasts sharply with that defended by Alan Goldman in the subsequent selection.

Reading Questions

1. Scruton asks whether there is such a thing as sexual virtue; what is his answer? Why does he speak of sexual *virtue*? In what ways is his approach an *Aristotelian* approach to sexual morality?

2. According to Scruton, in what way should sexual virtue have the character of a mean (in the Aristotelian sense)? What are the extremes to be avoided in relation to sexual desire? How is this mean to be achieved?

3. What is the role of moral education on Scruton's view? How should sexual desire in children be subject to training and education?

4. On Scruton's view, how are love and sexual desire related? Is it possible to properly experience the latter without the former? What dangers does Scruton see in separating sexual desire from love?

Sexual Morality

ROGER SCRUTON

THE SUBJECT OF THIS CHAPTER is of such importance that my treatment must inevitably limit itself to first suggestions. I hope that those who disagree with my conclusions will at least find, in the supporting arguments, a procedure whereby to refute them. My purpose is not to provide a comprehensive philosophy of morals, but to show how a plausible account of moral reasoning may, when combined with the foregoing theory of sexual desire, lead to an intuitively persuasive sexual morality.

Reprinted with permission of The Free Press, a Division of Simon & Schuster, from Roger Scruton, "Sexual Morality," in Sexual Desire: A Moral Philosophy of the Erotic *(New York: Free Press, 1986), pp. 322–347.* © 1986.

Morality, in its fundamental meaning, is a condition upon practical reasoning. It is a constraint upon reasons for action, which is felt by most rational beings and which is, furthermore, a normal consequence of the possession of a first-person perspective. Morality must be understood, therefore, in first-person terms: in terms of the reasoning that *leads* to action.

Our life is limited by what is forbidden, and fulfilled in what is valuable. Kantian philosophy, which subsumes both those facts under the idea of duty, has been of enormous appeal, partly because it imposes a coherent and unified structure on moral thought, and partly because it shows moral thinking to be a necessary consequence of rational agency, and an expression of the first-person perspective that defines our condition. It is now evident, however, that Kant's attempt to derive morality from the categorical imperative, and the categorical imperative from the first-person perspective (the perspective that forces on us the idea of a "transcendental freedom"), is unlikely to succeed. For Kant, the sympathy that we feel for the virtuous, and the benevolent emotions that prompt us to do what virtue commands, are not genuine expressions of morality, but merely "empirical determinations," which intrude into the realm of practical reason only to deflect it from its categorical purposes. Many have entirely rejected Kant's theory on account of this, while others have tried to modify it, reinterpreting the categorical imperative, either as a special kind of *thought* contained within the moral emotions, or as a kind of normative emotion, which may perhaps grow from human sympathy, but which spreads its charge over the whole human world. Those modifications of Kant's view retain what I believe to be its central idea: that moral reasoning expresses the view of ourselves which is imposed on us by our existence as persons, and by our interaction with others of our kind. Moral reasoning is the formal recognition of the strictures placed upon us by our interpersonal attitudes, from which in turn our existence as persons derives....

Kant's approach is the most beautiful and thorough of all the theories which try to find the basis of morality in the first-person perspective, and its failure must serve as a warning. We should, I believe, follow the path of those philosophers—notably Aristotle—who have looked for the grounds of first-person practical reason outside the immediate situation of the agent. Kant's principal opponent—Hume—was such a philosopher. But his skepticism, and his grotesque caricature of the human mind, render him a doubtful authority. I propose, like Hume's predecessors,

Shaftesbury and Hutcheson, to return to the philosophical intuitions of Aristotle, and to refurbish them for the needs of a modern moral perspective.

The weakness of the Kantian position lies in its attribution of a "motivating force" to reason—in its denial of Hume's principle that reason alone cannot be a motive to action. The Aristotelian position involves no commitment to the idea of a "pure practical reason." It recognizes that practical reasoning concludes in action only because it begins in desire....

Aristotle's strategy, in the *Nicomachean Ethics*, is not easy to grasp, and is open to many interpretations. The strategy I shall propose may or may not be identical with Aristotle's; at least, it is inspired by Aristotle's and leads to similar conclusions. I suggest that Aristotle's invocation of happiness, as the final end of human conduct, is essentially correct. Happiness is the single final answer to the question "why do that?" the answer which survives the conflict with every rival interest or desire. In referring to happiness we refer, not to the satisfaction of impulses, but to the fulfillment of the person. We all have reason to want this fulfillment, and we want it reasonably, whatever our other desires, and whatever our circumstances. In moral education this alone is certain: that the child ought to be happy, and hence that whatever disposition is essential to happiness is a disposition that he has reason to acquire....

The Aristotelian approach offers hope to those who seek for a secular morality of sexual conduct. Not only does it place in the forefront of moral thinking the crucial practice through which sexual morality arises—the practice of moral education; it also gives cogency to prohibitions and privations—something that a secular morality seems otherwise incompetent to do. Thus, in the same way as the sacrifice of the brave man in battle may be shown to be supremely reasonable, so too might we justify such peculiar practices as chastity, modesty and sexual hesitation. Although these block the road to present pleasure, and seen from the immediate first-person point of view, are wholly irrational, they may yet be justified in terms of the disposition from which they spring. It may be in the long-term interests of the rational agent that he acquire just this kind of control over his sexual impulses....

We must now attempt to apply the Aristotelian strategy to the subject-matter of this [chapter], and ask whether there is such a thing as sexual virtue, and, if so, what is it, and how is it acquired? Clearly, sexual desire, which is an interpersonal attitude with the most far-reaching consequences for those who are joined by it, cannot be morally neutral. On the contrary, it is in the experience of sexual desire that we are most vividly conscious of the distinction between virtuous and vicious impulses, and most vividly aware that, in the choice between them, our happiness is at stake.

The Aristotelian strategy enjoins us to ignore the actual conditions of any particular person's life, and to look only at the permanent features of human nature. We know that people feel sexual desire; that they feel erotic love, which may grow from desire; that they may avoid both these feelings, by dissipation or self-restraint. Is there anything to be said about desire, other than that it falls within the general scope of the virtue of temperance, which enjoins us to desire only what reason approves?

The first, and most important, observation to be made is that the capacity for love in general, and for erotic love in particular, is a virtue. . . . Erotic love involves an element of mutual self-enhancement; it generates a sense of the irreplaceable value, both of the other and of the self, and of the activities which bind them. To receive and to give this love is to achieve something of incomparable value in the process of self-fulfillment. It is to gain the most powerful of all interpersonal *guarantees*; in erotic love the subject becomes conscious of the full reality of his personal existence, not only in his own eyes, but in the eyes of another. Everything that he is and values gains sustenance from his love, and every project receives a meaning beyond the moment. All that exists for us as mere hope and hypothesis—the attachment to life and to the body—achieves under the rule of *erōs* the aspect of a radiant certainty. Unlike the cold glances of approval, admiration and pride, the glance of love sees value precisely in that which is the source of anxiety and doubt: in the merely contingent, merely "empirical," existence of the flesh, the existence which we did not choose, but not which we are condemned. It is the answer to man's fallen condition—to his *Geworfenheit*.[1]

To receive erotic love, however, a person must be able to give it: or if he cannot, the love of others will be a torment to him, seeking from him that which he cannot provide, and directing against him the fury of a disappointed right. It is therefore unquestionable that we have reason to acquire the capacity for erotic love, and, if this means bending our sexual impulses in a certain direction, that will be the direction of sexual virtue. Indeed, . . . the development of the

sexual impulse toward love may be impeded: there are sexual habits which are vicious, precisely in neutralizing the capacity for love. The first thing that can be said, therefore, is that we all have reason to avoid those habits and to educate our children not to possess them. . . .

Love, I have argued, is prone to jealousy, and the object of jealousy is defined by the thought of the beloved's desire. Because jealousy is one of the greatest of psychical catastrophes, involving the possible ruin of both partners, a morality based in the need for erotic love must forestall and eliminate jealousy. It is in the deepest human interest, therefore, that we form the habit of fidelity. This habit is natural and normal; but it is also easily broken, and the temptation to break it is contained in desire itself—in the element of generality which tempts us always to experiment, to verify, to detach ourselves from that which is too familiar in the interest of excitement and risk. Virtuous desire is faithful; but virtuous desire is also an artifact, made possible by a process of moral education which we do not, in truth, understand in its complexity.

If that observation is correct, a whole section of traditional sexual morality must be upheld. The fulfillment of sexual desire defines the nature of desire: *to telos phuseis estin*. And the nature of desire gives us our standard of normality. There are enormous varieties of human sexual conduct, and of "common-sense" morality: some societies permit or encourage polygamy, others look with indifference upon premarital intercourse, or regard marriage itself as no more than an episode in a relation that preexists and perhaps survives it. But no society, and no "common-sense" morality—not even, it seems, the morality of Samoa—looks with favor upon promiscuity or infidelity, unless influenced by a doctrine of "emancipation" or "liberation" which is dependent for its sense upon the very conventions which it defies. Whatever the institutional forms of human sexual union, and whatever the range of permitted partners, sexual desire is itself inherently "nuptial": it involves concentration upon the embodied existence of the other, leading through tenderness to the "vow" of erotic love. It is a telling observation that the civilization which has most tolerated the institution of polygamy—the Islamic—has also, in its erotic literature, produced what are perhaps the interesting and most poignant celebrations of monogamous love, precisely through the attempt to capture, not the institution of marriage, but the human datum of desire.

The nuptiality of desire suggests, in its turn, a natural history of desire: a principle of development

[1]Editor's note: *Geworfenheit* is Heidegger's term for our state of being in the world; it means "throwness," or literally "being thrown into."

which defines the "normal course" of sexual education. "Sexual maturity" involves incorporating the sexual impulse into the personality, and so making sexual desire into an expression of the subject himself, even though it is, in the heat of action, a force which also overcomes him. If the Aristotelian approach to these things is as plausible as I think it is, the virtuous habit will also have the character of a "mean": it will involve the disposition to desire what is desirable, despite the competing impulses of animal lust (in which the intentionality of desire may be demolished) and timorous frigidity (in which the sexual impulse is impeded altogether). Education is directed toward the special kind of temperance which shows itself, sometimes as chastity, sometimes as fidelity, sometimes as passionate desire, according to the "right judgment" of the subject. In wanting what is judged to be desirable, the virtuous person wants what may also be loved, and what may therefore be obtained without hurt or humiliation.

Virtue is a matter of degree, rarely attained in its completion, but always admired. Because traditional sexual education has pursued sexual virtue, it is worthwhile summarizing its most important features, in order to see the power of the idea that underlies and justifies it.

The most important feature of traditional sexual education is summarized in anthropological language as the "ethic of pollution and taboo." The child was taught to regard his body as sacred, and as subject to pollution by misperception or misuse. The sense of pollution is by no means a trivial side-effect of the "bad sexual encounter": it may involve a penetrating disgust, at oneself, one's body and one's situation, such as is experienced by the victim of rape. Those sentiments—which arise from our "fear of the obscene"—express the tension contained within the experience of embodiment. At any moment we can become "mere body," the self driven from its incarnation, and its habitation ransacked. The most important root idea of personal morality is that I am *in* my body, not (to borrow Descartes's image) as a pilot in a ship, but as an incarnate self. My body is identical with me, and sexual purity is the precious guarantee of this.

Sexual purity does not forbid desire: it simply ensures the status of desire as an interpersonal feeling. The child who learns "dirty habits" detaches his sex from himself, sets it outside himself as something curious and alien. His fascinated enslavement to the body is also a withering of desire, a scattering of erotic energy and a loss of union with the other. Sexual purity sustains the *subject* of desire, making

him present as a self in the very act which overcomes him. . . .

The child was traditionally brought up to achieve sexual fulfillment only *through* chastity, which is the condition which surrounds him on his first entering the adult world—the world of commitments and obligations. At the same time, he was encouraged to ponder certain "ideal objects" of desire. These, presented to him under the aspect of an idealized physical beauty, were never *merely* beautiful, but also endowed with the moral attributes that fitted them for love. This dual inculcation of "pure" habits and "ideal" love might seem, on the face of it, to be unworthy of the name of education. Is it not, rather, like the mere *training* of a horse or a dog, which arbitrarily forbids some things and fosters others, without offering the first hint of a reason why? And is it not the distinguishing mark of education that it engages with the rational nature of its recipient, and does not merely mold him indifferently to his own understanding of the process? Why, in short, is this moral education, rather than a transference into the sexual sphere—as Freud would have it—of those same processes of interdiction that train us to defecate, not in our nappies, but in a porcelain pot?

The answer is clear. The cult of innocence is an attempt to *generate* rational conduct, but incorporating the sexual impulse into the self-activity of the subject. It is an attempt to impede the impulse, until such a time as it may attach itself to the interpersonal project that leads to its fulfillment: the project of union with another person, who is wanted not merely for his body, but for the person who *is* this body. Innocence is the disposition to avoid sexual encounter, except with the person whom one may fully desire. Children who have lost their innocence have acquired the habit of gratification through the body alone, in a state of partial or truncated desire. Their gratification is detached from the conditions of personal fulfillment and wanders from object to object with no settled tendency to attach itself to any, pursued all the while by a sense of the body's obscene dominion. "Debauching of the innocent" was traditionally regarded as a most serious offense, and one that offered genuine *harm* to the victim. The harm in question was not physical, but moral: the undermining of the process which prepares the child to enter the world of *erōs*. (Thus Nabokov's Lolita, who passes with such rapidity from the childish provocativeness to a knowing interest in the sexual act, finds, in the end, a marriage devoid of passion, and dies without knowledge of desire.)

The personal and the sexual can become divorced in many ways. The task of sexual morality is to unite them, to sustain thereby the intentionality of desire, and to prepare the individual for erotic love. Sexual morality is the morality of embodiment: the posture which strives to unite us with our bodies, precisely in those situations when our bodies are foremost in our thoughts. Without such a morality the human world is subject to a dangerous divide, a gulf between self and body, at the verge of which all our attempts at personal union falter and withdraw. Hence the prime focus of sexual morality is not the attitude to others, but the attitude to one's own body and its uses. Its aim is to safeguard the integrity of our embodiment. Only on that condition, it is thought, can we inculcate either innocence in the young or fidelity in the adult. Such habits are, however, only one part of sexual virtue. Traditional morality has combined its praise of them with a condemnation of other things—in particular of the habits of lust and perversion. And it is not hard to find the reason for these condemnations.

Perversion consists precisely in a diverting of the sexual impulse from its interpersonal goal, or toward some act that is intrinsically destructive of personal relations and of the values that we find in them. The "dissolution" of the flesh, which the Marquis de Sade regarded as so important an element in the sexual aim, is in fact the dissolution of the soul; the perversions described by de Sade are not so much attempts to destroy the flesh of the victim as to rid his flesh of its personal meaning, to wring out, with the blood, the rival perspective. That is true in one or another of all perversion, which can be simply described as the habit of finding a sexual release that avoids or abolishes the *other*, obliterating his embodiment with the obscene perception of his body. Perversion is narcissistic, often solipsistic, involving strategies of replacement which are intrinsically destructive of personal feeling. Perversion therefore prepares us for a life without personal fulfillment, in which no human relation achieves foundation in the acceptance of the other, as this acceptance is provided by desire.

Lust may be defined as a genuine sexual desire, from which the goal of erotic love has been excluded, and in which whatever tends toward that goal—tenderness, intimacy, fidelity, dependence—is curtailed or obstructed. There need be nothing perverted in this. Indeed the special case of lust . . . of Don Juanism, in which the project of intimacy is constantly abbreviated by the flight toward another sexual object, provides one of our paradigms of desire. Nevertheless, the traditional condemnation of lust is far from arbitrary, and the associated contrast between lust and love far from a matter of convention. Lust is also a habit, involving the disposition to

give way to desire, without regard to any personal relation with the object. (Thus perversions are all forms of lust even though lust is not in itself a perversion.) Naturally, we all feel the promptings of lust, but the rapidity with which sexual acts become sexual habits, and the catastrophic effect of a sexual act which cannot be remembered without shame or humiliation, give us strong reasons to resist them, reasons that Shakespeare captured in these words:

Th'expence of Spirit in a waste of shame
Is lust in action, and till action, lust
Is perjur'd, murdrous, blouddy, full of blame,
Savage, extreame, rude, cruell, not to trust,
Injoyd no sooner but dispised straight,
Past reason hunted, and no sooner had,
Past reason hated as a swollowed bayt,
On purpose layd to make the taker mad:
Mad in pursuit and in possession so,
Had, having, and in quest to have, extreame,
A blisse in proofe, and prov'd, a very woe,
Before a joy proposd, behind, a dreame,
   All this the world well knowes, yet none
     knowes well
   To shun the heaven that leads men to this hell.

In addition to the condemnation of lust and perversion, however, some part of traditional sexual education can be seen as a kind of sustained war against fantasy. It is undeniable that fantasy can play an important part in all our sexual doings, and even the most passionate and faithful lover may, in the act of love, rehearse to himself other scenes of sexual abandon than the one in which he is engaged. Nevertheless, there is truth in the contrast (familiar, in one version, from the writings of Freud) between fantasy and reality, and in the sense that the first is in some way destructive of the second. Fantasy replaces the real, resistant, objective world with a pliant substitute—and that, indeed, is its purpose. Life in the actual world is difficult and embarrassing. Most of all it is difficult and embarrassing in our confrontation with other people, who, by their very existence, make demands that we may be unable or unwilling to meet. It requires a great force, such as the force of sexual desire, to overcome the embarrassment and self-protection that shield us from the most intimate encounters. It is tempting to take refuge in substitutes, which neither embarrass us nor resist the impulse of our spontaneous cravings. The habit grows, in masturbation, of creating a compliant world of desire, in which unreal objects become the focus of real emotions, and the emotions themselves are rendered incompetent to participate in the building of personal relations. The fantasy blocks the passage to reality, which becomes inaccessible to the will.

Even if the fantasy can be overcome so far as to engage in the act of love with another, a peculiar danger remains. The other becomes veiled in substitutes; he is never fully himself in the act of love; it is never clearly *him* that I desire, or *him* that I *possess*, but always rather a composite object, a universal body, of which he is but one among a potential infinity of instances. Fantasy fills our thoughts with a sense of the obscene, and the orgasm becomes, not the possession of another, but the expenditure of energy on his depersonalized body. Fantasies are private property, which I can dispose according to my will, with no answerability to the other whom I abuse through them. He, indeed, is of no intrinsic interest to me, and serves merely as my opportunity for self-regarding pleasure. For the fantasist, the ideal partner is indeed the prostitute, who, because she can be purchased, solves at once the moral problem presented by the presence of another at the scene of sexual release.

The connection between fantasy and prostitution is deep and important. The effect of fantasy is to "commodify" the object of desire, and to replace the law of sexual relationship between people with the law of the market. Sex itself can then be seen as a commodity: something that we pursue and obtain in quantifiable form, and which comes in a variety of packages: in the form of a woman or a man; in the form of a film or a dream; in the form of a fetish or an animal. In so far as the sexual act is seen in this way, it seems morally neutral—or, at best, impersonal. Such criticism as may be offered will concern merely the dangers for the individual and his partner of this or that sexual package: for some bring diseases and discomforts of which others are free. The most harmless and hygienic act of all, on this view, is the act of masturbation, stimulated by whatever works of pornography are necessary to prompt the desire for it in the unimaginative. This justification for pornography has, indeed, recently been offered.

As I have already argued, however, fantasy does not exist comfortably with reality. It has a natural tendency to realize itself: to remake the world in its own image. The harmless wanker with the video-machine can at any moment turn into the desperate rapist with a gun. The "reality principle" by which the normal sexual act is regulated is a principle of personal encounter, which enjoins us to respect the other person, and to respect, also, the sanctity of his body, as the tangible expression of another self. The world of fantasy obeys no such rule, and is governed by monstrous myths and illusions which are at war with the human

world—the illusions, for example, that women wish to be raped, that children have only to be awakened in order to give and receive the intensest sexual pleasure, that violence is not an affront but an affirmation of a natural right. All such myths, nurtured in fantasy, threaten not merely the consciousness of the man who lives by them, but also the moral structure of his surrounding world. They render the world unsafe for self and other, and cause the subject to look on everyone, not as an end in himself, but as a possible means to his private pleasure. In his world, the sexual encounter has been "fetishised," to use the apt Marxian term, and every other human reality has been poisoned by the sense of the expendability and replaceability of the other.

It is a small step from the preoccupation with sexual virtue, to a condemnation of obscenity and pornography (which is its published form). Obscenity is a direct assault on the sentiment of desire, and therefore on the social order that is based in desire and which has personal love as its goal and fulfillment. There is no doubt that the normal conscience cannot remain neutral toward obscenity, any more than it can remain neutral toward pedophilia and rape (which is not to say that obscenity must also be treated as a *crime*). It is therefore unsurprising that traditional moral education has involved censorship of obscene material, and a severe emphasis on "purity in thought, word and deed"—an emphasis which is now greeted with irony or ridicule.

Traditional sexual education was, despite its exaggerations and imbecilities, truer to human nature than the libertarian culture which has succeeded it. Through considering its wisdom and its shortcomings, we may understand how to resuscitate an idea of sexual virtue, in accordance with the broad requirements of the Aristotelian argument that I have, in this chapter, been presenting. The ideal of virtue remains one of "sexual integrity": of a sexuality that is entirely integrated into the life of personal affection, and in which the self and its responsibility are centrally involved and indissolubly linked to the pleasures and passions of the body.

Traditional sexual morality has therefore been the morality of the body. Libertarian morality, by contrast, has relied almost entirely on a Kantian view of the human subject, as related to his body by no coherent moral tie. Focusing as he does on an idea of purely personal respect, and assigning no distinctive place to the body in our moral endeavor, the Kantian inevitably tends toward permissive morality. No sexual act can be wrong merely by virtue of its physical character, and the ideas of obscenity, pollution and perversion have no obvious application. His attitude to homosexuality is conveniently summarized in this passage from a Quaker pamphlet:

> We see no reason why the physical nature of the sexual act should be the criterion by which the question whether it is moral should be decided. An act which (for example) expresses true affection between two individuals and gives pleasure to them both, does not seem to us to be sinful by reason *alone* of the fact that it is homosexual. The same criteria seem to apply whether a relationship is heterosexual or homosexual.

Such sentiments are the standard offering of the liberal and utilitarian moralities of our time. However much we may sympathize with their conclusions, it is not possible to accept the shallow reasoning that leads up to them, and which bypasses the great metaphysical conundrum to which all sexual morality is addressed: the conundrum of embodiment. Lawrence asserts that "sex is *you*," and offers some bad but revealing lines on the subject:

> And don't, with the nasty, prying mind, drag it
> out from its deeps
> And finger it and force it, and shatter the rhythm
> it keeps
> When it is left alone, as it stirs and rouses and
> sleeps.

If anything justifies Lawrence's condemnation of the "nasty, prying mind," it is the opposite of what he supposes. Sex "sleeps" in the soul precisely because, and to the extent that, it is buried there by education. If sex is you, it is because you are the product of that education, and not just its victim. It has endowed you with what I have called "sexual integrity": the ability to be *in* your body, in the very moment of desire.

The reader may be reluctant to follow me in believing that traditional morality is largely justified by the ideal of sexual integrity. But if he accepts the main tenor of my argument, he must surely realize that the ethic of "liberation," far from promising the release of the self from hostile bondage, in fact heralds the dissipation of the self in loveless fantasy: th'expence of Spirit, in a waste of shame.

Discussion and Reflection Questions

1. Scruton links love and sexual desire throughout his essay. What connection is there, or should there be, between love and sexual desire?

2. How does Scruton respond to the claim that prostitution, pornography, sexual fantasizing, and masturbation are all harmless, because there is no victim involved in partaking in any of these things? Is there a victim in any of these activities? Can one victimize *oneself*?

3. What role does the concept of "human nature" play in Scruton's account? What is Scruton's view of human nature? What role should the concept of "human nature" play in one's view of sexual morality?

4. What are Scruton's specific criticisms of Kantian and utilitarian approaches to sexual morality? Has Scruton convinced you that an Aristotelian approach to sexual morality is superior to them?

Alan H. Goldman, Plain Sex

In the following reading, Alan Goldman sets out a "minimal" view of sexual desire and activity, that is, a view of sex that includes only those elements essential to it. The point of doing so is to distinguish what is essential to sex from other elements that are incorrectly associated with it. It is these other elements that give rise to mistaken beliefs about sexual morality. Once the essential features of sex are identified, Goldman argues, one is in a position to reject views that place unnecessary and undesirable restrictions on sexual desire and activity. Goldman thus articulates what might be called the "liberal" view of sexual morality.

Reading Questions

1. What does Goldman mean by "means-end analyses" and why does he find this way of thinking defective for understanding sex? What fault does he locate in this way of viewing sex? What is Goldman's alternative "simple" view of sexual desire? According to Goldman, what is the goal of sexual desire and activity?

2. Why does Goldman reject the view that the purpose of sexual activity is reproduction? How does he handle the objection that sexual activity apart from reproductive activity is "unnatural"?

3. According to Goldman, in what ways is love different from sexual desire? What do these differences suggest about the relationship between love and sexual desire?

4. According to Goldman, what are the moral consequences of his view of sex? Is there a distinctive "sexual ethic" on his view? Which view does he find better supported by reflections on sex: utilitarianism or a Kantian view? Why?

Plain Sex

ALAN H. GOLDMAN

I

Several recent articles on sex herald its acceptance as a legitimate topic for analytic philosophers (although it has been a topic in philosophy since Plato). One might have thought conceptual analysis unnecessary in this area; despite the notorious struggles of judges and legislators to define pornography suitably, we all might be expected to know what sex is and to be able to identify at least paradigm sexual desires and activities without much difficulty. Philosophy is nevertheless of relevance here if for no other reason than that the concept of sex remains at the center of moral and social consciousness in our, and perhaps any, society. Before we can get a sensible view of the relation of sex to morality, perversion, social regulation, and marriage, we require a sensible analysis of the concept itself; one which neither understates its animal pleasure nor overstates its importance within a theory or system of value. I say "before," but the order is not quite so clear, for questions in this area, as elsewhere in moral philosophy, are both conceptual and normative at the same time. Our concept of sex will partially determine our moral view of it, but as philosophers we should formulate a concept that will accord with its proper moral status. What we re-

quire here, as elsewhere, is "reflective equilibrium," a goal not achieved by traditional and recent analyses together with their moral implications. Because sexual activity, like other natural functions such as eating or exercising, has become imbedded in layers of cultural, moral, and superstitious superstructure, it is hard to conceive it in its simplest terms. But partially for this reason, it is only by thinking about plain sex that we can begin to achieve this conceptual equilibrium.

I shall suggest here that sex continues to be misrepresented in recent writings, at least in philosophical writings, and I shall criticize the predominant form of analysis which I term "means-end analysis." Such conceptions attribute a necessary external goal or purpose to sexual activity, whether it be reproduction, the expression of love, simple communication, or interpersonal awareness. They analyze sexual activity as a means to one of these ends, implying that sexual desire is a desire to reproduce, to love or to be loved, or to communicate with others. All definitions of this type suggest false views of the relationship of sex to perversion and morality by implying that sex which does not fit one of these models or fulfill one of these functions is in some way deviant or incomplete.

Alan H. Goldman, "Plain Sex," Philosophy and Public Affairs, *vol. 6, no. 3 (Spring 1977), pp. 267–287.*
Copyright © 1977 by Princeton University Press. Reprinted by permission of Princeton University Press.

The alternative, simpler analysis with which I will begin is that sexual desire is desire for contact with another person's body and for the pleasure which such contact produces; sexual activity is activity which tends to fulfill such desire of the agent. Whereas Aristotle and Butler were correct in holding that pleasure is normally a byproduct rather than a goal of purposeful action, in the case of sex this is not so clear. The desire for another's body is, principally among other things, the desire for the pleasure that physical contact brings. On the other hand, it is not a desire for a particular sensation detachable from its causal context, a sensation which can be derived in other ways. This definition in terms of the general goal of sexual desire appears preferable to an attempt to more explicitly list or define specific sexual activities, for many activities such as kissing, embracing, massaging, or holding hands may or may not be sexual, depending upon the context and more specifically upon the purposes, needs, or desires into which such activities fit. The generality of the definition also represents a refusal (common in recent psychological texts) to overemphasize orgasm as the goal of sexual desire or genital sex as the only norm of sexual activity (this will be hedged slightly in the discussion of perversion below).

Central to the definition is the fact that the goal of sexual desire and activity is the physical contact itself, rather than something else which this contact might express. By contrast, what I term "means-end analyses" posit ends which I take to be extraneous to plain sex, and they view sex as a means to these ends. Their fault lies not in defining sex in terms of its general goal, but in seeing plain sex as merely a means to other separable ends. I term these "means-end analyses" for convenience, although "means-separable-end analyses," while too cumbersome, might be more fully explanatory. The desire for physical contact with another person is a minimal criterion for (normal) sexual desire, but is both necessary and sufficient to qualify normal desire as sexual. Of course, we may want to express other feelings through sexual acts in various contexts; but without the desire for the physical contact in and for itself, or when it is sought for other reasons, activities in which contact is involved are not predominantly sexual. Furthermore, the desire for physical contact in itself, without the wish to express affection or other feelings through it, is sufficient to render sexual the activity of the agent which fulfills it. Various activities with this goal alone, such as kissing and caressing in certain contexts, qualify as sexual even without the presence of genital symptoms of sexual excitement. The latter are not therefore necessary criteria for sexual activity.

This initial analysis may seem to some either over- or underinclusive. It might seem too broad in leading us to interpret physical contact as sexual desire in activities such as football and other contact sports. In these cases, however, the desire is not for contact with another body per se, it is not directed toward a particular person for that purpose, and it is not the goal of the activity—the goal is winning or exercising or knocking someone down or displaying one's prowess. If the desire is purely for contact with another specific person's body, then to interpret it as sexual does not seem an exaggeration. A slightly more difficult case is that of a baby's desire to be cuddled and our natural response in wanting to cuddle it. In the case of the baby, the desire may be simply for the physical contact, for the pleasure of the caresses. If so, we may characterize this desire, especially in keeping with Freudian theory, as sexual or protosexual. It will differ nevertheless from full-fledged sexual desire in being more amorphous, not directed outward toward another specific person's body. It may also be that what the infant unconsciously desires is not physical contact per se but signs of affection, tenderness, or security, in which case we have further reason for hesitating to characterize its wants as clearly sexual. The intent of our response to the baby is often the showing of affection, not the pure physical contact, so that our definition in terms of action which fulfills sexual desire *on the part of the agent* does not capture such actions, whatever we say of the baby. (If it is intuitive to characterize our response as sexual as well, there is clearly no problem here for my analysis). The same can be said of signs of affection (or in some cultures polite greeting) among men or women: these certainly need not be homosexual when the intent is only to show friendship, something extrinsic to plain sex although valuable when added to it.

Our definition of sex in terms of the desire for physical contact may appear too narrow in that a person's personality, not merely her or his body, may be sexually attractive to another, and in that looking or conversing in a certain way can be sexual in a given context without bodily contact. Nevertheless, it is not the contents of one's thoughts per se that are sexually appealing, but one's personality as embodied in certain manners of behavior. Furthermore, if a person is sexually attracted by another's personality, he or she will desire not just further conversation, but actual sexual contact. While looking at or conversing with someone can be interpreted as sexual in given contexts it is so when intended as preliminary to, and hence parasitic upon, elemental sexual interest. Voyeurism or viewing a pornographic movie qualifies as a sexual activity, but only as an imaginative substitute for the real thing (otherwise a deviation from the norm as expressed in our definition). The same is true of masturbation as a sexual activity without a partner.

That the initial definition indicates at least an ingredient of sexual desire and activity is too obvious to argue. We all know what sex is, at least in obvious cases, and do not need philosophers to tell us. My preliminary analysis is meant to serve as a contrast to what sex is not, at least, not necessarily. I concentrate upon the physically manifested desire for another's body, and I take as central the immersion in the physical aspect of one's own existence and attention to the physical embodiment of the other. One may derive pleasure in a sex act from expressing certain feelings to one's partner or from awareness of the attitude of one's partner, but sexual desire is essentially desire for physical contact itself: it is a bodily desire for the body of another that dominates our mental life for more or less brief periods. Traditional writings were correct to emphasize the purely physical or animal aspect of sex; they were wrong only in condemning it. This characterization of sex as an intensely pleasurable physical activity and acute physical desire may seem to some to capture only its barest level. But it is worth distinguishing and focusing upon this least common denominator in order to avoid the false views of sexual morality and perversion which emerge from thinking that sex is essentially something else.

II

We may turn then to what sex is not, to the arguments regarding supposed conceptual connections between sex and other activities which it is necessary to conceptually distinguish. The most comprehensible attempt to build an extraneous purpose into the sex act identifies that purpose as reproduction, its primary biological function. While this may be "nature's" purpose, it certainly need not be ours (the analogy with eating, while sometimes overworked, is pertinent here). While this identification may once have had a rational basis which also grounded the identification of the value of morality of sex with that applicable to reproduction and childrearing, the development of contraception rendered the connection weak. Methods of contraception are by now so familiar and so widely used that it is not necessary to dwell upon the changes wrought by these develop-

ments in the concept of sex itself and in a rational sexual ethic dependent upon that concept. In the past, the ever present possibility of children rendered the concepts of sex and sexual morality different from those required at present. There may be good reasons, if the presence and care of both mother and father are beneficial to children, for restricting reproduction to marriage. Insofar as society has a legitimate role in protecting children's interests, it may be justified in giving marriage a legal status, although this question is complicated by the fact (among others) that children born to single mothers deserve no penalties. In any case, the point here is simply that these questions are irrelevant at the present time to those regarding the morality of sex and its potential social regulation. (Further connections with marriage will be discussed below.)

It is obvious that the desire for sex is not necessarily a desire to reproduce, that the psychological manifestation has become, if it were not always, distinct from its biological roots. There are many parallels, as previously mentioned, with other natural functions. The pleasures of eating and exercising are to a large extent independent of their roles in nourishment or health (as the junk-food industry discovered with a vengeance). Despite the obvious parallel with sex, there is still a tendency for many to think that sex acts which can be reproductive are, if not more moral or less immoral, at least more natural. These categories of morality and "naturalness," or normality, are not to be identified with each other, as will be argued below, and neither is applicable to sex by virtue of its connection to reproduction. The tendency to identify reproduction as the conceptually connected end of sex is most prevalent now in the pronouncements of the Catholic church. There the assumed analysis is clearly tied to a restrictive sexual morality according to which acts become immoral and unnatural when they are not oriented toward reproduction, a morality which has independent roots in the Christian sexual ethic as it derives from Paul. However, the means-end analysis fails to generate a consistent sexual ethic: homosexual and oral-genital sex is condemned while kissing or caressing, acts equally unlikely to lead in themselves to fertilization, even when properly characterized as sexual according to our definition, are not.

III

Before discussing further relations of means-end analyses to false or inconsistent sexual ethics and concepts of perversion, I turn to other examples of these analyses. One common position views sex as essentially an expression of love or affection between the partners. It is generally recognized that there are other types of love besides sexual, but sex itself is taken as an expression of one type, sometimes termed "romantic" love. Various factors again ought to weaken this identification. First, there are other types of love besides that which it is appropriate to express sexually, and "romantic" love itself can be expressed in many other ways. I am not denying that sex can take on heightened value and meaning when it becomes a vehicle for the expression of feelings of love or tenderness, but so can many other usually mundane activities such as getting up early to make breakfast on Sunday, cleaning the house, and so on. Second, sex itself can be used to communicate many other emotions besides love, and, as I will argue below, can communicate nothing in particular and still be good sex.

On a deeper level, an internal tension is bound to result from an identification of sex, which I have described as a physical-psychological desire, with love as a long-term, deep emotional relationship between two individuals. As this type of relationship, love is permanent, at least in intent, and more or less exclusive. A normal person cannot deeply love more than a few individuals even in a lifetime. We may be suspicious that those who attempt or claim to love many love them weakly if at all. Yet, fleeting sexual desire can arise in relation to a variety of other individuals one finds sexually attractive. It may even be, as some have claimed, that sexual desire in humans naturally seeks variety, while this is obviously false of love. For this reason, monogamous sex, even if justified, almost always represents a sacrifice or the exercise of self-control on the part of the spouses, while monogamous love generally does not. There is no such thing as casual love in the sense in which I intend the term "love." It may occasionally happen that a spouse falls deeply in love with someone else (especially when sex is conceived in terms of love), but this is relatively rare in comparison to passing sexual desires for others; while the former often indicates a weakness or fault in the marriage relation, the latter does not.

If love is indeed more exclusive in its objects than is sexual desire, this explains why those who view sex as essentially an expression of love would again tend to hold a repressive or restrictive sexual ethic. As in the case of reproduction, there may be good reasons for reserving the total commitment of deep love to the context of marriage and family—the normal personality may not withstand additional divi-

sions of ultimate commitment and allegiance. There is no question that marriage itself is best sustained by a deep relation of love and affection; and even if love is not naturally monogamous, the benefits of family units to children provide additional reason to avoid serious commitments elsewhere which weaken family ties. It can be argued similarly that monogamous sex strengthens families by restricting and at the same time guaranteeing an outlet for sexual desire in marriage. But there is more force to the argument that recognition of a clear distinction between sex and love in society would help avoid disastrous marriages which result from adolescent confusion of the two when sexual desire is mistaken for permanent love, and would weaken damaging jealousies which arise in marriages in relation to passing sexual desires. The love and affection of a sound marriage certainly differs from the adolescent romantic variety, which is often a mere substitute for sex in the context of a repressive sexual ethic.

In fact, the restrictive sexual ethic tied to the means-end analysis in terms of love again has failed to be consistent. At least, it has not been applied consistently, but forms part of the double standard which has curtailed the freedom of women. It is predictable in light of this history that some women would not advocate using sex as another kind of means, as a political weapon or as a way to increase unjustly denied power and freedom. The inconsistency in the sexual ethic typically attached to the sex-love analysis, according to which it has generally been taken with a grain of salt when applied to men, is simply another example of the impossibility of tailoring a plausible moral theory in this area to a conception of sex which builds in conceptually extraneous factors.

I am not suggesting here that sex ought never to be connected with love or that it is not a more significant and valuable activity when it is. Nor am I denying that individuals need love as much as sex and perhaps emotionally need at least one complete relationship which encompasses both. Just as sex can express love and take on heightened significance when it does, so love is often naturally accompanied by an intermittent desire for sex. But again love is accompanied appropriately by desires for other shared activities as well. What makes the desire for sex seem more intimately connected with love is the intimacy which is seen to be a natural feature of mutual sex acts. Like love, sex is held to lay one bare psychologically as well as physically. Sex is unquestionably intimate, but beyond that the psychological toll often attached may be a function of the restrictive sexual ethic itself, rather than a legitimate apology for it. The intimacy involved in love is psychologically consuming in a generally healthy way, while the psychological tolls of sexual relations often including embarrassment as a correlate of intimacy, are too often the result of artificial sexual ethics and taboos. The intimacy involved in both love and sex is insufficient in any case in light of previous points to render a means-end analysis in these terms appropriate. . . .

V

I have now criticized various types of analysis sharing or suggesting a common means-end form. I have suggested that analyses of this form relate to attempts to limit moral or natural sex to that which fulfills some purpose of function extraneous to basic sexual desire. The attempts to brand forms of sex outside the idealized models as immoral or perverted fail to achieve consistency with intuitions that they themselves do not directly question. The reproductive model brands oral-genital sex a deviation, but cannot account for kissing or holding hands; the communication account holds voyeurism to be perverted but cannot accommodate sex acts without much conscious thought or seductive nonphysical foreplay; the sex-love model makes most sexual desire seem degrading or base. The first and last condemn extramarital sex on the sound but irrelevant grounds that reproduction and deep commitment are best confined to family contexts. The romanticization of sex and the confusion of sexual desire with love operate in both directions: sex outside the context of romantic love is repressed; once it is repressed, partners become more difficult to find and sex becomes romanticized further, out of proportion to its real value for the individual.

What all these analyses share in addition to a common form is accordance with and perhaps derivation from the Platonic-Christian moral tradition, according to which the animal or purely physical element of humans is the source of immorality, and plain sex in the sense I defined it is an expression of this element, hence in itself to be condemned. All the analyses examined seem to seek a distance from sexual desire itself in attempting to extend it conceptually beyond the physical. The love and communication analyses seek refinement or intellectualization of the desire; plain physical sex becomes vulgar, and too straightforward sexual encounters without an aura of respectable cerebral communicative content are to be avoided. [Robert C.] Solomon explicitly argues that sex cannot be a "mere" appetite, his argument being that if it were, subway exhibitionism and other vul-

gar forms would be pleasing. This fails to recognize that sexual desire can be focused or selective at the same time as being physical. Lower animals are not attracted by every other member of their species, either. Rancid food forced down one's throat is not pleasing, but that certainly fails to show that hunger is not a physical appetite. Sexual desire lets us know that we are physical beings and, indeed, animals; this is why traditional Platonic morality is so thorough in its condemnation. Means-end analyses continue to reflect this tradition, sometimes unwittingly. They show that in conceptualizing sex it is still difficult, despite years of so-called revolution in this area, to free ourselves from the lingering suspicion that plain sex as physical desire is an expression of our "lower selves," that yielding to our animal natures is subhuman or vulgar.

VI

Having criticized these analyses for the sexual ethics and concepts of perversion they imply, it remains to contrast my account along these lines. To the question of what morality might be implied by my analysis, the answer is that there are no moral implications whatever. Any analysis of sex which imputes a moral character to sex acts in themselves is wrong for that reason. There is no morality intrinsic to sex, although general moral rules apply to the treatment of others in sex acts as they apply to all human relations. We can speak of a sexual ethic as we can speak of a business ethic, without implying that business in itself is either moral or immoral or that special rules are required to judge business practices which are not derived from rules that apply elsewhere as well. Sex is not in itself a moral category, although like business it invariably places us into relations with others in which moral rules apply. It gives us opportunity to do what is otherwise recognized as wrong, to harm others, deceive them or manipulate them against their wills. Just as the fact that an act is sexual in itself never renders it wrong or adds to its wrongness if it is wrong on other grounds (sexual acts towards minors are wrong on other grounds, as will be argued below), so no wrong act is to be excused because done from a sexual motive. If a "crime of passion" is to be excused, it would have to be on grounds of temporary insanity rather than sexual context (whether insanity does constitute a legitimate excuse for certain actions is too big a topic to argue here). Sexual motives are among others which may become deranged, and the fact that they are sexual has no bearing in itself on the moral character, whether negative or exculpatory, of the actions deriving from them. Whatever might be true of war, it is certainly not the case that all's fair in love or sex.

Our first conclusion regarding morality and sex is therefore that no conduct otherwise immoral should be excused because it is sexual conduct, and nothing in sex is immoral unless condemned by rules which apply elsewhere as well. The last clause requires further clarification. Sexual conduct can be governed by particular rules relating only to sex itself. But these precepts must be implied by general moral rules when these are applied to specific sexual relations or types of conduct. The same is true of rules of fair business, ethical medicine, or courtesy in driving a car. In the latter case, particular acts on the road may be reprehensible, such as tailgating or passing on the right, which seem to bear no resemblance as actions to any outside the context of highway safety. Nevertheless their immorality derives from the fact that they place others in danger, a circumstance which, when avoidable, is to be condemned in any context. This structure of general and specifically applicable rules describes a reasonable sexual ethic as well. To take an extreme case, rape is always a sexual act and it is always immoral. A rule against rape can therefore be considered an obvious part of sexual morality which has no bearing on nonsexual conduct. But the immorality of rape derives from its being an extreme violation of a person's body, of the right not to be humiliated, and of the general moral prohibition against using other persons against their wills, not from the fact that it is a sexual act.

The application elsewhere of general moral rules to sexual conduct is further complicated by the fact that it will be relative to the particular desires and preferences of one's partner (these may be influenced by and hence in some sense include misguided beliefs about sexual morality itself). This means that there will be fewer specific rules in the area of sexual ethics than in others areas of conduct, such as driving cars, where the relativity of preference is irrelevant to the prohibition of objectively dangerous conduct. More reliance will have to be placed upon the general moral rule, which in this area holds simply that the preferences, desires, and interests of one's partner or potential partner ought to be taken into account. This rule is certainly not specifically formulated to govern sexual relations; it is a form of the central principle of morality itself. But when applied to sex, it prohibits certain actions, such as molestation of children, which cannot be categorized as violations of the rule without at the same time being classified as sexual. I believe this last case is the closest we can come to an action which is

wrong *because* it is sexual, but even here its wrongness is better characterized as deriving from the detrimental effects such behavior can have on the future emotional and sexual life of the naive victims, and from the fact that such behavior therefore involves manipulation of innocent persons without regard for their interests. Hence, this case also involves violation of a general moral rule which applies elsewhere as well.

Aside from faulty conceptual analyses of sex and the influence of the Platonic moral tradition, there are two more plausible reasons for thinking that there are moral dimensions intrinsic to sex acts per se. The first is that such acts are normally intensely pleasurable. According to a hedonistic, utilitarian moral theory they therefore should be at least prima facie morally right, rather than morally neutral in themselves. To me this seems incorrect and reflects unfavorably on the ethical theory in question. The pleasure intrinsic to sex acts is a good, but not, it seems to me, a good with much positive moral significance. Certainly I can have no duty to pursue such pleasure myself, and while it may be nice to give pleasure of any form to others, there is no ethical requirement to do so, given my right over my own body. The exception relates to the context of sex acts themselves, when one partner derives pleasure from the other and ought to return the favor. This duty to reciprocate takes us out of the Kantian moral framework, the central principles of which call for just such reciprocity in human relations. Since independent moral judgments regarding sexual activities constitute one area in which ethic theories are to be tested, these observations indicate here, as I believe others indicate elsewhere, the fertility of the Kantian, as opposed to the utilitarian, principle in reconstructing reasoned moral consciousness.

It may appear from this alternative Kantian viewpoint that sexual acts must be at least prima facie wrong in themselves. This is because they invariably involve at different stages the manipulation of one's partner for one's own pleasure, which might appear to be prohibited on the formulation of Kant's principle which holds that one ought not to treat another as a means to such private ends. A more realistic rendering of this formulation, however, one which recognizes its intended equivalence to the first universalizability principle, admits no such absolute prohibition. Many human relations, most economic transactions for example, involve using other individuals for personal benefit. These relations are immoral only when they are one-sided, when the benefits are not mutual, or when the transactions are not freely and rationally endorsed by all parties. The same holds true of sexual acts. The central principle governing them is the Kantian demand for reciprocity in sexual relations. In order to comply with the second formulation of the categorical imperative, one must recognize the subjectivity of one's partner (not merely by being aroused by her or his desire, as Nagel describes). Even in an act which by its nature "objectifies" the other, one recognizes a partner as a subject with demands and desires by yielding to those desires, by allowing oneself to be a sexual object as well, by giving pleasure or ensuring that the pleasures of the acts are mutual. It is this kind of reciprocity which forms the basis for morality in sex, which distinguishes right acts from wrong in this area as in others. (Of course, prior to sex acts one must gauge their effects upon potential partners and take these longer range interests into account.)

VII

I suggested earlier that in addition to generating confusion regarding the rightness or wrongness of sex acts, false conceptual analyses of the means-end form cause confusion about the value of sex to the individual. My account recognizes the satisfaction of desire and the pleasure this brings as the central psychological function of the sex act for the individual. Sex affords us a paradigm of pleasure, but not a cornerstone of value. For most of us it is not only a needed outlet for desire but also the most enjoyable form of recreation we know. Its value is nevertheless easily mistaken by being confused with that of love, when it is taken as essentially an expression of that emotion. Although intense, the pleasures of sex are brief and repetitive rather than cumulative. They give value to the specific acts which generate them, but not the lasting kind of value which enhances one's whole life. The briefness of these pleasures contributes to their intensity (or perhaps their intensity makes them necessarily brief), but it also relegates them to the periphery of most rational plans for the good life.

By contrast, love typically develops over a long term relation; while its pleasures may be less intense and physical, they are of more cumulative value. The importance of love to the individual may well be central in a rational system of value. And it has perhaps an even deeper moral significance relating to the identification with the interests of another person, which broadens one's possible relationships with others as well. Marriage is again important in preserving this relation between adults and children, which seems as important to the adults as it is to the children in broadening concerns which have a tendency to become selfish. Sexual desire, by contrast, is desire for another which is nevertheless essentially self-regarding. Sexual pleasure is certainly good for the individual, and for many it may be necessary in order for them to function in a reasonably cheerful way. But it bears little relation to those other values just discussed, to which some analyses falsely suggest a conceptual connection.

VIII

While my initial analysis lacks moral implications in itself, as it should, it does suggest by contrast a concept of sexual perversion. Since the concept of perversion is itself a sexual concept, it will always be defined relative to some definition of normal sex; and any conception of the norm will imply a contrary notion of perverse forms. The concept suggested by my account again differs sharply from those implied by the means-end analyses examined above. Perversion does not represent a deviation from the reproductive function (or kissing would be perverted), from a loving relationship (or most sexual desire and many heterosexual acts would be perverted), or from efficiency in communicating (or unsuccessful seduction attempts would be perverted). It is a deviation from a norm, but the norm in question is merely statistical. Of course, not all sexual acts that are statistically unusual are perverted—a three-hour continuous sexual act would be unusual but not necessarily abnormal in the requisite sense. The abnormality in question must relate to the *form of the desire* itself in order to constitute sexual perversion; for example, desire, not for contact with another, but for merely looking, for harming or being harmed, for contact with items of clothing. This concept of sexual abnormality is that suggested by my definition of normal sex in terms of its typical desire. However, not all unusual desires qualify either, only those with the typical physical sexual effects upon the individual who satisfies them. These effects, such as erection in males, were not built into the original definition of sex in terms of sexual desire, for they do not always occur in activities that are properly characterized as sexual, say, kissing for the pleasure of it. But they do seem to bear a closer relation to the definition of activities as perverted. (For those who consider only genital sex sexual, we could build such symptoms into a narrower definition, then speaking of sex in a broad sense as well as "proper" sex.)

. . . I do not deny that the term "perverted" is often used evaluatively (and purely emotively for that matter), or that it has a negative connotation for the average speaker. I do deny that we can find a norm, other than that of statistically usual desire, against which all and only activities that properly count as sexual perversions can be contrasted. Perverted sex is simply abnormal sex, and if the norm is not to be an idealized or romanticized extraneous end or purpose, it must express the way human sexual desires usually manifest themselves. Of course not all norms in other areas of discourse need be statistical in this way. Physical health is an example of a relatively clear norm which does not seem to depend upon the numbers of healthy people. But the concept in this case achieves its clarity through the connection of physical health with other clearly desirable physical functions and characteristics, for example, living longer. In the case of sex, that which is statistically abnormal is not necessarily incapacitating in other ways, and yet these abnormal desires with sexual effects upon their subject do count as perverted to the degree to which their objects deviate from usual ones. The connotations of the concept of perversion beyond those connected with abnormality or statistical deviation derive more from the attitudes of those likely to call certain acts perverted than from specifiable features of the acts themselves. These connotations add to the concept of abnormality that of *sub*normality, but there is no norm against which the latter can be measured intelligibly in accord with all and only acts intuitively called perverted.

The only proper evaluative norms relating to sex involve degrees of pleasure in the acts and moral norms, but neither of these scales coincides with statistical degrees of abnormality, according to which perversion is to be measured. The three parameters operate independently (this was implied for the first two when it was held above that the pleasure of sex is a good, but not necessarily a moral good). Perverted sex may be more or less enjoyable to particular individuals than normal sex, and more or less moral, depending upon the particular relations involved. Raping a sheep may be more perverted than raping a woman, but certainly not more condemnable morally. It is nevertheless true that the evaluative connotations attaching to the term "perverted" derive partly from the fact that most people consider perverted sex highly immoral. Many such acts are forbidden by long standing taboos, and it is sometimes difficult to distinguish what is forbidden from what is immoral. Others, such as sadistic acts, are genuinely immoral, but again not at all because of their connection with sex or abnormality. The principles which condemn these acts would condemn them equally if they were common and nonsexual. It is not true that we properly could continue to consider acts perverted which were found to be very common practice across societies. Such acts, if harmful, might continue to be condemned properly as immoral, but it was just shown that the immorality of an act does not vary with its degree of perversion. If not harmful, common acts previously considered abnormal might continue to be called perverted for a time by the moralistic minority; but the term when applied to such cases would retain only its emotive negative connotation without consistent logical criteria for application. It would represent merely prejudiced moral judgments.

To adequately explain why there is a tendency to so deeply condemn perverted acts would require a treatise in psychology beyond the scope of this paper. Part of the reason undoubtedly relates to the tradition of repressive sexual ethics and false conceptions of sex; another part is the fact that all abnormality seems to disturb and fascinate us at the same time. The former explains why sexual perversion is more abhorrent to many than other forms of abnormality; the latter indicates why we tend to have an emotive and evaluative reaction to perversion in the first place. It may be, as has been suggested according to a Freudian line, that our uneasiness derives from latent desires we are loathe to admit, but this thesis takes us into psychological issues I am not competent to judge. Whatever the psychological explanation, it suffices to point out here that the conceptual connection between perversion and genuine or consistent moral evaluation is spurious and again suggested by misleading means-end idealizations of the concept of sex.

The position I have taken in this paper against those concepts is not totally new. Something similar to it is found in Freud's view of sex, which of course was genuinely revolutionary, and in the body of writings deriving from Freud to the present time. But in his revolt against romanticized and repressive conceptions, Freud went too far—from a refusal to view sex as merely a means to a view of it as the end of all human behavior, although sometimes an elaborately disguised end. This pansexualism led to the thesis (among others) that repression was indeed an inevitable and necessary part of social regulation of any form, a strange consequence of a position that began by opposing the repressive aspects of the means-end view. Perhaps the time finally has arrived when we can achieve a reasonable middle ground in this area, at least in philosophy if not in society.

Discussion and Reflection Questions

1. How would a natural-law theorist like Aquinas respond to Goldman's rejection of means-end analysis regarding sex?

2. Goldman locates the goal of sexual desire and activity in physical contact rather than in some other goal such as expressing love, communicating, or achieving intimacy. Do you think that men and women typically differ on the goals they associate with sexual activity? Could you conduct a survey to find out? What would you predict as the outcome of such a survey?

3. Is there a special morality associated with sexual activity? Or should sexual activity be governed by the same moral principles that pertain to other areas of human experience?

4. Goldman defends a Kantian approach to sexual desire and activity, and rejects a utilitarian approach. Do you agree with this position? Are there other moral perspectives that could be applied to sex?

Chung M. Tse, Confucianism and Contemporary Ethical Issues

In the following reading selection Chung M. Tse explains his interpretation of the Confucian view of sexual morality. At the center of Confucian ethics is the concept of *jen*-mind. As Tse emphasizes, the concept of *jen* is a central concept in Confucian ethics, referring alternatively to magnanimity, benevolence, perfect virtue, compassion, human-heartedness, kindness, love, and so on, or to all of these collectively. One's vocation on earth is to actualize the *jen*-mind's activity in oneself and to assist others in actualizing their own *jen*-mind. The ultimate purpose of such *jen*-mind cultivation is to bring about a world of morally perfect individuals, or the realization of the Great Harmony. Confucianism thus provides a general conceptual framework for assessing moral issues. Tse applies this framework especially to issues involving sexual activity. The result is a set of guidelines designed to respect the *jen*-mind and basic human dignity of each person.

Reading Questions

1. What do Confucians mean by the term "*jen*-mind"? What role does this concept play in Confucian philosophy? What is the purpose of the physical body in relation to *jen*-mind? Which is more important in Confucian moral philosophy, motive or consequence? Why? What does Tse mean when he says that "Confucian ethics is not teleological or rule-governed; it is more a theory of act-deontology"?

2. What are the three fundamental and general principles proposed by Confucian ethics? What directives for living do each of these principles provide? How do these principles attempt to include both concern for oneself and concern for others? According to these principles, what is the ultimate purpose of human life?

3. What does Tse mean when he says that "the Confucian position on sexual morality is unambiguously conservative"? On this view, what is the purpose of sexual intercourse? In what ways is sexual intercourse viewed as a manifestation of Heavenly creation? Why is intercourse, on this view, essentially connected with serious moral considerations? What implications does this view have for the range of morally acceptable conditions for sexual activity?

4. What are the Confucian views on incest, bestiality, rape, child molestation, homosexuality, premarital sex, and extramarital sex? What grounds are mentioned for arriving

at moral judgments concerning each of these issues? How do such judgments reflect broader themes in Confucian moral philosophy? What does Tse mean when he says that "Confucianism does allow a *reasonable* outlet for natural desires"?

Confucianism and Contemporary Ethical Issues

CHUNG M. TSE

Introduction

Confucianism has been associated, invariably and rightly, with the name of Confucius (551–479 B.C.), its mentor. But today's Confucianism as it now stands is the result of elaborations, interpretations, speculations and additions by Confucians of later historic periods. From its early form of moral admonitions in the *Analects*, Confucianism has now evolved into a system of thought penetrating the areas of ethics, metaphysics and religion. The term Confucianism should no longer be taken to stand for a particular ethical theory alone; it rather refers to a body of ideas and beliefs about morality, reality, and the Supreme Being. But it is still true that the ethical remains the ultimate concern and foundation of Confucianism. . . .

Confucian Metaphysics

BASIC MORAL CONCEPTS

The concept of *jen* is basic to Confucianism because it defines or explains nearly all other Confucian concepts, providing unity to the various dimensions of Confucian thought. The concept of *jen* invariably bears upon the Confucian concepts of man, God, natural and supernatural realities, and morality. It is therefore imperative to begin with an elucidation of the concept of *jen* as a structural element of the framework of Confucianism.

There have been a number of English translations of the term *jen*. Some popular ones are: magnanimity, benevolence, perfect virtue (James Legge), moral life, moral character (ku Hung-ming), true manhood, compassion (Lin Yutang), human-heartedness (Derk Bodde), man-to-manness (E. R. Hughes), love, altruism, kindness, and hominity (Boodberg). These ren-

derings, though helpful in identifying some of the meanings of *jen*, are at best partial characterizations of the concept. The concept of *jen* certainly includes the meaning of love, yet it embraces more than that. It is basically an ethical concept, yet it carries rich metaphysical connotations.

In the *Analects* the term *jen* is employed in a number of different ways without providing an explicit definition. Sometimes it is placed in juxtaposition with names of other specific virtues; at other times it suggests a particular conduct; on other occasions it vaguely refers to love, filial piety, or benevolence. Despite this vagueness and ambiguity, several kinds of meanings are distinguishable. First, the term *jen* may refer to a particular virtue of character roughly equivalent to benevolence or love. It is, then, a name of a particular virtue. Second, it stands for a class of virtues, for example, wisdom, courage, confidence, gravity, forgiveness, trustworthiness, earnestness, kindness, etc., and *jen*-virtues. Some of the virtues of the class are more characteristic of and essential to the concept. The virtues of faithfulness, reciprocity (*shu*), and filial piety, are cases in point. In this capacity, the term *jen* is a generic name. Third, *jen* may also refer to a very special quality in its own right, namely, the quality of moral perfection. By moral perfection is meant, negatively, the quality of having no moral deficiency, and, positively, the ideal state of possessing all possible moral virtues or the state of being absolutely good. The notion of moral perfection defines the ideal of sageness, the highest goal of moral cultivation in Confucianism. In this sense, *jen* is the Confucian ideal.

The three kinds of meaning listed above are clusters of ethical connotations typical of the concept. The roster of meanings, however, could be longer. Often

From Chung M. Tse, "Confucianism and Contemporary Ethical Issues," in World Religions and Global Ethics, *edited by S. Cromwell Crawford (New York: Paragon House, 1989), pp. 91, 92–105. Reprinted by permission of Paragon House.*

Confucius gave different answers to different students who asked the same question—what *jen* is. *Jen* was variously referred to as: "the subduing of one's selfish ego and restoration of propriety"; "[behaving to everyone in such a way that] when you leave home you act as if you were receiving an honorable guest; when you employ people you act as if you were performing a sacrificial ritual; and you do not do to others as you would not wish done to yourself"; "[a mannerism] of cautious and thoughtful speech"; "[being] sedately grave in private life, and reverently serious in handling affairs, and strictly sincere in dealing with people"; and many others. Among the indispensable manifestations of *jen* are love and the "Golden Rule"—"Do unto others as you would wish done to yourself." In general, the concept comprehends nearly all other ethical concepts about human conduct, moral quality, and character that are deemed desirable in Confucianism. As to the question of where the limits of its range lie and what the sufficient and necessary conditions of its applications are, there are no obvious and definitive answers. But the concept of *jen* is invariably associated with the idea of moral goodness and perfection.

The Metaphysics of Jen

The ethical concept of *jen* covers the arena of individual and social morality concerning motive, action, character, and feeling. However, the true spirit of Confucianism does not so much consist in *jen* being understood in behavioral or dispositional terms, but in being understood as the ground of morality. For it is in terms of the metaphysical signification of the concept that the idea of man (humanity) and the ultimate ground of morality are construed. This being the case, Confucian ethics is distinguished from ethical naturalism that includes various forms of empiricism, (heteronomous) authoritarianism, and social conventionalism, and from religious supernaturalism that posits a distinct deity to account for the origin of morals requiring faith in that deity, logically and practically, to precede morality. While it is frequently said that Confucianism is a type of ethical humanism, the label "humanism" cannot be taken without qualification. Although Confucianism posits the ground of morality in humanity itself, it does so in that particular part of humanity that transcends nature while immanent in it. Confucianism maintains that there is an essential constituent of man, defining man as man, that transcends the system of natural causality, and has its own causality, effectually materialized, or to be materialized, in nature.

This statement briefly summarizes the transcendental humanism of Confucianism.

In the orthodox Confucian tradition, man is thought of as a composite being consisting of two elements in a unique way. In Mencius (371–289 B.C.?), one of the elements is called the greater *ti*, the other, the lesser *ti*. By the lesser *ti* Mencius means the physical body with all its attachments and derivatives. Thus, for example, the human intellect and all sensuous desires belong to this category. The concept of physical body is simply a subconcept of the general concept of nature (*Ch'i*), to be explained later. Man has a share in this natural world and, as such, he is subject to the rule of natural laws. Mencius says, "For the mouth to desire [sweet] tastes, the eye to desire [beautiful] colors, the ear to desire [pleasant] sound, the nose to desire [fragrant] odors, and the four limbs to desire ease and rest—these things are natural." To this extent, man lives in the same kingdom as other animals.

By the greater *ti* Mencius means the moral mind (*hsin*, *jen*-mind). Mencius's doctrine of mind represents a cornerstone in the development of Confucianism, inaugurating a line of moral philosophical thought uniquely Confucian, culminating with Wang-ming's philosophy of *Liang-Chih* (Good Knowledge). The Confucian concept of mind must be carefully distinguished from other popular concepts. The moral mind posited by Confucianism is not to be understood as a thinking substance *per se*, or a storehouse for sensible ideas, or a bundle of impressions and ideas, or a complex of behavioral dispositions, or a sort of phenomenal consciousness. The Confucian concept of mind is interwoven with metaphysical, ethical, and functional meanings. Mencius thinks that the (moral) mind is given, not biologically or chronologically, but logically and metaphysically, *a priori*. Logically speaking, the mind must be posited before moral precepts and moral conduct are possible. Wang-ming later makes this thesis clearer and more specific, saying, "Only if there is the mind that sets itself for loving the parents, there is the principle of filial piety; and if there is no such mind, there is no such principle." To say that the mind is metaphysically *prior* is to say that the mind is not to be defined in empirical or naturalistic terms; it is not conceived to be part of, or derived from, nature, although it is supposed to operate through and on nature.

The mind's being consists in its activity (function); it *is* the activity. The mind is defined as nothing but a creatively active faculty for originating moral precepts and principles alone, and commanding and discriminating, accordingly. In order to comprehend such a Confucian concept of mind, the duality of substratum and activity must be eliminated. The mind is the very activity itself, apart from which there is no other entity posited as a substratum. The manifestation of the mind, or, in other words, the effects of this activity itself, occur in the natural world as moral feelings, moral conduct and acts, and moral principles and discriminations. Among the principles that the mind gives rise to are *jen* (in a narrow sense), righteousness, propriety, and wisdom (in an ethical sense), and correspondingly, there are moral feelings of commiseration, of disgrace and disgust, of modesty and yielding, and the sense of right and wrong. These principles and feelings are among the fundamental outcomes to the mind. To illustrate the workings of the mind, Mencius cites an anecdote which has become a classical example:

> When I say that all men have a mind which cannot bear [to see the sufferings of] others . . . if men suddenly see a child about to fall into a well, they will without exception experience a feeling of alarm and distress. [They will feel so], not as a ground on which they may seek the praise of their neighbors and friends, nor from a dislike to the reputation of having been unmoved by such a thing.

The feeling of commiseration in this particular situation appears as a feeling of alarm and distress. In other situations, as with the ruler of a country, the feeling appears as a love for his subjects. The feeling of commiseration is identified with reference to the actual occasions in which it occurs. Similarly, other moral feelings affected by the mind are explained in like manner.

The orthodox "Mencian" school of thought with Wang Yang-ming and Lu Hsiang-shan as chief proponents, faithfully following Mencius, holds that *jen* is the mind. This identification gives a new twist, reciprocally, to the concept of *jen* and the concept of mind. *Jen* in its ethical sense primarily refers to a group of moral entities, including conduct, principle, character, and quality, but not to a metaphysical entity; it is not a "thing" name, so to speak. The concept of mind, in contrast, refers to an entity—an active moral faculty; it is by analogy a "thing" name. The identification of *jen* and mind results in a compound concept that requires an adequate referent. A reality is the referent, which is an active moral faculty and, at the same time, the most general active moral principle itself. The description, "the active moral reason (or *logos*)," could be helpful to indicate the nature of this reality. In Confucian literature, this reality is gener-

ally referred to as the *jen*-mind. Sometimes the term *jen* or the term "mind" alone suffices to carry the messages with the other side of the conjugation understood. The *jen*-mind, then, is a metaphysical reality whose entire essence is the activity of originating moral precepts and principles, and commanding and discriminating accordingly. To use an analogy, the *jen*-mind is like an office of both moral legislation and judiciary that, having its own principle of activity, presents itself as an excelling and commanding entity in relation to the executive.

The Confucian philosophy of *jen*-mind is consummated with Wang Yang-ming's Doctrine of *Liang-Chih* (Good Knowledge), summed up in his renowned "Teaching of Four Lines": the mind in itself is over and above the distinction between good and evil (i.e., the mind is absolutely good), the volition in its exercises may tend to the good or to evil, that which discriminates the good from the evil is the mind of good-knowledge, to have always observed the good and eliminated the evil is called the rectification of the volition in its direction. Note that the volition is a faculty of desire given by nature whereas the mind is a metaphysical being.

THE CONCEPT OF THE SUPREME BEING

Throughout Confucian literature, the concept of the Supreme Being bears a multitude of names and descriptions. Most frequently seen are Heaven, Tao, God, the Lord, the Heavenly Tao, the Great Tao, the Heavenly Principle, the One, the Ultimate One, the Supreme Vacuity, the Heavenly Mind, the Divine Mind. Some of the names and descriptions are suggestive, some are merely symbolic, while some are misleading. In spite of the diversity, these names and descriptions do help indicate some of the attributes of the Supreme Being as conceived by the Confucians. The term Heaven, for example, is symbolic of what is above, transcending, all-covering, and above all, superhuman. The term mind excludes corporeality and materiality; and the term One may suggest unity, simplicity, originality, or priority. The most widely used term, Tao, may denote a certain way (of doing things), a well-defined process, a normative principle, or a cosmic norm.

The orthodox Confucian notion of Heaven stems from Mencius's saying, "He who cultivates [or extends] his *jen*-mind to the utmost knows his [essential] nature. He who knows his [essential] nature knows Heaven. To attend to one's mind and to nourish one's nature, is the way to serve Heaven." There is a wealth of presuppositions and implications that can be unearthed from this saying of Mencius. For the present purpose it is sufficient to concentrate on one relevant point—a doctrine that has developed from this saying, namely, the doctrine of Man-Heaven Continuum. The doctrine holds that man, as far as his essential reality is concerned, is continuous with Heaven. By continuity is meant that there is no ontological, essential difference between man and Heaven; that man and Heaven, insofar as their essential reality is concerned, are a unity. But, of course, there is some sense in which man and Heaven are distinguishable. The distinction can be drawn in the following ways. Man in his ideal essence is Heaven-in-concreto; he is Heaven in individualized form. To say that man is Heaven is not to say that man, as such, is *de facto* Heaven itself, but only that the ideal essence of man is Heaven-in-concreto. The doctrine of Man-Heaven Continuum, then, can be expressed as: there resides in man an infinite divinity (Heaven) as his essential reality. Man can be actually and fully identical with Heaven only when he has fully actualized this infinite divinity in him. In the *Doctrine of the Mean* the ideal "Heavenly Man" is admired with the exclamations, "Does he depend on anything else? How earnest and sincere—he is *jen*! How deep and unfathomable—he is abyss! How vast and great—he is Heaven!"

The doctrine of Man-Heaven Continuum is very important for apprehending the Confucian concept of Heaven (God). Now the question as to what the Confucian God is, is explicable with reference to the Confucian view of Man. Confucianism approaches Heaven, the Supreme Being, and man-in-his essence, reciprocally. The concept of Heaven, by its formal definition, refers to that which is creative, supreme, ultimate, transcendental, universal, and, in short, to a being that is the subject of all infinite attributes. However, the concept is still indeterminate as to its content (object), for these formal predicates of supremacy, ultimacy, universality, etc., are all analytical of the concept of God as the Highest Being. Nothing is said about what God really is. Confucianism takes a humanistic, moral approach to furnish the concept with contents to give a material definition to the concept. Heaven is defined as the *jen*-mind in its infinite self, as man is essentially defined as the *jen*-mind in individuality.

One may recall what Mencius has said: "He who knows his [essential] nature knows Heaven." To know what Heaven is consists in knowing what one's true, essential self is. The knowledge is not gained through philosophical speculation, religious revelation, scriptural doctrine, discursive thinking, or by logical arguments. Rather, knowledge of Heaven comes as a result of diligent cultivation and discipline of the moral self to its fullness. Figuratively speaking, knowledge of Heaven is "lived out," not "thought out," nor "handed down from above." Such cultivation and discipline aim at fully actualizing the *jen*-mind—expanding and extending the activity of the *jen*-mind to its infinite limit where it is unfettered, uninfluenced, unblocked by any alien factors, particularly sensuous desires and selfish calculations. To summarize, Confucian reality is nothing other than the *jen*-mind. Considered in its infinity, it is Heaven; considered in its particularity, it is man's essence.

THE CONCEPT OF PHYSICAL NATURE

Nature as a system of physical existents is explained in terms of *Ch'i*. The concept is not altogether transparent and takes on added obscurities when rendered in Western terminology. Attempts have been made to find an equal concept in contemporary vocabulary. It has been variously said, for example, the *Ch'i* is an ether-like substance, or a material substance (matter), or cosmic substance, or material force. What *Ch'i* is exactly may be an interesting topic for philosophical discussion, but the popular opinion tends to define *Ch'i* as cosmic material force.

Despite its obscurity, the concept of *Ch'i* has been utilized to explain the configuration and development of the physical universe. Some Neo-Confucians, such as Chou Tun-i (1017–1073) and Chang Tsai (1021–1077), have constructed, by giving interpretations to the symbolic scheme and text of the *Book of Change*, a neat cosmogony depicting the origin and becoming of the physical universe in terms of *Ch'i*. The cosmogony consists of such key notions as the *Yin* and *Yang* (the two opposing but complementary modes of *Ch'i*) and the Five Elements of Process: metal, wood, water, fire, and earth that are the five basic configurations of *Ch'i*. The cosmogony pictures the universe as an orderly, balanced, and internally harmonious structure, changing and transforming in rhythmic patterns.

Apart from its role in Confucian cosmology, the concept of *Ch'i* bears important implications for Confucian ethical theory and practice. *Ch'i* accounts for the origin of evil, and it is the instrument or vehicle for the actualization of moral existents.

The human body, or in Mencius's word, the lesser *ti*, is conceived of as a special configuration of *Ch'i*—a proposition generally assumed by the Neo-Confucians. *Ch'i*, in the form of the human body, displays many of its dispositions known as man's natural qualities and capacities. Thus, man has emotions, senses, desires, temperament, and instincts as parts of his phenomenal existence. Man in his physical existence—as a configuration of *Ch'i*—is not inherently evil. For *Ch'i* in itself is not an evil being. Evil begins when individuals follow their dispositions of *Ch'i* to the extent that they defy, or become indifferent to, the bounds of morality prescribed by the *jen*-mind. Mencius believes that they are likely to do moral wrongs when they let their lesser *ti* rule over their greater *ti*. For the Neo-Confucians, unchecked selfish desire is the centerpiece of all moral evils.

In contradistinction to the *jen*-mind, *Ch'i* is the category that comprehends all things, occurrences, properties, and events that are not immediately explainable by virtue of the concept of the *jen*-mind in any of its capacities. While the concept of the *jen*-mind accounts for the ground and origin of morality, the concept of *Ch'i* accounts for all those things that are morally indeterminate.

In one of its relations to Heaven (the cosmic *jen*-mind), *Ch'i* serves as a necessary instrument. Heaven is in a constant process of self-actualization. To actualize itself is to materialize itself into concrete particulars that require a principle of individuation. Ch'eng I puts it this way: "The mind is the principle of production. As there is the mind, a *body* must be provided for it so it can produce." The instrumentality of *Ch'i* consists in its being a vehicle with which the cosmic *jen*-mind actualizes itself.

Heaven's self-actualization process translates itself into a process of purposive change and transformation of *Ch'i*. The movement follows a dialectical pattern. Hence, there is the principle of complementary opposites understood from the Confucian perspective. *Ch'i* is thought to differentiate itself into two opposing forces, the *Yin* and the *Yang*, acting, reacting, and interacting on each other. This dynamic opposition is not mutually destructive but complementary as things and events emerge from, and pass into, the process. Ch'eng Hao epitomizes this productive opposition, saying, "Nevertheless, there cannot be anything without the distinction between rising and falling, and between birth and extinction."

The *Yin* and *Yang* are the most general concepts for specific complementary opposites: female and male, winter and summer, night and day, death and life, submission and domination, passivity and activity, receptivity and spontaneity. The principle is employed to explain not only natural things and events but human affairs as well. Hence, there are such opposing but complementary pairs as people and government, worker and employer, wife and husband,

the weak and the strong, the emotional and the rational. It is relevant to note that the principle of complementary opposites is supposed to be a normative principle governing human affairs as much as an explanatory principle descriptive of natural process.

SUMMARY OF THE CONFUCIAN MORAL METAPHYSICS AND A TRANSITION TO ITS APPLICATION

The concept of *jen*-mind is the first principle of orthodox Confucian philosophy. The *jen*-mind is a moral activity-relating, creating, in the manner of self-actualization, existents either immediately good or conducive to goodness. Considered in itself, the *jen*-mind is the Supreme Being—Heaven or God. Considered in its most primary and excellent locus, it is the *jen*-mind in man as the essence of humanity. The *jen*-mind in man acts and affects an outflow of moral feelings, principles, and precepts that result in moral conduct. Among these feelings of commiseration, of disgrace and disgust, of modesty and yielding, and the sense of right and wrong are most typical and fundamental. Although man has the *jen*-mind as his defining essence, he also has a physical body. The physical body at its best is the vehicle or instrument for the *jen*-mind's activity—self-actualization. The physical body is paradigmatic of (physical) nature.

The Confucian metaphysics of (physical) nature is constructed on the concepts of *Ch'i*—a cosmic, material force. The configurations and motions of *Ch'i* constitute the physical, phenomenal universe of which the human body is a part. Man, as far as his physical constitution is concerned, naturally possesses dispositions originated from *Ch'i*. Although such dispositions are not inherently evil, they can become causes of moral evil if they are not properly contained. Excessive selfish desire is the core of all moral impurities, according to Confucian ethics. *Ch'i* is, however, a necessary instrument for the self-actualization of the *jen*-mind, serving as a principle of individuation. The process of the actualization of the *jen*-mind translates itself as incessant transformation of *Ch'i*. The transformation proceeds by way of interaction between opposing forces.

For Confucianism, the ultimate judge of morality is the *jen*-mind ideally unfettered, unbiased, undistorted, and uninfluenced by selfish desires and natural inclinations that are inherent properties of *Ch'i*. As he stands, man is a composite being of the *jen*-mind embodied in a configuration of *Ch'i*; his acts either spring from the *jen*-mind or from dispositions of *Ch'i*. That which is from the *jen*-mind is categorically good, whereas that which is from *Ch'i* is either morally agreeable, indifferent, or objectionable and evil. Hence, the motive of an act carries the most weight when the act is subject to moral judgment; consequences of the act count less toward its morality or immorality. The *jen*-mind responds and reacts to each moral occasion, and it does so in correspondence to the uniqueness of each situation. In Confucianism there are no rigid rules of morality specifying the right and the wrong for all circumstances. Confucian ethics is not teleological or rule-oriented; it is more a theory of act-deontology.

However, there are at least three fundamental and general principles proposed by Confucian ethics. (1) Since man is a *jen*-being in essence, it is therefore his Heavenly vocation and duty fully to actualize the *jen*-mind's activity in his own person and to help do so with other people. More explicitly, it is man's duty to follow the dictates of the *jen*-mind and to help others to do the same, with the final end of realizing a world of Great Harmony—a world where every person is a morally perfect individual. This is Heaven actualized. Moral self-abandonment is a vice, for it is a relinquishment of one's Heavenly duty. (2) If a man is to live up to the name of being human, he must respect his own person and that of others. To be respectful is to be respectful of the essence of humanity. Negatively stated, this means that he is not to act and treat himself and others in a way that erases the essential distinction between man and beast. Knowingly or unknowingly he is not to denigrate the dignity of humanity. (3) The cosmic *jen*-mind is in a constant process of self-actualization, and this results in the coming into being of individuals (i.e., things and persons) underlaid by a moral purpose. Among all the creatures, living human beings are *par excellence* the highest, for it is in a living human being that the *jen*-mind can be truly said to have a locus of actualization. Every individual living person is potentially Heaven-in-particular. Nothing should be done unto a person by oneself or others which might suppress, subvert, or destroy the Heavenly potentiality he has.

The ultimate concern of Confucianism does not lie in the metaphysical as much as in the ethical. Matters of morality—the ground, the ideal, the justification, the principles, the method—are what the philosophy is basically interested in, with the aim to better the world and humanity morally. It does not presume to be able to give final solutions to all ethical problems that emerge out of this ever-changing world, but it provides a way of ethical thinking, along with a conceptual framework for the assessment of problems and affairs that call for moral consideration.

Confucian Response to Contemporary Ethical Issues

MORALITY OF SEX

That animate beings, human or nonhuman, have sexual desires, presumably for procreation purposes, and that they are naturally and normally disposed to derive pleasure from engaging in sex, is an indisputable biological and psychological fact. It should be added, that sexual contact is an intimate way of expressing love. Looked upon from these perspectives, sexual activity is quite justifiable and perfectly legitimate. But in the human community, some sorts of sexual behavior call for special considerations that do not apply to the animal kingdom. When activities such as rape, incest, child molestation, extramarital sex, premarital sex, homosexuality, and bestiality occur, then problems of morality arise.

The Confucian position of sexual morality is unambiguously conservative. It views human sexual intercourse as primarily for the purpose of the continuation of the species by means of procreation. Sexual intercourse is the initial act of procreation and is read as an individualized act of creation of the cosmic *jen*-mind (Heaven), in and through human beings. The whole process, from intercourse to the completion of an individual, is regarded as the most basic and highest mode of Heavenly creation. The act of intercourse instantiates many great virtues of the cosmic *jen*-mind and exemplifies the way the cosmic *jen*-mind actualizes itself. In the sex act there is caring, love, intimacy, union, dynamic harmony, exchange of vital energy, give-and-take, joyful consummation, and, above all, creativity. Viewed as such, sexual intercourse is divinely moral, both in itself and in respect to its *telos* (goal).

Although the process of procreation may be said to begin with the act of intercourse, it does not end with it, but ends rather, with the coming into existence of an individual human being. This extended view of the sexual act places solemn responsibilities upon the couple involved. According to Confucianism, Heavenly creation does not essentially consist in the bringing forth of individuals (particulars) who are at least potentially Heaven-*in-concreto*. An individual is one who possesses this moral potentiality. Thus, the process of generation that begins with the act of intercourse is followed by conception and all the steps necessary to nurture, care, cultivate, and educate this being, ending finally in the formation of an individual capable of moral undertakings.

The generating process requires a couple to start and bring it to fruition. Hence, sexual activity occupies the highest place in the Confucian scheme of life. Normatively, sexual intercourse must occur for the purpose of procreation and is to be engaged in only by couples of the opposite sex who are permanently bonded, in order to carry through the process of procreation. Simply stated, sexual activity should occur between husband and wife for the purpose of raising a family for which they are willing and able to provide in a manner that meets all needs adequately.

Sexual relationships deviating from this norm are considered in a realm extending anywhere from morally tolerable to downright evil, depending on the nature and degree of the deviation. Incest and bestiality are condemned as evils. The party engaged in incest virtually denies the moral order within the family that Confucianism regards as an extended individualization of the cosmic *jen*-mind, not to mention the social or genetic consequences of the act. The party engaged in bestiality annihilates the dignity of humanity, completely destroying the distinction between man and beast. This is so because the individual through this act assimilates with an animal and treats it in the same intimate way one would treat a human being.

Both rape and child molestation are morally reprehensible. Rape is sexual contact by force, against another person's will, and is, therefore, both contradictory to the idea of harmonious union, and the source of grave pain to its victim. The latter implies a denial of *jen*-love, i.e., the feeling of commiseration. The attacker not only witnesses the suffering of another, he even derives pleasure from making the person suffer. Child molestation is reprehensible because it is an impediment to the normal process of growth of a child into an individual. It distorts and hinders a particular locus of actualization of the cosmic *jen*-mind.

Consensual homosexuality is morally indefensible, not because the act is antisocial though glossed over as an "alternative life style," but because it countervails the manifest way of Heaven—the way of complementary opposites. It is therefore counterproductive of the Heavenly cause. Homosexual con-

tact by force is blameworthy on two counts, being a combination of rape and homosexuality.

Premarital sex may be morally excusable, provided that the parties engaged in the act do it in good faith, with sincere intention eventually to establish a permanent and normal sexual relationship and to assume all the consequential responsibilities. But there is a kind of premarital sex that is for no other purpose except pleasure. Sexual behavior for the sole sake of pleasure cannot be criticized, for pleasure-seeking is morally tolerable. But excessive, unrestrained seeking of sexual pleasure, whether premarital or marital, is morally degrading because, in Confucian ethics, it virtually reduces a person to the low position of being an attendant to the lesser *ti*, i.e., sensuous desires. On the whole, premarital sex, though socially questionable, or unbecoming, or even unacceptable in some social settings, is either morally excusable or tolerable, if restrained.

Extramarital sex, in the majority of cases, is morally objectionable for two reasons. First, extramarital sex almost inevitably presupposes or entails other unethical acts, such as deception, cheating, infidelity, unchastity, and, in particular, a conscious disregard for the spouse's right to sexual exclusivity, tacitly implied in a marriage. Second, extramarital sex is mostly for added sexual excitement or pleasure. As far as the motive is concerned, a person who engages in extramarital sex is servile to sensuous desires, and is, therefore, subject to the same criticism as the excessive, unrestrained seeking of sexual pleasure. There is a sense, however, in which extramarital sex may be defended from the above criticisms. Extramarital sex may be negotiated when, for example, the spouse voluntarily waives the right to sexual exclusivity so that extramarital sex need not entail duplicity. It is also permissible when actual circumstances or physical conditions do not allow normal sexual behavior between a husband and wife. In general, there is much rationalism in Confucianism, but not to the extent that there is in Stoicism. Confucianism does allow a *reasonable* outlet for natural desires. . . .

Discussion and Reflection Questions

1. How does the Confucian notion of the *jen*-mind endow individuals with a special dignity, nobility, and worth? Why, on this view, are the activities of the body subservient to the *jen*-mind's activity? How does this emphasis on the importance of cultivating the *jen*-mind relate to moral decisionmaking? Do you find this to be an attractive view? Explain.

2. According to Confucianism, why does each of us have a moral obligation to try to actualize the *jen*-mind in ourselves and in others? How does this view treat individuals as actors in a much larger drama of humanity? In what ways does the Confucian view give human beings an especially privileged place in the world? What are the attractions of this view? How might one go about criticizing this view of individuals and humanity?

3. If, as Tse says, the Confucian view of sexual intercourse is that it is for the sake of procreation, does this mean that (on this view) one should only engage in sexual activity for the sake of achieving pregnancy? Can this view be squared with his claim that "in the sex act there is caring, love, intimacy, union, dynamic harmony, exchange of vital energy, give-and-take, joyful consummation, and, above all, creativity"? Doesn't this latter claim imply that there are goods associated with sexual activity that need not be connected with procreation? How would Confucianism view sexual intimacy between two people who do not desire to achieve pregnancy?

4. Looking over the Confucian judgments concerning incest, bestiality, rape, child molestation, homosexuality, and premarital and extramarital sex, do you find any that you disagree with? If so, why? Are there some that you agree with, but not for the reasons Tse mentions? In light of the above, do you agree that Confucianism allows a reasonable outlet for natural desires?

Geoffrey Parrinder, Chinese Yin and Yang

The proper relationship between the sexes and sexual morality more generally have been a concern of Chinese thinkers since the earliest recorded documents of China. In "Chinese Yin and Yang," Geoffrey Parrinder explores some of the forms this concern has taken. Fundamental to any discussion of Chinese views of sexual activity are the twin concepts of yin and yang. Yin, associated with the female element, is described as dark, black, deep, and receptive. Yang, the element associated with the male, is described as bright, high, celestial, and penetrating. These elements characterize both the universe as a whole and human relationships in particular (the macrocosm-microcosm idea). The Taoist view of sex, intimately connected as it is with the concepts of yin and yang, sees human sexual activity as essentially associated with the balancing of principles necessary for human health, strength, and longevity. This view of the purpose of sex gives rise to specific sexual practices designed to insure these results. As Parrinder points out, however, these practices were often criticized by the rival Chinese thought systems of Confucianism and Buddhism, which sought to place more severe strictures on sexual activity. Although these latter views are perhaps closer to views common in the West, the Taoist view here explained is worth considering for its concern with the philosophical aspects of sex.

Reading Questions

1. According to traditional Chinese symbolism, how are the processes of nature and the processes of sex and procreation similar? Why might such analogies be useful for understanding both nature and human sexual activity?

2. How are yin and yang described? What are the properties of each? Which is associated with the female, which with the male? What is supposed to be the relationship between these two elements? How is this relationship illustrated in the symbol of the *t'ai chi t'u*?

3. In traditional Chinese thinking, what are the two main purposes of sexual intercourse? Is *love* a necessary, or even important, factor in accomplishing either of these purposes?

4. What is the Taoist view of celibacy and sexual abstinence? What sort of explanation do Taoists give for their view? Why was this view opposed by Confucians and Buddhists? What are some features of the Taoist view of male-female relationships, marriage, and sexual activity that conflict with the Confucian view described earlier by Tse?

Chinese Yin and Yang

GEOFFREY PARRINDER

Female and Male

The duality of the sexes is one of the oldest and most usual ways of representing universal powers and relationships. This symbolism was used in many cultures: Father Heaven and Mother Earth, Zeus and Demeter, Dyaus and Prithivi, Shiva and Shakti, Yang and Yin. But Chinese symbolism developed in particular ways owing to its virtual isolation, and even after the coming of Buddhism in the first century A.D. the new influences tended to be absorbed into indigenous patterns.

In Chinese inscriptions that remain from prehistoric times, pictographs, that were the basis for later writing, represented a woman as a figure with large breasts, and a mother figure had added nipples. The character for man was a square picture of cultivated land with a sign meaning work. These suggest that woman was chiefly the nourishing mother and man the farmer, and that perhaps ancient Chinese society was matriarchal.

Further, the color red was associated with woman, creative ability, and sexual power, and the marriage ceremony was later called the "Red Affair," with all the presents and decorations in this auspicious color. But the color white indicated sexual weakness and death, and a funeral was the "White Affair." In later Chinese alchemical and erotic literature woman was called red and man white, and pictures often showed them in these colors. In ancient times children seem often to have been named after their mothers, and in old myths women had magical powers, while in

handbooks of sex women were the teachers of sexual knowledge.

This early matriarchal rule was reversed by the Chou dynasty, which ruled from about 1100 to 221 B.C., and the patriarchal system then imposed was reinforced by the teachings of the Confucians, which emphasized the strength and superiority of man who was the leader and head of the family. Yet powerful counter-currents remained, especially in Taoism, with concepts of the Great Mother, and the potent female who in sexual intercourse fed man's limited life-force from her inexhaustible supply. The negative was praised above the positive, and inactivity above activity. In classical Taoist texts mystical terms like "the deep Valley" and "the mysterious Doorway" were interpreted in sexological texts as womb and vulva. A famous chapter of the classical Taoist scripture, the *Tao Te Ching*, could be taken in this symbolical manner:

> The Valley Spirit never dies.
> It is named the Mysterious Female.
> And the Doorway of the Mysterious Female
> Is the base from which Heaven and Earth sprang.

The alternation of day and night, summer and winter, youth and age, led the Chinese to believe in the interaction of dual cosmic forces. Mankind functioned in the same way as the universe, and human sexual intercourse was like the union of heaven and earth which mate during rainstorms. The Chinese thought of the clouds as the ova of the earth, which were fertilized by the sperm of heaven in rain. Much of the symbolism of sun and moon, or heaven and earth, came to be replaced by the formal terms of Yang and Yin, but the symbol of the mating of heaven and earth in storms remained, and to this day "clouds and rain" is a standard expression for sexual intercourse.

A classical story expressed this idea in an account of a king who went on an excursion and fell asleep during the daytime. He dreamt of a woman who said, "I am the Lady of the Wu mountain and wish to share pillow and couch with you." They had sexual intercourse and on parting she said, "I live on the southern slope of the mountain. In the morning I am the clouds and in the evening I am the rain." The story transformed the old picture of the mating of heaven and earth, and it was the woman who made the sexual advances.

In addition to "clouds and rain," later literature wrote of "the Wu mountain" or the "southern slopes of the Wu mountain," as elegant terms for coition. In sexological writing the "clouds" were explained as both ova and vaginal secretions, and "rain" as semen. Expressions such as "the reverse clouds and the inverted rain" were used for male homosexual acts.

Yin and Yang

The terms Yin and Yang appeared in Chinese philosophy from the fourth century B.C., though archaeologists trace their symbolism to a much earlier time. The origin of the characters for Yin and Yang is not known, but they were interpreted as "the dark side" and "the sunny side" of a hill, and from that there developed the indication of vital energies: dark and light, weak and strong, female and male. The female was therefore dark, black, deep, and receptive; and the male was bright, high, celestial, and penetrating. Yet they were complementary rather than opposing, since all Yin had some Yang in it, and all Yang some Yin.

Yin and Yang have been compared to the Dark and Light of Zoroastrianism, and the dualism of evil and good that arose therefrom. But Yin and Yang were not opposed, they were interdependent, like woman and man. The aim was not the triumph of one over the other, but a perfect balance of two principles.

Later Chinese philosophers gave much time to speculation about the beginning of things. The ultimate unity, as in Indian, Persian, and Greek notions of the undivided male and female, was represented in China by the symbol of a circle. From the eleventh century A.D. Neo-Confucian scholars represented this concept by the undivided circle known as *t'ai chi t'u*,

"the supreme ultimate." The circle was divided into two pear-shaped halves of dark and light, Yin and Yang. The dark half of Yin contained a white dot indicating the Yang embryo within in, and the light half Yang had a black dot designating the Yin element in it.

Although the philosophical interpretation came late, the design itself went back to ancient times with circles found on ancient bronzes. It remains to this day in decorations on gates and houses, utensils and furnishings, and in sexual and exorcist symbols. The circle with its pear-shaped halves is also found in India and Europe, and it appears in patterns popularly known as Kashmir or Paisley.

Different and more complex magical symbols were developed in China in combinations of horizontal lines, which were interpreted in books of divination. Among these the *I Ching*, the *Book of Changes*, came to supersede all others. This book became so important in daily life that it was considered as a "Confucian" classic, though it was not adopted by followers of Confucius until well after his time. Tradition credited a mythical emperor with the invention of eight basic trigrams of horizontal lines; broken lines representing Yin and continuous lines being Yang. The eight trigrams were again combined into pairs and formed sixty-four hexagrams. Arranged in a circle, symbol of heaven, the trigrams corresponded to the directions of the compass, the seasons of the year and the times of day.

The *I Ching* described Yin and Yang as the dual cosmic forces that perpetuate the universe in a chain of permutations, a concept that was worked out into a philosophical system, so that the *I Ching* was used by both philosophers and diviners. Here we are only concerned with passages that consider the relationship of the sexes. Thus it was said that "the constant intermingling of Heaven and Earth gives shape to all things, and the sexual union of man and woman gives life to all things." Again, "the interaction of one Yin and one Yang is called Tao," and this was later interpreted to mean one woman and one man.

Hexagram 63 was considered to symbolize sexual union, for it consisted of the trigram meaning "water," "clouds," and "woman" on top, and beneath it the trigram meaning "fire," "light," and "man." Thus the harmony of woman and man was expressed and their complementary nature was depicted by the perfect alternation of Yin and Yang lines, and such harmony was regarded as the basis of a happy sex life. "The transition from confusion to order is completed, and everything is in its proper place even in particulars. The strong lines are in the strong places, the weak lines in the weak places. This is a very favorable outlook."

Nearly all later Chinese handbooks of sex speculated on this hexagram and pictures showed scholars meditating on the perfect balance of the male and female elements here. It is significant that the element for woman occupied the upper part, and as to the symbols of fire and water medical treatises said that man was like fire which flared up easily but was extinguished by female water which heated and cooled slowly, as in human sexual experience.

Tao

Theories developed from the *I Ching* influenced Chinese ideas on sexual intercourse, but with the rise of Taoism in the second half of the Chou dynasty much wider currents of thought came to the fore. The concept of Tao was basic to much of Chinese thought and art, religion and sex. This complex word has many shades of meaning: way, power, principle, and it was beyond meaning: "The Tao that can be defined is not the ultimate Tao, it existed before Heaven and Earth, it is the ancestor of all doctrines, the mystery of mysteries."

Philosophical Taoism, exemplified in the classic *Tao Te Ching*, spoke of Tao as like an empty vessel, a mysterious female, an uncarved block, water which takes the lowest way but benefits all creatures. The sage similarly overcame by "wordless teaching, actionless activity, discarding formal knowledge and morality." It seemed likely that a man who followed nature and did what he wanted would enjoy sex without limitations, unless he was seeking a higher stage of trance. Perhaps this is what was meant by an obscure passage: "An infant has power, its bones are soft, but its grip is strong. It does not yet know the union of male and female, but it may have an erection and show the height of vital force, which means that harmony is at its perfection." So the sage may use continence like a child, to help him concentrate his energies and attain a tranquil state.

Popular Taoism was the religion of the masses in China, and its symbolism appeared in mythology, art, medicine, magic, and sex. Common symbols of Tao were twisted or hollow stones, which were sought by collectors from rivers and lakes, and kept in gardens and houses. The stone could represent both the kidney shape of the female Yin vulva, and the mountain shape of the male phallic Yang in harmony. In carvings gods and pilgrims going to their temples could be fashioned inside the same stones. Taoist ideas brought objects into contact with each other, or arranged them to influence one another, so that the aroused Yin and Yang would be in balance.

Yin and Yang symbolism was seen by Taoists in countless objects, patterns, pictures, vessels, public and domestic altars. Yang was thought to dominate in stallion, dragon, Feng-bird, cock, ram, horned animals, mountains, summer, and the south. Yin dominated in fungus, whirling clouds, water, valleys, winter, north, vase, peach, female dragon with divided tail, fish, peony, and chrysanthemum. The peach, with its deep cleft, was a favorite symbol of the vulva. Harmonic combinations showed a Fend-bird flying into a garden of peony flowers, a dragon among swirling clouds, a woman with a ram, or a plate with subdued red and blue flowers melting together to show the reconciliation of color opposites. Chinese art was imbued throughout with mystical and sexual symbolism, and to understand it is to learn an unspoken language.

Popular Taoist myths used sexual symbolism in accounts of the gods. A favorite deity was Hsi Wang Mu, the Royal Mother of the Western Air, or the Golden Mother of the Tortoise, the counterpart of the god Mu Kung who was sovereign of the Eastern Air. She was the passive or female Yin to his Yang, and by their union all beings in heaven and earth were born. Hsi Wang Mu lived on a jade mountain in a palace with a Heavenly Peach Garden and a magic tree that ripened every six thousand years. Then it was the birthday of the goddess and all the immortals were invited to the Peach Festival, at which they ate the fruit that gave them immortality. A famous Buddhist story of "Monkey" told how he stole the food and pills of immortality when he gate-crashed this festival. Hsi Wang Mu was depicted in art in brilliant dress, accompanied by a phoenix and bearing a dish of fruit. In other pictures the immortals appeared outside the golden rampart of her palace hoping to enter, while others were already seated on an island in her garden lake feasting on the immortal peaches.

Among other gods the star deity Shou Hsing or Shou Lao was the prototype of male success. As the Old Man of the South Pole, his influence brought peace to mankind. In pictures and carvings he was characterized by a very high forehead and bald pate, like a mountain to show his great power, and a peach which he carried in his hand indicated long life. He was a happy god, carrying a long staff to which were attached a gourd and a scroll which with the peach were symbols of longevity.

There were countless Taoist gods and divinized human beings, each with individuality and eccentricity. Legendary immortals were said to ride through the air, on dragons or in chariots, and some lived in caves on mountains where they sought the food of immortality and passed on their discoveries to favorite pupils. Most of their images and temples have disappeared, outwardly at least in China, though traces survive in other places of Chinese influence, and in works of art in galleries and museums all over the world.

The search for long life or immortality was a constant aim of Taoists. They practiced breathing exercises, like Indian yogis, but making breathing quiet and holding it as long as possible, with the aim of returning to the manner of respiration in the womb. They practiced sun-bathing (only recently recognized as valuable in the West), while holding in the hand a character of the sun within a border. But women had to expose themselves to the moon, holding a piece of yellow paper with the moon in a black border. Those who sought the "outer elixir" were alchemists looking for magical potions, drinking dew, hanging from trees, returning to nature, or setting off for the islands of the immortals. In such a search a Taoist might abandon sex altogether, or restrict orgasm so as not to lose the precious fluid. But those who pursued the "inner elixir" tried by self-control and proper techniques to achieve perfect coordination of body and soul.

Tao in Sex

"Of all the ten thousand things created by Heaven, man is the most precious. Of all things that make man prosper none can be compared to sexual intercourse. It is modeled after Heaven and takes its pattern by Earth, it regulates Yin and rules Yang. Those who understand its significance can nurture their nature and prolong their years; those who miss its true meaning will harm themselves and die before their time." So wrote the scholar Tung-hsüan, perhaps in the seventh century A.D. in his *Art of Love*.

From the highest to the lowest levels of Chinese society followers of Tao sought to cultivate sexual energy and unite Yin and Yang. In sexual play these powers were aroused and in orgasm they were released from the body and passed into the partner of the other sex, male into female and female into male. Such mutual exchange of Yin and Yang essences was thought to produce perfect harmony, and sexual intercourse, instead of declining with age, was believed to increase vigor and bring long life.

Tung-hsüan said again:

Truly Heaven revolves to the left and Earth revolves to the right. Thus the four seasons succeed each other, man calls and woman follows, above there is action and below compliance; this is the natural order of all things. . . . Man and woman must move according to their cosmic orientation, the man should thrust from above and woman receive below. If they unite in this way, it can be called Heaven and Earth in even balance.

Sexual intercourse in China had two main purposes. The first was the procreation of children, especially healthy males, when the man's Yang essence was at its highest strength, so that the family would be continued, the ancestors cared for, and the order of the universe maintained. But male semen was supposed to be strictly limited, while woman had an inexhaustible supply of Yin essence.

The second purpose therefore was to strengthen male vitality by absorption of female Yin essence. The Yin essence was supposed to be in the vaginal juices which the man absorbed, but a further element was added by *coitus reservatus*, coition without ejaculation, so that the Yang would be supplemented by the Yin. If this was done with several partners, prolonging coitus as much as possible without orgasm, then the Yang would be augmented and strengthened. Although Taoism stressed the importance of the cooperation of Yin and Yang, this did not necessarily lead to love and equality between two partners. In rich families, at least, there were numerous concubines, and since the dominant male could not often ejaculate every time, limitation of emission helped to solve the problem, with the belief that retained semen aided health.

Some of the sexual techniques of the Taoists were greatly opposed by Confucians and Buddhists. Taoism considered continence to be against the rhythm of nature, and celibacy to lead to neurosis, whereas the Buddhists advocated monastic celibacy. Further, Taoists taught not only *coitus reservatus* by mental discipline, but by physical methods. Ejaculation was prevented by pressing the seminal duct with the fingers, thus diverting the fluid into the bladder. But Taoist theory, like Indian Yogic and Tantric, held that the semen (*ching*) would "flow upwards" along the spinal column to "nourish the brain" and the entire system, the male Yang essence having been intensified by contact with the female Yin.

Chinese literature on sex emphasized that semen was a man's most precious possession, and every emission must be compensated by acquiring an equivalent amount of Yin essence from the woman. While he should give the woman complete satisfaction at every act of coition, he should only ejaculate on certain occasions. If they wished the woman to conceive then the most favorable time was thought to be five days after menstruation.

Reprehensible Taoist practices, in the eyes of other religions, were public ceremonies of sexual intercourse which flourished in the early Christian centuries and resembled Indian left-handed Tantra. After a liturgical dance the two chief celebrants might copulate in the presence of the congregation, or members would do the same in chambers along the sides of the temple courtyard. Sexual intercourse was sacralized, and the human union harmonized with that of the universe, with careful attention to the seasons, the weather, the phases of the moon, and the astrological situation.

Sexual handbooks were compiled from ancient times in China, often written as dialogues. The mythical Yellow Emperor, Huang-ti, figured largely in handbooks from the early centuries asking questions of female guardians of the mysteries of sex. One of the chief of these was the Plain Girl, Su-nü, said to have been a river-goddess who could take the shape of a shell, a fertility symbol in China. A story is told of a poor but virtuous man who found a large shell on a river bank and took it home, whereupon every time he went out he found the house cleaned and food prepared on his return. He watched secretly and saw a beautiful young girl emerge from the shell, who said she was Su-nü sent to look after him by the Heavenly Emperor. She disappeared, but the shell remained and was always full of rice.

The Plain Girl was said to have explained the arts of sexual intercourse, along with two others, the Dark Girl and the Elected Girl. The Elected Girl is a rather nebulous figure, though she is also said to have been a goddess. But it was reported that, "The Yellow Emperor learned the Art of the Bedchamber from the Dark Girl. It consists of suppressing emissions, absorbing the woman's fluid, and making the semen return to strengthen the brain, thereby to obtain longevity."

It is clear that in the early centuries there existed a number of handbooks of sexual relations, written as dialogues between the Yellow Emperor and one of these Girls. These manuals were illustrated with pictures of various positions of coitus, their methods were widely known by husbands, wives, and dancing girls, and formed part of a bride's trousseau. They not only taught how to maintain satisfactory sexual relations, but also how to benefit health and prolong life.

In the second century a well known poet Chang Heng described a bride addressing her husband. She swept the pillow and bedmat, lit the lamp and filled the burner with incense. She locked the door, shed her robes, and rolled out the picture scroll to take the Plain Girl as her instructor as taught to the Yellow Emperor, "so that we can practice all the variegated postures, those that an ordinary husband has but rarely seen."

Master Tung-hsüan, quoted at the beginning of this section, said, "The methods of sexual intercourse as taught by the Dark Girl have been transmitted since antiquity; but they give only a general survey of this subject, they do not exhaust its subtle mysteries." He gave many more details therefore of embracing, kissing, petting, licking, biting, thrusting, intervals, times, and seasons.

Thirty main positions were described for sexual intercourse, each with a metaphorical name: Unicorn's Horn, Winding Dragon, Pair of Swallows, Fluttering Butterflies, Reversed Flying Ducks, Bamboos near the Altar, Galloping Steed, Jumping White Tiger, Phoenix in a Cinnabar Crevice, and so on. Here and in other writings descriptive names were given to the sexual organs. The male was the Jade Stalk, the Positive Peak, the Swelling Mushroom, the Turtle Head or the Dragon Pillar. The female was the Jade Gate, the Open Peony, the Golden Lotus, the Receptive Vase, the Lute Strings, the Golden Gully, the Deep Vale, the Chicken's Tongue. The most powerful symbolical natural substance was Cinnabar, a rosy-purple crystalline stone, which represented the energies of joined Yin and Yang.

Handbooks of sex continued to be popular in China with the centuries. Sometimes numerous items on the Art of the Bedchamber were listed under Taoist Classics, and lists of medical books also included works on sex, such as *Classic of the Secret Methods of the Plain Girl, Handbook of Sex of the Dark Girl, Summary of the Secrets of the Bedchamber, Principles of Nurturing Life, Poetical Essay on the Supreme Joy.* By the time of the T'ang dynasty, from the seventh to the ninth centuries, sexual instruction was classified as a branch of medical science, and many handbooks had a special section on it.

The most famous of these medical works was *Priceless Recipes* by the seventh-century physician Sun Szu-mo. In a section on "healthy sex life," Sun wrote that after his fortieth year a man's potency decreased and he needed to acquire a knowledge of the Art of the Bedchamber. Sexual techniques should be learnt because in youth man does not understand Tao, and in old age he may be too weak or sick to benefit by it. *Si jeunesse savait, si vieillesse pouvait.*[1] Sexual inter-

[1]Editor's note: *If youth knew, if age could.*

course should not be indulged in simply to satisfy lust, but it should be controlled to nurture the vital essence.

Sun pointed out the importance of preliminary sex play, rousing the woman's passion and drinking her Jade Fluid, her saliva. It did not matter if the woman was beautiful, as long as she was young, but the ideal was to copulate on one night with ten different women, without emitting semen once. Women should be changed, since by intercourse with one only her Yin essence would become weak and of little benefit to her partner. Ejaculation should be controlled by holding the breath and pressing the urethra, so that semen would ascend to the brain "thus lengthening one's span of life."

Sun told a story which was often quoted by others. A peasant of over seventy told him that his Yang was exuberant and he made love to his wife several times a day. Sun replied that this was most unfortunate, it was a last flare-up of fire, and the peasant should have abstained from intercourse long ago. Six weeks later the peasant died, and this was a warning to control sexual relations.

"Man cannot do without woman," said Sun, "and woman cannot do without man," but the passions should not be indulged freely for that would rob the man of his vital essence. Men should nurture their vital power when they notice that is particularly strong, and in advancing years if a man restrained himself this was like adding oil to a lamp that was about to go out. A strong man of over sixty may feel that his thoughts are still composed after not having copulated with a woman for a month or so, and if he can control himself for so long then he could continue longer. The dominant aim was to conserve the precious semen and prolong life, and the feelings of the woman or women were of less concern, though their Yin essence would be stimulated by coition, even without emission.

Confucian Morality

Taoists, Confucians, and Buddhists have been followers of three traditional "ways" in China. These were not separate "religions," and even when opposed they often supplemented each other. The Confucian scholar-gentleman was depicted as a conscientious official, a responsible citizen, and a good family man. The Taoist was often the same man in private life, with his loves and his search for the things of the spirit.

Taoist legends spoke of the abasement of Confucius before their mythical founder Lao Tzu, but they were obviously partisan. Both sages, or the writings attributed to them, spoke of Tao but in different ways. Many Chinese accepted the treatments of Tao as complementary, but some Confucians attacked Taoist teachings as narrow, making light of humanity and righteousness. Taoists had said that robbers would not disappear until the accepted sages died off, but this was thoughtless, for if there had been no sages in the past morality would have perished. Taoists and Buddhists had taught men to reject order, and seek for personal purity and nirvana. But to regulate families one must first cultivate one's own person.

Confucius said little about women and nothing of physical sexual relationships. In one verse he remarked: "Women and people of low birth are very hard to deal with. If you are friendly with them, they get out of hand, and if you keep your distance, they resent it." The followers of Confucius developed this attitude to ensure the lower place of women; their foremost duty was to obey their husband and his parents, to look after the house, and to bear healthy male children. Procreation was primary, and enjoyment of sex secondary; the ideal woman was "she who is within," concentrating on the household tasks. Chastity was essential for the woman, but not for the man.

Confucian teaching was that of the Mean, the moral ideal of balance in society and harmony with the universe. This was to be practiced in the Five Relationships which concern everybody; the relations of ruler and subject, father and son, husband and wife, older and younger brother, and friend with friend.

The Confucians advocated the separation of the sexes, in order to maintain the purity of family life. The *Book of Rites*, a collection of early and later dates, took this separation to extremes: "In the dwelling house, outside and inside are clearly divided; the man lives in the outer, the women in the inner apartments. The latter are located at the back of the house, the doors are kept locked and guarded by eunuchs." Husband and wife should not even use the same clothes-rack, they should not bathe together, share the same sleeping-mat, or borrow each other's articles of dress. If the husband was absent the wife should lock his bedding away. She should not receive anything from another man directly. "When a woman goes out she shall veil her face . . . Walking in the street the men shall keep to the right, the women to the left."

In the first and second centuries A.D., Lady Pan Chao, greatly honored for her chastity and learning, advocated elementary education for girls as well as boys. But she wrote *Women's Precepts*, which has been called "one of the most bigoted books in Chinese literature," though Confucians took it as a shining example of womanhood. Education, thought Lady Pan, should teach woman her inferiority and absolute obedience to her husband.

> The Tao of husband and wife represents the harmonious blending of Yin and Yang, it establishes man's communion with the spirits, it reaffirms the vast significance of Heaven and Earth, and the great order of human relationships. . . . Yin and Yang are fundamentally different, hence man and woman differ in behavior. Strength is the virtue of Yang, yielding constitutes the use of Yin. Man is honored for his power, woman is praised for her weakness. . . . To be reverent and obedient, that is the golden rule of wifehood.

And again, "According to the *Rites* man has the right to marry more than one wife, but woman shall not follow two masters. . . . Modesty is the cornerstone of virtue, obedience the proper conduct of a wife."

Lady Pan's precepts were ideal, but it seems that they were not often followed. Other writers speak of women going out to pleasures, by day and night, visiting Buddhist temples for festivals and organizing picnics. In the home visitors would tease their host until he brought out his womenfolk, and then they would sit together, sing and dance, and exchange unseemly conversation.

Confucian teachings determined the place of man and woman in society and the family, but in the privacy of the bedchamber they would follow Taoist teaching, and there the woman was not infrequently the teacher of sexual mysteries. Physical contact of husband and wife was confined to the marriage bed, which was often a small room. Even here the Lady Pan maintained that "Dalliance in the bedchamber will only create lewdness; lewdness will induce idle talk; idle talk will generate moral laxity; and moral laxity will breed contempt for her husband in the wife. The root of all these evils is their inability to learn moderation [in their sexual relations]." It must be said that Lady Pan had married when she was fourteen, but her husband died young and she never remarried though she lived to a great age.

Confucians, like Taoists, and they were often the same persons, thought that sexual intercourse was good, necessary for all men and women, and essential to the continuation of the race. Some teachers disliked sexual dalliance out of fear that it might disrupt family life, and especially hinder procreation by superfluous amorous play. They considered woman to be inferior to man, just as Earth was inferior to Heaven, but they did not despise women or sex, as did teachers in some world-denying religions.

According to Confucian ideas, a man's interest in his wife as a human being ceased when she left his bed. Since women were not supposed to share their husband's intellectual interests, or interfere in their outside activities, little was done for the education of girls. Most women were illiterate, even in upper-class families where they were only taught sewing and weaving. Only courtesans and singing girls learnt to read and write as part of their training.

In Confucian China the relations of the sexes were formal in public. An upright man would show no sign of intimacy with any woman before others, not even with his wife, for that would be detrimental to filial piety, since the primary duty in life was toward the parents. The mother-in-law problem was extended to other relatives of her husband's. Lady Pan said: "How must a wife gain the affection of her parents-in-law? There is no other way than complete obedience. If her mother-in-law says 'It is not' while it is so, the wife must still obey her. . . . And in order to obtain the affection of her parents-in-law, she must first secure that of her brothers- and sisters-in-law."

For a woman to be attractive to men was regarded as unnatural, equivalent to sexual offense, and even attractiveness to the husband should not be displayed publicly. It was good manners to avoid talking to a husband intimately in public, and tender feelings were banned from open company. On the other hand, the husband might, and often did, take a concubine. Very often this would be if the wife was barren, and she might even encourage him to take such a woman to continue the family line. Or a concubine might be acquired if a bridegroom did not like the bride whom he had first met at the wedding ceremony.

Concubinage was an accepted custom in China, though no woman wanted to be a concubine. Girls were sold for money, or sometimes because they had lost their virginity, but even poor families did not like to admit that their daughter might become a concubine and it was said that concubines came from some distant region. A concubine might be well treated if the wife was not jealous or the husband was strong-minded, but her life would be miserable if that was not so. If she failed to give birth to a son she might come to be ignored, while the husband would get other women to ensure the family succession. Since they were often young girls, concubines tended to outlive their husbands and then the family might neglect or scorn them and they would have no relatives to fall back on.

For the husband, possession of concubines or several wives meant increased sexual activity; he would go from one to another of them, on the same or successive nights. On Taoist theory his Yang would be weakened by loss of semen, but by practicing *coitus reservatus* he was supposed to satisfy the sexual needs of his wives and concubines, and be strengthened by the passage of their Yin essence to him.

Marriage

The *Book of Rites* attributed to Confucius the saying, "If Heaven and Earth were not mated, the ten thousand things would not have been born. It is by means of the great rite of marriage that mankind subsists throughout the myriad generations." Thus marriage was extolled, even when the wife was regarded as inferior. Every woman, however poor or ugly, could claim the right to a husband, and it was the duty of a householder to provide husbands for all the women in his employ; while among the poor and peasants it was the obligation of the community to find a husband for every girl.

In early China marriage among the ruling classes was exogamic, and marrying a woman with the same surname was completely taboo. Peasants also had taboos, though many were not recorded, but the family-name taboo still applies today. Marriages were arranged by a go-between, and the couple did not meet until marriage presents had been exchanged, the selection being decided by the parents. In country communities, in ancient times, young men and girls met at spring festivals, danced and sang together often in erotic ways, and then had sexual intercourse with chosen partners. Such unions would be regularized by the community. The Confucians were shocked by such traditional matings, and ordered that all unions should be supervised and registered by a "middleman," though how far this was done is debated.

There is frequent reference in later literature to a custom called "making a row in the bridal chamber" or "ragging the bride." After the wedding banquet the guests would take the couple to the bridal chamber and tease and make fun of them without restraint. Course questions and offensive behavior, sometimes even with whipping, were applied to the "happy" couple by drunken guests. To some degree the custom subsisted until modern times, perhaps preserving the ancient purpose of defloration of the bride and consummation of the marriage.

The preliminary viewing of the future pair traditionally took place after family agreement, though from the time of the Ming dynasty this viewing did not happen until the bride's veil was removed in the ceremony in the ancestral hall. Courtesans often acted as matchmakers, and they would lead the bride to the nuptial room, where the couple exchanged a wedding-cup and locks of their hair were knotted together.

In ancient China a wife as well as a husband could ask for a divorce and she did not thereby surrender her independence, but Confucians in the Sung dynasty forbade any female remarriage, for "to die in starvation is a minor matter, but to lose one's chastity by remarriage is very serious." The *Book of Rites* had already forbidden widows to wail at night, and it even prohibited people making friends with the sons of widows. For the sake of Confucian decorum young women were forced to remain widows, had no freedom, and lived restricted lives in ladies' chambers that came to be called locked-up prisons.

Until the T'ang dynasty Chinese women exposed their throats and bosoms, and girls often danced with naked breasts. But from the Sung dynasty, from the tenth century, the high collar became the distinctive feature of women's dress that it remained till modern times, and communist boilersuits perpetuate this covering. The binding of women's feet, introduced in the tenth century, designed to make women more attractive, was the cause of great suffering and has been abolished.

Buddhist Influences

According to tradition Buddhism, in its all-embracing Mahayana form, entered China in the first Christian century. Although Mahayana could easily absorb native Chinese deities under the guise of Bodhisattvas, "beings of enlightenment," some Buddhist beliefs and practices aroused criticism as alien to China. The foreign origins of Buddhism were objectionable, as was the claimed superiority of monks to rulers and even to the emperor. The celibacy of monks was one of the greatest obstacles to the native adoption of the new religion, since childlessness was regarded in China as the most unfilial conduct. Buddhist apologists replied that "Wives, children and property are the luxuries of the world . . . but the monk accumulates goodness and wisdom instead."

Buddhists found that the Chinese were interested in magical spells and charms, such as were already used in Taoism, and they translated Indian works which included these and teachings about sex. Moreover women had a leading role in Indian sex books, often being the instructors in sexual mysteries, so that Buddhism enhanced the position of women, and joined in this with Taoism generally against the Confucian subordination of women. In the early periods Buddhist texts on love-making were abbreviated to spare Confucian feelings, but when Buddhism was flourishing erotic Tantric texts were widely published. Then under later Neo-Confucian reformers they were expurgated again.

Women, in particular, were attracted by Buddhism. Its creed of universal compassion implied the equality of all beings and answered the spiritual needs of women. The favorite Mahayana scripture was the Lotus Sutra which presented the Bodhisattva Avalokiteshvara, the "lord of looking or regard," who became in China the compassionate goddess Kwanyin, the lady giver of children (in Japan she became Kwannon or Kannon). Kwanyin was often depicted carrying the peach of sex, she gave children and helped in distress, and the dazzling ceremonies of her temples brought color into the monotony of daily life.

The most popular Buddhist sect was the Pure Land, the religion of faith and grace. It was ruled over by Amitabha, The Buddha of Boundless Light in his Western Paradise which could be entered by anyone who uttered his name in sincere devotion. The Chinese version of Amitabha was O-mi-t'o-fo, which became a favorite exclamation of astonishment or delight for Chinese women. The Pure Land has remained the most popular of Buddhist sects in Japan, and was for long so in China.

Buddhist nuns were popular among many Chinese women, for they had free access to the women's quarters of houses and became advisors on personal problems. They held prayer-meetings for recovery of sick children or curing of sterility, and for healing female diseases. Nuns also taught girls to read and write, and other feminine skills. But Confucians were shocked at the sight of women forsaking their sacred duty of producing children and satisfying their husbands, and scurrilous novels were written about monks and nuns. Poems were written against monks who were charged with having changed the Pure Land into a sea of lust, like leeches sucking blood; they called a maiden to feel for an opening and revealed the true shape of the Buddha's Tooth.

Some Chinese girls became nuns no doubt for sincere reasons of religious conviction, while others were vowed by their parents as protection against evil, and other wives and concubines escaped to nunneries from cruel husbands or families. Critics said that they practiced unnatural vices in the monasteries and nunneries, or they provided love philters for women and acted as go-betweens in illicit affairs. If nunneries were ruled by women of strong personality the discipline was probably strict, but laxity might give some room for suspicion. An erotic text of the T'ang dynasty accused nuns of having sexual intercourse with Chinese and Indian monks, and "when

they are with those lovers the nuns forget the Law of the Buddha and play absent-mindedly with their rosaries." Others maintained that nunneries were havens for loose women who did not wish to register as prostitutes, but they held dinners and drinking bouts there while the religious authorities made good profits out of the food and wine.

Mahayana Buddhist philosophical systems included speculations about male and female cosmic principles, which were developed in Tantra and resembled Yin and Yang. In the Vajrayana, the "thunder bolt vehicle," in which the thunderbolt was a phallic symbol, there was taught the attainment of supreme bliss by the union of male and female, a mystical marriage which overcame sexual duality in a hermaphroditic unity. Buddhist Tantrists practiced this method either alone in imagination or in real sexual embrace with a woman, but most texts stated that the partner should be a live woman because "Buddha-hood abides in the *yoni*." The yogic method of breath-control worked on the man's rising semen so that it was not emitted but rose upwards, and the woman's energy stimulated and blended with his, to produce from the unshed semen a new and powerful essence which rose up through the nerve centers to the "Lotus on top of the head."

Taoist sexual practices were no doubt influenced by Indian Tantrism, but it is possible that Indian texts in their turn were affected by Chinese teachings. Buddhist Tantrism arrived in China relatively late, about the eighth century, and since a sexual mysticism of making "translated semen return" had already flourished in China for several centuries, and had perhaps not been long known in India, there may have been a two-way traffic of religious and sexual practices. An Indian Tantric text, Rudra-yamala, told of a sage who practiced austerities for ages without seeing the supreme goddess, whereupon he was advised to obtain the "Chinese discipline" in which the goddess delighted. She sent him to China where he saw the Buddha surrounded by naked adepts who drank wine, ate meat, and engaged in sexual intercourse with beautiful women. The sage was greatly disturbed by this sight, until the Buddha taught him the true meaning of the sexual rites.

Vajrayana became practically extinct in India by the twelfth century, but its teachings had been reimported into Tibet and China. There was opposition to it, and a shocked Confucian scholar in the Sung dynasty described a "Buddha-mother Hall" in Peking in which Tibetan male and female deities were represented by statues locked in sexual embrace. These were regarded as repulsive foreign practices, without any recognition that they might have depicted ancient

Taoist disciplines. Earlier such "Joyful Buddhas" had been used to instruct princes and princesses in sexual matters, but Neo-Confucianism tried to suppress "immoral cults," and description of the sexual mysticism of Chinese Tantrism was partly preserved in Japan.

Variations

Since the Chinese believed that a man's semen was his most precious possession, and every emission would diminish his vital force unless compensated by acquiring an equivalent amount of Yin essence from a woman, it followed that certain sexual variants were reprehended. Male masturbation was forbidden, for it implied a complete loss of vital essence, and it was only condoned when a man was away for long from female company and the "devitalized semen" might clog his system. Even involuntary emissions in sleep were viewed with concern, and might be thought to be induced by evil female succubi stealing the man's vital powers. If they came from seeing a woman in a dream, the man should beware of meeting her in waking life for she might be a vampire or foxspirit. Female masturbation, however, was viewed with tolerance, since the Yin supply of woman is unlimited. The texts mention dildos used for self-satisfaction by women, and pictures show them, but warning was given against excessive use which might damage "the lining of the womb."

Male homosexuality was not mentioned in sexual handbooks, since they were concerned with conjugal relations. From other sources it appears that it was rare in early times, flourished in the Middle Ages, and was not unusually frequent later. Homosexuality was tolerated among adults because intimate contact between two Yang elements could not result in loss of vital force. Some of the emperors had catamites, but also female concubines, and some T'ang poets seem to have been homosexual, though the affectionate language they used of their friends need not imply sexual intercourse. Male friendship was one of the Confucian virtues, and was often expressed in warm terms. A seventh-century story tells of an official and his wife spying on men bathing together, ostensibly to see if they had double ribs, but probably to observe how intimate they were together. Foreign observers in the nineteenth century said that pederasty was rampant in China, but social etiquette tolerated men walking hand in hand and homosexuals acted women's parts in theaters. There was probably a shortage of women in the ports where foreigners traded, and they would not see heterosexual relationships which were strictly private.

Female homosexuality was common and tolerated, and considered bound to prevail in women's quarters. Women could satisfy each other naturally or with artificial means, such as double dildos, or "exertion bells" or "tinkling balls" used for masturbation. The Chinese said that such artificial sexual aids were foreign: "Burmese Bells," "Tarter pastures," "barbarian soldiers," just as Europeans spoke of "French letters" and "lettres anglaises."

Heterosexual intercourse, we see from the sexual manuals, was prepared and performed carefully, so as to activate the Yin essence. Kissing was important, along with further movement of lips and tongue in preliminary play. Foreigners thought that the Chinese did not kiss, because it was an act reserved for the bedchamber, and when the Chinese saw western women kissing in public they thought they were the lowest kind of prostitutes since even regular prostitutes would only kiss in private.

The sexual handbooks gave great detail of the various positions that could be adopted in sexual intercourse. Cunnilingus was approved, especially in Taoist texts, since it procured Yin essence for the man. But anal penetration and fellatio should only be used as preliminaries and if there was no complete male emission.

Single and married men were thought to be entitled to association with prostitutes, but it was different from conjugal intercourse as not designed for procreation and so it was not discussed in sexual manuals. Name-taboos did not apply, as the man did not know the prostitute's surname. Some writers thought that intercourse with a prostitute did not waste the male semen, since the woman from her profession had an abundant supply of Yin essence and gave back more than he lost to her patron. After the sixteenth century syphilis was identified and medical treatises warned of the dangers of association with prostitutes. Medical and sex books laid great stress on eugenics, in order to produce the best offspring.

Incest was rare, and to be punished according to the penal code as an "inhuman crime" deserving death in a severe form, though some early imperial officials had incestuous relations with their sisters and other female relatives. Bestiality was also rare, though mentioned in connection with debauched rulers. Apart from sexual manuals, which were not pornographic, at least in intention, scatological material was rare and only found in some novels which delighted in exaggerated detail of male and female organs and secretions. The ancient Chinese had few inhibitions, though Confucian decorum sought to regulate natural functions. . . .

Discussion and Reflection Questions

1. The relationship between yin and yang is central to Chinese thought about nature and human relationships. What does this relationship suggest about the proper relationships between women and men? What characteristics ought to be present in such relationships?

2. In traditional Chinese thinking, the two main purposes of sexual intercourse are procreation and the increase of male energy. How do these views differ from views prevalent in the West? What other purposes of sexual intercourse are emphasized in the West? What is your own view of the relative importance of each of these purposes? Which is most important? Which is least important? Why?

3. Certain kinds of sexual activity (sexual intercourse before marriage, outside of marriage, in public, etc.) are condemned by most Western religions but apparently are accepted by Taoism. Which view seems more reasonable to you? Is it possible to comparatively evaluate these two views without taking into account the larger philosophical and religious contexts of which they are parts?

4. How do Taoist, Confucian, Buddhist, and Western views of male-female relationships, marriage, and sexual activity differ? What do you find to be the most, and least, attractive features of each of these views? How would you describe your ideals concerning each of these things?

Suggestions for Further Reading

Philosophical works on sex are a fairly recent phenomenon. Here are some good places to continue your exploration of the issues raised above: Raymond A. Bellicotti, "Sex," in *A Companion to Ethics*, edited by Peter Singer (Oxford: Basil Blackwell, 1991), pp. 315–326; see also his "A Philosophical Analysis of Sexual Ethics," *Journal of Social Philosophy* 10 (1979): 8–11; R. Baker and F. Elliston, eds., *Philosophy and Sex* (Buffalo, N.Y.: Prometheus Books, 1984); J. F. M. Hunter, *Thinking About Sex and Love: A Philosophical Inquiry* (New York: St. Martin's Press, 1980); Alan Soble, ed., *Philosophy of Sex*, 2nd ed. (Totowa, N.J.: Rowman and Littlefield, 1991); Russell Vannoy, *Sex Without Love: A Philosophical Exploration* (Buffalo, N.Y.: Prometheus Books, 1980). A good general reader in the realm of sexual ethics is *The Ethics of Sex*, edited by Mark D. Jordan (Oxford: Blackwell Religious Ethics, 2001). Buddhist perspectives on sexual morality are articulated in *Buddhism, Sexuality, and Gender*, edited by Jose I. Cabezon (Albany: State University of New York Press, 1992). For a Kantian analysis of "unnatural sex" see Lara Denis' "Kant on the Wrongness of 'Unnatural' Sex," *History of Philosophy Quarterly* 16 (1999): 225–248. Piers Benn explores an Aristotelian perspective on sexual morality in "Is Sex Morally Special?" *Journal of Applied Philosophy* 16 (1999): 235–245. Another resource for Greek Virtue Ethic perspectives on sexual morality is Raja Fouad Halwani's "Virtue Ethics and Adultery," *Journal of Social Philosophy* 29 (1998): 5–18. For essays that describe the views on homosexuality found in different religious traditions, see Arlene Swidler, ed., *Homosexuality and World Religions* (Valley Forge, Pa.: Trinity Press International, 1993).

InfoTrac

sexual ethics, "sex and ethics", love, friendship, sexual orientation, sex crimes

Chapter 10

Abortion

Introduction: The Problem of Abortion

The problem of abortion surely ranks as one of the most important and divisive moral issues of our time. Watching television news or opening a newspaper on any given day, you are likely to encounter the very public and passionate arguments characterizing this issue. It is also, and perhaps more fundamentally, a *personal* issue that will very likely affect you, at least indirectly, at some point in your life. There are, as one might expect, a number of different principled perspectives on this issue. Some of these are represented in the readings below. The first two readings approach the issue of abortion from Western perspectives. Don Marquis argues that abortion is almost always wrong. Judith Jarvis Thomson, on the other hand, argues that abortion is not necessarily wrong and is sometimes morally permissible. Although there is some room for agreement between these two writers, they nonetheless present essentially opposing viewpoints on the morality of abortion. The second two readings represent Eastern perspectives, or at least perspectives that arise from the distinctive situations of Eastern societies. Ren Zong Qiu, Chun Zhi Wang, and Yuan Gu adopt a consequentialist perspective in reflecting on the morality of abortion in China and argue that in some circumstances late-term abortion is morally permissible. R. E. Florida explores Buddhist approaches to abortion and finds that it is almost always morally wrong. What is perhaps especially interesting about these latter two articles is the role of circumstantial factors in evaluating the morality of abortion in specific cases. Thus this issue brings out sharply the different approaches taken by Western and Eastern thinkers.

Don Marquis, Why Abortion Is Immoral

In the first reading selection, Don Marquis sets out to show "that abortion is, except possibly in rare cases, seriously immoral" and that it is "in the same moral category as killing an innocent adult human being." In both cases, he says, killing someone deprives that person of his or her future, and this is what makes such killing immoral. Marquis is careful to distinguish his account from other antiabortion accounts and to show how his view succeeds where others fail. In light of his arguments, he concludes that the problem of the ethics of abortion is solvable.

Reading Questions

1. Marquis gives two reasons in support of his claim that killing is wrong because it entails the loss of the victim's future. What are these reasons?

2. Marquis identifies four implications of his view concerning the wrongness of killing that support this view. What are these four implications?

3. How does Marquis's theory of what makes killing wrong differ from "sanctity of life" or "personhood" theorists? What advantages does Marquis see for his theory over these others?

4. According to Marquis, why does his account *not* entail viewing contraception as immoral?

Why Abortion Is Immoral

DON MARQUIS

THE VIEW THAT ABORTION is, with rare exceptions, seriously immoral has received little support in the recent philosophical literature. No doubt most philosophers affiliated with secular institutions of higher education believe that the antiabortion position is either a symptom of irrational religious dogma or a conclusion generated by seriously confused philosophical argument. The purpose of this essay is to undermine this general belief. This essay sets out an argument that purports to show, as well as any argument in ethics can show, that abortion is, except possibly in rare cases, seriously immoral, that it is in the same moral category as killing an innocent adult human being.

The argument is based on a major assumption. Many of the most insightful and careful writers on the ethics of abortion—such as Joel Feinberg, Michael Tooley, Mary Anne Warren, H. Tristram Engelhardt, Jr., L. W. Sumner, John T. Noonan, Jr., and Philip Devine—believe that whether or not abortion is morally permissible stands or falls on whether or not a fetus is the sort of being whose life it is seriously wrong to end. The argument of this essay will assume, but not argue, that they are correct.

Also, this essay will neglect issues of great importance to a complete ethics of abortion. Some antiabortionists will allow that certain abortions, such as abortion before implantation or abortion when the life of a woman is threatened by a pregnancy or abortion after rape, may be morally permissible. This essay will not explore the casuistry of these hard cases. The purpose of this essay is to develop a general argument for the claim that the overwhelming majority of deliberate abortions are seriously immoral.

I

A sketch of standard antiabortion and pro-choice arguments exhibits how those arguments possess certain symmetries that explain why partisans of those positions are so convinced of the correctness of their own positions, why they are not successful in convincing their opponents, and why, to others, this issue seems to be unresolvable. An analysis of the nature of this standoff suggests a strategy for surmounting it.

Consider the way a typical antiabortionist argues. She will argue or assert that life is present from the

Don Marquis, "Why Abortion Is Immoral," Journal of Philosophy, *vol. 86, no. 4 (April 1989), pp. 183–202. Reprinted by permission of the author and publisher.*

moment of conception or that fetuses look like babies or that fetuses possess a characteristic such as a genetic code that is both necessary and sufficient for being human. Antiabortionists seem to believe that (1) the truth of all these claims is quite obvious, and (2) establishing any of these claims is sufficient to show that abortion is morally akin to murder.

A standard pro-choice strategy exhibits similarities. The pro-choicer will argue or assert that fetuses are not persons or that fetuses are not rational agents or that fetuses are not social beings. Pro-choicers seem to believe that (1) the truth of any of these claims is quite obvious, and (2) establishing any of these claims is sufficient to show that an abortion is not a wrongful killing.

In fact, both the pro-choice and the antiabortion claims do seem to be true, although the "it looks like a baby" claim is more difficult to establish the earlier the pregnancy. We seem to have a standoff. How can it be resolved?

As everyone who has taken a bit of logic knows, if any of these arguments concerning abortion is a good argument, it requires not only some claim characterizing fetuses, but also some general moral principle that ties a characteristic of fetuses to having or not having the right to life or to some other moral characteristic that will generate the obligation or the lack of obligation not to end the life of a fetus. Accordingly, the arguments of the antiabortionist and the pro-choicer need a bit of filling in to be regarded as adequate.

Note what each partisan will say. The antiabortionist will claim that her position is supported by such generally accepted moral principles as "It is always prima facie seriously wrong to take a human life" or "It is always prima facie seriously wrong to end the life of a baby." Since these are generally accepted moral principles, her position is certainly not obviously wrong. The pro-choicer will claim that her position is supported by such plausible moral principles as "Being a person is what gives an individual intrinsic moral worth" or "It is only seriously prima facie wrong to take the life of a member of the human community." Since these are generally accepted moral principles, the pro-choice position is certainly not obviously wrong. Unfortunately, we have again arrived at a standoff.

Now, how might one deal with this standoff? The standard approach is to try to show how the moral principles of one's opponent lose their plausibility under analysis. It is easy to see how this is possible. On the one hand, the antiabortionist will defend a moral principle concerning the wrongness of killing which tends to be broad in scope in order that even

fetuses at an early stage of pregnancy will fall under it. The problem with broad principles is that they often embrace too much. In this particular instance, the principle "It is always prima facie wrong to take a human life" seems to entail that it is wrong to end the existence of a living human cancer-cell culture, on the grounds that the culture is both living and human. Therefore, it seems that the antiabortionist's favored principle is too broad.

On the other hand, the pro-choicer wants to find a moral principle concerning the wrongness of killing which tends to be narrow in scope in order that fetuses will *not* fall under it. The problem with narrow principles is that they often do not embrace enough. Hence, the needed principles such as "It is prima facie seriously wrong to kill only persons" or "It is prima facie wrong to kill infants or young children or the severely retarded or even perhaps the severely mentally ill." Therefore, we seem again to have a standoff. The antiabortionist charges, not unreasonably, that pro-choice principles concerning killing are too narrow to be acceptable; the pro-choicer charges, not unreasonably, that antiabortionist principles concerning killing are too broad to be acceptable.

Attempts by both sides to patch up the difficulties in their positions run into further difficulties. The antiabortionist will try to remove the problem in her position by reformulating her principle concerning killing in terms of human beings. Now we end up with: "It is always prima facie seriously wrong to end the life of a human being." This principle has the advantage of avoiding the problem of the cancer-cell culture counterexample. But this advantage is purchased at a high price. For although it is clear that a fetus is both human and alive, it is not at all clear that a fetus is a human *being*. There is at least something to be said for the view that something becomes a human being only after a process of development, and that therefore first trimester fetuses and perhaps all fetuses are not yet human beings. Hence, the antiabortionist, by this move, has merely exchanged one problem for another.

The pro-choicer fares no better. She may attempt to find reasons why killing infants, young children, and the severely retarded is wrong which are independent of her major principle that is supposed to explain the wrongness of taking human life, but which will not also make abortion immoral. This is no easy task. Appeals to social utility will seem satisfactory only to those who resolve not to think of the enormous difficulties with a utilitarian account of the wrongness of killing and the significant social costs of preserving the lives of the unproductive. A pro-choice strategy that extends the definition of "person" to infants or even to young children seems just as arbitrary as an antiabortion strategy that extends the definition of "human being" to fetuses. Again, we find symmetries in the two positions and we arrive at a standoff.

There are even further problems that reflect symmetries in the two positions. In addition to counterexample problems, or the arbitrary application problems that can be exchanged for them, the standard antiabortionist principle "It is prima facie seriously wrong to kill a human being," or one of its variants, can be objected to on the grounds of ambiguity. If "human being" is taken to be a *biological* category, then the antiabortionist is left with the problem of explaining why a merely biological category should make a moral difference. Why, it is asked, is it any more reasonable to base a moral conclusion on the number of chromosomes in one's cells than on the color of one's skin? If "human being," on the other hand, is taken to be a *moral* category, then the claim that a fetus is a human being cannot be taken to be a premise in the antiabortion argument, for it is precisely what needs to be established. Hence, either the antiabortionist's main category is a morally irrelevant, merely biological category, or it is of no use to the antiabortionist in establishing (noncircularly, of course) that abortion is wrong.

Although this problem with the antiabortionist position is often noticed, it is less often noticed that the pro-choice position suffers from an analogous problem. The principle "Only persons have the right to life" also suffers from an ambiguity. The term "person" is typically defined in terms of psychological characteristics, although there will certainly be disagreement concerning which characteristics are most important. Supposing that this matter can be settled, the pro-choicer is left with the problem of explaining why *psychological* characteristics should make a *moral* difference. If the pro-choicer should attempt to deal with this problem by claiming that an explanation is not necessary, that in fact we do treat such a cluster of psychological properties as having moral significance, the sharp-witted antiabortionist should have a ready response. We do treat being both living and human as having moral significance. If it is legitimate for the pro-choicer to demand that the antiabortionist provide an explanation of the connection between the biological character of being a human being and the wrongness of being killed (even though people accept this connection), then it is legitimate for the antiabortionist to demand that the pro-choicer provide an explanation of the connection between psycho-

logical criteria for being a person and the wrongness of being killed (even though that connection is accepted).

Feinberg has attempted to meet this objection (he calls psychological personhood "commonsense personhood"):

> The characteristics that confer commonsense personhood are not arbitrary bases for rights and duties, such as race, sex or species membership; rather they are traits that make sense out of rights and duties and without which those moral attributes would have no point or function. It is because people are conscious; have a sense of their personal identities; have plans, goals, and projects; experience emotions; are liable to pains, anxieties, and frustrations; can reason and bargain, and so on—it is because of these attributes that people have values and interests, desires and expectations of their own, including a stake in their own futures, and a personal well-being of a sort we cannot ascribe to unconscious or nonrational beings. Because of their developed capacities they can assume duties and responsibilities and can have and make claims on one another. Only because of their sense of self, their life plans, their value hierarchies, and their stakes in their own futures can they be ascribed fundamental rights. There is nothing arbitrary about these linkages.

The plausible aspects of this attempt should not be taken to obscure its implausible features. There is a great deal to be said for the view that being a psychological person under some description is a necessary condition for having duties. One cannot have a duty unless one is capable of behaving morally, and a being's capability of behaving morally will require having a certain psychology. It is far from obvious, however, that having rights entails consciousness or rationality, as Feinberg suggests. We speak of the rights of the severely retarded or the severely mentally ill, yet some of these persons are not rational. We speak of the rights of the temporarily unconscious. The New Jersey Supreme Court based their decision in the Quinlan case on Karen Ann Quinlan's right to privacy, and she was known to be permanently unconscious at that time. Hence, Feinberg's claim that having rights entails being conscious is, on its face, obviously false.

Of course, it might not make sense to attribute rights to a being that would never in its natural history have certain psychological traits. This modest connection between psychological personhood and moral personhood will create a place for Karen Ann Quinlan and the temporarily unconscious. But then it makes a place for fetuses also. Hence, it does not serve Feinberg's pro-choice purposes. Accordingly, it seems that the pro-choicer will have as much difficulty bridging the gap between psychological personhood and personhood in the moral sense as the antiabortionist has bridging the gap between being a biological human being and being a human being in the moral sense.

Furthermore, the pro-choicer cannot any more escape her problem by making person a purely moral category than the antiabortionist could escape by the analogous move. For if person is a moral category, then the pro-choicer is left without the resources for establishing (noncircularly, of course) the claim that a fetus is not a person, which is an essential premise in her argument. Again, we have both a summary and a standoff between pro-choice and antiabortion views.

Passions in the abortion debate run high. There are both plausibilities and difficulties with the standard positions. Accordingly, it is hardly surprising that partisans of either side embrace with fervor the moral generalizations that support the conclusions they preanalytically favor, and reject with disdain the moral generalizations of their opponents as being subject to inescapable difficulties. It is easy to believe that the counterexamples to one's own moral principles are merely temporary difficulties that will dissolve in the wake of further philosophical research, and that the counterexamples to the principles of one's opponents are as straightforward as the contradiction between *A* and *O* propositions in traditional logic. This might suggest to an impartial observer (if there are any) that the abortion issue is unresolvable.

There is a way out of this apparent dialectical quandary. The moral generalizations of both sides are not quite correct. The generalizations hold for the most part, for the usual cases. This suggests that they are all *accidental* generalizations, that the moral claims made by those on both sides of the dispute do not touch on the *essence* of the matter.

This use of the distinction between essence and accident is not meant to invoke obscure metaphysical categories. Rather, it is intended to reflect the rather atheoretical nature of the abortion discussion. If the generalization a partisan in the abortion dispute adopts were derived from the reason why ending the life of a human being is wrong, then there could not be exceptions to that generalization unless some special case obtains in which there are even more powerful countervailing reasons. Such generalizations would not be merely accidental generalizations; they would point to, or be based upon, the essence of the wrongness of killing, what it is that makes killing wrong. All this suggests that a necessary condition of resolving the abortion controversy is a more theoretical account of the wrongness of killing. After all, if we merely believe, but do not understand, why killing adult human beings such as ourselves is wrong, how could we conceivably show that abortion is either immoral or permissible?

II

In order to develop such an account, we can start from the following unproblematic assumption concerning our own case: it is wrong to kill *us*. Why is it wrong? Some answers can be easily eliminated. It might be said that what makes killing us wrong is that a killing brutalizes the one who kills. But the brutalization consists of being inured to the performance of an act that is hideously immoral; hence, the brutalization does not explain the immorality. It might be said that what makes killing us wrong is the great loss others would experience due to our absence. Although such hubris is understandable, such an explanation does not account for the wrongness of killing hermits, or those whose lives are relatively independent and whose friends find it easy to make new friends.

A more obvious answer is better. What primarily makes killing wrong is neither its effect on the murderer nor its effect on the victim's friends and relatives, but its effect on the victim. The loss of one's life is one of the greatest losses one can suffer. The loss of one's life deprives one of all the experiences, activities, projects, and enjoyments that would otherwise have constituted one's future. Therefore, killing someone is wrong, primarily because the killing inflicts (one of) the greatest possible losses on the victim. To describe this as the loss of life can be misleading, however. The change in my biological state does not by itself make killing me wrong. The effect of the loss of my biological life is the loss to me of all those activities, projects, experiences, and enjoyments which would otherwise have constituted my future personal life. These activities, projects, experiences, and enjoyments are either valuable for their own sakes or are means to something else that is valuable for its own sake. Some parts of my future are not valued by me now, but will come to be valued by me as I grow older and as my values and capacities change. When I am killed, I am deprived both of what I now value which would have been part of my future personal life, but also what I would come to value.

Therefore, when I die, I am deprived of all of the value of my future. Inflicting this loss on me is ultimately what makes killing me wrong. This being the case, it would seem that what makes killing *any* adult human being prima facie seriously wrong is the loss of his or her future.

How should this rudimentary theory of the wrongness of killing be evaluated? It cannot be faulted for deriving an "ought" from an "is," for it does not. The analysis assumes that killing me (or you, reader) is prima facie seriously wrong. The point of the analysis is to establish which natural property ultimately explains the wrongness of the killing, given that it is wrong. A natural property will ultimately explain the wrongness of killing, only if (1) the explanation fits with our intuitions about the matter and (2) there is no other natural property that provides the basis for a better explanation of the wrongness of killing. This analysis rests on the intuition that what makes killing a particular human or animal wrong is what it does to that particular human or animal. What makes killing wrong is some natural effect or other of the killing. Some would deny this. For instance, a divine-command theorist in ethics would deny it. Surely this denial is, however, one of those features of divine-command theory which renders it so implausible.

The claim that what makes killing wrong is the loss of the victim's future is directly supported by two considerations. In the first place, this theory explains why we regard killing as one of the worst of crimes. Killing is especially wrong, because it deprives the victim of more than perhaps any other crime. In the second place, people with AIDS or cancer who know they are dying believe, of course, that dying is a very bad thing for them. They believe that the loss of a future to them that they would otherwise have experienced is what makes their premature death a very bad thing for them. A better theory of the wrongness of killing would require a different natural property associated with killing which better fits with the attitudes of the dying. What could it be?

The view that what makes killing wrong is the loss to the victim of the value of the victim's future gains additional support when some of its implications are examined. In the first place, it is incompatible with the view that it is wrong to kill only beings who are biologically human. It is possible that there exists a different species from another planet whose members have a future like ours. Since having a future like that is what makes killing someone wrong, this theory entails that it would be wrong to kill members of such a species. Hence, this theory is op-

posed to the claim that only life that is biologically human has great moral worth, a claim which many antiabortionists have seemed to adopt. This opposition, which this theory has in common with personhood theories, seems to be a merit of the theory.

In the second place, the claim that the loss of one's future is the wrong-making feature of one's being killed entails the possibility that the futures of some actual nonhuman mammals on our own planet are sufficiently like ours that it is seriously wrong to kill them also. Whether some animals do have the same right to life as human beings depends on adding to the account of the wrongness of killing some additional account of just what it is about my future or the futures of other adult human beings which makes it wrong to kill us. No such additional account will be offered in this essay. Undoubtedly, the provision of such an account would be a very difficult matter. Undoubtedly, any such account would be quite controversial. Hence, it surely should not reflect badly on this sketch of an elementary theory of the wrongness of killing that it is indeterminate with respect to some very difficult issues regarding animal rights.

In the third place, the claim that the loss of one's future is the wrong-making feature of one's being killed does not entail, as sanctity-of-human-life theories do, that active euthanasia is wrong. Persons who are severely and incurably ill, who face a future of pain and despair, and who wish to die will not have suffered a loss if they are killed. It is, strictly speaking, the value of a human's future which makes killing wrong in this theory. This being so, killing does not necessarily wrong some persons who are sick and dying. Of course, there may be other reasons for a prohibition of active euthanasia, but that is another matter. Sanctity-of-human-life theories seem to hold that active euthanasia is seriously wrong even in an individual case where there seems to be good reason for it independently of public policy considerations. This consequence is most implausible, and it is a plus for the claim that the loss of a future of value is what makes killing wrong that it does not share this consequence.

In the fourth place, the account of the wrongness of killing defended in this essay does straightforwardly entail that it is prima facie seriously wrong to kill children and infants, for we do presume that they have futures of value. Since we do believe that it is wrong to kill defenseless little babies, it is important that a theory of the wrongness of killing easily account for this. Personhood theories of the wrongness of killing, on the other hand, cannot straightforwardly account for the wrongness of killing infants and young children. Hence, such theories must add special ad hoc accounts of the wrongness of killing the young. The plausibility of such ad hoc theories seems to be a function of how desperately one wants such theories to work. The claim that the primary wrong-making feature of a killing is the loss to the victim of the value of its future accounts for the wrongness of killing young children and infants directly; it makes the wrongness of such acts as obvious as we actually think it is. This is a further merit of this theory. Accordingly, it seems that this value-of-a-future-like-ours theory of the wrongness of killing shares strengths of both sanctity-of-life and personhood accounts while avoiding weaknesses of both. In addition, it meshes with a central intuition concerning what makes killing wrong.

The claim that the primary wrong-making feature of a killing is the loss to the victim of the value of its future has obvious consequences for the ethics of abortion. The future of a standard fetus includes a set of experiences, projects, activities, and such which are identical with the futures of adult human beings and are identical with the futures of young children. Since the reason that is sufficient to explain why it is wrong to kill human beings after the time of birth is a reason that also applies to fetuses, it follows that abortion is prima facie seriously morally wrong.

This argument does not rely on the invalid inference that, since it is wrong to kill persons, it is wrong to kill potential persons also. The category that is morally central to this analysis is the category of having a valuable future like ours; it is not the category of personhood. The argument to the conclusion that abortion is prima facie seriously morally wrong proceeded independently of the notion of person or potential person or any equivalent. Someone may wish to start with this analysis in terms of the value of a human future, conclude that abortion is, except perhaps in rare circumstances, seriously morally wrong, infer that fetuses have the right to life, and then call fetuses "persons" as a result of their having the right to life. Clearly, in this case, the category of person is being used to state the *conclusion* of the analysis rather than to generate the *argument* of the analysis.

The structure of this antiabortion argument can be both illuminated and defended by comparing it to what appears to be the best argument for the wrongness of the wanton infliction of pain on animals. This latter argument is based on the assumption that it is prima facie wrong to inflict pain on me (or you, reader). What is the natural property associated with the infliction of pain which makes such infliction wrong? The obvious answer seems to be that the infliction of pain causes suffering and that suffering is a misfortune. The suffering caused by the infliction of pain is what makes the wanton infliction of pain on me wrong. The wanton infliction of pain on other adult humans causes suffering. The wanton infliction of pain on animals causes suffering. Since causing suffering is what makes the wanton infliction of pain wrong and since the wanton infliction of pain on animals causes suffering, it follows that the wanton infliction of pain on animals is wrong.

This argument for the wrongness of the wanton infliction of pain on animals shares a number of structural features with the argument for the serious prima facie wrongness of abortion. Both arguments start with an obvious assumption concerning what it is wrong to do to me (or you, reader). Both then look for the characteristic or the consequence of the wrong action which makes the action wrong. Both recognize that the wrong-making feature of these immoral actions is a property of actions sometimes directed at individuals other than postnatal human beings. If the structure of the argument for the wrongness of the wanton infliction of pain on animals is sound, then the structure of the argument for the prima facie serious wrongness of abortion is also sound, for the structure of the two arguments is the same. The structure common to both is the key to the explanation of how the wrongness of abortion can be demonstrated without recourse to the category of person. In neither argument is that category crucial.

This defense of an argument for the wrongness of abortion in terms of a structurally similar argument for the wrongness of the wanton infliction of pain on animals succeeds only if the account regarding animals is the correct account. Is it? In the first place, it seems plausible. In the second place, its major competition is Kant's account. Kant believed that we do not have direct duties to animals at all, because they are not persons. Hence, Kant had to explain and justify the wrongness of inflicting pain on animals on the grounds that "he who is hard in his dealings with animals becomes hard also in his dealing with men." The problem with Kant's account is that there seems to be no reason for accepting this latter claim unless Kant's account is rejected. If the alternative to Kant's account is accepted, then it is easy to understand why someone who is indifferent to inflicting pain on animals is also indifferent to inflicting pain on humans, for one is indifferent to what makes inflicting pain wrong in both cases. But, if Kant's account is accepted, there is no intelligible reason why one who is hard in his dealings with animals (or crabgrass or stones) should also be hard in his dealings with men.

After all, men are persons: animals are no more persons than crabgrass or stones. Persons are Kant's crucial moral category. Why, in short, should a Kantian accept the basic claim in Kant's argument?

Hence, Kant's argument for the wrongness of inflicting pain on animals rests on a claim that, in a world of Kantian moral agents, is demonstrably false. Therefore, the alternative analysis, being more plausible anyway, should be accepted. Since this alternative analysis has the same structure as the antiabortion argument being defended here, we have further support for the argument for the immorality of abortion being defended in this essay.

Of course, this value-of-a-future-like-ours argument, if sound, shows only that abortion is prima facie wrong, not that it is wrong in any and all circumstances. Since the loss of the future to a standard fetus, if killed, is, however, at least as great a loss as the loss of the future to a standard adult human being who is killed, abortion, like ordinary killing, could be justified only by the most compelling reasons. The loss of one's life is almost the greatest misfortune that can happen to one. Presumably abortion could be justified in some circumstances, only if the loss consequent on failing to abort would be at least as great. Accordingly, morally permissible abortions will be rare indeed unless, perhaps, they occur so early in pregnancy that a fetus is not yet definitely an individual. Hence, this argument should be taken as showing that abortion is presumptively very seriously wrong, where the presumption is very strong—as strong as the presumption that killing another adult human being is wrong.

III

How complete an account of the wrongness of killing does the value-of-a-future-like-ours account have to be in order that the wrongness of abortion is a consequence? This account does not have to be an account of the necessary conditions for the wrongness of killing. Some persons in nursing homes may lack valuable human futures, yet it may be wrong to kill them for other reasons. Furthermore, this account does not obviously have to be the sole reason killing is wrong where the victim did have a valuable future. This analysis claims only that, for any killing where the victim did have a valuable future like ours, having that future by itself is sufficient to create the strong presumption that the killing is seriously wrong.

One way to overturn the value-of-a-future-like-ours argument would be to find some account of the wrongness of killing which is at least as intelligible and which has different implications for the ethics of abortion. Two rival accounts possess at least some degree of plausibility. One account is based on the obvious fact that people value the experience of living and wish for that valuable experience to continue. Therefore, it might be said, what makes killing wrong is the discontinuation of that experience for the victim. Let us call this the *discontinuation account*. Another rival account is based upon the obvious fact that people strongly desire to continue to live. This suggests that what makes killing us so wrong is that it interferes with the fulfillment of a strong and fundamental desire, the fulfillment of which is necessary for the fulfillment of any other desires we might have. Let us call this the *desire account*.

Consider first the desire account as a rival account of the ethics of killing which would provide the basis for rejecting the antiabortion position. Such an account will have to be stronger than the value-of-a-future-like-ours account of the wrongness of abortion if it is to do the job expected of it. To entail the wrongness of abortion, the value-of-a-future-like-ours account has only to provide a sufficient, but not a necessary, condition for the wrongness of killing. The desire account, on the other hand, must provide us also with a necessary condition for the wrongness of killing in order to generate a pro-choice conclusion on abortion. The reason for this is that presumably the argument from the desire account moves from the claim that what makes killing wrong is interference with a very strong desire to the claim that abortion is not wrong because the fetus lacks a strong desire to live. Obviously, this inference fails if someone's having the desire to live is not a necessary condition of its being wrong to kill that individual.

One problem with the desire account is that we do regard it as seriously wrong to kill persons who have little desire to live or who have no desire to live or, indeed, have a desire not to live. We believe it is seriously wrong to kill the unconscious, the sleeping, those who are tired of life, and those who are suicidal. The value-of-a-human-future account renders standard morality intelligible in these cases; these cases appear to be incompatible with the desire account.

The desire account is subject to a deeper difficulty. We desire life, because we value the goods of this life. The goodness of life is not secondary to our desire for it. If this were not so, the pain of one's own premature death could be done away with merely by an appropriate alteration in the configuration of one's desires. This is absurd. Hence, it would seem that it is the loss of the goods of one's future, not the interference with the fulfillment of a strong desire to live, which accounts ultimately for the wrongness of killing.

It is worth noting that, if the desire account is modified so that it does not provide a necessary, but only a sufficient, condition for the wrongness of killing, the desire account is compatible with the future-like-ours account. The combined accounts will yield an antiabortion ethic. This suggests that one can retain what is intuitively plausible about the desire account without a challenge to the basic argument of this paper.

It is also worth noting that, if future desires have moral force in a modified desire account of the wrongness of killing, one can find support for an antiabortion ethic even in the absence of a value-of-a-future-like-ours account. If one decides that a morally relevant property, the possession of which is sufficient to make it wrong to kill some individual, is the desire at some future time to live—one might decide to justify one's refusal to kill suicidal teenagers on these grounds, for example—then, since typical fetuses will have the desire in the future to live, it is wrong to kill typical fetuses. Accordingly, it does not seem that a desire account of the wrongness of killing can provide a justification of a pro-choice ethic of abortion which is nearly as adequate as the value of a human-future justification of an antiabortion ethic.

The discontinuation account looks more promising as an account of the wrongness of killing. It seems just as intelligible as the value-of-a-future-like-ours account, but it does not justify an antiabortion position. Obviously, if it is the continuation of one's activity, experiences, and projects, the loss of which makes killing wrong, then it is not wrong to kill fetuses for that reason, for fetuses do not have experiences, activities, and projects to be continued or discontinued. Accordingly, the discontinuation account does not have the antiabortion consequences that the value-of-a-future-like-ours accounts has. Yet, it seems as intelligible as the value-of-a-future-like-ours account, for when we think of what would be wrong with our being killed, it does seem as if it is the discontinuation of what makes our lives worthwhile which makes killing us wrong.

Is the discontinuation account just as good an account as the value-of-a-future-like-ours account? The discontinuation account will not be adequate at all, if it does not refer to the *value* of the experience that may be discontinued. One does not want the discontinuation account to make it wrong to kill a patient who begs for death and who is in severe pain that cannot be relieved short of killing. (I leave open the question of whether it is wrong for other reasons.) Accordingly, the discontinuation account must be more than a bare discontinuation account. It must make some reference to the positive value of the patient's experiences. But, by the same token, the value-of-a-future-like-ours account cannot be a bare future account either. Just having a future surely does not itself rule out killing the above patient. This account must make some reference to the value of the patient's future experiences and projects also. Hence, both accounts involve the value of experiences, projects, and activities. So far we still have symmetry between the accounts.

The symmetry fades, however, when we focus on the time period of the value of the experiences, etc., which has moral consequences. Although both accounts leave open the possibility that the patient in our example may be killed, this possibility is left open only in virtue of the utterly bleak future for the patient. It makes no difference whether the patient's immediate past contains intolerable pain, or consists in being in a coma (which we can imagine is a situation of indifference), or consists in a life of value. If the patient's future is a future of value, we want our account to make it wrong to kill the patient. If the patient's future is intolerable, whatever his or her immediate past, we want our account to allow killing the patient. Obviously, then, it is the value of that patient's future which is doing the work in rendering the morality of killing the patient intelligible.

This being the case, it seems clear that whether one has immediate past experiences or not does not work in the explanation of what makes killing wrong. The addition the discontinuation account makes to the value-of-a-human-future account is otiose. Its addition to the value-of-a-future account plays no role at all in rendering intelligible the wrongness of killing. Therefore, it can be discarded with the discontinuation account of which it is a part.

IV

The analysis of the previous section suggests that alternative general accounts of the wrongness of killing are either inadequate or unsuccessful in getting around the antiabortion consequences of the value-of-a-future-like-ours argument. A different strategy for avoiding these antiabortion consequences involves limiting the scope of the value-of-a-future argument. More precisely, the strategy involves arguing that fetuses lack a property that is essential for the value-of-a-future argument (or for any antiabortion argument) to apply to them.

One move of this sort is based upon the claim that a necessary condition of one's future being valuable is that one values it. Value implies a valuer. Given this one might argue that, since fetuses cannot value their futures, their futures are not valuable to them. Hence, it does not seriously wrong them deliberately to end their lives.

This move fails, however, because of some ambiguities. Let us assume that something cannot be of value unless it is valued by someone. This does not entail that my life is of no value unless it is valued by me. I may think, in a period of despair, that my future is of no worth whatsoever, but I may be wrong because others rightly see value—even great value—in it. Furthermore, my future can be valuable to me even if I do not value it. This is the case when a young person attempts suicide, but is rescued and goes on to significant human achievements. Such young people's futures are ultimately valuable to them, even though such futures do not seem to be valuable to them at the moment of attempted suicide. A fetus's future can be valuable to it in the same way. Accordingly, this attempt to limit the antiabortion argument fails.

Another similar attempt to reject the antiabortion position is based on Tooley's claim that an entity cannot possess the right to life unless it has the capacity to desire its continued existence. It follows that, since fetuses lack the conceptual capacity to desire to continue to live, they lack the right to life. Accordingly, Tooley concludes that abortion cannot be seriously prima facie wrong.

What could be the evidence for Tooley's basic claim? Tooley once argued that individuals have a prima facie right to what they desire and that the lack of the capacity to desire something undercuts the basis of one's right to it. This argument plainly will not succeed in the context of the analysis of this essay, however, since the point here is to establish the fetus's right to life on other grounds. Tooley's argument assumes that the right to life cannot be established in general on some basis other than the desire for life. This position was considered and rejected in the preceding section of this paper.

One might attempt to defend Tooley's basic claim on the grounds that, because a fetus cannot apprehend continued life as a benefit, its continued life cannot be a benefit or cannot be something it has a right to or cannot be something that is in its interest. This might be defended in terms of the general proposition that, if an individual is literally incapable of caring about or taking an interest in some X, then one does not have a right to X or X is not a benefit or X is not something that is in one's interest.

Each member of this family of claims seems to be open to objections. As John C. Stevens has pointed out, one may have a right to be treated with a certain medical procedure (because of a health insurance policy one has purchased), even though one cannot conceive of the nature of the procedure. And, as Tooley himself has pointed out, persons who have been indoctrinated, or drugged, or rendered temporarily unconscious may be literally incapable of caring about or taking an interest in something that is in their interest or is something to which they have a right, or is something that benefits them. Hence, the Tooley claim that would restrict the scope of the value-of-a-future-like-ours argument is undermined by counterexamples.

Finally, Paul Bassen has argued that, even though the prospects of an embryo might seem to be a basis for the wrongness of abortion, an embryo cannot be a victim and therefore cannot be wronged. An embryo cannot be a victim, he says, because it lacks sentience. His central argument for this seems to be that, even though plants and the permanently unconscious are alive, they clearly cannot be victims. What is the explanation of this? Bassen claims that the explanation is that their lives consist of mere metabolism and mere metabolism is not enough to ground victimizability. Mentation is required.

The problem with this attempt to establish the absence of victimizability is that both plants and the permanently unconscious clearly lack what Bassen calls "prospects" or what I have called "a future life like ours." Hence, it is surely open to one to argue that the real reason we believe plants and the permanently unconscious cannot be victims is that killing them cannot deprive them of a future life like ours; the real reason is not their absence of present mentation.

Bassen recognizes that his view is subject to this difficulty, and he recognizes that the case of children seems to support this difficulty, for "much of what we do for children is based on prospects." He argues, however, that, in the case of children and in other such cases, "potentiality comes into play only where victimizability has been secured on other grounds."

Bassen's defense of his view is patently question-begging, since what is adequate to secure victimizability is exactly what is at issue. His examples do not support his own view against the thesis of this essay. Of course, embryos can be victims: when their lives are deliberately terminated, they are deprived of their future value, their prospects. This makes them victims, for it directly wrongs them.

The seeming plausibility of Bassen's view stems from the fact that paradigmatic cases of imagining someone as a victim involve empathy, and empathy requires mentation of the victim. The victims of flood, famine, rape, or child abuse are all persons with whom we can empathize. That empathy seems to be part of seeing them as victims.

In spite of the strength of these examples, the attractive intuition that a situation in which there is victimization requires the possibility of empathy is subject to counterexamples. Consider a case that Bassen himself offers: "Posthumous obliteration of an author's work constitutes a misfortune for him only if he had wished his work to endure." The conditions Bassen wishes to impose upon the possibility of being victimized here seem far too strong. Perhaps this author, due to his unrealistic standards of excellence and his low self-esteem, regarded his work as unworthy of survival, even though it possessed genuine literary merit. Destruction of such work would surely victimize its author. In such a case, empathy with the victim concerning the loss is clearly impossible.

Of course, Bassen does not make the possibility of empathy a necessary condition of victimizability; he requires only mentation. Hence, on Bassen's actual view, this author, as I have described him, can be a victim. The problem is that the basic intuition that renders Bassen's view plausible is missing in the author's case. In order to attempt to avoid counterexamples, Bassen has made his thesis too weak to be supported by the intuitions that suggested it.

Even so, the mentation requirement of victimizability is still subject to counterexamples. Suppose a severe accident renders me totally unconscious for a month, after which I recover. Surely killing me while I am unconscious victimizes me, even though I am incapable of mentation during that time. It follows that Bassen's thesis fails. Apparently, attempts to restrict the value-of-a-future-like-ours argument so that fetuses do not fall within its scope do not succeed.

V

In this essay, it has been argued that the correct ethic of the wrongness of killing can be extended to fetal life and used to show that there is a strong presumption that any abortion is morally impermissible. If the ethic of killing adopted here entails, however, that contraception is also seriously immoral, then there would appear to be a difficulty with the analysis of this essay.

But this analysis does not entail that contraception is wrong. Of course, contraception prevents the actualization of a possible future of value. Hence, it follows from the claim that futures of value should be maximized that contraception is prima facie immoral. This obligation to maximize does not exist, however; furthermore, nothing in the ethics of killing in this paper entails that it does. The ethics of killing in this essay would entail that contraception is wrong only if something were denied a human future of value by contraception. Nothing at all is denied such a future by contraception, however.

Candidates for a subject of harm by contraception fall into four categories: (1) some sperm or other, (2) some ovum or other, (3) a sperm and an ovum separately, and (4) a sperm and an ovum together. Assigning the harm to some sperm is utterly arbitrary, for no reason can be given for making a sperm the subject of harm rather than an ovum. Assigning the harm to some ovum is utterly arbitrary, for no reason can be given for making an ovum the subject of harm rather than a sperm. One might attempt to avoid these problems by insisting that contraception deprives both the sperm and the ovum separately of a valuable future like ours. On this alternative, too many futures are lost. Contraception was supposed to be wrong, because it deprived us of one future of value, not two. One might attempt to avoid this problem by holding that contraception deprives the combination of sperm and ovum of a valuable future like ours. But here the definite article misleads. At the time of contraception, there are hundreds of millions of sperm, one (released) ovum and millions of possible combinations of all of these. There is no actual combination at all. Is the subject of the loss to be a merely possible combination? Which one? This alternative does not yield an actual subject of harm either. Accordingly, the immorality of contraception is not entailed by the loss-of-a-future-like-ours argument simply because there is no nonarbitrarily identifiable subject of the loss in the case of contraception.

VI

The purpose of this essay has been to set out an argument for the serious presumptive wrongness of abortion subject to the assumption that the moral permissibility of abortion stands or falls on the moral status of the fetus. Since a fetus possesses a property, the possession of which in adult human beings is sufficient to make killing an adult human being wrong, abortion is wrong. This way of dealing with the problem of abortion seems superior to other approaches to the ethics of abortion, because it rests on an ethics of killing which is close to self-evident, because the crucial morally relevant property clearly applies to fetuses, and because the argument avoids the usual equivocations on "human life," "human being," or "person." The argument rests neither on religious claims nor on Papal dogma. It is not subject to the objection of "speciesism." Its soundness is compatible with the moral permissibility of euthanasia and contraception. It deals with our intuitions concerning young children.

Finally, this analysis can be viewed as resolving a standard problem—indeed, *the* standard problem—

concerning the ethics of abortion. Clearly, it is wrong to kill adult human beings. Clearly, it is not wrong to end the life of some arbitrarily chosen single human cell. Fetuses seem to be like arbitrarily chosen single human cells in some respects and like adult humans in other respects. The problem of the ethics of abortion is the problem of determining the fetal property that settles this moral controversy. The thesis of this essay is that the problem of the ethics of abortion, so understood, is solvable.

Discussion and Reflection Questions

1. Marquis argues that what makes killing morally wrong is that it deprives someone of the value of his or her (or its) future life. Do you agree that this is what makes killing wrong?

2. Having now examined the four implications of his view that Marquis claims lend support to this view, do you agree with him? Do the implications *support* or *weaken* Marquis's theory? Why?

3. Marquis constructs an argument about inflicting pain on animals as part of his argument in support of his view of what makes killing wrong. How does he do this? Do you find this argument convincing? Does it lend support to his view about what makes killing wrong?

4. Marquis argues that his view about the wrongness of abortion does not render contraception immoral. Why not? Does it make sense to talk about depriving eggs and sperm of future lives? Do you find any weaknesses in Marquis's argument?

Judith Jarvis Thomson, A Defense of Abortion

In the next reading selection, Judith Jarvis Thomson argues that abortion is sometimes morally permissible. Thomson does not take up the question of whether the fetus is a person. For the sake of the argument she is willing to set aside her view and go along with the idea of the fetus's personhood, a view held by those who wish to argue that abortion is immoral. Nonetheless, she argues that abortion is not necessarily wrong. Her claim is that even if a fetus has a right to life, it may still lack a right to use the mother's body. She defends this conclusion by constructing a number of "thought-experiments" in which she duplicates important features of various situations in which the problem of abortion arises and then asks what is morally permissible in each of these cases. The answers are then used to shed light on the morality of abortion.

Reading Questions

1. What is the point of Thomson's example of the "unconscious violinist"? How is this example supposed to bear on the issue of abortion?

2. What is the "extreme" antiabortion view that Thomson discusses? What is her assessment of this argument? Why does Thomson insist on considering the morality of

abortion when the mother's life is at stake by taking the point of view of the woman carrying the fetus, rather than the perspective of a "third party"?

3. How does Thomson understand the notion of a "right to life"? Does having a "right to life" mean that one has a right to whatever one needs to continue living? Does it mean that one has the right not to be killed by anybody? Does it mean that one has the right not to be killed *unjustly*?

4. How does Thomson deal with cases in which a woman is responsible for becoming pregnant and is considering an abortion? Does the fact that the woman is responsible for the fetus entail that aborting that fetus is immoral? How does she use the example of the burglar who enters one's home to make her point?

A Defense of Abortion

JUDITH JARVIS THOMSON

MOST OPPOSITION TO abortion relies on the premise that the fetus is a human being, a person, from the moment of conception. The premise is argued for, but, as I think, not well. Take, for example, the most common argument. We are asked to notice that the development of a human being from conception through birth into childhood is continuous; then it is said that to draw a line, to choose a point in this development and say "before this point the thing is not a person, after this point it is a person" is to make an arbitrary choice, a choice for which in the nature of things no good reason can be given. It is concluded that the fetus is, or anyway that we had better say it is, a person from the moment of conception. But this conclusion does not follow. Similar things might be said about the development of an acorn into an oak tree, and it does not follow that acorns are oak trees, or that we had better say they are. Arguments of this form are sometimes called "slippery slope arguments"—the phrase is perhaps self-explanatory—and it is dismaying that opponents of abortion rely on them so heavily and uncritically.

I am inclined to agree, however, that the prospects for "drawing a line" in the development of the fetus look dim. I am inclined to think also that we shall probably have to agree that the fetus has already become a human person well before birth. Indeed, it comes as a surprise when one first learns how early in its life it begins to acquire human characteristics.

By the tenth week, for example, it already has a face, arms and legs, fingers and toes; it has internal organs, and brain activity is detectable. On the other hand, I think that the premise is false, that the fetus is not a person from the moment of conception. A newly fertilized ovum, a newly implanted clump of cells, is no more a person than an acorn is an oak tree. But I shall not discuss any of this. For it seems to me to be of great interest to ask what happens if, for the sake of argument, we allow the premise. How, precisely, are we supposed to get from there to the conclusion that abortion is morally impermissible? Opponents of abortion commonly spend most of their time establishing that the fetus is a person, and hardly any time explaining the step from there to the impermissibility of abortion. Perhaps they think the step too simple and obvious to require much comment. Or perhaps instead they are simply being economical in argument. Many of those who defend abortion rely on the premise that the fetus is not a person, but only a bit of tissue that will become a person at birth; and why pay out more arguments than you have to? Whatever the explanation, I suggest that the step they take is neither easy nor obvious, that it calls for closer examination than is commonly given, and that when we do give it this closer examination we shall feel inclined to reject it.

I propose, then, that we grant that the fetus is a person from the moment of conception. How does

Judith Jarvis Thomson, "A Defense of Abortion," Philosophy and Public Affairs, *vol. 1, no. 1 (Fall 1971), pp. 47–66. Copyright © 1971 by Princeton University Press. Reprinted by permission of Princeton University Press.*

the argument go from here? Something like this, I take it. Every person has a right to life. So the fetus has a right to life. No doubt the mother has a right to decide what shall happen in and to her body; everyone would grant that. But surely a person's right to life is stronger and more stringent than the mother's right to decide what happens in and to her body, and so outweighs it. So the fetus may not be killed; an abortion may not be performed.

It sounds plausible. But now let me ask you to imagine this. You wake up in the morning and find yourself back to back in bed with an unconscious violinist. A famous unconscious violinist. He has been found to have a fatal kidney ailment, and the Society of Music Lovers has canvassed all the available medical records and found that you alone have the right blood type to help. They have therefore kidnapped you, and last night the violinist's circulatory system was plugged into yours, so that your kidneys can be used to extract poisons from his blood as well as your own. The director of the hospital now tells you, "Look, we're sorry the Society of Music Lovers did this to you—we would never have permitted it if we had known. But still, they did it, and the violinist now is plugged into you. To unplug you would be to kill him. But never mind, it's only for nine months. By then he will have recovered from his ailment, and can safely be unplugged from you." Is it morally incumbent on you to accede to this situation? No doubt it would be very nice of you if you did, a great kindness. But do you *have* to accede to it? What if it were not nine months, but nine years? Or longer still? What if the director of the hospital says, "Tough luck, I agree, but you've now got to stay in bed, with the violinist plugged into you, for the rest of your life. Because remember this. All persons have a right to life, and violinists are persons. Granted you have a right to decide what happens in and to your body, but a person's right to life outweighs your right to decide what happens in and to your body. So you cannot ever be unplugged from him." I imagine you would regard this as outrageous, which suggests that something really is wrong with that plausible sounding argument I mentioned a moment ago.

In this case, of course, you were kidnapped; you didn't volunteer for the operation that plugged the violinist into your kidneys. Can those who oppose abortion on the ground I mentioned make an exception for a pregnancy due to rape? Certainly. They can say that persons have a right to life only if they didn't come into existence because of rape; or they can say that all persons have a right to life, but that some have less of a right to life than others, in particular,

that those who come into existence because of rape have less. But these statements have a rather unpleasant sound. Surely the question of whether you have a right to life at all, or how much of it you have, shouldn't turn on the question of whether or not you are the product of a rape. And in fact the people who oppose abortion on the ground I mentioned do not make this distinction, and hence do not make an exception in case of rape.

Nor do they make an exception for a case in which the mother has to spend the nine months of her pregnancy in bed. They would agree that would be a great pity, and hard on the mother; but all the same, all persons have a right to life, the fetus is a person, and so on. I suspect, in fact, that they would not make an exception for a case in which, miraculously enough, the pregnancy went on for nine years, or even the rest of the mother's life.

Some won't even make an exception for a case in which continuation of the pregnancy is likely to shorten the mother's life; they regard abortion as impermissible even to save the mother's life. Such cases are nowadays very rare, and many opponents of abortion do not accept this extreme view. All the same, it is a good place to begin: a number of points of interest come out in respect to it.

1. Let us call the view that abortion is impermissible even to save the mother's life "the extreme view." I want to suggest first that it does not issue from the argument I mentioned earlier without the addition of some fairly powerful premises. Suppose a woman has become pregnant, and now learns that she has a cardiac condition such that she will die if she carries the baby to term. What may be done for her? The fetus, being a person, has a right to life, but as the mother is a person too, so has she a right to life. Presumably they have an equal right to life. How is it supposed to come out that an abortion may not be performed? If mother and child have an equal right to life, shouldn't we perhaps flip a coin? Or should we add to the mother's right to life her right to decide what happens in and to her body, which everybody seems to be ready to grant—the sum of her rights now outweighing the fetus's right to life?

The most familiar argument here is the following. We are told that performing the abortion would be directly killing[1] the child, whereas doing nothing would

---

[1]The term "direct" in the arguments I refer to is a technical one. Roughly what is meant by "direct killing" is either killing as an end in itself, or killing as a means to some end, for example, the end of saving someone else's life. See Note 4 below for an example of its use.

not be killing the mother, but only letting her die. Moreover, in killing the child, one would be killing an innocent person, for the child has committed no crime, and is not aiming at his mother's death. And then there are a variety of ways in which this might be continued. (1) But as directly killing an innocent person is always and absolutely impermissible, an abortion may not be performed. Or, (2) as directly killing an innocent person is murder, and murder is always and absolutely impermissible, an abortion may not be performed.[2] Or, (3) as one's duty to refrain from directly killing an innocent person is more stringent than one's duty to keep a person from dying, an abortion may not be performed. Or, (4) if one's only options are directly killing an innocent person or letting a person die, one must prefer letting the person die, and thus an abortion may not be performed.[3]

Some people seem to have thought that these are not further premises which must be added if the conclusion is to be reached, but that they follow from the very fact that an innocent person has a right to life.[4] But this seems to me to be a mistake, and perhaps the simplest way to show this is to bring out that while we must certainly grant that innocent persons have a right to life, the theses in (1) through (4) are all false. Take (2), for example. If directly killing an innocent person is murder, and thus is impermissible, then the mother's directly killing the innocent person inside her is murder, and thus is impermissible. But it cannot seriously be thought to be murder if the mother performs an abortion on herself to save her life. It cannot seriously be said that she *must* refrain, that she *must* sit passively by and wait for her death. Let us look again at the case of you and the violinist. There you are, in bed with the violinist, and the director of the hospital says to you, "It's all most distressing, and I deeply sympathize, but you see this is putting an additional strain on your kidneys, and you'll be dead within the month. But you *have* to stay where you are all the same. Because unplugging you would be directly killing an innocent violinist, and that's murder, and that's impermissible." If anything in the world is true, it is that you do not commit murder, you do not do what is impermissible, if you reach around to your back and unplug yourself from that violinist to save your life.

The main focus of attention in writings on abortion has been on what a third party may or may not do in answer to a request from a woman for an abortion. This is in a way understandable. Things being as they are, there isn't much a woman can safely do to abort herself. So the question asked is what a third party may do, and what the mother may do, if it is mentioned at all, is deduced, almost as an afterthought, from what it is concluded that third parties may do. But it seems to me that to treat the matter in this way is to refuse to grant to the mother that very status of person which is so firmly insisted on for the fetus. For we cannot simply read off what a person may do from what a third party may do. Suppose you find yourself trapped in a tiny house with a growing child. I mean a very tiny house, and a rapidly growing child—you are already up against the wall of the house and in a few minutes you'll be crushed to death. The child on the other hand won't be crushed to death; if nothing is done to stop him from growing he'll be hurt, but in the end he'll simply burst open the house and walk out a free man. Now I could well understand it if a bystander were to say, "There's nothing we can do for you. We cannot choose between your life and his, we cannot be the ones to decide who is to live, we cannot intervene." But it cannot be concluded that you too can do nothing, that you cannot attack it to save your life. However innocent the child may be, you do not have to wait passively while it crushes you to death. Perhaps a pregnant woman is vaguely felt to have the status

[2]Cf. *Encyclical Letter of Pope Pius XI on Christian Marriage*, St. Paul Editions (Boston, n.d.), p. 32: "However much we may pity the mother whose health and even life is gravely imperiled in the performance of the duty allotted to her by nature, nevertheless what could be ever a sufficient reason for excusing in any way the direct murder of the innocent? This is precisely what we are dealing with here." Noonan (*The Morality of Abortion*, p. 43) reads this as follows: "What cause can ever avail to excuse in any way the direct killing of the innocent? For it is a question of that."

[3]The thesis in (4) is in an interesting way weaker than those in (1), (2), and (3): They rule out abortion even in cases in which both mother *and* child will die if the abortion is not performed. By contrast, one who held the view expressed in (4) could consistently say that one needn't prefer letting two persons die to killing one.

[4]Cf. the following passage from Pius XII, *Address to the Italian Catholic Society of Midwives*: "The baby in the maternal breast has the right to life immediately from God. Hence there is no man, no human authority, no science, no medical, eugenic, social, economic or moral 'indication' which can establish or grant a valid juridical ground for a direct deliberate disposition of an innocent human life, that is a disposition which looks to its destruction either as an end or as a means to another end perhaps in itself not illicit. The baby, still not born, is a man in the same degree and for the same reason as the mother" (quoted in John T. Noonan, Jr., "An Almost Absolute Value in History," in *The Morality of Abortion*, ed. John T. Noonan, Jr. [Cambridge, Mass., 1970], p. 45).

of [a] house, to which we don't allow the right of self-defense. But if the woman houses the child, it should be remembered that she is a person who houses it.

I should perhaps stop to say explicitly that I am not claiming that people have a right to do anything whatever to save their lives. I think, rather, that there are drastic limits to the right of self-defense. If someone threatens you with death unless you torture someone else to death, I think you have not the right, even to save your life, to do so. But the case under consideration here is very different. In our case there are only two people involved, one whose life is threatened, and one who threatens it. Both are innocent: the one who is threatened is not threatened because of any fault, the one who threatens does not threaten because of any fault. For this reason we may feel that we bystanders cannot intervene. But the person threatened can.

In sum, a woman surely can defend her life against the threat to it posed by the unborn child, even if doing so involves its death. And this shows not merely that the theses in (1) through (4) are false; it shows also that the extreme view of abortion is false, and so we need not canvass any other possible ways of arriving at it from the argument I mentioned at the outset.

2. The extreme view could of course be weakened to say that while abortion is permissible to save the mother's life, it may not be performed by a third party, but only by the mother herself. But this cannot be right either. For what we have to keep in mind is that the mother and the unborn child are not like two tenants in a small house which has, by an unfortunate mistake, been rented to both; the mother *owns* the house. The fact that she does adds to the offensiveness of deducing that the mother can do nothing from the supposition that third parties can do nothing. But it does more than this: it casts a bright light on the supposition that third parties can do nothing. Certainly it lets us see that a third party who says "I cannot choose between you" is fooling himself if he thinks this is impartiality. If Jones has found and fastened on a certain coat, which he needs to keep from freezing, but which Smith also needs to keep him from freezing, then it is not impartiality that says "I cannot choose between you" when Smith owns the coat. Women have said again and again, "This body is *my* body!" and they have reason to feel angry, reason to feel that it has been like shouting into the wind. Smith, after all, is hardly likely to bless us if we say to him, "Of course it's your coat, anybody would grant that it is. But no one may choose between you and Jones who is to have it."

We should really ask what it is that says "no one may choose" in the face of the fact that the body that houses the child is the mother's body. It may be simply a failure to appreciate this fact. But it may be something more interesting, namely the sense that one has a right to refuse to lay hands on people, even where it would be just and fair to do so, even where justice seems to require that somebody do so. Thus justice might call for somebody to get Smith's coat back from Jones, and yet you have a right to refuse to be the one to lay hands on Jones, a right to refuse to do physical violence to him. This, I think, must be granted. But then what should be said is not "no one may choose," but only "*I* cannot choose," and indeed not even this, but "*I* will not *act*," leaving it open that somebody else can or should, and in particular that anyone in a position of authority, with the job of securing people's rights, both can and should. So this is no difficulty. I have not been arguing that any given third party must accede to the mother's request that he perform an abortion to save her life, but only that he may.

I suppose that in some views of human life the mother's body is only on loan to her, the loan not being one which gives her any prior claim to it. One who held this view might well think it impartiality to say "I cannot choose." But I shall simply ignore this possibility. My own view is that if a human being has any just, prior claim to anything at all, he has a just, prior claim to his own body. And perhaps this needn't be argued for here anyway, since, as I mentioned, the arguments against abortion we are looking at do grant that the woman has a right to decide what happens in and to her body.

But although they do grant it, I have tried to show that they do not take seriously what is done in granting it. I suggest the same thing will reappear even more clearly when we turn away from cases in which the mother's life is at stake, and attend, as I propose we now do, to the vastly more common cases in which a woman wants an abortion for some less weighty reason than preserving her own life.

3. Where the mother's life is not at stake, the argument I mentioned at the outset seems to have a much stronger pull. "Everyone has a right to life, so the unborn person has a right to life." And isn't the child's right to life weightier than anything other than the mother's own right to life, which she might put forward as ground for an abortion?

This argument treats the right to life as if it were unproblematic. It is not, and this seems to me to be precisely the source of the mistake.

For we should now, at long last, ask what it comes to, to have a right to life. In some views having a right to life includes having a right to be given at least the bare minimum one needs for continued life. But suppose that what in fact *is* the bare minimum a man needs for continued life is something he has no right at all to be given? If I am sick unto death, and the only thing that will save my life is the touch of Henry Fonda's cool hand on my fevered brow, then all the same, I have no right to be given the touch of Henry Fonda's cool hand on my fevered brow. It would be frightfully nice of him to fly in from the West Coast to provide it. It would be less nice, though no doubt well meant, if my friends flew out to the West Coast and carried Henry Fonda back with them. But I have no right at all against anybody that he should do this for me. Or again, to return to the story I told earlier, the fact that for continued life that violinist needs the continued use of your kidneys does not establish that he has a right to be given the continued use of your kidneys. He certainly has no right against you that *you* should give him continued use of your kidneys. For nobody has any right to use your kidneys unless you give him such a right; and nobody has the right against you that you shall give him this right—if you do allow him to go on using your kidneys, this is a kindness on your part, and not something he can claim from you as his due. Nor has he any right against anybody else that *they* should give him continued use of your kidneys. Certainly he had no right against the Society of Music Lovers that they should plug him into you in the first place. And if you now start to unplug yourself, having learned that you will otherwise have to spend nine years in bed with him, there is nobody in the world who must try to prevent you, in order to see to it that he is given something he has a right to be given.

Some people are rather stricter about the right to life. In their view, it does not include the right to be given anything, but amounts to, and only to, the right not to be killed by anybody. But here a related difficulty arises. If everybody is to refrain from killing that violinist, then everybody must refrain from doing a great many different sorts of things. Everybody must refrain from slitting his throat, everybody must refrain from shooting him—and everybody must refrain from unplugging you from him. But does he have a right against everybody that they shall refrain from unplugging you from him? To refrain from doing this is to allow him to continue to use your kidneys. It could be argued that he has a right against us that *we* should allow him to continue to use your kidneys. That is, while he had no right against us that we should give him the use of your kidneys, it might be argued that he anyway has a right against us that

we shall not now intervene and deprive him of the use of your kidneys. I shall come back to third-party interventions later. But certainly the violinist has no right against you that *you* shall allow him to continue to use your kidneys. As I said, if you do allow him to use them, it is a kindness on your part, and not something you owe him.

The difficulty I point to here is not peculiar to the right to life. It reappears in connection with all the other natural rights; and it is something which an adequate account of rights must deal with. For present purposes it is enough just to draw attention to it. But I would stress that I am not arguing that people do not have a right to life—quite to the contrary, it seems to me that the primary control we must place on the acceptability of an account of rights is that it should turn out in that account to be a truth that all persons have a right to life. I am arguing only that having a right to life does not guarantee having either a right to be given the use of or a right to be allowed continued use of another person's body—even if one needs it for life itself. So the right to life will not serve the opponents of abortion in the very simple and clear way in which they seem to have thought it would.

4. There is another way to bring out the difficulty. In the most ordinary sort of case, to deprive someone of what he has a right to is to treat him unjustly. Suppose a boy and his small brother are jointly given a box of chocolates for Christmas. If the older boy takes the box and refuses to give his brother any of the chocolates, he is unjust to him, for the brother has been given a right to half of them. But suppose that, having learned that otherwise it means nine years in bed with that violinist, you unplug yourself from him. You surely are not being unjust to him for you gave him no right to use your kidneys, and no one else can have given him any such right. But we have to notice that in unplugging yourself, you are killing him; and violinists, like everybody else, have a right to life, and thus in the view we were considering just now, the right not to be killed. So here you do what he supposedly has a right you shall not do, but you do not act unjustly to him in doing it.

The emendation which may be made at this point is this: the right to life consists not in the right not to be killed, but rather in the right not to be killed unjustly. This runs a risk of circularity, but never mind; it would enable us to square the fact that the violinist has a right to life with the fact that you do not act unjustly toward him in unplugging yourself, thereby killing him. For if you do not kill him unjustly, you do not violate his right to life, and so it is no wonder you do him no injustice.

But if this emendation is accepted, the gap in the argument against abortion stares us plainly in the face: it is by no means enough to show that the fetus is a person, and to remind us that all persons have a right to life—we need to be shown also that killing the fetus violates its right to life, i.e., that abortion is unjust killing. And is it?

I suppose we may take it as a datum that in a case of pregnancy due to rape the mother has not given the unborn person a right to the use of her body for food and shelter. Indeed, in what pregnancy could it be supposed that the mother has given the unborn person such a right? It is not as if there were unborn persons drifting about the world, to whom a woman who wants a child says, "I invite you in."

But it might be argued that there are other ways one can have acquired a right to the use of another person's body than by having been invited to use it by that person. Suppose a woman voluntarily indulges in intercourse, knowing of the chance it will issue in pregnancy, and then she does become pregnant; is she not in part responsible for the presence, in fact the very existence, of the unborn person inside her? No doubt she did not invite it in. But doesn't her partial responsibility for its being there itself give it a right to the use of her body? If so, then her aborting it would be more like the boy's taking away the chocolates, and less like your unplugging yourself from the violinist—doing so would be depriving it of what it does have a right to, and thus would be doing it an injustice.

And then, too, it might be asked whether or not she can kill it even to save her own life: If she voluntarily called it into existence, how can she now kill it, even in self-defense?

The first thing to be said about this is that it is something new. Opponents of abortion have been so concerned to make out the independence of the fetus, in order to establish that it has a right to life, just as its mother does, that they have tended to overlook the possible support they might gain from making out that the fetus is *dependent* on the mother, in order to establish that she has a special kind of responsibility for it, a responsibility that gives it rights against her which are not possessed by any independent person—such as an ailing violinist who is a stranger to her.

On the other hand, this argument would give the unborn person a right to its mother's body only if her pregnancy resulted from a voluntary act, undertaken in full knowledge of the chance a pregnancy might result from it. It would leave out entirely the unborn person whose existence is due to rape. Pending the availability of some further argument, then, we would be left with the conclusion that unborn persons whose existence is due to rape have no right to the use of their mothers' bodies, and thus that aborting them is not depriving them of anything they have a right to and hence is not unjust killing.

And we should also notice that it is not at all plain that this argument really does go even as far as it purports to. For there are cases and cases, and the details make a difference. If the room is stuffy, and I therefore open a window to air it, and a burglar climbs in, it would be absurd to say, "Ah, now he can stay, she's given him a right to the use of her house—for she is partially responsible for his presence there, having voluntarily done what enabled him to get in, in full knowledge that there are such things as burglars, and that burglars burgle." It would be still more absurd to say this if I had had bars installed outside my windows, precisely to prevent burglars from getting in, and a burglar got in only because of a defect in the bars. It remains equally absurd if we imagine it is not a burglar who climbs in, but an innocent person who blunders or falls in. Again, suppose it were like this: people-seeds drift about in the air like pollen, and if you open your windows, one may drift in and take root in your carpets or upholstery. You don't want children, so you fix up your windows with fine mesh screens, the very best you can buy. As can happen, however, and on very, very rare occasions does happen, one of the screens is defective; and a seed drifts in and takes root. Does the person-plant who now develops have a right to the use of your house? Surely not—despite the fact that you voluntarily opened your windows, you knowingly kept carpets and upholstered furniture, and you knew that screens were sometimes defective. Someone may argue that you are responsible for its rooting, that it does have a right to your house, because after all you *could* have lived out your life with bare floors and furniture, or with sealed windows and doors. But this won't do—for by the same token anyone can avoid a pregnancy due to rape by having a hysterectomy, or anyway by never leaving home without a (reliable!) army.

It seems to me that the argument we are looking at can establish at most that there are *some* cases in which the unborn person has a right to the use of its mother's body, and therefore *some* cases in which abortion is unjust killing. There is room for much discussion and argument as to precisely which, if any. But I think we should sidestep this issue and leave it open, for at any rate the argument certainly does not establish that all abortion is unjust killing.

5. There is room for yet another argument here, however. We surely must all grant that there may be cases in which it would be morally indecent to detach a person from your body at the cost of his life. Suppose you learn that what the violinist needs is not nine years of your life, but only one hour: all you need do to save his life is to spend one hour in that bed with him. Suppose also that letting him use your kidneys for that one hour would not affect your health in the slightest. Admittedly you were kidnapped. Admittedly you did not give anyone permission to plug him into you. Nevertheless it seems to me plain you *ought* to allow him to use your kidneys for that hour—it would be indecent to refuse.

Again, suppose pregnancy lasted only an hour, and constituted no threat to life or health. And suppose that a woman becomes pregnant as a result of rape. Admittedly she did not voluntarily do anything to bring about the existence of a child. Admittedly she did nothing at all which would give the unborn person a right to the use of her body. All the same it might well be said, as in the newly emended violinist story, that she *ought* to allow it to remain for that hour—that it would be indecent in her to refuse.

Now some people are inclined to use the term "right" in such a way that it follows from the fact that you ought to allow a person to use your body for the hour he needs, that he has a right to use your body for the hour he needs, even though he has not been given that right by any person or act. They may say that it follows also that if you refuse, you act unjustly toward him. This use of the term is perhaps so common that it cannot be called wrong; nevertheless it seems to me to be an unfortunate loosening of what we would do better to keep a tight rein on. Suppose that that box of chocolates I mentioned earlier had not been given to both boys jointly, but was given only to the older boy. There he sits, stolidly eating his way through the box, his small brother watching enviously. Here we are likely to say "You ought not to be so mean. You ought to give your brother some of those chocolates." My own view is that it just does not follow from the truth of this that the brother has any right to any of the chocolates. If the boy refuses to give his brother any, he is greedy, stingy, callous—but not unjust. I suppose that the people I have in mind will say it does follow that the brother has a right to some of the chocolates, and thus that the boy does act unjustly if he refuses to give his brother any. But the effect of saying this is to obscure what we should keep distinct, namely the difference between the boy's refusal in this case and the boy's refusal in the earlier case, in which the box was given to both

boys jointly, and in which the small brother thus had what was from any point of view clear title to half.

A further objection to so using the term "right" that from the fact that A ought to do a thing for B, it follows that B has a right against A that A do it for him, is that it is going to make the question of whether or not a man has a right to a thing turn on how easy it is to provide him with it; and this seems not merely unfortunate, but morally unacceptable. Take the case of Henry Fonda again. I said earlier that I had no right to the touch of his cool hand on my fevered brow, even though I needed it to save my life. I said it would be frightfully nice of him to fly in from the West Coast to provide me with it, but that I had no right against him that he should do so. But suppose he isn't on the West Coast. Suppose he has only to walk across the room, place a hand briefly on my brow—and lo, my life is saved. Then surely he ought to do it, it would be indecent to refuse. Is it to be said, "Ah, well, it follows that in this case she has a right to the touch of his hand on her brow, and so it would be an unjustice in him to refuse"? So that I have a right to it when it is easy for him to provide it, though no right when it's hard? It's rather a shocking idea that anyone's rights should fade away and disappear as it gets harder and harder to accord them to him.

So my own view is that even though you ought to let the violinist use your kidneys for the one hour he needs, we should not conclude that he has a right to do so—we should say that if you refuse, you are, like the boy who owns all the chocolates and will give none away, self-centered and callous, indecent in fact, but not unjust. And similarly, that even supposing a case in which a woman pregnant due to rape ought to allow the unborn person to use her body for the hour he needs, we should not conclude that he has a right to do so; we should conclude that she is self-centered, callous, indecent, but not unjust, if she refuses. The complaints are no less grave; they are just different. However, there is no need to insist on this point. If anyone does wish to deduce "he has a right" from "you ought," then all the same he must surely grant that there are cases in which it is not morally required of you that you allow that violinist to use your kidneys, and in which he does not have a right to use them, and in which you do not do him an injustice if you refuse. And so also for mother and unborn child. Except in such cases as the unborn person has a right to demand it—and we were leaving open the possibility that there may be such cases—nobody is morally *required* to make large sacrifices, of health, of all other interests and concerns, of all other duties and commitments, for nine years, or even for nine months, in order to keep another person alive.

6. We have in fact to distinguish between two kinds of Samaritan: the Good Samaritan and what we might call the Minimally Decent Samaritan. The story of the Good Samaritan, you will remember, goes like this:

A certain man went down from Jerusalem to Jericho, and fell among thieves, which stripped him of his raiment, and wounded him, and departed, leaving him half dead.

And by chance there came down a certain priest that way; and when he saw him, he passed by on the other side.

And likewise a Levite, when he was at the place, came and looked on him, and passed by on the other side.

But a certain Samaritan, as he journeyed, came where he was; and when he saw him he had compassion on him.

And went to him, and bound up his wounds, pouring in oil and wine, and set him on his own beast, and brought him to an inn, and took care of him.

And on the morrow, when he departed, he took out two pence, and gave them to the host, and said unto him, "Take care of him; and whatsoever thou spendest more, when I come again, I will repay thee."

(Luke 10:30–35)

The Good Samaritan went out of his way, at some cost to himself, to help one in need of it. We are not told what the options were, that is, whether or not the priest and the Levite could have helped by doing less than the Good Samaritan did, but assuming they could have, then the fact they did nothing at all shows they were not even Minimally Decent Samaritans, not because they were not Samaritans, but because they were not even minimally decent.

These things are a matter of degree, of course, but there is a difference, and it comes out perhaps most clearly in the story of Kitty Genovese, who, as you will remember, was murdered while thirty-eight people watched or listened, and did nothing at all to help her. A Good Samaritan would have rushed out to give direct assistance against the murderer. Or perhaps we had better allow that it would have been a Splendid Samaritan who did this, on the ground that it would have involved a risk of death for himself. But the thirty-eight not only did not do this, they did not even trouble to pick up a phone to call the police. Minimally Decent Samaritanism would call for doing at least that, and their not having done it was monstrous.

After telling the story of the Good Samaritan, Jesus said, "Go, and do thou likewise." Perhaps he meant that we are morally required to act as the Good Samaritan did. Perhaps he was urging people to do more than is morally required of them. At all events it seems plain that it was not morally required of any of the thirty-eight that he rush out to give direct assistance at the risk of his own life, and that it is not morally required of anyone that he give long stretches of his life—nine years or nine months—to sustaining the life of a person who has no special right (we were leaving open the possibility of this) to demand it.

Indeed, with one rather striking class of exceptions, no one in any country in the world is *legally* required to do anywhere near as much as this for anyone else. The class of exceptions is obvious. My main concern here is not the state of the law in respect to abortion, but it is worth drawing attention to the fact that in no state in this country is any man compelled by law to be even a Minimally Decent Samaritan to any person; there is no law under which charges could be brought against the thirty-eight who stood by while Kitty Genovese died. . . . This doesn't by itself settle anything one way or the other, because it may well be argued that there should be laws in this country—as there are in many European countries—compelling at least Minimally Decent Samaritanism. But it does show that there is a gross injustice in the existing state of the law. And it shows also that the groups currently working against liberalization of abortion laws, in fact working toward having it declared unconstitutional for a state to permit abortion, had better start working for the adoption of Good Samaritan laws generally, or earn the charge that they are acting in bad faith.

I should think, myself, that Minimally Decent Samaritan laws would be one thing, Good Samaritan laws quite another, and in fact, highly improper. But we are not here concerned with the law. What we should ask is not whether anybody should be compelled by law to be a Good Samaritan, but whether we must accede to a situation in which somebody is being compelled—by nature, perhaps—to be a Good Samaritan. We have, in other words, to look now at third-party interventions. I have been arguing that no person is morally required to make large sacrifices to sustain the life of another who has no right to demand them, and this even where the sacrifices do not include life itself; we are not morally required to be Good Samaritans or anyway Very Good Samaritans to one another. But what if a man cannot extricate himself from such a situation? What if he appeals to us to extricate him? It seems to me plain that there are cases in which we can, cases in which a Good Samaritan would extricate him. There you are, you were kidnapped, and nine years in bed with that violinist lie ahead of you. You have your own life to lead. You are sorry, but you simply cannot see giving up so much of your life to the sustaining of his. You cannot extricate yourself, and ask us to do so. I should have thought that—in light of his having no right to the use of your body—it was obvious that we do not have to accede to your being forced to give up so much. We can do what you ask. There is no injustice to the violinist in our doing so.

7. Following the lead of the opponents of abortion, I have throughout been speaking of the fetus merely as a person, and what I have been asking is whether or not the argument we began with, which proceeds only from the fetus's being a person, really does establish its conclusion. I have argued that it does not.

But of course there are arguments and arguments, and it may be said that I have simply fastened on the wrong one. It may be said that what is important is not merely the fact that the fetus is a person, but that it is a person for whom the woman has a special kind of responsibility issuing from the fact that she is its mother. And it might be argued that all my analogies are therefore irrelevant—for you do not have that special kind of responsibility for that violinist. Henry Fonda does not have that special kind of responsibility for me. And our attention might be drawn to the fact that men and women both *are* compelled by law to provide support for their children.

I have in effect dealt (briefly) with this argument in Section 4 above; but a (still briefer) recapitulation now may be in order. Surely we do not have any such "special responsibility" for a person unless we have assumed it, explicitly or implicitly. If a set of parents do not try to prevent pregnancy, do not obtain an abortion, and then at the time of birth of the child do not put it out for adoption, but rather take it home with them, then they have assumed responsibility for it, they have given it rights, and they cannot *now* withdraw support from it at the cost of its life because they now find it difficult to go on providing for it. But if they have taken all reasonable precautions against having a child, they do not simply by virtue of their biological relationship to the child who comes into existence have a special responsibility for it. They may wish to assume responsibility for it, or they may not wish to. And I am suggesting that if assuming responsibility for it would require large sacrifices, then they may refuse. A Good Samaritan would not refuse—or anyway, a Splendid Samaritan, if the sacrifices that had to be made were enormous. But then so would a Good Samaritan assume responsibility for that violinist; so would Henry Fonda, if he is a Good Samaritan, fly in from the West Coast and assume responsibility for me.

8. My argument will be found unsatisfactory on two counts by many of those who want to regard abortion as morally permissible. First, while I do argue that abortion is not impermissible, I do not argue that it is always permissible. There may well be cases in which carrying the child to term requires only Minimally Decent Samaritanism of the mother, and this is a standard we must not fall below. I am inclined to think it a merit of my account precisely that it does *not* give a general yes or a general no. It allows for and supports our sense that, for example, a sick and desperately frightened fourteen-year-old schoolgirl, pregnant due to rape, may *of course* choose abortion, and that any law which rules this out is an insane law. And it also allows for and supports our sense that in other cases resort to abortion is even positively indecent. It would be indecent in the woman to request an abortion, and indecent in a doctor to perform it, if she is in her seventh month, and wants the abortion just to avoid the nuisance of postponing a trip abroad. The very fact that the arguments I have been drawing attention to treat all cases of abortion, or even all cases of abortion in which the mother's life is not at stake, as morally on a par ought to have made them suspect at the outset.

Secondly, while I am arguing for the permissibility of abortion in some cases, I am not arguing for the right to secure the death of the unborn child. It is easy to confuse these two things in that up to a certain point in the life of the fetus it is not able to survive outside the mother's body; hence removing it from her body guarantees its death. But they are importantly different. I have argued that you are not morally required to spend nine months in bed, sustaining the life of that violinist; but to say this is by no means to say that if, when you unplug yourself, there is a miracle and he survives, you then have a right to turn around and slit his throat. You may detach yourself even if this costs him his life; you have no right to be guaranteed his death, by some other means, if unplugging yourself does not kill him. There are some people who will feel dissatisfied by this feature of my argument. A woman may be utterly devastated by the thought of a child, a bit of herself, put out for adoption and never seen or heard of again. She may therefore want not merely that the child be detached from her, but more, that it die. Some opponents of abortion are inclined to regard this as beneath contempt—thereby showing insensitivity to what is surely a powerful source of despair. All the same, I agree that the desire for the child's death is not one which anybody may gratify, should it turn out to be possible to detach the child alive.

At this place, however, it should be remembered that we have only been pretending throughout that the fetus is a human being from the moment of conception. A very early abortion is surely not the killing of a person, and so is not dealt with by anything I have said here.

Discussion and Reflection Questions

1. Thomson's argument against the "extreme" antiabortion view assumes that the right to self-defense permits us to kill an innocent person if doing so is necessary to preserve our own life. Is this true? Use an example (outside of the context of abortion) to support your answer.

2. Thomson argues that "having a right to life does not guarantee having either a right to be given the use of or a right to be allowed continued use of another person's body." What, then, does having a "right to life" consist in? How would you explain this notion?

3. How does Thomson distinguish between the Good Samaritan and the Minimally Decent Samaritan? What is the point of this distinction? On your view, does morality require us to be Good Samaritans or only Minimally Decent Samaritans? How would you apply your answer to this to the problem of abortion?

4. Why does Thomson reject the view that one should either condemn or permit all abortions? In what ways is her view sensitive to the specific factors involved in each case? In your view, is this a weakness of her view or a strength? What does your answer imply about the nature of moral theories? What should an adequate moral theory be like?

Ren Zong Qiu, Chun Zhi Wang, and Yuan Gu, Can Late Abortion Be Ethically Justified?

The population of the People's Republic of China is over one billion people. If population levels continue to increase, that country's efforts at modernization will be jeopardized. The Chinese government has thus instituted a "one-child policy" in an attempt to curb population growth. What this means is that there are severe penalties for women or families that have more than one child. This unique situation puts the problem of abortion in a special context in that country and forces us to consider the morality of abortion in relation to various social factors that may be involved. In the reading selection that follows, Ren Zong Qiu, Chun Zhi Wang, and Yuan Gu explore the problem of abortion in China. Taking a consequentialist perspective, they argue that in some circumstances late-term abortion is morally permissible.

Reading Questions

1. According to the authors, how has the Confucian cultural tradition contributed to people's desire to have more children in China? How has this desire contributed to ethical dilemmas concerning abortion? How do the "national interests" of China play an important role in the issue of abortion in China? How is this different from the situation in America and other Western nations?

2. In what ways is the Chinese policy of "one couple, one child" a reflection of utilitarian or consequentialist thinking? How are the relative interests of individuals and society weighed in this policy? How does the policy of penalizing a group for the choices of individuals reflect an additional element that must be taken account of in a consequentialist evaluation of the morality of abortion in China? What "conflict of values" does this situation create?

3. What sorts of dilemmas do physicians in China face concerning abortions? How do their moral obligations to the state sometimes come into conflict with their moral obligations to pregnant women and their fetuses?

4. How do the authors frame the issue of "individual interests" and "social goods"? Which of these, in their view, should take priority, and why? How does this view differ from views that are prominent in the West?

Can Late Abortion Be Ethically Justified?

REN ZONG QIU, CHUN ZHI WANG, AND YUAN GU

I. Thorny Cases

Miss A is a 25-year-old unmarried woman working in a factory. She lived with her boyfriend and became pregnant. She was not aware of her condition in the early stage of her pregnancy, because she lacked education in reproduction. After she realized that she was pregnant, she was afraid to undergo an abortion. She used a cloth to bind her waist to hide her illegitimate pregnancy from others, and she was burdened with anxieties every day. Her pregnancy was revealed when the fetus was eight months old. Responsible men in her factory escorted her to the hospital and asked the physician to perform an abortion. The physician agreed, because the young woman did not want the child, and because she had no birth quota as an unmarried woman.[1] The physician performed the abortion using an intraamniotic injection of Huangyan Flower,[2] and a 2800 g. dead baby was expelled the next day.

Mrs. B is another story. She is a 30-year-old accountant, the wife of an army officer. She has been pregnant two times, but only gave birth once, to a girl, and was given a "One Child" certificate.[3] When she became aware of being pregnant the third time, she felt a physical difference, and she inferred that the fetus might possibly be a boy. Her husband was performing his duty outside Beijing at that time. She made every effort to hide the truth for seven months. During this period she economized on food and clothing, and she worked very hard to save money for the penalty fine;[4] both courses of action jeopardized her health. When her husband came home to visit, he persuaded her to give up the fetus in the interests of their family and country. Mrs. B agreed, and was escorted by her husband to the hospital to undergo an abortion. After examination, the physician found her malnourished, dropsical, Hgb 4 g., heart rate 120/min., fetal heart beat quite weak. She was given supportive treatment first, and then an intraamniotic injection of Rivanol several days later. A 1800 g. dead baby was born the next day.

The experience of Mrs. C is somewhat different. She is a 40-year-old worker in a state-owned factory, with two daughters and one son from five pregnan-

[1]Every married woman gets a birth quota before pregnancy; also see Note 5.
[2]The extraction from an herb used as an effective drug to induce abortion.

[3]Whoever has such a certificate enjoys favored treatment, such as additional rewards at the factory, enrollment in a kindergarten for their child, etc.
[4]If you give birth to a second child, you will be fined about 1000 yuan ($270), which can be about one year's wages.

Ren Zong Qiu, Chun Zhi Wang, and Yuan Gu, "Can Late Abortion Be Ethically Justified?" From Journal of Medicine and Philosophy, *vol. 14 (1989), pp. 343–350. Reprinted by permission of the Journal of Medicine and Philosophy and Kluwer Academic Publishers.*

cies. She wanted more children. When she conceived the sixth time, she succeeded in covering the truth until seven months later, when the cadres of her factory discovered her condition. The cadres asked her to give up the fetus, but she refused, because she believed the Chinese maxim "More children, more happiness." She said she did not care if she were fined. One month later she was persuaded to undergo an abortion, but the physician refused to perform the operation. The cadres of her factory complained that if she gave birth to a fourth child, the rewards of all the workers would be diminished, because they had broken the birth quota assigned to the factory.[5] Finally the physician was convinced, and he performed that abortion with an intraamniotic injection of Huangyan Flower. The next day a 3000 g. live baby was born, and later adopted by an infertile couple.

II. Reasons for Late Abortions

From the cases described above we know that there are two groups of pregnant women who undergo late abortion: the unmarried woman, and those who want more than one child but who are convinced at a late date to forgo the fetus.

The rate of pregnancy in unmarried women has increased in recent decades. With the wide application and free distribution of contraceptives and the opening of the door to foreign cultures, China is undergoing its own form of the "sexual revolution." But sex education is still unavailable to young men, including knowledge on how to use contraceptives. According to one study in nine villages of Jiangbei County in the Sichuan Province, the average rate of illegitimate pregnancies was 50–82%. In one village it was as high as 90%; and in another village the rates in 1979, 1980, and 1981 were 44%, 53%, and 71% respectively (Hua, 1984). We think that the figures may not be representative, but only indicative. In a region of Shanghai city, among the pregnant women who underwent abortion, the rate of unmarried women was 8.4%; but in recent years it has been as high as 40% in some hospitals in Beijing and other cities.

In the early stages of pregnancy, these unmarried women made every effort to hide the truth from others. However, it is hardly possible for them to raise a child by themselves, for moral and economic reasons.

The average income of a young woman is below 100 yuan ($27) per month. And changes in the moral environment lag behind the change in the sexual behavior of youth. In Chinese public opinion, premarital sexual relations are still considered unethical, an illegitimate pregnancy even more so. In some cities, abortion in hospitals was allowed only for married women, in an attempt to decrease or put an end to illegitimate pregnancies. As a result, however, there was an increase in the rate of late and illegal abortions which usually led to the death of both mother and fetus.

In our opinion, appropriate sex and reproductive education should be provided to young people, and there should be a change of attitude toward premarital sexual relations and illegitimate pregnancies. We believe that the attitude should be more lenient, in order to make it easier for pregnant girls to tell the truth and to have an abortion earlier and more safely, if they do not want to carry the pregnancy to term.

The case of pregnancy in a woman who already has a child is much more complicated. It is the Confucian cultural tradition which encourages the Chinese to have more children. Confucius said, "Among the three vices that violate the principle of filial piety, the biggest is to be without offspring." The Chinese turned this negative warning into a positive maxim: "More children, more virtues." In the case of Mrs. B. she wanted a male child. Chinese tradition values male children more highly than females, because genealogy is continued through the male. But the desire to have more children, or a male child, often conflicts with the state policy of "one couple, one child." In Mrs. C's case, it also conflicted with the interests of her colleagues in the factory where she worked. However, Mrs. B and Mrs. C were finally persuaded to agree to undergo an abortion in the interest of their country and their colleagues. Can this be ethically justified?

III. Conflicts of Values

There are conflicts of values around the ethical issue of late abortion which cannot be solved exclusively by deontological theory. The Chinese Ministry of Health has promulgated a regulation to prohibit late abortions after 28 weeks, with the purpose of protecting the health and life of the mother as well as of the fetus. But at the same time, since the beginning of the 1980s, the Chinese government has promulgated a regulation of birth control which permits a couple to have only one child. These two regulations are in conflict, but the latter is the more powerful. It is

---

[5]Every factory, school, or institute has a birth quota set by the authorities. Female workers are allowed to give birth to only a certain number per year, and the quotas are assigned to the married women on the basis of consultation with them each year.

argued that this regulation ("one couple, one child") is in the maximum interest of the maximum number of people. Rewards in a factory are connected not only with one's work performance, but also with one's reproductive behavior.

If you give birth to a second child, you will be fined *and* the rewards of all of your colleagues will be deducted. This practice forces a fertile married woman to consider the consequences of her reproductive behavior for others before making a decision. Some married women, most of whom are professionals and intellectuals, do not want more than one child. A few of them do not even want to get married. Some want more than one child, but they are reluctant to be in a position to be fined, or they think they should put the interest of their country first by carrying out the birth control policy. But there are still a few women who insist on having another child. The outcome is usually that they are finally persuaded to undergo an abortion, or they give birth to the child in spite of the financial or psychological pressures from their colleagues or their employers.

In our opinion, it is difficult to say which conduct is moral or immoral. For a woman not to have any more children, for whatever reason, may be labeled praiseworthy conduct; but if a woman wants more than one child, it is not a vicious desire. "Moral" or "immoral" may be too strong a label to apply in such cases.

But value conflicts exist. In preceding years, when the technology for late abortion was underdeveloped and no third party intruded, the balance would usually incline toward rejecting late abortion in the interest of protecting the mother and the viable fetus. Now the scale is more evenly stacked. On the one side is the presumed interest of the viable fetus; on the other are the interests of a big third party: the country, the factory and colleagues, and the family. If the mother stands on the latter side, she tips the balance against the fetus. If she insists on giving birth, or if the late abortion would jeopardize the mother's life, the scale could be a match, or the interests of the fetus could even prevail.

IV. Physicians' Dilemmas

In two of the three cases described above, the physician did not hesitate to perform a late abortion. In the third case the physician was persuaded to perform the abortion by cadres of the factory where the pregnant woman worked.

There is a schism between physicians, ethicists, and the public over late abortions.

The first to explicitly defend prohibiting abortions after seven months was an obstetrician, Dr. J. K. Liu, at the 2nd National Conference on Medical Ethics. We have asked our obstetrician friends their opinions on this issue. They always say, "I don't know what I should do." Some of them prefer not to perform late abortions except for women with particularly troubled pregnancies. Others take their responsibility to society into account first, and perform late abortions with less hesitation. The overwhelming majority of Chinese physicians are employed by state-owned hospitals; they are labeled "state cadres" and have the responsibility of carrying out state policy. But all of them are perplexed; either way they harm one side, either the mother and fetus or society. Especially thorny is the case in which the aborted fetus is alive. Although the infertility rate is increasing now in China, and infertile couples are willing to adopt such a baby, should the physician tell the truth to the mother who had expressed a desire to give up the fetus? In some cases physicians do not do so, because they are afraid that the mother might change her mind and keep the baby.

The author of *An Outline of Medical Moral Theory* claims that in some cases, because a woman was coerced into an abortion in order to keep the birth rate low, the physician was coerced to perform late abortions, thereby violating both policy and medical morality. But the author of *Essential Medical Ethics* claims that "when the perinatal care comes into conflict with birth control and eugenics, it must be subordinated to the needs of the latter, because these are in the interest of the whole nation and the whole of mankind, as well as in accord with the greatest morality."

A questionnaire showed that 16% of the respondents assented to performing late abortions on women with second pregnancies, in order to conform with the state policy. 7% supported respect for the woman's free will without any interference, and 77% believed the late abortion should not be performed, but that a fine should be imposed. As for the question of who should make the decision on late abortion, 32% supported the pregnant woman and her family as the primary decision makers, 32% the physician, 9% the responsible men of the unit (factory, school, institute, etc.) where the woman was working; and 27% an ethical committee.

When making the decision to undergo or perform a late abortion, should the responsible parties take into account the interests of the third party, or only the interest of the woman, or only the interest of the fetus?

V. Social Good

Even as a member of an individualist society, one should be concerned about the social good, although more attention might be paid to individual rights or interests. If you are a carrier of the AIDS virus, do you have the right to have sex freely and spread the disease to others? No. A socialist country operating under the guiding ideology of Marxism favors a holistic social philosophy which asserts that a society is not merely the sum of its members but a nonadditive whole which is more than the sum. Every member should put the interest of society as a whole in the first position and subordinate his or her interest to that of society. The problem is, who is the representative of society and its interests, and how is the interest of a society as a whole known? Usually, someone claims that he is the representative, and it later turns out that this is not the case. However, in China the "one couple, one child" policy has been accepted by the majority of the Chinese people as in the best interest of the society as a whole. Of course, birth control is not the only factor, but it is one of the most important factors in modernizing underdeveloped countries in Asia, Africa, and Latin America. In a sense, the success or failure of development depends on the use of birth control. Everyone, including the married couple and the physician, should take this into account.

But we should practice birth control in a more human way. We should make every effort to avoid late abortions, i.e., to use effectively the contraceptives and to perform the abortions earlier. In the case of a late abortion, voluntary consent of the mother is indispensable. The physician should determine whether the late abortion would cause any harm to the mother's health or endanger her life, and he should refuse to perform it if there is a high risk

In preceding years the second pregnancy was treated with more leniency and flexibility than at present. If a couple in a rural area had a child who was disabled, or if they lived in a rural area that had a birth rate lower than the quota, they were permitted to give birth to a second child. But this flexibility in policy has raised the birth level, and an upsurge of second births amongst China's rural families is jeopardizing the attempt to limit the population to 1.2 billion by the year 2000. The State Statistics Bureau reports that 40% of rural women have given birth to three or more children over the past several years. Compared with 1985, the number of second births last year climbed by 1.37 million people to 6.92 million, and the number of third or more births topped 2.88 million, 240,000 more than the previous year.

VI. Conclusion

Our conclusion is that the late abortion can be justified ethically in China: 1) if the "one couple, one child" policy is justifiable; 2) if the couple and the physician take the social good into account; 3) if the mother expresses her voluntary consent, no matter whether the decision is made on the basis of her own original desire or after persuasion by others that is not coercive; and 4) if the late abortion will entail only a low risk to the mother's health or life.

Discussion and Reflection Questions

1. What does the situation in China described by Qiu, Wang, and Gu suggest about the importance of context in thinking about a moral problem like abortion? Is it possible, or desirable, to consider proposed solutions to moral problems apart from their consequences for society as a whole?

2. Given the penalties colleagues suffer when a women has a child out of wedlock or has more than one child, what should a pregnant woman in China do? How should she weigh her obligations to her colleagues and to her unborn fetus? Is it possible to resolve this dilemma by performing a utilitarian calculation of benefits and harms?

3. Do physicians who are employed by the state have moral obligations to the state? Do they have moral obligations to their patients? To unborn fetuses? When these obligations

come into conflict, which one should take priority? When a woman gives up a fetus to be aborted but the fetus unexpectedly lives, should physicians notify the mother of this fact? Are they morally obligated to do so?

4. Qiu, Wang, and Gu conclude that late abortion can be ethically justified in China if a number of conditions are met. What are these conditions? Do you agree that if these conditions are met, abortion is morally justified? Is it possible that abortion might be morally justified in one society but not in another, if the conditions in these societies are different? If so, what does this suggest about the contextual nature of moral judgments?

R. E. Florida, Buddhist Approaches to Abortion

In the following reading selection, R. E. Florida explores Buddhist approaches to abortion. As Florida points out, within Buddhism morality is a relative notion that is a part of, and hence secondary to, religious aims. Foremost among these is cultivating right motivations as a means of improving one's karma, and hence of promoting one's spiritual advancement. Because permitting abortions is usually accompanied by motivations of "greed, hatred, and delusion," abortion is morally wrong. As Florida is careful to point out, however, in practice Buddhists often take a more lenient attitude toward abortion and emphasize the need to exercise compassion, both for the aborted fetus and for the woman who has had the abortion. Florida concludes his article with the verses of a Buddhist ceremony for the death of an unborn child (included below) which reveals something of the deeper perspective on abortion provided by a Buddhist approach.

Reading Questions

1. According to Florida, what basic Buddhist principles form the wider context into which the question of abortion must be put? What does it mean to consider ethical problems as problems in "co-conditioned causality"?

2. What are the two major Buddhist ideals? How do these ideals bear on the problem of abortion? What is the role of morality in Buddhism? In what sense are moral precepts held to be relative in Buddhism?

3. What is the role of motivational factors in the Buddhist analysis of morality? What kinds of motivations are considered "skillful"? What kinds of motivations are considered "unskillful"? What kinds of motivations does Florida believe usually precede a decision to have an abortion?

4. According to the Buddhist sources Florida quotes, how is the problem of abortion connected with the larger sphere of "living unmindfully"? What does this suggest about the proper conception of abortion as a moral problem? Can this problem be treated separately from considerations concerning ways of life?

Buddhist Approaches to Abortion

R. E. FLORIDA

Introduction

As we all know, bioethics is currently one of the most active areas in Western religious and philosophical discourse. Although Eastern countries are facing the same bioethical issues as we are in the West, on the whole, Eastern religious leaders have not systematically dealt with the problems raised by the collision between ancient traditions and explosively advancing medical techniques. In Buddhist circles, for example, the work is just beginning. . . .

. . . This paper is an attempt to advance the discussion by presenting some Buddhist theoretical and practical responses to the ethical and religious problems raised concerning abortion. It is based both on textual study and on field observations and interviews in Hawaii, Japan, the People's Republic of China, Taiwan, and Thailand from 1987 through 1989.

Some Buddhist Ethical Principles

Let us begin with some basic Buddhist principles to put the question of abortion in a wider context. First, anything that exists, exists only in relationship with everything else that exists. That is, nothing has independent self-being. You and I—anything that is—exists only as the result of temporary, contingent causal relationships with other similarly changing, insubstantial, suffering beings. Therefore, all ethical problems must be considered globally and rationally as problems in co-conditioned causality.

The Buddha's great insight into the interrelatedness of all phenomena (co-conditioned causality), which is perhaps the first principle of Buddhism, has two major expressions. First is the ultimate truth that all things are fundamentally empty, which leads inevitably to the second, relative truth, compassion. The wise person, knowing the truth of the contingency and complete interdependence of all beings, can only regard their frenzied grasping for selfish ends with compassion. Practically, wisdom leads to selfless action for the sake of others. Thus *prajñā* or wisdom and

karuṇā or compassion are the two major Buddhist ideals, the first relating to the realm of ultimacy and the second to the world of day-to-day existence. Without ultimate wisdom one will be defective in *upāya* or skillful means for helping others. Witless compassion, the bungling attempt to do good without the wisdom to effect it, is extremely dangerous.

Moral behavior in Buddhist systems then, is not an absolute in itself; it is a means toward a religious end, the transcendence of those selfish cravings which bind all beings to an unending round of suffering. Accordingly all moral acts are understood either to be *kuśala karma*, skillful deeds which are beneficial to self and others, or *akuśala karma*, unskillful deeds which harm self and others. Everything in the phenomenal world is relative. Human behavior, therefore, is to be judged not on an absolute scale of good and evil but rather on a relative scale of skillful and unskillful. Skillfulness, of course, is understood in regard to the ascent of the path of the Buddha out of this world of suffering.

This means that the precepts of morality laid down by the Buddha also are not absolute commandments. They are clearly understood as "rules of training" which the individual undertakes in order to advance along the religious path. In fact, so little are they absolute commandments, that the precepts have been used since the earliest days of the Buddhist community as temporary vows, freely assumed by individuals for specified lengths of time. A lay meditator, for example, might follow the rule of training to abstain from the misuse of sensual pleasures for the period of a retreat. The relativity of the precepts is further demonstrated by the fact that there are traditionally five for the ordinary person, eight for the advanced laity, and 10 for monks and nuns.

It is taught that, for advanced Mahayana practitioners and especially for Vajrayāna adepts, the precepts can be violated if done for the benefit of others. However, it is cautioned that it takes a very wise person, far along in *prajñā*, to make this judgment. Others had better stick with the rules or they will reap

R. E. Florida, "Buddhist Approaches to Abortion," Asian Philosophy, *vol. 1, no. 1 (1991) pp. 39–50.*
Reprinted by permission of Carfax Publishing Company.

the whirlwind. Although Buddhist morality is contextual and relative, it is not generally antinomian.

On the level of relative truth, one's deeds or karma obey fixed laws of causality which determine one's destiny. Basically the moral consequences of an act are determined by the will or motivation (cetanā) of the actor. If the will behind an act is driven by greed, hatred, or delusion, which Buddhists understand as the three fundamental aspects of selfish craving, then the act is akuśala or unskillful.

It works in the following way. Every act involves body, speech, and mind working in conjunction. Mind starts a train of activity, and if mind is motivated by greed, hatred, or delusion, then the speech and bodily activity which follow are doomed to be unskillful. Unskillful acts always have negative consequences for the actor and generally for the recipient of the act. The precepts are designed to provide guidelines for skillful activity and when followed will minimize negative karmic consequences. From the Buddhist vantage point of the middle way, there are two basic errors one could fall into on this issue. If one denies the reality of karmic consequences, one has adopted the nihilistic extreme view, which tends towards antinomianism. The eternalistic extreme view would involve the reification of moral precepts, resulting in inflexible dogmatic positions.

Application to Abortion

From the very earliest days, the theory of co-conditioned causality, or pratītyasamutpāda, the doctrine of the interrelatedness of all phenomena, was interpreted embryologically. In the form which came to be the standard, dependent origination was expressed as a circle of 12 causal factors or links, which seem to operate simultaneously. As applied to the fetal development of an individual, the first three links of the chain are ignorance, which gives rise to the karma foundations, which in turn give rise to consciousness or vijñāna.

Vasubandhu, an outstandingly brilliant fourth or fifth century exegete, clarifies this very well:

> Avidyā [ignorance] is in the previous life the condition of passion. . . . All the passions in effect accompany ignorance, entering into activity through ignorance. It is just the same as they say, "When the king comes, you understand that his courtesans accompany him."

> Samskāras [karma foundations] are in the previous life the condition of the act. The series of the previous existence, in so far as it accomplished a

good act or a bad one and so on, is what is understood by the karma foundations.

> Vijñāna [consciousness] is the skandhas [the physical and mental components of a being] at conception. The five skandhas, within the womb, at the moment of reincarnation or of birth-of-existence.

Thus, vijñāna in this context is sometimes translated as "rebirth consciousness." In short, what all this boils down to is that Buddhists traditionally have understood that the human being begins at the instant of conception when sperm, egg, and vijñāna come together. As Taniguchi puts it, "there is no qualitative difference between an unborn fetus and a born individual."

Therefore, the precept against taking life applies in the case of abortion. Buddhaghosa, a fifth century Theravāda commentator who is Vasubandhu's only equal though of another school, has an extensive commentary on this precept:

> "I undertake to observe the rule to abstain from taking life." . . . "Taking life" means to murder anything that lives. It refers to the striking and killing of living beings. . . . "Taking life" is then the will to kill anything that one perceives as having life, to act so as to terminate the life-force in it, in so far as the will finds expression in bodily action or in speech. With regard to animals it is worse to kill large ones than small. Because a more extensive effort is involved. Even where the effort is the same, the difference in substance must be considered. In the case of humans the killing is the more blameworthy the more virtuous they are. Apart from that, the extent of the offense is proportionate to the intensity of the wish to kill.

Considered externally, then, abortion is a serious unskillful act as it involves violence against a presumably virtuous fetal human being.

From the point of view of motivation, the most important factor in Buddhist ethical evaluation, abortion again involves several grievous errors. Greed, hatred, and delusion, the three root drives of unskillful men and women, seem to apply all too well to abortion decisions. Greed, that is passionate attachment, would lie behind persons' considering only their own interests or pleasures in the situation. It would also solidify the notion that an "I" owned the fetus and could do with it what "I" would. Hatred would motivate one to strike out to eliminate the perceived cause of discomfort, the fetus. Delusion might cloud one's understanding and lead to denial that the fetus is a living being. It also could result in a condition of apathy where one, avoiding responsibility for oneself, followed advice to terminate the pregnancy. Underlying these three "poisons" of greed, hatred, and delusion are even more fundamental errors. The three poisons arise through lack of insight into the interconnectedness of all beings, a misguided sense of difference between I and other. When *prajñā* is so lacking, then so too *karuṇā* or compassion will also fall short, and *upāya* or skillful means will not be conspicuous.

In light of co-conditioned causality, the moral consequences of abortion do not only concern the relationship between the pregnant woman and the fetus. Abortion also entails physical and mental trauma to the woman and has karmic consequences on the technicians, advisors, friends, and family involved.

Additionally the situation which leads one to consider abortion is often caused by some previous error involving the precept concerning sexuality, which as explained by Buddhaghosa is:

> "I undertake to observe the rule to abstain from sensuous misconduct." . . . The offense is the more serious, the more moral and virtuous the person transgressed against. Four factors are involved: someone who should not be gone into, the thought of cohabiting with that one, the actions which lead to such cohabitation, and its actual performance. There is only one way of carrying it out: with one's own body.

Sensuous misconduct leads to an awkward pregnancy, which leads to abortion being contemplated. One unskillful act tends to lead to another as long as one lives unmindfully.

This leads us back to the religious context of this discussion. What Buddhists aim to do is to perfect themselves by following the path that the Buddha blazed for them. It involves replacing unwholesome roots of action, namely the selfish drives of greed, hatred, and delusion, with wholesome motives: loving-kindness, compassion, joy for others, and equanimity. Morality, meditation, and wisdom constantly work together in this path of *prajñā* and *karuṇā*. From this point of view any pregnancy could be taken as an opportunity to help one in perfecting selfless compassion. Ratanakul closes his book with a very fine reminder of the high religious ideals of the "voluntary sacrifice of one's claims or rights" that are at the heart of Buddhism and Christianity. At any rate, whatever one does, one's acts will ripen, with those skillful acts that are beneficial to self and others bearing good fruit while those unskillful acts that harm self and others yielding bad fruit.

It should also be mentioned that contraception, if the methods used do no harm to fetus or the lovers, is considered to be skillful means. Obviously, then, from the Buddhist point of view, preventing unwanted pregnancies is far better than terminating them.

Abortion and Buddhism in Thailand

Buddhism is generally depicted as an extremely tolerant tradition which does not seek to impose its teachings on individuals. On March 20, 1988, the CBC interviewed Dr. Sugunasari, the President of the Buddhist Council of Canada, to solicit a Buddhist view on the current national abortion dilemma. Dr. Sugunasari noted that although abortions involve lack of skill in two of the fundamental Buddhist precepts, the abstention from taking life and the abstention from going astray in sensual pleasures, Buddhists do not think that the state should intervene in matters of conscience. Further he advocated compassion for the individuals involved.

In Thailand, a Theravāda kingdom where Buddhism is the state religion, there is a very complex and intricate interrelationship amongst the king, the military, the government, the universities, the religious orders, and the people. The Thais, unlike the Canadian Buddhists, are not shy about trying to build their legal system on Buddhist principles. As they recognize the fetus as a human being from the moment of conception and take the precept against killing as primary, their law against abortion is quite restrictive. Abortions are legal only when there is a serious threat to the health of the mother and in cases of rape. Strictly speaking, it would seem to me that even the outrage of rape, even though it includes both violence and sensuous misconduct, should not be adequate grounds to allow abortion, which always involves killing a relatively innocent sentient being. That is, one unskillful act does not justify another. The point is to break the chain. At any rate, the vast majority of Thais think that abortion is *akuśala karma* and are pleased with the restrictive law. Legal abortions are very rare; only five per year on average were reported in the mid 1960s.

Nonetheless, the law is widely broken. Virginity is highly valued and there is a heavy social stigma against unmarried mothers so that fear and shame drive many single pregnant women to illegal abortions. They are unable to face the social consequences of their situation and thus sacrifice their Buddhist principles against taking life. Some rationalize that a very small fetus is not yet conscious and thus an abortion does not involve killing. However, as we have seen, this is contrary to the traditional Buddhist understanding. Some medical professionals more or less discreetly advertise for abortion business, but many abortionists are untrained, which leads to the usual dreadful consequences.

The Buddhist community in Thailand is divided on the abortion issue. Some leaders like Major General Chamlong Srimunang, the political head of Bangkok, are firmly opposed to any liberalization of the abortion law, basing their position on the absolute sanctity of life in the Buddhist tradition. Others, including some monastic leaders, take a much more global view, pointing out that in Buddhist morality the intent of the action has much to do with the karmic result of the act. Therefore, in some cases, for example when the mother's life is endangered by the pregnancy, abortion could be a skillful act. Dr. Pinit Ratanakul's study *Bioethics*, while it does not offer a complete Buddhist discussion on the abortion question, looks at issues in subtle and complex ways. While the precept against killing counsels against easy abortion decisions, many factors have to be taken in account in coming to a skillful judgment.

Professor Siralee Sirilai of the Faculty of Social Sciences and Humanities at Mahidol University, Bangkok, points out that the main Buddhist criterion for moral decisionmaking is whether or not the act has wholesome motivation. A skillful deed should work against greed, hatred, and delusion, and thus will be for the good of self and others. However, there are also secondary criteria such as "wholesome-unwholesome, usefulness-unusefulness, trouble-untrouble, admirability-blameworthiness." She thinks that for the world renouncers, only the first criterion can be taken into account, but that for the Buddhist layperson the secondary can also come into play. Therefore, in some circumstances, abortion could perhaps be morally permissible.

Abortion and Buddhism in China

In Taiwan, where Chinese Buddhism is currently in a very strong resurgence, abortion is condemned in Buddhist theory, for the same reasons as mentioned earlier. However, in traditional Buddhist thought abortion was less culpable than other forms of taking human life. The law in Taiwan is very restrictive, with induced abortion being illegal for any reason and with strong penalties for both the technician and woman involved. Since chastity for unmarried people is very highly valued in both theory and prac-

tice, abortions, therefore, are mainly confined to married women who already have the desired number of children. Although illegal, abortion is both widespread and tolerated. It does not seem to be of particular public concern in Taiwan to Buddhists.

In mainland China, from my observations, Buddhism has been reduced to an adjunct to the tourist industry. Chinese traditional religions are permitted only the most marginal sort of half life, and all religious bodies are expected to restrict themselves to ritual activities within the confines of their buildings. Religious participation in political or legal issues has been unthinkable. Indeed, very few citizens have any interest in traditional Buddhist thought. Therefore, Buddhist objections to abortion are neither voiced nor would they be listened to in the People's Republic of China, and the government has a free hand in its one-child policy which relies on abortion for enforcement. Incidentally, the People's Republic and Taiwan are very similar in their attitudes toward sexual chastity.

Abortion in Japan

Since 1948 Japan has had a liberal abortion law and has had a rather high rate of legal abortions, in 1980 running at 22.5 per 1000 women of child-bearing age. In the same year, for comparison, that rate in the USA was 29.3, Canada 11.5, and the Soviet Union 180, the world's highest. As is true in many countries, it is thought that the actual rate of medically supervised procedures is much higher than the officially reported rate, and there are still an unknown number of illegal abortions. Although contraception is increasing in Japan, abortion remains the major form of birth control. In part, this is because the government has refused to certify the pill and IUDs as medically safe. Cynics argue that the medical profession has opposed these means of contraception to protect their highly lucrative abortion trade, but it is true that the pill and IUDs do involve medical risks.

Buddhist Responses to Abortion in Japan

In 1987 I visited Kamakura, one of the great centers of Buddhist culture. It was in the grounds of one of Kamakura's exquisite temples, the Hasedera dedicated to Kannon (also known as Kanzeon in Japanese, Kuan Yin in Chinese, Bodhisattva Avalokiteśvara in Sanskrit) and containing a monumental wooden statue of him, that I came across an extraordinary sight. There were thousands of statues of Jizo Bosatsu lining the walkways and filling courtyards. Stone, porcelain, and plastic Jizos of various sizes were grouped together. None of particular artistic merit, they came in about a half dozen varieties. The mass of these little statuettes was somehow very touching, and the pathetic effect was greatly intensified by the way many of them were decorated. Very often they were dressed with a red bib or a little red hand-knit cap. Some had soothers on a ribbon around their necks, some had pinwheels or rattles to play with.

What was going on here? My friend, an American who had been in Kamakura for several years as a Zen student, explained that the Hasedera temple was one of several around the country that specialized in memorializing miscarried and aborted fetuses—*mizuko* or water-babies—or very young children who had died. The vast majority of the statues are for aborted *mizuko*. At this particular temple, so many women commissioned statues that they continually were clearing away old ones to make room for the new. A major part of the income of the temple came from these services. The cheapest figurine cost the equivalent of US $80 and memorial services, which many clients ordered, were extra. In the literature given out by Hasedera temple, the images of Jizo were explained as commemorating stillborn and miscarried children, but not aborted ones, even though they did note that Jizo was the protector of aborted fetuses.

Jizo Bosatsu's connection with aborted fetuses in Japan has a revealing history. Originating in India as the Bodhisattva Kṣitigarbha (womb of the earth, or earth-store), Jizo vowed to roam all six realms of existence in this dark time between Gautama, the historical Buddha, and Maitreya, the Buddha of the future. Because of this vow, in Japan his images sometimes appear in groups of six slightly different statues, each one representing his activities in one of the realms of reincarnation. In his wandering, Jizo aids all suffering creatures toward their ultimate salvation.

Although introduced to China and Japan as one of the celestial Bodhisattvas of Vajrayāna or esoteric Buddhism, he became very popular in the folk religion due to his connection with the hells. In Japan he become connected with a folk belief concerning the fate of water-babies and very young children who die. Such youngsters are neither good enough to enter a paradise nor bad enough for a hell, so they find themselves on a deserted riverbank called Sai-no-kawara in Meido, the ghostly realm of gloom. During the day there, they try to make the best of it and play with the pebbles they find, stacking them into the form of little pagodas. This play is more than it seems as their building pagodas, for the benefit of their surviving relatives, is a powerful act of merit. However, when night falls, they become cold and afraid of the dark, and to make things worse malicious demons come and destroy their little structures.

Jizo, who has vowed to help all creatures no matter how sad the circumstances, then appears. He is pictured as dressed in the robes of a monk and carrying a staff with six jingling rings on it, each ring representing one of the six realms that he constantly patrols. The jingling of the rings reassures the children, and they are comforted by sheltering in his robe, which gently glows, dispelling the dark. This scene is the subject of many folk tales and songs:

Be not afraid, little dear ones,
You were so little to come here,
All the long journey to Meido!
I will be Father and Mother,
Father and Mother and Playmate
To all the children in Meido!

Then he caresses them kindly,
Folding his shining robes round them,
Lifting the smallest and frailest
Into his bosom, and holding
His staff for the stumblers to clutch.

To his long sleeves cling the infants,
Smile in response to his smiling,
Glad in his beauteous compassion.

Although the image of Kannon in the Hasedera temple was the art treasure that drew the tourists, it was the Jizos in the courtyard that fulfilled a religious need of the people.

In dedicating a statuette and commissioning services for their aborted fetuses believers can accrue religious merit. Donations to temples and performing services are excellent ways to improve one's karma, to compensate for the unskillfulness in sexual conduct and violence that accompany an act of abortion. Also, whether taken literally or metaphorically, the notion of Jizo comforting the lost *mizuko* would be very comforting to the mourning survivors. Jizo has a very large place in the hearts of the Japanese, and little shrines to him appear all over the country, often in unexpected sites; I recall one image nestled amongst a display of valves and piping in a plumber's display window. Often they have little stacks of pebbles before them, recalling the meritorious play of the departed water-babies.

The outdoors votive images of Jizo tend to be very simple, stylized figures with him dressed as a Hinayana monk. Although I did not notice it at the time, these figures have an undoubtedly phallic appearance. Indeed, when the Japanese adopted Jizo, he partly supplanted the ancient indigenous Dosojin, Earth Ancestor Deity or Road Ancestor Deity, a god of sexuality in the form of a husband-and-wife couple, who previously had the function of protecting children. His images were often carved onto ancient phallic representations of Dosojin and, to my eye at least, his usual folk form reflects this origin. In this light, the little images in the courtyard of the Hasedera temple, dedicated to so many *mizuko* are even more poignant as symbols of human frailty and futility. Religion's wonderful power to express our deepest illusions, as in this case that sexuality can conquer death, is no doubt one of the reason it has such a hold on humanity.

Not all temples display their votive Jizo figures in the casual mode of Hasedera, where they almost seem like mushrooms growing in profusion from the soil. In 1989 I observed a very different style at the Kannon memorial temple in Kyoto. In this modern temple, which dates from the 1950s, the Jizos are encased neatly in numbered rows in glass cases. All of the figures are the same, and the overall effect reminded me of a sterile department store. However, there were rows of pinwheels for the *mizuko* as well as racks for toys, in which one also sees some of the more traditional Jizo images.

An American Buddhist Response to Abortion

In Honolulu I attended and eventually joined the Diamond Sangha, a Zen group led by an American Roshi, Robert Aitken. He is a leading figure in the "engaged Buddhism" movement, an informal grouping of North American Buddhists who are trying to formulate theory and practice for applying Buddhist insights and traditions to the social situation of North American practitioners. Roshi Aitken's reflections on abortion are found in the context of his discussion of the first precept, to abstain from killing:

> Perhaps the most intimate and agonizing test is faced by the woman considering abortion. Oversimplified positions of pro-life and pro-choice do not touch the depths of dilemma. Usually she experiences distressing conflict between her sexual/reproductive drive and the realities of her life; . . . and indeed, she faces such realities for any child she may bring to term. . . .

> I get the impression that when a woman is sensitive to her feelings, she is conscious that abortion is killing a part of herself and terminating the ancient process, begun anew within herself, or bringing life into being. Thus she is likely to feel acutely miserable after making a decision to have an abortion. This is time for compassion for the woman, and for her to be compassionate with herself and for her unborn child. If I am consulted, and we explore the options carefully and I learn that the decision is definite, I encourage her to go through the act with the consciousness of a mother who holds her dying child in her arms, lovingly nurturing it as it passes from life. . . . Once the decision is made, there is not blame, but rather acknowledgment that sadness pervades the whole universe, and this bit of life goes with our deepest love.

This position seems to hold them to the middle way very skillfully. The moral consequences of the precepts are fully recognized, but the persons involved are treated compassionately rather than judgmentally.

For those who so desire, the Diamond Sangha marks these deaths with a public ceremony [see Appendix] based on the Japanese funeral services for *mizuko*. From my experience I believe that this or a similar ceremony could be very useful in dealing with such a loss, which in our culture usually remains hidden and difficult to resolve.

Here it should be mentioned that in Japan, due to the disgrace surrounding abortion, both as a function of sexual misconduct and killing, such services do not seem to involve a public, community recognition of the unhappy event. In Thailand and Taiwan there also is no formalized religious consolation for people involved in abortions. It is a private hidden grief. Furthermore, in Theravāda countries there is no tradition of revering Bodhisattva Kṣitigarbha. In China this bodhisattva, known as Ti-tsang, is neither widely worshipped, nor is he particularly connected with "water-babies."

Finally, my research confirms earlier studies. Where religious prohibitions result in highly restrictive abortion laws, illegal abortions are frequent. When social pressure to limit family size or to avoid the disgrace of unmarried pregnancy conflicts with religious principles against abortion, religion loses out. It seems that the gaps between religious theory and practice are often fruitful places for investigation.

Appendix
The Diamond Sangha Ceremony on the Death of an Unborn Child

1. Three full bows.
2. *Vandana* and *Ti Sarana* in Pali, or *Taking Refuge* in English.
3. *Enmei Jikku Kannon Gyo*, or other short sutra in Japanese or English.
4. Leader:

We gather today to express our love and support for _____, and for _____[names of parents], and to _____, who appeared just as we all do, from the undifferentiated mind, as that mind, and who passed away after a few moments of flickering life, just as we all do.

In our culture, we place great emphasis upon maintaining life, but truly death is not a fundamental matter, but an incident, another wave. Bassui Zenji speaks of it as clouds fading in the sky. Mind essence, Bassui says, is not subject to birth or death. It is neither being nor nothingness, neither emptiness nor form and color.

It is, as Yamada Koun Roshi has said, infinite emptiness, full of possibilities, at once altogether at rest and also charged with countless tendencies awaiting the fullness of karma. Here _____ is in complete repose, at one with the mystery that is our own birth and death, our own no-birth and no-death.

5. *Heart Sutra* in Japanese or English, as parents, leader, and friends offer incense.
6. Leader:

Buddha nature pervades the whole universe, existing right here now;
with our reciting of Enmei Jikku Kannon Gyo let us unite with
the Ancient Seven Buddhas,
Fully Realized Sākyamuni Buddha,
Great Compassion Avalokiteśvara Bodhisattva,
Earth Treasury Kṣitigarbha Bodhisattva,
all Founding Teachers, past, present, future.
We especially dedicate our love and our prayerful
     thoughts to you_____.
May you rest in perfect peace.
Let true Dharma continue—
Sangha relations become complete.

All:

All Buddhas throughout space and time,
all Bodhisattvas, Mahāsattvas,
the Great Prajñāpāramitā.

7. *Great Vows for All* in English
8. Three full bows.

Discussion and Reflection Questions

1. Given Buddhism's emphasis on motivational factors in judging the morality of actions, how would you classify the Buddhist approach to abortion? In considering the morality of abortion, are Buddhists more concerned with the "rights" of the fetus or the karma of the persons associated with permitting an abortion? What does this reveal about the relationship between religion and morality in Buddhism?

2. Florida says that "greed, hatred, and delusion . . . seem to apply all too well to abortion decisions." Do you think that this claim is true? Do you find his defense of this claim well supported?

3. Florida writes that "the outrage of rape, even though it includes both violence and sensuous misconduct, should not be adequate grounds to allow abortion." What is his reasoning here? Are there any grounds that a Buddhist would assent to that could be used to oppose this reasoning?

4. Near the end of his article Florida discusses several religious ceremonies related to abortion and to the death of unborn or young children more generally. What function do these ceremonies serve? How do they relate to the primary ideals of Buddhism? How do such ceremonies help place abortion into a wider context of life and the human experience of suffering? Is there something valuable to be learned from this practice? What?

Suggestions for Further Reading

Probably few moral issues have received as much philosophical attention as abortion. The following represent just a fraction of the recent writings on the ethical dimensions of abortion: Robert L. Armstrong, "The Right to Life," *Journal of Social Philosophy*, vol. 8, no. 1 (January 1977); Martha Brandt Bolton, "Responsible Women and Abortion Decisions," in *Having Children: Philosophical and Legal Reflections on Parenthood*, edited by Onora O'Neill and William Ruddick (New York: Oxford University Press, 1979); Robert M. Baird and Stuart E. Rosenbaum, eds., *The Ethics of Abortion: Pro-Life vs. Pro-Choice* (Buffalo, N.Y.: Prometheus Books, 1989); Joel Feinberg, ed., *The Problem of Abortion*, 2nd ed. (Belmont, Cal.: Wadsworth, 1984); Hyman Rodman, et al., *The Abortion Question* (New York: Columbia University Press, 1987); Jane English, "Abortion and the Concept of a Person," and "On the Moral and Legal Status of Abortion," both in *Social Ethics: Morality and Social Policy*, 3rd ed., edited by Thomas Mappes and Jane Zembaty (New York: McGraw-Hill, 1987); L. W. Sumner, *Abortion and Moral Theory* (Princeton, N.J.: Princeton University Press, 1981). *Liquid Life: Abortion and Buddhism in Japan*, edited by William R. LaFleur (Princeton, N.J.: Princeton University Press, 1992) and Roy W. Perrett's "Buddhism, Abortion and the Middle Way," *Asian Philosophy* 10 (2000): 101–114, both examine Buddhist ethical perspectives on abortion. Susan Feldman gives a Kantian analysis of abortion in "From Occupied Bodies to Pregnant Persons: How Kantian Ethics Should Treat Pregnancy and Abortion," in *Autonomy and Community*, edited by Jane E. Kneller (Albany: State University of New York Press, 1998). Earl Conee's "Metaphysics and the Morality of Abortion," *Mind* 108 (1999): 619–646, explores the concept of "persons" in the metaphysical doctrines of several philosophers to see if an ethical exploration of abortion can be informed by these doctrines.

InfoTrac

abortion, "women's rights and abortion", right to life, pro-choice movement, "personhood and fetus"

Chapter 11

Suicide and Euthanasia

Introduction: Facing Death

You will die. This is not meant as a threat but rather simply as a statement of fact. In a world full of uncertainties, there is one thing that each of us can count on with absolute certainty: that someday the processes of life that enable us to read books like this, or to do anything connected with having a functioning physical body, will cease. Although many people, religious and nonreligious alike, believe in an afterlife of some sort, this is where we enter the realm of uncertainty. Perhaps we survive physical death in some fashion, perhaps we do not. But that each of us will undergo physical death is as certain as that the sun will rise tomorrow. In fact, it is even *more* certain, because if the sun does *not* rise tomorrow we shall all certainly be dead!

Although the fact of death is a certainty, the issue of when it is best to die is the subject of much controversy and debate. Only a person who has not reflected much on the kinds of life situations one can find oneself in would think that no matter what, he should try to live as long as possible. Perhaps, all other things being equal, each of us should attempt to live as long as possible, but in life all other things are rarely equal. All sorts of events may alter our perceptions of when it is best to go on living and when it is best to make a graceful departure from this world.

The need to reflect on this issue has become even more pronounced in recent years. As medical technology has advanced, we have acquired the ability to sustain the life of individuals who, just a few years previously, would have been expected to die. Our understanding of the ethical implications of these developments, however, has not kept pace. That is, we know more than we did about how to sustain a person's life, but we don't necessarily have a better understanding of the conditions under which doing so is desirable.

The twin issues of suicide and euthanasia raise the same issue, albeit in slightly different ways. Suicide is the intentional taking of one's own life. Euthanasia (which literally means "good death") is the termination of another person's life, usually because that person's life is considered to be no longer worth living and because such termination is considered preferable, for that person, than is continued life. What the two kinds of actions have in common, therefore, is the termination of a person's life, either one's own or another's, when it seems to be in that person's best interests to do so. Suicide, thus construed, is distinct from self-sacrifice, where one willingly sacrifices one's own life for the sake of someone or something else.

Suicide is legal in many countries. In the United States its legality differs from one state to the next. Euthanasia has a similarly complex legal status. Be that as it may, it is important to remember that law and morality need not coincide. That is, the mere fact that something is illegal does not necessarily entail that it is morally wrong. Nor does the fact that something is morally wrong require that it be made illegal. What this means is that the morality of suicide and euthanasia need to be assessed without simply assuming that the morality of such actions corresponds to their legality. The morality of such actions can only be determined by examining the arguments given for specific positions on these issues. The reading selections below are designed to help you begin to reflect carefully on these important ethical issues.

John Hardwig, Is There a Duty to Die?

Some people claim that human beings possess an inherent and inalienable "right to life." Others oppose such a claim. Much less discussed is whether there is a *duty to die*. But this is precisely the issue John Hardwig takes up in this essay. According to him, there are circumstances when we have a duty to die. Ironically, the very advances in medical technology that permit one to stay alive may at the same time create the circumstances in which the duty to die becomes necessary. According to Hardwig, the common belief that there is no duty to die stems in part from "the individualistic fantasy" according to which how one lives, and what decisions one makes, have no effect on the lives of others. But since this is clearly false, there can arise circumstances in which morality requires that one end one's life rather than choose to prolong it. In the end, he suggests, embracing the idea of a duty to die may be the best, and only, way to render death meaningful.

Reading Questions

1. According to Hardwig, "there are circumstances when we have a duty to die." What are those circumstances?

2. Why does Hardwig reject the idea that our wealth and technological sophistication have rendered us exempt from the duty to die that might be present for some other cultures? Why might these features of our society force us to consider more seriously whether there might be a duty to die?

3. What does Hardwig mean by "the individualistic fantasy"? How is this related to the question of a duty to die?

4. Hardwig raises a number of objections to the view he advocates. Which one do you find most powerful? How does he respond to this objection? Do you find his response satisfactory?

Is There a Duty to Die?

JOHN HARDWIG

MANY PEOPLE WERE OUTRAGED when Richard Lamm claimed that old people had a duty to die. Modern medicine and an individualistic culture have seduced many to feel that they have a right to health care and a right to live, despite the burdens and costs to our families and society. But in fact there are circumstances when we have a duty to die. As modern medicine continues to save more of us from acute illness, it also delivers more of us over to chronic illnesses, allowing us to survive far longer than we can take care of ourselves. It may be that our technological sophistication coupled with a commitment to our loved ones generates a fairly widespread duty to die.

When Richard Lamm made the statement that old people have a duty to die, it was generally shouted down or ridiculed. The whole idea is just too preposterous to entertain. Or too threatening. In fact, a fairly common argument against legalizing physician-assisted suicide is that if it were legal, some people might somehow get the idea that they have a duty to die. These people could only be the victims of twisted moral reasoning or vicious social pressure. It goes without saying that there is no duty to die.

But for me the question is real and very important. I feel strongly that I may very well some day have a duty to die. I do not believe that I am idiosyncratic, morbid, mentally ill, or morally perverse in thinking this. I think many of us will eventually face precisely this duty. But I am first of all concerned with my own duty. I write partly to clarify my own convictions and to prepare myself. Ending my life might be a very difficult thing for me to do.

This notion of a duty to die raises all sorts of interesting theoretical and metaethical questions. I intend to try to avoid most of them because I hope my argument will be persuasive to those holding a wide variety of ethical views. Also, although the claim that there is a duty to die would ultimately require theoretical underpinning, the discussion needs to begin on the normative level. As is appropriate to my attempt to steer clear of theoretical commitments, I will use "duty," "obligation," and "responsibility" interchangeably, in a pretheoretical or preanalytic sense.[1]

Circumstances and a Duty to Die

Do many of us really believe that no one ever has a duty to die? I suspect not. I think most of us probably believe that there is such a duty, but it is very uncommon. Consider Captain Oates, a member of Captain Scott's expedition to the South Pole. Oates became too ill to continue. If the rest of the team stayed with him, they would all perish. After this had become clear, Oates left his tent one night, walked out into a raging blizzard, and was never seen again.[2] That may have been a heroic thing to do, but we might be able to agree that it was also no more than his duty. It would have been wrong for him to urge—or even to allow—the rest to stay and care for him.

This is a very unusual circumstance—a "lifeboat case"—and lifeboat cases make for bad ethics. But I expect that most of us would also agree that there have been cultures in which what we would call a duty to die has been fairly common. These are relatively poor, technologically simple, and especially nomadic cultures. In such societies, everyone knows that if you manage to live long enough, you will eventually become incapacitated. Then you will need to decide on a time to die. The old people in these societies regularly did precisely that. Their cultures prepared and supported them in doing so.

Those cultures could be dismissed as irrelevant to contemporary bioethics; their circumstances are so different from ours. But if that is our response, it is instructive. It suggests that we assume a duty to die is irrelevant to us because our wealth and technological sophistication have purchased an exemption for us . . . except under very unusual circumstances like Captain Oates's.

be the most appropriate word. Nevertheless, I often use "duty" despite its legalistic overtones, because Lamm's famous statement has given the expression "duty to die" a certain familiarity. But I intend no implication that there is a law that grounds this duty, nor that someone has a right corresponding to it.

[2]For a discussion of the Oates case, see Tom L. Beauchamp, "What Is Suicide?" in *Ethical Issues in Death and Dying*, ed. Tom L. Beauchamp and Seymour Perlin (Englewood Cliffs, N.J.: Prentice-Hall, 1978).

[1]Given the importance of relationships in my thinking, "responsibility"—rooted as it is in "respond"—would perhaps

John Hardwig, "Is There a Duty to Die?," From Hastings Center Report, *vol. 27, no. 2 (1997), pp. 34-42. Reprinted by permission of the Hastings Center and the author.*

But have wealth and technology really exempted us? Or are they, on the contrary, about to make a duty to die common again? We like to think of modern medicines as all triumph with no dark side. Our medicine saves many lives and enables most of us to live longer. That is wonderful, indeed. We are all glad to have access to this medicine. But our medicine also delivers most of us over to chronic illnesses and it enables many of us to survive longer than we can take care of ourselves, longer than we know what to do with ourselves, longer than we even are ourselves.

The costs—and these are not merely monetary—of prolonging our lives when we are no longer able to care for ourselves are often staggering. If further medical advances wipe out many of today's "killer diseases"—cancers, heart attacks, strokes, ALS, AIDS, and the rest—then one day most of us will survive long enough to become demented or debilitated. These developments could generate a fairly widespread duty to die. A fairly common duty to die might turn out to be only the dark side of our life-prolonging medicine and the uses we choose to make of it.

Let me be clear. I certainly believe that there is a duty to refuse life-prolonging medical treatment and also a duty to complete advance directives refusing life-prolonging treatment. But a duty to die can go well beyond that. There can be a duty to die before one's illnesses would cause death, even if treated only with palliative measures. In fact, there may be a fairly common responsibility to end one's life in the absence of any terminal illness at all. Finally, there can be a duty to die when one would prefer to live. Granted, many of the conditions that can generate a duty to die also seriously undermine the quality of life. Some prefer not to live under such conditions. But even those who want to live can face a duty to die. These will clearly be the most controversial and troubling cases; I will, accordingly, focus my reflections on them.

The Individualistic Fantasy

Because a duty to die seems such a real possibility to me, I wonder why contemporary bioethics has dismissed it without serious consideration. I believe that most bioethics still shares in one of our deeply embedded American dreams: the individualistic fantasy. This fantasy leads us to imagine that lives are separate and unconnected, or that they could be so if we chose. If lives were unconnected, things that happened in my life would not or need not affect others. And if others were not (much) affected by my life, I would have no duty to consider the impact of my decisions on others. I would then be free morally to live

my life however I please, choosing whatever life and death I prefer for myself. The way I live would be nobody's business but my own. I certainly would have no duty to die if I preferred to live.

Within a health care context, the individualistic fantasy leads us to assume that the patient is the only one affected by decisions about her medical treatment. If only the patient were affected, the relevant questions when making treatment decisions would be precisely those we ask: What will benefit the patient? Who can best decide that? The pivotal issue would always be simply whether the patient wants to live like this and whether she would consider herself better off dead.[3] "Whose life is it, anyway?" we ask rhetorically.

But this is morally obtuse. We are not a race of hermits. Illness and death do not come only to those who are all alone. Nor it is much better to think in terms of the bald dichotomy between "the interests of the patient" and "the interests of society" (or a third-party payer), as if we were isolated individuals connected only to "society" in the abstract or to the other, faceless members of our health maintenance organization.

Most of us are affiliated with particular others and, most deeply, with family and loved ones. Families and loved ones are bound together by ties of care and affection, by legal relations and obligations, by inhabiting shared spaces and living units, by interlocking finances and economic prospects, by common projects and also commitments to support the different life projects of other family members, by shared histories, by ties of loyalty. This life together of family and loved ones is what defines and sustains us; it is what gives meaning to most of our lives. We would not have it any other way. We would not want to be all alone, especially when we are seriously ill, as we age, and when we are dying.

But the fact of deeply interwoven lives debars us from making exclusively self-regarding decisions, as the decisions of one member of a family may dramatically affect the lives of all the rest. The impact of my decisions upon my family and loved ones is the source of many of my strongest obligations and also

---

[3]Most bioethicists advocate a "patient-centered ethics"—an ethics which claims only the patient's interests should be considered in making medical treatment decisions. Most health care professionals have been trained to accept this ethic and to see themselves as patient advocates. For arguments that a patient-centered ethics should be replaced by a family-centered ethics see John Hardwig, "What About the Family?" *Hastings Center Report,* 20, no. 2 (1990): 5–10; Hilde L. Nelson and James L. Nelson, *The Patient in the Family* (New York: Routledge, 1995).

the most plausible and likeliest basis of a duty to die. "Society," after all, is only very marginally affected by how I live, or by whether I live or die.

A Burden to My Loved Ones

Many older people report that their one remaining goal in life is not to be a burden to their loved ones. Young people feel this, too: When I ask my undergraduate students to think about whether their death could come too late, one of their very first responses always is, "Yes, when I become a burden to my family or loved ones." Tragically, there are situations in which my loved ones would be much better off—all things considered, the loss of a loved one notwithstanding—if I were dead.

The lives of our loved ones can be seriously compromised by caring for us. The burdens of providing care or even just supervision twenty-four hours a day, seven days a week, are often overwhelming.[4] When this kind of caregiving goes on for years, it leaves the caregiver exhausted, with no time for herself or life of her own. Ultimately, even her health is often destroyed. But it can also be emotionally devastating simple to live with a spouse who is increasingly distant, uncommunicative, unresponsive, foreign, and unreachable. Other family members' needs often go unmet as the caring capacity of the family is exceeded. Social life and friendships evaporate, as there is no opportunity to go out to see friends and the home is no longer a place suitable for having friends in.

We must also acknowledge that the lives of our loved ones can be devastated just by having to pay for health care for us. One part of the recent SUPPORT study documented the financial aspects of caring for a dying member of a family. Only those who had illnesses severe enough to give them less than a 50 percent chance to live six more months were included in this study. When these patients survived their initial hospitalization and were discharged about one-third required considerable caregiving from their families; in 20 percent of cases a family member had to quit work or make some other major lifestyle change; almost one-third of these families lost all their savings; and just under 30 percent lost a major source of income.[5]

If talking about money sounds venal or trivial, remember that much more than money is normally at stake here. When someone has to quit work, she may well lose her career. Savings decimated late in life cannot be recouped in the few remaining years of employability, so the loss compromises the quality of the rest of the caregiver's life. For a young person, the chance to go to college may be lost to the attempt to pay debts due to an illness in the family, and this decisively shapes an entire life.

A serious illness in a family is a misfortune. It is usually nobody's fault; no one is responsible for it. But we face choices about how we will respond to this misfortune. That's where the responsibility comes in and fault can arise. Those of us with families and loved ones always have a duty not to make selfish or self-centered decisions about our lives. We have a responsibility to try to protect the lives of loved ones from serious threats or greatly impoverished quality, certainly an obligation not to make choices that will jeopardize or seriously compromise their futures. Often, it would be wrong to do just what we want or just what is best for ourselves; we should choose in light of what is best for all concerned. That is our duty in sickness as well as in health. It is out of these responsibilities that a duty to die can develop.

I am not advocating a crass, quasi-economic conception of burdens and benefits, nor a shallow, hedonistic view of life. Given a suitably rich understanding of benefits, family members sometimes do benefit from suffering through the long illness of a loved one. Caring for the sick or aged can foster growth, even as it makes daily life immeasurably harder and the prospects for the future much bleaker. Chronic illness or a drawn-out death can also pull a family together, making the care for each other stronger and more evident. If my loved ones are truly benefiting from coping with my illness or debility, I have no duty to die based on burdens to them.

But it would be irresponsible to blithely assume that this always happens, that it will happen in my family, or that it will be the fault of my family if they cannot manage to turn my illness into a positive experience. Perhaps the opposite is more common: a hospital chaplain once told me that he could not think of a single case in which a family was strengthened or brought together by what happened at the hospital.

---

[4] A good account of the burdens of caregiving can be found in Elaine Brody, *Women in the Middle: Their Parent-Care Years* (New York: Springer, 1990). Perhaps the best article-length account of these burdens is Daniel Callahan, "Families as Caregivers; the Limits of Morality" in *Aging and Ethics: Philosophical Problems in Gerontology,* ed. Nancy Jecker (Totowa, N.J.: Humana Press, 1991).

[5] Kenneth C. Covinsky et al., "The Impact of Serious Illness on Patients' Families," *Journal of the American Medical Association,* 272 (1994): 1839–44.

Our families and loved ones also have obligations, of course—they have the responsibility to stand by us and to support us through debilitating illness and death. They must be prepared to make significant sacrifices to respond to an illness in the family. I am far from denying that. Most of us are aware of this responsibility and most families meet it rather well. In fact, families deliver more that 80 percent of the long-term care in this country, almost always at great personal cost. Most of us who are a part of a family can expect to be sustained in our time of need by family members and those who love us.

But most discussions of an illness in the family sound as if responsibility were a one–way street. It is not, of course. When we become seriously ill or debilitated, we too may have to make sacrifices. To think that my loved ones must bear whatever burdens my illness, debility, or dying process might impose upon them is to reduce them to means to my well-being. And that would be immoral. Family solidarity, altruism, bearing the burden of a loved one's misfortune, and loyalty are all important virtues of families, as well. But they are all also two-way streets.

Objections to a Duty to Die

To my mind the most serious objections to the idea of a duty to die lie in the effects on my loved ones of ending my life. But to most others, the important objections have little or nothing to do with family and loved ones. Perhaps the most common objections are: (1) there is a higher duty that always takes precedence over a duty to die; (2) a duty to end one's own life would be incompatible with a recognition of human dignity or the intrinsic value of a person; and (3) seriously ill, debilitated, or dying people are already bearing the harshest burdens and so it would be wrong to ask them to bear the additional burden of ending their own lives.

These are all important objections; all deserve a thorough discussion. Here I will only be able to suggest some moral counterweights—ideas that might provide the basis for an argument that these objections do not always preclude a duty to die.

An example of the first line of argument would be the claim that a duty to God, the giver of life, forbids that anyone take her own life. It could be argued that this duty always supersedes whatever obligations we might have to our families. But what convinces us that we always have such a religious duty in the first place? And what guarantees that it always supersedes our obligations to try to protect our loved ones?

Certainly, the view that death is the ultimate evil cannot be squared with Christian theology. It does not reflect the actions of Jesus or those of his early followers. Nor is it clear that the belief that life is sacred requires that we never take it. There are other theological possibilities.[6] In any case, most of us—bioethicists, physicians, and patients alike—do not subscribe to the view that we have an obligation to preserve human life as long as possible. But if not, surely we ought to agree that I may legitimately end my life for other-regarding reasons, not just for self-regarding reasons.

Secondly, religious considerations aside, the claim could be made that an obligation to end one's own life would be incompatible with human dignity or would embody a failure to recognize the intrinsic value of a person. But I do not see that in thinking I had a duty to die I would necessarily be failing to respect myself or to appreciate my dignity or worth. Nor would I necessarily be failing to respect you in thinking that you had a similar duty. There is surely also a sense in which we fail to respect ourselves if, in the face of illness or death, we stoop to choosing just what is best for ourselves. Indeed, Kant held that the very core of human dignity is the ability to act on a self-imposed moral law, regardless of whether it is in our interest to do so.[7] We shall return to the notion of human dignity.

A third objection appeals to the relative weight of burdens and thus, ultimately, to considerations of fairness or justice. The burdens that an illness creates for the family could not possibly be great enough to justify an obligation to end one's life—the sacrifice of life itself would be a far greater burden than any involved in caring for a chronically ill family member.

But is this true? Consider the following case:

An 87-year-old woman was dying of congestive heart failure. Her APACHE score predicted that

[6]Larry Churchill, for example, believes that Christian ethics takes us far beyond my present position: "Christian doctrines of stewardship prohibit the extension of one's own life at a great cost to the neighbor. . . . And such a gesture should not appear to us a sacrifice, but as the ordinary virtue entailed by a just, social conscience." Larry Churchill, *Rationing Health Care in America* (South Bend, Ind.: Notre Dame University Press, 1988), p. 112.
[7]Kant, as is well known, was opposed to suicide. But he was arguing against taking your life out of self-interested motives. It is not clear that Kant would or we should consider taking your life out of a sense of duty to be wrong. See Hilde L. Nelson, "Death with Kantian Dignity," *Journal of Clinical Ethics*, 7 (1996): 215–21.

she had less than a 50 percent chance to live for another six months. She was lucid, assertive, and terrified of death. She very much wanted to live and kept opting for rehospitalization and the most aggressive life-prolonging treatment possible. That treatment successfully prolonged her life (though with increasing debility) for nearly two years. Her 55-year-old daughter was her only remaining family, her caregiver, and the main source of her financial support. The daughter duly cared for her mother. But before the mother died, her illness had cost the daughter all of her savings, her home, her job, and her career.

This is by no means an uncommon sort of case. Thousands of similar cases occur each year. Now, ask yourself which is the greater burden:

(a) To lose a 50 percent chance of six more months of life at age 87?
(b) To love all your savings, your home, and your career at age 55?

Which burden would you prefer to bear? Do we really believe the former is the greater burden? Would even the dying mother say that (a) is the greater burden? Or has she been encouraged to believe that the burdens of (b) are somehow morally irrelevant to her choices?

I think most of us would quickly agree that (b) is a greater burden. That is the evil we would more hope to avoid in our lives. If we are tempted to say that the mother's disease and impending death are the greater evil, I believe it is because we are taking a "slice of time" perspective rather than a "lifetime perspective."[8] But surely the lifetime perspective is the appropriate perspective when weighing burdens. If (b) is the greater burden, then we must admit that we have been promulgating an ethics that advocates imposing greater burdens on some people in order to provide smaller benefits for others just because they are ill and thus gain our professional attention and advocacy.

A whole range of cases like this one could easily be generated. In some, the answer about which burden is greater will not be clear. But in many it is. Death—or ending your own life—is simply not the greatest evil or the greatest burden.

---

[8]Obviously, I owe this distinction to Norman Daniels, *Am I My Parents' Keeper? An Essay on Justice Between the Young and the Old* (New York: Oxford University Press, 1988). Just as obviously, Daniels is not committed to my use of it here.

This point does not depend on a utilitarian calculus. Even if death were the greatest burden (thus disposing of any simple utilitarian argument), serious questions would remain about the moral justifiability of choosing to impose crushing burdens on loved ones in order to avoid having to bear this burden oneself. The fact that I suffer greater burdens than others in my family does not license me simply to choose what I want for myself, nor does it necessarily release me from a responsibility to try to protect the quality of their lives.

I can readily imagine that, through cowardice, rationalization, or failure of resolve, I will fail in this obligation to protect my loved ones. If so, I think I would need to be excused or forgiven for what I did. But I cannot imagine it would be morally permissible of me to ruin the rest of my partner's life to sustain mine or to cut off my sons' careers, impoverish them, or compromise the quality of their children's lives simply because I wish to live a little longer. This is what leads me to believe in a duty to die.

Who Has a Duty to Die?

Suppose, then, that there can be a duty to die. Who has a duty to die? And when? To my mind, these are the right questions, the questions we should be asking. Many of us may one day badly need answers to just these questions.

But I cannot supply answers here, for two reasons. In the first place, answers will have to be very particular and contextual. Our concrete duties are often situated, defined in part by the myriad details of our circumstances, histories, and relationships. Though there may be principles that apply to a wide range of cases and some cases that yield pretty straightforward answers, there will also be many situations in which it is very difficult to discern whether one has a duty to die. If nothing else, it will often be very difficult to predict how one's family will bear up under the weight of the burdens that a protracted illness would impose on them. Momentous decisions will often have to be made under conditions of great uncertainty.

Second and perhaps even more importantly, I believe that those us with family and loved ones should not define our duties unilaterally, especially not a decision about a duty to die. It would be isolating and distancing for me to decide without consulting them what is too much of a burden for my loved ones to bear. That way of deciding about my moral duties is not only atomistic, it also treats my family and loved ones paternalistically. They must be allowed to speak for themselves about the burdens my life imposes on them and how they feel about bearing those burdens.

Some may object that it would be wrong to put a loved one in a position of having to say, in effect, "You should end your life because caring for you is too hard on me and the rest of the family." Not only will it be almost impossible to say something like that to someone you love, it will carry with it a heavy load of guilt. On this view, you should decide by yourself whether you have a duty to die and approach your loved ones only after you have made up your mind to say goodbye to them. Your family could then try to change your mind, but the tremendous weight of moral decision would be lifted from their shoulders.

Perhaps so. But I believe in family decisions. Important decisions for those whose lives are interwoven should be made together, in a family discussion. Granted, a conversation about whether I have a duty to die would be a tremendously difficult conversation. The temptations to be dishonest could be enormous. Nevertheless, if I am contemplating a duty to die, my family and I should, if possible, have just such an agonizing discussion. It will act as a check on the information, perceptions, and reasoning of all of us. But even more importantly, it affirms our connectedness at a critical juncture in our lives and our life together. Honest talk about difficult matters almost always strengthens relationships.

However, many families seem unable to talk about death at all, much less a duty to die. Certainly most families could not have this discussion all at once, in one sitting. It might well take a number of discussions to be able to approach this topic. But even if talking about death is impossible, there are always behavioral clues—about your caregiver's tiredness, physical condition, health, prevailing mood, anxiety, financial concerns, outlook, overall well-being, and so on. And families unable to talk about death can often talk about how the caregiver is feeling, about finances, about tensions within the family resulting from the illness, about concerns for the future. Deciding whether you have a duty to die based on these behavioral clues and conversation about them honors your relationships better than deciding on your own about how burdensome you and your care must be.

I cannot say when someone has a duty to die. Still, I can suggest a few features of one's illness, history, and circumstances that make it more likely that one has a duty to die. I present them here without much elaboration or explanation.

1. A duty to die is more likely when continuing to live will impose significant burdens—emotional burdens, extensive caregiving, destruction of life plans, and, yes, financial hardship—on your family and loved ones. This is the fundamental insight underlying a duty to die.

2. A duty to die becomes greater as you grow older. As we age, we will be giving up less by giving up our lives, if only because we will sacrifice fewer remaining years of life and a smaller portion of our life plans. After all, it's not as if we would be immortal and live forever if we could just manage to avoid a duty to die. To have reached the age of, say, seventy-five or eighty years without being ready to die is itself a moral failing, the sign of a life out of touch with life's basic realities.[9]

3. A duty to die is more likely when you have already lived a full and rich life. You have already had a full share of the good things life offers.

4. There is greater duty to die if your loved ones' lives have already been difficult of impoverished, if they have had only a small share of the good things that life has to offer (especially if through no fault of their own).

5. A duty to die is more likely when your loved ones have already made great contributions—perhaps even sacrifices—to make your life a good one. Especially if you have not made similar sacrifices for their well-being or for the well-being of other members of your family.

6. To the extent that you can make a good adjustment to your illness or handicapping condition, there is less likely to be a duty to die. A good adjustment means that smaller sacrifices will be required of loved ones and there is more compensating interaction for them. Still, we must also recognize that some diseases—Alzheimer or Huntington chorea—will eventually take their toll on your loved ones no matter how courageously, resolutely, even cheerfully you manage to face that illness.

7. There is less likely to be a duty to die if you can still make significant contributions to the lives of others, especially your family. The burdens of family members are not only or even primarily financial, neither are the contributions to them. However, the old and those who have terminal illnesses must also bear in mind that the loss their family members will feel when they die cannot be avoided, only postponed.

8. A duty to die is more likely when the part of you that is loved will soon be gone or seriously com-

[9]Daniel Callahan, *The Troubled Dream of Life* (New York: Simon & Schuster, 1993).

promised. Or when you soon will no longer be capable of giving love. Part of the horror of dementing disease is that it destroys the capacity to nurture and sustain relationships, taking away a person's agency and the emotions that bind her to others.

9. There is a greater duty to die to the extent that you have lived a relatively lavish lifestyle instead of saving for illness or old age. Like most upper middle-class Americans, I could easily have saved more. It is a greater wrong to come to your family for assistance if your need is the result of having chosen leisure or a spendthrift lifestyle. I may eventually have to face the moral consequences of decisions I am now making.

These, then, are some of the considerations that give shape and definition to the duty to die. If we can agree that these considerations are all relevant, we can see that the correct course of action will often be difficult to discern. A decision about when I should end my life will sometimes prove to be every bit as difficult as the decision about whether I want treatment for myself.

Can the Incompetent Have a Duty to Die?

Severe mental deterioration springs readily to mind as one of the situations in which I believe I could have a duty to die. But can incompetent people have duties at all? We can have moral duties we do not recognize or acknowledge, including duties that we never recognized. But can we have duties we are unable to recognize? Duties when we are unable to understand the concept of morality at all? If so, do others have a moral obligation to help us carry out this duty? These are extremely difficult theoretical questions. The reach of moral agency is severely strained by mental incompetence.

I am tempted to simply bypass the entire question by saying that I am talking only about competent persons. But the idea of a duty to die clearly raises the specter of one person claiming that another— who cannot speak for herself—has such a duty. So I need to say that I can make no sense of the claim that someone has a duty to die if the person has never been able to understand moral obligation at all. To my mind, only those who were formerly capable of making moral decisions could have such a duty.

But the case of formerly competent persons is almost as troubling. Perhaps we should simple stipulate that no incompetent person can have a duty to die, not even if she affirmed belief in such a duty in an advance directive. If we take the view that formerly competent people may have such a duty, we

should surely exercise extreme caution when claiming a formerly competent person would have acknowledged a duty to die or that any formerly competent person has an unacknowledged duty to die. Moral dangers loom regardless of which way we decide to resolve such issues.

But for me personally, very urgent practical matters turn on their resolution. If a formerly competent person can no longer have a duty to die (or if other people are not likely to help her carry out this duty), I believe that my obligation may be to die while I am still competent, before I become unable to make and carry out the decision for myself. Surely it would be irresponsible to evade my moral duties by temporizing until I escape into incompetence. And so I must die sooner than I otherwise would have to. On the other hand, if I could count on others to end my life after I become incompetent, I might be able to fulfill my responsibilities while also living out all my competent or semi-competent days. Given our society's reluctance to permit physicians, let alone family members, to perform aid-in-dying, I believe I may well have a duty to end my life when I can see mental incapacity on the horizon.

There is also the very real problem of sudden incompetence—due to a serious stroke or automobile accident, for example. For me, that is the real nightmare. If I suddenly become incompetent, I will fall into the hands of the medical-legal system that will conscientiously disregard my moral beliefs and do what is best for me, regardless of the consequences for my loved ones. And that is not at all what I would have wanted!

Social Policies and a Duty to Die

The claim that there is a duty to die will seem to some a misplaced response to social negligence. If our society were providing for the debilitated, the chronically ill, and the elderly as it should be, there would be only very rare cases of a duty to die. On this view, I am asking the sick and debilitated to step in and accept responsibility because society is derelict in its responsibility to provide for the incapacitated.

This much is surely true: there are a number of social policies we could pursue that would dramatically reduce the incidence of such a duty. Most obviously, we could decide to pay for facilities that provided excellent long-term care (not just health care!) for all chronically ill, debilitated, mentally ill, or demented people in this country. We probably could still afford to do this. If we did, sick, debilitated, and dying people might still be morally required to make sacrifices for their families. I might, for example, have a duty to forgo personal care by a family member who knows me and really does care for me. But these sacrifices would only rarely include the sacrifice of life itself. The duty to die would then be virtually eliminated.

I cannot claim to know whether in some abstract sense a society like ours should provide care for all who are chronically ill or debilitated. But the fact is that we Americans seem to be unwilling to pay for this kind of long-term care, except for ourselves and our own. In fact, we are moving in precisely the opposite direction—we are trying to shift the burdens of caring for the seriously and chronically ill onto families in order to save costs for our health care system. As we shift the burdens of care onto families, we also dramatically increase the number of Americans who will have a duty to die.

I must not, then, live my life and make my plans on the assumption that social institutions will protect my family from my infirmity and debility. To do so would be irresponsible. More likely, it will be up to me to protect my loved ones.

A Duty to Die and the Meaning of Life

A duty to die seems very harsh, and often it would be. It is one of the tragedies of our lives that someone who wants very much to live can nevertheless have a duty to die. It is both tragic and ironic that it is precisely the very real good of family and loved ones that gives rise to this duty. Indeed, the genuine love, closeness, and supportiveness of family members is a major source of this duty: we could not be such a burden if they did not care for us. Finally, there is deep irony in the fact that the very successes of our life-prolonging medicine help to create a widespread duty to die. We do not live in such a happy world that we can avoid such tragedies and ironies. We ought not to close our eyes to this reality or pretend that it just doesn't exist. We ought not to minimize the tragedy in any way.

And yet, a duty to die will not always be as harsh as we might assume. If I love my family, I will want to protect them and their lives. I will not want to make choices that compromise their futures. Indeed, I can easily imagine that I might want to avoid compromising their lives more than I would want anything else. I must also admit that I am not necessarily giving up so much in giving up my life: the conditions that give rise to a duty to die would usually already have compromised the quality of the life I am required to end. In any case, I personally must confess that at age fifty-six, I have already lived a very good life, albeit not yet nearly as long a life as I would like to have.

We fear death too much. Our fear of death has led to a massive assault on it. We still crave after virtually any life-prolonging technology that we might conceivably be able to produce. We still too often feel morally impelled to prolong life—virtually any form of life—as long as possible. As if the best death is the one that can be put off longest.

We do not even ask about meaning in death, so busy are we with trying to postpone it. But we will not conquer death by one day developing a technology so magnificent that no one will have to die. Nor can we conquer death by postponing it ever longer. We can conquer death only by finding meaning in it.

Although the existence of a duty to die does not hinge on this, recognizing such a duty would go some way toward recovering meaning in death. Paradoxically, it would restore dignity to those who are seriously ill or dying. It would also reaffirm the connections required to give life (and death) meaning. I close now with a few words about both of these points.

First, recognizing a duty to die affirms my agency and also my moral agency. I can still do things that make an important difference in the lives of my loved ones. Moreover, the fact that I still have responsibilities keeps me within the community of moral agents. My illness or debility has not reduced me to a mere moral patient (to use the language of the philosophers). Though it may not be the whole story, surely Kant was onto something important when he claimed that human dignity rests on the capacity for moral agency within a community of those who respect the demands of morality.

By contrast, surely there is something deeply insulting in a medicine and an ethic that would ask only what I want (or would have wanted) when I become ill. To treat me as if I had no moral responsibilities when I am ill or debilitated implies that my condition has rendered me morally incompetent. Only small children, the demented or insane, and those totally lacking in the capacity to act are free from moral duties. There is dignity, then, and a kind of meaning in moral agency, even as it forces extremely difficult decisions upon us.

Second, recovering meaning in death requires an affirmation of connections. If I end my life to spare the futures of my loved ones, I testify in my death that I am connected to them. It is because I love and care for precisely these people (and I know they care for me) that I wish not to be such a burden to them. By contrast, a life in which I am free to choose whatever I want for myself is a life unconnected to others. A bio-ethics that would treat me as if I had no serious moral responsibilities does what it can to marginalize, weaken, or even destroy my connections with others.

But life without connections is meaningless. The individualistic fantasy, though occasionally liberating, is deeply destructive. When life is good and vitality seems unending, life itself and life lived for yourself may seem quite sufficient. But if not life, certainly death without connection is meaningless. If you are only for yourself, all you have to care about as your life draws to a close is yourself and your life. Everything you care about will then perish in your death. And that—the end of everything you care about—is precisely the total collapse of meaning. We can, then, find meaning in death only through a sense of connection with something that will survive our death.

This need not be connections with other people. Some people are deeply tied to land (for example, the family farm), to nature, or to a transcendent reality. But for most of us, the connections that sustain us are to other people. In the full bloom of life, we are connected to others in many ways—through work, profession, neighborhood, country, shared faith and worship, common leisure pursuits, friendship. Even the guru meditating in isolation on his mountain top is connected to a long tradition of people united by the same religious quest.

But as we age or when we become chronically ill, connections with other people usually become much more restricted. Often, only ties with family and close friends remain and remain important to us. Moreover, for many of us, other connections just don't go deep enough. As Paul Tsongas has reminded us, "When it comes time to die, no one says, 'I wish I had spent more time at the office.'"

If I am correct, death is so difficult for us partly because our sense of community is so weak. Death seems to wipe out everything when we can't fit it into the lives of those who live on. A death motivated by the desire to spare the futures of my loved ones might well be a better death for me than the one I would get as a result of opting to continue my life as long as there is any pleasure in it for me. Pleasure is nice, but it is meaning that matters.

I don't know about others, but these reflections have helped me. I am now more at peace about facing a duty to die. Ending my life if my duty required might still be difficult. But for me, a far greater horror would be dying all alone or stealing the futures of my loved ones in order to buy a little more time for myself. I hope that if the time comes when I have a duty to die, I will recognize it, encourage my loved ones to recognize it too, and carry it out bravely.

Discussion Questions

1. Did Hardwig convince you that there is, at least under some circumstances, a duty to die? Explain.

2. Under what sorts of conditions (if any) do you believe you would be morally obligated to end your own life?

3. If you were to find yourself suffering from a terminal disease, how many other people would be affected by your misfortune? How does your answer relate to what Hardwig calls "the individualistic fantasy"?

4. At one point Hardwig asks the following question: Which of the following would be a greater burden to bear: (a) To lose a 50 percent chance of six more months of life at age 87? (b) To lose all your savings, your home, and your career at age 55? He claims that most of us would agree that (b) is the greater burden. Do you agree? How can one go about rationally weighing the burdens in such cases?

Richard B. Brandt, The Morality and Rationality of Suicide

Richard B. Brandt's aim in the reading selection that follows is to identify the factors determining the morality and rationality of suicide. In particular, he tries to determine the conditions under which suicide is morally blameworthy, the value of arguments for and against suicide, and the moral obligations of others toward a person contemplating suicide.

According to Brandt, although one might identify reasons for concluding that there is always *some* moral obligation not to commit suicide, the decision to commit suicide may, in certain circumstances, be both rational and morally permissible. Traditional arguments against suicide under any conditions therefore fail. It would not follow, however, that if one desires to commit suicide, one should immediately go through with it. Brandt identifies the various factors that can cloud judgment concerning the rationality of committing suicide, and draws appropriate cautionary lessons from this. He concludes with some practical advice for those facing the difficult task of counseling someone contemplating suicide. Brandt's essay is especially useful for its balanced and insightful discussion of many complex factors interwoven in this issue.

Reading Questions

1. Explain Brandt's distinction between an action's being morally wrong and an action's being morally reprehensible. What would be an example of an action that is morally wrong but *not* morally reprehensible? Why does Brandt make this distinction? What purpose does it serve in his argument?

2. Brandt claims that the view that holds every form of suicide to be morally wrong is absurd and obviously false. How does his example of a pilot support his claim?

3. Why does Brandt discuss the importance for the person contemplating suicide of considering between alternative possible "future world-courses"? According to Brandt, when is a decision to commit suicide rational? How does he support this view? What obstacles to making a rational decision about suicide does Brandt discuss? What is his advice concerning the best way to deal with these obstacles?

4. According to Brandt, what is the moral obligation of other persons to those who are contemplating suicide? How does the state of mind of the person contemplating suicide affect the kind of help one should give?

The Morality and Rationality of Suicide

RICHARD B. BRANDT

From the point of view of contemporary philosophy, suicide raises the following distinct questions: whether a person who commits suicide (assuming that there is suicide if and only if there is intentional termination of one's own life) is morally blameworthy, reprehensible, sinful in all circumstances; whether suicide is objectively right or wrong, and in what circumstances it is right or wrong, from a moral point of view; and whether, or in which circumstances, suicide is the best or the rational thing to do from the point of view of the agent's personal welfare.

The Moral Blameworthiness of Suicide

In former times the question of whether suicide is sinful was of great interest because the answer to it was considered relevant to how the agent would spend eternity. At present the practical issue is not as great, although a normal funeral service may be denied a person judged to have committed suicide sinfully. The chief practical issue now seems to be that persons may disapprove of a decedent for having committed suicide, and his friends or relatives may wish to defend his memory against moral charges.

The question of whether an act of suicide was sinful or morally blameworthy is not apt to arise unless it is already believed that the agent morally ought not to have done it: for instance, if he really had very poor reason for doing so, and his act foreseeably had catastrophic consequences for his wife and children. But, even if a given suicide is morally wrong, it does not follow that it is morally reprehensible. For, while asserting that a given act of suicide was wrong, we may still think that the act was hardly morally blameworthy or sinful if, say, the agent was in a state of great emotional turmoil at the time. We might then say that, although what he did was wrong, his action is *excusable,* just as in the criminal law it may be decided that, although a person broke the law, he should not be punished because he was *not responsible,* that is, was temporarily insane, did what he did inadvertently, and so on.

The foregoing remarks assume that to be morally blameworthy (or sinful) on account of an act is one thing, and for the act to be wrong is another. But, if we say this, what after all does it *mean* to say that a person is morally blameworthy on account of an action? We cannot say there is agreement among philosophers on this matter, but I suggest the following account as being safe from serious objection: "X is morally blameworthy on account of an action A" may be taken to mean "X did A, and X would not have done A had not his character been in some respect below standard; and in view of this it is fitting or justified for X to have some disapproving attitudes including remorse toward himself, and for some other persons Y to have some disapproving attitudes toward X and to express them in behavior." . . .

In case the foregoing definition does not seem obviously correct, it is worthwhile pointing out that it is usually thought that an agent is not blameworthy or sinful for an action unless it is a *reflection on him;* the definition brings this fact out and makes clear why.

If someone charges that a suicide was sinful, we may now properly ask, "What defect of character did it show?" Some writers have claimed that suicide is blameworthy because it is *cowardly;* and since being cowardly is generally conceded to be a defect of character, if an act of suicide is admitted to be both objectively wrong and also cowardly, the claim to blameworthiness might be warranted in terms of the above definition. Of course, many people would hesitate to call taking one's own life a cowardly act, and there will certainly be controversy about which acts are cowardly and which are not. But at least we can see part of what has to be done to make a charge of blameworthiness valid.

The most interesting question is the general one: which types of suicide in general are ones that, even if objectively wrong (in a sense to be explained below), are not sinful or blameworthy? Or, in other words, when is a suicide *morally excused* even if it is objectively wrong? We can at least identify some types that are morally excusable.

1. Suppose I *think* I am morally bound to commit suicide because I have a terminal illness and continued medical care will ruin my family financially. Suppose, however, that I am mistaken in this belief, and that suicide in such circumstances is not right. But surely I am not morally blameworthy; for I may be doing, out of a sense of duty to my family, what I would personally prefer not to do and is hard for me to do. What defect of character might my action show? Suicide from a genuine sense of duty is not blameworthy, even when the moral conviction in question is mistaken.

2. Suppose that I commit suicide when I am temporarily of unsound mind, either in the sense of the M'Naghten rule that I do not know that what I am doing is wrong, or of the Durham rule that, owing to a mental defect, I am substantially unable to do what is right. Surely, any suicide in an unsound state of mind is morally excused.

3. Suppose I commit suicide when I could not be said to be temporarily of unsound mind, but simply because I am not myself. For instance, I may be in an extremely depressed mood. Now a person may be in a very depressed mood, and commit suicide on account of being in that mood, when there is nothing the matter with his character—or, in other words, his character is not in any relevant way below standard. What are other examples of being "not myself," of emotional states that might be responsible for a person's committing suicide, and that might render the suicide excusable even if wrong? Being

frightened; being distraught; being in almost any highly emotional frame of mind (anger, frustration, disappointment in love); perhaps just being terribly fatigued.

So there are at least three types of suicide which can be morally excused even if they are objectively wrong. The main point is this: Mr. X may commit suicide and it may be conceded that he ought not to have done so, but it is another step to show that he is sinful, or morally blameworthy, for having done so. To make out that further point, it must be shown that his act is attributable to some substandard trait of character. So, Mrs. X after the suicide can concede that her husband ought not to have done what he did, but she can also point out that it is no reflection on his character. The distinction, unfortunately, is often overlooked. St. Thomas Aquinas, who recognizes the distinction in other places, seems blind to it in his discussion of suicide.

The Moral Reasons for and Against Suicide

Persons who say suicide is morally wrong must be asked which of two positions they are affirming: Are they saying that *every* act of suicide is wrong, *everything considered;* or are they merely saying that there is always *some* moral obligation—doubtless of serious weight—not to commit suicide, so that very often suicide is wrong, although it is possible that there are *countervailing considerations* which in particular situations make it right or even a moral duty? It is quite evident that the first position is absurd; only the second has a chance of being defensible.

In order to make clear what is wrong with the first view, we may begin with an example. Suppose an army pilot's single-seater plane goes out of control over a heavily populated area; he has the choice of staying in the plane and bringing it down where it will do little damage but at the cost of certain death for himself, and of bailing out and letting the plane fall where it will, very possibly killing a good many civilians. Suppose he chooses to do the former, and so, by our definition, commits suicide. Does anyone want to say that his action is morally wrong? Even Immanuel Kant, who opposed suicide in all circumstances, apparently would not wish to say that it is; he would, in fact, judge that this act is not one of suicide, for he says, "It is no suicide to risk one's life against one's enemies, and even to sacrifice it, in order to preserve one's duties towards oneself." St. Thomas Aquinas, in his discussion of suicide, may

seem to take the position that such an act would be wrong, for he says, "It is altogether unlawful to kill oneself," admitting as an exception only the case of being under special command of God. But I believe St. Thomas would, in fact, have concluded that the act is right because the basic intention of the pilot was to save the lives of civilians, and whether an act is right or wrong is a matter of basic intention.

In general, we have to admit that there are things with some moral obligation to avoid which, on account of other morally relevant considerations, it is sometimes right or even morally obligatory to do. There may be some obligation to tell the truth on every occasion, but surely in many cases the consequences of telling the truth would be so dire that one is obligated to lie. The same goes for promises. There is some moral obligation to do what one has promised (with a few exceptions); but, if one can keep a trivial promise only at serious cost to another person (i.e., keep an appointment only by failing to give aid to someone injured in an accident), it is surely obligatory to break the promise.

The most that the moral critic of suicide could hold, then, is that there is *some* moral obligation not to do what one knows will cause one's death; but he surely cannot deny that circumstances exist in which there are obligations to do things which, in fact, will result in one's death. If so, then in principle it would be possible to argue, for instance, that in order to meet my obligation to my family, it might be right for me to take my own life as the only way to avoid catastrophic hospital expenses in a terminal illness. Possibly the main point that critics of suicide on moral grounds would wish to make is that it is never right to take one's own life *for reasons of one's own personal welfare,* of any kind whatsoever. Some of the arguments used to support the immorality of suicide, however, are so framed that if they were supportable at all, they would prove that suicide is *never* moral.

One well-known type of argument against suicide may be classified as *theological.* St. Augustine and others urged that the Sixth Commandment ("Thou shalt not kill") prohibits suicide, and that we are bound to obey a divine commandment. To this reasoning one might first reply that it is arbitrary exegesis of the Sixth Commandment to assert that it was intended to prohibit suicide. The second reply is that if there is not some consideration which shows on the merits of the case that suicide is morally wrong, God has no business prohibiting it. It is true that some will object to this point, and I must refer them elsewhere for my detailed comments on the divine-will theory of morality.

Another theological argument with wide support was accepted by John Locke, who wrote: "Men being all the workmanship of one omnipotent and infinitely wise Maker; all the servants of one sovereign Master, sent into the world by His order and about His business; they are His property, whose workmanship they are made to last during His, not one another's pleasure. Every one . . . is bound to preserve himself, and not to quit his station willfully." And Kant: "We have been placed in this world under certain conditions and for specific purposes. But a suicide opposes the purpose of his Creator; he arrives in the other world as one who has deserted his post; he must be looked upon as a rebel against God. So long as we remember the truth that it is God's intention to preserve life, we are bound to regulate our activities in conformity with it. This duty is upon us until the time comes when God expressly commands us to leave this life. Human beings are sentinels on earth and may not leave their posts until relieved by another beneficent hand." Unfortunately, however, even if we grant that it is the duty of human beings to do what God commands or intends them to do, more argument is required to show that God does *not* permit human beings to quit this life when their own personal welfare would be maximized by so doing. How does one draw the requisite inference about the intentions of God? The difficulties and contradictions in arguments to reach such a conclusion are discussed at length and perspicaciously by David Hume in his essay "On Suicide," and in view of the unlikelihood that readers will need to be persuaded about these, I shall merely refer those interested to that essay.

A second group of arguments may be classed as arguments *from natural law*. St. Thomas says: "It is altogether unlawful to kill oneself, for three reasons. First, because everything naturally loves itself, the result being that everything naturally keeps itself in being, and resists corruptions so far as it can. Wherefore suicide is contrary to the inclination of nature, and to charity whereby every man should love himself. Hence suicide is always a mortal sin, as being contrary to the natural law and to charity." Here St. Thomas ignores two obvious points. First, it is not obvious why a human being is morally bound to do what he or she has some inclination to do. (St. Thomas did not criticize chastity.) Second, while it is true that most human beings do feel a strong urge to live, the human being who commits suicide obviously feels a stronger inclination to do something else. It is as natural for a human being to dislike, and to take steps to avoid, say, great pain, as it is to cling to life.

A somewhat similar argument by Immanuel Kant may seem better. In a famous passage Kant writes that the maxim of a person who commits suicide is "From self-love I make it my principle to shorten my life if its continuance threatens more evil than it promises pleasure. The only further question to ask is whether this principle of self-love can become a universal law of nature. It is then seen at once that a system of nature by whose law the very same feeling whose function is to stimulate the furtherance of life should actually destroy life would contradict itself and consequently would not subsist as a system of nature. Hence this maxim cannot possibly hold as a universal law of nature and is therefore entirely opposed to the supreme principle of all duty." What Kant finds contradictory is that the motive of self-love (interest in one's own long-range welfare) should sometimes lead one to struggle to preserve one's life, but at other times to end it. But where is the contradiction? One's circumstances change, and, if the argument of the following section in this chapter is correct, one sometimes maximizes one's own long-range welfare by trying to stay alive, but at other times by bringing about one's demise.

A third group of arguments, a form of which goes back at least to Aristotle, has a more modern and convincing ring. These are arguments to show that, in one way or another, a suicide necessarily does harm to other persons, or to society at large. Aristotle says that the suicide treats the *state* unjustly. Partly following Aristotle, St. Thomas says: "Every man is part of the community, and so, as such, he belongs to the community. Hence by killing himself he injures the community." Blackstone held that a suicide is an offense against the king "who hath an interest in the preservation of all his subjects," perhaps following Judge Brown in 1563, who argued that suicide cost the king a subject—"he being the head has lost one of his mystical members." The premise of such arguments is, as Hume pointed out, obviously mistaken in many instances. It is true that Freud would perhaps have injured society had he, instead of finishing his last book, committed suicide to escape the pain of throat cancer. But surely there have been many suicides whose demise was not a noticeable loss to society; an honest man could only say that in some instances society was better off without them.

It need not be denied that suicide is often injurious to other persons, especially the family of a suicide. Clearly it sometimes is. But, we should notice what this fact establishes. Suppose we admit, as generally would be done, that there is some obligation not to perform any action which will probably or certainly be injurious to other people, the strength of the obligation being dependent on various factors, notably the seriousness of the expected injury. Then there is *some* obligation not to commit suicide, when that act would probably or certainly be injurious to other people. But, as we have already seen, many cases of *some* obligation to do something nevertheless are *not* cases of a duty to do that thing, *everything considered.* So it could sometimes be morally justified to commit suicide, even if the act will harm someone. Must a man with a terminal illness undergo excruciating pain because his death will cause his wife sorrow—when she will be caused sorrow a month later anyway, when he is dead of natural causes? Moreover, to repeat, the fact that an individual has some obligation not to commit suicide when that act will probably injure other persons does not imply that, everything considered, it is wrong for him to do it, namely, that in all circumstances suicide *as such* is something there is some obligation to avoid.

Is there any sound argument, convincing to the modern mind, to establish that there is (or is not) *some moral obligation* to avoid suicide *as such,* an obligation, of course, which might be overridden by other obligations in some or many cases? (Captain Oates may have had a moral obligation to commit suicide as such, but his obligation not to stand in the way of his comrades getting to safety might have been so strong that, everything considered, he was justified in leaving the polar camp and allowing himself to freeze to death.)

To present all the arguments necessary to answer this question convincingly would take a great deal of space. I shall, therefore, simply state one answer to it which seems plausible to some contemporary philosophers. Suppose it could be shown that it would maximize the long-run welfare of everybody affected if people were taught that there is a moral obligation to avoid suicide—so that people would be motivated to avoid suicide just because they thought it wrong (would have anticipatory guilt feelings at the very idea), and so that other people would be inclined to disapprove of persons who commit suicide unless there were some excuse (such as those mentioned in the first section). One might ask: how could it maximize utility to mold the conceptual and motivational structure of persons in this way? To which the answer might be: feeling in this way might make persons who are impulsively inclined to commit suicide in a bad mood, or a fit of anger or jealousy, take more time to deliberate; hence, some suicides that have bad effects generally might be prevented. In other words, it might be a good thing in its effects for people to feel about suicide in the way they feel about breach of promise or injuring others, just as it might be a good thing for people to feel a moral obligation not to smoke, or to wear seat belts. However, it might be that negative moral feelings about suicide as such would stand in the way of action by those persons whose welfare really is best served by suicide and whose suicide is the best thing for everybody concerned.

When a Decision to Commit Suicide Is Rational from the Person's Point of View

The person who is contemplating suicide is obviously making a choice between future world-courses: the world-course that includes his demise, say, an hour from now, and several possible ones that contain his demise at a later point. One cannot have precise knowledge about many features of the latter group of world-courses, but it is certain that they will all end with death some (possibly short) finite time from now.

Why do I say the choice is between *world*-courses and not just a choice between future life-courses of the prospective suicide, the one shorter than the other? The reason is that one's suicide has some impact on the world (and one's continued life has some impact on the world), and that conditions in the rest of the world will often make a difference in one's evaluation of the possibilities. One *is* interested in things in the world other than just oneself and one's own happiness.

The basic question a person must answer, in order to determine which world-course is best or rational for him to choose, is which he *would* choose under conditions of optimal use of information, when *all* of his desires are taken into account. It is not just a question of what we prefer *now,* with some clarification of all the possibilities being considered. Our preferences change, and the preferences of tomorrow (assuming we can know something about them) are just as legitimately taken into account in deciding what to do now as the preferences of today. Since any reason that can be given today for weighting heavily today's preference can be given tomorrow for weighting heavily tomorrow's preference, the preferences of any time-stretch have a rational claim to an equal vote. Now the importance of that fact is this: we often know quite well that our desires, aversions, and preferences may change after a short while. When a person is in a state of despair—perhaps brought about by a rejection in love or discharge from a long-held position—nothing but the thing he cannot have seems desirable; everything else is turned to ashes. Yet we know quite well that the passage of time is likely to reverse all this; replacements may be found or other types of things that are available to us may begin to look attractive. So, if we were to act on the preferences of today alone, when the emotion of despair seems more than we can stand, we might find death preferable to life; but, if we allow for the preferences of the weeks and years ahead, when many goals will be enjoyable and attractive, we might find life much preferable to death. So, if a choice of what is best is to be determined by what we want not only now but later (and later desires on an equal basis with the present ones)—as it should be—then what is the best or preferable world-course will often be quite different from what it would be if the choice, or what is best for one, were fixed by one's desires and preferences now.

Of course, if one commits suicide there are no future desires or aversions that may be compared with present ones and that should be allowed an equal vote in deciding what is best. In that respect the course of action that results in death is different from any other course of action we may undertake. I do not wish to suggest the rosy possibility that it is often or always reasonable to believe that next week "I shall be more interested in living than I am today, if today I take a dim view of continued existence." On the contrary, when a person is seriously ill, for instance, he may have no reason to think that the preference-order will be reversed—it may be that tomorrow he will prefer death to life more strongly.

The argument is often used that one can never be *certain* what is going to happen, and hence one is never rationally justified in doing anything as drastic as committing suicide. But we always have to live by probabilities and make our estimates as best we can. As soon as it is clear beyond reasonable doubt not only that death is now preferable to life, but also that it will be every day from now until the end, the rational thing is to act promptly.

Let us not pursue the question of whether it is rational for a person with a painful terminal illness to commit suicide; it is. However, the issue seldom arises, and few terminally ill patients do commit suicide. With such patients matters usually get worse slowly so that no particular time seems to call for action. They are often so heavily sedated that it is impossible for the mental processes of decision leading to action to occur; or else they are incapacitated in a hospital and the very physical possibility of ending their lives is not available. Let us leave this grim topic and turn to a practically more important problem: whether it is rational for persons to commit suicide for some reason other than painful terminal physical

illness. Most persons who commit suicide do so, apparently, because they face a nonphysical problem that depresses them beyond their ability to bear.

Among the problems that have been regarded as good and sufficient reasons for ending life, we find (in addition to serious illness) the following: some event that has made a person feel ashamed or lose his prestige and status; reduction from affluence to poverty; the loss of a limb or of physical beauty; the loss of sexual capacity; some event that makes it seem impossible to achieve things by which one sets store; loss of a loved one; disappointment in love; the infirmities of increasing age. It is not to be denied that such things can be serious blows to a person's prospects of happiness.

Whatever the nature of an individual's problem, there are various plain errors to be avoided—errors to which a person is especially prone when he is depressed—in deciding whether, everything considered, he prefers a world-course containing his early demise to one in which his life continues to its natural terminus. Let us forget for a moment the relevance to the decision of preferences that he may have tomorrow, and concentrate on some errors that may infect his preference as of today, and for which correction or allowance must be made.

In the first place, depression, like any severe emotional experience, tends to primitivize one's intellectual processes. It restricts the range of one's survey of the possibilities. One thing that a rational person would do is compare the world-course containing his suicide with his *best* alternative. But his best alternative is precisely a possibility he may overlook if, in a depressed mood, he thinks only of how badly off he is and cannot imagine any way of improving his situation. If a person is disappointed in love, it is possible to adopt a vigorous plan of action that carries a good chance of acquainting him with someone he likes at least as well; and if old age prevents a person from continuing the tennis game with his favorite partner, it is possible to learn some other game that provides the joys of competition without the physical demands.

Depression has another insidious influence on one's planning; it seriously affects one's judgment about probabilities. A person disappointed in love is very likely to take a dim view of himself, his prospects, and his attractiveness; he thinks that because he has been rejected by one person he will probably be rejected by anyone who looks desirable to him. In a less gloomy frame of mind he would make different estimates. Part of the reason for such gloomy probability estimates is that depression tends to repress one's memory of evidence that supports a nongloomy prediction. Thus, a rejected lover tends to forget any cases in which he has elicited enthusiastic response from ladies in relation to whom he has been the one who has done the rejecting. Thus his pessimistic self-image is based upon a highly selected, and pessimistically selected, set of data. Even when he is reminded of the data, moreover, he is apt to resist an optimistic inference.

Another kind of distortion of the look of future prospects is not a result of depression, but is quite normal. Events distant in the future feel small, just as objects distant in space look small. Their prospect does not have the effect on motivational processes that it would have if it were of an event in the immediate future. Psychologists call this the "goal-gradient" phenomenon; a rat, for instance, will run faster toward a perceived food box than a distant unseen one. In the case of a person who has suffered some misfortune, and whose situation now is an unpleasant one, this reduction of the motivational influence of events distant in time has the effect that present unpleasant states weigh far more heavily than probable future pleasant ones in any choice of world-courses.

If we are trying to determine whether we now prefer, or shall later prefer, the outcome of one world-course to that of another (and this is leaving aside the questions of the weight of the votes of preferences at a later date), we must take into account these and other infirmities of our "sensing" machinery. Since knowing that the machinery is out of order will not tell us what results it would give if it were working, the best recourse might be to refrain from making any decision in a stressful frame of mind. If decisions have to be made, one must recall past reactions, in a normal frame of mind, to outcomes like those under assessment. But many suicides seem to occur in moments of despair. What should be clear from the above is that a moment of despair, if one is seriously contemplating suicide, ought to be a moment of reassessment of one's goals and values, a reassessment which the individual must realize is very difficult to make objectively, because of the very quality of his depressed frame of mind.

A decision to commit suicide may in certain circumstances be a rational one. But a person who wants to act rationally must take into account the various possible "errors" and make appropriate rectification of his initial evaluations.

The Role of Other Persons

What is the moral obligation of other persons toward those who are contemplating suicide? The question of their moral blameworthiness may be ignored and what is rational for them to do from the point of view of personal welfare may be considered as being of secondary concern. Laws make it dangerous to aid or encourage a suicide. The risk of running afoul of the law may partly determine moral obligation, since moral obligation to do something may be reduced by the fact that it is personally dangerous.

The moral obligation of other persons toward one who is contemplating suicide is an instance of a general obligation to render aid to those in serious distress, at least when this can be done at no great cost to one's self. I do not think this general principle is seriously questioned by anyone, whatever his moral theory; so I feel free to assume it as a premise. Obviously the person contemplating suicide is in great distress of some sort; if he were not, he would not be seriously considering terminating his life.

How great a person's obligation is to one in distress depends on a number of factors. Obviously family and friends have special obligations to devote time to helping the prospective suicide—which others do not have. But anyone in this kind of distress has a moral claim on the time of any person who knows the situation (unless there are others more responsible who are already doing what should be done).

What is the obligation? It depends, of course, on the situation, and how much the second person knows about the situation. If the individual has decided to terminate his life if he can, and it is clear that he is right in this decision, then, if he needs help in executing the decision, there is a moral obligation to give him help. On this matter a patient's physician has a special obligation, from which any talk about the Hippocratic oath does not absolve him. It is true that there are some damages one cannot be expected to absorb, and some risks which one cannot be expected to take, on account of the obligation to render aid.

On the other hand, if it is clear that the individual should not commit suicide, from the point of view of his own welfare, or if there is a presumption that he should not (when the only evidence is that a person is discovered unconscious, with the gas turned on), it would seem to be the individual's obligation to intervene, prevent the successful execution of the decision, and see to the availability of competent psychiatric advice and temporary hospitalization, if necessary. Whether one has a right to take such steps when a clearly sane person, after careful reflection over a period of time, comes to the conclusion that an end to his life is what is best for him and what he wants, is very doubtful, even when one thinks his conclusion a mistaken one; it would seem that a man's own considered decision about whether he wants to live must command respect, although one must concede that this could be debated.

The more interesting role in which a person may be cast, however, is that of advisor. It is often important to one who is contemplating suicide to go over his thinking with another, and to feel that a conclusion, one way or the other, has the support of a respected mind. One thing one can obviously do, in rendering the service of advice, is to discuss with the person the various types of issues discussed above, made more specific by the concrete circumstances of his case, and help him find whether, in view, say, of the damage his suicide would do to others, he has a moral obligation to refrain, and whether it is rational or best for him, from the point of view of his own welfare, to take this step or adopt some other plan instead.

To get a person to see what is the rational thing to do is no small job. Even to get a person, in a frame of mind when he is seriously contemplating (or perhaps has already unsuccessfully attempted) suicide, to rec-ognize a plain truth of fact may be a major operation. If a man insists, "I am a complete failure," when it is obvious that by any reasonable standard he is far from that, it may be tremendously difficult to get him to see the fact. But there is another job beyond that of getting a person to see what is the rational thing to do; that is to help him *act* rationally, or *be* rational, when he has conceded what would be the rational thing.

How either of these tasks may be accomplished effectively may be discussed more competently by an experienced psychiatrist than by a philosopher. Loneliness and the absence of human affection are states which exacerbate any other problems; disappointment, reduction to poverty, and so forth, seem less impossible to bear in the presence of the affection of another. Hence simply to be a friend, or to find someone a friend, may be the largest contribution one can make either to helping a person be rational or see clearly what is rational for him to do; this service may make one who was contemplating suicide feel that there is a future for him which it is possible to face.

Discussion and Reflection Questions

1. Brandt gives three examples of an action's being morally wrong and that action's being morally reprehensible. He takes it for granted that in each of the cases he describes, the action taken (i.e., suicide) *is* morally wrong. Do you agree? How might one argue for the claim that if an action is not morally reprehensible, it should therefore not be considered morally wrong either? What would be the implication of such an argument?

2. Brandt considers, and attempts to refute, various arguments against suicide based on theology, on natural law, and on the obligation not to harm others. Do you find his responses to these arguments persuasive? Has he overlooked any arguments against suicide that would make it always impermissible?

3. Given the various factors that Brandt mentions that can cloud a person's judgment when he or she is contemplating suicide, is it reasonable to believe that a person contemplating suicide can ever make a rational decision to end his or her life? Given an answer to the foregoing question, what policy ought one to adopt toward the prevention of suicide, either of oneself or of another?

4. Suppose that an acquaintance, friend, or relative told you that they were thinking about committing suicide. What would you do? Would you attempt to talk them out if it? If they convinced you that they were rational and that it was in their best interests, all things considered, to end their life, and asked for your assistance in doing so, what would you do?

Carl B. Becker, Buddhist Views of Suicide and Euthanasia

In the reading selection that follows, Carl B. Becker is concerned with the current state of thinking about bioethical issues, especially suicide and euthanasia, in Japan. He compares traditional Japanese thought with contemporary Japanese thought on suicide and euthanasia and then contrasts both with the Buddhist perspective on these issues. He finds the Buddhist perspective to be vastly superior to other views popular in Japan. He grounds his defense of Buddhist perspectives on suicide and euthanasia by examining first the attitude of the Buddha to voluntary death, and then Buddhist-influenced thought in later Japanese tradition, such as samurai customs. Central to this tradition is the importance placed on death with dignity. People should be allowed complete responsibility for their own deaths. This may involve selecting the place, means, and timing of ending one's own life. Because death represents passing on to another state of existence, determined in part by the person's state of mind at the moment of death, cultivating the proper state of mind at death is seen as all-important, and every effort should be made to insure that one dies with the right thoughts. Becker believes that adoption of this Buddhist perspective will lead bioethics in a more humanitarian direction.

Reading Questions

1. According to Becker, what is the basis for the widespread Japanese rejection of brain-death criteria for death? What problems does he find with this view? How might this rejection of brain-death criteria be grounded in a Buddhist view of life and death?

2. How have Confucian ideas influenced Japanese views and practices concerning organ transplantation, autopsies, and burial? According to Becker, has this been a positive influence?

3. Explain Becker's distinction between "bodies of value to others" and "subjects of value to themselves." What is the significance of this distinction for attitudes toward suicide and euthanasia?

4. What is the Buddhist attitude toward suicide? Under what conditions did the Buddha condone suicide? Is being terminally ill a sufficient justification for committing suicide?

Buddhist Views of Suicide and Euthanasia

CARL B. BECKER

Bioethics and Brain Death: The Recent Discussion in Japan

Japanese scholars of ethics and religions have been slow to come to grips with issues of bioethics, suicide, and death with dignity. Although the practical problems are frequently addressed in the popular press, and scattered citizen groups are beginning to draw at-

tention to the issues, few people outside of the medical community have seriously addressed these issues. As one recent representative example of this situation, consider the 39th annual meeting of the Japan Ethics Association (the academic association of ethicists from the entire country) held at Waseda University in October of 1988. The title of the annual meeting, in

Carl B. Becker, "Buddhist Views of Suicide and Euthanasia," Philosophy East & West, *vol. 40 (1990), pp. 543–556. Reprinted by permission of* Philosophy East & West.

deference to the late Emperor's ailing condition and the growing urgency of bioethical issues, was "Life and Ethics." Ostensibly, this was a chance to further the discussion among medical, religious, and philosophical ethicists on topics such as euthanasia and death with dignity. In fact, more than half of the presentations discussed classical views of life, such as those of Hippocrates, Confucius, Vico, Kant, Nietzsche, and so forth. The periods planned for open discussion were entirely usurped by the panelists' overtime reading of such papers. To their credit, however, there were a few Japanese scholars who boldly attempted to establish some more-Japanese views on the topics in bioethics, particularly euthanasia and death with dignity. While not without their problems, these presentations displayed less a Buddhist than a popular Japanese approach to the issue. The majority agreed with Anzai Kazuhiro's early presentation that brain death should not be equated with human death. Anzai's reasoning runs as follows: If brain death implies human death, then, by contraposition, human life must imply conscious (brain) life. Now there are clearly segments of our lives in which we are alive but not always conscious. Therefore it is wrong to conclude that a human is dead because he or she lacks consciousness. Of course, this argument can be faulted for collapsing conscious life and brain life, and for failing to distinguish periods of unconsciousness with the expectation of future revival (like deep sleep) from periods of unconsciousness with no expectation of future revival (like irreversible coma). But it is representative of a widely seen Japanese rejection of brain-death criteria.

This rejection comes partly from the Japanese association of brain-death criteria with organ transplantation. Many Japanese continue to manifest a distaste for organ transplantation, a distaste which dates back to Confucian teachings that the body, a gift from heaven and from one's parents, must be buried whole, and never cut. For this reason, dissections and autopsies were late in coming to Japan, not widely permitted until the nineteenth century. The modern Japanese practices of universal cremation, of surgical operations, and of flying to other countries to have organ transplants all have superseded the old Confucian prejudice against body-cutting. However, there remains a fear that if brain-death criteria were widely accepted, less conservative elements of society might abuse it for the sake of the "distasteful" practice of organ transplantation.

In his keynote address about Buddhist ethics, Tsukuba Professor Shinjō Kawasaki implied that this rejection of brain-death criteria may also be grounded

in a Buddhist view of life and death. He cited the *Visuddhimagga*, which indicates that life energy (*ayus*) is supported by body warmth and conscious faculties (broadly interpretable to include reflexes). If either body heat or reflexes remain, then a person cannot be considered dead. Now Buddhism admits situations (such as meditative trances or hypothermia) in which neither body warmth nor reflexes are externally detectable, but the subject is not yet dead. So lack of warmth and reflexes is a necessary but not sufficient indicator of death; if either persists, it can be said that the body is not yet dead. In other words, Buddhism does not equate life with warmth and reflexes, but holds that body heat and reflexes are the "supports" of life, and therefore life cannot be empirically measurable except through such variables. Kawasaki also reaffirms the widespread Japanese Buddhist view that death is not the end of life, but merely a brief transition to another state, commonly thought to last for forty-nine days, intermediate between life in this body and life in the next. The reluctance to dismiss a body as "dead" prior to its loss of warmth and reflexes is not based on a fear of personal extinction or annihilation, but rather on a Buddhist view of the basic components of the life system.

Chiba's Iida Tsunesuke expands this view by arguing that "persons are not merely the meaningless 'subjects of rights,' but personalities, 'faces' embodying the possibilities of fulfilling the dreams of their parents or loved ones . . . recipients of love, and therefore worthy of honoring." This argument begs the question of "possibilities," since in the case of brain-dead victims, it is precisely such possibilities which are missing. Logically speaking, the "possibilities" argument has long ago been laid to rest by philosophers like Mary Anne Warren, who have demonstrated that we need not treat potential presidents as presidents, potential criminals as criminals, or potential humans as humans. (Japanese society might differ in this respect; until recently, suspicion of crime or likelihood of committing crime were sufficient grounds for arrest, and children of nobles [potential lords] were often honored or killed as real lords.)

However, Iida's argument is important less for its logical persuasion than for its revelation of the Japanese attitude: that persons are not subjects with rights and individual free wills, but rather objects of the attentions of others. (Japanese treatment of infants and children reinforces this view that Japanese children are seen not as persons but as possessions of their parents; this was the legal as well as philosophical status of women and servants as well as children prior to the twentieth century.)

This position is further developed by Ohara Nobuo, who argues that "although a body may be treated as a 'thing' or a corpse by physicians, it remains a body of value and meaning, and in that sense, a *person,* to members of its family. . . . In this sense, even vegetative humans and brain-dead corpses can give joy to other people." Of course this point of view is pregnant with problems which Ohara himself seems loath to acknowledge. Only in the most metaphorical of senses can a corpse "give" anything to anyone; rather, it is the family who may *derive* some sense of joy by beholding the face of one dear to them, even though that person is incapable of ever being conscious in that body again.

This attitude is akin to the Japanese reverence for pictures, sculptures, and myths; it provides no useful guidelines whatsoever to the medical faculty as to when to continue or desist from what kinds of treatment for the patient. To the question "When does a body stop being a person?" the Oharan answer, "It never stops being a person to those who love it," may be psychologically correct for some people, but is a dead end in medical ethics, for it fails to answer the question, "When should a body be treated not as a living person but as a dead body?"

Moreover, even if it were thought to have some utility in the case where relatives or "significant others" remain alive and concerned with the fate of the deceased, it values the person (or corpse) entirely in terms of his value *to others.* In cases where old people die alone and uncared for, the absence of concerned others leaves the medical practitioner utterly without guidelines. (This is consistent with the frequently noted proposition that Japanese without social contexts seem morally at a loss.)

This position also presumes a wishful naiveté on the part of the parent or family, a failure to distinguish between a living human with a potential for interaction and a dead body with only the resemblance of a loved one. This may not bother many Japanese parents, for whom children are indeed "objects." In fact, there are "rehabilitation hospitals" in Japan in which anencephalic infants are cared for and raised for as many years as their parents' finances and interest dictate; they are propped up and made to "greet" their parents whenever the parents desire to visit.

Such unwillingness to admit the finality of death or the fundamental suffering of the human condition runs counter to the basic tenets of Buddhism. We are reminded of the famous story of the woman who asked the Buddha to revive her baby. In response, the Buddha instructed her to ask for food from any house in which no one had died. In the process of asking around the entire village, the woman came to realize that all humans must die and deal with death. In this way she gained enlightenment, stopped grieving for her dead child, and became a follower of the Buddha. The relatives who refuse to pronounce dead a relative as long as he has a "face," or the parents who insist on artificially prolonging the appearance of life of an anencephalic infant, cannot claim to understand Buddhism.

A much larger misunderstanding lurks behind the whole discussion between "brain-death advocates" and "brain-death opposers" in Japan. The real issue is not whether or not every body should immediately be scavenged for spare parts as soon as its brain is isoelectric, as some opponents would purport. Rather, the question is whether it is ever acceptable to desist from treatment after brain death (turning the hospital's valuable and limited resources to other waiting patients). In the absence of brain-death criteria, many otherwise hopeless bodies remain on artificial support systems almost indefinitely. Even if brain-death criteria were accepted, nothing would prevent families from finding hospitals which would preserve the bodies of their beloved on artificial support systems indefinitely, nor would anything require organ donation if the patient and family did not desire it. Thus the issue, like that of suicide and euthanasia, is not "Should everyone be forced to follow these criteria?" but rather "May people who desire it be allowed to follow these criteria?" Groundless fears of widespread organ sales or piracy have made this issue into a much greater hobgoblin than it ever needed to become.

This is not merely to criticize the recently voiced positions of Japanese ethicists. Rather, I introduce this body of evidence to demonstrate the slow growth of Japanese thought in bioethics, and particularly their concerns with *bodies of value to others* rather than with *subjects of value to themselves.* This concern finds no support either in Japanese Buddhism or in samurai teaching, but on the level of popular belief, it may have serious ramifications for Japanese bioethics for many generations to come.

The World Federation of the Right to Die Society held an International Conference in Nice (France) in 1984. Although many Japanese attended this conference, apparently none of them contributed to the West's understanding of Buddhist views of euthanasia. When the President of the Society published a book on world attitudes on euthanasia the following year, only 2 percent (2.5 out of 150 pages) was about Buddhist attitudes, and those ideas were gained from California Buddhists, not from Japanese Buddhists at Nice.

Buddhists have a big contribution to make to the humanization and naturalization of medicine and bioethics. I may not speak for all of Japanese Buddhism, but I shall be happy if this article inspires further dialogue and contributions from the Japanese Buddhist side.

Early Buddhist Views of Death, Suicide, and Euthanasia

Japan has long been more aware of and sensitive to the dying process than modern Western cultures. Moreover, Japan already has its own good philosophical and experiential background to deal effectively with "new" issues of bioethics, such as euthanasia. Japanese Buddhists have long recognized what Westerners are only recently rediscovering: that the manner of dying at the moment of death is very important. This fundamental premise probably predates Buddhism itself, but is made very explicit in the teachings of the Buddha. In his meditations, the Buddha noticed that even people with good karma were sometimes born into bad situations, and even those with bad karma sometimes found inordinately pleasant rebirths. Buddha declared that the crucial variable governing rebirth was the nature of the consciousness at the moment of death. Thereafter, Buddhists placed high importance on holding the proper thoughts at the moment of death. Many examples of this idea can be found in two works of the Theravāda canon, the *Petavatthu* and the *Vimānavatthu* ("Stories of the Departed"). Indeed, in many sutras, monks visit laymen on their deathbeds to ensure that their dying thoughts are wholesome, and the Buddha recommends that lay followers similarly encourage each other on such occasions.

Buddhism sees death as not the end of life, but simply a transition; suicide is therefore no escape from anything. Thus, in the early *saṅgha* (community of followers of the Buddha), suicide was in principle condemned as an inappropriate action. But the early Buddhist texts include many cases of suicide which the Buddha himself accepted or condoned. For example, the suicides of Vakkali and of Channa were committed in the face of painful and irreversible sickness. It is significant, however, that the Buddha's praise of the suicides is *not* based on the fact that they were in terminal states, but rather that their minds were selfless, desireless, and enlightened at the moments of their passing.

This theme is more dramatically visible in the example of Godhika. This disciple repeatedly achieved an advanced level of *samādhi*, bordering on *parinirvāṇa*, and then slipped out of the state of enlightenment into normal consciousness again. After this happened six times, Godhika at last vowed to pass on to the next realm while enlightened, and quietly committed suicide during his next period of enlightenment. While cautioning his other disciples against suicide, the Buddha nonetheless blessed and praised Godhika's steadiness of mind and purpose, and declared that he had passed on to *nirvāṇa*. In short, the acceptability of suicide, even in the early Buddhist community, depended not on terminal illness alone, but upon the state of selfless equanimity with which one was able to pass away. It is interesting in passing that all these suicides were committed by the subject knifing himself, a technique which came to be standardized in later Japanese ritual suicide.

When asked about the morality of committing suicide to move on to the next world, the Buddha did not criticize it. He emphasized that only the uncraving mind would be able to move on toward *nirvāṇa*, and that, conversely, minds desiring to get free of or flee something by their death might achieve nothing. Similarly, there are stories in the Jātaka tales of the Buddha giving his own body (in former lives) to save other beings, both animals and humans. Thus death out of compassion for others is also lauded in the Scriptures. It is also well known that in the Jain tradition, saints were expected to fast until their deaths, and thereafter there have been those in both China and Japan who have followed this tradition.

In China, it is believed that a disciple of Zendō's jumped out of a tree in order to kill himself and reach the Pure Land. Zendō's response was not that the action of suicide was right or wrong in and of itself, but that the disciple who wanted so strongly to see the Pure Land was doubtless ready to reach it. Other more recent examples may be found in the Buddhist suicides of the Vietnamese monks protesting against the Vietnam government. Whether or not these stories are all historical fact is not at issue here. The point is that they demonstrate the consistent Buddhist position toward suicide: there is nothing intrinsically wrong with taking one's own life, if it is not done in hate, anger, or fear. Equanimity or preparedness of mind is the main issue.

In summary, Buddhism realizes that death is not the end of anything, but a transition. Buddhism has long recognized persons' rights to determine when they should move on from this existence to the next. The important consideration here is not whether the body lives or dies, but whether the mind can remain at peace and in harmony with itself. The Jōdo (Pure Land) tradition tends to stress the continuity of life, while the Zen tradition tends to stress the importance of the time and manner of dying. Both of these ideas are deeply rooted in the Japanese consciousness.

Religious Suicide and Death with Dignity in Japan

Japanese Buddhists demonstrated an unconcern with death even more than their neighbors. Japanese valued peace of mind and honor of life over length of life. While the samurai often committed suicide on the battlefield or in court to preserve their dignity in death, countless commoners chose to commit suicide in order to obtain a better future life in the Pure Land. On some occasions, whole masses of people committed suicide at the same time. In others, as in the situation depicted in Kurosawa's famous film *Red Beard*, a poverty-stricken family would commit suicide in order to escape unbearable suffering in this life and find a better life in the world to come. Often parents would kill their children first, and then kill themselves; this kind of *shinjū* can still be seen in Japan today. The issue for us today is: how does Buddhism appraise such suicide in order to gain heavenly rebirth?

On a popular level, the desire to "leave this dirty world and approach the Pure Land" *(Enri edo, gongu jōdo)* was fostered by wandering itinerant monks such as Kūya in the Heian period, and Ippen in the Kamakura period. The tradition of committing suicide by entering a river or west-facing seashore apparently began in the Kumano area, but rapidly spread throughout the nation along with the Pure Land faith upon which it was based. The common tradition was to enter the water with a rope tied around one's waist, held by one's retainers or horse. If one's nerve and single-minded resolution failed, then one would not achieve rebirth in the Pure Land as desired. In such an instance, either the suicide himself, or his retainers (judging from his countenance), might pull him out of the water and save him from dying with inappropriate thoughts. However, if the suicide retained a peaceful and unperturbed mind and countenance throughout the drowning, the retainers were to let him die in peace, and simply retain the body for funeral purposes. Such situations clearly demonstrate that what is at stake here is not the individual's right to die, but rather his ability to die with peace of mind. If death with a calm mind is possible, then it is not condemned.

A paradigmatic example of this situation can be found in the records of Saint Ippen. Ajisaka Nyūdō, a Pure Land aspirant possibly of noble descent, gave up his home and family to follow the teachings of Saint Ippen. For unclear reasons, Ippen refused him admission to his band of itinerant mendicants, but advised him that the only way to enter the Pure Land was to die holding the Nembutsu (name and figure of Amida) in mind. Nyūdō then committed suicide by drowning himself in the Fuji River.

The scene is vividly depicted in the scroll paintings. Here, Ajisaka is seen with a rope around his waist. His attendants on the shore hold one end of the rope. As he bobs above the current, he is seen perfectly preserving the gasshō position, at peace and in prayer. Music is heard from the purple clouds above him, a common sign of Ojō, or rebirth in the Pure Land.

When Ippen heard of this suicide, he praised Ajisaka's faith, interpreting the purple clouds and Ajisaka's unruffled demeanor as proof of his attainment of rebirth in the Pure Land. At the same time, he warned his other disciples, repeating Ajisaka's last words *(nagori o oshimuna)*, not to grieve over their master's passing.

When Ippen himself died, six of his disciples also committed suicide in sympathy, hoping to accompany their master to the Pure Land. This occasioned some debate about the propriety of "sympathy suicide." Shinkyō, Ippen's disciple and second patriarch of the Ji School, declared that the disciples had failed to obtain rebirth in the Pure Land, for their action was seen as "self-willed," and Pure Land faith relies entirely on the power and will of Amida Buddha. Assertion of self-will is seen as running counter to the reliance on other power demanded by the Amida faith.

Several important points can be learned from these examples. First, suicide is never condemned per se. Rather it is the state of mind which determines the rightness or wrongness of the suicide situation. The dividing line between choosing one's own time and place of death with perfectly assured peace of mind, and self-willing one's own death at the time of one's master's death is perhaps a thin gray one, but this should not obscure the criteria involved: death with desire leads not to rebirth in the Pure Land, but death with calm assurance does. Even the method of water suicide, using a rope as a preventive backup, stresses the importance of the state of mind in this action.

Secondly, Ajisaka's famous phrase, "Nagori o oshimuna," means that Buddhists are not to kill themselves in "sympathy" when others die. A literal translation would be that we are not to cling to what remains of the name or person, but to let the deceased go freely on to the next world. In other words, when someone dies with an assured state of mind, it is not for those who remain either to criticize or to wish that he had not died in this situation. Those who are left behind are to respect and not resent, reject, or grieve for a death which might seem to them untimely.

It is not coincidental that the word for euthanasia in Japanese is *anrakushi,* a term with Buddhist meanings. In Buddhist terminology, *anrakukoku* is another name for the Pure Land, the next world of Amida Bodhisattva, to which each Japanese expects to go after death. German-educated doctor and historical novelist Mori Ogai's famous book *Takasebune* specifically deals with *anrakushi;* it is the story of Yoshisuke killing his sickly young brother who wants to die but lacks the strength to kill himself. Many famous twentieth-century Japanese authors wrote of suicide, and some, such as Akutagawa, Dazai, Kawabata, and Mishima, actually committed suicide. Following the deaths of each emperor (Meiji, Taishō, and, last year, Shōwa), faithful retainers have also committed suicide in sympathy with their departed leaders. While some of these suicides are not Buddhistic (they show anger, pessimism, nihilism, and so forth), they are still reminders that the Japanese Buddhist worldview does not condemn suicide.

Japanese law does not criminalize suicide, and European law is slowly beginning to follow the Japanese model in this regard. However, Japanese law does hold it to be a crime to assist or encourage a suicide. In normal situations, this is only wise and prudent, for healthy people should be encouraged to live and make the most of their lives. But in the situations where *songenshi* (death with dignity) is requested, it is precisely because the person is facing imminent death that it is morally acceptable to assist his suicide, particularly if the motive is mercy.

Samurai, Seppuku, *and Euthanasia*

Among the warrior elite, who usually followed Zen Buddhism, suicide was considered an honorable alternative to being killed by others or continuing a life in shame or misery. Beginning with the famous *seppuku* of Minamoto no Tametomo and Minamoto no Yorimasa in 1170, *seppuku* became known as the way that a vanquished but proud Buddhist warrior would end his life. Soon thereafter, headed by Taira Noritsune and Tomomori, hundreds of Taira warriors and their families committed suicide in the battle of Dannoura of 1185. Famous suicides included that of Kusunoki Masashige in 1336, in the battle between Nitta and Hosokawa, and that of Hideyori Toyotomi, under siege by Tokugawa Ieyasu in 1615. In the Tokugawa period, love suicides were dramatized in a dozen plays by Chikamatsu Monzaemon, including *Sonezaki shinjū, Shinjū ten no Amijima,* and *Shinjū mannenso.* The forty-seven Akō rōnin, who committed suicide after avenging their master's death, was another famous true story, dramatized in the Chūshingura plays and films. The samurai's creed, to be willing to die at any moment, was dramatically spelled out by the *Hagakure.* According to the *Hagakure,* the important concern was not whether one lived or died, but (1) being pure, simple, single-minded, (2) taking full responsibility for doing one's duty, and (3) unconditionally serving one's master, without concern for oneself.

Although *seppuku* may seem like a violent death to the observer, it was designed to enable the samurai to die with the greatest dignity and peace.

It is particularly noteworthy that the samurai's code of suicide included a provision for euthanasia: the *kaishakunin* (attendant). Cutting of the *hara* alone was very painful, and would not lead to a swift death. After cutting their *hara,* few samurai had enough strength to cut their own necks or spines. Yet without cutting their necks, the pain of the opened *hara* would continue for minutes or even hours prior to death. Therefore, the samurai would make arrangements with one or more *kaishakunin* to assist his suicide. While the samurai steadied his mind and prepared to die in peace, the *kaishakunin* would wait by his side. If the samurai spoke to the *kaishakunin* before or during the *seppuku* ceremony, the standard response was *"go anshin"* (set your mind at peace). All of the interactions and conversations surrounding an officially ordered *seppuku* were also fixed by tradition, so that the suicide might die with the least tension and greatest peace of mind. After the samurai had finished cutting to the prearranged point, or gave some other signal, it was the duty of the *kaishakunin* to cut the neck of the samurai to terminate his pain by administering the coup de grâce.

Many samurai suicides were in fact the moral equivalent of euthanasia. The reasons for a samurai's suicide were either (1) to avoid an inevitable death at the hands of others, or (2) to escape a longer period of unbearable pain or psychological misery, without being an active, fruitful member of society. These are exactly the sorts of situations when euthanasia is desired today: (1) to avoid an inevitable death at the hands of others (including disease, cancer, or bacteria), (2) to escape a longer period of pain or misery without being a fruitful, active member of society.

In regard to (1), most Japanese are now cut down in their seventies by the enemies of cancer and other diseases, rather than in their youth on a battlefield. Regardless of whether the person is hopelessly surrounded by enemies on a battlefield, or hopelessly defeated by enemy organisms within his body, the morality of the situation is the same. In regard to (2), it might be argued that there is a difference between the pain or misery of the permanent incapacitation of a samurai, and the pain or misery of the permanent incapacitation of a hospital patient. But if anything, the hospital patient is in even less of a position to contribute to society or feel valued than is the samurai, so he has even more reason to be granted the option of leaving this arena (world) when he chooses. The samurai tradition shows that the important issue is not the level of physical pain, but the prospect for meaningful and productive interaction with other members of society. If there are no prospects for such interactions, then samurai society claimed no right to prevent the person from seeking more meaningful experiences in another world.

Now in both cases, there may be relatives or retainers in the area who do not wish to see their friend die. The issue in these cases is not whether or not the besieged person will die; it is only a question of how soon, and in what manner. From ancient times, Japanese have respected the right of the individual to choose the moment and manner of dying. This Buddhist principle ought to apply equally well to the modern medical battles against the enemies of the body. The argument that if a body still has a face, it is still a person to those around him, is a basically un-Buddhist failure to understand (a) the difference between body and life, (b) the importance of each person's determination of his own mental states, and (c) the importance of placing mercy over desire in Buddhism.

Of course there need to be safeguards in such situations, and those safeguards have already been spelled out by the decision of the Nagoya High Court. In a case of euthanasia, the Nagoya High Court (22 December 1962) defined certain conditions under which euthanasia could be considered acceptable:

(1) The disease is considered terminal and incurable by present medicine.
(2) The pain is unbearable—both for the patient and those around him.

(3) The death is for the purpose of his peaceful passing.
(4) The person himself has requested the death, while conscious and sane.
(5) The killing is done by a doctor.
(6) The method of killing is humane.

If these safeguards are followed, it seems there is no moral reason that Buddhists should oppose euthanasia.

Conclusions

There are Japanese who hold that the Japanese lack the independent decision-making abilities of Western people, and that therefore doctors should make the decisions for their patients. This logic is backwards. The reason patients cannot make good independent judgments is because the doctors refuse them the information and freedom to do so, not because they lack the mental abilities or personal characteristics to make judgments. Buddhism has always recognized the importance of individual choice, despite social pressures; examples range from the Buddha himself, through Kūkai, Hōnen, Shinran, and Nagamatsu Nissen. The ability of Japanese to take personal responsibility for important decisions in times of stress, danger, or anguish has been repeatedly shown in the historical examples of these bold Buddhist reformers.

In order for the patient to make an intelligent decision about when and how he wants to die, he needs to know the facts about the nature of his disease, not only its real name, but the realistic prospects and alternative outcomes of all available forms of treatment. This means renouncing the paternalistic model held by present Japanese medicine, and granting substantial freedom to the patient in deciding his own case. Some Japanese doctors have argued that (1) patients do not really want to know the bad news about themselves, that (2) knowing the truth may harm their conditions, and that (3) the physician can judge more intelligently than the patient. However, studies in the West show that none of these claims is true. As Bok points out, "The attitude that what [the patient] doesn't know won't hurt him is proving unrealistic—it is rather what patients do not know but vaguely suspect that causes them corrosive (destructive) worry." People recover faster from surgery and tolerate pain with less medication when they understand their own medical problems and what can and cannot be done about them. In any case, doctors' withholding of information from patients is based not on statistical proof or ethical principles, but on the physicians' desires to retain control over patients. This is a situation that clear-thinking Buddhists naturally oppose. There is no reason to believe that these findings, long known and supported in Western medicine, should prove any different for the Japanese.

One important question for Buddhists today remains: what, if any, are the differences between suicide and euthanasia? Obviously one important difference is in the case where the person receiving euthanasia is unconscious. In this case, we have no way of knowing whether the patient genuinely desires euthanasia, unless he or she has previously made a declaration of wishes in a living will. On the other hand, once the consciousness has permanently dissociated itself from the body, there is no reason in Buddhism to continue to nourish or stimulate the body, for the body deprived of its *skandhas* is not a person. The Japan Songenshi Kyōkai (Association for Death with Dignity) has done much to improve the ability of the individual Japanese to choose his time and manner of death.

Another issue is the relation of pain-killing to prolonging life and hastening death itself. The Japan Songenshi Kyōkai proposes the administering of pain-killing drugs even if they hasten the death of the patient. Buddhists would agree that relief of pain is desirable, and whether the death is hastened or not is not the primary issue. However, consider a case where the pain is extreme and only very strong drugs will stop the pain. Here there may be a choice between: (a) no treatment at all, (b) pain-killing which only blurs or confuses the mind of the patient, and (c) treatment which hastens the end while keeping the mind clear. In such a situation, the Buddhist would first prefer the most natural way of (a) no treatment at all. But if his mind were unable to focus or be at peace because of the great pain, the Buddhist would choose (c) over (b), because clarity of consciousness at the moment of death is so important in Buddhism.

Doctors who do not like the idea of shortening a person's life would prefer to prolong the material life-processes, regardless of the mental quality of that life. This is where Buddhists disagree with materialistic Western medicine. But there need be no conflict between Buddhism and medicine. There is no reason to assign the doctor the "responsibility" for the death of the patient. Following the guidelines of the Nagoya court, patients potentially eligible for euthanasia are going to die soon anyway, so that is not the fault of the doctor. And the patient has the right to determine his own death. The fact that he is too weak to hold a sword or to cut short his own life is not morally significant. If his mind is clear, calm, and ready for death, then the one who understands and compassionately assists that person is also following Buddhist morality. In summary, the important issue for Buddhists here is whether or not the person will be allowed responsibility for his own life and fate. The entire Buddhist tradition, and particularly that of suicide within Japan, argues that personal choice in time and manner of death is of extreme importance, and anything done by others to dim the mind or deprive the dying person of such choice is a violation of Buddhist principles. Japanese Buddhists may respect this decision more than Western cultures, and lead humanitarian bioethics in a different perspective toward dignified death.

Discussion and Reflection Questions

1. How does the common Japanese attitude that "persons are not subjects with rights and individual free wills, but rather objects of the attention of others" bear on issues of suicide and euthanasia? How does this attitude differ from the typical Western (e.g., American) view of persons? What problems does Becker find with the Japanese attitude? How is this attitude in conflict with the teachings of Buddhism?

2. What was the samurai attitude toward suicide (including assisted suicide)? Under what conditions would a suicide be seen as justified? How does Becker compare such conditions with those now facing many terminally ill patients? Is this comparison a fair one?

3. According to Becker, under what conditions is suicide to end terminal illness justified? Do you agree with these conditions? How might someone develop a criticism to using these conditions as criteria for terminating life?

4. Becker obviously favors the Buddhist view toward suicide and euthanasia. What is his main argument in support of this view? How does one go about showing that one moral perspective is better than another? How does Becker attempt to do this? Has he convinced you? Why or why not?

Katherine K. Young, Traditional Hindu Views on Planned Self-Willed Death and Euthanasia

As Katherine K. Young points out, Hindu views of the moral permissibility of self-willed death did not remain static, but instead continued to change in response to circumstances. She distinguishes several types of self-willed death, and discusses each in the context of Hindu spirituality and customs. A particular concern of her essay is to consider whether permitting self-willed death under some circumstances might lead to a "slippery slope" in which self-willed death becomes far too common. Lessons from the Hindu tradition might well help us to think more clearly about this issue as it affects contemporary society.

Reading Questions

1. According to Young's interpretation, in the Hindu tradition is it morally acceptable to intentionally take one's own life? If so, under what conditions?

2. How did early Hindu ethicists distinguish legitimate self-willed death from illegitimate suicide? On what was this distinction based?

3. What is meant by a "slippery slope," and why might it be considered dangerous in considering the moral permissibility of self-willed death?

4. According to Young, how might familiarity with the history of self-willed death in the Hindu tradition help us to think about suicide and euthanasia in the present?

Traditional Hindu Views on Planned Self-Willed Death and Euthanasia

KATHERINE K. YOUNG

IS IT MORALLY ACCEPTABLE to intentionally take one's own life? If so, under what conditions? The Hindu view is an important case study because it initially rejected the idea of legitimate, self-willed death (which was distinguished from suicide), then it religiously endorsed it but placed strict restrictions on the practice in the classical period (about sixth century B.C.E. to sixth C.E.), and then it rejected it again in some circles in the tenth century because a slippery slope was perceived (though only during British rule was self-willed death made a criminal offense and the practice, by and large, came to an end). Recovery of the Indian history of self-willed death will be a major step in understanding how it differs from the history

Katherine K. Young, "Traditional Hindu Views on Planned Self-Willed Death and Euthanasia." Reprinted by permission of the author.

of self-willed death in the West and other civiliza-tions, and how it may inform the contemporary dis-cussion of euthanasia. Whereas self-willed death was found in Hinduism from the classical period but was eliminated in the early modern period, self-willed death in the sense of "freedom to leave" was rarely found in the West after the Greco-Roman period, al-though today its merits are increasingly debated in the context of physician-assisted suicide (euthanasia) and one country—the Netherlands—has legalized it.

For clarity, it is worthwhile to distinguish be-tween several types of self-willed death: (1) suicide, here defined as an event motivated by overwhelm-ing despair, fear, rage, or passion, often described as spontaneous, irrational, and unfortunate; (2) as-sisted suicide, involving the help of a physician and considered illegitimate by those in authority; (3) le-gitimate self-willed death, a planned death moti-vated by one or more supposedly good reasons that have been accepted by religious, philosophical, le-gal, or political authorities within very specific boundaries; (4) assisted, legitimate self-willed death; (5) death that is indirectly caused by withholding or withdrawal of treatment when treatment is not ben-eficial; and (6) death that is indirectly caused by medication to relieve pain but which may uninten-tionally shorten life. Today the term euthanasia would be applied to #2 where it is not legalized and to #3 where it is legalized (the Netherlands).

Self-willed death had become an issue in Indian society after sixth century B.C.E. One Indian religion, Jainism, legitimated it for monks and nuns as a way to culminate a spiritual life of asceticism and medita-tion, and another, Theravada Buddhism, made the experience of unbearable pain in the process of dying an exception to natural death (though it discouraged the practice by an extremely high spiritual require-ment—the person could not cling to bodily existence and desire for rebirth, which implied that the person had achieved liberation from the cycles of existence). But Hinduism initially refused to legitimate planned self-willed death in any circumstance (this is made evident by *Īśa Upaniṣad* 2–3, which promoted the old Vedic ideal life-span of one hundred years and warned that people who are slayers of the self [*ātmahatya*] will go to hell [*asurya-loka*]). It is striking that a principle of nonviolence or the sanctity of life was enshrined in Hinduism (and the other two Indic religions, Jainism and Buddhism) at the same time that legitimate, self-willed death developed. A few other exceptions to nonviolence were allowed such as self-defense (saving the life of a mother over the fe-tus) or a just war (to be waged by the warrior caste).

When one approaches the topic of death in the classical Hindu context, one encounters three basic types of death: natural, unnatural (being killed), and self-willed (killing oneself). With reference to natural death we find that there continued to be a strong Hindu prescription to live a hundred years or at least to the end of the natural life span. The funeral or *śrāddha* rites were performed for those who died a natural death. Those men who died naturally became the ancestors who were sustained through ritual of-ferings, ostensibly until they were reborn. The offer-ings also ensured that they became gods (*viśvadeva*) as part of the process, thereby creating a double buffer against the idea of death as annihilation. Un-natural death by being killed in battle, by murder, or by accident was viewed as violent and not to be marked by *śrāddha*. Such a violent death, especially that of a warrior killed in battle, was not perceived negatively, however. It was religiously powerful, for it led to heaven or deification. (This idea is echoed even today in contemporary folk cults that deify vic-tims of murder or accident).

Besides natural death and unnatural violent death, there also developed the category of self-willed death. This included three different types: sui-cide and what I term heroic, voluntary death (*mors voluntaria heroica*) and religious, self-willed death (*mors voluntaria religiosa*). The following features dis-tinguish these three types. Suicide, which was pro-hibited, was self-willed death prompted by passion, depression, or uncontrollable circumstance. *Mors voluntaria heroica*, found mainly in the milieu of the warriors, was: (1) a way to avoid calamity, as when a warrior avoided capture and a woman avoided rape or slavery by a conqueror; (2) a substitute for heroic death in battle (which automatically resulted in heaven) by aged warriors who survived all battles; and (3) a way to allow peaceful succession to the throne, by encouraging old kings to withdraw to the forest. Closely related both historically and conceptu-ally to heroic, self-willed death was *mors voluntaria religiosa*.

The latter emphasized *dharma* (duties to ensure an ethical and ordered society), heaven, or liberation. It was carefully distinguished from suicide. Whereas religious, self-willed death was legitimate, suicide was illegitimate in the sense that the authorities did not officially condone such deaths as a solution to problems, though they might have felt compassion for the individual concerned. We can understand the motivation of *dharma* better by looking to the ritual logic of Mīmāṃsā. Because these duties were dhar-mic and required, the non-performance of them would ordinarily create bad *karma*. But because the incapacitated person could not perform mandatory, religious duties because of circumstances beyond control, it was necessary to create an exception to the general rule regarding required acts. Nonperformance of obligatory action by an incapacitated person was to be considered dharmic. If nonperformance of obligatory rituals was dharmic for an incapacitated person, and self-willed death was permitted to an incapacitated person, then self-willed death could also be considered dharmic. If self-willed death was dharmic, then, in Hindu terms, it was righteous and religious. Finally, if self-willed death was dharmic and therefore religious, it belonged to the category of *mors voluntaria religiosa* and was definitively different from suicide. This was the logic. Moreover, to will death was so powerful it could burn up bad *karma* and thereby expiate sin. It could produce good *karma* and thereby direct destiny, including a visit to (lower) heaven. And it could even dramatically influence the course of destiny—either by eliminating all *karmas* that cause bondage thereby triggering salvation or enlightenment, or by appealing to the Supreme Deity to recognize and reward this supreme self-sacrifice by helping the person to attain the highest heaven.

To distinguish legitimate self-willed death from illegitimate suicide, Hindu ethicists proposed a number of constraints for the former and punishments to discourage the latter. (1) To discourage suicide, which was considered a sin, they said that the *śrāddha* or funeral rituals should not be performed for those who committed suicide because of rage, fear, affliction, or pride by means such as fire, water, beating the head, poison, or hanging. (2) The prescription that one's duties (*dharma*) had to be fulfilled was a deterrent against the premature desire for self-willed death on the part of the individual who had social and religious responsibilities (*dharma* in Hinduism included everything from spousal duties in marriage to raising children to mandatory rituals). Self-willed death in the case of illness could occur only if the person was incapacitated and could not perform religious duties. In the case of old age, it was an option only if the condition of the extremely aged person was such that there was no desire for pleasure (in the terminology of modern gerontology, this would be a case of disengagement). (3) Self-willed death could also be done when a person no longer could perform the rites of bodily purification in cases of extreme illness or extreme old age. (4) If someone announced that they intended to perform self-willed death, others were to try to talk the person out of it to guard

against rash actions caused by depression. (5) A formal and publicly expressed intention (saṃkalpa), which was intimately related to the goal (*artha*) through the power created by the will, helped to separate the phenomenon of *mors voluntaria religiosa* from suicide. People were to actively discourage suicide.

Once good boundaries and reasons for self-willed death had been given by the authorities, the decision for legitimate, self-willed death was primarily the responsibility of the individual. The Law of Karma was the key to individual responsibility. It was important for an individual to consider the various criteria for legitimate self-willed death and to determine whether the particular desire to die fulfilled these or whether it was a case of suicide. The distinction was crucial, for the latter generated bad *karma* and led to hell. Despite the individualism of the Law of Karma, Hindus recognized that human lives were interconnected in the social order. Practices such as self-willed death were also viewed critically in social terms so that the welfare of society was taken into consideration. Once these criteria had been met, then an individual was free to perform self-willed death.

In general, however, it seems that brahmins were reluctant to endorse self-willed death for brahmin ascetics or those liberated in this life (*jīvanmuktas*) (unless, following Manu's views, it was done toward the very end of the natural life span). The famous Hindu thinker Sankara (788–833 C.E.), for example, argued that one must live out one's life to allow the *karmas* to come to fruition. He implied that for the virtually enlightened person the moment of natural death signals the moment when there are no more *karmas* that create bondage.

> We should understand that right knowledge is the cause which renders all actions impotent. But the action by which this body has been brought into existence will come as an end only when their effects will have been fully worked out; for, those actions have already commenced their effects. Thus wisdom can destroy only such actions as have not yet begun to produce their effects, whether they are actions done in this birth before the rise of knowledge and along with knowledge, or those done in the many previous births. (Sankara's commentary on *Bhagavad Gītā* 4.37[1])

---

[1]A. Mahadeva Sastri, trans. *The Bhagavad Gītā: With the Commentary of Śrī Śaṅkarācārya* (Madras: V. Ramaswamy Sastrulu & Sons, 1972), p. 150.

The brahmins' desire to live out the natural life span is most apparent in the theory of the four distinct stages of life (*āśramas*), which is expounded in the Dharmasatras (the books on right behavior, ethics, and law). This theory was grafted onto the ancient Vedic idea of the long life. The ideal of a hundred years remained, presumably to allow time for the stages of studentship (*brahmācārya*), householdership (*gṛhastha*), retirement to the forest (*vānaprastha*), and wandering alone (*saṃnyāsa*). This plan may be seen as the Hindu version of the Buddhist middle path, for it was a synthesis of householder and ascetic orientations. The old Vedic values of prosperity and progeny were incorporated into the stage of being a householder. The value of longevity was promoted in the concept of the full allotment of time needed to accomplish all goals. The prescriptions of the Ayurvedic or medical texts were to be followed to ensure a long, healthy life (mentally, as well as physically, through proper diet, exercise, and discipline). The ideal of *vānaprastha* was an acknowledgement of the ascetic's customary withdrawal to the forest and the royal custom of withdrawal to provide for a peaceful succession. As such, *vānaprastha* might have served the purpose of disengagement (a phenomenon observed by cross-cultural gerontologists). Moreover, liberation or heaven was incorporated as a goal for the last two stages of life. Individuals were to cultivate a life-affirming attitude with a yogic discipline introduced in the very first stage of the life cycle and pursued seriously in the last two stages to nurture disengagement and achieve enlightenment.

My question in this essay is whether there is any evidence of a slippery slope when self-willed death was legitimated in Hinduism. Slippery slope here refers to the *probability* that once there is legitimization of self-willed death, this may lead under certain social conditions to more types of self-willed death, involving other motives, means, and groups. A slippery slope implies that there is a relation among the examples. These may be due to some of the following: (1) cultural contact or inter-religious competition leading to the exchange of ideas and practices, especially in a shared social, economic, and political milieu that causes common problems; (2) the psychological tendency for people to assimilate cases, even when they involve "fallacious assimilation, mistaken use of precedent, and unwarranted cause,"[2] if they fulfill some need or satisfy some desire, or express some central value of the society; (3) interested

agents who help to popularize the practice; (4) the use of reiterative arguments to include more and more examples; (5) vague concepts leading to more applications; and (6) the need to treat similar cases consistently and to avoid faulty analogies and bad precedents.

The textual approach used here shows that the philosophical arguments that dismiss claims of the possibility of a slippery slope may not be relevant in the real world (ordinary people do not think like philosophers). I have found that a slippery slope did occur in Hinduism. Even though there was an attempt in Hinduism to create firm boundaries around "legitimate" self-willed death and to limit the types of motives, methods, and people who were allowed to do this (and therefore the numbers) and even though the brahmins, who were the religious leaders whom others emulated, did not encourage the practice for themselves, there is textual evidence of a slippery slope.

Self-willed death began with warriors and ascetics (about the sixth century B.C.E., a time of rapid social and political change, when new ideas could be introduced without much debate). Gradually, it was extended from these circles to other groups such as the very old and the very ill. The lawgiver Atri (about the second century B.C.E.) stated, for example, that

> if one who is very old (beyond 70) cannot observe the rules of bodily purification (owing to extreme weakness), is so ill that no medical help can be given, kills himself by throwing himself from a precipice or into a fire or water or by fasting, mourning should be observed for him for three days and *śrāddha* [funeral rituals] may be performed for him (Atri 218–219).[3]

The inclusion of the very old and ill might have been a response to an aging population (with slow degenerative illnesses that caused great suffering); a new social reality of population explosion in the Gangetic valley; and a new empirical perspective on medicine in which physicians were not to treat the dying (so that they could build their reputation as healers and thereby distinguish themselves from quacks). Aparāka (who lived about 1110–1200 C.E.) said much the same thing as Atri centuries before:

> He who is suffering from serious illness [and] cannot live, or who is very old, who has no desire

---

[2] T. Govier, "What's Wrong with Slippery Slope Arguments?" (1982) 12 *Canadian Journal of Philosophy*, p. 316.

[3] Cited in P. V. Kane, *History of Dharmaśāstra: Ancient and Mediaeval Religious and Civil Law*. Government Oriental Series Class B, no. 6, Poona: Bhandarkar Oriental Research Institute, 2: 926.

left for the pleasures of any of the senses and who has carried out his tasks, may bring about his death at pleasure by resorting to *mahāprasthāna* [walking in a giant circle and fasting until dropping dead], by entering fire or water or by falling from a precipice. By so doing he incurs no sin and his death is far better so than *tapas* (asceticism), and one should not desire to live vainly (without being able to perform the duties laid down by the *śāstra*).[4]

It is important to note that once the ethicists created scope for self-willed death, they allowed easy means, such as jumping from a precipice or into fire and water, unlike the Jains, whose method of fasting to death was more arduous. It is likely that these faster and easier means contributed to a slippery slope. Promotion of these easy means to the supreme goal was related, in turn, to competition among the Indic religions—Hinduism, Jainism, and Buddhism. In addition, the motivation was made more attractive; self-willed death was now said to be equivalent to asceticism and meditation as the means to the supreme goal of enlightenment (see *Kūrma-purāṇa* 1:37; 16:39; *Padma-purāṇa*, sṛṣṭi 60:65; *Brahma-purāṇa* 177:25).

By the early medieval period, many others—not just warriors, ascetics, and very ill and very old people—were encouraged to perform self-willed death by jumping into a holy river (such as the confluence of the Gaṅgā and Yamunā) and so forth. And this inspired new types of Hindu groups, whose identity was premised on the idea of self-willed death such as a class of heroes (*tuḷilāl*), a class of servants (*veḷevāḷi*), and a class of women (*satī*). The latter were women whose husband had died and who had vowed to join him through self-immolation on his funeral pyre. In addition, self-willed death was now being performed by *groups* of ascetics. For instance, according to tradition, Jñānadeva (1275–1296 C.E.), a Marathi brahmin, voluntarily ended his life in his twenties along with his two brothers and sister. They felt that they had accomplished their mission in life.[5] Another interesting case is the tradition about the Kashmiri savant Abhinavagupta (10th–11th century). It is said that by the time Abhinavagupta started to write his magnun opus, he had attained liberation (*jīvanmukti*). The last scene of his earthly existence, upon the completion of his life's work, involved walking with twelve hundred disciples into the

Bhairava cave never to be seen again. R. C. Pandey visited this cave and discovered that the area was large enough to accommodate forty to fifty people. He concluded that it is plausible that Abhinavagupta went into the cave with some followers to perform self-willed death.[6] In the nineteenth century, British officials observed that some low caste Hindus were sacrificing children by hurling them into the sea from an island (Sagara) where the Ganga river meets the sea or were taking their own lives there in fulfillment of a vow. Moreover, now lepers were offered obsequies (otherwise denied) if they consented to burial alive. All this suggests that groups rather than individuals and different types of groups (often including vulnerable people) were performing "legitimate," self-willed death.

Even though the idea of restrictions around the practice of self-willed death continued—*satīs*, for example, could not be pregnant nor have young children; had to make a formal, public vow (*saṃkalpa*); had to have their finger burnt by a priest to see if they showed no emotion (a sign of the voluntary nature of their decision and an indication of their fortitude to carry out the act); and had to have relatives try to dissuade them—it was obvious that the practice was abused. At the very least, this was because if a woman's husband died before her, this was blamed on her bad *karma*. Moreover, although the practice of legitimate, self-willed death was ostensibly voluntary, we cannot rule out possible motivations of despair or the feeling of being a burden. From British records in the modern period we also know that the number of *satīs* increased at times of famine.

Thus, it seems that a slippery slope occurred in Hinduism after self-willed death was legitimated. This is indicated by an increase in the types of means (easier ones), motives (loyalty, encouraged by those with power, or desire for the supreme goals of life, namely heaven or liberation) and groups (especially more vulnerable ones) mentioned in the texts. Some of the contributing factors include a time of rapid political and social change; an increase in the life span (more people living into old age and dying from slow diseases, which incapacitated them, and physicians refusing to care for the dying); and interreligious competition (among Hindus, Buddhists, and Jains which encouraged a promotion of easy means to salvation).

Today, some social conditions that may contribute to a slippery slope such as a large aging population,

[4]Kane 2: 926.
[5]Benjamin Walker, *Hindu World: An Encyclopedia Survey of Hinduism* [1968] (New Delhi: Indus, 1995) 2: 505.

[6]Kanti Chandra Pandey, *Abhivanagupta: An Historical and Philosophical Study* (Varanasi, India: Chowkhamba Sanskrit Series Office, 1963), p. 25.

legitimization associated with a central societal value (in this case, freedom and autonomy), and rapid social change are already present. No society can rule out the possibility of a slippery slope developing after legitimization of self-willed death, because no society can rule out future situations that contribute to such slopes. Even if a society does not take the extreme step of moving from self-willed death to other-willed death (as happened in Nazi Germany), this does not mean that serious problems can be avoided. This suggests that it may prove better in the long run not to legitimate self-willed death, even though compassion for those who are suffering extreme pain or recognition of a person's autonomy might seem initially to be a good reason for a society to take this step.

Although it is beyond the scope of the present chapter, there is evidence that a slippery slope in the motives, means, and types of people allowed to perform self-willed death also occurred in Jainism and Buddhism in India (though not to the same degree) and that similar slopes occurred in China and Japan as well as ancient Greece and Rome.[7] But it is important to point out that the aid of physicians and drugs was virtually never mentioned in Asian texts as a means to help an individual carry out an act of planned, self-willed death. Even though this might have occurred behind the scenes, it was probably recognized that this would make the means just too easy and would contribute to abuse (even the use of hemlock in ancient Greece and Rome was viewed as an ignoble means of self-willed death and discouraged for the elite). Physicians no doubt also recognized that it might destroy their status (at a time when they were trying to distinguish themselves from quacks who caused death through negligence and ignorance). For instance, Hindu physicians were warned by Caraka and Suśruta[8] in no uncertain terms not to use their skills and medicines to help people die just as Hippocrates did in the West.

Modern Western supporters of euthanasia have also placed restrictions on the practice of self-willed death. They have argued, for instance, that euthanasia should be allowed only when one is no longer able to live with dignity and comfort and when the quality of life is intolerably undermined. And they have argued that restrictions have been necessitated by the considerable overlap between what had been condoned as legitimate forms of self-willed death (especially the difficulties of old age) and the desire to commit suicide proper. For, not only were they both forms of self-willed death, they also could be prompted by extreme emotion, depression, or uncontrollable circumstance.

Are there any lessons to be learned from this history? Some people argue that it is irrelevant to look to history for answers to modern problems. Because there have been tremendous social and technological changes, they claim, there can be no meaningful analogies with the past. I would argue, however, that we need first to do our homework on a cross-cultural and historical basis. As this study has shown, there are many conditions in traditional texts that sound very similar to ones encountered today: from the common human problem of suffering in the dying process; to a time of rapid political, social, economic, and technological changes; to the existence of an aging population; to the exploitation of vulnerable groups; to the claims of freedom and rational choice to determine the time, place, and mode of death. This suggests that there may be some meaningful analogies.

It is important to realize, however, that even though slippery slopes existed in those societies that legitimized self-willed death, the existence of a phenomenon or even its popularity does not determine whether it is good or bad. This is the problem of deriving an ought from an "is," known as the naturalist fallacy. There must be good reasons why an act should not be done. In the final analysis, such good reasons might include the following.

- Humans have freedom of behavior (including the ability to kill other humans and themselves). This contributes to their ability to adapt and therefore to survive as a species. But they must use culture to limit this freedom so that it does not become destructive, especially at times of personal or social crises when people are filled with despair and see no reason to live. Therefore, cultural systems consciously promote the value of life-affirmation to prevent the abuse of human freedom, even though they recognize that in the final analysis they still have to deal with the basic paradox of life: that we have to eat and therefore kill some living creatures in order to live and that for self-defense, it is sometimes necessary to kill, even train people to kill, others.
- Suicide out of despair has never been viewed as a positive thing but as an extremely regrettable event which societies have tried hard to prevent.

[7]See Katherine K. Young, "A Cross-Cultural Historical Case Against Planned Self-Willed Death and Assisted Suicide," *McGill Law Journal,* Oct. Vol. 39, no. 3, 1994, 657–707.

[8]Katherine K. Young, "Hindu Bioethics," in *Religious Methods and Resources in Bioethics* (Dordrecht: Kluwer Academic Publishers, 1994), pp. 3–30.

- Even when planned self-willed death was legitimated in some societies, it was certainly not a blanket endorsement of the freedom to die at any time or by any means or with help. On the contrary, the choices were very carefully limited. Obviously, religious communities were seeking to balance the interests of the society and the individual.
- Societies acknowledge, moreover, that human beings are interdependent. Because human beings have phases of dependency (for example, infancy, childhood, and old age) or particular situations of dependency or despair (for example, devastating illness, extreme mental depression, or abject poverty), they need the protection of others at critical points in their lives. Because of the unpredictability of illness, the inherent ambiguity in any quality-of-life arguments (By who's standard? Will it always be this way?), and the fact that the moment of death itself is always unknown, it has been important to encourage life-affirmation to sustain people through difficult periods in their lives. Because it may not be in the immediate self-interest of others to offer such protection or support, human beings have been culturally encouraged to be altruistic to protect others when they are dependent so that there is a general cultural presumption that they themselves will be protected, in turn, when they are dependent. This is, in effect, a kind of human life-insurance policy that becomes encoded into cultural systems. Such altruism is a duty and responsibility. Sometimes when it is beyond the call of duty, it is a gift. But the wise will see that it is also important for an individual on a long-term basis, not to mention the well-being of the individual, the family, the community, and even the species. Culture, which is the collective wisdom of a human society, has built these insights into its codes of behavior, ethics, or law so that the ethical wheel does not have to be reinvented by each person or each generation (a precarious proposition), though sometimes there is need for reform or even a new ethical position because of new technologies or changed circumstances.
- The reluctance of many societies to endorse self-willed death, and especially physician-assisted suicide, can be attributed to the problem of determining the real intention or motive of a person's act when there are genuine conflicts of interest. Despite the importance of altruism for

human communities and the cultural norms to encourage it, there is always the possibility that individuals will be short-sighted or conveniently forget cultural norms and act selfishly for their own immediate benefits and goals. Some parents may abandon a handicapped newborn, for example, and some couples may not provide physical or emotional support for an old in-law who becomes temporarily ill. It is only realistic to acknowledge that in extremely difficult human situations there may be a tug-of-war between selfish and altruistic motives. Moreover, selfish ones may be denied or disguised by seemingly altruistic ones. Because it is so difficult to determine what are the real intentions of an individual, societies have tended to act very conservatively where ambiguity can occur, especially when intentions become a matter of life and death. In general, complex societies have encouraged a principle of nonviolence or sanctity of life and then have made only a few exceptions (for example, self-defense or a just war).

To conclude, the legitimization of self-willed death in certain circumstances was an experiment that was tried because there seemed to be good reasons for such an exception, such as compassion to those who are in extreme pain. This proved problematic for the society as a whole in the long run because of a slippery slope that involved an increase in the types of motives, methods, and groups. In the final analysis, the boundary between unplanned, irrational suicide and planned, rational self-willed death has always been fuzzy. Desperate people who committed suicide often thought about how to accomplish the act; they too planned. Moreover, they too often thought about the reasons, and came to the conclusion that they had good ones. And we should not forget the ambiguity involved even in cases of self-willed death that ostensibly had no help or encouragement from others. It is just too difficult to know what thinking is truly independent from general cultural values taught to an individual from childhood. In other words, there are good reasons for any human society to protect the life of its members through cultural norms, ethics, and laws. The fact that planned, self-willed death created a slippery slope in those complex societies that experimented with its being an exception to the general rule of nonviolence or the sanctity of life is, moreover, an additional reason why this should not be done today. If there have been problems of abuse even when the decision has been that of the individual and there have been strict criteria, perhaps societies should be even more wary when the decisions are made by others as in the case of physician-assisted, self-willed death. In sum, the State should avoid legitimizing planned, self-willed death.

Discussion and Reflection Questions

1. In your view, is it ever morally acceptable to intentionally take one's own life? If so, under what conditions?

2. How would you distinguish legitimate self-willed death from illegitimate suicide? What considerations or arguments could be developed to defend this distinction?

3. Do you believe that if some self-willed death is permitted, that this will lead to a "slippery slope," with the result that suicide and euthanasia will become far more common than is morally desirable? Explain your view.

4. What did you learn from this essay? In what ways might our views of the moral acceptability of a practice be informed (or influenced) by the culture(s) in which we live?

Suggestions for Further Reading

A useful contrast to Brandt's article included above is Thomas E. Hill, Jr.,'s "Self-Regarding Suicide: A Modified Kantian View," in his *Autonomy and Self-Respect* (Cambridge: Cambridge University Press, 1991). A useful collection of essays on suicide may be found in *Suicide: Right or Wrong?*, edited by John Donnelly (Buffalo, N.Y.: Prometheus Books, 1990). A collection of studies examining how suicide is viewed in different social and cultural contexts is Norman L. Farberow, ed., *Suicide in Different Cultures* (Baltimore: University Park Press, 1975). For more on euthanasia, see Helga Kuhse, "Euthanasia," in *A Companion to Ethics*, edited by Peter Singer (Oxford: Blackwell, 1991), pp. 294–302. See also her book *The Sanctity-of-Life Doctrine in Medicine—A Critique* (Oxford: Oxford University Press, 1987). Other treatments include D. Humphry and A. Wickett, *The Right to Die—Understanding Euthanasia* (New York: Harper & Row, 1986), and J. Glover, *Causing Death and Saving Lives* (Harmondsworth: Penguin, 1987). See *Principles of Biomedical Ethics*, edited by Tom L. Beauchamp and James F. Childress (New York: Oxford University Press, 1994); *Bioethics: An Anthology*, edited by Helga Kuhse and Peter Singer (Boston: Blackwell Publishers, 1999); and *A Companion to Bioethics*, edited by Helga Kuhse and Peter Singer (Boston: Blackwell Publishers, 1998) for an examination of the ethical questions involved in euthanasia and other medical procedures. Eric Matthews examines the views of St. Thomas Aquinas and Immanuel Kant, as well as a host of other philosophers, on suicide and euthanasia in "Choosing Death: Philosophical Observations on Suicide and Euthanasia," in *Philosophy, Psychiatry, and Psychology* 5 (1998): 107–111. *Hindu Ethics: Purity, Abortion, and Euthanasia*, by Harold G. Coward, Julius J. Lipner, and Katherine K. Young (New York: State University of New York Press, 1989) gives a good account of Hindu perspectives on the issues of both euthanasia and abortion.

InfoTrac

euthanasia, assisted suicide, right to die, "death, moral and ethical aspects", suicide and ethics

Chapter 12

Morality within the Family

Introduction: The Moral Obligations of Parents and Children

A standard principle of much contemporary Western moral theory is the principle of impartiality. This principle states that the interests and welfare of each person are as important as those of any other. Another way of putting this is that from the moral point of view, there are no privileged persons. This principle has two important consequences: (1) We cannot justifiably regard *ourselves* as having special moral status, and (2) we cannot justifiably treat others differently in virtue of morally insignificant properties. That is, we cannot justifiably make an exception of ourselves (for example, by claiming, "Stealing is wrong for others, but not for me"), nor may we discriminate on the basis of irrelevant characteristics. (We would not be justified, for instance, in treating someone differently because of their racial identity, or the color of their eyes, or the size of their nose, which are morally irrelevant characteristics.) The principle of impartiality is important because it directs us to be fairer in our treatment of others.

Although the principle of impartiality is an important assumption in much moral theorizing, a moment's reflection indicates that it is highly problematic and, when applied in some fairly common cases, has quite counterintuitive consequences. Not only *do* we practice partiality when it comes to deciding what to do, but in many cases it seems that this is the *right* thing to do. This is especially the case with the second consequence identified above. So, for instance, if you have enough income to support one additional person besides yourself, and your elderly parent is in need of such support, you might consider it quite reasonable to support your elderly parent, rather than a total stranger. People will spend huge sums of money to support and care for their own children and only a small fraction of this amount to provide food for starving children in distant lands. People who did just the opposite (letting their own children go hungry) would likely be considered morally deficient rather than morally praiseworthy. Here extreme partiality seems to be accepted. Likewise, if you are competing with others for some valuable prize (a job, a mate, a scholarship, etc.) it would be bizarre, rather than highly moral, to be indifferent to the issue of who obtains the valued prize in question. In such situations we normally act as if we have a right, or indeed a special obligation, to do our best to secure good things for ourselves. This is, of course, to show a great deal of partiality and hence to violate the principle of impartiality. Yet such behavior seems quite unexceptional and is not the sort of thing for which anyone is likely to morally condemn you. This suggests that our obligations to others are not to be discharged in a completely impartial manner, but that some people merit or deserve our attention and assistance more than others.

Next to (or even above) ourselves, many of us consider our families to have the greatest claim to our concern and assistance. Certainly our close family members have a greater call on us than do people who are related to us more remotely or not at all. As everyone who has grown up in a family knows only too well, there are special moral considerations that pertain to the members of one's immediate family that do not (or do not necessarily) extend to those outside this circle. This is where a great many of the most difficult moral problems arise. If we assume that our close family members have some claim to our assistance, how are we to measure this claim? Under what conditions does meeting the needs and desires of our families take precedence over meeting our own needs and desires or those of unrelated persons? What are we to do when conflicts arise between what we believe is good for us and what is good for close relations?

Western and Eastern ethicists often have very different views on this issue, especially in the matter of obligations of children to their parents. Their views reflect differences found in Western and Eastern cultures. Often, Asian parents have much greater expectations of assistance and deference due to them by their children than do Western parents. Likewise, it is common for grown children in the West to feel less responsibility for their parents than children might feel in Asia. Although there are many exceptions to these generalities, they are noticeable characteristics nonetheless, rooted in the very different philosophical and cultural ideals of East and West. Kantian moral theory, for example, recommends treating all rational beings, in virtue of their rationality, as equally deserving of our consideration. Confucianism, on the other hand, is at odds with Kantianism on this point. Confucius (and his follower Mencius) accepted an ideal of graded love, according to which the strength of moral obligations to others is directly related to their familial relationship to oneself. Another way of putting this is to note that whereas Kant proposes universally binding moral prescriptions, according to which one has equal moral obligations to all rational beings, Confucius promotes a hierarchical order of moral obligations, according to which one owes more to one's close relatives than to strangers. Remarkably, here an Eastern perspective seems to be more in keeping with the way people actually form their moral judgments in the West than does the view developed by one of the West's most powerful thinkers.

Some of these different perspectives are evident in the reading selections below. You might think about the moral issues that arise within your *own* family situations as you read these selections and ask yourself how the ideas developed in these readings might assist you in making wise moral decisions in these cases.

Jane English, What Do Grown Children Owe Their Parents?

What do grown children owe their parents? According to Jane English, they "owe" their parents absolutely nothing at all. Although there are many things that children *ought* to do for their parents, talk of owing in this context, she argues, is inappropriate and misleading. The duties of grown children to their parents result from love, affection, and friendship between them. Where these feelings are missing, so too are any duties. It follows that when parents tell their children that the children "owe" it to them to take care of them (or obey them or support them) because of all the sacrifices made on their behalf, they are simply mistaken. One should not conclude from this, however, that children have no obligations toward their parents. English's aim is to clarify the sense in which children have obligations to their parents and to identify the correct bases for such obligations.

Reading Questions

1. English describes two examples in which Nina provides help to Max. What is the essential difference between these two cases? What conclusions about obligation does English draw from them? How do favors and voluntary sacrifices differ? According to English, why does receiving a favor create a debt that must be discharged, whereas being the recipient of a voluntary sacrifice does not?

2. What is the distinction between mutuality and reciprocity that English appeals to? Why does she think that mutuality, rather than reciprocity, characterizes friendship? How is the example of Alfred and Beatrice used to establish the claim that talk of "owing" is out of place in friendship?

3. How does English apply the distinction between mutuality and reciprocity in developing her view of the appropriate relationship between parents and children? According to English, under what conditions do grown children have obligations toward their parents? What point is English making with the example of Cecile and Dana?

4. According to English, how does basing children's obligations to their parents on mutual love, rather than on perceived debts owed, affect our understanding of the nature of parent-child relationships? Why is effecting such a change in our understanding desirable?

What Do Grown Children Owe Their Parents?

JANE ENGLISH

WHAT DO GROWN CHILDREN owe their parents? I will contend that the answer is "nothing." Although I agree that there are many things that children *ought* to do for their parents, I will argue that it is inappro-priate and misleading to describe them as things "owed." I will maintain that parents' voluntary sacrifices, rather than creating "debts" to be "repaid," tend to create love or "friendship." The duties of

Jane English, "What Do Grown Children Owe Their Parents?" in Onora O'Neill and William Ruddick, eds., Having Children *(New York: Oxford University Press, 1979), pp. 351–356.*

grown children are those of friends and result from love between them and their parents, rather than being things owed in repayment for the parents' earlier sacrifices. Thus, I will oppose those philosophers who use the word "owe" whenever a duty or obligation exists. Although the "debt" metaphor is appropriate in some moral circumstances, my argument is that a love relationship is not such a case.

Misunderstandings about the proper relationship between parents and their grown children have resulted from reliance on the "owing" terminology. For instance, we hear parents complain, "You owe it to us to write home (keep up your piano playing, not adopt a hippie lifestyle), because of all we sacrificed for you (paying for piano lessons, sending you to college)." The child is sometimes even heard to reply, "I didn't ask to be born (to be given piano lessons, to be sent to college)." This inappropriate idiom of ordinary language tends to obscure, or even to undermine, the love that is the correct ground of filial obligation.

1. Favors Create Debts

There are some cases, other than literal debts, in which talk of "owing," though metaphorical, is apt. New to the neighborhood, Max barely knows his neighbor, Nina, but he asks her if she will take in his mail while he is gone for a month's vacation. She agrees. If, subsequently, Nina asks Max to do the same for her, it seems that Max has a moral obligation to agree (greater than the one he would have had if Nina had not done the same for him), unless for some reason it would be a burden far out of proportion to the one Nina bore for him. I will call this a *favor*: when A, at B's request, bears some burden for B, then B incurs an obligation to reciprocate. Here the metaphor of Max's "owing" Nina is appropriate. It is not literally a debt, of course, nor can Nina pass this IOU on to heirs, demand payment in the form of Max's taking out her garbage, or sue Max. Nonetheless, since Max ought to perform one act of similar nature and amount of sacrifice in return, the term is suggestive. Once he reciprocates, the debt is "discharged"—that is, their obligations revert to the condition they were in before Max's initial request.

Contrast a situation in which Max simply goes on vacation and, to his surprise, finds upon his return that his neighbor has mowed his grass twice weekly in his absence. This is a voluntary sacrifice rather than a favor, and Max has no duty to reciprocate. It would be nice for him to volunteer to do so, but this would be supererogatory on his part. Rather than a favor, Nina's action is a friendly gesture. As a result, she might expect Max to chat over the back fence, help her catch her straying dog, or something similar—she might expect the development of a friendship. But Max would be chatting (or whatever) out of friendship, rather than in repayment for mown grass. If he did not return her gesture, she might feel rebuffed or miffed, but not unjustly treated or indignant, since Max has not failed to perform a duty. Talk of "owing" would be out of place in this case.

It is sometimes difficult to distinguish between favors and nonfavors, because friends tend to do favors for each other, and those who exchange favors tend to become friends. But one test is to ask how Max is motivated. Is it "to be nice to Nina" or "because she did *x* for me"? Favors are frequently performed by total strangers without any friendship developing. Nevertheless, a temporary obligation is created, even if the chance for repayment never arises. For instance, suppose that Oscar and Matilda, total strangers, are waiting in a long checkout line at the supermarket. Oscar, having forgotten the oregano, asks Matilda to watch his cart for a second. She does. If Matilda now asks Oscar to return the favor while she picks up some tomato sauce, he is obliged to agree. Even if she had not watched his cart, it would be inconsiderate of him to refuse, claiming he was too busy reading the magazines. He may have a duty to help others, but he would not "owe" it to her. But if she has done the same for him, he incurs an additional obligation to help, and talk of "owing" is apt. It suggests an agreement to perform equal, reciprocal, canceling sacrifices.

2. The Duties of Friendship Versus Debts

The terms "owe" and "repay" are helpful in the case of favors, because the sameness of the amount of sacrifice on the two sides is important; the monetary metaphor suggests equal quantities of sacrifice. But friendship ought to be characterized by *mutuality* rather than reciprocity: friends offer what they can give and accept what they need, without regard for the total amounts of benefits exchanged. And friends are motivated by love rather than by the prospect of repayment. Hence, talk of "owing" is singularly out of place in friendship.

For example, suppose Alfred takes Beatrice out for an expensive dinner and a movie. Beatrice incurs no obligation to "repay" him with a goodnight kiss or a return engagement. If Alfred complains that she "owes" him something, he is operating under the assumption that she should repay a favor, but on the contrary his was a generous gesture done in the hopes of developing a friendship. We hope that he would not want her repayment in the form of sex or attention if this was done to discharge a debt rather than from friendship. Since, if Alfred is prone to reasoning in this way, Beatrice may well decline the invitation or request to pay for her own dinner, his attitude of expecting a "return" on his "investment" could hinder the development of a friendship. Beatrice should return the gesture only if she is motivated by friendship.

Another common misuse of the "owing" idiom occurs when the Smiths have dined at the Joneses' four times, but the Joneses at the Smiths' only once. People often say, "We owe them three dinners." This line of thinking may be appropriate between business acquaintances, but not between friends. After all, the Joneses invited the Smiths not in order to feed them or to be fed in turn, but because of the friendly contact presumably enjoyed by all on such occasions. If the Smiths do not feel friendship toward the Joneses, they can decline future invitations and not invite the Joneses; they owe them nothing. Of course, between friends of equal resources and needs, roughly equal sacrifices (though not necessarily roughly equal dinners) will typically occur. If the sacrifices are highly out of proportion to the resources, the relationship is closer to servility than to friendship.

Another difference between favors and friendship is that after a friendship ends, the duties of friendship end. The party that has sacrificed less owes the other nothing. For instance, suppose Elmer donated a pint of blood that his wife Doris needed during an operation. Years after their divorce, Elmer is in an accident and needs one pint of blood. His new wife, Cora, is also of the same blood type. It seems that Doris not only does not "owe" Elmer blood, but that she should actually refrain from coming forward if Cora has volunteered to donate. To insist on donating not only interferes with the newlyweds' friendship, but it belittles Doris and Elmer's former relationship by suggesting that Elmer gave blood in hopes of favors returned instead of simply out of love for Doris. It is one of the heart-rending features of divorce that it attends to quantity in a relationship previously characterized by mutuality. If Cora could not donate, Doris's obligation is the same as that for any former spouse in need of blood; it is not increased by the fact that Elmer similarly aided her. It *is* affected by the degree to which they are still friends, which in turn may (or may not) have been influenced by Elmer's donation.

In short, unlike the debts created by favors, the duties of friendship do not require equal quantities of sacrifice. Performing equal sacrifices does not cancel the duties of friendship, as it does the debts of favors. Unrequested sacrifices do not themselves create debts, but friends have duties regardless of whether they requested or initiated the friendship. Those who perform favors may be motivated by mutual gain, whereas friends should be motivated by affection. These characteristics of the friendship relation are distorted by talk of "owing."

3. Parents and Children

The relationship between children and their parents should be one of friendship characterized by mutuality rather than one of reciprocal favors. The quantity of parental sacrifice is not relevant in determining what duties the grown child has. The medical assistance grown children ought to offer their ill mothers in old age depends upon the mothers' need, not upon whether they endured a difficult pregnancy, for example. Nor do one's duties to one's parents cease once an equal quantity of sacrifice has been performed, as the phrase "discharging a debt" may lead us to think.

Rather, what children ought to do for their parents (and parents for children) depends upon (1) their respective needs, abilities, and resources and (2) the extent to which there is an ongoing friendship between them. Thus, regardless of the quantity of childhood sacrifices, an able, wealthy child has an obligation to help his needy parents more than does a needy child. To illustrate, suppose sisters Cecile and Dana are equally loved by their parents, even though Cecile was an easy child to care for, seldom ill, while Dana was often sick and caused some trouble as a juvenile delinquent. As adults, Dana is a struggling artist living far away, while Cecile is a wealthy lawyer living nearby. When the parents need visits and financial aid, Cecile has an obligation to bear a higher proportion of these burdens than her sister. This results from her abilities, rather than from the quantities of sacrifice made by the parents earlier.

Sacrifices have an important causal role in creating an ongoing friendship, which may lead us to assume incorrectly that it is the sacrifices that are the source of the obligation. That the source is the friendship instead can be seen by examining cases in which the sacrifices occurred but the friendship, for some reason, did not develop or persist. For example, if a woman gives up her newborn child for adoption, and if no feelings of love ever develop on either side, it seems that the grown child does not have an obligation to "repay" her for her sacrifices in pregnancy. For that matter, if the adopted child has an unimpaired love relationship with the adoptive parents, he or she has the same obligations to help them as a natural child would have.

The filial obligations of grown children are a result of friendship, rather than owed for services rendered. Suppose that Vance married Lola despite his parents' strong wish that he marry within their religion, and that as a result, the parents refuse to speak to him again. As the years pass, the parents are unaware of Vance's problems, his accomplishments, the birth of his children. The love that once existed between them, let us suppose, has been completely destroyed by this event and thirty years of desuetude. At this point, it seems, Vance is under no obligation to pay his parents' medical bills in their old age, beyond his general duty to help those in need. An additional, filial obligation would only arise from whatever love he may still feel for them. It would be irrelevant for his parents to argue, "But look how much we sacrificed for you when you were young," for that sacrifice was not a favor but occurred as part of a friendship which existed at that time but is now, we have supposed, defunct. A more appropriate message would be, "We still love you, and we would like to renew our friendship."

I hope this helps to set the question of what children ought to do for their parents in a new light. The parental argument, "You ought to do x because we did y for you," should be replaced by, "We love you and you will be happier if you do x," or "We believe you love us, and anyone who loved us would do x." If the parents' sacrifice had been a favor, the child's reply, "I never asked you to do y for me," would have been relevant; to the revised parental remarks, this reply is clearly irrelevant. The child can either do x or dispute one of the parents' claims: by showing that a love relationship does not exist, or that love for someone does not motivate doing x, or that he or she will not be happier doing x.

Seen in this light, parental requests for children to write home, visit, and offer them a reasonable amount of emotional and financial support in life's crises are well founded, so long as a friendship still exists. Love for others does call for caring about and caring for them. Some other parental requests, such as for more sweeping changes in the child's lifestyle or life goals, can be seen to be insupportable, once we shift the justification from debts owed to love. The terminology of favors suggests the reasoning, "Since we paid for your college education, you owe it to us to make a career of engineering, rather than becoming a rock musician." This tends to alienate affection even further, since the tuition payments are depicted as investments for a return rather than done from love, as though the child's life goals could be "bought." Basing the argument on love leads to different reasoning patterns. The suppressed premise, "If A loves B, then A follows B's wishes as to A's lifelong career" is simply false. Love does not even dictate that the child adopt the parents' values as to the desirability of alternative life goals. So the parents' strongest available argument here is, "We love you, we are deeply concerned about your happiness, and in the long run you will be happier as an engineer." This makes it clear that an empirical claim is really the subject of the debate.

The function of these examples is to draw out our considered judgments as to the proper relation between parents and their grown children, and to show how poorly they fit the model of favors. What is relevant is the ongoing friendship that exists between parents and children. Although that relationship developed partly as a result of parental sacrifices for the child, the duties that grown children have to their parents result from the friendship rather than from the sacrifices. The idiom of owing favors to one's parents can actually be destructive if it undermines the role of mutuality and leads us to think in terms of quantitative reciprocal favors.

Discussion and Reflection Questions

1. English claims that if Nina does a favor for Max, he is obligated to return the favor to her in some way, whereas if Nina simply does something for Max without having been asked to do so (i.e., she performs a voluntary sacrifice), Max owes her nothing in return. Do you agree?

2. According to English, friendship is characterized by mutuality rather than reciprocity. She writes, "Friends offer what they can give and accept what they need, without regard for the total amounts of benefits exchanged. . . . Hence 'owing' is out of place in friendship." Is it a fair criticism to claim that this represents an overly idealized view of friendship? How might English respond to such a criticism?

3. Whether children love their parents or not may change considerably as they mature and have additional life experiences. Does this mean that children's obligations toward their parents similarly change? If, as English argues, love between parents and children creates mutual obligations, but sacrifices made do not, couldn't a child simply escape his obligations by claiming (or actually bringing it about) that he no longer loves his parents?

4. English believes that basing obligations toward one's parents on mutuality rather than reciprocity would have positive consequences for parent-child relationships. Do you agree? Can you think of any possible negative consequences of this view? Has English convinced you of her position?

Christina Hoff Sommers, Filial Morality

In the reading that follows, Christina Hoff Sommers argues for a strong thesis of filial obligation. She explicitly addresses the impartiality thesis endorsed by Kantians and utilitarians and finds this thesis to be severely deficient. In place of what she calls the "equal pull thesis," she proposes the "differential pull thesis" that would dictate that more is owed to those to whom we are more intimately related. She also criticizes those moral theorists (like Jane English) who focus on the feelings of love and friendship between parents and children, arguing that it is an insufficient basis for grounding parent-child morality. Ultimately, she argues for a conception of filial obligation not unlike that proposed by Confucius, namely, the view that children have special obligations toward their parents that are of a kind that they do not have for other, unrelated, individuals. Sommers's view is therefore in strong opposition to the view developed by English in the previous reading.

Reading Questions

1. What point is Sommers trying to establish with the first three examples she provides? What is it about these examples that suggests that grown children have special obligations toward their parents?

2. What is the "Jellyby fallacy" Sommers identifies? How does the behavior of someone like Mrs. Jellyby represent the "impartialist point of view"? What is the "equal pull thesis," and how does it relate to the impartialist point of view? What is the "thesis of differential pull"?

3. What two conditions does Sommers identify for determining when a special positive obligation arises for a moral agent? Given these two conditions, what are some of the filial obligations she identifies?

4. How does Sommers characterize those moralists she calls "sentimentalists"? How do sentimentalists differ from "deontologists"? What are Sommers's major criticisms of sentimentalist moral theories? What crucial mistake do sentimentalists make?

Filial Morality

CHRISTINA HOFF SOMMERS

We not only find it hard to say exactly how much a son owes his parents, but we are even reluctant to investigate this.

—HENRY SIDGWICK, *THE METHODS OF ETHICS*[1]

WHAT RIGHTS DO PARENTS have to the special attentions of their adult children? Before this century there was no question that a filial relationship defined a natural obligation; philosophers might argue about the nature of filial obligation, but not about its reality. Today, not a few moralists dismiss it as an illusion, or give it secondary derivative status. A. John Simmons expresses "doubts . . . concerning the existence of 'filial' debts," and Michael Slote seeks to show that the idea of filial obedience is an illusion whose source is the false idea that one owes obedience to a divine being. Jeffrey Blustein argues that parents who have done no more than their duty may be owed nothing, and Jane English denies outright that there are any filial obligations not grounded in mutual friendship.

The current tendency to deny or reconstrue filial obligation is related to the more general difficulty that contemporary philosophers have when dealing with the special duties. An account of the special obligations to one's kin, friends, community or country puts considerable strain on moral theories such as Kantianism and utilitarianism, theories that seem better designed for telling us what we should be doing for everyone impartially than for explaining something like filial obligation. The moral philosopher of a utilitarian or Kantian persuasion who is concerned to show that it is permissible to give some biased vent to family feeling *may* go on to become concerned with the more serious question of accounting for what appears to be a special obligation to care for and respect one's parents—but only as an afterthought. On the whole, the question of special agent-relative duties has not seemed pressing. In what follows I shall be arguing for a strong notion of filial obligation, and more generally I shall be making a case for the special moral

[1] *The Methods of Ethics* (New York: Dover, 1966), p. 243.

relations. I first present some anecdotal materials that illustrate the thesis that a filial duty to respect one's parents is not an illusion.

I. The Concrete Dilemmas

I shall be concerned with the filial duties of adult children and more particularly with the duty to honor and respect. I have chosen almost randomly three situations, each illustrating what seems to be censurable failure on the part of adult children to respect their parents or nurturers. It would not be hard to add to these cases, and real life is continually adding to them.

1. An elderly man was interviewed on National Public Radio for a program on old age. This is what he said about his daughter.

   I live in a rooming house. I lost my wife about two years ago and I miss her very much. . . . My little pleasure was to go to my daughter's house in Anaheim and have a Friday night meal. . . . She would make a meal that I would enjoy. . . . So my son-in-law got angry at me one time for a little nothing and ordered me out of the house. That was about eight months ago. . . . I was back once during the day when he was working. That was about two and a half or three months ago. I stayed for about two hours and left before he came home from work. But I did not enjoy the visit very much. That was the last time I was there to see my daughter.

2. An eighty-two-year-old woman (call her Miss Tate) spent thirty years working as a live-in housekeeper and baby-sitter for a judge's family in Massachusetts. The judge and his wife left her a small pension which inflation rendered inadequate. After her employers died, she lost contact with the children whom she had virtually brought up. One day Miss Tate arranged for a friend of hers to write to the children (by then

Christina Hoff Sommers, "Filial Morality," Journal of Philosophy, *vol. 83, no. 8 (August 1986), pp. 439–456.*
Reprinted by permission of the author and Journal of Philosophy.

middle-aged) telling them that she was sick and would like to see them. They never got around to visiting her or helping her in any way. She died last year without having heard from them.

3. The anthropologist Barbara Meyerhoff did a study of an elderly community in Venice, California. She tells about the disappointment of a group of elders whose children failed to show up at their graduation from an adult education program:

> The graduates, 26 in all, were arranged in rows flanking the head table. They wore their finest clothing bearing blue and white satin ribbons that crossed the breast from shoulder to waist. Most were solemn and flushed with excitement. . . . No one talked openly about the conspicuous absence of the elders' children.

I believe it may be granted that the father who had dined once a week with his daughter has a legitimate complaint. And although Miss Tate was duly salaried throughout her long service with the judge's family, it seems clear that the children of that family owe her some special attention and regard for having brought them up. The graduation ceremony is yet another example of wrongful disregard and neglect. Some recent criticisms of traditional conceptions of filial duty (e.g., by Jane English and John Simmons) make much of examples involving unworthy parents. One may agree that exceptional parents can forfeit their moral claims on their children. (What, given his behavior, remains of Fyodor Karamazov's right to filial regard?) But I am here concerned with what is owed to the average parent who is neglected or whose wishes are disregarded when they could at some reasonable cost be respected. I assume that such filial disregard is wrong. Although the assumption is dogmatic, it can be defended—though not by any quick maneuver. Filial morality is but one topic in the morality of special relations. The attempt to understand filial morality will lead us to a synoptic look at the moral community as a whole and to an examination of the nature of the rights and obligations that bind its members.

II. Shifting Conceptions

Jeffrey Blustein's *Parents and Children* contains an excellent historical survey of the moral issues in the child-parent relationship. For Aristotle the obligation to serve and obey one's parents is like an obligation to repay a debt. Aquinas too explains the commandment to honor one's parents as "making a return for benefits received." Both Aristotle and Aquinas count life itself as the first and most important gift that the child is given.

With Locke the topic of filial morality changes: the discussion shifts from a concern with the authority and power of the parent to concern with the less formal, less enforceable, right to respect. Hume was emphatic on the subject of filial ingratitude, saying, "Of all the crimes that human creatures are capable, the most horrid and unnatural is ingratitude, especially when it is committed against parents." By Sidgwick's time the special duties are beginning to be seen as problematic: "The question is on what principles . . . we are to determine the nature and extent of the special claims of affection and kind services which arise out of . . . particular relations of human beings." Nevertheless, Sidgwick is still traditional in maintaining that "all are agreed that there are such duties, the nonperformance of which is ground for censure," and he is himself concerned to show how "our common notion of Justice [is] applicable to these no less than to other duties."

If we look at the writings of a contemporary utilitarian such as Peter Singer, we find no talk of justice or duty or rights, and *a fortiori*, no talk of special duties or parental rights. Consider how Singer, applying a version of R. M. Hare's utilitarianism, approaches a case involving filial respect. He imagines himself about to dine with three friends when his father calls saying he is ill and asking him to visit. What shall he do?

> To decide impartially I must sum up the preferences for and against going to dinner with my friends, and those for and against visiting my father. Whatever action satisfies more preferences, adjusted according to the strength of the preferences, that is the action I ought to take.

Note that the idea of a special obligation does not enter here. Nor is any weight given to the history of the filial relationship which typically includes some two decades of parental care and nurture. According to Singer, "adding and subtracting preferences in this manner" is the only rational way of reaching ethical judgment.

Utilitarian theory is not very accommodating to the special relations. And it would appear that Bernard Williams is right in finding the same true of Kantianism. According to Williams, Kant's "moral point of view is specially characterized by its impartiality and its indifference to any particular relations to particular persons." In my opinion, giving no special consideration to one's kin commits what might be called the *Jellyby fallacy*. Mrs. Jellyby, a character in

Charles Dickens' *Bleak House,* devotes all of her considerable energies to the foreign poor to the complete neglect of her family. She is described as a "pretty diminutive woman with handsome eyes, though they had a curious habit of seeming to look a long way off. As if they could see nothing nearer than Africa." Dickens clearly intends her as someone whose moral priorities are ludicrously disordered. Yet by some modern lights Mrs. Jellyby could be viewed as a paragon of impartial rectitude. In the next two sections I will try to show what is wrong with an impartialist point of view and suggest a way to repair it.

III. The Moral Domain

By a *moral domain* I mean a domain consisting of what G. J. Warnock calls "moral patients." Equivalently, it consists of beings that have what Robert Nozick calls "ethical pull." A being has *ethical pull* if it is ethically "considerable"; minimally, it is a being that should not be ill treated by a moral agent and whose ill treatment directly wrongs it. The extent of the moral domain is one area of contention (Mill includes animals; Kant does not). The nature of the moral domain is another. But here we find more uniformity. Utilitarians and deontologists are in agreement in conceiving of the moral domain as constituted by beings whose ethical pull is equal on all moral agents. To simplify matters, let us consider a domain consisting only of moral patients that are also moral agents. (For Kant, this is no special stipulation.) Then it is as if we have a gravitational field in which the force of gravitation is not affected by distance and all pairs of objects have the same attraction to one another. Or, if this sort of gravitational field is odd, consider a mutual admiration society no member of which is, intrinsically, more attractive than any other member. In this group, the pull of all is the same. Suppose that Buridan's ass was not standing in the exact middle of the bridge but was closer to one of the bags of feed at either end. We should still say that he was equally attracted to both bags, but also that he naturally would choose the closer one. So too does the utilitarian or Kantian say that the ethical pull of a needy East African and that of a needy relative are the same, but we can more easily act to help the relative. This theory of equal pull but unequal response saves the appearances for impartiality while acknowledging that, in practice, charity often begins and sometimes ends at home.

This is how the principle of impartiality appears in the moral theories of Kant and Mill. Of course their conceptions of ethical pull differ. For the Kantian any

being in the kingdom of ends is an embodiment of moral law whose force is uniform and unconditional. For the utilitarian, any being's desires are morally considerable, exerting equal attraction on all moral agents. Thus Kant and Mill, in their different ways, have a common view of the moral domain as a domain of moral patients exerting uniform pull on all moral agents. I shall refer to this as the *equal-pull (EP) thesis.* It is worth commenting on the underlying assumptions that led Kant and Mill to adopt this view of the moral domain.

It is a commonplace that Kant was concerned to free moral agency from its psychological or "anthropological" determinations. In doing so he offered us a conception of moral agents as rational beings which abstracts considerably from human and animal nature. It is less of a commonplace that utilitarian theory, in its modern development, tends also to be antithetical to important empirical aspects of human nature. For the Kantian, the empirical demon to be combated and exorcised lies within the individual. For the utilitarian it is located within society and its customs, including practices that are the sociobiological inheritance of the species. According to an act utilitarian like Singer, reason frees ethical thought from the earlier moralities of kin and reciprocal altruism and opens it to the wider morality of disinterestedness and universal concern: "The principle of impartial consideration of interests . . . alone remains a rational basis for ethics." The equal-pull thesis is thus seen to be entailed by a principle of impartiality, common to Kantian and utilitarian ethics, which is seen as liberating us from the biased dictates of our psychological, biological, and socially conventional natures.

IV. Differential Pull

The doctrine of equal ethical pull is a modern development in the history of ethics. It is certainly not attributable to Aristotle or Aquinas, nor, arguably, to Locke. Kant's authority gave it common currency and made it, so to speak, foundational. It is, therefore, important to state that EP is a dogma. Why should it be assumed that ethical pull is constant regardless of circumstance, familiarity, kinship and other special relations? The accepted answer is that EP makes sense of impartiality. The proponent of the special duties must accept this as a challenge: alternative suggestions for moral ontology must show how impartiality can be consistent with differential ethical forces.

I will refer to the rival thesis as the *thesis of differential pull (DP).* According to the DP thesis, the ethical pull of a moral patient will always partly depend on how the moral patient is related to the moral agent on whom the pull is exerted. Moreover, the "how" of relatedness will be determined in part by the social practices and institutions in which the agent and patient play their roles. This does not mean that every moral agent will be differently affected, since it may be that different moral agents stand in the same relation to different moral patients. But where the relations differ in certain relevant ways, there the pull will differ. The relevant factors that determine ethical pull are in a broad sense circumstantial, including the particular social arrangements that determine what is expected from the moral agent. How particular circumstances and conventions shape the special duties is a complex question to which we cannot here do justice. We shall, however, approach it from a foundational standpoint which rejects EP and recognizes the crucial role of conventional practice, relationships, and roles in determining the nature and force of moral obligation. The gravitational metaphor may again be suggestive. In DP morality the community of agents and patients is analogous to a gravitational field, where distance counts and forces vary in accordance with local conditions.

V. Filial Duty

Filial duty, unlike the duty to keep a promise, is not self-imposed. But keeping the particular promise one has made is also a special duty, and the interplay of impartiality and specific obligation is more clearly seen in the case of a promise. We do well, therefore, to look at the way special circumstances shape obligations by examining more carefully the case of promise making.

A. I. Melden has gone into the morality of promise keeping rather thoroughly, and I believe that some features of his analysis apply to the more general description of the way particular circumstances determine the degree of ethical pull on a moral agent. Following Locke, Melden assumes the natural right of noninterference with one's liberty to pursue one's interests (including one's interest in the well-being of others) where such pursuit does not interfere with a like liberty for others. Let an interest be called *invasive* if it is an interest in interfering with the pursuit of someone else's interests. Then the right that every moral patient possesses is the right not to be interfered with in the pursuit of his or her noninvasive interests. (In what follows "interest" will mean noninvasive interest.)

According to Melden, a promiser "gives the promisee the action as his own." The promise-breaking failure to perform is then "tantamount to interfering with or subverting endeavors he [the promisee] has a right to pursue." The promisee is "as entitled to [the action] as he is, as a responsible agent, to conduct his own affairs." What is special about this analysis is the formal grounding of the special positive duty of promise keeping in the minimalist negative obligation of noninterference. The negative, general, and indiscriminate obligation not to interfere is determined by the practice of promise making as a positive, specific, and discriminate obligation to act. Note how context here shapes and directs the initial obligation of noninterference and enhances its force. Given the conventions of the practice of promise making, the moral patient has novel and legitimate expectations of performances caused by the explicit assurances given by the promiser, who, in effect, has made over these performances to the promisee. And given these legitimate expectations, the agent's nonperformance of the promised act is invasive and tantamount to active interference with the patient's rights to its performance.

It is in the spirit of this approach to make the attempt to analyze other special obligations in the same manner. We assume a DP framework and a minimal universe deontological principle (the duty to refrain from interfering in the lives of others). This negative duty is refracted by the parochial situation as a special duty which may be positive in character, calling on the moral agent to act or refrain from acting in specific ways toward specific moral patients. This view of the special obligations needs to be justified. But for the present I merely seek to state it more fully.

The presumption of a special positive obligation arises for a moral agent when two conditions obtain: (1) In a given social arrangement (or practice) there is a specific interaction or transaction between moral agent and patient, such as promising and being promised, nurturing and being nurtured, befriending and being befriended. (2) The interaction in that context gives rise to certain conventional expectations (e.g., that a promise will be kept, that a marital partner will be faithful, that a child will respect the parent). In promising, the content of the obligation is verbally explicit. But this feature is not essential to the formation of other specific duties. In the filial situation, the basic relationship is that of nurtured to nurturer, a type of relationship which is very concrete, intimate, and long-lasting and which is considered to be more morally determining than any other in shaping a variety of rights and obligations.

Here is one of Alasdair MacIntyre's descriptions of the denizens of the moral domain:

I am brother, cousin, and grandson, member of this household, that village, this tribe. These are not characteristics that belong to human beings accidentally, to be stripped away in order to discover "the real me." They are part of my substance, defining partially at least and sometimes wholly my obligations and my duties.

MacIntyre's description takes Aristotle's dictum that man is a social animal in a sociological direction. A social animal has a specific social role whose prerogatives and obligations characterize a particular kind of person. Being a father or mother is socially as well as biologically descriptive: it not only defines what one is; it also defines who one is and what one owes.

Because it does violence to a social role, a filial breach is more serious than a breach of promise. In the promise the performance is legitimately expected, being, as it were, explicitly made over to the promisee as "his." In the filial situation the expected behavior is implicit, and the failure to perform affects the parent in a direct and personal way. To lose one's entitlements diminishes one as a person. Literature abounds with examples of such diminishment; King Lear is perhaps the paradigm. When Lear first becomes aware of Goneril's defection, he asks his companion: "Who am I?" to which the reply is "A shadow." Causing humiliation is a prime reason why filial neglect is tantamount to active interference. One's sense of dignity varies with temperament. But dignity itself—in the context of an institution like the family—is objective, being inseparable from one's status and role in that context.

The filial duties of adult children include such things as being grateful, loyal, attentive, respectful and deferential to parents (more so than to strangers). Many adult children, of course, are respectful and attentive to their parents out of love, not duty. But, as Melden says: "The fact that, normally, there is love and affection that unites the members of the family . . . in no way undercuts the fact that there is a characteristic distribution of rights and obligations within the family circle."

The mutual understanding created by a promise is simplicity itself when compared with the range of expected behavior that filial respect comprises. What is expected in the case of a promise is clearly specified by the moral agent, but with respect to most other special duties there is little that is verbally explicit. Filial obligation is thus essentially underdetermined, although there are clear cases of what counts as disrespect—as we have seen in our three cases. The complexity and nonspecificity of expected behavior which is written into the domestic arrangements do not affect what the promissory and the filial situation have in common: both may be viewed as particular contexts in which the moral agent must refrain from behavior that interferes with the normal prerogatives of the moral patient.

By taking promising as a starting point in a discussion of special duties, one runs the risk of giving the impression that DP is generally to be understood as a form of social-contract theory. But a more balanced perspective considers the acts required by any of the special duties as naturally and implicitly "made over" within the practices and institutions that define the moral agent in his particular role as a "social animal." Within this perspective promising and other forms of contracting are themselves special cases and not paradigmatic. Indeed, the binding force of the obligation to fulfill an explicit contract is itself to be explained by the general account to be given to special duties in a DP theory.

VI. Grateful Duty

One group of contemporary moral philosophers, whom I shall tendentiously dub *sentimentalists*, has been vocal in pointing out the shortcomings of the mainstream theories in accounting for the morality of the special relations. But they would find my formal and traditional approach equally inadequate. The sentimentalists oppose deontological approaches to the morality of the parent-child relationship, arguing that *duties* of gratitude are paradoxical, that the "owing idiom" distorts the moral ideal of the parent-child relationship, which should be characterized by love and mutual respect. For them, each family relationship is unique, its moral character determined by the idiosyncratic ties of its members. Carol Gilligan has recently distinguished between an "ethic of care" and an "ethic of rights." The philosophers I have in mind are objecting to the aridity of the "rights perspective" and are urging moral philosophers to attend to the morality of special relations from a "care perspective." The distinction is suggestive, but the two perspectives are not necessarily exclusive. One may recognize one's duty in what one does spontaneously and generously. And just as a Kantian caricature holds one in greater esteem when one does what is right against one's inclination, so the idea of care, responsibility and personal commitment, without formal obligation, is an equally dangerous caricature.

Approaches that oppose care and friendship to rights and obligations can be shown to be sadly inadequate when applied to real-life cases. The following situation described in this letter to Ann Landers is not atypical:

> Dear Ann Landers:
> We have five children, all overachievers who have studied hard and done well. Two are medical doctors and one is a banker. . . . We are broke from paying off debts for their wedding and their education. . . . We rarely hear from our children. . . . Last week my husband asked our eldest son for some financial help. He was told "File bankruptcy and move into a small apartment." Ann, personal feelings are no longer a factor: it is a matter of survival. Is there any law that says our children must help out?

There are laws in some states that would require that these children provide some minimal support for their indigent parents. But not a few contemporary philosophers could be aptly cited by those who would advocate their repeal. A. John Simmons, Jeffrey Blustein, and Michael Slote, for example, doubt that filial duty is to be understood in terms of special moral debts *owed* to parents. Simmons offers "reasons to believe that [the] particular duty meeting conduct [of parents to children] does not generate an obligation of gratitude on the child." And Blustein opposes what he and Jane English call the "owing idiom" for services parents were obligated to perform. "If parents have any right to repayment from their children, it can only be for that which was either above and beyond the call of parental duty, or not required by parental duty at all." (The "overachievers" could not agree more.) Slote finds it "difficult to believe that one has a *duty* to show gratitude for benefits one has not requested." Jane English characterizes filial duty in terms of the duties one good friend owes another. "[A]fter a friendship ends, the duties of friendship end."

Taking a sentimentalist view of gratitude, these philosophers are concerned to remove the taint of onerous duty from what should be a spontaneous and free desire to be considerate of one's parents. One may agree with the sentimentalists that there is something morally unsatisfactory in being considerate of one's parents *merely* out of duty. The mistake lies in thinking that duty and inclination are necessarily at odds. Moreover, the *having* of certain feelings and attitudes may be necessary for carrying out one's duty. Persons who lack feeling for their parents may be morally culpable for that very lack. The sentimentalist objection that this amounts to a paradoxical duty to *feel* (grateful, loyal, etc.) ignores the extent to which people are responsible for their characters; to have failed to develop in oneself the capacity to be considerate of others is to have failed morally, if only because many duties simply cannot be carried out by a cold and unfeeling moral agent. Kant himself speaks of "the universal duty which devolves upon man of so ordering his life as to be fit for the performance of all moral duties." And MacIntyre, who is no Kantian, makes the same point when he says, "Moral education is an 'education sentimentale.'"

Sentimentalism is not harmlessly false. Its moral perspective on family relationships as spontaneous, voluntary, and duty-free is simply unrealistic. Anthropological observations provide a sounder perspective on filial obligation. Thus Corinne Nydegger warns of the dangers of weakening the formal constraints that ensure that obligations are met: "No society, including our own, relies solely on . . . affection, good will and enlightened self-interest." She notes that the aged in particular "have a vested interest in the social control of obligations."

It should be noted that the sentimentalist is arguing for a morality that is sensitive to special relations and personal commitment; this is in its own way a critique of EP morality. But sentimentalism ignores the extent to which the "care perspective" is itself dependent on a formal sense of what is fitting and morally proper. The ideal relationship cannot be "duty-free," if only because sentimental ties may come unraveled, often leaving one of the parties at a material disadvantage. Sentimentalism then places in a precarious position those who are not (or no longer) the fortunate beneficiaries of sincere personal commitments. If the EP moralist tends to be implausibly abstract and therefore inattentive to the morality of the special relations, the sentimentalist tends to err on the side of excessive narrowness by neglecting the impersonal "institutional" expectations and norms that qualify all special relations.

VII. DP Morality: Some Qualifications

It might be thought that the difference between EP and DP tends to disappear when either theory is applied to concrete cases, since one must in any case look at the circumstances to determine the practical response. But this is to underestimate how what one *initially* takes to be the responsibility of moral agents to patients affects the procedure one uses in making practical decisions in particular circumstances. Recall again how Peter Singer's EP procedure pits the preferences of the three friends against the preferences of the father, and contrast this with a differential-pull approach that assumes discriminate and focused obligations to the father. Similarly, the adult children of the graduating elders and the children raised by Miss Tate gave no special weight to filial obligation in planning their day's activities.

There are, then, significant practical differences between a DP and an EP approach to concrete cases. The EP moralist is a respecter of the person whom he sees as an autonomous individual but no respector of the person as a social animal within its parochial preserve. Moreover, a DP theory that grounds duty in the minimal principle of noninterference is sensitive to the distinction between strict duty and benevolence. Behaving as one is duty bound to behave is not the whole of moral life. But duty (in the narrow sense) and benevolence are not commensurate. If I am right, the Anaheim woman is culpably disrespectful. But it would be absurd if (in the manner of Mrs. Jellyby) she were to try to compensate for excluding her father by inviting several indigent gentlemen to dine in his stead.

I am arguing for a DP approach to the morality of the special relations. Williams, Nozick, MacIntyre, and others criticize utilitarianism and Kantianism for implausible consequences in this area. I believe that their objections to much of contemporary ethics are symptomatic of a growing discontent with the EP character of the current theories. It may be possible to revise the theories to avoid some of the implausible consequences. Rule utilitarianism seems to be a move in this direction. But, as they stand, their EP character leaves them open to criticism. EP is a dogma. But so is DP. My contention is that DP moral theories more plausibly account for our preanalytic moral judgments concerning what is right and wrong in a wide variety of real cases. Having said this, I will acknowledge that the proper antidote to the malaise Williams and others are pointing to will not be effectively available until DP moral theories are given a theoretical foundation as well worked out as those of the mainstream theories. Alasdair MacIntyre is a contemporary DP moralist who has perhaps gone furthest in this direction. Nozick and Williams are at least cognizant that a "particularistic" approach is needed.

The DP moral theory is in any case better able to account for the discriminate duties that correspond to specific social roles and expectations. But of course not all duties are discriminate: there are requirements that devolve on everyone. This not only includes the negative requirement to refrain from harming one's fellowman, but also, in certain circumstances, to help him when one is singularly situated to do so. I am, for example, expected to help a lost child find its parent or to feed a starving stranger at my doorstep. Failure to do so violates an understanding that characterizes the loosest social ties binding us as fellow human beings. The "solitariness" that Hobbes speaks of is a myth; we are never in a totally unrelated "state of nature." The DP moralist recognizes degrees of relatedness and graded expectations. The most general types of positive behavior expected of anyone as a moral agent obey some minimal principle of Good Samaritanism applicable to "the stranger in thy midst."

Perhaps the most serious difficulty facing the DP approach is that it appears to leave the door wide open to ethical relativism. We turn now to this problem.

VIII. DP and Ethical Relativism

A theory is nonrelativistic if it has the resources to pass moral judgments on whole societies. My version of DP moral theory avoids ethical relativism by adopting a deontological principle (noninterference) which may be deployed in assessing and criticizing the moral legitimacy of the traditional arrangements within which purportedly moral interactions take place. We distinguish between unjust and merely imperfect arrangements. Arrangements that are essentially invasive are unjust and do not confer moral legitimacy on what is expected of those who are party to them. To correct the abuses of an unjust institution like slavery or a practice like suttee is to destroy the institution or practice. By contrast, an institution like marriage or the family will often contain some unjust features, but these are usually corrigible, and the institution itself is legitimate and morally determining in a straightforward sense.

In any case the DP moralist is in a position to hold that not all social arrangements impose moral imperatives. It is not clear to me that DP can avoid relativism without *some* deontological minimal ground. But conceivably a principle other than noninterference might better serve as universal ground of the special duties. What is essential to any deontologically grounded DP morality is the recognition that the universal deontological principle is differentiated and specified by local arrangements that determine what is legitimately expected of the moral agent.

It may now be clear in what sense I believe DP theories to be plausible. A moral theory is plausible to the extent that it accounts for our pretheoretical moral judgments. Such intuitive judgments are admittedly idiosyncratic and prejudicial, being conditioned by our upbringing and the traditions we live by. The EP moralist nobly courts implausibility by jettisoning prejudice and confronting moral decisions anew. By contrast, the DP moralist jettisons only those prejudices which are exposed as rooted in and conditioned by an unjust social arrangement. But for those institutions which are not unjust, our common-sense judgments of "what is expected" (from parents, from citizens, from adult children) are generally held to be reliable guides to the moral facts of life.

The version of DP that I favor accepts the Enlightenment doctrine of natural rights in the minimal form of a universal right to noninterference and the correlative duty of moral agents to respect that right. MacIntyre's version of DP is hostile to Enlightenment "modernism," abjuring all talk of universal rights or deontic principles of a universal character. It is in this sense more classical. An adequate version of DP must nevertheless avoid the kind of ethical relativism that affords the moral philosopher no way to reject some social arrangements as immoral. MacIntyre appears to suggest that this can be achieved by accepting certain teleological constraints on good societies. Pending more detail, I am not convinced that a teleological approach can by itself do the critical job that needs to be done if we are to avoid an unacceptable ethical relativism. But other nondeontic approaches are possible. David Wong has argued for a Confucian condition of adequacy that grades societies as better or worse depending on how well they foster human flourishing. My own deontic approach is not opposed to teleological or Confucianist ways of judging the acceptability of social arrangements. If a given arrangement is degenerate, then that is in itself a good reason to discount its norms as morally binding. But conceivably even a flourishing society could be unjust; nevertheless its civic norms should count as morally vacuous and illegitimate. It seems to me, therefore, that MacIntyre's version of DP morality probably goes too far in its rejection of all liberal deontic principles.

I have argued that DP best explains what we intuitively accept as our moral obligations to parents and other persons who stand to us in special relations. And though my version of DP allows for criticizing unjust social arrangements, it may still seem unacceptably relativistic. For does it not allow that what is right for a daughter or son in one society is wrong for them in another? And does this not run afoul of the condition that what is right and wrong must be so universally? It should, I think, be acknowledged that the conservatism that is a feature of the doctrine of differential pull is somewhat hospitable to ethical

relativism. Put another way: differential pull makes sense of ethical relativism's large grain of truth, but it does so without losing claim to its ability to evaluate morally the norms of different societies and institutions. Institutions that allow or encourage interference with noninvasive interests are unjust, and we have noted that the adherent of differential pull is in as good a position to apply a universal principle in evaluating an institution as anyone of an EP persuasion. But application of DP will rule out some institutions while allowing *diverse* others to count as legitimate and just. Only a just institution can assign and shape a moral obligation for those who play their roles within it. However, there are many varieties of just institutions, and so, in particular, are there many ways in which filial obligations are determined within different social and cultural contexts. What counts as filial respect in one context may not count as filial respect in another context. It is a virtue of our account that it not only tolerates but shows the way to justify different moral norms.

IX. *Common Sense*

The sociologist Edward Shils warns about the consequences of the modern hostility to tradition in ways reminiscent of ecologists warning us about tampering with delicate natural systems that have taken millennia to evolve. The EP character of much of modern philosophy encourages a hasty style of playing fast and loose with practices and institutions that define the traditional ties binding the members of a family or community. And a duty-free sentimentalism is no kinder to traditional mores.

The appeal to common sense is often a way of paying proper attention to the way that particular circumstances and social practice enter into the shaping of obligations. This, to my mind, is Sidgwick's peculiar and saving grace. But many a moral philosopher lacks Sidgwick's firm appreciation of the role of accepted practice or common sense. I shall illustrate this by way of a final example.

Richard Wasserstrom in "Is Adultery Immoral?" raises the question of whether the (alleged) obligation not to commit adultery might be explained by reasons that would apply to any two persons generally. It is, for example, wrong for any person to deceive another. And he discusses the destructive effects adultery has on the love that the marital partners bear to one another. What is missing from Wasserstrom's account is any hint that the obligations of marriage are shaped by the institution as it exists and that being "faithful" is a legitimate institutional expectation informing the way that the partners may treat each other. Wasserstrom does say that "we ought to have reasons for believing that marriage is a morally desirable and just social institution." But what follows if it is? Wasserstrom does not say. What we want here is an account of how and why a married person who commits adultery may be wronging the partner. How, in particular, might an act of adultery be construed as unwarranted interference? The shift from the examination of an obligation that has its locus and form within a given institution to evaluating the institution itself is legitimate; but it is all too often a way of avoiding the more concrete and immediate investigation which is the bread and butter of normative ethics.

EP is ethics without ethos. So too is sentimentalism. Both have a disintegrative effect on tradition. Where EP and sentimentalism sit in judgment on ethos, DP respects it and seeks to rationalize it. The EP moralist is reformist in spirit, tending to look upon traditional arrangements as obstacles to social justice. John Rawls, for example, is led to wonder whether the family is ethically justifiable:

> It seems that even when fair opportunity (as it has been defined) is satisfied, the family will lead to unequal chances between individuals. Is the family to be abolished then? Taken by itself and given a certain primacy, the idea of equal opportunity inclines in this direction. But within the context of the theory of justice as a whole, there is less urgency to take this course.

Not urgent perhaps, but not unreasonable either. A defender of filial morality cannot with equanimity entertain the idea of abolishing the family. Here Sidgwick is the welcome antidote. For him the suggestion that ethical principles might require the elimination of something so central to "established morality" betrays a misconception of the job of ethics. Instead, Sidgwick demands of philosophers that they "repudiate altogether that temper of rebellion . . . into which the reflective mind is always apt to fall when it is first convinced that the established rules are not intrinsically reasonable."

Reporting on how he arrived at his way of doing moral philosophy, Sidgwick tells of his rereading of Aristotle:

> [A] light seemed to dawn upon me as to the meaning and drift of [Aristotle's] procedure. . . . What he gave us there was the Common Sense Morality of Greece, reduced to consistency by careful comparison: given not as something external to him but as what "we"—he and others—think, ascertained by reflection. . . . Might I not imitate this: do the same for *our* morality here and now, in the same manner of impartial reflection on current opinion?

Discussion and Reflection Questions

1. In the first three examples Sommers gives, she does not indicate the current state of affection or friendship between the grown children and the parents or caretaker in question. Would it make any difference to your moral assessment of these examples to learn that in each case the parent or caretaker was not especially lovable or deserving of consideration? In other words, are filial obligations related in any way to the current level of friendship between parents and children?

2. How does the existence of what Sommers calls "special duties" conflict with the moral principles defended by Kant and Mill? When faced with this sort of conflict, which should take precedence: our moral intuitions or our considered moral theories? Is there some way to reach a balance between the two?

3. Does Sommers think that the existence of special duties requires a new moral theory, or are such duties best addressed within a broadly duty-based ethical theory?

4. Sommers discusses Kantian, utilitarian, and "sentimentalist" approaches to the issue of filial morality. How would a Confucian perspective on this issue fare? Would Sommers be likely to accept a Confucian perspective? What is your own view of the obligations of children to their parents?

Chenyang Li, Grown Children's Filial Obligation

In "Grown Children's Filial Obligation," Chenyang Li defends a view of filial moral obligation associated with the Confucian moral tradition. He cites Confucius and Mencius as setting the historical foundation for his view. Although he puts forth several arguments for the claim that grown children should care for their aged parents, his central argument for this claim takes the position of Jane English as its point of departure. English argues that giving birth to and raising children is not a *favor* from parents to children, because children did not *ask* to be born. Li examines this claim more closely and argues that not all favors need be benefits resulting from an explicit request for assistance. Parental sacrifice for their children does, he argues, create an obligation on the part of children to care for their parents. Throughout the essay Li appeals to the Chinese, and especially Confucian, view of the natural and ideal relation between parents and children, according to which filial obligation is perhaps the strongest moral obligation a person can have in life.

Reading Questions

1. Li retells a story about a government official and his mother. What is the point of this story? What lesson does Li draw from it?

2. Li cites a recent case in which a ninety-year-old Chinese woman sued her two grown sons for failing in their filial duty to her. How, according to Li, is filial duty supported by Chinese social values?

3. Li claims that "filial obligation exists even if the grown children do not have love or friendship to their parents," and that parental sacrifices "do create a situation in which the children are obliged to reciprocate service or financial assistance when the aged parents are in need." Explain carefully his argument for this claim.

4. Li tells a story about Al lending a hand to Barbara in her time of need. What is the point of this example? How is it supposed to provide an objection to the claims made by Jane English in the article included above? In particular, what is Li's argument for the claim that obligation-incurring favors need not be the result of asking another person for assistance?

Grown Children's Filial Obligation

CHENYANG LI

WHEN I WAS LITTLE, my Chinese grandmother told me the following story. A long, long time ago, food was scarce. It was a custom that people over sixty were sent out to the mountains and put inside graves built on the ground. Without food and water they would soon die there. Because it was a common practice, no-body felt there was anything wrong with it. There was a government official who loved his aged mother so much that, although he had to follow the custom to send his mother to the mountain grave, he left a hole in the grave and kept sending food and water to feed his mother, year after year. One day, he brought his mother a big basketful of food and water and told his mother that was the last time he could send her food. "I am going to die," said the man. "The royal palace has been invaded by five strange animals. They are destroying everything. Nobody knows what they are and how to deal with them. Tomorrow is my deadline to subdue these animals. If I as a government official fail to perform my duty, I must die. Today I came to say good-bye." The extremely saddened mother said, "Son, tell me what these animals look like." The man gave her as specific descriptions of those animals as he could. Then the old woman said, "I know what they are and how to subdue them. They are huge rats. The last time I saw them was before you were born. They ate all kinds of food and destroyed clothes and furniture. They ran fast and men couldn't catch them. The only thing that subdued them was cats." "What are cats?" the man asked. "Because there have not been rats for a long time, all the cats have disappeared from town. But there may be some in the mountains." The old woman drew a picture of a cat for her son. "Go and find one and your problem is solved." With the picture the son finally found a cat and the cat caught all the rats in the royal palace. The emperor was overjoyed and offered to grant the man a wish. "I want my mother back home." He told the emperor how he had kept his mother alive and how she had helped him in solving the problem. With little hesitation the emperor issued a decree: "From now on old people are to stay home with their children as long as they live, and their children must take good care of them and treat them with respect and dignity." From then on, all old people lived happily with their families.

The story may not be literally true, but it tells us that old people deserve respect because of their experience and knowledge. Today in America many people love, care for, and are attentive to their aged parents. But many people send their aged parents away, not to graves in the mountains, but to nursing homes. Many people do this at the expense of society. In some states, an old person in a nursing home can cost the state as much as fifty to sixty thousand dollars a year. It would cost considerably less if their grown children took care of them at home, even with the aid of a part-time helper and some financial assistance from the state. And these old people are likely to be happier if they live at home with their family instead of in a nursing home. But the system is set up in such a way that many people will not do so.

The question I would like to raise and discuss here is, what responsibility, if any, do grown children have toward their aged parents?

The most natural relation among humans is between children and parents. By nature, parents generally care for their young. Even among animals, parents have a natural inclination to care for their young. But the natural inclination for adult children to care for their aged parents is much weaker. In animals this kind of care almost does not exist. Humans have morality. In many cultures an important function of morality is to nurture people's sense of filial obligation. For example, the Chinese have a strong tradition of respecting the old. Confucius made it clear that morality starts with respecting one's parents (*Analects*, 1:2). Mencius maintained that one criterion of a good society is that there are no people with gray hair (old people) carrying heavy burdens on the street (*Mencius*, 1A:3). They both believed that a moral person must take care of his or her aged parents and not leave them to hardship whenever it is possible. Tseng Tzu, a disciple of Confucius, was a classic exemplar of this notion of filial morality. When his father grew old and became weak, in order to make sure his father had enough food Tseng Tzu served his father separate meals before the rest of the family ate. He served his father meat and wine every day even though Tseng Tzu himself did not have meat and wine to eat and drink. In the Confucian view, a person's filial duty is not only to serve his or her aged parents, but also to do the best to serve them well. In order to perform this duty, Confucius believed, a person should not go far from home while his parents are alive; and if he has to go far from home, he should let his parents know his whereabouts in case they need him (*Analects*, 4:19). Needless to say, a son at home should never send his aged parents away, not to a nursing home, not anywhere. In the *People's Daily* (overseas edition) of August 25, 1993, there was a report that in the Shandong province of China a ninety-year-old woman sued her two sons for failing in their filial duty. The woman's husband died young and left her with two sons one and three years old. Through countless hardships she brought them both up. Now she is old and can do no more work. Neither of her two sons wanted to take care of her. The court took her case and ordered the sons to take full responsibility for her living and medical expenses. Given the Chinese culture this court decision is no surprise. It reflects the social values of the culture.

In the West many people feel the same way. But in some people the feeling does not seem as strong as in some other cultures. Some philosophers are openly opposed to the idea of filial obligation on the ground of biological ties. Jane English, for example, in her article "What Do Grown Children Owe Their Parents?"

maintains that love and friendship are the sole ground for filial obligation. When the children no longer have love and friendship toward their parents, filial obligation ceases to exist. She argues that parents' sacrifices for having children are not "favors" that are to be "repaid" by their children later, because the children never asked to be born or to be looked after when they were little. She writes, "I will maintain that parents' voluntary sacrifices, rather than 'debts' to be 'repaid,' tend to create love or 'friendship.' The duties of grown children are those of friends and result from love between them and their parents, rather than being things owed in repayment for the parents' earlier sacrifices" [pp. 428–429]. Thus, she believes that if the grown children have no love or friendship toward their parents, there is no filial obligation bonding the children and the parents.

I do not deny that parents' sacrifices for their children tend to create love and friendship in the children toward the parents. I contend, however, that grown children's filial obligation to their parents goes beyond obligations between friends or people who love each other. I contend that filial obligation exists even if the grown children do not have love or friendship to their parents. Although parents' earlier sacrifices for their children are not the sole ground for filial obligation to the children, these sacrifices do create a situation in which the children are obliged to reciprocate services or financial assistance when the aged parents are in need.

The Chinese traditionally believe that the greatest favor a person has ever received is from his parents, their giving him birth and bringing him up. This favor is so great that a person can never completely "repay" it. Thus he is in a lifetime obligation to serve his parents. Even though this is not the only ground for filial obligation, it is a considerable portion of it.

English does not deny that a person has a moral obligation to return or "repay" a favor done to her. But she argues that parents' earlier sacrifices for their children are not a favor to the children because the children did not ask for it. Therefore the children are not obliged to repay it when the parents are in need. A favor results, according to English, "when A, at B's request, bears some burden for B, then B incurs an obligation to reciprocate" [p. 429]. English illustrated as follows. "New to the neighborhood, Max barely knows his neighbor, Nina, but asks her if she will take in his mail while he is gone for a month's vacation. She agrees. If, subsequently Nina asks Max to do the same for her, it seems that Max has a moral obligation to agree (greater than the one he would have

had if Nina had not done the same for him), unless for some reason it would be a burden far out of proportion to the one Nina bore for him" [p. 429]. In this case, English maintains, Nina has done a favor to Max. But if "Max simply goes on vacation and, to his surprise, finds upon his return that his neighbor has mowed his grass twice weekly in his absence. This is a voluntary sacrifice rather than a favor, and Max has no duty to reciprocate" [p. 429]. In the latter case there is no favor done because, English suggests, Max did not request the service from his neighbor.

But is a request necessary for a favor to take place? I do not think so. Whether a favor is done has more to do with whether a person is in need and would like the thing done to or for her. Suppose on her way home to feed her three-year-old child, Barbara's car broke down, and Al happened to drive by and offered to give her a lift home or to call a tow truck. Even though Barbara did not request it, Al has done a favor for Barbara. If Barbara should see Al's car break down, she has a moral obligation to help, an obligation greater than if Al had not helped Barbara when her car broke down, as long as no burden much greater would result from helping Al. Perhaps Barbara would feel a stronger obligation if she had requested a lift home from Al. But in many cases favors are done without a request. Suppose Barbara's three-year-old accidentally falls into a pond. Al happens to pass by the pond and sees it. He jumps into the pond and saves the child's life. Even though she did not request it, it would be nevertheless outrageous if Barbara did not consider Al's sacrifice to have done her a great favor. It would be indecent if Barbara does not think she has a moral obligation to lend a hand if Al later needs some help from Barbara. Under these circumstances, whether a request has been made is irrelevant to the fact of a favor's having been done.

I assume that a normal person appreciates the fact that he has a life. I assume that a normal person appreciates the fact that his parents have endured hardship and sacrifices to bring him up. I assume that between being born and not being born a normal person would strongly prefer the former, and between being taken good care of and not when he was little, a normal person would strongly prefer the former. Then the person "owes" his parents a great favor for giving him life and bringing him up, even though he did not request either. And such a person is under moral obligation to reciprocate the favor he has received. When his parents are old and need assistance, he is obliged to help. Although how much help he can offer depends on circumstances, his moral obligation to help his aged parents is greater than his general duty to help other people in need.

A moral obligation is a moral obligation, regardless of whether a person likes it or not. If Barbara's life is in great danger and Al saves her life without being requested to, Al does Barbara a great favor. If Barbara does not appreciate the favor and does not feel grateful, we say that she has a very poor sense of appreciation or that she lacks a moral conscience. Even if she does not feel she "owes" Al a great favor, it does not change the fact that she is under moral obligation to reciprocate the favor in some appropriate way. Al, on the other hand, may gracefully "waive" any moral obligation Barbara has to him and not expect anything in return. But that is entirely Al's noble gesture. In the same way, parents have done a great favor to their children without being requested to, by giving them life and bringing them up. Grown children are under obligation to return the favor. Usually the best way to do so is to take care of their parents when they grow old and need care from their grown children. Although a grown child should have love and friendship for his parents, even if he does not, he is not exempt from his filial obligation. Similar to the case of Al's saving the life of Barbara's child without being appreciated, a person may not feel grateful for his parents' giving him life and bringing him up. But that only shows that he has a weak moral conscience. The lack of love and friendship on his part does not exempt him from his filial obligation to serve his aged parents. Morality demands that a person fulfill this obligation.

So, to the question, What responsibility do grown children have toward their aged parents? my answer is: when their aged parents become feeble or sick and need care, grown children have a responsibility to take care of their parents in the best way possible. At this point one may want to ask, What if grown children do not have a house large enough for their aged parents to live in? What if grown children do not make enough money to support their aged parents? I think the issue is first of all a matter of attitude. Have not people found themselves with fewer rooms in their house than children in the family? Have not people found their budget is tight because they have more children than their money can adequately support? Yes, of course they have. But they do not send their children away for these reasons, because they believe that it is their inescapable responsibility to take care of their own children. They may have to ask for financial assistance from the state or other sources. They may have to hire a house-helper. But they do manage it. Once people realize that they also have an inescapable obligation to take care of their aged parents, they will find ways to manage to take care of them. With the resources that society has been, and is still, spending on old people, by accepting their filial responsibility grown children will make their aged parents happier and the world will be a much better place for everyone.

Discussion and Reflection Questions

1. Li interprets the story of the government official and his aged mother to show that old people deserve respect because of their experience and knowledge. In the story the old woman possessed valuable information. But what would this principle suggest about old persons who do *not* possess such information? In other words, is there a danger in connecting respect for older persons with their knowledge or, more generally, their social utility?

2. Li cites a case from China in which a ninety-year-old woman sued her two sons for failing to care for her in her old age. Should American society *require*, perhaps under threat of legal sanctions, that grown children care for their elderly parents? What sorts of arguments could be given in support of such an idea?

3. Li claims that "the greatest favor a person has ever received is from his parents, their giving him birth and bringing him up. This favor is so great that a person can never completely 'repay' it. Thus he is in a lifetime obligation to serve his parents." Do you agree?

4. What connection does Li draw between the example of Barbara and Al and the obligations grown children have toward their parents? Are the cases similar? Is being born

best construed as a "favor" from one's parents? If it is, does it create the obligation Li says it does? Can this obligation ever be "repaid"? Does Li have much sympathy with the claim that taking care of one's aged parents might be a major "inconvenience"? What connection does he draw between one's responsibility for caring for one's aged parents and one's responsibility for caring for one's young children? Is this argument sound?

Brian K. Smith, Morality within the Family: The Hindu Tradition

Every day most of us interact with a range of different people, including friends, acquaintances, and strangers. But some of our most important relationships occur within the family. Within the family the relationship between husband and wife is central. In virtue of the marital bond, including the mutual promises and commitments made, distinctive marital obligations arise. But what do husbands and wives owe one another? This question is so important that major religious traditions often have much to say about it. In the Hindu tradition the mutual obligations of husbands and wives is specified in detail. In the following essay, Brian K. Smith examines some of the central themes in this tradition.

Reading Questions

1. In the Hindu tradition, how is the fulfillment of obligations to one's family related to the fulfillment of one's religious duties? How are "this-worldly" and "other-worldly" values related?
2. According to the Hindu tradition, what are the special moral obligations of the householder? How does a man's wife help him to fulfill these obligations?
3. What do husbands owe their wives? What are the chief virtues of a husband?
4. What do wives owe their husbands? What are the chief virtues of a wife?

Morality within the Family: The Hindu Tradition

BRIAN K. SMITH

IN HINDUISM, as in most other traditional world religions, a very high premium is placed on the family. It is by forming and maintaining a family that a man and a woman fulfill some of their most important religious duties—to themselves, to one another, to their ancestors, to society, and to posterity. Indeed, while families are obviously regarded as important in many societies (including our own, as is witnessed by the frequent political appeal to "family values"), in the Hindu religious tradition one's very salvation is often said to hinge on a timely and proper marriage and the production of offspring. Despite the fact that Hinduism has had a long tradition of world renunciation, asceticism, and chastity, these other-worldly values and practices are almost always set within a context of the prior fulfilling of one's obligations to the family.

The family in Hinduism is the essential germ of social and even cosmic order, the microcosm of stability, regularity, and propriety. The social and moral or-

Brian K. Smith, "Morality within the Family: The Hindu Tradition," in Ethics of Family Life, edited by Jacob Neusner (Belmont, Calif.: Wadsworth, 2001), pp. 91–109. Used by permission of Wadsworth.

der of things and beings (seen and unseen) depend on a correctly structured, hierarchically governed, and well-functioning family. Conversely, as we shall see below, when the family is threatened or ruined, the ramifications are severe and wide-ranging.

Another reason the family plays such a vital role in both society and the cosmos as a whole is because for most strands of Hinduism religious life revolves around the householder stage of life, during which one marries, reproduces, and raises children. It is in this stage of life that one's ritual obligations to the gods, the ancestors, and to one's fellow human beings are discharged. For this reason and others, the householder stage is said to be the best—better even than those stages of life in which one is pursuing the ultimate religious goal of final liberation from rebirth, or *moksha*. Furthermore, all other stages of life (those of the student, forest-dweller, and world renouncer) depend on the householder, in part because it is the householder who feeds and donates to them when they beg from him:

A householder alone offers sacrifices. A householder afflicts himself with austerities. Of the four stages of life, therefore, the householder is the best. As all rivers and rivulets ultimately end up in the ocean, so people of all stages of life ultimately end up with the householder. As all creatures depend on their mothers for their survival, so all mendicants depend on householders for their survival.[1]

Thus, as another text puts it, when "carried out with zeal" the householder stage of life procures both happiness in this life and heaven in the next:

Just as all living creatures depend on air in order to live, so do members of the other stages of life subsist by depending on householders. Since people in the other three stages of life are supported every day by the knowledge and food of the householder, therefore the householder stage of life is best. It must be carried out with zeal by the man who wants to win an incorruptible heaven (after death) and endless happiness here on earth. . . .[2]

Yet another reason for the emphasis on the family in Hinduism is the traditional importance placed on the begetting sons to carry on the family name and lineage. Already in some of the earliest and subsequently most authoritative sacred texts of the Hindu tradition, the Vedas (composed ca. 1200–400 B.C.E.), the critical and supreme importance of sons and the value of the wife who produces them is evident. In one such passage, composed of a discussion between a king named Hariscandra, who has one hundred wives but no sons, and a priest named Narada, the king asks, "What does one gain by a son? Tell me that, O Narada." The priest replies by enumerating the many benefits a son brings to his father:

A debt he pays in him,
And immortality he gains,
The father who sees the face
Of his son born and alive.
Greater than the delights
That earth, fire, and water
Bring to living beings
Is a father's delight in his son.
By means of sons have fathers ever
Crossed over the mighty darkness;
For one is born from oneself,
A ferry laden with food.
What is the use of dirt and deer skin?
What profit in beard and austerity?
Seek a son, O Brahmin,
He is the world free of blame.[3]

Narada, in this glorification of male offspring, begins with an articulation of a very common Hindu theme: it is through the production of sons that a man repays a "debt" he owes to his ancestors and thereby also wins a kind of immortality for himself. By creating a son a father perpetuates himself ("for one is born from oneself") and also "crosses over the mighty darkness." Furthermore, Narada contrasts the life of the family man to that of the ascetic or world renouncer (covered in "dirt and deer skin" practicing his austerities), and claims that it is through a son that a father wins a "world free of blame," that is, a pleasant and righteous life in both this world and the next.

Narada then goes on to specify yet more of the benefits and joys the birth of a son brings to the father, and expands his discussion to extol also the role the wife plays in a man's life as well:

[1]Vasistha Dharma Sutra 10.14–16. Translated in Patrick Olivelle, *The Asrama System: The History and Hermeneutics of a Religious Institution* (New York: Oxford University Press, 1993), 93.
[2]Manusmriti (hereafter abbreviated as Manu) 3.77–79. This and all other quotations from this text are taken from *The Laws of Manu*, translated by Wendy Doniger with Brian K. Smith (London: Penguin Books, 1991).

[3]Aitareya Brahmana 7.13. Translated in Olivelle, *The Asrama System*, 44.

Food is breath, clothes protect.
Gold is for beauty, cattle for marriage.
The wife is a friend, a daughter brings grief.
But a son is a light in the highest heaven.
The husband enters the wife;
Becoming an embryo he enters the mother.
Becoming in her a new man again,
He is born in the tenth (lunar) month.
A wife is called "wife,"
Because in her he is born again.
He is productive, she is productive,
For the seed is placed in her.
The gods and the seers
Brought to her great luster.
The gods said to men:
"She is your mother again."[4]

Here again we see the idea that one is reproduced in the form of one's son. A man is said to be born again in his wife's womb and thus, as another text puts it, "in your offspring you are born again; that, o mortal, is your immortality" (Satapatha Brahmana 1.5.5.6). If the son is a means of extending his own life into another generation, or, indeed, into a kind of "immortality," a man's wife is thus considered his second mother, "because in her he is born again." As such, as we shall see, both offspring and wife are to be revered by the man as the very agents of his happiness in this life and the next.

Thus, at all levels—cosmic, social, and individual—the family is at the center of religious life in Hinduism. Because of the prominence of family life in this religion, guidelines are set out for the proper establishment and maintenance of the family and to direct the relationships between husbands and wives and parents and children. These interrelationships are guided by a set of mutually obtaining obligations between the various members of the Hindu family.

What Do Husbands Owe Wives?

While Hindu texts of all sorts maintain that ultimately the supreme goal of religious life is reached through detachment from and renunciation of the world of family, work, and social ties, most also insist that this pursuit of final liberation from karma and rebirth must wait until one's obligations (or "debts") are fulfilled. Chief among these are the debts to the ancestors, paid off, as we have seen above, through the production of a son with one's wife. But other debts are also owed and are repaid by the study of

the sacred Veda and by sacrificial rituals, both of which are part and parcel of the householder's ritual routine and all of which are incumbent upon a man before he may renounce the world:

> When a man has paid his three debts, he may set his mind-and-heart on Freedom; but if he seeks Freedom when he has not paid the debts, he sinks down. When a man has studied the Veda in accordance with the rules, and begotten sons in accordance with his duty, and sacrificed with sacrifices according to his ability, he may set his mind-and-heart on Freedom. But if a twice-born man seeks Freedom when he has not studied the Vedas, and has not begotten progeny, and has not sacrificed with sacrifices, he sinks down. (Manu 6.35–37)

Another text makes a similar point and adds other obligatory duties to the list a man must perform as a householder before he is allowed to renounce: "No one but a man who has studied the Vedas, muttered prayers, fathered sons, given food (to guests and others in various rituals), maintained the sacred fires, and offered sacrifices according to his ability, may set his mind on renunciation."[5]

Thus, Hinduism demands that a man complete himself as a householder—a husband, father, and man-in-the-world—before pursuing final liberation. A man's responsibilities, if they are to be properly fulfilled, require that he, after a period as a student under the guidance of a teacher, select a suitable woman, marry her, and thus begin the stage of life of a householder. A wife not only enables a man to fulfill his spiritual and ritual obligations, playing as she does an indispensable role in those arenas; she also, it is said, completes the very being of a man: "A full half of one's self is one's wife. As long as one does not obtain a wife, therefore, for so long one is not reborn and remains incomplete. As soon as he obtains a wife, however, he is reborn and becomes complete" (Satapatha Brahmana 5.2.1.10). "When he finds a wife, therefore," it is said in another text, "a man considers himself to be, as it were, more complete" (Aitareya Aranyaka 1.2.5). It is as a pair that husband and wife participate in the sacrificial rituals and carry out other of the household's ritual duties. They are, therefore, jointly responsible for both the ritual obligation and for the merit that comes from fulfilling such duties. The wife is thus said in at least one text to be "qualified to perform sacrifices" because she assumes the responsibilities for carrying out the rituals on her own when her husband cannot:

---

[4]Ibid., 45.

[5]Yajnavalkya Dharmasmriti 3.56, in ibid., 143.

Together do these two (husband and wife) constitute a couple; together do these two maintain the sacred fires; together do these two procreate and obtain progeny. The eastern world pertains to the husband, the western world to the wife. Since the wife takes upon herself the responsibility of the vow (to maintain the sacrificial rites) of the husband who has gone out on a journey or who has become incapacitated, therefore she is entitled to half (of the ritual's benefits). Women are (thus) qualified to perform sacrifices. (Manava Srauta Sutra 8.23.10–14)

Because she will be so crucial to his future well-being, selecting a wife is a matter of great concern. She should, of course, come from the right caste and from a good family, but she should also possess good qualities and character: "One should examine the family (of the intended bride), those on the mother's side and on the father's side. . . . One should marry a girl who possesses the characteristics of intelligence, beauty, and good character, and who is free from disease" (Apastamba Grhya Sutra 1.5.1–3). Some texts, like the following, go into some detail about the type of woman one should seek as a wife and the types one should definitely avoid:

When he has received his guru's permission and bathed and performed the ritual for homecoming according to the rules (i.e., when he has completed the student stage of life), a twice-born man should marry a wife who is of the same class and has the right marks. A woman who does not come from the same blood line on her mother's side, nor belongs to the same ritual line on her father's side, and who is a virgin, is recommended for marriage to a twice-born man. When a man connects himself with a woman, he should avoid the ten following families, even if they are great or rich in cows, goats, sheep, property, or grain: a family that has abandoned the rites, or does not have male children, or does not chant the Veda; and those families in which they have hairy bodies, piles, consumption, weak digestion, epilepsy, white leprosy, or black leprosy. A man should not marry a girl who is a redhead or has an extra limb or is sickly or has no body hair or too much body hair or talks too much or is sallow; or who is named after a constellation, a tree, or a river, or who has a low-caste name, or is named after a mountain, a bird, a snake, or has a menial or frightening name. He should marry a woman who does not lack any part of her body and who has a pleasant name, who walks like a goose or an elephant, whose body hair and hair on the head is fine, whose teeth are not big, and who has delicate limbs. A wise man will not marry a woman who has no brother or whose father is unknown. . . . (Manu 3.4–11)

Later on, after a man has married a woman of his own caste, he may wed other women as well. Men "driven by desire" may take additional wives from castes other than their own caste, assuming the first wife has the proper pedigree. But the highest castes are prohibited under any circumstances from forming unions with women of the servant classes, for if they do they drag their own families down the caste ladder:

A woman of the same class is recommended to twice-born men for the first marriage; but for men who are driven by desire, these are the women, in progressively descending order: According to tradition, only a servant woman can be the wife of a servant; she and one of his own class can be the wife of a commoner; these two and one of his own class for a king; and these three and one of his own class for a priest. Not a single story mentions a servant woman as the wife of a priest or ruler, even in extremity. Twice-born men who are so infatuated as to marry women of low caste quickly reduce their families, including the descendants, to the status of servants. (Manu 3.12–15)

Having thus selected the right woman to wed, a man should marry her according to the proper rites of marriage laid out in the scriptures. When he has done so, the husband becomes her "master" but he also takes on certain duties vis-à-vis his new wife:

Benedictory verses are recited and a sacrifice to the Lord of Creatures is performed at weddings to make them auspicious, but it is the act of giving away (the bride by the father) that makes (the groom) her master. A husband who performs the transformative ritual (of marriage) with Vedic verses always makes his woman happy, both when she is in her fertile season and when she is not, both here on earth and in the world beyond. (Manu 5.152–153)

Note here that the husband has, according to the text, the responsibility to keep his wife happy and sexually fulfilled, even in times when she will not conceive.

In addition, however, and among the most important of all duties that husbands have to wives, is the obligation to impregnate them. In another passage we read of the exact times when a husband may and may not approach his wife for sex, and the type of offspring they will produce out of intercourse at different times of the month:

A man should have sex with his wife during her fertile season, and always find his satisfaction in his own wife; when he desires sexual pleasure he should go to her to whom he is vowed, except on the days at the (lunar) junctures. The natural fertile season of women is traditionally said to last for sixteen nights, though these include four special days that good people despise. Among these (nights), the first four, the eleventh, and the thirteenth are disapproved; the other ten nights are approved. On the even nights, sons are conceived, and on the uneven nights, daughters; therefore a man who wants sons should unite with his wife during her fertile season on the even nights. A male child is born when the semen of the man is greater (than the seed of a woman), and a female child when (the seed) of the woman is greater (than the semen of a man); if both are equal, a hermaphrodite is born, or a boy and a girl (i.e., fraternal twins). . . . (Manu 3.45–49)

A husband also has the obligation to support his wife and family materially; he must provide for their shelter and subsistence and other necessities of life. In the householder stage of life, in fact, one has the religious duty to pursue *artha*, "advantage" or "self-interest" as it pertains to the political and economic spheres of life. Such an obligation to work and provide for the wife continues even if a man is called upon to travel, although it appears that the husband needs to do more than just leave money behind—he should find an occupation to keep his wife busy so as to keep her honest:

A man may go away on a journey on business only after he has established a livelihood for his wife; for even a steady woman could be corrupted if she is starving for lack of livelihood. If he goes away on a journey after providing a livelihood, she should subject herself to restraints in her life; but if he goes away on a journey without providing for her, she may make her living by crafts that are not disapproved of. (Manu 9.74–75)

Furthermore, if a husband goes on such a journey (with or without making provisions for his wife) a woman need not wait forever for her husband to return before carrying on with her own life: "If the man has gone away on a journey to fulfill some duty, (she)

should wait for him for eight years; (if he has gone) for learning or fame, six; for pleasure, three years" (Manu 9.76).

A wife with whom one makes a family and who is and remains virtuous should be revered by her menfolk; she is equated with "the goddesses of good fortune" and becomes worthy of worship by her husband. The virtuous wife and mother becomes the linchpin for the proper performance of a householder's dharma or religious duty, which includes the procreation and care of children, the running of the household, and sexual pleasure (or *kama*, another of the prescribed "ends of life" for the Hindu in the householder stage of life), but also the attainment of heaven itself for the male householder and his ancestors:

There is no difference at all between the goddesses of good fortune who live in houses and women who are the lamps of their houses, worthy of reverence and greatly blessed because of their progeny. The wife is the visible form of what holds together the begetting of children, the caring for them when they are born, and the ordinary business of every day. Children, the fulfillment of duties, obedience, and the ultimate sexual pleasure depend upon a wife, and so does heaven, for oneself and one's ancestors. The woman who is not unfaithful to her husband but restrains her mind-and-heart, speech, and body reaches her husband's worlds (after death), and good people call her a virtuous woman. (Manu 9.26–29)

The good wife and "virtuous woman" is thus crucial to the success of the family as a whole and to the husband's welfare in particular. In the following text, it is said that women who fulfill such an ideal should be worshiped and revered, for through their virtue and the respect paid to them by their male family members the gods are pleased and the family thrives. Conversely, in homes where virtuous women are not so honored and become unhappy, the family is destroyed:

Fathers, brothers, husbands, and brothers-in-law who wish for great good fortune should revere these women and adorn them. The deities delight in places where women are revered, but where women are not revered all rites are fruitless. Where the women of the family are miserable, the family is soon destroyed, but it always thrives where the women are not miserable. Homes that are cursed by women of the family who have not been treated with due reverence are completely destroyed, as if struck down by witchcraft. Therefore men who wish to prosper should always revere these women with ornaments, clothes, and food at celebrations and festivals. There is unwavering good fortune in a family where the husband is always satisfied by the wife, and the wife by the husband. If the wife is not radiant she does not stimulate the man; and because the man is unstimulated the making of children does not happen. If the woman is radiant, the whole family is radiant, but if she is not radiant the whole family is not radiant. Through bad marriages, the neglect of rites, failure to study the Veda, and transgressing against priests, families cease to be families. (Manu 3.55–63)

Such then, is the supreme importance of the family in general and of the mutual respect between husbands and wives under ideal circumstances. The husband's duty to his wife is to care for her in all ways and to do his best to make her happy; the wife's duty to her husband, as we shall see shortly, is to please, honor, and obey him in all things. But certain texts also take into account the unfortunate possibility that a wife will, for one reason or another, not be satisfactory and will need to be, as the following passage puts it, "superseded" (i.e., replaced by another wife):

A husband should wait for one year for a wife who hates him; but after a year, he should take away her inheritance and not live with her. If she transgresses against a husband who is infatuated, a drunk, or ill, he may deprive her of her jewelry and personal property and desert her for three months. But if she hates him because he is insane, fallen, impotent, without semen, or suffering from a disease caused by his evil, she should not be deserted or deprived of her inheritance. A wife who drinks wine, behaves dishonestly, or is rebellious, ill, violent, or wasteful of money may be superseded at any time. A barren wife may be superseded in the eighth year; one whose children have died, in the tenth; one who bears (only) daughters, in the eleventh; but one who says unpleasant things (may be superseded) immediately. But if a woman who is kind and well-behaved becomes ill, she should be superseded (only) when she has been asked for her consent, and she should never be dishonored. And if a woman who has been superseded should leave the house in fury, she should be locked up immediately or deserted in the presence of the family. (Manu 9.77–83)

The ancient Indian equivalent of divorce (being "superseded"; however, this need not entail the ex-wife leaving the house, but merely losing her pride of place to another wife who succeeds her) is justified here on a number of different grounds. A wife may be replaced if she is cruel to her husband (even, it appears, if he deserves it), is herself undisciplined and ruled by vice, or if she cannot bear sons for the husband.

These reasons for "superseding" a wife point to traditional Hinduism's set of virtues for the ideal wife, and to what this wife owes her husband.

What Do Wives Owe Husbands?

A girl, a young woman, or even an old woman should not do anything independently, even in (her own) house. In childhood a woman should be under her father's control, in youth under her husband's, and when her husband is dead, under her sons'. She should not have independence. A woman should not try to separate herself from her father, her husband, or her sons, for her separation from them would make both (her own and her husband's) families contemptible. She should always be cheerful, and clever at household affairs; she should keep her utensils well polished and not have too free a hand in spending. When her father, or her brother with her father's permission, gives her to someone, she should obey that man while he is alive and not violate her vow to him when he is dead. (Manu 5.147–151)

Here we have a classic formulation of male dominance: a woman should be under a man's control and guidance at every stage of life. A girl's father should supervise her in her childhood, her husband in her youth and middle age, and if she survives her husband she should be placed under the care of her sons—such is the way to prevent families from becoming "contemptible." "Men must make their women dependent day and night," it is said in another passage, "and keep under their own control those who are attached to sensory objects. Her father guards her in childhood, her husband guards her in youth, and her sons guard her in old age. A woman is not fit for independence" (Manu 9.2–3).

The wife's duties to her husband are thus to obey him absolutely and to care for his home diligently; she is not only to be submissive but also wholly occupied with the pursuits of domesticity. She should, as the text cited above puts it, carefully but "cleverly" run the household affairs (under the supervision of a male) and keep herself focused on her chores. Marriage is for life, without the possibility of divorce for the woman, and remarriage should the husband die first is strictly forbidden. A wife should be loyal to her husband in this life and "not violate her vow to him when he is dead." She should "care for his body and perform the obligatory daily chores" (Manu 9.86) and if she remains faithful to him throughout his life she will join him in heaven. If, however, she is unfaithful an unsavory fate awaits her after death:

> The woman who is not unfaithful to her husband but restrains her mind-and-heart, speech, and body reaches her husband's worlds (after death), and good people call her a virtuous woman. But a woman who is unfaithful to her husband is an object of reproach in this world; (and after death) she is reborn in the womb of a jackal and is tormented by the diseases (born) of (her) evil. (Manu 9.29–30)

A woman should not leave her husband for another no matter how bad he is, for "A woman who abandons her own inferior husband and lives with a superior man becomes an object of reproach in this world; she is said the be 'previously had by another man'" (Manu 5.163).

This is the traditional (and, need it be said, patriarchal) standard for the Hindu wife: wholly dependent on her male family members and absolutely faithful to her husband (even if he is "inferior"), she is assigned her place in the home where she is charged with the production and proper upbringing of children and the supervision of domestic affairs. She is to remain restrained in mind and body and loyal and obedient to her husband, and, as we have seen, if she does so the husband is to regard her with respect and even veneration. The wife's role is pivotal both to the well-being of the family as a whole and to the fate of her husband, and she in turn should be accorded the good, if paternalistic, treatment she deserves.

In the following, taken from a famous play by the Sanskrit author Kalidasa, the dramatist has a young woman's father pass along some advice regarding how she should comport herself with her future royal husband. Later on in the passage, the daughter calls this "an excellent compendium, truly, of every wife's duties":

> Listen, then, my daughter. When thou reachest thy husband's palace, and art admitted into his family,
> Honour thy betters; ever be respectful
> To those above thee; and, should others share

> Thy husband's love, ne'er yield thyself a prey
> To jealousy; but ever be a friend,
> A loving friend, to those who rival thee
> In his affections. Should thy wedded lord
> Treat thee with harshness, thou must never be
> Harsh in return, but patient and submissive.
> Be to thy menials courteous, and to all
> Placed under thee, considerate and kind:
> Be never self-indulgent, but avoid
> Excess in pleasure; and, when fortune smiles,
> Be not puffed up. Thus to thy husband's house
> Wilt thou a blessing prove, and not a curse.[6]

This outline of the ideally humble, dependent, submissive, and utterly faithful wife is sketched on a background that assumes a rather different notion of the inherent nature of women. Left to her own devices, some texts assert, women will follow their intrinsic and evil proclivities. By nature, women are said to be lustful and unfaithful, unable to control their sexual desires; they must, therefore, be carefully guarded by their husbands. Such natural promiscuity is even said to be wholly indiscriminate:

> Good looks do not matter to them, nor do they care about youth; "A man!" they say, and enjoy sex with him, whether he is good-looking or ugly. By running after men like whores, by their fickle minds, and by their natural lack of affection these women are unfaithful to their husbands even when they are zealously guarded here. Knowing that their very own nature is like this, as it was born at the creation by the Lord of Creatures, a man should make the utmost effort to guard them. The bed and the seat, jewellery, lust, anger, crookedness, a malicious nature, and bad conduct are what Manu assigned to women. There is no ritual with Vedic verses for women; this is a firmly established point of law. For women, who have no virile strength and no Vedic verses, are falsehood; this is well established. (Manu 9.14–18)

Such an extremely unflattering view of women as "by nature" promiscuous, untrustworthy and evil—the very essence of "falsehood"—is replicated in a variety of ancient texts. "There exist no friendships with women," says the most ancient of Hindu texts, the Rig Veda, for "they have the hearts of hyenas" (Rig Veda 10.95.15). Elsewhere in that work we read that women are ineducable (Rig Veda 8.33.17), an

---

[6]From Kalidasa's *Sakuntala*, cited and translated in Ainslie T. Embree, editor, *The Hindu Tradition: Readings in Oriental Thought* (New York: Vintage Books, 1966), 167–168.

early sanction for the prohibition on teaching women the sacred texts of Hinduism. The somewhat later Mahabharata declares that "women are speakers of untruth," that "fickleness is the norm in women," that "women are the root of faults and have weak understanding," and that "nothing exists that is more wicked than women" (Mahabharata 1.68.72; 5.36.56; 13.38.1; 13.38.12).

These kinds of assumptions about women justify the insistence that a husband must guard and protect his wife from her own inborn proclivities. The following text claims this is in fact the husband's "supreme duty," and suggests the best way to guard one's wife is to keep her busy at home and indoctrinate her so thoroughly that she "guards herself":

> Women should especially be guarded against addictions, even trifling ones, for unguarded (women) would bring sorrow upon both families (her own and her husband's). Regarding this as the supreme duty of all the classes, husbands, even weak ones, try to guard their wives. For by zealously guarding his wife he guards his own descendants, practices, family, and himself, as well as his own duty. . . . No man is able to guard women entirely by force, but they can be entirely guarded by using these means: he should keep her busy amassing and spending money, engaging in purification, attending to her duty, cooking food, and looking after the furniture. Women are not guarded when they are confined in a house by men who can be trusted to do their jobs well; but women who guard themselves are well guarded. Drinking, associating with bad people, being separated from their husbands, wandering about, sleeping, and living in other peoples' houses are the six things that corrupt women. (Manu 9.5–7, 10–13)

The "well-guarded" wife will, in addition to tending to the children and household, help her husband carry out the family's ritual and religious ceremonies and duties. Women themselves, however, were specifically precluded from many of these regularly performed religious duties; they were not allowed to study or recite the Veda and therefore did not undergo the initiation ceremony that signified a "second birth" for young men. Those rites of passage that women did undergo were performed without the ritual accompaniment of recited verses from the Veda, for women were traditionally prohibited from even hearing the sound of this sacred text. Nevertheless, in the following passage certain of the important life-cycle rites, stages of life, and subsequent ritual duties of the male householder are equated to their supposed correlates in the woman's life:

> For women, this cycle (of rites of passage) should be performed without Vedic verses, leaving nothing else out, at the proper time and in the proper order, to perfect the body. The ritual of marriage is traditionally known as the Vedic initiation ritual for women; serving her husband is (the equivalent of) living with a guru, and household chores are the sacrificial rites of the fire. (Manu 2.66–67)

The domestic life of the dependent wife is here valorized by connecting it to the religious life of men: marriage is equated to the initiation ceremony, service to the husband is correlated to the study of the Veda under the tutelage of a guru, and household chores are regarded as the female equivalent of the sacrificial rituals performed by the husband.

The religious duties or dharma of a woman, under this view, revolve entirely around affairs of the home, the family, and the marriage; what she owes her God and what she owes her husband are thus conflated. In a summary of the "duty of the woman" (*stri-dharma*), one author wholly confounds the woman's religious duties with her "service to her husband":

> The husband is thus to be propitiated (by the wife as follows): by observing the rules of purification; by attending to the fire ritual; by paying homage to guests; by taking care of the household duties; by keeping close watch over the household (accounts), both income and expenditure; by attending to her husband's bodily comfort; by serving food to her husband's dependents, etc.; . . . by love-making and so on at night; by avoiding both those things which are forbidden to her and those which her husband does not like; by putting into practice both those things which are prescribed and those which her husband likes; . . . by obedient service to her husband; and by doing what he says. Propitiating him in this way is said to constitute true "service" to one's husband.[7]

In this traditional system, should a wife outlive her husband she is not allowed to remarry. A good widow should honor her husband's memory by her ascetic lifestyle, chastity, and loyalty.

---

[7]The *Stridharmapaddhati* of Tryambakayajvan, 86.4–88.1; translated in I. Julia Lessa, *The Perfect Wife: The Orthodox Hindu Woman according to the Stridharmapaddhati of Tryambakayajvan* (Delhi: Oxford University Press, 1989), 314–315.

A virtuous wife should never do anything displeasing to the husband who took her hand in marriage, when he is alive or dead, if she longs for her husband's world (i.e., heaven after her death). When her husband is dead she may fast as much as she likes, (living) on auspicious flowers, roots, and fruits, but she should not even mention the name of another man. She should be long-suffering until death, self-restrained, and chaste, striving (to fulfill) the unsurpassed duty of women who have one husband. (Manu 5.156–158)

Indeed, a widow should not remarry even if she has remained childless; such is the binding force of the marriage vow for her, and such is her obligation to her husband:

Many thousands of priests who were chaste from their youth have gone to heaven without begetting offspring to continue the family. A virtuous wife who remains chaste when her husband has died goes to heaven just like those chaste men, even if she has no sons. But a woman who violates her (vow to her dead) husband because she is greedy for progeny is the object of reproach here on earth and loses the world beyond. No (legal) progeny are begotten here by another man or in another man's wife; nor is a second husband ever prescribed for virtuous women. (Manu 5.159–162)

The tradition has presented another alternative for the wife whose husband dies before her. Among the most controversial elements of the traditional Hindu view of a wife's obligations to her husband is the ritual called sati. This practice, performed especially among the upper classes (and most especially among women from the warrior castes) from the eighth century C.E. onward, entailed the self-sacrifice of the widow who joined her deceased husband on his funereal pyre. Sati, which literally means the "virtuous woman," was regarded by some Hindu women as both the ultimate act of devotion to the husband and as a preferable alternative to life as a widow. The following depicts a queen's conversation with her son who was trying to prevent her from cremating herself in the fire:

If at this hour my regard is not towards you, it is that my lord's great condescension comes between us. Furthermore, dear son, I am not ever craving for the sight of another lord. I am the lady of a great house, born of stainless ancestry, one whose virtue is her dower. . . . Daughter, spouse,

mother of heroes, how otherwise could such a woman as I, whose price was valour, act? . . . I would die while still unwidowed. I cannot endure, like the widowed Rati, to make unavailing lamentations for a burnt husband. Going before, like the dust of your father's feet, to announce his coming to the heavens, I shall be high esteemed of the hero-loving spouses of the gods. Not to die, but to live at such a time would be unfeeling. Compared with the flame of wifely sorrow, whose fuel is imperishable love, fire itself is chilly cold. . . . Not in the body, dear son, but in the glory of loyal widows would I abide on earth. Therefore dishonour me no more, I beseech you, beloved son, with opposition to my heart's desire. . . . Having embraced her son and kissed his head, the queen went forth on foot from the women's quarter, and, though the heavens, filled with the citizen's lamentations, seemed to block her path, proceeded to the Sarasvati's banks. Then, having worshiped the fire with the blooming red lotus posies of a woman's timorous glances, she plunged into it, as the moon's form enters the adorable sun.[8]

The practice of sati became a major issue among both the British colonial rulers and Hindu reformers in the beginning of the early nineteenth century, and was officially outlawed in 1829. Nevertheless, satis have occurred occasionally since; one recent case in north India received much media attention and was the cause of great controversy.

What Do Parents Owe Their Children?

If one of the great obligations husbands and wives have to one another is to bring children into the world, it is certainly in part because of self-interest that they should be glad to do so. Children, and especially male children, provide all kinds of benefits to their parents—emotional, economic, and spiritual. A son who is "wise and virtuous" and has "good qualities" is capable of bringing good fortune to the entire family; his very existence has a salutary effect on the whole group:

A single son who is wise and virtuous, a lion among men, illuminates the family as the moon illuminates the sky. A single good tree, sweet-

---

[8] *The Harsacarita of Bana,* translated by E. B. Cowell and F. W. Thomas (London: Royal Asiatic Society, 1897), 153–155; reprinted in Embree, editor, *The Hindu Tradition,* 98–100.

smelling and in flower, perfumes the entire wood; so does a single good son perfume the family, a single son who has good qualities.[9]

For a woman, the birth of children (and especially the birth of sons) ensures that she will be supported throughout her life, even if she survives her husband. And for a man, the birth of a son, as we have seen, guarantees not only the continuity of his family and lineage but also confers upon the father immortality, for "in your offspring you are born again; that, o mortal, is your immortality" (Satapatha Brahmana 1.5.5.6). Elsewhere we read that "A man wins worlds through a son, and he gains eternity through a grandson, but he reaches the summit of the chestnut horse (i.e., the sun and the heavenly world associated with it) through the grandson of his son." Thus, this text continues, sons and grandsons (born of either the son or the daughter) are a man's salvation:

> Because the male child saves his father from the hell called *put*, therefore he was called a "son" (*putra*) by the Self-existent one himself. There is no distinction between a son's son and a daughter's son in worldly matters, for a daughter's son also saves him in the world beyond, just like a son's son. (Manu 9.137–39)

So it is that the production of sons, among other merit-making activities, is said to prepare a man's body for "ultimate reality" and salvation:

> By the study of the Veda, by vows, by offerings into the fire, by acquiring the triple learning, by offering sacrifices, by sons, and by the great sacrifices and the (other) sacrifices, this body is made fit for ultimate reality. (Manu 2.28)

In return for these benefits a son confers upon his parents, parents are obliged to care for and nurture him the first few years of his life—a parental obligation in Hindu India as in everywhere else where parents bring children into the world. The upbringing of a child involves, among other things, proper discipline, and although in general violence toward others is not condoned in Hindu texts, a man is allowed to beat "his son or pupil . . . for the sake of instruction" (Manu 4.164). Or again,

> If a wife, a son, a slave, a menial servant, or a full brother has committed an offence, they may be

beaten with a rope or with a split bamboo cane, but only on the back of the body, and never on the head; anyone who beats them anywhere else will incur the guilt of a thief. (Manu 8.299–300)

Proper upbringing also involves teaching the child how to read, for "The mother is an enemy and the father an opponent to their children if they do not teach them to read; without reading, a man cannot shine in the midst of the assembly, but is like a heron in the midst of swans."[10]

But beyond this, parents also have religious obligations to the son, and these tend to revolve around a series of rituals called the *samskaras*. The term *samskara* literally means "to make whole or perfect," and connotes a set of rites of passage that not only move the child from one status to another but transform or even construct a new and better being for the individual. For according to the Hindu texts, a child is born inherently defective and in a natural state of irresponsibility: "They do not put any restrictions on the acts of (a child) before the initiation, for he is on the level with a servant (no matter what his caste) before his (second) birth through the Veda" (Baudhayana Dharma Sutra 1.2.3.6).

Usually there are twelve of these life-cycle rites enumerated in the text. The first three concern the creation and proper formation of the embryo and begin at conception and continue at intervals through the woman's pregnancy. There are also a birth rite and a naming ritual, and a ritual in which the infant is taken out of the house for the first time, which is performed shortly after birth. During early childhood, rituals also mark the child's first eating of solid food and a ceremonial haircut. Later, one of the most important samskaras is performed for the young boy, the initiation ritual that inaugurates a period of study of the sacred Veda under the tutelage of the teacher. Two different rites of passage mark the end of the time of studentship, and the marriage ceremony (the final samskara) signals the beginning of the second stage of life as a householder.

These samskaras are meant not only as rites of passage but as the ritual means for constructing a strong, viable, and purified self for the boy who undergoes them. Several also act as healing rituals to counteract the impurities of biological birth, as the following indicates:

> The transformative rituals for the bodies of the twice-born, beginning with the rite of the infusion

---

[9]From the Garuda Purana, translated in Wendy Doniger O'Flaherty, editor and translator, *Textual Sources for the Study of Hinduism* (Manchester: Manchester University Press, 1988), 81.

[10]Ibid., 84.

(of semen, at conception), which purify them here on earth and after death, should be performed with excellent Vedic rites. The offerings into the fire (accompanying the *samskaras* performed) for the embryo, the birth rites, the ceremonial haircut (performed on a toddler) and the tying of the belt of rushes (one of the main features of the initiation rite), wipe away from the twice-born the guilt of the seed and the guilt of the womb. (Manu 2.26–27)

The samskara of initiation is of particular importance because, among other reasons, it is the occasion when the parents turn over their son to the care of a religious teacher, or guru, who becomes the boy's new father, for it is he that will give the boy a "second birth"—a male-produced ritual birth "out of the Veda," which is regarded as superior to the biological birth he received from his mother:

(The teacher) who fills (the pupil's) two ears with the Veda not in vain is to be known as his mother and his father, and he must not act with malice against him. . . . Between the one who gives him birth and the one who gives him the Veda, the one who gives the Veda is the more important father; for a priest's birth through the Veda is everlasting, both here on earth and after death. That his mother and father produced him through mutual desire, and he was born in the womb, he should regard as his mere coming into existence. But the birth that a teacher who has crossed to the far shore of the Veda produces for him through the verse to the sun-god, in accordance with the rules, is real, free from old age and free from death. . . . The priest who brings about the Vedic birth of an older person and who teaches him his own duties becomes his father, according to law, even if he is himself a child. (Manu 2.144, 146–148, 150)

According to the traditional law books, parents turn over their sons to the teacher at the age of eight or ten, and the boy lives with his new "father" until graduation in his late teens. At that point he is eligible for marriage, and his parents also have a duty to make sure he finds a suitable wife and has success starting up a new household. As for the daughter, however, the making of a good marriage is the parents' supreme obligation to her. (We will recall here that marriage is said to be the female equivalent of the male's initiation.) The father's responsibility is to give his daughter away in marriage, and if he does not do so "at the proper time" (i.e., when she has reached puberty) he is as blameworthy as other men who do not

fulfill their obligations to their women: "A father who does not give her away at the proper time should be blamed, and a husband who does not have sex with her at the proper time should be blamed; and the son who does not guard his mother when her husband is dead should be blamed" (Manu 9.40).

Elsewhere we read that it is critical for a father to give his daughter to a man with good qualities, and should such a potential husband appear she could be married even before puberty. But if the father does not fulfill this obligation to her, the young woman is allowed to make her own match:

A man should give his daughter, in accordance with the rules, to a distinguished, handsome suitor who is like her, even if she has not reached (the right age). But it would be better for a daughter, even after she has reached puberty, to stay in the house until she dies than for him to give her to a man who has no good qualities. When a girl has reached puberty she should wait for three years, but after that period she should find a husband like her. If she herself approaches a husband when she has not been given one, she commits no error, nor does the man whom she approaches. (Manu 9.88–91)

But it is better if the marriage is arranged properly, that is, with the father playing his role to the fullest. The offspring of unions formed in this way purifies the family for many generations:

The father may give away his daughter after decking her with ornaments and having first offered a libation of water: This is the *Brahma* form of marriage. A son born to her after such a marriage purifies twelve descendants and twelve ancestors on both her husband's and her own sides. The father may give her away after decking her with ornaments to an officiating priest while a Vedic sacrifice is being performed: that is the *Daiva* form of marriage. A son born of such a marriage purifies ten descendants and ten ancestors on both sides.[11]

What Do Children Owe Their Parents?

Children, first and foremost, owe their parents respect and obedience, for as the text below states, what they have gone through by having and raising children

[11]From the Asvalayana Grhya Sutra, cited and translated in Ainslie T. Embree, editor, *Sources of Indian Tradition, Volume One: From the Beginning to 1800,* 2nd ed. (New York: Columbia University Press, 1988), 226.

"cannot be redeemed even in a hundred years." Note also how the teacher is put on a par with the mother and father in the following passage, for as we have seen he becomes the boy's new father after initiation. These three figures—father, mother, and teacher—are to be revered and obeyed; they are the very form of cosmic powers and deities. By "loving devotion" to them, a son wins all three of the "worlds" of ancient Indian cosmology; no other duty is higher than revering and obeying them, and no other duties should be assumed by a man without first asking the permission of his parents and teacher. Such treatment of these three, it is said, is a man's "ultimate duty," and all other duties are subordinate to this one:

> A teacher, a father, mother, and older brother should not be treated with contempt, especially by a priest, not even by someone who has been provoked. The teacher is the physical form of ultimate reality, the father the physical form of the Lord of Creatures, the mother the physical form of the earth. The trouble that a mother and father endure in giving birth to human beings cannot be redeemed even in a hundred years. He should constantly do what pleases the two of them, and always what pleases his teacher. . . . Obedience to these three is said to be the supreme generation of inner heat; he should not assume any other duties without their permission. For they alone are the three worlds, they alone are the three stages of life, they alone are the three Vedas, and they alone are said to be the three sacrificial fires. . . . The householder who does not neglect these three conquers the three worlds; illuminated by his own body, like a god, he rejoices in heaven. By loving devotion to his mother he wins this world; by loving devotion to his father, the middle world; and by obedience to his guru the world of ultimate reality. A man who has deeply respected these has deeply respected all duties; but all rites are fruitless for the man who has not deeply respected these. As long as these three should live, he should not undertake any other (duties); he should constantly give them his obedience, taking pleasure in what pleases them and is good for them. . . . For by treating these three in this way a man accomplishes what ought to be done; this is the ultimate duty right before one's eyes, and any other is said to be a subordinate duty. (Manu 2.225–230; 232–235; 237)

A child should in particular treat his mother with respect and solicitation: "The teacher is more important than ten instructors, and the father more than a hundred teachers, but the mother more than a thousand fathers" (Manu 2.144). While all other elder female relations should be treated as a mother, the mother herself is the most important: "He should treat his father's sister, his mother's sister, and his own older sister like a mother; but his mother is more important than they are" (Manu 2.133).

The only or eldest son has a special responsibility at the time of the death of a parent, for it is he who with the help of specialized priests oversees the rituals designed to transform the deceased parent into an ancestor. Such rites begin with cremation at which time the skull is cracked in order to free the soul. Rituals involving the offering of rice balls, food, and gifts continue at intervals for a year; it is through these gifts and sacrifices that the spirit of the deceased parent becomes an ancestor. Death rites are thus conceived of as both a kind of last sacrifice to the gods (in which the body is the offering) and as a rebirth or transformation of the dead into a new life. But they also serve to ease the pain and discomfort of the recently departed and nourish the disembodied spirit; this, then, is the final duty of the son to his parents:

> When his corpse is being burnt, he experiences terrible burning; and when it is beaten he suffers too, and when it is cut he suffers intense agony. When a man's (body) stays wet for a very long time he suffers miserably, even if by the ripening of his own karma he has gone to another body. But whatever water, together with sesamum seeds, his relatives offer (in the rites for dead relatives), and whatever balls of rice they offer, he eats that as he is being led along. When his relatives rub his (dead) body with oil and massage his limbs, that nourishes and strengthens a man, and so does whatever his relatives eat. A dead man who does not (take the form of a ghost) and bother his relatives on earth too much when they are asleep and dreaming is nourished and strengthened by them as they give him gifts (in the form of offerings to his departed soul).[12]

[12]Markandeya Purana 10.47–87, translated in O'Flaherty, *Textual Sources*, 117.

Discussion Questions

1. How are the mutual obligations of husbands and wives related to the high value placed upon the family in the Hindu tradition?

2. How many of the attitudes and practices advocated in the Hindu tradition do you find attractive? Which ones would you agree with? Which ones would you disagree with? Why?

3. Smith describes the traditional Hindu view of a wife as embedded in a system that is "patriarchal" and "paternalistic." What does this mean? Do you consider this to be a strength or a weakness of the Hindu view?

4. Various elements of the Hindu tradition suggest that a person is "incomplete" unless they marry and become part of a household. Do you agree? Can a person be complete without a spouse and a household? What might being "complete" mean?

Suggestions for Further Reading

Additional discussions of moral issues arising from the parent-child relationship may be found in Hugh Lafollette, "Personal Relationships," in *A Companion to Ethics*, edited by Peter Singer (Oxford: Blackwell, 1991), pp. 327–332, and in James Rachels, "Morality, Parents, and Children," in *Person to Person*, edited by G. Graham and Hugh Lafollette (Philadelphia: Temple University Press, 1989). The most useful collection of articles on this subject is *Having Children: Philosophical and Legal Reflections on Parenthood*, edited by Onora O'Neill and William Ruddick (New York: Oxford University Press, 1979). Besides the article by Jane English (included above), it contains essays covering a wide spectrum of related issues. Tamar Schapiro explores the ethical responsibilities within a family in light of Kant's practical philosophy in "What Is a Child?" *Ethics* 109 (1999): 715–738. For a comparison of Confucian and Greek conceptions of filial piety, see Greg Whitlock's "Concealing the Misconduct of One's Own Father: Confucius and Plato on a Question of Filial Piety," *Journal of Chinese Philosophy* 21 (1994): 113–137. Carl Wellman critiques both Kantian and Millian conceptions of duty in "Relative Moral Duties," *American Philosophical Quarterly* 36 (1999): 209–223. Michael Collingridge and Seamus Miller examine several philosophical perspectives on filial piety in "Filial Responsibility and the Care of the Aged," *Journal of Applied Philosophy* 14 (1997): 119–128.

InfoTrac

family, filial piety, "parent and child", marriage, domestic relations

Chapter 13

Technology

Introduction: The Ethical Challenge of Technology

There can be little doubt that the world we live in has been radically transformed by the technologies we have created. For some it might be difficult to imagine living in a world without computers, the Internet, high-speed travel, and the wonders of modern medicine. Technology has not only transformed our world, it has dramatically affected both the length and quality of our lives in a number of ways that, most of the time, we might be only dimly aware of. One of the striking characteristics of advances in technology is that such advances make possible the acceleration of further advances, such that we live in a world in which technology is advancing faster than our ability to consider all its implications. Technology clearly brings with it the potential for tremendous good. The danger, however, is that our technology advances faster than our ability to adequately reflect on the moral implications of technology in its various guises. It is, however, worthwhile to pause and consider the ethical implications of technology. All the authors in this section encourage us to do so. According to Hans Jonas, with new technology comes a need to fundamentally rethink ethics. Perhaps so, but how should ethics be re-thought in light of our new capabilities? He attempts to point us in the new direction that ethics must take to keep pace with developments. If one had to point to the most significant piece of technology of the 20th century, the computer, and then the Internet, might easily top the list. How is this technology changing the ways in which people relate to one another? What are the cultural implications of technologies like the Internet? Robert Snyder and Mary I. Bockover consider such issues. And what about the incredible advances being made in medically related fields, like genetic engineering? We now have an unprecedented ability to manipulate life at the most fundamental level. We have the power. How should such power be used? James J. Walter considers such questions in light of Christian theology, while Swasti Bhattacharyya views such issues through the lens of classical Hindu scriptures. The advance of technology is inevitable and largely beyond our individual control. How we choose to use this technology, however, is both within our power and an important ethical responsibility.

Hans Jonas, Technology and Responsibility: Reflections on the New Task of Ethics

According to Hans Jonas, traditional ethical perspectives are no longer valid, because the new range of human actions made possible by modern technology necessitates a new ethics as well. Whereas in the past human interaction with nature was considered morally neutral, and only human-to-human interactions merited moral appraisal, with the advent of our ability to deeply alter nature itself comes new responsibilities. Traditional ethics is always focused on the present, whereas a new ethics would take into account the long-term impact of the decisions we make today. So, too, advances in medical technology raise questions about the value of life (and of death) that were simply inconceivable a generation before. Such developments, Jonas argues, call for "a new ethics of long-range responsibility, coextensive with the range of our power." Creating such an ethics is the challenge the author presents to the reader.

Reading Questions

1. According to Jonas, what sorts of presuppositions underlie traditional ethics? Why does he think that these presuppositions need to be replaced? What principles should replace them?

2. According to Jonas, how does modern technology force us to rethink our basic ethical principles?

3. Jonas discusses Kant's "categorical imperative" at length. According to him, why is Kant's formulation of this no longer adequate? How does Jonas propose that it ought to be updated in light of the situation we now find ourselves in?

4. What does Jonas mean when he says that our new situation, our newfound power over the world, calls for "a new kind of humility"?

Technology and Responsibility: Reflections on the New Task of Ethics

HANS JONAS

ALL PREVIOUS ETHICS—whether in the form of issuing direct enjoinders to do and not to do certain things, or in the form of defining principles for such enjoinders, or in the form of establishing the ground of obligation for obeying such principles—had these interconnected tacit premises in common: that the human condition, determined by the nature of man and the nature of things, was given once for all; that the human good on that basis was readily determinable; and that the range of human action and therefore responsibility was narrowly circumscribed. It will be the burden of my argument to show that these premises no longer hold, and to reflect on the meaning of this fact for our moral condition. More specifically, it will be my contention that with certain developments of our powers the *nature of human ac-*

tion has changed, and since ethics is concerned with action, it should follow that the changed nature of human action calls for a change in ethics as well: this not merely in the sense that new objects of action have added to the case material on which received rules of conduct are to be applied, but in the more radical sense that the qualitatively novel nature of certain of our actions has opened up a whole new dimension of ethical relevance for which there is no precedent in the standards and canons of traditional ethics.

I

The novel powers I have in mind are, of course, those of modern *technology*. My first point, accordingly, is to ask how this technology affects the nature of our acting, in what ways it makes acting under its dominion *different* from what it has been through the ages. Since throughout those ages man was never without technology, the question involves the human difference of *modern* from previous technology. Let us start with an ancient voice on man's powers and deeds which in an archetypal sense itself strikes, as it were, a technological note—the famous Chorus from Sophocles' *Antigone*.

Many the wonders but nothing more wondrous
  than man.
This thing crosses the sea in the winter's storm,
making his path through the roaring waves.
And she, the greatest of gods, the Earth—
deathless she is, and unwearied—he wears her
  away
as the ploughs go up and down from year to
  year
and his mules turn up the soil.

The tribes of the lighthearted birds he ensnares,
  and the races
of all the wild beasts and the salty brood of the
  sea,
with the twisted mesh of his nets, he leads captive, this clever man.
He controls with craft the beasts of the open air,
who roam the hills. The horse with his shaggy
  mane
he holds and harnesses, yoked about the neck,
and the strong bull of the mountain.

Speech and thought like the wind
and the feelings that make the town,
he has taught himself, and shelter against the
  cold,
refuge from rain. Ever resourceful is he.

He faces no future helpless. Only against death
shall he call for aid in vain. But from baffling
  maladies
has he contrived escape.

Clever beyond all dreams
the inventive craft that he has
which may drive him one time or another to well
  or ill.
When he honors the laws of the land the gods'
  sworn right
high indeed in his city; but stateless the man
who dares to do what is shameful.

This awestruck homage to man's powers tells of his violent and violating irruption into the cosmic order, the self-assertive invasion of nature's various domains by his restless cleverness; but also of his building—through the self-taught powers of speech and thought and social sentiment—the home for his very humanity, the artifact of the city. The raping of nature and the civilizing of himself go hand in hand. Both are in defiance of the elements, the one by venturing into them and overpowering their creatures, the other by securing an enclave against them in the shelter of the city and its laws. Man is the maker of his life *qua* human, bending circumstances to his will and needs, and except against death he is never helpless.

Yet there is a subdued and even anxious quality about this appraisal of the marvel that is man, and nobody can mistake it for immodest bragging. With all his boundless resourcefulness, man is still small by the measure of the elements: precisely this makes his sallies into them so daring and allows those elements to tolerate his forwardness. Making free with the denizens of land and sea and air, he yet leaves the encompassing nature of those elements unchanged, and their generative powers undiminished. Them he cannot harm by carving out his little dominion from theirs. They last, while his schemes have their short-lived way. Much as he harries Earth, the greatest of gods, year after year with his plough—she is ageless and unwearied; her enduring patience he must and can trust, and he must conform. And just as ageless is the sea. With all his netting of the salty brood, the spawning ocean is inexhaustible. Nor is it hurt by the plying of ships, nor sullied by what is jettisoned into its deeps. And no matter how many illnesses he contrives to cure, mortality does not bow to cunning.

All this holds because man's inroads into nature, as seen by himself, were essentially superficial, and powerless to upset its appointed balance. Nor is there a hint, in the *Antigone* chorus or anywhere else, that this is only a beginning and that greater things of artifice and power are yet to come—that man is embarked on an endless course of conquest. He had gone thus far in reducing necessity, had learned by his wits to wrest that much from it for the humanity of his life, and there he could stop. The room he had thus made was filled by the city of men—meant to enclose and not to expand—and thereby a new balance was struck within the larger balance of the whole. All the well or ill to which man's inventive craft may drive him one time or another is inside the human enclave and does not touch the nature of things.

The immunity of the whole, untroubled in its depth by the importunities of man, that is, the essential immutability of Nature as the cosmic order, was indeed the backdrop to all of mortal man's enterprises, between the abiding and the changing: the abiding was Nature, the changing his own works. The greatest of these works was the city, and on it he could offer some measure of abidingness by the laws he made for it and undertook to honor. But no long-range certainty pertained to this contrived abidingness. As a precarious artifact, it can lapse or go astray. Not even within its artificial space, with all the freedom it gives to man's determination of self, can the arbitrary ever supersede the basic terms of his being. The very inconstancy of human fortunes assures the constancy of the human condition. Chance and luck and folly, the great equalizers in human affairs, act like an entropy of sorts and make all definite designs in the long run revert to the perennial norm. Cities rise and fall, rules come and go, families prosper and decline; no change is there to stay, and in the end, with all the temporary deflections balancing each other out, the state of man is as it always was. So here too, in his very own artifact, man's control is small and his abiding nature prevails.

Still, in this citadel of his own making, clearly set off from the rest of things and entrusted to him, was the whole and sole domain of man's responsible action. Nature was not an object of human responsibility—she taking care of herself and, with some coaxing and worrying, also of man: not ethics, only cleverness applied to her. But in the city, where men deal with men, cleverness must be wedded to morality, for this is the soul of its being. In this intra-human frame dwells all traditional ethics and matches the nature of action delimited by this frame.

II

Let us extract from the preceding those characteristics of human action which are relevant for a comparison with the estate of things today.

1. All dealing with the non-human world, i.e., the whole realm of *techne* (with the exception of medicine), was ethically neutral—in respect both of the object and the subject of such action: in respect of the object, because it impinged but little on the self-sustaining nature of things and thus raised no question of permanent injury to the integrity of its object, the natural order as a whole; and in respect of the subject it was ethically neutral because *techne* as an activity conceived itself as a determinate tribute to necessity and not as an indefinite, self-validating advance to mankind's major goal, claiming in its pursuit man's ultimate effort and concern. The real vocation of man lay elsewhere. In brief, action on non-human things did not constitute a sphere of authentic ethical significance.

2. Ethical significance belonged to the direct dealing of man with man, including the dealing with himself: all traditional ethics is *anthropocentric*.

3. For action in this domain, the entity "man" and his basic condition was considered constant in essence and not itself an object of reshaping *techne*.

4. The good and evil about which action had to care lay close to the act, either in the praxis itself or in its immediate reach, and were not a matter for remote planning. This proximity of ends pertained to time as well as space. The effective range of action was small, the time-span of foresight, goal-setting, and accountability was short, control of circumstances limited. Proper conduct had its immediate criteria and almost immediate consummation. The long run of consequences beyond was left to chance, fate, or providence. Ethics accordingly was of the here and now, of occasions as they arise between men, of the recurrent, typical situations of private and public life. The good man was he who met these contingencies with virtue and wisdom, cultivating these powers in himself, and for the rest resigning himself to the unknown.

All enjoinders and maxims of traditional ethics, materially different as they may be, show this confinement to the immediate setting of the action. "Love thy neighbor as thyself"; "Do unto others as you would wish them to do unto you"; "Instruct your child in the way of truth"; "Strive for excellence by developing and actualizing the best potentialities of your being *qua* man"; "Subordinate your individual good to the common good"; "Never treat your fellow man as a means only but always *also* as an end in himself"—and so on. Note that in all those maxims the agent and the "other" of his action are sharers of a common present. It is those alive now and in some commence with me that have a claim on my conduct as it affects them by deed or omission. The ethical universe is composed of contemporaries, and its horizon to the future is confined by the foreseeable span of their lives. Similarly confined is its horizon of place, within which the agent and the other meet as neighbor, friend or foe, as superior and subordinate, weaker and stronger, and in all the other roles in which humans interact with one another. To this proximate range of action all morality was geared.

III

It follows that the *knowledge* that is required—besides the moral will—to assure the morality of action, fitted these limited terms: it was not the knowledge of the scientist or the expert, but knowledge of a kind readily available to all men of good will. Kant went so far as to say that "human reason can, in matters of morality, be easily brought to a high degree of accuracy and completeness even in the most ordinary intelligence";[1] that "there is no need of science or philosophy for knowing what man has to do in order to be honest and good, and indeed to be wise and virtuous. . . . [Ordinary intelligence] can have as good a hope of hitting the mark as any philosopher can promise himself";[2] and again: "I need no elaborate acuteness to find out what I have to do so that my willing be morally good. Inexperienced regarding the course of the world, unable to anticipate all the contingencies that happen in it," I can yet know how to act in accordance with the moral law.[3]

Not every thinker in ethics, it is true, went so far in discounting the cognitive side of moral action. But even when it received much greater emphasis, as in Aristotle, where the discernment of the situation and what is fitting for it makes considerable demands on experience and judgment, such knowledge has nothing to do with the science of things. It implies, of course, a general conception of the human good as such, a conception predicated on the presumed invariables of man's nature and condition, which may or may not find expression in a theory of its own. But

its translation into practice requires a knowledge of the here and now, and this is entirely non-theoretical. This "knowledge" proper to virtue (of the "where, when, to whom, and how") stays with the immediate issue, in whose defined context the action *as the agent's own* takes its course and within which it terminates. The good or bad of the action is wholly decided within that short-term context. Its moral quality shines forth from it, visible to its witnesses. No one was held responsible for the unintended later affects of his well-intentioned, well-considered, and well-performed act. The short arm of human power did not call for a long arm of predictive knowledge; the shortness of the one is as little culpable as that of the other. Precisely because the human good, known in its generality, is the same for all time, its relation or violation takes place at each time, and its complete locus is always the present.

IV

All this has decisively changed. Modern technology has introduced actions of such novel scale, objects, and consequences that the framework of former ethics can no longer contain them. The *Antigone* chorus on the *deinotes*, the wondrous power, of man would have to read differently now; and its admonition to the individual to honor the laws of the land would no longer be enough. To be sure, the old prescriptions of the "neighbor" ethics—of justice, charity, honesty, and so on—still hold in their intimate immediacy of the nearest, day-by-day sphere of human interaction. But this sphere is overshadowed by a growing realm of collective action where doer, deed, and effect are no longer the same as they were in the proximate sphere, and which by the enormity of its powers forces upon ethics a new dimension of responsibility never dreamt of before.

Take, for instance, as the first major change in the inherited picture, the critical *vulnerability* of nature to man's technological intervention—unsuspected before it began to show itself in damage already done. This discovery, whose shock led to the concept and nascent science of ecology, alters the very concept of ourselves as a causal agency in the larger scheme of things. It brings to light, through the effects, that the nature of human action has *de facto* changed, and that an object of an entirely new order—no less than the whole biosphere of the planet—has been added to what we must be responsible for because of our power over it. And of what surpassing importance an object, dwarfing all previous objects of active man! Nature as a human responsibility is surely a *novum* to

---

[1]Immanuel Kant, *Groundwork of the Metaphysic of Morals*, preface, translated by H. J. Paton (New York: Harper & Row, 1964).

[2]*Op. cit.*, Chapter 1.

[3]*Ibid.* (I have followed H. J. Paton's translation with some changes.)

be pondered in ethical theory. What kind of obligation is operative in it? Is it more than a utilitarian concern? Is it just prudence that bids us not to kill the goose that lays the golden eggs, or saw off the branch on which we sit? But the "we" that here sits and may fall into the abyss is all future mankind, and the survival of the species is more than a prudential duty of its present members. Insofar as it is the fate of *man*, as affected by the condition of nature, which makes us care about the preservation of nature, such care admittedly still retains the anthropocentric focus of all classical ethics. Even so, the difference is great. The containment of nearness and contemporaneity is gone, swept away by the spatial spread and time-span of the cause-effect trains which technological practice sets afoot, even when undertaken for proximate ends. Their irreversibility conjoined to their aggregate magnitude injects another novel factor into the moral equation. To this take their cumulative character: their effects add themselves to one another, and the situation for later acting and being becomes increasingly different from what it was for the initial agent. The cumulative self-propagation of the technological change of the world thus constantly overtakes the conditions of its contributing acts and moves through none but unprecedented situations, for which the lessons of experience are powerless. And not even content with changing its beginning to the point of unrecognizability, the cumulation as such may consume the basis of the whole series, the very condition of itself. All this would have to be co-intended in the will of the single action if this is to be a morally responsible one. Ignorance no longer provides it with an alibi.

Knowledge, under these circumstances, becomes a prime duty beyond anything claimed for it heretofore, and the knowledge must be commensurate with the causal scale of our action. The fact that it cannot really be thus commensurate, i.e., that the predictive knowledge falls behind the technical knowledge which nourishes our power to act, itself assumes ethical importance. Recognition of ignorance becomes the obverse of the duty to know and thus part of the ethics which must govern the ever more necessary self-policing of our outsized might. No previous ethics had to consider the global condition of human life and the far-off future, even existence, of the race. There now being an issue demands, in brief, a new concept of duties and rights, for which previous ethics and metaphysics provide not even the principles, let alone a ready doctrine.

And what if the new kind of human action would mean that more than the interest of man alone is to be considered—that our duty extends farther and the anthropocentric confinement of former ethics no longer holds? It is at least not senseless anymore to ask whether the condition of extra-human nature, the biosphere as a whole and in its parts, now subject to our power, has become a human trust and has something of a more claim on us not only for our ulterior sake but for its own and in its own right. If this were the case it would require quite some rethinking in basic principles of ethics. It would mean to seek not only the human good, but also the good of things extra-human, that is, to extend the recognition of "ends in themselves" beyond the sphere of man and make the human good include the care for them. For such a role of stewardship no previous ethics has prepared us—and the dominant, scientific view of *Nature* even less. Indeed, the latter emphatically denies us all conceptual means to think of Nature as something to be honored, having reduced it to the indifference of necessity and accident, and divested it of any dignity of ends. But still, a silent plea for sparing its integrity seems to issue from the threatened plenitude of the living world. Should we heed this plea, should we grant its claim as sanctioned by the nature of things, or dismiss it as a mere sentiment on our part, which we may indulge as fair as we wish and can afford to do? If the former, it would (if taken seriously in its theoretical implications) push the necessary rethinking beyond the doctrine of action, i.e., ethics, in the doctrine of being, i.e., metaphysics, in which all ethics must ultimately be grounded. On this speculative subject I will here say no more than that we should keep ourselves open to the thought that natural science may not tell the whole story about Nature.

V

Returning to strictly intra-human considerations, there is another ethical aspect to the growth of *techne* as a pursuit beyond the pragmatically limited terms of former times. Then, so we found, *techne* was a measured tribute to necessity, not the road to mankind's chosen goal—a means with a finite measure of adequacy to well-defined proximate ends. Now, *techne* in the form of modern technology has turned into an infinite forward-thrust of the race, its most significant enterprise, in whose permanent, self-transcending advance to ever greater things the vocation of man tends to be seen, and whose success of maximal control over things and himself appears as the consummation of his destiny. Thus the triumph of *homo faber* over his external object means also his triumph in the internal constitution of *homo sapiens*, of whom he used to be a subsidiary part. In other words, technology, apart from it objective works, assumes ethical significance by the central place it now occupies in human purpose. Its cumulative creation, the expanding artificial environment, continuously reinforces the particular powers in man that created it, by compelling their unceasing inventive employment in its management and further advance, and by rewarding them with additional success—which only adds to the relentless claim. This positive feedback of functional necessity and reward—in whose dynamics pride of achievement must not be forgotten—assures the growing ascendancy of one side of man's nature over all the others, and inevitably at their expense. If nothing succeeds like success, nothing also entraps like success. Outshining in prestige and starving in resources whatever else belongs to the fullness of man, the expansion of his power is accompanied by a contraction of his self-conception and being. In the image he entertains of himself—the potent self-formula which determines his actual being as much as it reflects it—man now is evermore the maker of what he has made and the doer of what he can do, and most of all the preparer of what he will be able to do next. But not your or I: it is the aggregate, not the individual doer or deed that matters here; and the indefinite future, rather than the contemporary context of the action, constitutes the relevant horizon of responsibility. This requires imperatives of a new sort. If the realm of making has invaded the space of essential action, then morality must invade the realm of making, from which it had formerly stayed aloof, and must do so in the form of public policy. With issues of such inclusiveness and such lengths of anticipation public policy has never had to deal before. In fact, the changed nature of human action changes the very nature of politics.

For the boundary between "city" and "nature" has been obliterated: the city of men, once an enclave in the non-human world, spreads over the whole of terrestrial nature and usurps its place. The difference between the artificial and the natural has vanished, the natural is swallowed up in the sphere of the artificial, and at the same time the total artifact, the works of man working on and through himself, generates a "nature" of its own, i.e., a necessity with which human freedom has to cope in an entirely new sense. Once it could be said *Fiat justitia, pereat mundus*, "Let justice be done, and may the world perish"—where "world," of course, meant the renewable enclave in the imperishable whole. Not even rhetorically can the like be said anymore when the perishing of the whole through the doings of man—be they just or unjust—

has become a real possibility. Issues never legislated on come into the purview of the laws which the total city must give itself so that there will be a world for the generations of man to come.

That there *ought* to be through all future time such a world fit for human habitation, and that it ought in all future time to be inhabited by a mankind worthy of the human name, will be readily affirmed as a general axiom or a persuasive desirability of speculative imagination (as persuasive and undemonstrable as the proposition that there being a world at all is "better" than there being none): but as a *moral* proposition, namely, a practical *obligation* toward the posterity of a distant future, and a principle of decision in present action, it is quite different from the imperatives of the previous ethics of contemporaneity; and it has entered the moral scene only with our novel powers and range of prescience.

The *presence of man in the world* had been a first and unquestionable given, from which all idea of obligation in human conduct started out. Now it has itself become an *object* of obligation—the obligation namely to ensure the very premise of all obligation, i.e., the *foothold* for a moral universe in the physical world—the existence of mere *candidates* for a moral order. The difference this makes for ethics may be illustrated in one example.

VI

Kant's categorical imperative said: "Act so that you *can* will that the maxim of our action be made the principle of a universal law." The "can" here invoked is that of reason and its consistency with itself: *Given* the existence of a community of human agents (acting rational beings), the action must be such that it can without self-contradiction be imagined as a general practice of that community. Mark that the basic reflection of morals here is not itself a moral but a logical one: The "I *can* will" or "I *cannot* will" expresses logical compatibility or incompatibility, not moral approbation or revulsion. But there is no self-contradiction in the thought that humanity would once come to an end, therefore also none in the thought that the happiness of present and proximate generations would be bought with the unhappiness or even non-existence of later ones—as little as, after all, in the inverse thought that the existence or happiness of later generations would be bought with the unhappiness or even partial extinction of present ones. The sacrifice of the future for the present is *logically* no more open to attack than the sacrifice of the present for the future. The difference is only that in the one case the series goes on, and in the other it does not. But that it *ought to go on*, regardless of the distribution of happiness or unhappiness, even with a persistent preponderance of unhappiness over happiness, nay, even of immorality over morality[4]—this cannot be derived from the rule of self-consistency *within* the series, long or short as it happens to be: it is a commandment of a very different kind, lying outside and "prior" to the series as a whole, and its ultimate grounding can only be metaphysical.

An imperative responding to the new type of human action and addressed to the new type of agency that operates it might run thus: "Act so that the effects of your action are compatible with the permanence of genuine human life"; or expressed negatively: "Act so that the effects of your action are not destructive of the future possibility of such life"; or simply: "Do not compromise the conditions for an indefinite continuation of humanity on earth"; or most generally: "In your present choices, include the future wholeness of Man among the objects of your will."

It is immediately obvious that no rational contradiction is involved in the violation of this kind of imperative. I *can* will the present good with sacrifice of the future good. It is also evident that the new imperative addresses itself to public policy rather than private conduct, which is not in the causal dimension to which that imperative applies. Kant's categorical imperative was addressed to the individual, and its criterion was instantaneous. It enjoined each of us to consider what would happen *if* the *maxim* of my present action were made, or at this moment already were, the principle of a universal legislation; the self-consistency of inconsistency of such a *hypothetical* universalization is made the test for my *private* choice. But it was no part of the reasoning that there is any probability of my private choice *in fact* becoming universal law, or that it might contribute to its becoming that. The universalization is a thought-experiment by the private agent not to test the immanent morality of his action. Indeed, real consequences are not considered at all, and the principle is one not of objective responsibility but of the subjective quality of my self-determination. The new imperative invokes a different consistency: not that of the act with itself, but that of its eventual *effects* with the continuance of human agency in times to come. And the "universalization" it contemplates is by no means hypothetical—i.e., a purely logical transference from the individual "me" to an imagi-

nary, causally unrelated "all" ("*if* everybody acted like that"); on the contrary, the actions subject to the new imperative—actions of the collective whole—have their universal reference in their actual scope of efficacy: they "totalize" themselves in the progress of their momentum and thus are bound to terminate in shaping the universal dispensation of things. This adds a *time* horizon to the moral calculus which is entirely absent from the instantaneous logical operation of the Kantian imperative: whereas the latter extrapolates into an ever-present order of abstract compatibility, our imperative extrapolates into a predictable real *future* as the open-ended dimension of our responsibility.

VII

Similar comparisons could be made with all the other historical forms of the ethics of contemporaneity and immediacy. The new order of human action requires a commensurate ethics of foresight and responsibility, which is as new as are the issues with which it has to deal. We have seen that these are the issues posed by the works of *homo faber* in the age of technology. But among those novel works we haven't mentioned yet the potentially most ominous class. We have considered *techne* only as applied to the non-human realm. But man himself has been added to the objects of technology. *Homo faber* is turning upon himself and gets ready to make over the maker of all the rest. This consummation of his power, which may well portend the overpowering of man, this final imposition of art on nature, calls upon the utter resources of ethical thought, which never before has been faced with elective alternatives to what were considered the definite terms of the human condition.

a. Take, for instance, the most basic of these "givens," man's mortality. Who ever before had to make up his mind on its desirable and *eligible* measure? There was nothing to choose about the upper limit, the "three score years and ten, or by reason of strength fourscore." Its inexorable rule was the subject of lament, submission, or vain (not to say foolish) wish-dreams about possible exceptions—strangely enough, almost never of affirmation. The intellectual imagination of a George Bernard Shaw and a Jonathan Swift speculated on the privilege of not having to die, or the curse of not being able to die. (Swift with the latter was the more perspicacious of the two.) Myth and legend toyed with such themes against the acknowledged background of the unalterable, which made the earnest man rather pray "teach

---

[4]On this last point, the biblical God changed his mind to an all-encompassing "yes" after the Flood.

us to number our days that we may get a heart of wisdom" (Psalm 90). Nothing of this was in the realm of doing, and effective decision. The question was only how to relate to the stubborn fact.

But lately, the dark cloud of inevitability seems to lift. A practical hope is held out by certain advances in cell biology to prolong, perhaps indefinitely extend, the span of life by counteracting biochemical processes of aging. Death no longer appears as a necessity belonging to the nature of life, but as an avoidable, at least in principle tractable and long-delayable, organic malfunction. A perennial yearning of mortal man seems to come nearer fulfillment. And for the first time we have in earnest to ask the questions: "How desirable is this? How desirable for the individual, and how for the species?" These questions involve the very meaning of our finitude, the attitude toward death, and the general biological significance of the balance of death and procreation. Even prior to such ultimate questions are the more pragmatic ones of who should be eligible for the boon: persons of particular quality and merit? of social eminence? those that can pay for it? everybody? The last would seem the only just course. But it would have to be paid for at the opposite end, at the source. For clearly, on a population-wide scale, the price of extended age must be a proportional slowing of replacement, i.e., a diminished access of new life. The result would be a decreasing proportion of youth in an increasingly aged population. How good or bad would that be for the general condition of man? Would the species gain or lose? And how right would it be to preempt the place of youth? Having to die is bound up with having been born: mortality is but the other side of the perennial spring of "a natality" (to use Hannah Arendt's term). This had always been ordained; now its meaning has to be pondered in the sphere of decision.

To take the extreme (not that it will ever be obtained): if we abolish death, we must abolish procreation as well, for the latter is life's answer to the former, and so we would have a world of old age with no youth, and of known individuals with no surprises of such that had never been before. But this perhaps is precisely the wisdom in the harsh dispensation of our mortality: that it grants us the eternally renewed promise of the freshness, immediacy, and eagerness of youth, together with the supply of otherness as such. There is no substitute for this in the greater accumulation of prolonged experience: it can never recapture the unique privilege of seeing the world for the first time and with new eyes, never relive the wonder which, according to Plato, is the be-

ginning of philosophy, never the curiosity of the child, which rarely enough lives on as thirst for knowledge in the adult, until it wanes there too. This ever renewed beginning, which is only to be had at the price of ever repeated ending, may well be mankind's hope, its safeguard against lapsing into boredom and routine, its chance of retaining the spontaneity of life. Also, the role of the *memento mori* in the individual's life must be considered, and what its attenuation to indefiniteness may do to it. Perhaps a non-negotiable limit to our expected time is necessary for each of us as the incentive to number our days and make them count.

So it could be that what by intent is a philanthropic gift of science to man, the partial granting of his oldest wish—to escape the curse of mortality—turns out to be to the detriment of man. I am not indulging in prediction and, in spite of my noticeable bias, not even in valuation. My point is that already the promised gift raises questions that had never to be asked before in terms of practical choice, and that no principle of former ethics, which took the human constants for granted, is competent to deal with them. And yet they must be dealt with ethically and by principle and not merely by the pressure of interest.

b. It is similar with all the other, quasi-utopian powers about to be made available by the advances of biomedical science as they are translated into technology. Of these, *behavior control* is much nearer to practical readiness than the still hypothetical prospect I have just been discussing, and the ethical questions it raises are less profound but have a more direct bearing on the moral conception of man. Here again, the new kind of intervention exceeds the old ethical categories. They have not equipped us to rule, for example, on mental control by chemical means or by direct electrical action of the brain via implanted electrodes—undertaken, let us assume, for defensible and even laudable ends. The mixture of beneficial and dangerous potentials is obvious, but the lines are not easy to draw. Relief of mental patients from distressing and disabling symptoms seems unequivocally beneficial. But from the relief of the *patient*, a goal entirely in the tradition of the medical art, there is an easy passage to the relief of *society* from the inconvenience of difficult individual behavior among its members: that is, the passage from medical to social application; and this opens up an indefinite field with grave potentials. The troublesome problems of rule and unruliness in modern mass society make the extension of such control methods to non-medical categories extremely tempting for social management. Numerous questions of human rights and dignity arise. The difficult question of preemption care versus enabling care insists on concrete answers. Shall we induce learning attitudes in school children by the mass administration of drugs, circumventing the appeal to autonomous motivation? Shall we overcome aggression by electronic pacification of brain areas? Shall we generate sensations of happiness or pleasure or at least contentment through independent stimulation (or tranquilizing) of the appropriate centers—independent, that is, of the objects of happiness, pleasure, or content and their attainment in personal living and achieving? Candidacies could be multiplied. Business firms might become interested in some of these techniques for performance-increase among their employees.

Regardless of the question of compulsion or consent, and regardless also of the question of undesirable side-effects, each time we thus bypass the human way of dealing with human problems, short-circuiting it by an impersonal mechanism, we have taken away something from the dignity of personal selfhood and advanced a further step on the road from responsible subjects to programmed behavior systems. Social functionalism, important as it is, is only one side of the question. Decisive is the question of what kind of individuals the society is composed of to make its existence valuable as a whole. Somewhere along the line of increasing social manageability at the price of individual autonomy, the question of the worthwhileness of the human enterprise must pose itself. Answering it involves the image of man we entertain. We must think it anew in light of the things we can do to it now and could never do before.

c. This holds even more with respect to the last object of a technology applied on man himself—the genetic control of future men. This is too wide a subject for cursory treatment. Here I merely point to this most ambitious dream of *homo faber*, summed up in the phrase that man will take his own evolution in hand, with the aim of not just preserving the integrity of the species but of modifying it by improvements of his own design. Whether we have the right to do it, whether we are qualified for that creative role, is the most serious question that can be posed to man finding himself suddenly in possession of such failed powers. Who will be the image-makers, by what standards, and on the basis of what knowledge? Also, the question of the moral right to experiment on future human beings must be asked. These and similar questions, which demand an answer before

we embark on a journey into the unknown, show most vividly how far our powers to act are pushing us beyond the terms of all former ethics.

VIII

The ethically relevant common feature in all the examples adduced is what I like to call the inherently "utopian" drift of our actions under the conditions of modern technology, whether it works on non-human or on human nature, and whether the "utopia" at the end of the road be planned or unplanned. By the kind and size of its snowballing effects, technological power propels us into goals of a type that was formerly the preserve of Utopias. To put it differently, technological power has turned what used and ought to be tentative, perhaps enlightening, plays of speculative reason into competing blueprints for projects, and in choosing between them we have to choose between extremes of remote effects. The one thing we can really know of them is their extremism as such—that they concern the total condition of nature on our globe and the very kind of creatures that shall, or shall not, populate it. In consequence of the inevitably "utopian" scale of modern technology, the salutary gap between everyday and ultimate issues, between occasions, is closing. Living now constantly in the shadow of unwanted, built-in, automatic utopianism, we are constantly confronted with issues whose positive choice requires supreme wisdom—an impossiblity in particular for contemporary man, who denies the very existence of its object: viz., objective value and truth. We need wisdom most when we believe in it least.

If the new nature of our acting then calls for a new ethics of long-range responsibility, coextensive with the range of our power, it calls in the name of that very responsibility also for a new kind of humility—a humility not like former humility, i.e., owing to the littleness, but owing to the excessive magnitude of our power, which is the excess of our power to act over our power to foresee and our power to evaluate and to judge. In the face of the quasi-eschatological potentials of our technological processes, ignorance of the ultimate implications becomes itself a reason for responsible restraint—as the second best to the possession of wisdom itself.

One other aspect of the required new ethics of responsibility for and to a distant future is worth mentioning: the insufficiency of representative government to meet the new demands on its normal principles and by its normal mechanics. For according to these, only *present* interests make themselves heard and felt and enforce their condition. It is to them that public agencies are accountable, and this is the way in which concretely the respecting of rights comes about (as distinct from their abstract acknowledgement). But the *future* is not represented, it is not a force that can throw its weight into the scales. The non-existent has no lobby, and the unborn are powerless. Thus accountability to them has no political reality behind it yet in present decision-making, and when they can make their complaint, then we, the culprits, will no longer be there.

This raises to an ultimate pitch the old question of the power of the wise, or the force of ideas not allied to self-interest, in the body politic. What *force* shall represent the future in the present? However, before *this* question can become earnest in practical terms, the new ethics must find its theory, on which dos and don'ts can be based. That is: before the question of what *force*, comes the question of what *insight* or value-knowledge shall represent the future in the present.

IX

And here is where I get stuck, and where we all get stuck. For the very same movement which put us in possession of the powers that have now to be regulated by norms—the movement of modern knowledge called science—has by a necessary complementarity eroded the foundations from which norms could be derived; it has destroyed the very idea of norm as such. Not, fortunately, the feeling for norm and even for particular norms. But this feeling, become uncertain of itself when contradicted by alleged knowledge or at least denied all sanction by it. Anyway and always does it have a difficult enough time against the loud clamors of greed and fear. Now it must in addition blush before the frown of superior knowledge, as unfounded and incapable of foundation. First, Nature has been "neutralized" with respect to value, then man himself. Now we shiver in the nakedness of a nihilism in which near-omnipotence is paired with near-emptiness, greatest capacity with knowing least what for. With the apocalyptic pregnancy of our actions, that very knowledge which we lack has become more urgently needed than at any other stage in the adventure of mankind. Alas, urgency is no promise of success. On the contrary, it must be avowed that to seek for wisdom today requires a good measure of unwisdom. The very nature of the age which cries out for an ethical theory makes it suspiciously look like a fool's errand. Yet we have no choice in the matter but to try.

It is a question whether without restoring the category of the sacred, the category most thoroughly destroyed by the scientific enlightenment, we can have an ethics able to cope with the extreme powers which we possess today and constantly increase and are almost compelled to use. Regarding those consequences imminent enough still to hit ourselves, fear can do the job—so often the best substitute for genuine virtue or wisdom. But this means fails us towards the more distant prospects, which here matter the most, especially as the beginnings seem mostly innocent in their smallness. Only awe of the sacred with its unqualified veto is independent to fit computations of mundane fear and the solace of uncertainty about distant consequences. But religion as a soul-determining force is no longer there to be summoned to the aid of ethics. The latter must stand on its worldly feet—that is, on reason and its fitness for philosophy. And while of faith it can be said that it either is there or is not, of ethics it holds that it must be there.

It must be there because men act, and ethics is for the reordering of actions and for regulating the power to act. It must be there all the more, then, the greater the powers of acting that are to be regulated; and with their size, the ordering principle must also fit their kind. Thus, novel powers to act require novel ethical rules and perhaps even a new ethics.

"Thou shalt not kill" was enunciated because man has the power to kill and often the occasion and even inclination for it—in short, because killing is actually done. It is only under the *pressure* of real habits of action, and generally of the fact that always action already takes place, without *this* having to be commanded first, that ethics as the ruling of such acting under the standard of the good or the permitted enters the stage. Such a *pressure* emanates from the novel technological powers of man, whose exercise is given with their existence. *If* they really are as novel in kind as here contended, and if by the kind of their potential consequences they really have abolished the moral neutrality which the technical commerce with matter hitherto enjoyed—then their pressure bids to seek for new prescriptions in ethics which are competent to assume their guidance, but which first of all can hold their own theoretically against that very pressure. To the demonstration of those premises this paper was devoted. If they are accepted, then we who make thinking our business have a task to last us for our time. We must do it in time, for since we act anyway we shall have some ethic or other in any case, and without a supreme effort to determine the right one, we may be left with a wrong one by default.

Discussion and Reflection Questions

1. Jonas apparently wants to replace the older, traditional ethical perspectives with new perspectives. Do you agree that such a replacement is necessary? Why or why not?

2. In your view, how does the development of modern technology affect the nature and scope of ethics? For example, what might be the ethical implications of the technological postponement (or even abolition) of death?

3. Do we have moral obligations to future generations, i.e., people who do not presently exist? Is there anything puzzling about having obligations to currently non-existing people?

4. Is this essay, is Jonas ultimately optimistic or pessimistic about our ability to forge a new ethics commensurate with the new world we find ourselves in? What about you? How would you go about designing a new ethics for this world?

Robert Snyder and Mary I. Bockover, The Internet East and West: A Moral Appraisal

Perhaps no form of technology has had a greater impact on how many of us in the Western world acquire information, purchase goods, and relate to one another than the Internet. Arguably part of the reason the Internet has had such a large influence in the West is because it embodies many fundamental Western values. According to Robert Snyder and Mary I. Bockover, this makes it a perfect format for comparing Eastern and Western views on autonomy, individual freedom, and the constituents of a good human life. They believe that the nature of the Internet as it exists is supported by both Kantian and utilitarian moral theories, and even see the information-acquiring power of the Internet as related to the natural desire to know, which is an important part of natural law ethics. The values that help to account for the success of the Internet in the West, however, are not present in some Asian countries where "freedom" as it is understood in the West is not seen as a fundamental value. In countries influenced by the Confucian tradition, for example, being part of a connected web of relationships is more essential for one's humanity than is enjoying personal freedom. This raises interesting, and difficult, questions about the value of the Internet in non-Western countries, and indeed of the values it promotes in Western countries.

Reading Questions

1. According to the authors, how does the Internet provide a perfect format for comparing Eastern and Western views on autonomy and individual freedoms?

2. Why does the Internet "epitomize the American ideals of individuals seeking life, liberty and happiness . . . in a minimally regulated environment"?

3. According to the authors, how might an Eastern view of "freedom" differ from a typically American understanding of this term? Why does understanding this difference matter?

4. Why do the authors think that central features of the Internet conflict with the traditional Chinese view of what it means to be human?

The Internet East and West: A Moral Appraisal

ROBERT SNYDER AND MARY I. BOCKOVER

Introduction

The Internet provides a perfect format for comparing eastern and western views on autonomy and individual freedoms that not only Americans but more and more of the world hold as fundamental to being truly human. The Internet is largely unregulated in terms of content, maximizes personal expression and can reach all over the world. It seems to be the perfect vehicle for individual entrepreneurs, struggling to get rich, that so typifies American society. The Internet, more than any other recent technology, embodies the individual freedoms that ground so much of the western way of life. In many non-western societies, however, individual freedoms, such as personal expression, are secondary to the needs of the tribe, family or society in general. Such freedoms are not seen as fundamental to human nature and in fact can be seen as detrimental to living a good life. In this article, the Internet will be used to explore this tension between some eastern and western views of whether autonomy and individual freedom are fundamental to human nature and to realizing our full potential as humans.

Section 1: The Internet in America— A Justification

The Internet is undoubtedly the fastest-growing technology in America, and probably the world, today. Some estimate that a billion people will be using the Internet by 2003 (Martin Stone, *ACM Tech News*, 3-24-2001). It maximizes freedom of expression, personal autonomy and individual efforts at capitalism—all goods from the American point of view. Some of these, like personal autonomy, are deeply grounded in western philosophy in general, while others, like capitalism, are more peculiarly American. This section will explore the philosophical justification for what the Internet symbolizes and for the lack of regulation that Internet users currently enjoy.

Individual freedom is arguably the most important good underlying American values today. It is a prerequisite for freedom of speech, freedom of religion and many of the other rights that Americans often take for granted. In its minimally regulated state, the Internet maximizes individual freedom. People can communicate rapidly, create their own Web pages and start e-businesses from home. There is little regulation of the content of Web sites even though anyone with a computer generally has access. Sexually oriented sites are a good example of how the Internet attempts to regulate access to content. Sites that do not charge membership fees post a warning that users should be 18 years or older in order to enter. It is left to the viewers' discretion whether or not to enter the site. Our government has resisted trying to ban sexual content on the Internet and yet has aggressively aimed at increasing Internet use for our children's education. Libraries, schools and parents in the United States continue to struggle with the problem of minors using these sexually explicit sites. At most, our government has tried to pass legislation that separates sites where our children are educated from sites where such things as sexually oriented businesses are located. What would justify this sort of autonomy for the Internet?

Much of American political practice is grounded in an instrumentalist view that sees government as a tool of the people; one which allows each of us to pursue our own interests in a climate of relative safety. John Locke, the British philosopher who is so important for American political theory, sees people ideally in

> . . . a state of perfect freedom to order their actions, and dispose of their possessions, and persons as they think fit, within the bounds of the Law of Nature, without asking leave, or depending upon the Will of any other man. (*Second Treatise on Government*—II.ii.4)

Individuals come first and the function of government is to safeguard our individual liberties from those who would make war against us. People enter into a social contract with others to form a government whose purpose is to guarantee safety and stability while interfering minimally with individual liberty. It is within this social structure that each of us is free to pursue life, liberty and happiness. In this context, the government would regulate the Internet only to the degree that it unjustly harms other people or their pursuit of the good life.

The primacy of individual freedom is fundamental to a number of different ethical theories that help justify not only our approach to politics but to a theory of basic human goods. Kant offers probably the best example of the necessity of individual autonomy for a theory of ethics. If we are going to praise (or blame) someone for an action, then that individual needs to be responsible for that action. He or she needs to have chosen to act in that way rather than in some other way. Ethics begins with freedom of choice, with personal autonomy. Another important part of Kant's ethical program is respect for persons. An ethical maxim, for Kant, is that we should always treat our humanity as an end (or good) in itself and not only as a means to some other goal. While Kant's view is complicated, an important part of respecting people, and treating humanity as an end, amounts to allowing people to choose what they want to do. This does not mean that we do not hold them responsible for their choices. If people choose badly, unethically, then they should be punished. The important point is that ethics is only possible because we have the freedom to choose, and this makes that freedom fundamental to our humanity. A concept of ethics is a large part of what separates us from the other animals. As far back as Aristotle we have been defined as rational animals. However, psychologists have since shown how complex rationality is and how many non-human animals exhibit complex traits of problem solving and communication. Regardless, the one trait that continues to stand out as peculiarly human is the ability to formulate general rules of conduct and choose whether or not to follow those rules. This is the sense of personal autonomy fundamental to ethical choice.

When do we restrict freedom of choice on an account like Kant's? When it unjustifiably harms others in serious and tangible ways that would be against their will. One cannot be free to cry fire in a crowded theater when he knows that doing so will result in the deaths of many innocent people. A good case can be made for the claim that much of the information found on the Internet harms others and therefore should be restricted. It is common knowledge that the Internet allows ready access to bomb making, targets for all sorts of potentially violent groups and instructions on how to complete terrorist missions.

Clearly this sort of information is likely to cause significant harm to persons if it falls into the hands of the wrong people. One way to justify free and open access to this sort of information is to argue that the persons harmed are not innocent. However, given the range of cases that have involved information on the Internet, from doctors that perform abortions to targets of eco-terrorism, it will be difficult to make this argument work. Surely some of these people are in fact innocent and are harmed unjustifiably. If the Internet facilitates the unjustifiable harm of innocent persons, wouldn't it be better to restrict access to such information, to ban it from the Internet? How you answer this question depends on a number of issues. Does the information or the individual using the information cause the harm? More importantly, should we, should society, regulate information on the Internet so that people are not faced with such choices? This is a fundamental question about the importance of personal autonomy.

Restricting access to information on the Internet would be one way to try to keep unstable individuals from harming others. However, because we don't know exactly who these individuals are we are going to have to restrict everyone's access to the relevant information. While this might seem like a good idea, the important point for someone like Kant is that in restricting access to information generally we are not treating Internet users as competent, rational adults who can make their own decisions. Instead, we are making their decisions for them. In effect we are treating them like children or other non-rational beings. Such treatment undermines the autonomy necessary for ethical decision making. It undermines our humanity. Parentalism is necessary for those who are not competent to make their own decisions but not for those who are. This is why it is appropriate for parents to use the screening software available to keep their children away from sexually oriented sites. This point about parentalism is particularly important because it emphasizes one of the major differences between Kant's approach to ethics and someone like Mill who is a utilitarian. We restrict access to information on a utilitarian account only if having that information would create more net unhappiness than happiness. In restricting information on the Internet we are, in effect, limiting individual choice for the good of society. Utilitarians are willing to sacrifice individual rights for the net happiness produced for society as a whole. For Kant, this means that you are using people's humanity, their autonomy, as a means to a better society. This is not respecting persons.

However, it is not just a Kantian account that supports access to information and the widely divergent views, which makes the Internet so interesting and controversial. Mill claims in *On Liberty* that "Over himself, over his own body and mind, the individual is sovereign" (68–69). Mill, like Kant, seems to be proclaiming that the individual is primary in any ethical or social system. It is the individual who seeks truth and, hopefully, through it finds happiness. That is the connection with utilitarianism. One way to make the connection between happiness and seeking the truth is through the doctrine of natural law, which holds that it is in our nature, as human beings, to seek the truth. Whatever helps you fulfill your nature is good and whatever hinders you from fulfilling your nature is bad. Again, an essential part of being human is being a rational, freely choosing animal. Interfering with the freedom of an individual, for the good of society, can only begin on a utilitarian account when his or her actions are aimed at others in society and not when those actions and beliefs essentially affect only the individual. Freedom of expression and toleration of differences become very important on this view. The justification is that the search for truth begins with the free interchange and evaluation of ideas. Without an unrestricted discussion of, and competition among, ideas people would be more easily fooled by the rhetoric of others, and thereby more likely to fail in their search for the truth. The Internet fits Mill's vision of the free competition of ideas very well. The Internet allows people to publish quickly, cheaply and broadly. Disseminating your views is only restricted by your ability to attract others to your Web site. In Mill's view, this allows us to weigh the different views and choose the strongest, the most reasonable from among the competitors. Through this competition, we come to hold justifiable beliefs. If someone is trying to mislead us, it will quickly become apparent in competing Web sites and then, as rational individuals interested in the truth, we will have to investigate further in order to justify our beliefs. Truth is more likely to emerge in this sort of setting than in one that restricts access to information.

The unrestricted capitalism, for which America is so famous, is more peculiarly American and because of this less well supported by western philosophy generally. Justifying capitalism, as it is currently practiced in America, from an ethical standpoint is problematic at best. If we set aside a justification of capitalism as an economic system and look instead at how it has and has not worked in America it quickly becomes apparent that the Internet provides something like the ideal for how the system should work. Our economic system, and much of the American way of life, is grounded in the idea that each of us has an equal opportunity to pursue the American dream. Our native abilities together with hard work determine who will and will not succeed. While this view has never been entirely true, it has become increasingly difficult to believe. Sociological studies suggest a number of disturbing patterns. For example, there is little movement among socio-economic classes. If you are born poor you are very likely to remain poor. If you come from a poor family you are far less likely to get a college education and, in this society, education is closely correlated with socio-economic status. A close examination of America is likely to reveal a society grounded more in socio-economic privilege than in equal opportunity. If this is true it undermines much that is fundamental to American values.

The Internet provides a vehicle that allows individuals to market their products and services to broad audiences at minimal costs. Because Web sites are so much less expensive than stores or the catalogs necessary in mail order businesses, more people are able to compete in the market and this dramatically advances the ideal of each of us having an equal opportunity to become successful capitalists. Our potential audience is worldwide and with such a large audience one need not market an expensive product or service to do well. All you need is an idea for a product or service that you can provide at competitive prices, a Web site for advertising and the ability to process orders. The diversity of products and services currently being offered on the Internet is boggling and a real testament to the ingenuity of entrepreneurs. Promoting the ideal of equal opportunity capitalism offers a strong argument for minimizing regulation and control of this expanding market. And this is exactly the approach that is currently being taken by legislators nationwide. Again, we come back to the idea of regulating the Internet only when significant direct harm to individuals that would be against their will can be established.

In many ways the Internet epitomizes the American ideals of individuals seeking life, liberty and happiness (property on Locke's account) in a minimally regulated environment. The Internet emphasizes the exchange of information, products and services at minimal effort and cost. We do not need to leave our homes to participate and anyone with computer access can join in the enterprise. The Internet is truly a remarkable phenomena that allows us to express our individuality in a world where being different is becoming increasingly difficult.

Section 2: The Internet in China in 2001— A Comparative Critique

At the beginning of the year 2000, 9 million people were online in China. What is remarkable about this figure is its increase: The number of Internet users in China only two years prior to that was a mere 650,000. Now China is a country of close to one and a half billion people, and the huge majority of Chinese are without televisions and phones, not to mention computers and Internet access. The most immediate reason for this is that China is still a third world country despite the staggering changes toward modernization that have occurred within the last two decades, since her posture toward capitalism and cooperation with the global economy has relaxed. China has had an incredibly long and remarkable history, to be sure, but it is difficult to envision her future. The effects of modernization are in large measure unpredictable, and so thinking more specifically about how the increasing presence of the Internet might figure into this change, having been brought into China only recently by businesses and universities, may not be easy to ascertain but is certainly worth our attention. The very least we can do is engage in some moral speculation about how the Internet stands in relation to the Chinese way of life and the philosophy it has reflected for several thousand years.

The most morally relevant consideration is that the Internet is regulated only on a local level, so there is no commerce for regulating the content of another server in another country, or even in the same town. Notice that this is not true for any other form of trade; commercial, political and even personal wares and behaviors are subject to screening from the very first moment they enter a foreign country. With the trading of information on the Internet, by way of contrast, one only has to put material out there to be an "author." There is no peer review or system for screening true information from the incredible bounty of fraudulent material that poses as true and could dupe even the savvy and intelligent user of this new technology. Consider the "urban legends," false warnings about computer viruses, and false pleas for help that require some kind of response on the part of the user. Since the original source of Internet information is often extremely difficult to verify, so is their truth. And the Internet wants to sell you something. It is downright distracting to deal with the advertisements that continuously pop up on all of the "dot coms." The user cannot select to have these advertisements cease, nor "fast-forward" through them. One can only choose to avoid commercial sites all together.

Anyone who has computer and Internet access can say anything and be heard, and even believed if the presentation is convincing enough. One of the distinguishing features of the Internet is the free expression that it allows; again, the restriction of Internet activity can only take place locally, and even then, it is extremely difficult to censor. According to the American way, our philosophy and our law, this may be acceptable. But it comes into conflict with the values and political systems of the Chinese. This is not to falsely identify the Chinese people with their government that is still very repressive by American standards. But it is to cite a deeper cultural difference: The Internet was at first an American creation, starting with U.S. military research and development, then moving out to our universities, and finally to our capitalist private sector. The Internet now embodies and perpetuates our constitutional right of free speech and principles of free trade and equal opportunity on a global level, freedoms that Americans now take to be basic human goods.

That such "basic human freedoms" are good or define "humanity" in any general way is questionable. Freedom is a various and complex concept even when it is an explicit principle of some philosophy: It can mean various things and have many applications, many of which can be quite abstract. A sufficient appreciation of how differently freedom can be defined and evaluated should give us pause about thinking of it as a singular principle with a universal application. It is not even central to most of the world's philosophies. Where it is—the Hindu concept of *moksha* and the Buddhist concept of *nirvana* come to mind—such "freedom" has nothing to do with the personal interest of autonomy found, say, in Kant or in the American philosophy grounding our politic and way of life. In America, for example, the concept of "freedom" has evolved from what our founding fathers envisioned and wrote in the Bill of Rights, a political document explicitly protecting personal rights, and even against the tyranny of a democratic majority. Some of what this document protects is the right to free speech, the freedom to practice the religion of one's choice, and the right to bear arms in order to protect against an oppressive government.

Now the average American simply takes for granted that these freedoms are basic or are rights "guaranteed" to us. But this is problematic. First, rights can be lost, and we run that risk if we take them for granted. Second, now, these rights are not seen by many to be culturally relative but instead are taken to be *universally* valid, a presumption that can rest philosophically on a number of inconclusive arguments.

The appeal to freedom found in our politic largely reflects the ideas of the British Empiricists (mainly Locke) and German philosopher Kant in the 18th century, where the moral ground for the concept of individual rights was really first formulated. We have already seen in the first section how Kant argues that the concept of freedom is "a priori" essential to our moral agency as human beings. Reason alone can not give us the ability to make moral choices, but only rational ones, and so freedom is what theoretically provides the bridge between reason and morality in the human will. This view also implies that absolute moral principles can be discovered, as well as expressed in terms of rights as duties. If one has an autonomy right, then every rational, moral agent has an obligation to uphold that right. This kind of presumption is also found in the Universal Declaration of Human Rights where the freedom that our founding fathers had to fight so hard for is taken to be a necessary good for all people. Freedom is a part of our nature, and must be protected as a concrete *human* reality.

The problem here is philosophical. Any view that holds some principle—any principle—to have such binding categorical force better have equally binding support of its own claims. But Kant's attempt to ground (the concept of) freedom in the human will only offers a "transcendental proof" which begs the question, and does so in a couple of directions. First, he defines our humanity *essentially* in terms of being rational and free, while casting all other features like the emotions as merely contingent psychological facts. But the "mere contingency" of compassion is precisely the "basic human feeling" that makes us moral according to Mencius, a classical Confucian who lived in China in the 3rd century B.C.E. Why think that freedom is more important than compassion when it comes to being moral? And why even think that freedom is essential to our humanity in the first place? Kant gave a transcendental argument because there is no other proof for what makes us moral beings, but only varying intuitions of what is more or less important. Conceiving of autonomy as being necessary (in order for moral agency to be possible) does not make it so. It may just be a big idea, without the theory or evidence needed to show that it *should* be conceived as universally binding. Nevertheless, it has ended up serving the interests of a select group of people in the first world who have enough power and money to "determine their own destiny," as well as to shape the future of others who are not so fortunate. But what follows from an absolute commitment to freedom as "autonomy rights for all" is that every sovereign nation not embracing the same philosophy, political structure, or way of life *should* guarantee to their people this kind of freedom. And these are issues that we have had extreme difficulty resolving even on our own soil.

The fact that a concerned body has to make a (democratic) decision about what these autonomy rights are, not to mention who should have them, shows how troublesome an absolute claim to freedom can be, even in the American case. For politically, legally, and morally we do limit autonomy. Free speech does not give us the right to slander or bear false witness against someone, and having a right to trade freely does not mean that we can sell illegal items or take them to another country for trade. Our American *carte blanche* regard for freedom ends up being a culturally chauvinist abstraction if we assume that the Chinese should have the "same freedoms" that we do. The American conflict between autonomy and regulation that has been with us since this country was first established shows us that our own values system is difficult enough to reconcile within our own cultural and political framework.

And the Internet tells us what we Americans value the most now—free expression and the ideas of free trade and equal opportunity. These values now color what we mean by freedom, and they have replaced the political and religious values that our forefathers had to fight so hard for. The point is that their fight was passionately motivated by a concept of freedom that at least in principle also entailed a concept of *justice* for all. Justice is another abstract concept, to be sure, but at least it demands consideration of what is right, true and fair, what is proper and in due measure. In contrast, Internet activity now embodies and perpetuates a view of freedom that has nothing to do with such concepts. A more subtle appreciation of our political system, for example, shows that even though each one of us is guaranteed a right to free speech, part of this right is protective and allows the individual due process, e.g., in case of slander. Free speech is restricted in the name of personal protection to speech that does not defame another's character. The Internet does not lend itself to such self-regulation, and so the concept of freedom that it now expresses is almost exclusively defined by the desire for economic freedom (to get rich) and personal freedom (to have an equal opportunity to do and say what one wants). Many Americans are now ignorant of the link between freedom and protection secured for us by our founding fathers, and given that only approximately 30% of the voting population actually exercise their democratic right to affect the politic, most do not seem to really care.

The Internet is the perfect new technology to frame a comparative discussion of "rights" and basic human values then. Most notably, the ideas of free expression, equality and free trade, embody a mentality that could be harmful to the close to one and a half billion people in China if not restricted. Americans may value such "absolute" freedom, even to the point of thinking it should be universally implemented, but in the traditional Chinese way of thinking, being moral has little or nothing to do with being an autonomous agent. Confucius, for example, conceived of morality as being grounded in our humanity, and of humanity as being cultivated in relation to others. The basic Confucian relationships show that he thought that being part of a family is what shapes our humanity—or teaches us to be moral—most essentially. First and foremost, we are children, learning mainly from our parents how to mature into adults. We have partners, husbands or wives—roles that we have also learned from the (hopefully) good example of our parents and others close to us. We have brothers or sisters, or are close to people who do. We are older than some, and younger than others are. We have grandparents, cousins, aunts and uncles, etc. These are the primary relations that "humanize" us.

We are also defined by our role(s) in the larger community. We are rulers because we have subjects, representatives because we have constituents, friends because we have friends, teachers because we have students, and the like. We are what we are *because* we stand in meaningful relation to others. The moral goal for Confucius then is to develop our humanity, which means that we learn to fulfill the responsibilities that we have to others. It means that we *want* to be good in this way and so this natural feeling to be meaningfully connected to others provides the impetus for developing our roles. In effect, one cultivates her humanity in cultivating her roles. One *becomes* a good mother, daughter, teacher, and friend, by living that life consistently and with the dedication that a human so naturally brings to the things that mean the most to her. But this must always be done in a social or relational context for Confucius: Humanity at its best (*jen*) occurs when the goal of promoting social harmony and cooperation is realized. This basic human goodness is thoroughly embedded in the world, in the relationships we have with others, but it also reflects the perfect integrity of the greater cosmos (*tao*). When the human way (*jen tao*) accords with the natural order and harmony of the greater cosmos (*tao*), all things will be right on earth and under heaven. This is how Chinese emperors and rulers kept the "mandate of heaven," and this is how families and communities can live peacefully together. These Confucian principles affect every aspect of daily living, and are still reflected strongly in the Chinese way of life.

The Internet is currently the most effective form of communication available to promote the first world value of consumerism, a value essentially based on the ideas of free expression, equal opportunity, and free trade. It is also quite clear that "modernization" in China translates to just this value. A visit to any major Chinese city shows that "prosperity" is taken not only to hinge on increased participation in the global economy, but also reflects a mentality of consumerism that a country like the United States epitomizes. But if modernization in this form is unrestricted in China (and in any third world country), the large majority of people will be increasingly alienated from their cultural roots and traditional life-sustaining practices. This is particularly problematic for the Chinese whose identity has already been sabotaged by the disasters of communism such as the Great Leap Forward and the Cultural Revolution. The little prosperity that the average Chinese person enjoys could be threatened by adopting such American values if the Chinese identity is not able to keep its bearing during this time of great social change. Real social stability has always been the result of values that place familial and social well being and harmony above all else. The Chinese regard for social integrity and the American regard for individual freedom *conflict*, for in China the individual is not taken to have personal and political autonomy. What it means to be an "individual" in China is to be a meaningful part of a larger social group—like a family, a neighborhood, or a nation. Personal roles are always socially defined. The concept of "individual" as being an autonomous, independent agent who stands outside of a social context is a western abstraction and not a Chinese reality. In China then, where the central moral goal has always been harmonious *inter-dependence* instead of the autonomous independence we pursue so devoutly in America, the Internet could present a threat to cultural identity and stability in being the perfect embodiment of current American values. And as these "democratic" values increasingly take hold, the Chinese government, whether we like it or not, has every "right" to protect their nation from what could be great internal turmoil.

The Internet now is quite at home in much of Europe and even Japan, but reflects and promotes the American love of free expression, our desire for financial gain, and our belief in equal opportunity, in an unprecedented way. Sadly, in 1989 we saw the effect of importing democratic values to China at

Tiananmen Square. What many Americans do not know is that a central demand that the Chinese students had was the right to stay in the modernized cities where they were educated instead of returning home to provinces that were very underdeveloped by comparison. But there can be no such equal opportunity in China; one cannot have a "right" to live and work where he or she wants because the infrastructure of the already staggeringly overpopulated cities cannot sustain it. This is not to be unsympathetic to those injured or killed. However, it is important for one to say that the demands that the students put on the government could not be met. The government could not just stand down with its tail between its legs, in front of the rest of China and the rest of the world (including America that has a vested political and economic interest in seeing "democracy" flourish). What the dramatic increase of Internet presence in China indicates then, at the very least, is this: There is an increase in business and academic activity using a new technology that passes distinctively American values on to people who could be harmed by them.

It would be simplistic to conclude that the argument here is against freedom, or against Internet use. This only misses the point; for clearly, autonomy rights as well as Internet use in the United States are central to how we live and what we value, which makes sense since both developed here in a form and to an extent found nowhere else. The argument here is only against the view that "freedom," defined as autonomy rights to the sorts of things that even Americans may or may not be entitled to (depending upon historical context, race, gender, age, sexual orientation, etc.), is an absolute or universally valid principle. This regard for autonomy so well reflected in the lack of regulation essential to Internet use (which may even become more of a problem in the United States) could threaten China and could present political conflict between us if cultural differences and national sovereignty are not respected. China must continue to regulate the flow of trade and ideas into that country. The over one billion people in China who are already very poor (by our standards) could face starvation and homelessness if she is not careful with her future. But if the business interests and personal freedoms of a few are put before the well being of the populace in general—by putting faith in the "trickle down" theory of economics—the prosperous may get richer, but the poor will get poorer. History has shown what such "freedom" offers the Chinese: not prosperity but potentially tragic western imperialism, and now American businesses in particular stand to make a killing off of it.

In conclusion, the Internet is not a value-neutral tool. It imports values that are practically impossible to regulate on it. Indeed, a final example of how a conflict of values may arise as the Internet becomes more prevalent in China results from the fact that the overwhelming use of Internet activity is pornographic. The word "overwhelming" is to be stressed in more than one way, for child pornography is a prominent feature of this (virtual or not). In China, pornography as well as prostitution are crimes punishable by death. This is not a moral argument against pornography, but it is a place where value conflicts and differences between China and other countries like the United States can surface. Currently, moral considerations of the Internet also relate to advertising, sex, violence, and a host of other morally controversial topics. And the objection that sex, violence, consumerism, etc. are not necessary features of the Internet can only go so far given that *whatever* it transmits is so hard to regulate. The Internet is the best form of telecommunication on the planet to engage in free, uncontrolled, and even anonymous expression. This may be consistent with the values of independence and autonomy that westerners, especially Americans, embrace. But it conflicts with the traditional Chinese view that sees our humanity as something to be cultivated and refined in the direction of sharing a community in a mutually beneficial way, instead of as a self-legislating "will" that drives personal, economic, and political interests.

To summarize, the difficulty in regulating its content makes the Internet the perfect American artifact: It allows the free exchange of ideas, including the ideas of free trade and equal opportunity, to occur in an unprecedented manner. These are the only "essentials" that attach to it. Therefore, three main moral problems arise in connection with the Internet in China. The first is subtle, but reveals the cultural bias surrounding almost all of our dealings with China. For it is hypocritical and culturally chauvinistic to think that China, despite her 5,000 years of history to the contrary, should adopt what has been even in the American case an ambiguous value of freedom. In the present case, we should not just presume that the sovereign nation of China should give its one and a half billion people the economic and personal freedoms that Americans now expect and that the Internet so aptly communicates. Importing our values into China could be dangerous, mainly in light of the fact that economic freedom has become unbridled consumerism in first world capitalistic countries. This *laissez faire* approach to economics could cripple China in widening the gap between the rich and the poor by alienating her great majority from their traditional life-sustaining practices, as well as by alienating the Chinese identity from it basic social and moral values. Consider how autonomy rights have translated into rampant pornography, violence, and fraud on the Internet. This is freedom without quality control, or without restrictions on what even Americans might consider to be basic human harms. China has *never* philosophically embraced such unrestricted liberty for the general population at any time during her incredibly long and rich history. The Internet, as a new and "progressive" technology, tells us more about who we are and what we value in America than virtually any other technology. And its underlying assumption is clear: Technology will be able to solve any of the problems it creates through its own advancement. Do you have such faith?

Section 3: Personal Freedom and the Internet—Concluding Remarks

While the preceding discussion raises a number of questions, the central issues revolve around the clash of eastern and western views on the importance and role of autonomy and individual freedoms. In America and most of the West such freedoms are taken as fundamental to being human and, more importantly, our ability to pursue the good life. Western nations disagree dramatically over such issues as capitalism, consumerism, and the extent to which society is responsible for its citizens. Differences in governmental programs among western countries are best understood in terms of a debate about how much support individuals need in order to be in a position to pursue a good life with equal opportunity. Sweden, in particular, and much of Europe, in general, are reluctant to embrace the sort of unregulated consumerism typified by America. Yet, they are leading participants in the Internet and all the diversity it has to offer. For all their differences, they agree that individual liberty is fundamental to leading a meaningful life.

China disagrees. The individual is defined within a relationship of family and community striving toward harmony. Family and community relationships are primary and individual freedoms are secondary. The good life is defined and pursued in terms of our relations among others, not in individual choices about what we want to do with our lives. An individual's choice about what he or she ought to do will always be in the context of how to promote familial, community, and national unity. This requires sacrifices of the individual that western countries would never require of its citizens. One can certainly choose to sacrifice oneself for others but generally this is not ethically required of us. Certainly such obligations exist in cases where we are responsible for children but rarely to extended families, the community or society (except, perhaps, in times of war). Because individual autonomy is not fundamental, there is no reason for the Chinese government to consider, for example, the wishes of the rebellious students over the needs of the country. On this view the Internet should promote social harmony and well-being and to the extent that it does not do this, it should be restricted and controlled.

The important difference is not so much in the final outcomes of our choices—they may be the same—but in the choice itself. Many of us in America choose to define ourselves through our relationships. It can also be argued that if we really understood the obligations that arise from such relationships we would be much less individualistic than we are today. One of the most important contributions of feminist philosophy is to emphasize that our relationships to our friends and family should be fundamental to our ethical viewpoints. In promoting individualism we tend to ignore the obligations that arise from the relationships we cultivate. However, as adults we choose these relationships. An individual may certainly pursue the good life by building a life with meaningful relationships. However, one is not compelled to make such choices and one has great latitude in how to make such choices. If your family is dysfunctional, you are not compelled to subordinate yourself to it in an effort to promote harmony and familial well-being. You may want to leave and try to develop other, more suitable, relationships with friends or a new family. This seems to fly in the face of traditional Confucian morality, where violating basic familial obligations, such as respecting and caring for parents, marks a deficiency in one's own humanity.

The real question is how to argue for or establish that individual autonomy is more fundamental than integrity of the family, tribe or community in pursuing a good or fulfilling life. We have seen the arguments of both the East and West and it is not easy to gain an independent, objective vantage point from which to judge these issues. Often these sorts of disputes come down to "reflective equilibrium" arguments in which we bring our beliefs and ethical principles into equilibrium by discarding some and modifying others. For example, in considering the conflict between the ethical principle that family unity is more important than the belief in the pursuit of individual happiness, one may modify the ethical principle, narrowing its focus to dependent members of one's family, and retain the belief. Or one may modify the ethical principle by conceiving of family unity or harmony more in terms of overall emotional well-being—consider the peace of mind and increased civility that results when one leaves a dysfunctional family and finds a more suitable one. One need not sacrifice his or her own happiness for familial well-being unless *choices* are made that obligate one to make this sacrifice. However, someone else might resolve this conflict by discarding the belief that we have a right to pursue individual happiness, especially when it conflicts with what is good for the larger social group. Both bring the conflict of principles and beliefs into reflective equilibrium but do so differently. It is not clear that one is right and the other is wrong.

So long as we can agree on which way to resolve these disputes, as we do generally in the West, then we rarely question the justification. Of course individual autonomy is primary and from this it follows that the Internet functions, by and large, as it should. It is only when large groups start resolving these disputes differently that we are forced to examine the justification of our most fundamental beliefs. For the Chinese, individual autonomy is not fundamental and the Internet should, therefore, be regulated to the degree that it infringes on social integrity, and so potentially, on everyone's well-being in the end. How, if at all, we resolve such disputes is one of the fundamental questions in philosophy. In the meantime, we see social and political considerations of global significance resurface between China and the West once again from the advent of yet another new technology.

Discussion and Reflection Questions

1. The authors suggest that what Americans typically take to be "basic human goods" is questionable when viewed from a broader (global) perspective. Why? Do you agree with them?

2. The authors emphasize the role of the Internet as a medium of capitalistic activity, i.e., to advertise goods and services, and thus to promote consumerism. What other roles does or might the Internet play? Do the authors take into account these other roles?

3. Why do the authors claim that "the Internet is not a value-neutral tool"? What danger do they see in this aspect of the Internet? Do you think they are right in identifying this danger?

4. At the end of their essay, the authors ask whether faith that technology will be able to solve any problems that it creates is justified. How would you answer this question? Why?

James J. Walter, "Playing God" or Properly Exercising Human Responsibility? Some Theological Reflections on Human Germ-Line Therapy

There is little doubt that religious convictions are often central to arguments for and against the development and application of novel biomedical technologies. A very common objection to the use of certain kinds of medical technology is that we have no right to "play God." In this essay James J. Walter, a bioethicist and theologian, examines this and related ideas in relation to the developing technology of human germ-line therapy. After briefly describing the sorts of technical issues in question, he turns to the moral (and theological) issues that arise in thinking about the acceptability of applying such technology, especially in relation to five fundamental Christian doctrines: creation, fall, incarnation, redemption, and eschatology. Based on this analysis, he cautiously suggests that human germ-line therapy need not violate any fundamental theological or moral strictures, and that, if developed responsibly, might actually have the potential to become ways of participating in God's redemptive activities toward humanity.

Reading Questions

1. According to Walter, how are the moral judgments that religious believers arrive at on issues of genetic manipulation informed by specifically theological beliefs?

2. What are the main arguments for and against germ-line therapy identified in the essay?

3. Walter asks the following question: "Is performing germ-line therapy on humans contrary to God's intentions and purposes, and therefore an act of usurping God's rights over creation?" How does he answer this question?

4. According to Walter, how are the Christian doctrines of creation, fall, incarnation, redemption, and eschatology related to the issue of human germ-line therapy?

"Playing God" or Properly Exercising Human Responsibility? Some Theological Reflections on Human Germ-Line Therapy

JAMES J. WALTER

Introduction

The two concerns of this essay are primarily theological in nature and scope, although both entail ethical issues. First, I want to show that the *moral* judgments that religious believers arrive at on issues of genetic manipulation are informed by and at least partially dependent on specifically theological beliefs about God and about the nature and destiny of humanity. The second theological concern is to decide whether we are really "playing God" by manipulating our genetic code or whether such interventions are only another way of properly exercising human responsibility.

The U.S. Department of Energy inaugurated its Human Genome Initiative in fiscal year 1987, and the National Institutes of Health began its project in 1988. The official starting date of the combined Human Genome Project, however, was October 1, 1990, and James Watson was appointed its first director. The stated objective of this fifteen-year project is to map and sequence the entire human genome. The genome

is comprised of all the genetic material in the forty-six chromosomes, which contain the human's full complement of 100,000 genes found in three billion base pairs. The research in recombinant DNA a decade earlier had made it possible for scientists to think of isolating and mapping the DNA molecule. The cost of the project is $3 billion, which is a dollar to map each base pair. In December 1993 the French reported that they had already completed a full, but very rough, map of the human genome. It is estimated that this achievement by the French will speed up by a factor of ten the final mapping of the human genetic blueprint.

Director James Watson recognized from the beginning that there were many issues of a non-scientific nature connected with the genome project. He urged that at least 3 percent of the genome funds ($90 million) should be spent on examining these important issues. He succeeded in his efforts, and so the Joint Working Group on the Ethical, Legal and Social Issues Relative to Mapping and Sequencing the Hu-

James J. Walter, " 'Playing God' or Properly Exercising Human Responsibility? Some Theological Reflections on Human Germ-Line Therapy." Originally published in New Theology Review *10 (November 1997), pp. 39–59. Reprinted by permission of Kenneth Himes.*

man Genome (ELSI) was formed and began its work in September 1989. Watson was indeed correct about the relevance of the ethical issues connected to this initiative. The scientific breakthroughs that are being made today because of this research, and those that will be made in the future, present us with extraordinarily important and far-reaching moral questions. Before addressing some of these questions, I will quickly review the various types of genetic manipulation that will likely be possible by mapping and sequencing the human genome.

Medical scientists could conceivably develop four different types of genetic manipulation from the results produced in the Human Genome Project. The first two types are therapeutic in nature because their intent is to prevent or to correct some genetic defect that causes disease. The other two types are not therapies at all. Rather, they are concerned with improving either various genetic aspects of the patient him/herself (somatic cell) or with permanently enhancing or engineering the genetic endowment of the patient's children (germ line).

The first kind of genetic manipulation is somatic cell therapy in which a genetic defect in a body cell of a patient could be corrected by using various enzymes (restriction enzymes and ligase) and retroviruses to splice out the defect and to splice in a healthy gene. Medical scientists have already used a variation of this technique to help children who suffer from severe combined immune deficiency (ADA) by modifying bone-marrow cells. Estimates are that there are between three to four thousand different genetic diseases controlled by one gene, and these diseases afflict approximately 2 percent of all live births. It is clear that the ability to correct these defects would benefit many patients and save billions of dollars in healthcare costs over the lifetime of these patients. Second, there is germ-line gene therapy in which either a genetic defect in the reproductive cells—egg or sperm cells—of a patient would be repaired or a genetic defect in a fertilized ovum would be corrected *in vitro* before it is transferred to its mother's womb. In either case the patient's future children would be free of the defect by permanently altering their genetic code.

Next are the two kinds of non-therapeutic genetic manipulation. The first is enhancement somatic engineering. In this type a particular gene could be inserted to improve a specific trait, for example, either by adding a growth hormone to increase the height of a patient or by genetically enhancing a worker's resistance to industrial toxins. Second, there is germ-line genetic engineering in which existing genes would be altered or new ones inserted into either germ cells or into a fertilized ovum such that these genes would then be permanently passed on to improve or enhance the patient's offspring. In this last form of genetic manipulation parents could design their children according to their own desires.

Moral Dimensions

Before addressing the specifically theological issues that serve as the context for moral decision making on genetic manipulation, it might be helpful to review briefly some of the moral dimensions of this topic. Most authors and most national and international commissions/councils of a civil or religious nature have argued morally against any form of enhancement genetic engineering (somatic or germ-line). In addition, most of the same authors and commissions/councils have argued in favor of pursuing research and implementation of somatic cell therapy for serious genetic diseases. Morally the most contentious form of genetic manipulation, then, concerns therapeutic interventions aimed at preventing or curing a genetic defect of either the reproductive cells or of the zygote before transfer to the mother's womb. Clearly, the controversy cuts across several areas beyond ethical considerations. For example, it necessarily involves the medical and scientific fields because it is not clear whether this technique is technologically feasible without doing great harm to either the patient or his/her progeny. It is also a social or public policy issue because we must be concerned with whether or not we could ever reach a consensus as a society on the implications of such research and medical interventions that would permanently change our genetic code. Finally, as I have suggested above, it involves a theological problem of whether or not we have now entered the realm of "playing God" by using this technology.

Eric Juengst (1991) has helpfully summarized the moral arguments for and against germ-line therapy. There are five arguments against such interventions. First, there is scientific uncertainty and clinical risks involved with these techniques. Germ-line therapy of either form—sex cells or zygote—would involve too many unpredictable, long-term iatrogenic risks and harms to the altered patients and their offspring to be justifiable. Second, there is the inevitable slippery slope to forms of genetic enhancement engineering. Therapy on the germ line would soon open the door to nontherapeutic experiments to improve our progeny, and so we should never move onto the slope that will eventually lead us down to these enhancement techniques. Third, the future generations that would be experimented on are unable to give their informed consent. Thus, such interventions would violate one of the most sacred moral principles in human experimentation, viz., the principle of informed consent. Next, there is the moral issue of allocation of scarce resources. Germ-line gene therapy will never be cost effective enough to justify the expense of these techniques in the face of alternative approaches to the genetic problems, e.g., somatic cell therapy. Finally, there is the issue of the integrity of genetic patrimony. All germ-line gene therapy would violate the moral rights of subsequent generations to inherit a genetic endowment that has not been intentionally altered.

There are also five arguments in favor of such therapeutic interventions. First, there is the issue of medical utility in which such techniques would offer a true cure for many genetic diseases. Therapeutic interventions at any level above the causal gene would only be palliative or symptomatic. Second, this form of genetic intervention may be the only effective way of medically addressing some genetic diseases, and thus it is an argument for medical necessity. Next, there is the argument about prophylactic efficiency. By preventing the passing on of disease-causing genes, germ-line therapy would bypass the need to perform costly, risky somatic cell therapy in multiple generations. Fourth, there is the moral need to have respect for parental autonomy. Medicine should accept, and respond to, reproductive health needs of prospective parents, including any requests for germ-line therapy. Finally, there is the moral argument to respect scientific freedom aimed at developing such therapeutic techniques, as long as these techniques are pursued within the boundaries of acceptable research on human subjects.

Theological Reflections

Two decades before the Human Genome Project officially began, the theologian Paul Ramsey warned us about the possible developments in genetic engineering. He claimed with great confidence that "Men ought not to play God before they learn to be men, and after they have learned to be men they will not play God" (1970, 138). For Ramsey, "to play God" certainly meant to convey a negative moral connotation, and his theological statement was aimed at limiting human efforts in the entire arena of genetic manipulation. For others, "to play God" means to appropriate for ourselves various functions and tasks that properly belong only to the divine. For some this phrase might mean a reaction to the realization that

humans are now on the threshold of understanding how the very building blocks of life work. Such understanding would indeed be awesome and thus could justify the description of being "God-like." The phrase could also mean either changing, and thus violating, God's created order by using this new technology or it could mean imitating the creator by fabricating new life forms through germ-line engineering. Finally, the phrase is sometimes construed within the theological context of usurping the rights of God over creation, and thus "to play God" is to act from a lack of a right (*ex defectu juris in agente*) in a certain area of life. In this last sense the phrase connotes affective and attitudinal responses of caution and restraint with respect to God's sovereignty over all creation.

Considering these various meanings of "playing God" the theological question that I would like to pursue is the following: Is performing germ-line therapy on humans contrary to God's intentions and purposes, and therefore an act of usurping God's rights over creation? An affirmative answer to the question would almost inevitably translate into an absolute moral prohibition against all germ-line therapeutic interventions. On the other hand, a negative response to this question *might* morally permit these genetic interventions, but it need not result in such a moral judgment. A negative answer might only be a judgment that such therapeutic actions would not be prohibited on strictly theological grounds alone. Therefore, an action could be judged in general as permissible on strictly theological grounds, i.e., it is not contrary to God's intentions and purposes, but currently as impermissible on moral grounds, i.e., because of current scientific or technical limitations the action might violate the moral principle of non-maleficence because it harms either the patients themselves or their future progeny.

Like most moral judgments, an answer to the theological question posed above would have to be decided for believers within the broader context of a religious interpretation of experience. Christians, at least, have regularly thematized their experiences of the divine and expressed them through certain doctrinal themes in terms of creation, fall, incarnation, redemption, and eschatology. These doctrinal expressions themselves have been based on certain models of God and of how the divine relates to and acts in nature and history. In addition, these themes, which have conveyed the Christian interpretations of God, have also served as anthropological frameworks for understanding our moral obligations for both the present and the future. I will use the framework of these five-fold Christian mysteries to show how moral judgments on germ-line therapy rely on and are authorized by certain theological beliefs and interpretations. However, there is only space to develop the essential lineaments of the various positions under each Christian theme. I will formulate my own position on the question of whether or not these therapeutic interventions are contrary to God's purposes by stating under each theological theme the position I adopt.

Creation

The doctrine of creation is actually a complex set of interpretations of who God is and how the divine directs human history and acts within it (divine providence). These theological interpretations have anthropological counterparts that attempt to understand both how we as created beings stand in the image of God (*imago dei*) and how we are to evaluate the significance of physical nature and our bodily existence.

Two different theological models of God, creation and divine providence, have been historically used in the great Christian tradition. Currently, Christians have used both models as a theological context in arguing morally for or against germ-line interventions to cure serious diseases.

In one perspective God is viewed as the creator of both the material universe and humanity and the one who has placed universal, fixed laws into the very fabric of creation. This view of creation obviously favors Parmenides' interpretation of reality as fixed and static, and it assumes that God's purposes for humanity, which are forever unchangeable, can be known by reflecting on the universal laws governing nature and humanity. As sovereign ruler over the created order, God directs the future through divine providence. As Lord of life and death, God possesses certain rights over creation, which in some cases have not been delegated to humans for their exercise. When humans take it upon themselves to exercise God's rights, for example, those divine rights to decide the future or to change the universal laws that govern biological nature, they usurp divine authority and thus they act contrary to God's purposes in creation. If one adopted the theological positions held in this model, one would likely judge as human arrogance the attempt to alter permanently the genetic structure of the human genome even to cure a serious disease. This assessment is confirmed in a *TIME/ CNN* Poll on people's reaction to genetic research. Not only were many respondents ambivalent about genetic research but a substantial majority of the respondents (58 percent) thought that altering human genes *in any way* was against the will of God.

In the second theological model, which I adopt, God is not interpreted as the one who has created both physical nature and humanity in their complete and final forms. Rather, the divine continues to create in history (*creatio continua*). Consequently, God is not understood as having placed universal, fixed laws into the fabric of creation, and so the divine purposes are not as readily discernible as in the first model. God's actions both in creation and in history continue to influence the world process, which is open to new possibilities and even spontaneity. Divine providence is understood as God providing ordered potentialities for specific occasions and responding creatively and in new ways to the continually changing needs of history (Barbour 1966, 449). Though there is some stable order in the universe, like Heraclitus' view of all reality, creation is not finished, and history is indeterminate. Because creation was not made perfect from the beginning, one can discern certain elements in the created order, like genetic diseases, that are disordered. Because these disordered aspects of creation cause great human suffering, they are judged to be contrary to God's final purposes and so can be corrected by human intervention.

As an anthropological counterpart to their interpretations of the divine, Christians, like Jews, have consistently understood all humanity to be created in the image and likeness of God (Gen. 1:26–27). However, the great Christian tradition has used at least two different interpretations of how humans stand in that image, and these diverse models almost inevitably lead to different moral evaluations about therapeutic interventions into the human genome.

The first interpretation defines humanity as a steward over creation. Our moral responsibility, then, is primarily to protect and to conserve what the divine has created and ordered. Stewardship is exercised by respecting the limits placed by God in the orders of biological nature and society. It is easy to see how this model is consistent with the understanding of God as the creator who has placed universal, fixed laws into the very fabric of creation. If we are only stewards over both creation and our own genetic heritage, then our moral responsibilities do not include the alteration of what the divine has created and ordered. Our principal moral duties are to remain faithful to God's original creative will and to respect the laws that are both inherent in creation and function as limits to human intervention.

The second interpretation of the *imago dei* defines humans as co-creators or participants with God in the continual unfolding of the processes and patterns of creation. As created co-creators we are both utterly dependent on God for our very existence and simultaneously responsible for creating the course of human history. Though we are not God's equals in the act of creating, we do play a significant role in bringing creation and history to their completion. Because I adopt this position, I would argue that part of our responsibility in bringing creation to its completion might even include permanently overcoming the defects in biological nature that remain contrary to God's purposes.

A Christian interpretation of the significance and value of both physical nature and our bodily existence also plays an important role in arriving at moral judgments on genetic therapy. There are several different models of material nature that can shape one's moral position on genetic manipulation. Each model attempts not only to interpret the nature of all material reality but also to understand the extent to which we can use human freedom to change permanently our biological processes for therapeutic purposes.

Daniel Callahan has argued that one of the most influential models of nature that operates in contemporary society is the power-plasticity model. In this view, material nature possesses no inherent value, and it is viewed as independent of and even alien to humans and their purposes. All material reality is simply plastic to be used, dominated and ultimately shaped by human freedom. Thus, the fundamental purpose of the entire physical universe, including human biological nature, is to serve human purposes. What is truly human and valuable are self-mastery, self-development, and self-expression through the exercise of freedom. The body is subordinated to the spiritual aspect of humanity, and humans view themselves as possessing an unrestricted right to dominate and shape not only the body but also its future genetic heritage.

The view of nature at the opposite extreme is the sacral-symbiotic model in which material nature is viewed as created by God and thus considered as sacred. As created and originally ordered by God, human biological nature is static and normative in this understanding, and the laws inherent in it must be respected. We are not masters over nature but stewards who must live in harmony and balance with our material nature. Biological nature remains our teacher that shows us how to live within the boundaries established by God at creation. Since physical nature is considered sacrosanct and inviolate, any permanent alteration of the human genetic code,

even to cure a serious genetic disease, would probably be morally prohibited.

I am a proponent of the final model, which construes material nature as evolving. Whereas there is some stability to nature and there are some laws that do govern material reality, neither this stability nor these laws are considered absolutely normative in moral judgments. Change and development are considered more normative than other aspects of nature, and history is seen as linear rather than cyclic or episodic. The relation between material nature and human freedom appears as a dialogue that dynamically evolves over time. It is within this dialogue that humans learn how to use responsibly material reality as the medium of their own creative self-expression. This model would seem to grant to humans the freedom and responsibility to intervene into our evolving biological nature to correct serious diseases at the germ-line level. The reason is because such human efforts would not necessarily be judged as usurping God's final prerogatives or purposes in creation.

Fall

The Christian tradition has taught that, though creation is essentially good, humans have misused their freedom and have acted irresponsibly. This teaching, then, refers to a fall that has infected all human history. However, there have been different interpretations about the depth of human depravity and about the connection between this fall and all disease, including genetic diseases. In one way, this doctrine functions as a way of assessing the extent to which humans can be morally trusted with the awesome powers to alter permanently the human genome even for therapeutic reasons.

One view of the human fall, which was adopted by many early Protestant reformers and continues in the thought patterns of some contemporary theologians, is that all aspects of the human person are deeply affected by sinfulness. This interpretation has led some to distrust that humanity will ever use genetic interventions only for moral ends, e.g., to cure disease. Consequently, proponents of this view regularly try to limit the extension of human control over the genetic heritage of individuals and of their progeny for fear that this therapy will inevitably slide down the slope to improper genetic engineering. This view does judge that genetic diseases are contrary to God's original purposes in creation. However, it also tends to connect causally the origin of these diseases with the misuse of human freedom.

At the opposite end of the spectrum religious advocates almost entirely forget about the fall of humanity. They look upon the fall as insignificant and inconsequential, and they consider only the possibilities open to human ingenuity and rational control. Consequently, these proponents regularly support efforts to manipulate the human genome. By downplaying the effects of the fall on humanity, these proponents extol human freedom and control over physical nature and the future.

I adopt an alternate view to these two extremes. This position, which has been historically consistent with Roman Catholic thought, could be described as a moderately optimistic assessment of the human condition. Though fallen, humanity remains essentially good and can know and do the moral good with the grace of God. Unlike the excessively optimistic view in the second interpretation, adherents of this view recognize that the human capacities to reason and will the moral good continue to be affected by sin. Consequently, they are cautious about putting too much trust in humanity's ability to use modern technology solely for moral ends. However, they do not necessarily view therapeutic interventions into the human germ line as violations of God's sovereignty over creation, nor do they judge these efforts to the contrary to divine purposes. In addition, genetic diseases are viewed fundamentally as natural to the unfinished created order and so they do not necessarily originate with human irresponsibility in the fall. These disorders have always been and continue to be contrary to divine purposes for humans, and so therapeutic manipulations of the human germ-line to cure them are not in themselves wrong on theological grounds.

Incarnation

The fact that God took on human bodily form in the person of Jesus Christ has several implications for the discussion of genetic medicine. First, this doctrine serves as a context both for assessing the relation between body and spirit and for evaluating the significance of the body in moral decision making. In turn, these considerations have an impact on the question of what we judge to be the normatively or uniquely human in moral analysis. Both issues function as presuppositions to moral judgments about the permissibility of germ-line therapy.

If one separates, or even grossly distinguishes, body and spirit, there is the tendency to view our spiritual part as more important or even as the solely unique characteristic of the human person. In addition, such a view will tend to hold that permanent alterations of the body, e.g., through genetic manipulation of the germ line, do not and cannot actually change the fundamental nature of humans. The influential physician-research biochemist W. French Anderson once remarked that he had been worried for years that we might end up altering our very humanness by methods of genetic engineering. However, he has recently decided that Plato was correct to view the soul and the body as two distinct entities (1994, 758). By adopting this Platonic framework Anderson now believes that we cannot alter our fundamental humanness because, as much as we might permanently change our biological genetic code, we cannot change that which is uniquely human about us, viz., our soul or that which is beyond our "physical hardware" (759). Some contemporary theologians who have addressed this issue of gene therapy have also adopted a similar position on the nature of the human. For example, G. R. Dunstan (1991, 236) has argued that only if gene therapy intervened at the level of the cerebral cortex and the central nervous system to alter the capacities of self-consciousness, inquiry, rational ordering and analysis, moral judgment and choice would human nature really be changed.

An opposing view is the position that holds that there is an intimate relation between body and soul. I would argue that we are embodied spirits or ensouled bodies. As Paul Ramsey once phrased it, "We need rather the biblical comprehension that man is as much the body of his soul as he is the soul of his body" (1970, 133). Such a view, then, would be far more cautious than the first about making a claim that we cannot permanently alter the nature of humanity through genetic manipulation. The relation of body and spirit is one, but not the only, element of what makes up our fundamental human nature. Thus to alter radically this relation would imply the possibility of changing our nature in this view. However, since the intent in germ-line therapy is to prevent or to cure disease and not to enhance or engineer the human subject, I would conclude there is much less risk that we will change this aspect of our human nature, i.e., the body-spirit relation, through this intervention.

Redemption

Christians believe not only that we are created yet fallen beings but that we are redeemed by God through the suffering, death, and resurrection of

Jesus Christ. Thus, besides God's creative purposes the divine also has redeeming purposes for all creation. Christians have sometimes grossly separated the creative and redeeming purposes of God. One way to understand the relation between these divine activities has been to interpret redemption as not only a continuation of creation but the means by which creation itself is brought to completion by God. This framework raises the question of whether the technology to alter the genetic code for therapeutic purposes can ever be viewed as potential participation in God's redeeming actions toward humanity. Since Christians have interpreted humankind as created in the divine image, it has been possible to view genetic interventions as possible acts of co-*creation* with the divine. However, now the question is whether it is also possible theologically to view our technological activities as potential participations in or mediations of God's *redemptive* purposes? To answer this question requires a brief discussion of various theological evaluations of technology in general.

There are several evaluations of modern technology that could serve as the context for our moral judgments on therapeutic techniques to cure serious genetic diseases. First, there is the rather pessimistic view of technology, an example of which the late Jacques Ellul (1964) adopted. Its characteristics include a very skeptical attitude toward any real benefits from technology and a great sensitivity to the potential evils that will come from its development and use. Technology is viewed as a threat, impersonal, manipulative and alienating, and thus it does not and cannot possess the inherent potential to share in the divine purposes of redemption, which are personal, salvific and wholistic.

The opposite extreme is an overly optimistic view of technology and its potential achievements. Its hallmarks are a focus on the liberating function of technology through progress and human fulfillment and an emphasis on greater freedom and creative expression. Some, like the Jesuit paleontologist Pierre Teilhard de Chardin, have closely linked technology and spiritual development and thus have viewed technology as clearly possessing the potential to cooperate with God's work.

The final position is what Ian Barbour has called "technology as instrument of power" (1993, 15–20), which is a moderate position between the two extremes above. Similar to the first view, proponents are cautious about and critical of many features of modern technology. However, like the second view these proponents also offer hope that technology must be redirected in its uses for these ends to be re-alized. The Protestant theologian Ronald Cole-Turner (1993, 80–97) has adopted a position similar to this one. He has argued, convincingly in my mind, that modern technological developments in genetics can have the potential for participating in God's redemptive activities. I too would argue that, when this technology is aimed at preventing or curing serious genetic diseases that are deemed contrary to God's final purposes because they cause great human suffering, this technology can participate in God's redemptive purposes by making whole and healthy what was once disordered and destructive.

Eschatology

The great Christian tradition has affirmed that all creation is called to a future beyond this history, i.e., to an eschatological era as the final end of human history. This future is variously called the "reign of God," the "kingdom of God" or "God's absolute future." However one names it, Christians believe that it is God who inaugurates this future and brings it to final consummation. Interpretations of the relation between our human history and God's eschatological future function as the background context for discerning our moral responsibilities toward the human future. Thus, various eschatological visions will contextualize differently the discernment of our moral obligations to improve our genetic heritage through germ-line interventions.

Harvey Cox (1967) identified three strains of eschatology that traditionally have been used in Judeo-Christian theologies: the apocalyptic, the teleological, and the prophetic. He argued that all three can be found both in ancient religious traditions and in modern secularized forms. Each religious strain has a different understanding of God's eschatological future and how God will inaugurate that future. Consequently, each strain will construe quite differently the relation of humanity's future to God's absolute future, and each will variously formulate what our moral responsibilities are for making sure human history turns out right.

The apocalyptic eschatology, whose origins are in ancient near-eastern dualism, always judges the present as somehow unsatisfactory. In both its religious and secularized forms, this eschatology negatively evaluates this world and its history and it foresees imminent catastrophe. The religious form of this eschatology always draws a sharp distinction between God's absolute future in the kingdom and the conditions of our human history, and thus it generally argues for a great discontinuity between this world and the next. On the other hand, the teleological eschatology, whose origins are Greek but was adopted by Christians, views the future as the "unwinding of a purpose inherent in the universe itself or in its primal stuff, the development of the world toward a fixed end" (38). All creation, then, is moving toward some final end, for example, beatific vision with God. Consequently, there is some continuity between present human history and God's future. The last interpretation of eschatology, which I adopt, is the prophetic strain. Its origins are Hebrew in nature, and it views the future as the open area of human hope and responsibility. In the Hebrew scriptures, the prophets did not foretell the future; rather, "they recalled Yahweh's promise as a way of calling the Israelites into moral action in the present" (38). In its biblical form, then, the future is not known in advance, but it is radically open and its actualization lies in the hands of humans who must take up responsibility for it. In its modern secularized form, the prophetic eschatology places great hope in human responsibility for the future, and it views the future with its manifold possibilities as unlocking the determinations of the past.

One of the most notable theologians who had adopted the apocalyptic eschatology and then applied it to issues in genetic research was the late Paul Ramsey. He regularly emphasized the discontinuity between this world and the next, and thus he always urged us to remain faithful to God's future as that is represented in the divine covenant between humanity and God. Ramsey argued that we do not have any moral obligation to safeguard the future of humanity through genetic research because he believed that "religious people have never denied, indeed they affirm, that God means to kill us all in the end, and in the end He is going to succeed" (1970, 27). It is this apocalyptic view, which interprets human history as coming to an abrupt end through divine activity, that influenced Ramsey's interpretation of both our general moral responsibilities for the future and his specific moral prohibitions against genetic research that would permanently alter our genetic code. Our primary moral responsibility, in his view, was to remain faithful to what God has given us; it was not to act as if we had the moral responsibility to save our future offspring from genetic disease.

If one adopted either a teleological or a prophetic eschatology, one would be inclined to accept morally certain genetic interventions into the human germ line to cure serious disease. Both strains emphasize human responsibility for the future, although each does this differently. Both understand that the future is open and somewhat indeterminate. Consequently, these eschatologies could serve as warrants for morally justifying germ-line therapy. Neither view would necessarily judge that such interventions would be contrary to God's creative and redemptive purposes, and thus neither would necessarily judge that these techniques would be wrong on theological grounds alone.

Conclusion

My theological interests in this topic of germ-line therapy have been twofold. I have sought to show how Christian moral decision making on the new genetics is contextualized by specifically theological beliefs. I have also posed the theological question of whether therapeutic interventions into the human germ line to prevent or to cure serious disease are acts of "playing God" or whether such actions are within the boundaries of authentic human responsibility. An answer to this question must be decided within the broader context of several theological affirmations or doctrinal themes that are interpretations of religious experience.

Significant scientific and technical difficulties remain to be solved with both types of germ-line therapy and there continue to be public policy difficulties with these genetic technologies as well. In addition, I am not convinced that all the moral arguments in favor of these therapeutic efforts are completely satisfying as they stand. Consequently, the ethical conclusion I reach is that *at the present time* we should not attempt to perform these therapies on either gametes or on fertilized ova before transferring them to their mothers' wombs. However, this essay has hopefully advanced the debate about germ-line therapy from a theological perspective. I would argue on theological grounds that once the scientific, public policy and moral difficulties can be resolved, we may cautiously move forward with this type of genetic therapy. In other words, based on my theological interpretations of both the five-fold Christian themes and their anthropological counterparts, I conclude that these therapies are not fundamentally contrary to God's creative and redemptive purposes. To use them is not necessarily to arrogate to ourselves various functions and tasks that properly belong only to the divine. If developed and applied responsibly, these genetic interventions neither usurp God's rights over creation, nor do they represent improper attempts "to play God." On the contrary, I consider these therapeutic technologies to have the potential of becoming mediations of or participations in God's very redemptive activities toward humanity. Consequently, their use for the moral ends of preventing or curing serious genetic diseases can be a means of properly exercising human responsibility.

References

Anderson, W. French. "Human Gene Therapy: Why Draw a Line?" *The Journal of Medicine and Philosophy* (December 1989), 681–693.

Barbour, Ian G. *Issues in Science and Religion.* New York: Harper & Row, 1966.

———. *Ethics in an Age of Technology.* San Francisco: Harper-Collins, 1993.

Cole-Turner, Ronald. *The New Genesis: Theology and the Genetic Revolution.* Louisville: Westminster/ John Knox, 1993.

Cox, Harvey. "Evolutionary Progress and Christian Promise" in Johannes B. Metz, ed. *Concilium* Vol. 26: *The Evolving World and Theology.* New York: Paulist, 1967, 35–47.

Dunstan, Professor the Reverend Canon G. R. "Gene Therapy, Human Nature and the Churches." *International Journal of Bioethics* 2 (1991) 235–240.

Ellul, Jacques. *The Technological Society.* New York: Knopf, 1964.

Juengst, Eric T. "The NIH 'Points to Consider' and the Limits of Human Gene Therapy." *Human Gene Therapy* 1 (1990) 425–433.

Ramsey, Paul. *Fabricated Man: The Ethics of Genetic Control.* New Haven: Yale University, 1970.

Discussion and Reflection Questions

1. Walter identifies a number of arguments for and against germ-line therapy. Which of these arguments do you find most and least convincing? Why?

2. How might acceptance of the theological doctrine of *creatio continua* (continued divine creation in history) lead to an acceptance of the moral permissibility of germ-line therapy?

3. What role, if any, do you think that theological considerations ought to play in the moral question of determining the acceptability of human germ-line therapy? Why? Are there insights that non-Christians might glean from such reflections?

4. Do you agree with Walter that, with the qualifications he states, germ-line therapy is not fundamentally contrary to God's creative and redemptive purposes? Why?

Swasti Bhattacharyya, Reproductive Technology and Cloning through Hindu Perspectives

Recent advances in biomedical and reproductive technology have made possible medical and therapeutic interventions that would have been almost unimaginable even a few decades ago. It might therefore seem surprising that religious texts written thousands of years ago could have anything to say about the ethical issues that arise from reflection on these sorts of issues. Remarkably, however, the writers of the ancient Hindu texts grappled with many of the same general ethical issues associated with reproduction that arise from contemporary technological advances. In the following essay, Swasti Bhattacharyya explores many of these issues, bringing ancient wisdom to bear on contemporary ethical problems.

Reading Questions

1. How does the story of the Pandavas family illustrate a problem associated with reproduction? In the story, how is this problem overcome? How might the same problem be solved through technological means today?

2. What ethical insights does Bhattacharyya glean from the story of the Pandavas family? How might such insights be applied to this problem using contemporary technology?

3. How does the story of the Kauravas family illustrate a problem associated with reproduction? In the story, how is this problem overcome? How might the same problem be solved through technological means today?

4. What ethical insights does Bhattacharyya glean from the story of the Kauravas family? How might such insights be applied to this problem using contemporary technology?

Reproductive Technology and Cloning through Hindu Perspectives

SWASTI BHATTACHARYYA

Introduction

Those involved with modern medical technology are on a fast track in their attempts to conquer various difficulties that plague human beings. Reproductive technology is in the forefront of these medical advances. While in the past, intercourse and surrogacy were the primary methods of conception, today people have additional options which include various medications, artificial insemination, in vitro fertilization (IVF), gamete intra-fallopian transfer (GIFT), zygote intra-fallopian transfer (ZIFT) and variations on all the above. More recently, some scientists are attempting to add cloning to this list as well. These attempts to circumvent human infertility are on the cutting edge of modern medicine, both in terms of the techniques developed for medical practice and in terms of the issues that arise in current bioethical debates. In North America, these ethical discussions, though primarily influenced by perspectives grounded in various Jewish and Christian traditions, are taking place in pluralistic societies. A diversity of worldviews is now local and pluralism is no longer simply a theory, but an increasingly recognized reality. With this diversity of ideologies come challenges: challenges that the field of bioethics needs to address.

While there are those who see a plethora of worldviews and argue there is no common ground from which to relate, there are others who attempt to collapse the diversity into a meaningless unity that ultimately neither relates to nor satisfies anyone. While retaining the differences, yet engaging in a discussion, this essay examines how various Hindu perspectives frame, view, and deal with issues relating to reproductive technology and cloning. Hinduism, like other religious traditions, does not speak with one monolithic voice, therefore this chapter is not speaking for all of Hinduism. Rather it is highlighting voices within Hinduism.

We begin by focusing on two birth narratives in the *Mahābhārata*, a formative text that encapsulates not only the whole of India, but the whole of human history. Many benefits are to be gained by examining this ancient Indian text when discussing modern reproductive technology and cloning. First, it is said that within the pages of the *Mahābhārata* everything that ever was and ever will be is discussed—reproductive technology and cloning are no exception. Though these paradigmatic stories do not contain actual one-to-one correlations between antiquity and modernity, they do record creative means of overcoming infertility. Though the specific technology of modern medicine may be new and innovative, an examination of these narratives indicates that the ideas and related ethical issues are not. The struggles, concerns, and ethical dilemmas that faced Kuntī and

Swasti Bhattacharyya, "Reproductive Technology and Cloning through Hindu Perspectives." Reprinted by permission of the author.

Gāndhārī reflect those confronting contemporary individuals. These queens overcome major obstacles by utilizing their version of what today may be accomplished through various forms of reproductive technology. While they sought aid from the gods, contemporary couples seek aid from medical doctors. What the *Mahābhārata* deals with in the realm of the divine, modern medicine brings into the realm of human beings. Through an examination of these two birth stories, this essay extrapolates some Hindu responses to issues relating to reproductive technology and cloning.

Second, it is important to note that Hinduism is a tradition where religion, philosophy, and the conduct of daily life are all tightly interwoven. Generally speaking, there is no separate category of "ethics" within Hindu thought or literature. There is no formal discipline that presents the standard western view of ethics as "an internally consistent rational system in which patterns of human conduct are justified with reference to ultimate norms and values" (Holdrege 1991, 12). Nevertheless, this does not mean that Hindus do not know about ethics or that they are immoral. It simply indicates that there is neither a discipline within Indian thought that separates ethics out from the activities of daily life nor that focuses exclusively on it (Narayanan 2001, 177). Hindu "ethics," its principles, morals, and values are present within the tradition and are tightly interwoven in the practical aspects of life. The narratives within the *Mahābhārata* provide more than thrilling stories, profound crises, and discussions on cosmology, philosophy, theology, and ethics, they also legitimize and inculcate ethical and political patterns fundamentally important to "Hindu" civilization. These stories are treasure mines that upon excavation will reveal, among other things, the jewels of Hinduism's ethical ideology. Thus, through a careful examination of these paradigmatic narratives, this chapter uncovers various Hindu perspectives on reproductive technology and cloning.

The "Cases"

The intricate stories of two related royal families, the Pāṇḍavas and Kauravas, form the warp of the *Mahābhārata* (abbreviated: *MBh.*). Here I will focus on the birth stories of Kuntī's and Gāndhārī's children. Kuntī and Gāndhārī, the matriarchs of these two clans, are married to two brothers: Pāṇḍu, head of the Pāṇḍavas, and Dhṛtarāṣṭra, patriarch of the Kauravas. Through a complicated and tenuous line of succession, these brothers rule over the land of the Kurus: an area that is located near the upper Ganges River, just below the foothills of the Himalayan range.

KUNTĪ AND PĀṆḌU

Sometime after Kuntī and Pāṇḍu are married, the king goes on a hunting exposition and kills a buck that is mating with its doe. Unknown to Pāṇḍu, the buck is a powerful holy man, who along with his wife, had taken on the forms of the animals. As the ascetic lay dying, he places a curse on the king: Since Pāṇḍu thoughtlessly aimed to kill the buck while it was engaged in the most sacred of activities, Pāṇḍu will suffer likewise. When he is engulfed by love and has sex, Pāṇḍu will die (*MBh.* I.109.5–30).

Pāṇḍu is overwhelmed with grief. Though he is married to two wise and beautiful women (his second wife is Mādrī), he has no children: no heirs for the throne. After consulting with his wives, Pāṇḍu decides to forfeit his rule to Dhṛtarāṣṭra and the three of them renounce the world and wander in the forests. After years of living like a hermit and practicing austerities, Pāṇḍu is troubled by the idea that for him, a childless man, there is no door to heaven. He discusses his concerns with Kuntī and implores her to have children for him through the traditional practice of *niyoga*, an ancient Indian custom that allows a woman to have sexual intercourse with a man in order to provide heirs for her husband. Kuntī, unable to bear the thought of being with any other man, yet wanting to have children and please her husband, chooses this time to inform Pāṇḍu of a boon she received long ago. As a child she was charged with honoring the guests that came to her home. On one occasion, she greatly pleased Durvāsas, a powerfully divine sage. He chose to reward her efforts by granting her a boon: a mantra that when used would result in a son engendered by whichever god she chose to call upon (*MBh.* I.110.25–113.35). Kuntī informs Pāṇḍu of this boon.

Pāṇḍu is thrilled by the news that Kuntī has the ability to provide him with sons, and together they carefully decide which god she should call upon first. They desire a son who will be righteous and good, so after much deliberation they select Dharma, the god of justice and order. Kuntī invokes Dharma and in time she gives birth to a son, Yudhiṣṭhira. Following the birth of their first son, they again consider which attributes they desire for other sons. After much deliberation, Kuntī summons Vāyu, the god of wind and then Indra, the king of gods. These divine unions result in the births of Bhīma and Arjuna, respectively, (*Mbh.* I.114.1-35).

When Pāṇḍu approaches Kuntī for a fourth time, she chastises him for his greediness and reminds him that the law of *niyoga* does not provide for a fourth son. According to the *Mahābhārata*, this law permits a woman to sleep with up to two males to provide heirs. *Niyoga* is not a license for illicit sex. Thus the laws governing its practice limit the number of partners a woman may legitimately have: it identifies a woman as "loose" if she sleeps with three men and "a harlot" if she has sexual intercourse with a fourth. Not willing to take on the label of "harlot," and not wanting to act outside of the law, Kuntī refuses to call upon a fourth god. It is at this point that Pāṇḍu's second wife Mādrī implores him to speak to Kuntī on her behalf so that she too may have a child. Kuntī agrees to allow Mādrī a one-time use of her boon. Thinking carefully and cunningly, Mādrī calls upon the twin gods, the Aśvins. From them she gives birth to her twin sons, Nakula and Sahadeva. Kuntī, furious and feeling deceived by Mādrī, refuses Pāṇḍu's second request on behalf of Mādrī (*MBh.* I.114.65-115.24). Thus, through Kuntī's boon, she and Mādrī are able to circumvent the curse placed on Pāṇḍu and provide him with the five Pāṇḍava brothers—the heroes of the *Mahābhārata*.

GĀNDHĀRĪ AND DHṚTARĀṢṬRA

Gāndhārī's situation is different. Prior to her marriage to Dhṛtarāṣṭra, Gāndhārī comforts and attends to Vyāsa, great sage and legendary author of the *Mahābhārata*. Due to her kindness he grants her a boon: She will have 100 sons that will be of equal station to her husband and herself. After some time, Gāndhārī marries Dhṛtarāṣṭra and becomes pregnant with his child. By the time Kuntī gives birth to her first-born son Yudhiṣṭhira, Gāndhārī has endured pregnancy for two years. Upon hearing of the birth of Yudhiṣṭhira, she feels the hardness of her belly, is exceedingly frustrated, miserable, and inconsolable from worry. She has patiently endured the physical and mental challenges of her extended pregnancy, she even forfeited the opportunity of giving birth to the first son of both clans, and now more than ever she desires the birth of her baby. With great effort and the help of her maid, she successfully expels the product of conception. She delivers a mass of flesh—a dense ball of clotted blood. She is totally distraught; after two years of being pregnant, how is it that all she has is a bloody mass—what happened to the promise of her 100 sons?

Vyāsa, divinely seeing what had just taken place, comes swiftly to her aid. Upon his questioning, Gāndhārī admits she was about to dispose of the ball of flesh. She reminds him of his promise, and questions the worth of his boon. Vyāsa reassures her that his words are never for naught; from her product of conception she will have one daughter in addition to her 100 sons. Following Vyāsa's instructions, Gāndhārī collects 101 clay pots and fills them with *ghee* (clarified butter). Then they sprinkle the ball of bloody flesh with cold water. Upon doing this, it falls apart into 101 pieces, each an embryo, the size of a thumb joint. Each embryo is placed in the ghee-filled pots and are incubated in a warm, well-guarded place. After some time, the first of Gāndhārī's sons, Duryodhana, is born (*MBh.* I.107.5-35). Thus through extraordinary means the 101 Kaurava children, antagonists of the *Mahābhārata*, are born to Gāndhārī and Dhṛtarāṣṭra.

NARRATIVE AS A SOURCE FOR ETHICS: POINTS OF CONTACT

Through the narratives of Kuntī and Gāndhārī, one catches a glimpse of how this Hindu text portrays issues relating to infertility and the means of overcoming its challenges. These stories contain several "points of contact" between antiquity and modernity. Extrapolating from the text, one may observe a number of precursors to modern medical practices. Kuntī rejects Pāṇḍu's suggestion that she participate in *niyoga*, a pre-IVF form of sperm donation, and instead informs him of her secret boon. By utilizing Kuntī's mantra to call upon the various gods, she and Mādrī are able to overcome Pāṇḍu's infertility by accessing a "divine sperm bank," so to speak.

They also participate in a form of gene selection. Consider Pāṇḍu's desire for his first born; he wants a son who "shall become the standard of Law for the Kurus," thus he implores Kuntī first to summon Dharma for "having been given by Dharma, his mind will not rejoice in lawlessness. . . ." Dharma is selected because of the particular attributes Pāṇḍu desires in his firstborn son. He wants a son who will set the "standard of Law" for the clan and who will "not rejoice in lawlessness." At the birth of Yudhiṣṭhira, a disembodied voice declares, "He shall of a certainty be the greatest of the upholders of the Law, Pāṇḍu's firstborn son. . . . He shall be a celebrated king, widely renowned in all three worlds, . . ." (*MBh.* I.113.40). As the *Mahābhārata* unfolds, Yudhiṣṭhira is respected, by friends and foe alike, for his truthfulness and lawfulness. Kuntī and Pāṇḍu's selection of Dharma is based on a calculated decision. They desire particular attributes in their son, thus they choose the god most likely to bestow those attributes.

The same careful selection process is utilized for choosing the gods who will father Kuntī's second and third sons. Being of the *kṣatriya* (warrior) caste, Pāṇḍu wants a son whose strength will find no match. Thus Vāyu, the god of wind, is summoned and the resulting union leads to the birth of Bhīma, one whose strength subdues humans and demons alike. Next Pāṇḍu desires a son who will be superior to all. Therefore, after a year of austerities, Kuntī calls up Indra, the king of the gods. This brings about the birth of Arjuna: the greatest warrior and hero of the *Bhagavad Gītā*. Mādrī also selects her divine "sperm donor" with great care. She is well aware that Kuntī's generosity has limits. Kuntī instructs Mādrī, "Think, for this once, of a deity and of certainty you shall have a child by him" (*MBh.* I.115.5). Therefore, desiring to maximize her one-time opportunity, Mādrī deliberately calls upon the Aśvins. Consequently her use of the mantra results in her twins. Again, the gods are not being called upon randomly; each one is carefully selected because of the particular attribute he will bestow on the promised son. As previously stated, where the narratives in the *Mahābhārata* fight infertility with the magic and power from the realm of the divine, modern medicine combats infertility with scientific technology.

In this modern world, options abound for individuals dealing with infertility or desiring a baby. Some will visit medical doctors specializing in infertility, others will visit fertility clinics and sperm banks. When choosing a sperm donor, individuals and couples consider the attributes they desire for their potential baby. They seek answers to all sorts of questions: What race is the sperm donor? Where is he from? What are his physical characteristics? What is his IQ? Grade point average? How much schooling has he completed? What is his current profession? These same questions, and others, are asked of women willing to donate their eggs. Similar to the ancient characters of Kuntī and Pāṇḍu, contemporary individuals put much thought and consideration into the particular attributes they desire in a potential child, and they select a particular sperm or egg donor accordingly.

One could argue that Gāndhārī's situation is equally intriguing and somewhat more contemporary than that of Kuntī and Mādrī. The manner in which Gāndhārī has her children is interesting and it brings to mind some controversial issues regarding reproductive technology and cloning. Recall how Gāndhārī's product of conception is divided into 101 thumb-size embryos. These embryos all originate from the same substance—the same genetic material. Gāndhārī and Vyāsa's actions could be considered crude analogies to modern attempts of "cloning," or at least "embryonic manipulation." Again, in terms of cloning, their actions differ from the actual procedures of cloning: they did not retrieve human eggs from Gāndhārī or some other women and extract the nucleus from the eggs. Nor did they gather cells from her or her husband and electronically fuse them with the harvested DNA-free eggs. However, they did take the same genetic material, as it were, and divided it up to produce 101 embryos.

Following Vyāsa's instructions, Gāndhārī does more than participate in something akin to "embryonic manipulation." Though the fertilization of Gāndhārī's fetuses occurred *in utero*, their gestation was *in vitro*, so to speak. Gāndhārī and Vyāsa take each zygote (fertilized human egg) and "implant" it into the *ghee*-filled clay pots. These pots become more then "test-tubes," they become "artificial wombs" that gestate the developing embryos until they are term—a feat yet to be accomplished by modern medicine.

Questions and concerns regarding multiple-gestational pregnancy is another issue that arises from an examination of Gāndhārī's story. She goes beyond the conventional methods of producing offspring, and takes action that results in her having 101 children. The complications associated with multiple-gestational pregnancies are all too familiar to contemporary users of reproductive technology. The use of Clomid (clomiphene citrate), IVF, GIFT, ZIFT, and other procedures often result in the development of multiple embryos. This situation leads to increased physical risks to the mother and developing fetuses. It also raises questions regarding the abilities (physical, psychological, and financial) of parents to care for these children of multiple births. Not every family with multiple-gestational pregnancies receive the international media attention, and subsequent commercial sponsorships, as did the McCaughey and Chukwu families.

These are but a few examples of how the birth narratives of Gāndhārī's and Kuntī's children contain ideas that are somewhat similar, or are at least precursors, to modern-day practices utilized in reproductive technology and cloning. Beyond containing these "points of contact" that indicate the *Mahābhārata*'s relevancy to contemporary bioethical discussions, this text records how individuals struggle with infertility and how they employ various methods to overcome its limitations. The text clearly indicates that progeny is a priority. It also demonstrates that some women play active roles in, and have control over, their fertility. Additionally, the epic appears to have few, if any, limitations on what methods may be employed when attempting to bring about the birth of children. Along with recording imaginative stories of how individuals conquer infertility, these narratives contain principles that may be applied to, and benefit, contemporary bioethical discussions.

Application of the Narrative

Hinduism is a religion overflowing with options, alternatives, and divergent beliefs. Its traditions neither owe their origin to a single religious leader or prophet nor do they have a single determinate creed or centralized hierarchical structure. This, combined with the fact that Hindu traditions do not establish clear distinctions between philosophy and life itself, leads to the development of multifaceted traditions that embrace a variety of voices. Hinduism is a "blend of independently held beliefs" (Barlingay 1998, 2). It is said that Hindus welcome pluralism and are bothered by attempts to eliminate alternative views. Sharma asserts that Hinduism is a "religion of options rather than prescriptions, of propositions rather than dogmas; a religion which prefers the article a (a truth) to the (the truth); a religion of guidelines rather than rules, and a religion which allows for more variations of the basic positions than its own Kama Sutra" (Sharma 2001, 98). Obviously these pluralistic, syncretistic traditions would not have a monolithic perspective on any topic. Though one will not find the Hindu perspective on reproductive technology and cloning, this does not mean that Hindu ideas and insights do not exist. Though the ancient Indian seers may not have constructed systematic, all-encompassing philosophical arguments, they did leave behind great mythologies—stories whose heroes and heroines provide role models for how individuals ought to live and how society ought to function.

Through an examination of Kuntī's and Gāndhārī's situations, various principles may be extrapolated and applied to contemporary discussions. From the previous section in this essay, one can clearly argue that the Mahābhārata not only permits the use of sperm donation, participation in gene selection, embryonic manipulation or cloning, it condones these practices. According to this text, none of the gods hesitate when they are called upon to fulfill Kuntī's mantra. The text records no condemnation of Kuntī, Pāṇḍu, or Mādrī for utilizing the mantra.

(Kuntī is not disparaged when, out of curiosity, she calls upon the sun god to ascertain if and how the mantra actually works. This union results in the birth of Karṇa). Gāndhārī is not criticized for her actions, even though her eldest son becomes a driving force behind the Great War that brings devastation to the clan and nation as a whole. These accounts imply that the methods, or "technology," utilized to bring about the birth of children are of themselves not necessarily an issue; their use is arguably ethically acceptable for those within Hinduism.

This is significant especially when the implications of these formative, though not "scriptural," Hindu narratives are juxtaposed to those found in the Hebrew Bible. The Hebrew Bible does not record instances where people are manipulating the products of conception to produce offspring. Throughout the Hebrew Bible one finds narratives depicting people praying and beseeching God to enable them to have children. Take for example Isaac and Rebekah; Genesis 25:21 reads: "Isaac prayed to the LORD for his wife, because she was barren; and the LORD granted his prayer, and his wife Rebekah conceived." Elsewhere in the Bible, Hannah, the barren but most favored wife of Elkanah, bitterly cries and prays to God for a son at the Shiloh temple. In due time, "the Lord remembered her," and she conceives and bears Samuel (I Samuel 1:17–20). Genesis 16:1–4 records how after Sarah and Abraham are promised a son, Sarah pro-actively presents her slave-girl, Hagar, to Abraham in order that she may obtain a child through her servant. Beyond this type of "surrogacy" and practices similar to niyoga (see the story of Tamar in Genesis 38:1–11 and the narrative of Ruth in the book of Ruth), the Hebrew Bible does not record extraordinary human actions in the process of procreation: There are no Biblical stories where the product of conception is being divided up and fetuses are developing ex-utero.

In the Hebrew Bible, people pray to God for children and God opens or closes women's wombs. Genesis 30:1–2 records how Rachel, Jacob's beloved wife, cries out "Give me children, or I shall die!" Jacob angrily retorts, "Am I in the place of God, who has withheld from you the fruit of the womb?" Jacob is at a loss; there is nothing he or Rachel can do other than pray to God and wait. Eventually, God hears their cries and opens Rachel's womb (Genesis 30:22–23). Genesis 20 records another situation where God "closed fast all the wombs of the house of Abimelech" because King Abimelech had taken Sarah into his palace. Upon his relinquishing Sarah to Abraham, and the latter's prayers to God, God healed the women of Abimelech's household. In the Hebrew Bible, and in the New Testament, though humans are involved, God is ultimately in control of human procreation. The official teachings of the Roman Catholic Church directly states, "the task of transmitting life, they [humans] are not free, therefore, to proceed at will, as if they could determine with complete autonomy the right paths to follow; but *they must conform their actions to the creative intention of God*. . ." (Pope Paul VI 1978, 10, emphasis added).

Unlike the stories in the Hebrew Bible, the birth narratives in the *Mahābhārata* reflect an attitude toward procreation where gods and humans share in this procreative process. Though gods may be involved in this process of procreation, they are neither the ones in ultimate control nor are they always dictating the terms. True, Kuntī is dependent upon the power within her mantra; however, Kuntī and Pāṇḍu select which god they desire to call upon. The chosen god is then obligated to impregnate her. Though Gāndhārī is dependent upon the supernatural powers of Vyāsa, she is the one who determines they should act. The Hindu perspectives reflected in these *Mahābhārata* narratives reveal an attitude that encourages human beings to employ imaginative means to produce children.

Humans are free to take control of their reproduction and implement various "technologies" toward the goal of having children. Though sexual intercourse did precede procreation in the narratives examined in the *Mahābhārata*, according to other stories within the text, procreation is not necessarily dependent upon sexual intercourse. Consider the circumstances surrounding the conception of Satyavatī, Pāṇḍu and Dhṛtarāṣṭra's grandmother. Thinking upon the loveliness of his wife, King Vasu inadvertently ejaculates. Eventually his sperm ends up in the river Yamunā where it is swallowed by a fish. One day, fishermen catch this fish and upon cutting her belly, they find Satyavatī and her twin brother (*Mbh.* I.57.35–55). Stories such as this demonstrate this epic places no limitations on how children are conceived.

Not only does the Hebrew Bible and *Mahābhārata* present different ideas regarding the issue of human procreation, the religious traditions grounded in these different texts do as well. Various Hindu perspectives stand in stark contrast to some of those within Roman Catholicism. While Hinduism does not have a central authoritative figure, as demonstrated in the story above, generally there is neither an insistence that procreation and sexual intercourse go hand in hand nor are there objections to the use of various forms of reproductive technology. However, the official teachings of the Roman Catholic Church take a clear stance on this issue. In the *Humanae Vitae*, Pope Paul VI argues that procreation is inextricably linked to sexual intercourse and that these sexual relations are to occur within a marriage relationship. Concerning marriage he writes, "Marriage is not, then, the effect of chance or the product to the evolution of blind natural forces; it is a wise institution of the Creator to realize in mankind his design of love" (8). Regarding the inseparable aspects of sex and procreation he says, "This teaching, set forth by the Magisterium on numerous occasions, is founded upon the inseparable connection, willed by God and which man may not break on his own initiative, between the two-fold significance of the conjugal act: the unitive significance and the procreative significance. . ." (11). Officially the Vatican places procreation in a context where individuals are called to follow the path of God, to "conform their actions to the creative intention of God." The *Humanae Vitae* quotes the Second Vatican Council as saying, "Marriage and conjugal love are by their nature ordained to the begetting and rearing of children" (9). According to the official teachings of the Church, procreation, sex, and marriage are all inextricably linked.

This required connection between sexual intercourse and conception, or at least the possibility of conception, provides the grounds upon which the Magisterium (official teaching of the Roman Catholic Church) builds one of their objections to the prohibition against such activities as sperm donation and IVF. Since sperm is usually obtained through the use of a condom and/or masturbation, sperm donation is prohibited. IVF also separates the act of sexual intercourse from fertilization; therefore it too is prohibited.

The belief of immediate hominization, a belief that the soul immediately enters the zygote at the moment of conception, is another reason these procedures are found to be problematic. The Vatican declares the teaching of immediate hominization in the following: "In reality, respect for human life is called for *from the time that the process of generation begins. From the time that the ovum is fertilized,* a life is begun which is neither that of the father nor of the mother; *it is rather the life of a new human being* with his or her own growth. . . ." The Magisterium continues that ensoulment occurs at the time the "process of generation begins" (*Declaration on Abortion* 3.12, emphasis added). Through IVF, ZIFT, and other such technologies, a greater number of zygotes are produced and frozen than are actually implanted. Thus the Church argues that in essence these procedures are imprisoning a number of human souls. Additionally, in the process of cryopreservation and implantation embryos are destroyed, resulting in the death of the destroyed ensouled zygotes. Finally, after individuals utilize these reproductive technologies, oftentimes there are "left-over" embryos. If one believes in immediate hominization, one is left with a dilemma of how to dispose of these extra ensouled embryos. Such official and definite teachings as found in the Roman Catholic Church do not find their equivalent within Hinduism.

Though the *Mahābhārata* encourages creativity and displays an openness to the process of procreation, it does not argue for a "free for all." Kuntī 's case highlights a particularly relevant and important issue to modern reproductive technology and cloning: that of designating limits of use. Kuntī willingly calls upon three different gods to provide Pāṇḍu with three sons. Upon his request for a fourth son, she refuses him. According to the passage, the law places limits on the number of partners a woman may have. Even in times of distress, when children may be vulnerable and more likely to die, *niyoga* does not allow for a fourth partner. Kuntī's objection to using her mantra a fourth time is related to her desires both to stay within the limits of the law and not to be branded a harlot. Her refusal to call upon a fourth god is not due to an impotency of the mantra itself, nor is it because she does not desire more children.

Kuntī's reaction to Mādrī's use of her mantra indicates that she would have welcomed more children. When Pāṇḍu approaches her to share her mantra with Mādrī a second time, Kuntī responds "I said to her, 'For this once,' and she got two! I was deceived! I fear that she will best me. That is the way of women! I had not known, the more fool I, that by invoking two Gods the fruit would be doubled . . ." (*Mbh.* I.115.23–34). Kuntī is angry with Mādrī. She feels deceived and threatened by the idea that, if given the opportunity, Mādrī could give birth to more sons than she did. Thus she refuses Pāṇḍu's request for her to allow Mādrī a second use of the mantra. The power within this mantra does not appear to have any limitations of its own. Theoretically, Kuntī could provide Pāṇḍu with an endless number of sons, while not being labeled a harlot, by simply calling upon the same gods a second or third time. This, however, is not her chosen course of action. Though the power in the mantra is unbridled and limitless, Kuntī is careful not to misuse or abuse it. She carefully controls its use and distribution.

Kuntī and Pāṇḍu's careful deliberation on how to implement her boon and the human/divine participation in procreation also reflects an underlying Hindu metaphysical understanding of an interconnectedness of all life. The *Upanishads, Bhagavad Gītā,* Vedantic philosophy, and other literature and schools of thought within Hindu traditions teach that there is an underlying unity amongst all. Emphasizing this point the *Gītā* records: "He who truly knows My manifested lordship and power is united with Me by unwavering devotion, of this there is no doubt. *I am the source of everything, from Me everything evolves.* Knowing this, the wise worship Me, endowed with faith" (*Bhagavad Gītā* 10.7–8, emphasis added). Ultimately everything is Brahman—the underlying reality, the spiritual essence, of all. Kuntī and Pāṇḍu's concerns with legality and their desire to act in conjunction with the needs of society, reflect this belief that ultimately Brahman is all.

This belief strongly influences how they decide to utilize Kuntī's boon for the first time. Through her mantra, Kuntī has access to the entire pantheon of gods, all who would be compelled to sire a son for her should she choose to call upon them. As noted, the power within this mantra is not taken lightly; she and Pāṇḍu utilized it only after careful consideration. Theirs is not a haphazard, random decision. Pāṇḍu selects Dharma because, "he among the Gods partakes of merit. For Dharma would not join yoke with us if it were not lawful, and people will now think that this is the Law" (*MBh.* I.1 13.40). Dharma is chosen because he is a god of merit, and more importantly, if what they want to do is unlawful, Pāṇḍu is convinced that Dharma would refuse to participate. Concurrently, if Dharma obliges their request, then it is assumed that the rest of society will look upon their actions as lawful.

Through their concerns, the *Mahābhārata* highlights the important role society plays in individual decision-making. Rather than acting immediately to satisfy their own needs by ignoring questions of legality and appropriateness, Kuntī and Pāṇḍu carefully consider the social context in which they live. They could easily argue that using the boon is similar to *niyoga.* Through the mantra they are placed in an applicable, yet different situation. It is applicable because *niyoga* is already a socially accepted practice. Kuntī and Pāṇḍu are in a different situation because those upon whom she will call on are divine, not human. Their actions of not simply using the mantra and later justifying its use indicate that they appreciate this difference and are committed to acting within the laws of society. Even Pāṇḍu's desire for an assurance of heaven is not outweighed by the constraints of society. In order to be assured that their actions are within the law and are considered legitimate by society, Kuntī summons Dharma first.

As mentioned above, Dharma is the god of justice, law and order. *Dharma* is also a complex term that has no direct English equivalent. When the topic of Hindu ethics is broached, it inevitably includes a discussion on *dharma*. Though ideas of *dharma* intersect with ethics, it is not its equivalent (Narayanan 2001, 179). Definitions of this term are context-specific and include, but are not limited to, the following: "the customary observances of a caste . . . practice; religious or moral merit; virtue; righteousness; duty; justice; piety; morality; sacrifice, and more" (Narayanan 2001, 178). *Dharma* has both a universal and individual level and refers to issues relating to religion, ethics, and moral behavior of individuals and groups alike. For Kuntī and Pāṇḍu, acting according to *dharma*, both in terms of the deity as well as the range of meanings just presented, is of utmost importance. Before they even begin to act, they want assurances that what they do is done in accordance to their *dharma*—in accordance to their privileges, duties, and obligations to society.

When this concern for society, seen in Kuntī's story, is juxtaposed to the narrative of Gāndhārī and Dhṛtarāṣṭra, another key principle of Hinduism comes to light. In traditions, such as those of Hinduism, that focus on the complexities of life, it is not surprising to find flexibility and the ability to hold a great amount of ambiguity. Traditions within Hinduism recognize that norms and values differ for those from different geographical areas, castes, gender, age, etc. There is also recognition that life is ever-changing and dynamic, and that no text, law, or philosophy could ever capture life in its entirety. Hindu traditions have foundational and formative texts (*Vedas, Upanishads*, etc.); however, these texts do not share the same kind of religious authority afforded to the religious texts of other traditions (i.e., Hebrew Bible, New Testament, Koran) (Narayanan 2001, 193). This tendency of these Hindu traditions to focus on the reality of life accentuates their fluidity and mercurial nature.

While Kuntī and Pāṇḍu allow the needs of society to influence their decisions, Gāndhārī and Dhṛtarāṣṭra choose to act in their own interests. The latter couple is warned of the coming doom and destruction if Duryodhana, their firstborn, is allowed to develop and live. At Duryodhana's birth, Dhṛtarāṣṭra calls a council of his advisors; they tell him, "Clearly this son of yours will spell the death of the dynasty! In abandoning him there is appeasement, great disaster in fostering him!" They remind the king that he will still have ninety-nine sons and a daughter, and that he will secure the world and his dynasty if this baby is not allowed to develop. The counselors cite the law "For the family, abandon one son; for the village, abandon a family; for the country, abandon a village; for the soul, abandon the earth!" (*MBh.* I.107.30–35). In spite of their warnings and utilitarian justifications for abandoning the infant, the parent's love for their son trumps the future of their dynasty and even society as a whole. Since many of the narratives within the *Mahābhārata* underscore the importance of society and argue that individuals ought to act with the best interest of society in mind, one could assume that the text would condemn Gāndhārī and Dhṛtarāṣṭra for doing just the opposite. However, the text does not. The narratives record no criticism of this royal couple. People find themselves in arduous situations where difficult decisions have to be made. In its silence the *Mahābhārata* acknowledges the complexity of life and demonstrates an understanding of the realities of the struggles in life.

Though the *Mahābhārata* does not criticize Gāndhārī and Dhṛtarāṣṭra for choosing their son over the needs of society, it also makes no apologies for their actions and it does not "let them off the hook." Throughout its verses, this text clearly portrays the results of their, as well as others', decisions. As Duryodhana matures, he envies the five sons of Pāṇḍu and is never dissuaded from his desire to take over as the ruling king. His persistent hatred for his cousins and his desire for the throne eventually leads to the Great War. At the conclusion of this war, practically everyone from both clans—family, friends, leaders, teachers, etc.—dies. The entire text records not only the decisions and actions of individuals and groups, it painstakingly records the consequences of those decisions and actions. This highlights yet another primary element within Hinduism—*karma*.

While linguistically *karma* simply means "action" (Chapple 1986, 2), the theories of *karma* not only involve action—past, present, and future—they also relate to individual, family, and group actions. Though the theories of *karma* vary and can be quite complicated, for the purposes of this discussion, suffice it to say that *karma* refers to actions that are always accompanied by consequences (either in this life or perhaps a future one). All, regardless of social status, will reap the seeds planted by their actions. For many, such as Yudhiṣṭhira in the *Mahābhārata* and Mahatma Gandhi of more recent times, this principle of *karma*, along with the other principles and characteristics discussed above, leads to a commitment of *ahimsa*, of non-violent action. Actions based on *ahimsa* can encapsulate the above Hindu principles and characteristics.

Let us demonstrate how these Hindu principles of *karma, dharma,* and characteristics of focusing on society can directly contribute to contemporary discussion on reproductive technology and cloning. The "Georgetown mantra" of Tom Beauchamp and James Childress is widely used in bioethical debates. Their mantra is composed of four basic principles: autonomy, nonmaleficence, beneficence, and justice. The principle of autonomy underlies many individuals' aggressive pursuits of reproductive technologies: they desire children and they believe they ought to be able to have them. Sometimes it appears as if the original intended parents did not consider the ramifications of their desires and actions implemented to fulfill them. This is evident in the types and number of legal cases that come before various courts throughout the United States (for example, see the situations surrounding the births of baby M, Jaycee Buzzanca, Judith Hart, and others).

Consider the particular case of Ed and Nancy Hart. After four years of marriage and unsuccessful attempts to have children, Ed was diagnosed with esophageal cancer. Prior to receiving treatment for his cancer, Ed deposited sperm samples in a fertility clinic to be utilized by his wife Nancy. Following Ed's death in June 1990, Nancy became pregnant with his sperm and Judith was born a year after her father's death. The state of Louisiana refused to recognize the baby as Ed's child because Ed was not alive when the child was conceived. This began years of legal battles between Nancy and state and federal governments. When Judith was five years old her entitlement to Social Security benefits was finally recognized. Fenwick asks the probing question, Should society be willing to underwrite survivors' benefits for children who did not actually survive their father's death but rather came into existence after death? (Fenwick 1998, 195–198). A similar situation regarding twins born two years following their biological father's death is currently working its way through the American court system.

When the principle emphasized by many Hindu traditions, namely the importance of acting with the needs and goods of society in mind and *ahimsa,* are incorporated with the principle of autonomy, perhaps a different situation may arise. The traditions reflected in the narratives of the *Mahābhārata* would not dispel the importance of autonomy; however, they might temper individual autonomy by also focusing on the needs of society. Additionally, a commitment to *ahimsa* would require the individuals to

consider the violence (not just physical, but mental and psychological as well) potentially experienced by the children, and others directly and indirectly involved. One has to wonder if the intended parents of Jaycee Buzzanca, a baby conceived with donor gametes through *in vitro* fertilization and carried by a surrogate mother, considered the personal and societal impact of their decisions. Unable to have children on their own, John and Luann obtained donor gametes and signed a surrogate contract with a woman willing to carry the baby to term. A month prior to Jaycee's birth John filed for divorce and denied Luann's request for child support. At one point in the legal proceedings of Jaycee's case, she was referred to as "a reproductive technology created orphan" (Crockin 1999). (See Donna Foote's *Newsweek* article, "And Baby Makes One," for a brief write-up on this case.) Autonomy is important, especially in the United States; however, one needs never to lose sight of the fact that "no man is an island, entire of itself. Every man is a piece of the continent, a part of the main" (Donne 1993, 1123). This is true even in decisions that seem so personal such as one's own reproductive choices. Nancy Hart exercised her autonomy in choosing to have a child, now society is obligated to support the child she bore. Her choice was personal, but it has an impact on society. The same is true for many other situations regarding reproductive technology and cloning.

Conclusion

From this brief discussion of two narratives in the *Mahābhārata,* one recognizes that this formative Hindu text contains elements that can be extrapolated to relate to ideas that underlie modern reproductive technologies and cloning. The *Mahābhārata's* claim has been proven true yet again: "Whatever is here, on Law, on Profit, on Pleasure, and on Salvation, that is found elsewhere. But what is not here is nowhere else" (*MBh.* I.56.35). More than providing "points of contact" between antiquity and modernity, these narratives contain Hindu principles that can enrich contemporary bioethical discussions in North America.

Selected Bibliography

Barlingay, S. S. *A Modern Introduction to Indian Ethics: My Impressions of Indian Moral Problems and Concepts.* Delhi: Penman Publishers, 1998.

Chapple, Christopher. *Karma and Creativity.* New York: State University of New York Press, 1986.

Coward, Harold G., Julius J. Lipner, and Katherine K. Young. *Hindu Ethics: Purity, Abortion, and Euthanasia.* New York: State University of New York Press, 1989.

Crawford, Cromwell S. *Dilemmas of Life and Death: Hindu Ethics in a North American Context.* New York: State University of New York Press, 1995.

———. "Hindu Developments in Bioethics." In *Bioethics Yearbook.* Vol. 5, *Theological Developments in Bioethics: 1992–1994,* ed. Andrew Lustig. Boston: Kluwer Academic Publishers, 1997.

Declaration on Abortion: Sacred Congregation for the Doctrine of the Faith. Washington, D.C.: Office of Publishing and Promotion Services, United States Catholic Conference, 1974.

Desai, Prakash N. *Health and Medicine in the Hindu Tradition: Continuity and Cohesion.* New York: Crossroad, 1989.

Fenwick, Lynda Beck. *Private Choices, Public Consequences: Reproductive Technology and the New Ethics of Conception, Pregnancy, and Family.* New York: Dutton, 1998.

Fitzgerald, James. "India's 5th Veda: The *Mahābhārata*'s Presentation of Itself." In *Essays on the Mahābhārata,* ed. Arvind Sharma (p. 154). Netherlands: E. J. Brill, 1991.

Holdrege, Barbara A. "Hindu Ethics." In *A Bibliographic Guide to the Comparative Study of Ethics,* ed. John Carman and Mark Juergensmeyer (pp. 12–69). New York: Cambridge University Press, 1991.

Matilal, Bimal Krishna. *Moral Dilemmas in the Mahābhārata.* New Delhi: Shri Jainendra Press, 1989.

Narayanan, Vasudha. "Hindu Ethics and Dharma." In *Ethics in the World Religions,* ed. Joseph Runzo and Nancy M. Martin (pp. 177–195). Oxford: Oneworld, 2001.

Pope Paul VI. *Humanae Vitae.* San Francisco: Ignatius Press, 1978.

Sharma, Arvind. *Essays on the Mahābhārata.* Netherlands: E. J. Brill, 1991.

"When It Comes to Karma." In *Ethical Issues in Human Cloning: Cross-Disciplinary Perspectives,* ed. Michael C. Brannigan (pp. 98–99). New York: Seven Bridges Press, 2001.

Sukthankar, Vishnu S. *The Adiparvan: Being the First Book of the Mahābhārata the Great Epic of India.* Poona, India: Bhandarkar Oriental Research Institute, 1933.

Sullivan, Bruce M. "The Religious Authority of the *Mahābhārata:* Vyāsa and Brahma in the Hindu Scriptural Tradition." *Journal of the American Academy of Religion* 62:2 (Summer 1994): 377–402.

Van Buitenen, J. A. *The Mahābhārata: I. The Book of the Beginning.* Chicago: University of Chicago, 1973.

Discussion and Reflection Questions

1. Apparently there is no ethical proscription in the Hindu tradition against what would now be called sperm donation, gene selection, and cloning. How might this attitude differ from that of other religious traditions (e.g., Judaism and Christianity)?

2. To what degree should humans be allowed to take control of their own reproduction, including using novel technological procedures? How might religious principles help us to make wise choices in these matters?

3. Bhattacharyya emphasizes that a key principle of Hinduism is its flexibility with regard to geographical area, castes, gender, age, etc. To what extent do you think that ethical principles should be adapted to present circumstances, rather than being stable and unchanging over time? Are there elements of ethics that should change in light of recent technological developments, or should we rather apply traditional ethical principles to these new technologies?

Suggestions for Further Reading

Society, Ethics, and Technology, edited by Morton E. Winston and Ralph D. Edelbach (Belmont, Calif.: Wadsworth Publishing Co., 2000), is an excellent source for an overview of the various topics in ethics and technology. For further investigation into the ethical questions raised by emerging computer technologies, see *Computer Ethics,* edited by Deborah G. Johnson (Englewood Cliffs, N.J.: Prentice Hall, 1985) and *Computers and Ethics in the Cyberage,* edited by D. Micah Hester and Paul J. Ford (Upper Saddle River, N.J.: Prentice Hall, 2001). *Responsible Science or Technomadness? Cloning,* edited by Michael Ruse and

Aryne Sheppard (New York: Prometheus Books, 2001), and *The Human Cloning Debate*, edited by Glenn McGee (Berkeley: Berkeley Hills Books, 2000), provide a series of insightful articles with respect to the ethical dilemmas of cloning. Raymond Spier gives an interesting account of the consideration of cloning as a tool in "An Approach to the Ethics of Cloning Humans via an Examination of the Ethical Issues Pertaining to the Use of Any Tool," *Science and Engineering Ethics* 5 (1999): 17–32. There are also a number of texts articulating Hindu ethical perspectives on technology: *A Modern Introduction to Indian Ethics: My Impressions of Indian Moral Problems and Concepts*, by S.S. Barlingay (Delhi: Penman Publishers, 1998); Cromwell S. Crawford, *Dilemmas of Life and Death: Hindu Ethics in a North American Context* (New York: State University of New York Press, 1995); "Hindu Developments in Bioethics," *Bioethics Yearbook* vol. 5, *Theological Developments in Bioethics: 1992–1994*, edited by Andrew Lustig (Boston: Kluwer Academic Publishers, 1997); *Health and Medicine in the Hindu Tradition: Continuity and Cohesion* by Prakash N. Desai (New York: Crossroad, 1989); Barbara A. Holdrege, "Hindu Ethics" in *A Bibliographic Guide to the Comparative Study of Ethics*, edited by John Carman and Mark Juergensmeyer (New York: Cambridge University Press, 1991); Bruce M. Sullivan, "The Religious Authority of the *Mahabharata*: Vyasa and Brahma in the Hindu Scriptural Tradition," *Journal of the American Academy of Religion* 62 (1994): 377–402. To supplement an investigation of the ethical problems developed in the current advancement of medical technology see Eric L. Krakauer's "Prescriptions: Autonomy, Humanism and the Purpose of Health Technology," *Theoretical Medicine and Bioethics* (1998): 525–545; Reins Vos and Dick L. Willems' "Technology in Medicine: Ontology, Epistemology, Ethics and Social Philosophy at the Crossroads," *Theoretical Medicine and Bioethics*, 1–7 (January 2000); LeRoy Walters' "Ethical Issues in Human Gene Therapy," *The Journal of Clinical Ethics* 2 (1991) 257–274; W. French Anderson's "Human Gene Therapy: Why Draw a Line?" *The Journal of Medicine and Philosophy* (December 1989): 681–693; "The Ethics of Genetic Manipulation," by Pope John Paul II, *Origins* 13 (1983): 385, 387–389; Eric T. Juengst, "Germ-Line Therapy: Back to Basics," *The Journal of Medicine and Philosophy* 16 (1991): 587–592; Ted Peters, "'Playing God' and Germline Intervention," *The Journal of Medicine and Philosophy* 20 (1995): 365–386; Allen Verhey, "'Playing God' and Invoking a Perspective," *The Journal of Medicine and Philosophy* 20 (1995): 347–364; and *The New Genesis: Theology and the Genetic Revolution*, by Ronald Cole-Turner (Louisville: Westminster/John Knox, 1993).

InfoTrac

"technology and ethics", "reproductive technology, moral and ethical aspects", bioethics, cloning, stem cell research

Chapter 14

Ethics in the Media

Introduction: Morality and the Media

The "media" have come to represent the diverse ways of delivering information and images to us: television, radio, films, the Internet, print, etc. Much of this is driven by the goal of advertisers to make us notice their products, and then to redistribute some of our financial resources to them (i.e., to get us to buy whatever they are selling). Clearly this can take any of a number of different forms, some of them more ethically benign than others. But why should ethical matters enter at all into an area such as advertising? Does truthfulness, for example, matter in the marketing of items? What about honesty? Should advertising be seen as communicating reliable information, or instead as a form of entertainment? The essays by A. David Gordon and Carol Reuss address such issues. Whereas Gordon argues that truth is and should be secondary in advertising, Reuss believes that advertising, no less than other forms of communication, should be informed by the value of honesty. Persuading us to buy things is one way that the media affects us. But there are other, more encompassing effects of the media as well. Advertising not only influences us to buy things, it sometimes also influences the way we think about ourselves and about the world at a fundamental level. Peter D. Hershock explores this "colonization of consciousness" from a Buddhist perspective, while Steven DeCaroli examines the implications of the media for issues surrounding personal privacy.

A. David Gordon, Truth as an Unnecessary Ethical Standard in Advertising

Should advertisers adhere to ethical standards? More specifically, should advertisers be required to only make truthful claims in their advertisements? In the following essay, A. David Gordon suggests that, apart from the requirements that advertisers not deliberately deceive consumers, they have no special ethical obligation to be truthful in their advertisements. Advertising, he emphasizes, is neither news nor entertainment, and thus should not be ethically assessed according to the standards appropriate for each. Advertising, he suggests, should be seen as a kind of "commercial poetry" exempt from the requirement of truthfulness. If he is right, then it is primarily up to consumers, rather than advertisers, to distinguish between the factual and persuasive elements of advertisements. *Caveat emptor.*

Reading Questions

1. Gordon suggests that advertising should be seen as creative (and persuasive) rather than as factual (and informative). Why? What is this distinction, and how is it related to the central argument of his essay?

2. Gordon believes that there are some ethical standards that advertisers must adhere to. What are these? Why are these ethical standards necessary?

3. Why does Gordon believe truth is not an appropriate ethical norm to apply to advertising?

4. What does he mean by describing advertising as "commercial poetry"? How is this idea related to the central argument of his essay?

Truth as an Unnecessary Ethical Standard in Advertising

A. DAVID GORDON

Everyone understands that the function of advertising is to create images that sell products and services, and there is therefore no need for it to adhere to truth as an ethical standard.

ARGUING THAT ADVERTISING is creative rather than factual, and persuasive more than informative, does not automatically mean that it should have absolutely *no* concerns for ethics. Rather, this ought to lead one to consider carefully which ethical standards should apply to advertising and how any such standards should differ from the ones applied to the news, information, and entertainment media.

This is especially important for advertising students to ponder because mass communication education too often fails to differentiate among its various subfields. Thus, when the talk turns to ethics, that discussion often is centered on what the standards should be for the news media—if for no other reason

than that we are all news media consumers—with too little attention paid to the other parts of the wide-ranging mass communication field.

Dealing with this issue more generally will also lead to a careful consideration of what ethical standards should *not* apply to advertising communication. I believe that chief among such inapplicable standards is "truth"—an elusive enough concept when applied to the news media, but one that is both irrelevant and nearly impossible to define when applied to advertising.

Supreme Court justices, among others, have written that although the truth of factual statements may be ascertained, one cannot prove the "truth" of an opinion. The same might be said for persuasive communication such as advertising, where the validity of many claims is subject to opinion rather than to factual proof. The Federal Trade Commission (FTC) has had a great deal to say about outright deception in ads. That is a legal issue as well as an ethical one, and we'll proceed here on the assumption that advertisements must adhere to the requirement not to make false statements in an effort to deceive, for legal if not for ethical reasons.

Beyond that minimum requirement, however, there is no need for ads to be "truthful" in the same sense that the news must be accurate or truthful. News reporters are supposed to provide a fair, accurate, and complete account in the stories they present. Advertising practitioners have a responsibility to do the best job they can to persuade potential customers of the value of a product (or an idea) while avoiding the kind of deception the FTC has banned. Such persuasion usually requires that the advertising communicator emphasize the strong or appealing points of the product and omit or conceal the weaknesses. A full, fair, balanced picture is *not* what is intended.

I believe that the *public* has a responsibility to be aware of this, to understand the conventions of advertising, and to use advertising as it is intended—as an attempt at persuasion that often can and does provide useful information. To help produce this increased public awareness and understanding, the advertising profession might well commit *itself* to do a better job of explaining to the public just how it works and what might fairly be expected (and *not* expected) from it. (Such consumer education is also very much needed in regard to the news media, but that's a different argument. . . .)

The early 1990s use of greater realism in television advertising spots, particularly in regard to the people who appear in those commercials, illustrates strikingly that ads and advertisers can't be held to the same standards of "truth" that exist for news people. A 1993 article in *The New York Times* noted that this "so-called real people school casting eschews the glamour and glitz of actors and models for the genuineness and imperfections of ordinary consumers" (Elliott, 1993).

This approach has its roots in the desire to persuade more effectively, rather than in concerns about ethics. It has to do with the ways in which the purveyors of the persuasive messages are perceived, not with the truth or completeness of the message itself. And this is appropriate for the advertising field. These "documercials" supposedly have "a more persuasive credibility, particularly among younger, more sales-resistant consumers. Such ads can then overcome the skepticism that so often results when professionals deliver paid pitches" (Elliott, 1993).

This phenomenon may reinforce the general notion that ethical practices and procedures can also be good business, in advertising as in other parts of the mass media world. But we must remember that the appeal of realism in TV ads has bottom-line rather than ethical roots. Its goal of presenting a bit of "purity amid a world of puffery" (Elliott, 1993) is driven by marketing forces, and would (and should) be abandoned if it proves ineffective. Here, also, it is the public's responsibility to provide the feedback that will determine whether this "realism" content should continue in advertising. Indeed, it also falls to the public to "regulate" advertising that goes beyond acceptable ethical limits simply by conveying its displeasure to the sponsor or the ad agency involved (directly, or by refusing to buy the product).

An Argument for Applying Ethical Standards

Richard Johannesen has made an interesting argument for the application of "ethical standards rooted in truthfulness and rationality" to advertising's efforts to argue "the actual nature or merit of a product." He suggests that "the evidence and reasoning supporting the claim [must be] clear, accurate, relevant, and sufficient in quantity," and that any emotional (or motivational) appeals must be directly relevant to the product being promoted (1996, pp. 129–130).

But advertising, as Johannesen notes, is inherently not necessarily an exercise in rational communication. Rather, it is persuasive communication, and I'd suggest that it should be given free rein as long as it remains within the legal boundaries regulating blatant deception. Indeed, Johannesen himself questions whether the truthfulness/rationality standards should still apply when advertising is aimed not at product quality, but simply seeks to get the attention of the reader or viewer in order to create awareness of the particular product (p. 130). This distinction between emphasis on product quality and "mere" attention-getting efforts seems to lack a clear dividing line, and strikes me as somewhat irrelevant when one considers the basic persuasive and pervasive nature of advertising.

Indeed, one observer argued more than two decades ago that advertising is a form of commercial poetry, and both advertisers and poets use "creative embellishment—a content which cannot be captured by literal description alone" (Levitt, 1970, p. 86). Accepting this approach would allow for some poetic license in the creation of advertising that, nonetheless, remained ethical.

Advertising and public relations have also been described as having "the goal of creating metaphors that resonate in the minds of the target publics: 'The Good Hands People,' 'The Friendly Skies,'" and so forth (Blewett, 1994, p. 42). Creating metaphors is clearly an approach to which standards of truth cannot and should not be applied in the usual ways.

The "commercial poetry" approach goes further, and sees advertisements as symbols of human aspirations that "are not the real things, nor are they intended to be, nor are they accepted as such by the public" (Levitt, 1970, p. 90). If, indeed, this perception about the audience is correct, there is clearly no need to hold advertising to the same standards of truth and accuracy that are required for the news media. Alternatively, if the audience *does* see ads as reality, the advertising industry—and perhaps the educational system as well—should take steps to ensure that the public comes to understand better the role, practices, and "commercial poetry" of advertising.

Sissela Bok, though holding that truth is clearly preferable to lies except under very special circumstances, nonetheless suggests that it is better to focus on being "truthful" rather than on always telling the exact truth (Bok, 1979). Applying this to advertising could mean that literal truth is not required as long as outright deception is avoided, and it would seem to sanction the "poetry" concept of advertising copy.

Some people have seen political or ideological advertising as a special case, and therefore subject to a different set of ethical (and legal) expectations. Ads extolling or attacking political candidates serve a different purpose than do product ads, and may be more important to society. Critics in recent decades have often lamented the tendency of political ads to deal with images rather than substance, and at least one TV station has tried a short-lived experiment in which it refused to run political ads of less than five minutes. Although the goal of forcing political candidates to deal with serious issues rather than stressing only quick imagery and soundbites in their ads was a laudable one, opposition from both politicians and the public doomed the experiment.

And that's not necessarily bad. Political ads should no more be subject to a standard of "truth" or "substance" than should the general rhetoric of political campaigns. It's a nice goal in the abstract, but both difficult and dangerous to try to implement.

The goal of advertising—perhaps especially political ads—is persuasion. If political ads sometimes stray from the truth, or concentrate on image rather than substance, then the best remedy is neither legal restrictions nor efforts to impose an ethical standard of truth. Rather, the remedy lies in further comment and discussion, either by opposing candidates or—as has been taking place increasingly in the 1990s—by news media materials that discuss the truthfulness, content, validity, and perceived effectiveness of political ads. Once more, it seems to be the responsibility of the public to sort out political as well as product ads and to send its own ballot-box signals about how effectively they persuade—a responsibility that may weigh more heavily as advertising, political and otherwise, spreads to the Internet.

In considering ideological ads, we can look at one of the most extreme cases imaginable in pondering whether such ads should be held to some standard of truth. Ads denying the existence of the Holocaust surfaced in many college and university newspapers in the late 1980s and into the 1990s. Arguments raged on every campus where this took place—and usually in the surrounding community as well—as to whether such ads should be accepted, or whether it was appropriate to reject them on the grounds that they were attempting to perpetrate a monstrous lie.

Some school newspapers wound up running these ads—often while attacking them editorially—and others refused them on various grounds, often including the fact that they distorted or perverted historical truths. Certainly, I have no sympathy whatever for the ideological position taken in these ads, and would much prefer that they never appeared. But I am uneasy with the position that they should be rejected because they fail to adhere to a standard of truth. If that stance is taken, we are opening ourselves up to an endless series of arguments as to just how "truthful" a political or ideological ad must be in order to be permitted to see the light of day. In these situations, as in so many others, I believe that we are better off worrying less about the truthfulness of an ad, and concentrating instead on somehow making sure that those who disagree with the contents have an ample opportunity to respond. More speech, rather than regulation of content (including the truth or falsity of the ad), seems to be a remedy far better suited to an open, democratic society—and this should be true for ideological and commercial ads as well as for other forms of communication in such a society. (For a thoughtful argument to the contrary, see the essay by Stephen Klaidman in Knowlton, 1997, pp. 167–169.)

Ads for Harmful Products

Observers over the years have articulated ethical concerns about advertising for products that might be harmful in some way to the users. Indeed, some legal restrictions on that score are already in place, such as the prohibition since 1971 of cigarette ads on television, and the 1997 and 1998 tentative settlements under which the tobacco companies agreed to major restrictions on their advertising and marketing activities. Advertising acceptability standards and practices of individual media—and retail—outlets can also sharply curtail the freedom to advertise, quite aside from any legal restrictions, and this opens up a different set of ethical issues.

The question comes down to whether it is proper, in the name of ethics and social responsibility, to restrict or prevent advertising about products that may be legally sold but that some people regard as harmful to society or to potential users. Might it be better to make additional information about these products available to the public so people can make up their own minds? The late 1980s argument over whether radio and TV stations should run condom advertising illustrates both the acceptability issue and the impact that increasing public acceptance can have on such standards.

The acceptability problem is complicated immeasurably by the "commercial speech" doctrine under which the Supreme Court historically has excluded a considerable portion of advertising from First Amendment protection. In essence, what the Court has done under this doctrine is to equate the non-protected parts of commercial communication with obscene communication, in that neither category is protected by the First Amendment. This seems to be unfair, unrealistic, and unwise because most if not all advertising conveys at least a kernel of potentially useful information (the "redeeming social value" of advertising, to carry the obscenity parallel just a small step further). Such restrictions also convey a very paternalistic view of an audience that is deemed to be incapable of making its own decisions or resisting advertising blandishments.

A much more pragmatic approach would hold that if a product is legal, it should be advertisable. That would appropriately shift the focus of any disagreements from the advertising sphere to the question of whether harmful products should be made illegal. As is, the opponents of particular products such as tobacco, alcohol, guns, and X-rated movies don't necessarily have to face up to the underlying issue of whether the use of that product should be allowed. Instead, they can shift the concern to the backs of the mass media and their advertisers, in the hope that by restricting or eliminating the ads, they can reduce product usage.

The 1990s flap over the successful use of the Joe Camel symbol by the R. J. Reynolds Tobacco Company illustrates the problem well. Attempts to ban the Joe Camel character, because of its reputed appeal to children, raised both legal and ethical issues. As *The Boston Globe* asked, "Are we to tell advertising firms that they can do their work as long as they are not too good or too successful?" The paper went on to note that this (laudable) attempt to protect children from being influenced to start smoking conceivably could be extended to some unlikely areas, such as banning the movie *Casablanca*:

> As John Banville wrote in *The New York Review of Books*, Humphrey Bogart, who died of throat cancer, was the "emblematic smoker" of his day. "No doubt many an adolescent boy bought his first pack of smokes after seeing a Bogart movie." ("Joe Camel's Rights," 1994)

As it happened, in 1997, "Joe Camel" was sent to pasture from RJR's ads as part of the tentative legal settlement between the tobacco industry and many states that had sued the industry over Medicaid costs.

On balance, it seems to me, the issues of advertising acceptability and the legality of ads for certain products pose far more serious ethical concerns for the advertising field than does the issue of adhering strictly to "truth."

Another area where advertising *should* be concerned about ethical standards has to do with its separation from the news portions of print and broadcast journalism. This is an ethical problem that applies as much to the news as to the business side of the enterprise. Although there is no need for advertising content to adhere to journalistic standards of truth, there is a clear need for news and information content to do so. The advertising side of the operation should remain completely separate from the news, and not try to water down or eliminate news content even if that material might induce advertisers to pull their ads. Aside from the highly questionable ethic of knuckling under, it often isn't good business because standing up to advertiser pressures can pay major dividends in the form of credibility and public trust and thereby produce a stronger audience base to sell to future advertisers. "Newspaper and television lore is burdened with examples of managers who caved in" to such pressures, but there are also examples where principle won out and produced long-run benefits even if there were short-term income losses (Fink, 1988, pp. 128–129).

One unusual example of caving in to advertiser pressure was a 1994 column written by the publisher of the *Mercury-News* in San Jose, California. His apology left the paper's automobile writer hanging out to dry in the face of strong complaints from area auto dealers (i.e., advertisers!) about an earlier story—fairly innocuous, by my standards—providing guidance to prospective auto buyers. After threats from the dealers to pull their ads, the publisher wrote a public apology for the original story, apparently fending off potential revenue loss but producing at least a few raised eyebrows among journalists.

A related concern is the so-called advertorial or infomercial, which should be clearly distinguished from news copy in printed publications or on the air, as Carol Reuss indicates. Unmistakable identification of the material as paid advertising is needed, in fairness to the readers, viewers, or listeners. But once that is ensured, the content can ethically be aimed at persuading the audience, without concern over news media standards of truth, objectivity, or fairness.

Ethical Frameworks Regarding Advertising

Edmund Lambeth (1992) has set forth a framework of five principles that he recommends as the basis for news media ethics. One of these—humaneness—might be argued as a principle that should also apply to advertising communication. This seems to require that ads avoid exploitation, that they not degrade individuals or groups, and, in general, "do no direct, intentional harm to others" (p. 30). But as Lambeth points out, the idea of avoiding direct harm to others is more of a universal *human* ethical principle than one that applies particularly to journalists or to advertisers. As for the balance of the humaneness principle, if advertising does not adhere to it, that's perhaps unfortunate, but (*possibly* with the single exception of ads that exploit young children) no more so—and no more preventable—than such occurrences are in the news and entertainment media.

It can be argued that it is up to parents rather than the advertising industry to control what their children watch. If, as Reuss says, children are in the "line of fire" of ads aimed at different and more mature audiences, that's unfortunate but it's hardly the fault of the advertisers. The sponsors, in fact, would unquestionably prefer that their ads reach the target audiences they're paying the media to reach, rather than being seen by children and others who are not potential customers for the advertised products or services.

In addition to humaneness, and to truth—which has been discussed previously at length—Lambeth discussed freedom, justice, and stewardship. These other three principles don't seem directly applicable to advertising, although Reuss appears to favor considerable stewardship on the part of advertisers. There are also a number of other ethical standards that don't apply here. For instance, Aristotle's Golden Mean, by definition, is not going to be useful concerning persuasive communication that is trying to achieve a nonbalanced goal.

Given the role advertising plays in the media and society as a whole, a utilitarian argument for wide-open advertising might be mounted. This argument would posit that both in economic terms and in terms of helping people to fill their needs and gratify their desires, the greatest good is achieved by giving considerable latitude to advertisements, particularly if the public is knowledgeable about the conventions of advertising. But this approach must also contend with the nagging question of how one judges what advertising practices or restraints produce the greatest good (or the most pleasure) for the largest portion of society, and that question seemingly defies a conclusive rational answer and therefore weakens the utilitarian approach to this topic.

Kantian absolutes seem inappropriate formulations to apply to advertising concerns. Rawl's concern for the most vulnerable members of society appears to be a less applicable approach (again, with the possible exception of ads aimed at young children, which he would likely regard as inherently unfair) than the goal of educating the public to understand advertising and to take it for what it really is: an effort to make them aware of products and services and to persuade them to buy.

The special case of television advertising directed at young children is one where arguing the need for ethical concerns may be valid. However, the Children's Television Act of 1990 seems to have preempted the ethical perspective on this by establishing some minimum legal requirements aimed at preventing advertisers from exploiting young viewers. It therefore seems sensible to treat this area of concern similarly to the way the FTC dealt legally with deception in advertising and just accept those rules as a given rather than arguing about their ethical dimensions.

The controversy over the appropriateness of exposing school children to ads beamed into their classrooms over Channel One raises some of the same ethical (and economic) questions. This venture, launched in 1990 by Whittle Communications, may have reached as many as 40% of American high school students before running into serious financial problems originating largely in other parts of Whittle's holdings and resulting in its sale in 1994 (Stewart, 1994).

Channel One was criticized on the grounds that the students were a captive audience and that it was unfair to expose them to ads in a school setting. The counter-arguments were that the 12-minute news and informational program (including 2 minutes of advertising) on Channel One provided more exposure to news than the students would otherwise receive, and that Channel One's donation of TV sets, VCRs, and satellite dishes to the schools receiving its broadcasts enhanced the opportunities for improved educational experiences for all their students.

I'd suggest that for students living in a society where advertising is so prominent, exposure to ads in a school setting is not appreciably more of a problem than such exposure in the rest of their lives. It has also been argued that Channel One provided an excellent opportunity for teachers to discuss with their students advertising's role in the economy and to help educate the students to have an increased understanding of advertising. All in all, taking a utilitarian approach to this specific problem, one might conclude that, on balance, Channel One produced greater benefits for more people than its absence would have done.

The same can be said for the general role played by advertising even if it is not held to ethical standards of truth. One can certainly argue cogently, as Reuss does, that it is *better* for the society as a whole if advertising adheres to certain overall ethical standards concerned primarily with the welfare of society. One can even argue for the benefits of advertising codes of ethics, bland and unenforceable as they often are, or for the plausibility that Reuss supports.

Although I don't disagree with these positions in the abstract, I much prefer to let the audience determine whether ads are plausible. I find it totally unrealistic to think about requiring (or even advocating) an ethical stance that focuses on truth as long as advertising serves the purposes it does in our society—namely, as a provider of important commercial information and as the economic engine that drives (or "drive$") the media. That engine must be free to attempt to persuade and to serve the needs of the clients who are paying for that persuasion, subject to the basic legal standards acknowledged previously.

Any other approach runs the risk of making advertising less effective in the name of imposing such ethical standards as plausibility or literal truthfulness. Such results would diminish not only the effectiveness of the advertising-driven economy but also the economic viability and the independence of the American mass media. Advertising, after all, is the major alternative to having the media financed (and controlled) by the government, or to placing the entire burden of paying for the media on the shoulders of the consumers. Although advertising arguably should not be beyond the reach of some ethical principles, it certainly should not be saddled with such excess ethical baggage as concerns for truth, which are really not relevant to its function in society.

Discussion Questions

1. In what way(s) is advertising like and unlike the delivery of news? What bearing (if any) should this have on the need for advertisers to adhere to the ethical standard of truth?

2. In what way(s) is advertising like and unlike entertainment? What bearing (if any) should this have on the need for advertisers to adhere to the ethical standard of truth?

3. Do you agree with Gordon that truth is generally not an appropriate ethical norm to apply to advertising? Why or why not?

4. Gordon suggests that for persuasive communication, such as advertising, truth is largely irrelevant, in part because it is not susceptible to factual proof in such a case. Do you agree? Do advertisers make at least some claims that could be shown to be either true or false? Should the *difficulty* of establishing the truth of a claim made in advertising have any bearing on the ethics of making claims in advertising?

Carol Reuss, The Need for Honesty in Advertising

Should advertisers adhere to ethical standards? In contrast to A. David Gordon in the previous essay, Carol Reuss argues that the need for ethical standards is no less critical in advertising than in any other area of human activity, and that honesty and a lack of deception, in particular, should be serious ethical concerns for advertisers. She argues that while it is true that people have to learn how to interpret advertising, sifting fact from persuasion, nonetheless the public does not bear all of the responsibility for interpreting the accuracy of advertisements. Advertisers have an ethical responsibility to the "three Ds" of dishonesty, deception, and duplicity. If her recommendations were enacted, they might substantially change the character of much advertising.

Reading Questions

1. According to Reuss, what ethical standards should advertisers adhere to? Why?

2. What does Reuss mean by the pitfalls of the "three Ds"—dishonesty, deception, and duplicity—in the context of advertising?

3. How might Reuss' view reflect a Kantian (rather than utilitarian) approach to ethics?

4. According to Reuss, what are some of the tensions present between advertising for persuasive effect (and financial gain), and adhering to basic ethical standards? How does she propose to resolve such tensions?

The Need for Honesty in Advertising

CAROL REUSS

Advertising, no less than news or public relations, should be held to standards of honesty and other ethical principles.

WITH FEW EXCEPTIONS, mass media in capitalistic societies are entwined with advertising—paid messages that promote products, services, and causes. Among the notable exceptions are the renewed *Ms.* magazine and public broadcasting, both of which actively solicit individuals and organizations for financial support. The New York tabloid *PM* was founded as an advertising-free newspaper in 1940, but changed that policy in 1946.

There are many strong arguments for advertising in mass media. At the top of the list is the fact that advertisers pay roughly $90 billion a year for media time and space. Those dollars support most broadcasting and augment the newsstand and subscription dollars that print readers pay. Until audiences are willing to pay directly the total costs of the media they use, advertising will remain the fiscal foundation for U.S. mass media, even those that aggressively and critically cover advertisers and advertising.

Not everyone agrees that advertising is useful to society. Critics such as former adman Jerry Mander, who proposes that advertising be eliminated, often cite its negative aspects. They overlook the positive effects of advertising, especially the fact that advertising dollars support the mass media. Mander's "Four Arguments for the Elimination of Advertising" makes a direct attack:

All advertising is a gross invasion of privacy.

All advertising is political propaganda representing the rich to the detriment of everyone else.

Advertising is dependent upon economic growth, which further concentrates wealth and power while destroying the planet.

All advertising encourages the centralization of feeling, destroys diversity of experience, and corrupts human interaction. (1993, p. 125)

Other critics of advertising, before and after Mander, are a shade more accepting. Typically, they recognize that people need *some* advertising—from information about "good" books and book stores and job openings to necessities such as health and plumbing services.

Directly opposed to Mander's broad attack against advertising is the libertarian view that there should be no limits on advertising. That view pushes the concept of *caveat emptor*—let the buyer beware—to an untenable extreme. It should not be an excuse for advertiser irresponsibility, nor should it excuse advertisers, the mass media, *and* the public from responsibilities related to advertising. If advertisers and the mass media that accept advertising cannot be socially responsible, individuals, groups, and even government should be prepared to intervene.

I agree with David Gordon that people have to learn how to interpret advertising, but I do not agree that the public bears all responsibility for interpreting the appropriateness, honesty, and accuracy of advertisements. The advertising industry should be the first guardian against the pitfalls of the three Ds: dishonesty, deception, and duplicity.

When we look at the ethics of advertising from two perspectives, the advertiser's and the mass media's, by implication we include a third—audiences, both targeted audiences and all others who might be affected by advertising. The latter might include underage teens who are influenced by advertisements for alcoholic products and find ways to get them, or people of any age who are frustrated by the desire for products they cannot possibly afford. Advertisers, the media, and the public share responsibilities for all of these people.

Dishonesty, Deception, and Duplicity in Ads

Advertisements are created for one purpose: to persuade audiences to do something—to buy a product, for example, or to like or dislike a person or concept or to support a cause. The appeals vary, and so do media, ad sizes, designs, words, and illustrations, as well as the opportunities for dishonesty, deception, and duplicity. For example, I believe that advertisements targeted to students and offering "term paper services" are dishonest. The purpose of assigning term papers and similar reports is to get students involved in the research and writing process. This is subverted when students buy papers and turn them in as their own work. Students who succumb to buying the advertised products are as dishonest as the service offered—and do not receive the education for which they are paying tuition.

Gullible people can be caught with other kinds of dishonest advertisements. Ads that offer to help a person who has been a poor credit risk get a credit card, or buy "government surplus" property, or get a government job are often scams. They usually require either a deposit or credit card payment in advance. There is no guarantee that the buyer will get the help or the product offered or that the credit card information will not be misused. These ads capitalize on half-truths, at best. People who have been cheated by them are often too embarrassed to admit their gullibility and seek redress, or decide that the amount they have lost is not worth the cost of pursuing the advertisers.

Unethical deception in advertisements can take many forms, including basing sales messages on incomplete evidence or engaging in bait-and-switch tactics—whereby the product or service advertised grabs people's attention, but when they ask, they are told it isn't available and they are steered toward a more expensive version or product.

Other potentially deceptive practices are the use of "enhanced" illustrations and testimonials. Any illustration can now be altered by a computer, making this a much easier form of deception. . . . Some deceptive testimonials were produced at a time when there was little or no concern about the health hazards connected with smoking, and capitalized on testimonials by opera stars and athletes to promote the pleasure of smoking. Some "pseudotestimonial" used actors, dressed in lab coats to imply that they were medical professionals, to recommend the pain-killing or other beneficial properties of over-the-counter remedies. Pseudotestimonials are getting more sophisticated; it takes very careful analysis before one realizes that a "slice of life" commercial, or a newspaper ad may be featuring, for example, actors or models and an invented company rather than the CEO of a small firm that supposedly is benefiting from a bank's services.

More prevalent today are advertising messages presented in the guise of news or entertainment, advertisements that show violence or demeaning behavior as acceptable behavior, product promotions disguised as teaching aids, and obvious displays of brand-name products in movies and television programs. The list could go on and on.

There are so many products and services advertised in so many ways that it is impractical to make any definitive list of the advertising practices that are ethical or not ethical. The first consideration for advertisers and media should be whether the product or service under consideration is legal. Then, is the appeal legitimate, or even plausible?

Look at the clothing and cosmetics ads in contemporary fashion magazines. Jeans and other apparel are sold by the millions, but how many in the sprite-sizes depicted in so many of the ads? Or ask the time-worn question: How many women fret aloud about rings around the collar or in the toilet bowl? Granted, the models and the poses are intended to grab attention and create the mystique for the merchandise, but how honest—indeed, how plausible—are such depictions?

Pay attention to ads on TV, radio, in newspapers and magazines and evaluate them yourself. Are the sales pitches for beverages, autos, appliances—you-name-it—honest and appropriate for the wide variety of audiences who watch TV, listen to radio, read publications? Do the media in which the ads appear promote social responsibility one minute, or on one page, and then allow depiction of antisocial behavior in the remaining time or space?

Advertisers need to evaluate message content and placement and anticipate the potential effects on audiences, including audiences the advertiser doesn't really want to reach but who might well be in the line of fire—children and immature adults, for example, or people who cannot afford the products being advertised. Persistent and persuasive messages about the *need* to have brand-name clothing or to drink alcoholic beverages are two examples. At best they ignite family arguments, at worst they spark criminal activities, including vicious thefts.

Some may argue that "creative" advertising might well be misinterpreted by vulnerable people; others might say that part of the intrigue of ads is the potential for double-meanings, which appeal to audiences. I agree, to a point: the point is when impressionable audiences suspend reality. Ads can be powerful teachers. The fear is that the lessons are not always appropriate to the audiences watching or reading or listening to the ads. "Miller time" is not

an entitlement for everyone, nor are expensive cars, clothing, or jewelry. Advertisers, and the media that carry the ads, are duplicitous when they hypocritically tout concern about the poor and then pitch appealing messages that tempt poor men and women to live well beyond their means. Although they are not their brother's keepers, they should have concern for the social implications of how their messages are received.

Advertisers can become involved in many other potentially unethical situations. Some, for example, pressure the mass media for special treatment, including favorable mentions in editorial sections or on-air. Some threaten television program content by canceling or avoiding advertising before, during, or even after programs that special-interest groups criticize. It matters little whether the interest group has previewed the program in question; the threat of dissatisfaction with a pending program can be enough to prompt advertisers to cancel contracts. The staff of *Ms.* magazine has said often that advertiser pressure was a major reason the magazine went ad-free, putting the burden of paying for the magazine on subscribers and organizations that are willing to pay the magazine's costs. The question here is whether it is right that only very strong and very determined media can withstand advertiser pressures.

The Mass Media and Advertising Ethics

Dishonesty, deception, and duplicity are not limited to advertisers and advertising. Look at some situations that advertising-supported media face—situations that can spell the life or death of media and of content presented in the media.

The mass media that accept advertising are tightrope performers. They have a big stake in the advertising they accept and they cannot be casual about accepting any that might be inappropriate, offensive, or unacceptable to major groups within the audiences they serve—the same audiences that attract advertisers.

Some media try to appear to be open and editorially independent. They accept advertisements for products and services but reserve the right to criticize the use of those products and services. Few advertisers take kindly to such policies, however, unless the particular medium offers them superb demographics—audiences composed of people who respond favorably to the advertised products and services. Here, again, very strong media can be critical of advertised products and services, but few are.

Questions that need to be asked regularly of the mass media and of advertisers include the following: Can a mass medium accept all advertising? Advertising that its own staff members condemn or criticize because they believe the products or services are contrary to their audience's needs or interests? Can an advertised product be acceptable of one audience and not another? For one time slot and not another? Is such accommodation honest or fair, or deceptive to advertisers, audiences, or both?

Although public radio and public television do not accept paid advertising, they do accept underwriting and carry out extensive fundraising activities. Their acknowledgment of these donations has become more obtrusive, prompting at least one question: Are credits for sponsorship really advertisements supporting stations that profess to be ad-free?

The few publications that are reader-supported have big subscription prices and they usually make appeals to individuals and organizations for memberships or underwriting funds. These publications do not want to alienate their readers, so they establish sponsor-acceptability standards.

There are other ethical pitfalls facing the mass media. For example, is it honest to undersell the published advertising rates? To "sell off the rate card"? To lower ad rates selectively for one advertiser or another? It is ethical for advertising sales people to coerce editorial staff to trade editorial or program space and time for ad contracts? To promise "puffs" in exchange for advertising contracts? Is it ethical to inflate audience numbers or to give false audience demographics to potential advertisers? I hope you will answer "No" to all of those questions—or have convincing arguments to defend questionable and unethical business practices.

Advertising rates are based on the audiences that the media draw. The media must give honest numbers to advertisers and potential advertisers and they must also have honest tactics for generating and retaining audiences. Circulation audits and audience studies help guard against misstatements. Circulation auditing services, such as the Audit Bureau of Circulation (ABC) for print and A. C. Nielsen for television, are retained by media to verify these numbers. These services are costly but advertisers and ad agencies want independent assurances that the media they pay offer the audiences they want to reach. Experience has convinced major advertisers that unaudited, unverified media don't deserve their serious attention—and dollars.

Few media people like to admit how advertising can directly affect mass media content. But television and radio networks and stations are very conscious of the fact that advertisers don't want their products to be connected with controversy, so broadcasters may refuse to air potentially controversial programs or ask producers to modify the content to make the programs less controversial. Publications are more specialized than network television but they are not immune from advertiser pressures. Audiences can be deprived of significant ideas when the media that pretend to be open arenas are not, and when advertisers assume the prerogatives of media content decision makers.

The mass media need to monitor and keep their own business and advertising activities ethical, and to guard against offending their audiences. To this end, they have practices and procedures for evaluating advertising before they accept it for publication or broadcast. Years ago, many newspapers prohibited advertising for alcoholic beverages. Some also prohibited advertisements for patent medicines, abortion clinics, and tobacco products. Some newspapers and magazines currently prohibit ads for guns, X-rated films, "gentlemen's clubs," products made from or tested by animals, personal care products, and controversial political and social organizations such as the Ku Klux Klan and neo-Nazi groups. Some media reject advertisements for foods and beauty products with ingredients they believe are unhealthy, or abortion clinics or pro-life counselors, or even term paper "consultants." To date, none of these prohibitions—except those against some controversial groups or ideas—has sparked serious complaints that an advertiser's freedom of the press has been infringed, or at least not complaints that the public was willing to support. Some other media companies accept any and all advertising because they just want the revenues or because they believe in the letter and spirit of the First Amendment. A few even editorialize against advertisements they carry, assured that their viewpoints are equally protected by the First Amendment but not, of course, from ad cancellations.

Television broadcasters, on the other hand, have been required by the government to reject cigarette advertising and to limit advertising, particularly during Saturday morning children's programs. Network advertising for other products and services is scrutinized for acceptability before it is allowed to be broadcast. Television and radio stations have their own standards for acceptability, usually based on whether the advertisement will violate viewers' or listeners' tastes—and those tastes vary by region, channel, and time of day. Anyone in doubt should analyze the ads on early-morning, daytime, early-evening, prime-time, and late-night television.

Standards of advertising acceptability have become more complicated than lists of products to be avoided. The men and women in charge of advertising acceptability must judge advertising messages as well as products, and they often have to negotiate on deadline. They fear last-minute contracts and late arrival (or withdrawal) of ad copy as much as they fear ads that mislead or misinform. They work to protect their reputations of the publications, networks, and stations they work for and to minimize controversy that might affect circulations or ratings. It would be nice to be able to say that standards of advertising acceptability are based on more virtuous foundations, but most are not. Libertarians equate acceptability standards with censorship. But considering the impact of advertising messages on the specific audiences of specific media, carefully developed acceptability standards are a mark of social responsibility and a way for media to describe clearly, to advertisers and audiences alike, what they stand for.

An advertising technique that concerns the media is the "advertorial," paid advertising that is prepared to look like editorial copy, entertainment, or feature programming. Although advertisers usually make sure that advertorials are labeled as such, many of them copy the newspaper or magazine's type and editorial format so thoroughly that readers find it hard to distinguish the advertising copy from the publications' editorial offerings. Magazine publishers have become especially concerned about advertorials that visually mimic their magazines' editorial pages, thus confusing readers; the Magazine Publishers Association (MPA) has issued guidelines for advertorials. The MPA is a voluntary organization, however; not all magazines belong to it and observance of the MPA guidelines thus is limited.

Veteran journalist Gilbert Cranberg has expressed fear that if the difference between advertising and editorial blurs further, especially if the advertising sections are prepared by a newspaper's editorial staff members, the traditional protections of the First Amendment may become eroded (Stein, 1993). His concern is probably welcome by newspaper staff members who dislike being asked to write promotional copy for advertising sections. One solution to both problems is to assign special advertising supplements or sections to a department and staff clearly separated from the paper's editorial department.

A natural question arises from this discussion: how obvious must the separation of editorial and advertising be? Both large and small mass media, because they are market-driven, often create departments and features that parallel advertising interests, such as travel or food sections. A magazine's editorial staff may regularly brief the advertising sales staff about pending editorial contents so that the latter can solicit advertising that matches editorial subjects. Many readers appreciate finding advertisements that complement the information contained in the articles they read. Others, however, may distrust the editorial content *because* of its association with the advertisement. Ethically, are editorial briefings good business practice because they eventually serve readers, or unethical conflicts of interest?

The television version of advertorials has begun to proliferate on cable channels and a few over-the-air stations. There is no reason to believe that other TV channels will be immune to them. The most deceptive among them, prepared by advertisers, appear to be interviews, demonstrations, or discussions. The production quality competes with network- and station-produced programs. However, they are prepared for one purpose—to promote or sell specific products and services, especially health and beauty products, home improvement products and tools, and food-processing equipment—and they are one-sided. Some of the programs are offered in videocassettes, too, in an attempt to increase direct sales.

Although the products and the program contents may not raise serious ethical questions, there is one problem: viewers might not realize that the programs they are watching have as their sole purpose the sale of a product or service. Video News Releases (VNRs) are common, and present many of the same problems.

The potential for deception increases with every new publication or channel. Cable television operators have added many channels in recent years, and will no doubt add more as will satellite delivery services. Viewers increasingly need to be informed when they are watching programs that are totally advertising, produced only to sell a specific manufacturer's product or a specific organization's services.

Advertising is important to the social, cultural, and economic life of the nation, to individuals as well as to groups, and to the mass media. If advertising and advertisers do not uphold high ethical standards, they and the nation suffer.

Discussion and Reflection Questions

1. Would requiring that advertising only include truthful claims be a form of *censorship*? Why or why not? If it would be a case of censorship, would this necessarily be a bad thing?

2. Reuss raises ethical questions about many of the practices associated with advertising. Which of these questions or concerns strike you as the most important ones requiring public discussion (and possibly legislative action)? Why?

3. Reuss claims that "If advertising and advertisers do not uphold high ethical standards, they and the nation suffer." Is this true? How should the desires of advertisers to sell their products and services be balanced against the common good?

4. If Reuss' recommendations were enacted, how might they substantially change the character of much advertising?

Peter D. Hershock, Media, Attention, and the Colonization of Consciousness: A Buddhist Perspective

The media plays an enormously influential role in our lives, whether we are devoted TV watchers or not. Not only does it deliver "content" to us (in the form of information of various sorts), but it also shapes the very way that we think about ourselves, others, and the world. In this sense it goes beyond merely delivering information: It also transforms us in various ways, not all of which are necessarily for the better. In this essay, Peter D. Hershock explores these issues in depth, using a Buddhist perspective to throw light on the actual (and possible) role of the media in our lives as individuals and as members of society. He proposes that much media ethics has focused too much on the content of the media, and has missed important truths about the ways in which the media itself shapes our thoughts and emotions. The media, on his view, make much deeper inroads into our consciousness than is often recognized, and he suggests that a Buddhist perspective on the media allows us to better understand the dangers this poses.

Reading Questions

1. Why does Hershock make a distinction between the *content* of media presentations and the media itself? How is this distinction important in his discussion?

2. What would it mean for the media to be "value-neutral"? Does Hershock believe that the media are value-neutral in this sense? Why does this matter?

3. According to Hershock, how might a Buddhist perspective help to illuminate the central issues of media ethics? How might the Buddhist prescription of "right speech" be applied to critiquing the media?

4. Why does Hershock distinguish between "tools" and "technologies"? Why does he think that the media are better viewed as the latter?

Media, Attention, and the Colonization of Consciousness: A Buddhist Perspective

PETER D. HERSHOCK

IGNORING MARSHALL MCLUHAN'S (1964) declaration that the "medium is the message," most attempts to ethically evaluate the media have taken for granted that content is critical and open to criticism, while the media conveying this content are not. In addition, private individuals are assumed to have a right to inform and entertain themselves however they want, so long as doing so neither directly infringes on others' rights nor seriously compromises social cohesion. More simply: the media are value-neutral, and evaluating the moral valence of their program content must finally be the responsibility of individuals, not the state or other comparable institutions.

The basic argument is a familiar one. The media are tools that can be put to a number of different uses. Whether these uses are benign or not is a function of *who* is using the media and *why*. Like the popular claim that, "guns don't kill, people do," there is an immediate plausibility to this argument. In the hands of a drug addict desperate for a fix, a gun can be used to commit armed robbery or murder. In the hands of a police officer, the "same" gun can be used to fight crime. The media have been used to incite ethnic hatred—as in Hitler's Germany—but they can also be used to educate for cross-cultural understanding.

Unfortunately, there are good reasons to question the premise that the media are tools that can be fully and adequately evaluated on the basis of individual patterns of use. Doing so from a Buddhist perspective and coming to grips with its implications for the scope of media ethics will be our primary occupation in this paper. Its conclusion will be a controversial one: the media have a significant (and finally troubling) moral valence, regardless of their program content. Far from being value-neutral, the media have come to play a pivotal role in an ongoing "colonization of consciousness" through which the attentive resources needed to meaningfully resolve our own troubles are being systematically depleted. Contrary to the intuitions of "common sense," the fundamental task of media ethics is not to critique what is currently "on the air," but to evaluate and provide alternatives to the history of progress through which the media have come about and which the media have, in turn, both sustained and deepened.

The Fence-Walk of Western Media Ethics

Over the past fifty years in media ethics, perhaps no issue has been so widely debated as the moral consequences of program content for (especially young) audiences. The first Congressional hearings about the psychological and social effects of televised violence were held in 1954. In the half-century since, the debate has been broadened to include the effects of gangsta rap recordings on urban youth, of Saturday morning cartoons on elementary aged children, and videogame playing on the first generations of the information age.

In spite of considerable evidence demonstrating powerful "links" between media content and long-term patterns in audience behavior, the debate continues. There are two major reasons for this. First, the debate addresses a deep tension—particularly in American society—between liberal ideals of individual freedom and communitarian ideals of social coherence, or between "what is good for *me*" and "what is good for *us*." Often, this tension is expressed in terms of questioning whether freedom of speech is absolute and whether there are (or should be) limits to the right of privacy. Second, the debate begs much broader questions about the relevance of our critical methods. In particular, it invites questioning whether complex social, economic, and cultural phenomena like the media can be adequately understood and addressed within any framework of linear, one-directional sequences of causes and effects.

To date, there has been no clear resolution of these tensions. And so, while legal steps have been taken to protect the privacy of individuals interested in reading or viewing "pornography" (at least when it does not involve the depiction of children in sexual

Peter D. Hershock, "Media, Attention, and the Colonization of Consciousness: A Buddhist Perspective."
Reprinted by permission of the author.

situations), standardized rating systems have been instituted to limit the freedom of media producers to market graphically violent or sexual program content. While legislation prohibiting "false advertising" has been passed to protect consumers from potential harm, the remarkably effective "Camel Joe" ad campaign was deemed legal by the Federal Trade Commission in spite of strong correlations between the cartoon campaign and rising child and adolescent tobacco use, and well-established links between tobacco use and a wide array of health risks. Media ethics continues to be a protracted "fence walk."

Although our ultimate aim is to free media ethics from its typical focus on program content, it is helpful first to examine why the debate about the effects of program content has resisted closure. Because they take patterns of interdependence (and not individually existing people and things) as most basic, Buddhist thought and practice are particularly well poised to contribute to such an examination. Indeed, they promise resources for bringing down the critical "fence" altogether.

A Buddhist Response

The most succinct statement of the early Buddhist thought and practice was given in the teaching of the Four Noble Truths: all this is troubled or suffering (*dukkha*); there is a pattern in the conditioned arising of trouble/suffering; there is a pattern in the dissolution of trouble/suffering; and there is a path by means of which such a resolution is possible. According to the fourth truth—the *practice* of the Noble Eight-fold Path—we can dissolve the pattern of conditions that brings about suffering by developing right view, right intention, right speech, right action, right livelihood, right effort, right mindfulness, and right concentration. In sum, the root of Buddhism lies in developing skillful insight into the interdependent origination of all things and, through this, redirecting the movement of our situation from *samsara* toward *nirvana*—that is, from cycles of chronic trouble and suffering toward release from those cycles.

Right speech would seem to provide a natural point of departure for developing a Buddhist critique of content-focused media ethics. Minimally, practicing right speech means communicating in such a way that new troubles and stresses do not arise and already existing ones are eased. The basis of this type of communication is compassion—literally, a relationship of shared feeling or emotion. Right speech

thus promotes *healing relationships* through the cultivation of felt interdependence.

Contrary to right speech are communicative practices that are harsh, false, untimely, connected with harm, focused on gossip, idle or purposeless, and characterized by inner hate or contempt. Such practices lead to weariness and disappointment (MN 21:11ff; 117:17). They make us aware, even painfully so, of troubling and unfulfilling relationships, but do nothing to revise them. On the contrary, "wrong" speech intensifies our inability to undertake the liberating revision of our relationships.

In light of this understanding of right speech, consider the following. In a remote Canadian town that was wired for television only in 1973, researchers observed that in just two years, first- and second-grade classes showed a 160% increase in hitting, biting, and shoving (Cannon, 1993). Global population studies over the past 50 years show that murder rates consistently double in the first 10 to 15 years after television is introduced to a society (Centerwall, 1989). Finally, longitudinal studies tracking the television viewing and behavior of individual males from age 8 to 30 indicate that levels of exposure to televised violence are the best predictors of adolescent delinquency and adult criminality—better than socio-economic setting, educational level attained, or ethnicity (June 12, 1995, Senate Committee on Commerce, Science and Transportation testimony by Dr. Leonard Eron).

From a Buddhist perspective, such studies make it clear that television viewing is part of a pattern of conditions that seriously compromises our capacity for resolving troubles or difficulties in a liberating fashion. While there are no grounds for claiming that television viewing makes it impossible to fully practice the Eight-fold path, it apparently fosters dispositions to "solve" daily problems in ways that compound those very problems and increase the sum total of suffering.

Of course, it can be objected that in the absence of a direct, causal link between program content and subsequent, long-term audience behavior, there is no way of discerning if televised violence gives rise to or simply reflects increasing violence in society. Do the patterns of delinquency and crime found among young males who consumed a steady diet of violent media programming point toward the influence of the media on their behavior, or do they simply point toward the "tastes" of people who are (perhaps genetically) disposed toward violence and crime?

Because they are committed to the metaphysical premises that being is more basic than value and that individually existing things are more basic than relationships, Western approaches to ethics can offer little more than guidance in continuing the critical "fence walk" between mere correlations and clear causal determinations. In fact, our indecisiveness about whether the media really cause behavioral changes or simply reflect them is rooted in the metaphysical blind-spot that results from insistently excluding the middle ground between what "is" and what "is-not." If we accept the Buddha's claim that "is" and "is-not" are the twin barbs on which all humankind is impaled, the belief that we can and should distinguish between these different (at least, possible) manifestations of the media is precisely what keeps us from being able to see how the media institutionalize suffering and what we might do to resist. In effect, we get stuck on a variant of the question, "which came first, the chicken or the egg?"

The first limb of the Eight-fold path—right view— involves cultivating opposite dispositions and cutting through such dilemmas. Summarized in the teaching of the "three marks," the practice of right view leads to seeing our situation as interdependently arisen, as irreducibly dynamic, and as to some degree troubled and yet always open to revision. Applied to the media, right view carries us toward seeing that while the media arise through and are sustained by both local and global social, political, and economic conditions, they also influence these very conditions. Although there are "causal" relations between the media and those conditions, and between the media and long-term human behavior, these relations are not—and could not be—one-way or linear.

The interdependence—or in Buddhist terms, the emptiness—of all things means that nothing has ultimate primacy or the status of an original cause. Rather, each thing contributes to the meaning of all other things. Having no fixed and essential nature is precisely what makes it possible for each thing to be radically open and responsive to all other things. Finally, "chickens" and "eggs" or "media-as-cause" and "media-as-mirror" can be seen as independently existing things only because of temporal, spatial, and conceptual horizons that we conventionally impose on the emptiness or interdependence of all things. That is, they do not announce the essence of these "things," but our own preferred patterns of ignorance.

For present purposes, we do well to focus on the interdependence among the media, the global economy of "commodity fetishism," and the advertising industry. Although advertising is also a forum for cultural production, its primary function is to stimulate consumer appetites. Advertising fosters a sense of lack or want for which it promises remedy: goods that have been produced by someone else (typically an anonymous "other"), somewhere else (usually very far away), and services rendered by trained professionals. Is there anything wrong with this?

When asked about the root conditions of suffering, the Buddha often singled out two for extended discussion: craving or heedless wanting, and ignoring the interdependence of all things, especially through the conceit of independent existence. Advertising effectively disposes us toward both. It fosters seeing ourselves as "freely choosing individuals" on whom the world economy ultimately pivots. Through fashion and the catechism of "the cutting edge," it guides us toward experiencing every aspect of our lives as open to substitution. No matter what we have, there is always more and better. And the means by which we acquire the goods and services through which we "better" ourselves? It is the almost weightless act of purchasing. We do not need to knowledgeably condition soil, deftly bury seeds, and carefully water and weed the garden beds for months to eat organic produce. We can ignore the interdependence among climate, landforms, plants and animals that are crucial in small-scale agriculture because a nearly instantaneous swipe of a debit card can "produce" a frozen gourmet meal for us to enjoy. As a crucial part of the global economy of commodity lust, advertising fosters a type of awareness through which our relationship with things is reduced to the act of taking possession. Critically assessed on Buddhist grounds, advertising and the media establish a feedback loop for institutionalizing suffering.

Media and the Restructuring of Awareness

Note that this assessment does not depend on advertising content. Lying at the root of advertising's moral status is not *what* we are instigated to want, but rather *how* it disposes us toward *wanting* and then *getting what we want*. Later, we will examine this cycle more closely through the Buddhist concept of karma. For now, it is enough to see that the Buddhist critique is not directed at *what is advertised*—whether private schools or pornographic videos—but at *how advertising effectively restructures awareness*.

Without this restructuring of awareness throughout a society, there would be no market for the great variety of experiential commodities conveyed by mass media. Without mass media, there would be no forum for advertising large populations into commodity fetishism. Mass media thus play a crucial role in consolidating a commodity-driven market economy that systematically undermines relational depth, breaking down the immediate and mutually helpful relationships through which members of a community contribute directly to one another's welfare and replacing them with a unilateral dependency on externally and generically supplied goods and services. Mass mediation trains populations to (passively) consume "meaningful" experiences rather than to directly engage in the (actively) shared production of meaning.

It must be stressed here that Buddhism understands awareness as a relationship, and not as something possessed by an individual. *As a relationship,* awareness *precedes* the separate existence of "aware organisms" and their "environments." Or put another way, "organisms" and "environments" are abstractions. In actuality, there is no absolute dividing line between them. Thus, the transformation of awareness is not merely a subjective or internal change. It is an alteration of the quality of our interrelatedness or situation as a whole. If the moral valence of the media rests on how it restructures awareness—not on program content—then it is inseparable from the morality of the global, historical processes of which they are integral parts.

At this point, two objections might be raised. First, given this critique from the effects of advertising on awareness, shouldn't media that don't depend on commercial advertising be free of any of its specific moral taint? Public radio and television in the U.S. and many of the media in Europe could then arguably be seen as effectively value-neutral. Indeed, they might provide a model for generally restoring the ethical integrity of the media. Secondly, how do we know that media-supported advertising creates a sense of want or lack rather than simply giving distinctive shape to an already existing condition? This is the "causing versus reflecting" rejoinder once again, but taken one step further. It is the nature of human beings to want, to desire something better. But most have no clear idea of *what* this means. Don't the media perform the positive function of giving attainable form and content to this innate sense of incompleteness?

As a way of answering these objections, placing the media in historical context, and decisively cutting through the ethical impasse created by the false distinction between what is a "cause" of social and psychological change and what is merely a "reflection" of it, I want to return to the question raised at the beginning of our conversation: should the media be seen and evaluated as tools?

The Media as Tools, the Media as Technologies

Tools are used and properly evaluated on the basis of their task-specific utility. Hammers are used to drive and pull nails. Computers are used to electronically process and transmit information. Tools quantitatively extend human abilities, and have greater utility the more precisely and powerfully they promote our interests. If tools don't work, we can put them away in the closet or the garage, we can cannibalize them to create other tools, or we can alter them to better suit our needs.

According to this definition, the media are clearly *not* tools. Although we may individually choose to not watch television, video broadcast and cable programming will continue to shape our everyday lives. It will shape the slang we use, the jokes we tell, the "news" we discuss, the music we listen to, the conversations we have with friends and family members, and, finally, how we imagine ourselves changing "for the better." We cannot put the media into storage. Indeed, in a very real sense, we live *within* them.

I would argue that the media are best seen as *complex systems of technologies.* While tools are built or manufactured out of basic raw materials and tools occupy strictly limited and precisely located amounts of space, technologies emerge as patterns of relationship or historical processes that institutionalize values across a wide range of human activities. Far from being task-specific, technologies generate new kinds of tasks, embodying broad strategies for realizing a certain kind of world or lived experience.

To give two concrete examples of technology—both implicated in the media—we might mention telecommunications and transportation. As technology, telecommunication consists of the full range of human conduct involved in institutionalizing the electronic transmission of information. Prominent in this range of conduct is the use of such tools as computers, fax machines, and telephones. But also included are the institutions by means of which these tools are produced, the evolving culture of their uses, the development of new vocabularies to capture these uses, and the marketing or advertising of the telecom lifestyle. Thus, telecommunications technology organizes a spectrum of human activities ranging from the mining of raw materials through the consumption and eventual disposal of information commodities.

Strictly speaking, technologies are not *used,* but consolidate transformative patterns in *how we conceive and promote our ends.* In other words, technologies institutionalize patterns of *moral valence.* They cannot be value neutral, and can only be evaluated karmically—that is, in terms of how they affect the meaning and quality of our interdependence as such.

Failing to recognize this has serious consequences. First and foremost is a tendency to fall into the fallacy that if something is good for each and every one of us, it must be good for all of us. Although it might be good for each and every one of us to drive a car to meet all our local transportation needs, if all six billion people on Earth were to do so, our cities would be in continuous gridlock, our global atmosphere would be deadly poisonous, and it would no longer be efficient to drive cars to school or work. What is good for each of us *as individuals* is not necessarily good for all of us *as communities*. Failing to counter this fallacy in evaluating either individual technologies or our technological lineage as a whole, we cannot avoid experiencing what Edward Tenner (1997) has referred to as the "revenge effects" resulting when technologies "bite back."

Less obviously, by restricting our "evaluation" of technologies to the utility of the tools they produce effectively blinds us to the fact that successful technologies are prone to so deeply institutionalizing their core values that they cross the "threshold of utility" to begin creating problems that only they are able to solve. This can be true even when each and every tool they produce continues to have clear and distinct utility. Having done so, they cease being useful and effectively become necessary. Stated generally, all technologies have thresholds of utility beyond which they begin producing the conditions of their own necessity and render us increasingly dependent on them.

The Buddhist teaching of karma enjoins us to see our experienced situation and its meaning as consonant with our own values and intentions. When a technology so thoroughly sediments its values throughout a society that it crosses the threshold of utility, it creates karma or experienced results that reflect these values. In evaluating a technology—or a lineage of technologies—we must assess how its values affect our individual and communal karma and thus the kind of interdependence we enjoy.

Through the core value of our now dominant technological lineage—control—we make karma for *experiencing independence from and power over our circumstances*. For the technologies of mass mediation, this means the power to determine the circumstances and nature of experience as such. These technologies have been successful enough that we now "enjoy" an historically unprecedented control over the kinds of entertainment we have available, the amount and

kind of information we can access, and the degree to which we remain (or elect to not remain) in contact with co-workers, family, and friends.

But, as control-biased technologies cross the threshold of utility, control becomes practically essential. We find ourselves experiencing our situation as increasingly in need of control or change. At the same time, this means we find ourselves living in increasingly controlled environments and, thus, increasingly *subject to control*. Technologies biased toward control allow us to experience what we want and to avoid what we do not want. But karmically, they establish and maintain a cycle of experiencing a lack or want, and then getting what we lacked or wanted. It is the entire cycle that is deepened with commitment to the value of control. And so, the better we get at getting what we want, the better we get at wanting; but the better we get at wanting, the better we get at getting what we want, although we won't want what we get.

Exporting Attention and the Colonization of Consciousness

As complexes of control-biased technologies, mass media deplete the attentive resources needed to appreciate the richness of our immediate situation. Indeed, the media restructure awareness in such a way that we experience a chronic "crisis of expectations"—an infinite spiral of rising demands and experiential poverty. Contrary to our common-sense intuitions, by intentionally engaging in satisfying our wants, we make karma for being increasingly *poorly situated*. Suffering an epidemic of boredom, restlessness, and dissatisfaction, we treat ourselves to and with yet more mass mediated consumption. Ironically, this leaves us only deeper in want. Our "cure" has started making us sick.

Calculated by sheer quantities of time involved, the greatest consumption of commodities in the new economy takes place through the media. Just to cite a few statistics, the average American watches just over 30 hours of television per week and, in the course of a year, is exposed to approximately 22,000 commercials. Listening to radio occupies approximately 20 hours per week. Internet use, averaged for all Americans, stands at roughly 4 hours per week since only about 60% of Americans currently go online. Given that 90% of Americans are expected to be online by 2003, a figure more reflective of the near future average would be that of seasoned users (3 or more years online), who typically spend 12–15 hours per week on the Web. Altogether, Americans will soon spend an *average* of 60% of their waking hours in direct media use. This does not include any media use required in the workplace or at school. Nor does it include the time spent reading magazines or books dedicated to media stars, or the hours we devote to conversations about favorite actors, movies, or sports teams and personalities. By tragic contrast, average American fathers spend less than three hours a week, one-on-one with their children. The time given to direct community service is much lower still.

The deep penetration of the media into our day-to-day lives marks a catastrophic export of attention from our families and local communities. This is true regardless of program content. Each hour spent consuming mass media commodities is an hour *not* spent attending our own immediate situation or actively and jointly improvising changes in its meaning. Like gardens, families and communities left untended will eventually go to ruin.

But distraction away from our immediate situation is not the sole consequence of intensive mass mediation. It has been argued that the information revolution has brought us great experiential variety, exposing us to ideas and cultural forms that would have been unknown to us without the media. But what conditions need to prevail for us to be open to this great volume of new experiences? Jerry Mander (1977) has argued that a signal characteristic of television viewing is its association with passive awareness. A common term for heavy television watching—"vegging out"—captures the essence of Mander's critique: as an experiential medium, television commands us to drop our critical alertness and simply accept what is given, as it is given. It is no accident that many people use television to fall asleep.

Although television supplies new experiences, it does so in such a way that we are discouraged from actively assessing their meaning for us. Television—and indeed each other form of mass media—is essentially a supply channel. It does not permit us to directly contribute to the content of our experience. Our choice is utterly digital: to watch or not to watch, to *pay attention* or not. The initial cost of this is severe enough: an atrophy of our capacity to actively and critically engage our perceptual field. But the longer-term cost is perhaps even more troubling: being trained to experience even the most intensely dramatic events as requiring *nothing more* than our attention. That is, we are being trained to *remain unmoved*, to feel no compulsion to take contributory action.

Thus, although we "get to know" the people and places to which the media provide access, we do not become truly intimate with them. Our relationship is, finally, voyeuristic. We may know as much or more about the lives of soap characters or sports figures as we do about many of our family members, friends, and neighbors—having followed their careers and read entire books about them. But we cannot help them in moments of need or, for that matter, harm them—not unless we cross into the transgressive terrain of groupie behavior or stalking. Our love affair with the media is, at bottom, a training program for narcissism and nihilism.

Spending over half of our waking hours in mass mediated modes of awareness is a training regimen that now rivals any military boot camp in terms of imposed discipline. Viewing television programs and films from the 60s and 70s, we are inclined to lose interest because of their slow pace, dramatic timidity, and lack of "realism." We have become acclimated to video production technology that permits such rapid cutting between scenes that our attention seldom rests on any image for more than a few seconds. In order to follow the "thread" of today's non-linear programming, it is imperative that we *not* stop to think about anything seen or heard. On the contrary, the sheer volume of information to which we typically expose ourselves cannot be taken in unless we unreflectively submit to its rush.

Contemporary video media in particular exercise a kind of temporal dictatorship or tyranny that prohibits ongoing critical reflection. Quite literally, the media determine when we pay attention and for precisely how long. Ideally, we are allowed no time for active acts of either criticism or imagination. Like new recruits into the military, we accept being commanded in this way because we would otherwise be punished—banished from what is "really current" and no longer "free" to "benefit" from the new experiences the media deliver.

In the era of material colonization, the efficient extraction of natural resources entailed engineering a breakdown of both the local economy and indigenous value systems. Otherwise, these resources could not have been "freed" for export and the colonized population could never have been rendered dependent on the colonial power for many of its subsistence needs. Likewise, the colonization of consciousness establishes a feedback loop that brings about a fragmentation of families and local communities without which attention could not be readily extracted and directed in ways beneficial to those controlling the circulation of goods in the global economy.

Rapid technology-driven globalization has not led to a homogenizing totalism as some early critics supposed. Rather, it has led to fragmentations of felt community and long-standing patterns of meaningful interdependence. Positively, this has freed many millions of people from traditional forms of order. For example, the global educational and employment opportunities for women have undergone tremendous growth. And for nearly all people, a technological globalization has made room for greatly increased experiential variety. But at the same time, the fragmentation of traditional patterns of meaning-making has not been matched by local and global means for consolidating the kinds of attentive resources and improvisational skills that would be needed for people to engage in revising the meaning of their lives and situations. On the contrary, their growing dependence on control-biased technologies and mass media practically insure that these resources will be further depleted and that the needed skills will remain undeveloped.

Increasing experiential variety has come at the cost of lost diversity. Like the species in a zoo or the goods in a shopping mall, we co-exist with one another, but are no longer fully interdependent. We have forfeited the dramatic commons on which we are able to immediately contribute to one another's welfare—the signal characteristic of any diverse community or environment. And, for the most part, we have done so quite willingly, insisting that it is an exercise of our freedom.

The media have played a crucial role in colonization of consciousness and this historical process of eliminating differences of the sort that allow us to truly *make a difference*. James Beniger (1986) has written an insightful technological history of the "control revolution" that underlies the birth of mass media, the information age, and the overall form of postmodern forms of globalization. This history begins taking clear shape from the 16th through 19th centuries—an era of material colonization when European powers developed technologies for commodifying natural resources and exerting global power over the distribution of manufactured goods. A transition occurred over the first half of the 20th century into the era of development economics in which labor was commodified and power exerted over patterns of consumption. Over the late 1970s and early 1980s, this gave way to a pattern of postindustrial economics in which information became the most basic commodity in the world market and in which power came to be exerted over knowledge flows and the production of conceptual capital. Finally, in the last decades of the 20th century, we have begun witnessing the colonization of consciousness itself. Through it, attention has become the prime export commodity and (largely corporate) power is being rapidly consolidated over the production of meaning.

Through the commodification of experience and the compromise of relational depth that takes place with an almost unrelenting export of attention out of our immediate situations, productively diverse communities are systematically reduced to consumer markets. Although consumers are often touted as key players in establishing the tenor and direction of the market, they are in fact the last stop before the garbage dump. In the global economy, consumers perform the necessary, but simple function of producing and eliminating waste.

Conclusion

A central Buddhist ideal is to be able to accord with any situation whatsoever and to respond as needed—in particular, to be able to orient it away from continued or intensified trouble or suffering. A steady diet of mass media does not and cannot permit developing such virtuosity. It affords us access to tremendous experiential variety, but exacts a very high price for the commodities it delivers and to which we have become effectively addicted. In spite of apparently benefiting each and every one of us, the new colonialism effectively erodes our potential for directly contributing to one another's welfare. If, as Buddhism suggests, we are irreducibly relational in nature, this means it erodes our ability to contribute to our own welfare as well.

Taken to an extreme, the mass mediated colonization of consciousness will lead to the realization of technotopia—a world in which we will know no galling hardship, no agonizing disappointments, no shortages, and no sense of loss. This will mean the end of "trouble" as we have known it until now. But it will also mean the end of compelling dramatic tensions, a collapse of our life stories into what we can refer to as maximum *dramatic entropy*—the collapse of all differences that might really make a difference. In such a state, experiences in infinite variety would be ours for the choosing, but we would have no compelling reason to choose one over any other. We would have realized unlimited freedom in choice. From a Buddhist perspective, realizing such a "utopia"—technologically or otherwise—would mean unbroken forgetfulness of even the possibility of enlightenment. It would signal our failure to counteract our dramatic impoverishment and attentive atrophy through vesting energy in alternative technologies aimed at realizing appreciative and contributory virtuosity. We would realize a "utopia," but it would be the worst thing to ever happen to us.

Works Cited

Andersen, P. B., et al. (eds.). *Downward Causation: Minds, Bodies, and Matter*. Aarhus, Denmark: Aarhus University Press, 2000.

Beniger, James. *The Control Revolution: Technological and Economic Origins of the Information Society*. Cambridge, Mass.: Harvard University Press, 1986.

Cannon, Carl M. "Honey, I Warped the Kids." *Mother Jones Magazine*, July/August, 1993.

Centerwall, B. S. "Exposure to Television as a Cause of Violence." In G. Comstock (ed.), *Public Communications as Behavior*. Orlando, Fla.: Academic Press, Inc., 1989.

Hershock, Peter. *Liberating Intimacy: Enlightenment and Social Virtuosity in Ch'an Buddhism*. Albany: SUNY Press, 1996.

Illich, Ivan. *Tools for Conviviality*. London: Calder and Boyars, 1973.

Majjhima-Nikaya, The Middle Length Discourses of the Buddha, translated by Bhikkhu Nanamoli and Bhikkhu Bodhi. Somerville, Mass.: Wisdom Publications, 1995.

Mander, Jerry. *Four Arguments for the Elimination of Television*. New York: Morrow, 1977.

McLuhan, Marshall. *Understanding Media: The Extensions of Man*. New York: McGraw-Hill, 1964.

Tenner, Edward. *Why Things Bite Back: Technology and the Revenge of Unintended Consequences*. New York: Knopf, 1996.

Discussion and Reflection Questions

1. Evaluate the following claim: "Private individuals have a right to inform and entertain themselves however they want, so long as doing so neither infringes on others' rights nor seriously compromises social cohesion."

2. Hershock points out that "advertising effectively restructures awareness." Describe three examples in which this might be illustrated.

3. Hershock notes that what is good for us as *individuals* is not necessarily good for us as *communities*. What examples might illustrate this claim? Why is understanding this important for assessing the role of the media in our society?

4. What does Hershock mean by "the colonization of consciousness" by the media? Why is this a danger? What is his positive proposal for combating this? Do you find it convincing?

Steven DeCaroli, Assuming Identities: Media, Security, and Personal Privacy

For many of us, the distinction between what is "private" and what is "public" is both obvious and critically important. What is private belongs to each of us as individuals, and *only* to each of us as individuals, whereas what is "public" is and ought to be accessible to everyone. Personal privacy as such is highly valued in a free society as one of the foundations of personal liberty. Often we simply take it for granted. Steven DeCaroli questions this complacency by examining these concepts in light of modern technology. Is the distinction between private and public really this clear-cut? How does the advent of modern technology begin to blur the line between the private and the public? Why might the individual goods associated with privacy sometimes have to be compromised in order to secure the public good? In the aftermath of the terrorist attacks in the United States in September 2001, the sorts of questions DeCaroli raises are particularly urgent. In its efforts to enhance security for its citizens, how much freedom should be given to the government to monitor phone lines, to access private email messages, to require that every citizen carry and display a government-issued identification card, and to employ other forms of surveillance in order to monitor their activities? Such questions have no easy answers. But it is critical that such questions be raised, and that the answers arrived at be subjected to careful examination.

Reading Questions

1. According to DeCaroli, how have technological innovations begun to "destablize" our conception of privacy? How have methods of gathering personal information through the use of computer technology begun to blur the distinction between what is "public" and what is "private"?

2. Why does DeCaroli believe that there is a (at least potential) dilemma between the desire to live in a society in which personal privacy is guaranteed, and to live in a society safe from criminal activity? What specific example(s) does he use to illustrate this claim?

3. DeCaroli notes that "security is always a matter of access." What does he mean by this? What sorts of problems are generated by the desire to make something (e.g., personal information) both secure and accessible?

4. What does DeCaroli mean by "forged membership"? Why does he believe that "many, if not most, security threats . . . can productively be understood as a form of forged membership"?

Assuming Identities: Media, Security, and Personal Privacy

STEVEN DECAROLI

I

A central organizing principle of Western political thought since classical antiquity has been the distinction between the public and the private. As far back as the Homeric epics, the Greek language has recognized a basic distinction between those activities of an individual performed for personal reasons and those actions undertaken by an individual in the service of a public office. When, in the *Odyssey*, Menelaus asks Telemachus if his quest is done for public or private reasons (*demion e idion*) Homer is making just such a distinction.[1] Here the Greek *idios* refers specifically to that which is "one's own," to that which "pertains to one's self," while the word

for public, *demios*, denotes that "having to do with the people [as a whole]."[2]

While there is much in the Greek terminology that overlaps with our modern usage of the terms public and private, it would be a mistake to assume that the meaning attributed to the terms of this dichotomy have remained stable. As Barrington Moore has shown, the use of the term for that which is private, *idios*, did not carry for the ancient Greeks the positive overtones that it would acquire, for instance, in the political writings of the Natural Law theorists of the seventeenth century.[3] In fact, evidence of the negative

[1]Homer, *Odyssey*, 4.314.

[2]Liddell and Scott, *Greek-English Lexicon* (Oxford: Oxford University Press, 1977).

[3]Barrington Moore, Jr., *Privacy: Studies in Social and Cultural History* (London: M. E. Sharpe, 1984), 82.

connotation that *idios* had for the ancient Greeks can be observed in the etymological history of its noun form, *idiotes*, which comprises the root of the English derogative, *idiot*. For the Greeks, private life was a derogatory designation directly associated with the laborer, the layman, and with those who did not hold public office and could not, therefore, participate in the political life of the *polis*. Today, however, in the United States at least, it is public life, that is to say, political life and its institutions, that often are considered a threat to private life insofar as actions taken on behalf of public interests are very often interpreted as encroachments into private matters.

The values attributed to the public and the private are, therefore, contingent upon the specific context in which they appear. Attempts to determine *a priori* the values associated with the private or the public are bound to fail, not only because the respective virtues of private life and public life vary greatly from culture to culture and epoch to epoch, but also because the specific content associated with each of these social jurisdictions cannot be abstractly determined. The most one can say is that, at a basic level, the private and the public are reciprocally determined concepts—in other words, that which is not considered to be public is, by and large, deemed to be private and that which is not private is considered public. Consequently, the content appropriate to the public and the private varies greatly from one community to another, for almost anything one can think of can be considered, at one time or another, or in one possible community or another, a matter of privacy or publicity. Those aspects of life that the modern West deem to be most private, bathing and defecation, for instance, were regularly performed in public in ancient Rome, often in the open air and visible to all. To simply say that in adopting these practices the Romans did not recognize privacy would clearly be mistaken. The point is simply that privacy does not correspond to a fixed content, but rather is the outcome of customs specific to individual communities. While life in all political communities is characterized by members who simultaneously inhabit public and private social jurisdictions, the explicit content of these jurisdictions, and particularly that of the latter, remains impossible to specify in the abstract.

Given that the value and meaning of privacy have undergone dramatic changes throughout Western history, it is worth considering how, and to what extent, current transformations in modern society continue to affect our basic understanding of privacy, and to estimate how this understanding influences the ethical and legal claims we make regarding it. But before discussing the contemporary relevance of privacy, or more specifically, before examining how technological innovations in data accumulation and filtering, coupled with the influence of rapid and pervasive media coverage, have begun to destabilize our conception of the term, it is important to first examine the modern genealogy of the concept so as to illustrate how privacy, in conjunction with its reciprocal concept, publicity, came to play a central role in the formation of modern liberalism. It is only after one has a clear sense of how the concept of privacy has been used in recent times that one can accurately identify the ways in which it is currently being altered.

Following a discussion of how modern liberalism established formal conditions for thinking about privacy, particularly through efforts to secure the safety of persons and property, I will consider how modern methods of gathering personal information through the use of computer technology have begun to blur the line between what is public and what is private. In the process, particular attention will be paid to issues raised by, on the one hand, the widespread desire to live in a society where robust individual privacy is guaranteed, and on the other hand, the equally common aspiration to live in a society safe from criminal (i.e., intentionally harmful) activity of all types. The dilemma that lies at the heart of these two demands arises from the fact that, in order to maintain the conditions necessary to fulfill the second demand, the goals of the first demand must be compromised. Creating a secure society requires, at some level, the use of surveillance not only to observe actions, but more essentially, to identify and keep track of individuals who perform these actions. The very means by which individuals are monitored, however—be it through security cameras and tax audits, or through the apparently more benign practices of issuing driver's licenses, passports, and even birth certificates—are precisely the means whereby individual privacy is intruded upon. In determining how much information ought to be gathered about individuals within a society, one is forced to weigh the harm, or potential harm, done by gathering such data against the harm prevented by gaining information which might assist in preventing certain harmful activities from occurring.

Due, however, to the exponential advancement and development of new technological means of surveillance and information analysis, it is becoming less and less clear where private life ends and where public life begins—particularly because marketing agencies, credit companies, commodity retailers, as well as the private media have, in numerous respects, surpassed the state in monitoring and analyzing our behaviors. With the appearance of ever more efficient means of gathering and processing information not only has it become less clear exactly how much personal information is actually being accumulated about us in the course of our regular, day-to-day activities, but non-governmental organizations are increasingly able to compete with the state in gathering together publicly available information into vast repositories of raw data. By sorting through this daunting amount of information with the assistance of sophisticated software, non-governmental organizations are able to extract greater and greater levels of informational value, or "resolution," about our lives from data which only a few decades ago would have been dismissed as random and meaningless. Since virtually every aspect of economic and social life in the United States generates a record, and is therefore subject to inclusion in an informational database, it is incumbent upon us to reassess the so-called "right to privacy" in terms of a number of difficult and increasingly urgent questions: Who has the right to access personal information? To what purposes ought this information be applied? Under what conditions does private information become public? Is personal information a type of property? And if so, how does one claim legitimate ownership? And finally, what level of risk, and *inconvenience*, are we willing to assume for the sake of maintaining our personal privacy?

II

In her essay, "Humankind as a System: Private and Public Agency at the Origins of Modern Liberalism,"[4] Daniela Gobetti explains how the modern concepts of the private and the public find their roots in the work of early modern Natural Law theorists who were the first both to formulate a conception of the "citizen" as the bearer of legal power, and to use the notion of harm, or injury, as a key criterion for distinguishing between the public and the private. According to Gobetti, Natural Law theorists employed a notion of injury derived from Roman law "to convey the idea that the violation of what belongs to a person according to the law of nature constitutes harm."[5] Conse-

quently, the social jurisdiction encompassed by the private sphere, conceived according to this principle of harm, includes all activities and possessions of an adult person which do not harm or threaten the safety of other private individuals. The social jurisdiction of the public sphere, on the other hand, while it overlaps with that of the private sphere in those instances where harm has taken place, is understood as being *in the service of* privacy. In other words, the public sphere corresponds to that collectively maintained authority which has the right to legitimately intrude upon a person's private jurisdiction either for the sake of preventing harm or to punish an injury already committed. It is, of course, government, acting in its capacity as an enforcer of common interests, that assumes this public role and regularly intrudes upon personal privacy. Ideally, governments should compromise individual privacy only as a way of ensuring the safety and well-being of private individuals and to ensure that these individuals retain the ability to act out private interests without unwarranted obstruction. In fact, it is precisely this limitation, applied to all governmental intrusions into private jurisdiction, that is expressed in Justice Louis Brandeis' consequential 1928 dissenting argument in *Olmstead v. U.S.* Here Brandeis asserts that, "they [the founders of the Constitution] conferred, as against the government, the right to be let alone—the most comprehensive of rights, the right most valued by civilized man. To protect that right, every *unjustifiable intrusion* by the government upon the privacy of the individual, whatever the means employed, must be deemed a violation of the fourth amendment."[6]

Of all the early contract theorists whose ideas comprise the foundation of modern liberalism, it was John Locke who first explicitly employed the concept of injury as a means of gauging the distinction between public and private jurisdictions. In *A Letter Concerning Toleration*, Locke states the case quite clearly. "The part of the Magistrate," he writes, "is only to take care that the Commonwealth receive no prejudice, and that there be no Injury done to any man, either in Life or Estate."[7] For Locke, the legiti-

---

[4]Daniela Gobetti, "Humankind as a System: Private and Public Agency at the Origins of Modern Liberalism," in *Public and Private in Thought and Practice: Perspectives on a Grand Dichotomy*, ed. Jeff Weintraub and Krishan Kumar (Chicago: University of Chicago Press, 1997), 103–132.
[5]Gobetti, "Humankind as a System," 103.

[6]*Olmstead v. U.S.*, 277 U.S. 438, 478 (1928) (Brandeis, J. dissenting). Quoted in Alexander Rosenberg, "Privacy as a Matter of Taste and Right," in *The Right to Privacy*, ed. Ellen Frankel Paul, Fred D. Miller, Jr. and Jeffrey Paul (Cambridge: Cambridge University Press, 2000), 84. Emphasis added.
[7]John Locke, *A Letter Concerning Toleration*, ed. J. Tully (Indianapolis: Hackett Publishing, 1983), 42. Quoted in Gobetti, "Humankind as a System," 103.

mate right to own property is *the* fundamental characteristic of private life, and it was to insure that the right to own property remained unbroken that the public institution of a government was established. For according to Locke, objects are bound to one in the form of property, not through nature or through God's will, but through one's own labor which is expended in the act of making something. As he famously writes in the *Second Treatise of Government*, "Whatsoever then he removes out of the state that nature hath provided, and left it in, he hath mixed his *labour* with, and joined to it something that is his own, and thereby makes it his *property*."[8] Property, Locke contends, is the consequence of an annexation of oneself, in the form of one's labor, to an object during the process of its creation. Through this activity one removes an object from that assembly of things which, by nature, are common to all people, and places it among those things which are considered private. Consequently, any uninvited attempt on the part of another person to lay claim to that which is legitimately constituted as private property is, for Locke, tantamount to a threat on one's own body. Since it is a person's labor which legitimates ownership, and because labor is the irreducible product of a person's inalienable body, the bonds that tie property to individuals are the same as those which bind bodies to the individuals whose lives reside within them. Defensive actions against such threats are, therefore, as legitimate as an individual's right to protect his or her own body from harm.

The right to protect one's body is, therefore, a basic principle of privacy, and its most profound expression in Western political thought actually appeared a generation before Locke in the writings of Thomas Hobbes who, in his *Leviathan*, spoke of what he called the "right of nature." At the beginning of Book XIV of *Leviathan*, Hobbes defines the right of nature, or *jus naturale*, as simply, "the liberty each man hath to use his own power, as he will himself, for the preservation of his own nature, that is to say, of his own life."[9] Once again, it is a universal threat—in this case, posed by those individuals who, in exercising their own right to survival, may willingly harm those around them—which brings about the need to form a government, that is to say, the need to construct a public body whose purpose it is to secure the safety of private bodies and their property.

What is important to recognize in all of this is that the formulation of modern political theory in the West is premised on the need to institutionalize a relationship between the public and the private, and more specifically, that this relationship is fundamentally one of *security*. The hypothetical decision on the part of those individuals living in Hobbes' fictional "state of nature" to relinquish a portion of their natural rights, namely, their right to do whatever they wish to serve their own interests, is strictly motivated by the fear that they may lose their lives. What the state of nature cannot provide to the completely autonomous individual is the security necessary to act freely without undue fear of harm. The apparent paradox at the root of political authority is that one must sacrifice a degree of autonomy in order to save it. The contractual decision on the part of sovereign individuals to willfully reduce their autonomy for the sake of safety neatly illustrates the abiding connection that exists between security and privacy. Autonomy, which is generally conceded to be intimately associated with privacy,[10] must remain hindered, at least to a degree, if a viable state of security is to be established. The establishment of a secure society requires that utterly sovereign individuals submit themselves to the authority of a sovereign whose power will be exercised in public—a sovereign whose very reason for being is a constant, though often innocuous, infringement on the private lives of individuals for the sake of greater security.

To the extent that this is true, the condition for the possibility of security for Hobbes is the institution of a form of *membership* which is entered into when individuals agree to certain common interests. The customary name given to this political agreement is, of course, the "social contract." In order to be a recipient of the security promised by Hobbes' political organization, individuals must join, through a contractual obligation, a group of other individuals who will, at the very least, hold one accountable for the terms of that contract. And it is precisely the enforcement of these obligations through a publicly exercised system of accountability in the form of a sovereign power that permits a state of security to prevail. Indeed, I will go so far as to say that, though often not immediately recognizable, *all forms of security involve some form of membership*, be they voluntary or involuntary, extensive or limited. And in each case, membership is

---

[8]John Locke, *Second Treatise of Government*, ed. C. B. Macpherson (Indianapolis: Hackett Publishing, 1980), 19.
[9]Thomas Hobbes, *Leviathan*, ed. Edwin Curley (Indianapolis: Hackett Publishing, 1994), 79.

[10]See Lloyd L. Weinreb, "The Right to Privacy," in *The Right to Privacy*, ed. Ellen Frankel Paul, Fred D. Miller, Jr. and Jeffrey Paul (Cambridge: Cambridge University Press, 2000), 25.

absolutely dependent upon the practical ability to establish and maintain the *identity* of its members. Regardless of the type of group or the specific means of establishing membership, each membership group is defined by its ability to identify those which properly belong to it. If a membership group cannot identify its members, there is simply no group. It is the act of monitoring membership through the establishment of credible identities that, on the one hand, compromises the privacy of the individuals involved, and on the other hand, produces the conditions for the possibility of implementing security. One need only consider the exponential growth in cases of so-called "identity theft" to recognize not only the importance of maintaining verifiable identities within a membership group, but also that the threat posed to institutions that provide security through membership is the increasingly likelihood that such institutions may not, in fact, know who their proper members are.

III

The model I am presenting here need not be as complicated as it may seem. A few examples will help clarify the point. Consider the most common of security devices, the padlock. The fact that I, as the owner of the lock, also possess the key which opens it, attributes to me a very specific identity with respect to the security provided by the lock. The lock, in effect, "recognizes" me as being the legitimate owner of the lock because I have a key which verifies my identity. The key, in other words, acts as what is known as an "identity token." However, if someone steals my key and uses it to open the lock without my permission, they have thwarted the security provided by the lock precisely by, at least as far as the lock is concerned, feigning my identity. Or put differently, they have feigned membership in the rather small security organization which includes myself and, say, the other members of my family who also have copies of the key. Admittedly, if someone breaks out a hammer and manages to bust the lock to pieces, the security provided by the lock has been compromised by means other than feigning identity, but my concern is not to prove that brute force is not a security risk, but rather to show that identity is always a significant component of security. When one opens a lock with a pick, he or she is, above all, feigning identity.

To take another somewhat clichéd example, consider the case of a spy. A spy spends years learning how to access classified information not by directly assaulting the safe in which the material is kept, but by accumulating the criteria, i.e., the "identity to-

kens," which allow him or her to fake membership and thereby gain access. Unlike the lock and key example, the case of the spy involves a far more complex set of factors. Not only does the spy need, for instance, a password or a key to access the secured information, he or she also needs to develop a wide range of often non-technical characteristics in order to gain access, for instance, to certain meetings or certain trusted conversations. The spy must breech security not only explicitly by acquiring a password, but implicitly by slowly developing trusted friendships and professional relationships with those who either possess the information themselves or represent a means to acquiring that information. The set of techniques used to enter the trust of another person are important aspects of any security system because at its most basic level the establishment of *trust*, when done disingenuously, is a common form of feigning membership.

To take an example from the world of computer hacking, it is too often assumed that malicious entry into a computer system is purely the result of programming skills. In fact, much of the information necessary to breech a computer system is accumulated by hackers directly from those who are fully authorized to access it. By feigning the identity of, say, a fellow employee schooled in the specific acronyms and terminology of a particular type of business, it is quite possible to casually convince a legitimate user to surrender his or her password. More often than not all that is needed is a simple phone call. Here, as with the spy example, the breech of security occurred *long before* the computer account was explicitly accessed. For instance, it was the feigning of membership—in a governmental institution and a private business—that led to direct access of secured material. This method for manufacturing the trust that legitimately exists between those associated by membership to a membership group has, at least in the world of hacking, a very specific and recognized name. It is called "social engineering."

Before moving on to my final example, it is important to say a word about a term that played a crucial part in the previous two examples, namely, *access*. Put simply, *security is always a matter of access*. Despite the seeming incongruity between securing and accessing, the two terms are inseparable, and not simply because they are reciprocally defined. An example I recently used with my students in a course on the subject makes this quite apparent. While sitting around our conference table I made the claim that security is first and foremost a question of access. After receiving quizzical looks from around the table I asked the students to play along with a simple scenario. Let us say I have a safe in front of me in which to secure some items of value. I asked my students what items we should secure and within a few moments we decided that it should be our money. So I asked them to give me their money (hypothetically, of course) so that I could place it in the safe. I then told them I would lock the safe and, to be sure it was totally secure, I would throw it into the nearby Chesapeake Bay. The point of the exercise reveals itself rather quickly. While the money would certainly be secure, for hundreds of years perhaps, it does us no good if we, the rightful owners, cannot access it. It is, in other words, easy to secure something if you never need to see it again. The difficulties arise precisely over the question of how an object can be both secure and accessible at the same time. And this is where identity within a membership group becomes essential. Only by being able to accurately identify who should, and who should not, be permitted to gain access to secured items can a secure system hope to be viable.

Turning now to my final and far less obvious example, an example which sits squarely in the gray area between that which is and that which is not a compromise of security, consider the all too familiar occurrence of a telemarketer's evening phone call. The goal of the telemarketer is, of course, not to steal anything from you (as was the case with the spy and the hacker), but to sell you a product. Thus, from the outset the stakes are different. But as we saw in the two preceding examples, the breech in security happened well before the spy accesses the documents or the hacker enters the computer. The breech, as I suggested, happened at the level of building a false sense of trust within a membership group of which one was not a legitimate member. Perhaps not surprisingly, the techniques used by the telemarketer to gain access to your wallet by persuading you to willingly part with your money are very similar to those used by the spy or the hacker, with the critical difference that the telemarketer must acquire *legitimate consent* from the customer. That is to say, the telemarketer must persuade the potential customer to give away his or her money in exchange for a product or service without falsely representing that product or service. In the case of the hacker, a password was freely given away and consent was freely given to access the information secured by that password, but the intentions of the hacker were not legitimately represented and therefore the consent can also be considered illegitimate. Telemarketing, and for that matter all permission-based marketing, functions by establishing a level of trust with customers based on more or less legitimate

representations of both products and intentions. To the extent that marketing campaigns can exaggerate or obscure information regarding either their products or their intentions (particularly with respect to personal information acquired from consumers), they can legally intrude deeply into personal privacy.

It is common for the telemarketer to use the first name of the person he or she is calling, for instance, "Hi Steve, this is Tom from Acme Insurance. How are you doing tonight, etc. etc." The salesperson uses this informal mode of address as a means of quickly achieving a level of familiarity with the person who answers the phone, thereby gaining trust, and with it an increased likelihood that the person will believe the sales pitch and purchase the product. Viewed from the vantage of what has been discussed above, however, this scenario is simply another example of an attempt to feign membership, in this case membership into that membership circle (usually characterized by deep trust and, therefore, substantial security) called friendship. That marketing agencies pursue this type of feigned familiarity is beyond doubt. One need only turn to Seth Godin's recently published book on direct-marketing, unambiguously entitled, *Permission Marketing: Turning Strangers into Friends and Friends into Customers,*[11] to get a strong idea of how marketing functions as a type of "social engineering." Godin, one of the world's foremost online promoters, argues that gaining *permission to market to a customer* is the key to sales. Persuaded with some kind of bait—a free sample, a supermarket discount card, a contest, an 800 number, or even just an opinion survey—once a customer *volunteers* his or her time, sales are more likely. Be it a spy, a hacker, or a direct marketer, the process of "turning strangers into friends" is central to feigning membership so as to exploit the power of trust. While the legitimate consent given by the consumer to have the salesperson debit his credit card account keeps this practice on the legal side of the security line, the techniques utilized in the process of making the sale are quite similar to those used to breech security in less legal endeavors.

The media by and large functions in a similar manner, with the added distinction that what the media sells is not a product or a service that *follows from* the establishment of a congenial, or to use Godin's terminology, a friendly relationship or trust, but is *that very relationship itself*. The media lives and dies by its audi-

[11]Consider a book by Seth Godin, a direct-marketing expert, entitled, *Permission Marketing: Turning Strangers into Friends and Friends into Customers* (New York: Simon & Schuster, 1999).

ence, e.g., its readership, viewership, etc., and consequently the very existence of the media is dependent upon the decision on the part of private individuals to "tune-in" to the stream of information or entertainment that is being offered. Unlike the sale of stoves and tennis racquets, however, the media has a uniquely important role to play with respect to the functioning of democracy. It is widely conceded that in order for a democracy to function properly, its citizenry must be kept reasonably informed of the important issues of the day. Democratic participation—making an informed judgment not only when voting, but also in local civil actions—necessitates the existence of a fair and relatively unbiased media whose duty it is to provide people with relevant information. To the degree that the media is also in the business of selling the relationship it has with its audience, however, the risk that the media is able to shape the views of its audience, due in part to their loyalty as members of this loosely conceived membership organization of viewers, remains significantly high. And this is especially worrisome when one realizes that the product the media is selling to its audience, the programming, is the very means by which the media attempts to establish a loyal viewership, i.e., a loyal membership of consumers. It is this "relationship of trust" that serves as the foundation of the media's dependable audience, but it is also this trust that presents the media with the dangerous opportunity to manipulate the opinions and desire of its audience by distributing leading or biased programming.

To sum up, then, it is my contention that many, if not most, security threats (not to mention successful marketing campaigns) can productively be understood as a form of forged membership. If one can convincingly become a member of a group without buying into the initial "contract" that establishes that group's legitimate members, then one poses a direct threat to the principles of stability that the contract seeks to maintain. A membership organization functions, first and foremost, by keeping track of its members. It is this monitoring, something which is a critical part of all security, that inevitably makes inroads into one's privacy. At the most basic levels, this trade-off is quite acceptable. In the case of political membership, we give up the complete autonomy bequeathed to us in the "state of nature" by becoming members of the state which in turn provides us with reasonable assurances of safety. But the trade-off becomes more difficult the more aggressive the state becomes in monitoring our behaviors, so much so that the information which once served as the very condition for security becomes a security risk itself. And

this is where the utilitarian consideration of harm arises. At what point does our desire for security become overshadowed by our desire for privacy? In the case of the Fourth Amendment, for instance, the state is barred from "unreasonable searches and seizures." While it would, given a trustworthy government, undoubtedly be a more secure society if the state could enter our private households at will to check for illegal property or potentially harmful activity, most of us recoil at such an idea. The reason for this is that our desire to maintain a high level of privacy within the space of our homes greatly outweighs the benefits that would result from unhindered governmental searches. In other words, the harm caused by the invasion of privacy convincingly outweighs any benefits that might be a consequence of such an intrusion. Thus, the amount of privacy and security we wish to have presents itself in the form of a classic moral dilemma in which these significantly contrary goods must be brought into balance. However, in the case of non-governmental organizations, and businesses and the media in particular, the trade-off is less clearly one between privacy and security. Indeed, if businesses and the media are concerned about security at all it is with *their own* financial security, which makes a business's or the media's intrusion into our private lives, as opposed to that of the state, far more risky than we often presume.

IV

As we have seen, the modern form of the Western nation state is based upon a security relationship which, at least in theory, seeks to preserve individual autonomy and the privacy that characterizes it. Individual privacy, in the form of both private property and one's own body, is that which is deemed worthy of being secured, while the public sphere is represented by an authority that enables security precisely through its right to legitimately intervene into the private sphere (both physically and informationally) to prevent, manage, or punish instances of intentional harm. The price paid by the individual for residing in this state of security is the regulated intrusion into his or her private affairs, as well as the requirement that one become and remain a member of a collective (i.e., a public) organization. Likewise the form of punishment very often incurred by those who injure others and thereby infringe upon their personal privacy is precisely a loss of their own personal privacy insofar as imprisonment entails, in conjunction with confinement, a continuous state of surveillance of personal activities.

While the United States Constitution does not explicitly recognize a right to privacy, two Amendments are often cited in support of such a right.[12] The First Amendment, which guarantees the freedom of religion, speech and assembly, appears to implicitly entail a right to privacy insofar as the freedom to engage in self-expression seems to presuppose that such expression is permissible out of view of the public gaze. The Fourth Amendment, on the other hand, has been shown to recognize privacy rights based on property in as much as it guarantees the "right of the people to be secure in their persons, houses, papers, and effects against unreasonable searches and seizures." The trouble with this claim is, of course, that the force of the argument turns on what exactly one considers property. In their 1890, groundbreaking article "The Right to Privacy," Samuel D. Warren and Louis D. Brandeis set forth the first fully conceived statement by the court concerning privacy rights. In the article, they argue that fundamental rights to life, liberty, and property must include not only the physical manifestations of these rights, but also their less tangible forms. As Warren and Brandeis put it, "the right to life has come to mean the right to enjoy life— the right to be let alone; the right to liberty secures the exercise of extensive civil privileges; and the term 'property' has grown to comprise every form of possession—intangible as well as tangible."[13] The upshot of their argument is that it pushes the law beyond a collection of torts, drawn largely from common law, which address specific issues of privacy, towards a recognition that the violation of privacy is a tort itself. In other words, to take an example from an article by A. M. Capron, instead of crafting a special provision to legally institute the prohibition against, for instance, eavesdropping (literally listening to a conversation within a private house by standing as close to the house as rain falling from the eaves), which had long been recognized in common law, the Warren-Brandeis documents distill all matters of privacy violation into four basic areas.[14] In an article written

many years after the Warren-Brandeis piece had become a benchmark for the courts, William L. Posser summarized the four basic categories of privacy as follows:

1. Intrusion upon the plaintiff's seclusion or solitude, or into his or her private affairs
2. Public disclosure of embarrassing private facts about the plaintiff
3. Publicity which places the plaintiff in a false light in the public eye
4. Appropriation, for the defendant's advantage, of the plaintiff's name or likeness[15]

The fourth category is of particular importance in as much as it speaks directly to the issue of assuming an identity for the sake of gaining access to the membership group the plaintiff is associated with. However, it is the first category that implies the most broad reaching violations of privacy rights.

While one would not have to work hard to convince most people that the government has no right to track the goods we buy or to monitor what television programs we watch without just cause, it is not so clear that non-governmental organizations, particularly businesses and private media consortiums, do not have such rights. As a matter of course, supermarkets, cable television operators, credit card companies, Internet service providers, and the like, all engage in activities which pry directly into the most private aspects of our lives—from the programs we watch to the food we eat. Each of these organizations, then, regularly intrudes upon what Posser referred to as our "private affairs." The "assumption of privacy" that many of us instinctively adopt when we are within the confines of our homes may not be as valid an assumption as it once was. When one is able to watch events in real time piped through cables into our living rooms, or when we are able to sit at home and access information stored thousands of miles away via an Internet connection, is it still reasonable to assume that these are private activities? By and large, Americans feel that the entertainment we engage in within our homes and the information we access for personal reasons ought to remain within the private sphere. We feel violated, in other words, when we realize that strangers know what programs we watched last night; we are troubled to know that

[12] In addition to these two Amendments, the Ninth Amendment, which claims that "the enumeration in the Constitution of certain rights shall not deny or disparage others retained by the people," is often cited in defense of privacy claims.

[13] Samuel D. Warren and Louis D. Brandeis, "The Right to Privacy," *Harvard Law Review* 4, no. 5 (1890), 193–220. Reprinted in *Philosophical Dimensions of Privacy: An Anthology*, ed. Ferdinand David Schoeman (Cambridge: Cambridge University Press, 1984), 75.

[14] A. M. Capron, "Genetics and Insurance: Accessing and Using Private Information" in *The Right to Privacy*, ed. Ellen

Frankel Paul, Fred D. Miller, Jr. and Jeffrey Paul (Cambridge: Cambridge University Press, 2000), 239.

[15] William L. Posser, "Privacy," *California Law Review* 48, no. 3 (1960), 389. Quoted in Capron, "Genetics and Insurance," 240.

Internet sites place "cookies" on our computers so as to better monitor our online behaviors. Ask people if they would feel comfortable with anyone knowing exactly what they purchased in the last six months and many would cringe. In the same way that many people feel that the government's right to search our private property ought to be limited by law, is it not reasonable to expect private corporations and media companies to adhere to similar, though perhaps less stringent, restrictions? Especially because unlike the government, businesses have no explicit mandate (no "social contract") to keep the best interests of their customers in mind.

Businesses and media conglomerates are growing increasingly inclined to gather as much information about their customers as possible and to use that information in complex ways, not only to tailor their inventory to the desires and habits of their customers, but, through direct marketing, to actively produce desires within certain predisposed demographics. As David Potter sagaciously argued in his 1954 book, *People of Plenty*, marketing is "the only institution which we have for instilling new needs, for training people to act as consumers, for altering men's values, and thus for hastening their adjustment to potential abundance."[16] Potter's statement could hardly be more relevant than it is today, not only because our level of abundance has never been higher, but because the means at the disposal of marketing firms to track, as well as shape, the behaviors of consumers has never been more powerful. While businesses and media companies have always sought to woo their customers and audiences by gathering information about their lives and their interests, the past several decades have seen this practice raised to a new level of efficiency, efficacy, and invasiveness. With the introduction of electronic means of data collection and information management it has now become feasible to track each transaction within a business, associate those transactions with specific customers, and then compare the information with databases collected by other businesses so as to build a relatively complete picture of a relevant customer base. Likewise, the media, by tracking each cable show we watch, and by measuring how long and how often we visit Web sites, will soon be able to tailor entertainment, as well as news and informational programming, to specific individuals and households. The traditional model of media "broadcasting"

is quickly being replaced by a new model, "narrowcasting," where streams of information are directed to both specific individuals and well-isolated demographics. *Time* magazine, to take but one example, already employs such a technique, called "cluster analysis," to group individuals according to behavioral and socio-economic similarities. It then uses the information gained in this process to target its publications, or more specifically the ads within its publications, to specific "market segments." Consequently, the issue of *Time* you receive at home does not contain the same advertisements as those received by other individuals identified as being within a different market segment.[17]

While media companies claim that target marketing is being done in the interest of providing the consumer a more "customized" array of services, and while this may, to some extent, be in fact true, it is not at all clear that the consumer, if he or she knew the amount of personal information which had been gathered about them, would be willing to trade this accumulation of private information for the convenience promised. Here, then, the relationship between privacy and security shifts to that between privacy and *convenience*, and I believe it is this trade-off that harbors for us the most important questions regarding the value of privacy for the new century. The question, in other words, is no longer how much privacy are we willing to sacrifice for the sake of security, but how much private information we are willing to sacrifice for convenience. The shift is a crucial one. In the case of the privacy/security trade-off, the state's intrusion into the private lives of individual citizens was done, at least in theory, for the sake of those citizens and their safety. The state, in other words, was established to protect people from unjustified harm in their private lives. In the case of nongovernmental businesses and media companies, however, the safety of individuals is not a primary concern. When a business gathers private information on its customers it is not doing so with the intention of protecting these customers from harm, so much as it is doing so to keep ahead of its competition and to generate sales revenues. It is ultimately for its own sake, for the sake of its own financial survival, which is to say, for the sake of its own security, that a business accumulates personal customer information, even though the consumer is quite often the recipient of certain benefits. Without a fundamental

---

[16]David M. Potter, *People of Plenty: Economic Abundance and the American Character* (Chicago: University of Chicago Press, 1954), 175.

[17]Oscar H. Gandy, Jr., *Operation the Panoptic Sort: A Political Economy of Personal Information* (Boulder: Westview Press, 1993), 88.

mandate to keep the consumer's interests in mind, that is to say, without being bound, like the state, to a "contract" which explicitly empowers the individual and his or her rights with respect to privacy, the risks of seeing one's personal information used to one's own disadvantage are significantly greater.

Consequently, as the debates about privacy move into the next century, it is primarily the trade-off between privacy and convenience that must be scrutinized. The terms of the debate which occupied thinkers such as Hobbes and Locke, namely, the balances of power between the individual and the state, have certainly not lost their relevance, but it is becoming increasingly clear that business and media interests must be directly factored into the discussion. When corporations can operate seamlessly across vast transnational territories in pursuit of their own institutional interests, it is essential to reevaluate the terms of the privacy debate with respect to the often incompatible interests of individuals, states, and corporations as well as to renegotiate the issues of membership and identity embedded within them.

Discussion and Reflection Questions

1. What is "privacy"? Is there a fundamental right to privacy? How might one argue for such a right? How might one argue that there are limits to an individual's right to privacy (e.g., when it conflicts with some greater common good)?

2. How might a conflict arise between (a) the desire to live in a society where individual privacy is guaranteed, and (b) the desire to live in a society safe from criminal activity? How might these two desires be balanced against one another to form the best compromise?

3. DeCaroli describes the "assumption of privacy" that many of us instinctively adopt when we are within the confines of our homes, and notes that it may not be as valid as it once was. Why not? How does modern technology call into question the idea that what we do in the "privacy" of our own homes is not really as private as we might like to think? Do you find this a cause for concern? Why or why not?

4. DeCaroli notes that in some ways the issue has shifted from how much privacy we are willing to sacrifice for security to "how much private information are we willing to sacrifice for convenience?" In the context of the examples he discusses, how would you answer this question?

Suggestions for Further Reading

For materials that work through a range of ethical considerations in mass media, see *Mass Media and the Moral Imagination*, edited by Philip J. Rossi and Paul A. Soukup (Kansas City, Mo.: Sheed and Ward, 1994); S. Klaidman and Tom L. Beauchamp, *The Virtuous Journalist* (New York: Oxford University Press, 1987); *Democracy and the Mass Media*, edited by J. Lichtenberg (Cambridge: Cambridge University Press, 1990); John M. Phelan, *Disenchantment: Meaning and Morality in the Media* (New York: Hastings House, 1980); Ralph L. Lowenstein and John C. Merrill, *Macromedia: Mission, Message, and Morality* (New York: Longman, 1990); *Communication Ethics and Universal Values*, edited by Clifford G. Christians and Michael Traber (Thousand Oaks, Calif.: Sage, 1997); Matthew Kieran, *Media Ethics: A Philosophical Approach* (Westport, Conn.: Praeger Publishers, 1997). To assist in the exploration of ethical issues in journalism, see *The Journalist's Moral Compass: Basic Principles*, edited by Stephen R. Knowlton and Patrick R. Parsons (Westport, Conn.: Praeger Publishers, 1994); *Committed Journalism: An Ethic for the Profession* (2nd edition), edited by Edmund B. Lambeth (Bloomington: Indiana University Press, 1992); *Moral Reasoning for Journalists: Cases and Commentaries*, by Stephen R. Knowlton (Westport, Conn.: Praeger Publishers, 1997); John C. Merrill, *Journalism Ethics: Philosophical Foundations for News Media* (New York:

St. Martin's Press, 1997); *The Dialectic in Journalism: Toward a Responsible Use of Press Freedom* (2nd edition), edited by John C. Merrill (Baton Rouge: Louisiana University Press, 1993); Jeffrey Olen, *Ethics in Journalism* (Old Tappan, N.J.: Prentice Hall, 1988); Elliot D. Cohen, *Philosophical Issues in Journalism* (New York: Oxford University Press, 1992). The following articles address various issues in the field of media ethics: J. J. Hemmer, Jr., "Hate Speech: The Egalitarian/Libertarian Dilemma," *The Howard Journal of Communications* 5 (1995): 307–330; J. J. Hemmer, Jr., "Ethics and Politics of the Media: The Quest for Quality," in *Ethical Issues in Journalism and the Media*, edited by Andrew Belsey and Ruth Chadwick (London: Routledge, 1992); Seamus Miller, "Freedom of the Media: A Philosophical Analysis," in *Quest* 9 (1995): 67–84.

InfoTrac

media ethics, journalistic ethics, freedom of information, false advertising, "privacy and mass media"

Chapter 15

Ethics in Business

Introduction: Money and Morality

The goal of business is to maximize profits (or at the very least to make a profit). But a single-minded focus on maximizing profits can easily blind one to the ethical issues at stake. How might one pursue business activity in a morally responsible manner? What sorts of values should be emphasized in business transactions? Is it even possible to articulate a coherent ethics for business? Is "business ethics" an oxymoron? How might a concern with profits and a concern with doing the right thing be harmonized? Difficult questions. Fortunately, there are substantial philosophical resources for tackling such questions. In the first essay below, Dennis P. McCann and Joanna Lam Kit Chun approach such questions from the perspective of Aristotelian ethics. In particular, they ask how Aristotle and his most illustrious disciple, St. Thomas Aquinas, viewed business activity, and the conditions under which one could virtuously engage in such activity. Although neither spent a great deal of time focusing on business ethics per se, the principles they developed have ready application to this area. Arguing that the profit motive need not result in ruthless profiteering, Richard McCarty explores the role of benevolence in formulating an acceptable business ethics. Having already explored Aristotelian approaches to business ethics, in the next essay, Dennis P. McCann and Joanna Lam Kit Chun turn their attention to Confucian perspectives. Finally, Xiusheng Liu reflects on Indian ethical views of economics and business. Business ethics is something of a boom industry in moral philosophy. Suggestions for further reading at the end of this chapter take the reader as far as she might like to go in exploring the fascinating issues in business ethics.

Dennis P. McCann and Joanna Lam Kit Chun, Aristotelian Perspectives on Business Ethics

In searching for the foundations of Western business ethics, an examination of the works of Aristotle (384–322 B.C.E.) and of St. Thomas Aquinas (1225–1274 C.E.) is

essential. Although they are separated in time by more than a thousand years,

Aquinas is commonly regarded as Aristotle's most illustrious disciple in premodern Europe. Their treatises—particularly, Aristotle's *Nichomachean Ethics* and *Politics*, and Aquinas' *Summa Theologiae*—profoundly shaped the premodern Western moral philosophy, and are once again having a significant influence on Western ethics, and not just in the moral theology of Roman Catholicism, where they have always been cherished. In this essay, Dennis P. McCann and Joanna Lam Kit Chun examine key texts from the Aristotelian tradition in order to identify fundamental moral perspectives on business activities as elaborated by both Aristotle himself and by his most influential disciple, St. Thomas Aquinas.

Reading Questions

1. According to McCann and Chun, how did Aristotle and Aquinas view the morality of market transactions? Did they see them as inherently immoral?

2. In the views of Aristotle and Aquinas, is the marketplace peripheral or central to a well-functioning social system? Why?

3. How did Aristotle and Aquinas view becoming a merchant, or buying and selling for a profit, as an occupation? Is it regarded as honorable or dishonorable?

4. In the views of Aristotle and Aquinas, is the government understood as having a moral responsibility to ensure that the outcomes of market activity are socially beneficial? If so, on what moral grounds; if not, why not?

Aristotelian Perspectives on Business Ethics

DENNIS P. McCANN AND JOANNA LAM KIT CHUN

Introduction

Entering imaginatively into the world opened up by the works of Aristotle and Aquinas means rediscovering a moral universe in which personal character counts, where social benevolence and the common good still define the purpose of the State, where moral education is rooted in narrative forms, and where personal example is still the most effective pedagogical strategy for communicating moral wisdom. It is to be grasped by a world in which personal and social behavior have cosmic significance, and the path of moral development consists not in the formulation of exceptionless rules but in the achievement of harmonies and a sense of balance that often defies rationalistic analysis. Compared to the dominant paradigms of modern Western rationalism in business ethics, a critical recovery of these traditions may provide important resources for understanding the broad contextual question regarding the appropriate relationship between politics and markets, or, in ethical terms, the relationship between propriety and profit, justice and self-interest. Society's basic moral attitude toward market institutions should not be determined by the understandable resentments of those who feel threatened by its dynamic capacities for producing and distributing wealth. A familiarity with premodern Western moral philosophy can alert us to the fact that market morality has been viewed with suspicion by elites as well as the masses, and that the motives of neither of these groups can be identified exclusively with either social benevolence or the common good. Such traditions hold out the possibility of moving beyond resentment to a balanced view, namely, that the ethical challenge is neither wealth

Dennis P. McCann and Joanna Lam Kit Chun, "Aristotelian Perspectives on Business Ethics." Reprinted by permission of the authors.

nor poverty as such, but greed, which may or may not be the decisive motive for those who engage in market transactions.

What, then, do these classics of the Western ethical tradition have to say about morality in the marketplace? More specifically, what basic moral attitudes are expressed toward the activity of market exchange, toward those who engage in such activities, and toward the role of government in relation to business? We approach each of these questions in turn.

Basic Moral Attitudes Toward the Activity of Market Exchange

Aristotle's world is the world of the Greek city-states in transition toward empire. His perspective is self-consciously aristocratic, elitist, and ideologically biased in favor of the ruling class. Aristotle accepts the aristocracy's self-definition as "rule by best people" (*aristoi*), that is, noble citizens, whose excellence in the management of their own households (*oikoi*) affords them both the leisure and the resources to rule disinterestedly on behalf of the common good. His *Nichomachean Ethics* may be regarded as a training manual of ethics for elite youth who will be called upon to govern the public affairs of the nation. Aristotle has been subject to ideological criticism, in the hope of determining whether his ethics contain any truth that transcends the limits of his own class interests. It is our view that they do.

Concerning the morality of marketplace activity as such, we find Aristotle strikingly ambivalent. On the one hand, no city-state can function without providing for a "trader's agora" or marketplace, since market exchanges or buying and selling will inevitably be necessary to acquire the things that the household or family estate (*oikos*) cannot best produce for itself. On the other hand, market activity itself seems incompatible with moral excellence or virtue, and a life devoted exclusively to trade, i.e., buying and selling for profit, is condemned unequivocally as unnatural and immoral:

> There are two sorts of wealth-getting, as I have said; one is a part of household management, the other is retail trade: the former is necessary and honorable, while that which consists in exchange is justly censured; for it is unnatural, and a mode by which men gain from one another. (*The Politics*, Book 1, Chapter 10)

Aristotle's reasons for condemning trade as a way of life are complex. They are partially rooted in his general views on the goal (*telos*) of human life, which

he defines as happiness or living well (*eudaimonia*). Living well, according to Aristotle, is the natural desire of all human beings. It is achieved by exercising all of our human capacities well, each of which has its own natural tendency, which define the moral limits to healthy human desires. Trade as an occupation requires single-minded devotion to profit-making. As such, it recognizes no natural limit to profit-seeking. Trade as an occupation is thus equated with unbridled greed, and is not to be confused with healthy self-love or self-interest. We can see his negative view of trade as an occupation (or business as one's profession) in the contrast he draws between those who seek wealth through buying and selling and the wealth-creating activities of the great landowners who practice the proper art of household management:

> But the art of wealth-getting which consists in household management, on the other hand, has a limit; the unlimited acquisition of wealth is not its business. And, therefore, in one point of view, all riches must have a limit; nevertheless, as a matter of fact, we find the opposite to be the case; for all getters of wealth increase their hoard of coin without limit. . . . Hence some persons are led to believe that getting wealth is the object of household management, and the whole idea of their lives is that they ought either to increase their money without limit, or at any rate not to lose it. The origin of this disposition in men is that they are intent upon living only, and not upon living well; and, as their desires are unlimited they also desire that the means of gratifying them should be without limit. (*The Politics*, Book 1, Chapter 9)

Householders enter the market only occasionally, and are motivated by gain only to the extent that they hope to acquire those goods for their families that they cannot produce efficiently on their own estates. Once they have obtained what they need, they cease trading and leave the marketplace. The professional trader, by contrast, relentlessly pursues profits for their own sake, and is indifferent to the qualities of any goods or any need for them, save their potential profitability.

Despite his ambivalent views on the morality of marketplace activity as such, Aristotle also offers the first sustained effort in Western moral philosophy to understand the morality of market exchange relations. In his treatise on justice, in Book 5 of *The Nichomachean Ethics*, Aristotle distinguishes two kinds of justice, distributive justice and commutative (or rectificatory) justice. Distributive justice occurs in the proportional distribution of public goods by the state, and commutative justice occurs primarily in private transactions by which buyers and sellers voluntarily exchange goods in the marketplace. Both kinds of justice are understood as forms of "equalization," that is, the disposition to make sure that everyone gets what he or she deserves or is owed, or whatever is "lawful and equal," with reference to both the common good and whatever particular goods are available.

But the "equalization"—Aristotle believes, contrary to modern theories of justice—is geometrically proportional in the one kind of justice, and arithmetically proportional in the other. Since Aristotle assumes that social hierarchy is natural, distributive justice is geometrically proportional, in that "treating equals equally" will mean giving one person proportionally more as his higher status demands it. Commutative justice, on the other hand, is arithmetically proportional, since private exchanges in the marketplace are determined not by the relative status of buyers and sellers, but by the desire on the part of both buyers and sellers to get what's coming to them in the exchange:

These names, both loss and gain, have come from voluntary exchange; for to have more than one's own is called gaining, and to have less than one's original share is called losing, e.g., in buying and selling and in all other matters in which the law has left people free to make their own terms; but when they get neither more nor less but just what belongs to themselves, they say that they have their own and that they neither lose nor gain. Therefore the just is intermediate between a sort of gain and a sort of loss, viz. those which are involuntary; it consists in having an equal amount before and after the transaction. (*Nichomachean Ethics*, Book 5, Chapter 4)

Commutative justice, like all virtues in Aristotle's thinking, thus exhibits a "golden mean." Equalization in a voluntary market exchange involves seeking the right balance between "loss" and "gain." Both parties are thus made whole in the transaction. Aristotle's analysis, from the perspective of modern economics, seems to imply a "zero-sum" view of market activity, as if exchange relations as such create no net gain in economic value. Nevertheless, his ethical insights can—and have been—rendered compatible with non-zero-sum views of the marketplace, a first hint of which we will see in his Medieval disciple, Aquinas.

In explaining how this equalization occurs in market exchanges, Aristotle touches upon two points that

were to become central to all subsequent economic theory, the division of labor and the role of money prices in facilitating exchanges. Aristotle's inability to distinguish them carefully testifies to their mutual entailment, both logically and historically:

All goods must therefore be measured by some one thing, as we said before. Now this unit is in truth demand, which holds all things together (for if men did not need one another's goods at all, or did not need them equally, here would be either no exchange or not the same exchange); but money has become by convention a sort of representative of demand; and this is why it has the name "money" (*nomisma*)—because it exists not by nature but by law (*nomos*) and it is in our power to change it and make it useless. There will, then, be reciprocity when the terms have been equated so that as farmer is to shoemaker, the amount of the shoemaker's work is to that of the farmer's work for which it exchanges. But we must not bring them into a figure of proportion when they have already exchanged (otherwise one extreme will have both excesses), but when they still have their own goods. Thus they are equals and associates just because this equality can be effected in their case. Let A be a farmer, C food, B a shoemaker, D his product equated to C. If it had not been possible for reciprocity to be thus affected, there would have been no association of the parties. That demand holds things together as a single unit is shown by the fact that when men do not need one another, i.e., when neither needs the other or one does not need the other, they do not exchange, as we do when some one wants what one has oneself, e.g., when people permit the exportation of corn in exchange for wine. This equation therefore must be established. And for the future exchange—that if we do not need a thing now we shall have it if ever we do need it—money is as it were our surety; for it must be possible for us to get what we want by bringing the money. (*Nichomachean Ethics*, Book 5, Chapter 5)

The division of labor makes market exchange transactions necessary and money prices make them possible. So far, so good. What Aristotle's analysis of market activity fails to see—as later in the history of Western moral philosophy, Adam Smith saw—was that, governments, by encouraging a further expansion in the division of labor, could actually promote economic growth through expanded trade. Aristotle, by contrast, simply observes the division of labor and the necessity of money for facilitating market exchanges. He could not imagine that either or both might become the object of economic and social policy.

Despite Aristotle's shortcomings in economic analysis, his ethical reflections on market activity clearly highlight the significance of the mutual consent between buyers and sellers considered as equals for determining the morality of exchange relations. In addition to defining commutative justice in terms of the voluntary character of exchange relations, Aristotle also recognizes that market transactions can be rendered involuntary, and hence must be judged immoral, when either violence (robbery) or deception (fraud) is involved (Book 5, Chapter 2). Aquinas will later clarify Aristotle's seminal thinking about exchange relations and state more clearly the moral distinction between justice in the marketplace and the injustices of involuntary forms of exchange. Aristotle's discussion of commutative justice, however, focuses primarily on understanding how and why both buyers and sellers usually come to an agreement that both parties regard as fair. His emphasis clearly is on free or voluntary exchanges that injure neither party, insofar as both parties render each other "equal," at least in relationship to the value of the goods exchanged. When either party is unsatisfied, and thinks he or she has been cheated, then an appeal to commutative justice may provide a basis for a legal case, that is, it may serve, in practical terms, as a moral guideline for judges called upon to settle disputes between buyers and sellers. In that sense, Aristotle rightly regards commutative justice as "rectificatory" justice.

Let us turn to Aristotle's most memorable Christian disciple, the Dominican friar, St. Thomas Aquinas. His compendium of Christian faith and practice, the *Summa Theologiae*, is both a summary of all previous theological inquiry in Western Europe and a groundbreaking attempt to crown theology "the Queen of the Sciences," by rationalizing theological inquiry on the basis of an Aristotelian understanding of science. So great is the authority of Aristotle in Aquinas' work that he is constantly invoked as "the Philosopher." Nevertheless, we shall see that while Aquinas preserves Aristotle's specific views on the morality of market activity, the moral character of traders and merchants, and the role of government regulation in the economy, he also departs from them in subtle but significant ways.

Consistent with his general understanding of the nature of Christian ethics, Aquinas' views are developed within the metaphysical framework provided by a distinctively Christian understanding of the moral life. In this Christian form of Aristotelianism, the virtue of justice is but a part of the human person's total response to God who, as Creator and Lord of the Universe, is the author of the objective moral order (*lex aeterna* or "eternal law") inscribed in humanity as the law of nature (*lex naturae*). The basic moral injunctions known through revelation and codified in the Bible (*lex divina* or "Divine law"), in Aquinas' view, simply confirm this law of nature, and help to make it explicit for those who are either too corrupt or too unreflective to grasp it rationally. Thus, for example, when Aquinas begins his discussion of commutative justice, he pointedly refers to the Biblical version of the "Golden Rule" as recorded in Jesus' Sermon on the Mount (Matthew 7:12): "Do unto others as you would have them do unto you." Commutative justice—which Aquinas, following Aristotle, understands as the kind of justice to be realized in market exchange relations—becomes in this Christian perspective another expression of what Jesus taught as a fitting summary of "the Law and the Prophets."

Aquinas' views on the morality of market transactions underscore the idea that buying and selling, like all human interactions, are subject to this comprehensive norm of justice. Thus Aquinas acknowledges Aristotle's condemnation of unrestricted profit-seeking. His description of trade, however, seems to soften Aristotle's denunciation: "Considered in itself, [trade has] a certain debasement attaching thereto, in so far as, by its very nature, it does not imply a virtuous or necessary end." (*Summa Theologiae II-II*, Q. 77, A.4) The nature of his hesitation is apparent later on in that same article, where he observes that, while the vices to which merchants are prone are common to all sinners, they are not intrinsic to the "craft" of trading as such:

> The greedy tradesman blasphemes over his losses; he lies and perjures himself over the price of his wares. But these are vices of the man, not of the craft, which can be exercised without these vices. Therefore trading is not itself unlawful. (Ibid.)

Since the sins typically committed in the marketplace are not intrinsic to business activity as such, one can practice the merchant's "craft" in principle "without [falling into] these vices."

How this is possible, Aristotle's prejudices to the contrary notwithstanding, is the burden of Aquinas' far more lucid and detailed exposition of the principle of commutative justice. Following Aristotle's emphasis on the voluntary character of exchange relations, Aquinas develops detailed arguments demonstrating the immorality of fraud and all other deceptive practices in the marketplace, as well as the moral obligation to make appropriate restitution in such cases. But then Aquinas adds an important point that departs from Aristotle's seemingly "zero-sum" thinking about the marketplace. In exploring the injustice involved in the various forms of cheating common in market transactions, Aquinas asks, "Whether it is lawful to sell a thing for more than it is worth?" Aristotle's answer to this question, of course, was "No"; and so is Aquinas'. But then in answer to the question, "Whether it is possible to sell a thing for more than one has paid for it?," Aquinas says "Yes"! The point is that these are two different questions. The only thing that Aquinas wants to condemn unequivocally is the vice of avarice, that is, the disposition to acquire, and especially to hoard money for its own sake. Thus Aristotle's condemnation of trade as such is narrowed to that which "seeks gain as a last end," that is, trade or profit-seeking that recognizes no moral limit, that will engage in any sharp practice, including fraud, so long as it maximizes profits. Aquinas sees no injustice in selling something for a higher price, provided that the value of the thing sold has been increased in some way, and if the profit realized is "lawfully intended, not as a last end, but for the sake of some other end which is necessary and virtuous," such as supporting one's family or enriching one's sovereign.

Among the ways in which the value of a thing for sale can be increased, Aquinas acknowledges that "the value of a thing has changed with the change of place or time, or on account of the danger [the merchant] incurs in transferring the thing from one place to another, or again in having it carried by another." Aquinas doesn't make the point explicitly, but the acceptance of such risks are a routine part of organized trading activity, and can be used to justify the markups that retailers routinely charge.

Finally, Aquinas deftly disposes of religious pseudo-arguments against trade, such as those offered by St. Jerome, the famed translator of the Bible into Latin. Jerome had offered an *a fortiori* argument for condemning trade, namely, that Christian clergy, at that time, were forbidden to engage in it. Aquinas, however, implicitly presupposes the Medieval distinction between clergy and laity, and concedes that clergy must avoid even the "appearance of evil." Nevertheless, he refuses to condemn business activity as unjust, but warns that it is inappropriate for priests and other religious to engage in it:

> [T]rading engages the mind too much with worldly cares, and consequently withdraws it from spiritual cares; wherefore the Apostle says: *No man being a soldier to God entangleth himself with secular businesses.* Nevertheless it is lawful for clerics to engage in the first mentioned kind of exchange, which is directed to supply the necessaries of life, either by buying or by selling. (Ibid.)

Some clerics, he shrewdly observes, will have to engage in business activities, as they carry out specific stewardship responsibilities toward the Church's own property. *A fortiori*—and contrary to Jerome—the same necessities will motivate the laity to engage in trade, provided that the unbridled pursuit of profit is not their final end or motive.

Basic Moral Attitudes Toward Businessmen

Returning now to Aristotle, concerning the moral character of traders or merchants, Aristotle's views can be treated very briefly. For they are implicit in what has already been said about the morality of market activity. Aristotle shares the prejudices of both landowners and peasants who, whatever their class differences, commonly regard traders and merchants as shady characters whose occupation leaves no room for moral excellence. (*The Politics*, Book 6, Chapter 4) Trading, therefore, is an occupation to be avoided by anyone who is serious about the practice of virtue. Aristotle specifically places retail traders among "the common people" in his view of the social hierarchy, along with husbandmen, mechanics, and laborers (*The Politics*, Book 6, Chapter 7). Indeed, Aristotle recommends that the best political constitution will specifically exclude them, along with others, from citizenship and its public responsibilities.

> Now, since we are here speaking of the best form of government, i.e., that under which the state will be most happy (and happiness, as has been already said, cannot exist without virtue), it clearly follows that in the state which is best governed and possesses men who are just absolutely, and not merely relatively to the principle of the constitution, the citizens must not lead the life of mechanics or tradesmen, for such a life is ignoble, and inimical to virtue. Neither must they be husbandmen, since leisure is necessary both for the development of virtue and the performance of political duties. (*The Politics*, Book 7, Chapter 9)

Aristotle's negative view of the moral character of traders and merchants can also be contrasted with the moral virtue claimed for those who possess wealth and use it well. These are the aristocratic landowners who have inherited wealth rather than earned it through money-making activities. Aristotle commends the virtue of "liberality" in the use of wealth and distinguishes it as another golden mean equidistant from the excesses of "prodigality," or wasteful extravagance, and "meanness" or miserliness. Taken with his remarks on "magnificence," liberality underscores the depth of Aristotle's feeling for the moral difference between wealth and money-making, i.e., between virtuous landowners and vicious merchants. But these two virtues of the wealthy also emphasize the aristocratic landowners' social responsibilities, who are expected to use their wealth to patronize various public festivals and events that increase public consumption without increasing public expenditures. Investing one's wealth in productive enterprises seems completely foreign to Aristotle's perspective.

When we consider Aquinas' views regarding the moral character of traders and merchants, we see subtle differences between his view and that of Aristotle. Perhaps Aquinas was influenced by his personal experience of the early urban renaissance that was then occurring in 13th century Italy, where some families organized trading companies in order to support themselves and their dependents. In any case, Aquinas acknowledged the possibility that traders and merchants could be motivated by honorable intentions, in a way that Aristotle would not and probably could not. The difference between the two is more than rhetorical, for Aquinas argues that commerce is no longer morally reprehensible, but morally indifferent as such. While one can engage in commerce for morally worthy reasons, those reasons, alas, are still seen by Aquinas as external to business activity itself:

> Nevertheless gain which is the end of trading, though not implying, by its nature anything virtuous or necessary, does not, in itself, connote anything sinful or contrary to virtue: wherefore nothing prevents gain from being directed to some necessary or even virtuous end, and thus trading becomes lawful. Thus, for instance, a man may intend the moderate gain which he seeks to acquire by trading for the upkeep of his household, or for the assistance of the needy: or again, a man may take to trade for some public advantage, for instance, lest his country lack the necessaries of life, and seek gain, not as an end, but as payment for his labors. (Ibid.)

Consequently, Aquinas departs in subtle ways from Aristotle's contemptuous suspicions about the character of traders and merchants. It is theoretically possible for a merchant to be virtuous, provided that he is motivated not by profit-seeking as such, but by some socially useful purpose, like supporting his family.

The difference between Aquinas and Aristotle, we believe, reflects the difference between Christian ethics and that of Hellenistic antiquity. In the perspective of Christian ethics, all persons are capable, through the grace of God, of becoming virtuous. Good intentions are morally significant indicators of one's openness to the grace of God. But however subtle the distinction between profit-seeking for its own sake and profit-seeking for some socially useful purpose, in Aquinas' view having the right intention is a powerful moral constraint. A properly motivated merchant will not engage in predatory practices, even when he stands to gain substantially from them.

Basic Moral Attitudes About the Role of Government

Concerning the ethical role of the state in managing the economy, Aristotle suggests a limited role for government intervention. The most prominent area of concern in *The Politics* is, of course, the question of a proper constitution for the state. While Aristotle favors aristocratic government, in which citizenship responsibilities are limited to "the best" people, who are also usually from the wealthy families, he is clear that property ownership should not be the test of citizenship. Indeed, he specifically criticizes both "oligarchy" and "democracy" for making property ownership central, and distinguishes them only insofar as the one is dominated by the rich and the other by the poor, both of whom are using the state to advance their own material interests.

Nevertheless, among the civil offices that are central to his ideal constitution are a number that have key functions relative to the overall supervision of the marketplace and the traders who operate within them. The first of these are "magistrates [who] should be appointed to inspect contracts and to maintain order" in the marketplace; second, "the city wardens," who are responsible essentially for the upkeep of public works, like roads and harbors, that are necessary for market activity to flourish; third, "receivers or treasurers" who collect taxes and distribute revenues to the government offices; fourth, "recorders" who register all private contracts, and decisions of the courts, all public indictments, and also all preliminary proceedings (*The Politics*, Book 6, Chapter 8). While this is a reasonably complete list of the offices required to carry out essential functions like adjudicating civil disputes arising from market transactions, providing economic infrastructure, recording property transfers, and collecting taxes, it does not envision a role for the government in managing market exchanges as such, either by monitoring prices or by timely government sales and purchases designed to moderate price fluctuations. This limited role for the government seems to presuppose that market activity will remain relatively small-scale, and that those who engage in it will remain relatively marginal socially.

The aristocratic household thus seems to form the core of Aristotle's moral universe. Its sons will have the benefit of a philosophical education that will inculcate the virtues necessary for the exercise of citizenship responsibility. Such an education will reinforce the aristocrat's natural disdain for commerce as well as servile labor, and will instill an ideal of happiness, both personal and social, that will render a life devoted to money-making particularly vulnerable to ridicule and condescension. As Aristotle observes in passing early on in *The Nichomachean Ethics*,

> The life of money-making is one undertaken under compulsion, and wealth is evidently not the good we are seeking; for it is merely useful and for the sake of something else. (Book 1, Chapter 5)

Aquinas' view regarding the role of government in regulating market activity and merchants can be dealt with very briefly. His remarks on the responsibilities of government—which is usually as local as it is rudimentary—are confined to the traditional security functions of legal administration and military protection. These are ordered, of course, by a cosmic and hierarchical understanding of law that explicitly links human laws and those who administer them, as we have already seen, with the eternal law, which is a direct expression of God's own self-understanding. The governments of Medieval Christendom were expected to enact and enforce human laws consistent with this Christian vision of the moral order of the universe. But the capacity to extend this aspiration into coherent economic policy on the part of a socially benevolent state, such as the Confucian classics urged Imperial China to become, was not to emerge in European history until early modern times.

Conclusions

Aquinas is relatively more open than Aristotle. For both, the pursuit of profit can only be regarded as moral when it is governed by the principle of justice. But Aquinas' relative openness to moral business is a reflection of the Biblical inheritance in Christian social ethics, which over the long term of Western history is radically subversive of the aristocratic posture of Hellenistic moral philosophy in so many ways. The decisive breakthrough toward business ethics in Christian ethics, however, would only come later in the Calvinistic tradition of the Protestant Reformation, as Max Weber pointed out nearly a century ago.

Discussion and Reflection Questions

1. In your view, is buying and selling for a profit, as such, morally good, bad, or indifferent? Does it depend on how much profit is at stake? What insights on these questions might be gained from Aristotle and Aquinas?

2. In our culture, how is going into business, becoming a merchant, or buying and selling for a profit regarded as an occupation? Is it regarded as honorable or dishonorable? How do Aristotle and Aquinas approach this?

3. Is choosing to become a businessperson necessarily in conflict with leading a morally exemplary life? Why or why not? What sorts of virtues should the businessperson especially strive to cultivate?

4. Should the government have a moral responsibility to ensure that the outcomes of market activity are socially beneficial? If so, on what moral grounds; if not, why not? What insights have you gained from Aristotle and Aquinas on these questions?

Richard McCarty, Business and Benevolence

Is "business ethics" an oxymoron? Is the selfish profit motive successful business requires intrinsically at odds with the requirements of morality? Must virtuous people abandon benevolent motives in their business activities, with the consequence that their profit motive becomes viciously selfish, or is there room in business for virtuous moral agents to act benevolently? In this essay Richard McCarty tackles such questions. After considering (and rejecting) two traditional moral defenses of business selfishness, he seeks to show how business and benevolence can be combined in profitable business activities that can also be morally virtuous. Virtuous persons, he argues, practice business not only within the limits set by laws and by others' moral rights, but also with a conscious commitment to perform at least some benevolent business activities, even if this means failing to maximize profits overall. "Business ethics" need not be a contradiction in terms.

Reading Questions

1. What is meant by "the profit motive"? According to McCarty, what is the first traditional justification of the profit motive, and why does he reject it?

2. What is the second traditional justification of the profit motive? Does McCarty think that this justification succeeds?

3. How does the example of Andrew Carnegie provide an example of coordinating the profit motive with genuine benevolence? What "moral danger" does the author see lurking in this example?

4. How does McCarty respond to the objection to his view that as long as benevolence is "tainted" by the profit motive, business cannot be fully ethical?

Business and Benevolence

RICHARD McCARTY

BUSINESS ACTIVITY, it seems, is the very model of cold, calculating, selfish conduct. Though some business persons sheepishly acknowledge this, many others openly celebrate ruthless selfishness, extolling the profit motive, even greed, as business virtues. Yet if selfishness is a business virtue, while selfless benevolence is a moral virtue, then it seems that good persons cannot be good at business, and that the successful business person is a moral failure. While this hasty conclusion ignores the ample room for benevolent activities in one's non-business, personal life, it nevertheless suggests that something about business is incompatible with morality. *Business ethics* is a contradiction in terms, according to a familiar jest; and perhaps a subtle truth underlying that quip is just that the selfish profit motive successful business requires is intrinsically at odds with part of the requirements of morality.

In order to take business ethics seriously, then, it is necessary to harmonize the apparent opposition between business selfishness and moral benevolence. Blending business and benevolence is the project of the present study, a project in which we shall find it fruitful to examine various traditional

Richard McCarty, "Business and Benevolence," Business and Professional Ethics Journal 7, no. 2 (1987), *pp. 63-83. Reprinted by permission of the author.*

moral defenses of business and the profit motive. Though often used in conjunction, two separate strategies for addressing this problem are prominent: one challenges the moral indictment of self-interest or selfishness, attempting to exonerate the profit motive; another tries to justify business selfishness through its beneficial consequences. Finding both traditional strategies ultimately unsatisfactory, I show in the end how business and benevolence can be combined in profitable business activities which can also be morally virtuous.

I. Self-Interest, Selfishness and Greed

The first traditional justification of the profit motive involves a defense of business selfishness; by demonstrating that self-interest need not be immoral, or vicious, it appears to follow that profit-seeking is morally blameless. Some variations on this theme see self-interest as amoral; ethical egoists see selfishness in business, and everywhere else, as morally praiseworthy.

Defenders of selfishness typically object to common tendencies to imbue the term with an immoral or vicious quality, condemning selfishness in advance through linguistic convention. It is better, they argue, to begin with a morally neutral definition, so that vicious selfishness may be distinguished from amoral, permissible or virtuous selfishness. To accommodate this suggestion, we shall begin with *self-interest* as an abstract kind of self-regard, and we shall stipulate the following morally neutral definition: *seeking satisfaction of one's desires or attainment of one's goals.* Now since it is plausible that people can have moral desires or seek moral goals, on this definition one can be both self-interested and morally good or virtuous. Indeed, since to be virtuous is to desire morally good states of affairs or to make the goals of morality one's own, self-interest so defined becomes a necessary condition for moral virtue, and also probably for life itself. In this neutral sense, *self-interest* can correctly characterize the profit motive as well as the moral saint's voluntary self-sacrifice.

Our morally neutral definition of *self-interest*, however, lacks any reference to the desires and goals of others. But both selfishness and selflessness seem to be essentially "other-related" characteristics. One could be neither selfish nor selfless on a deserted island, since there would be no one over whom to prefer oneself or for whom to sacrifice oneself. In solitude, one can be, at best, self-interested. *Selfishness,* then, seems more correctly defined in relation to others, as: *giving overriding importance to satisfying one's own desires or attaining one's own goals when doing so conflicts with proper desires and goals of others.* On this definition, then, the profit motive is selfish to the extent that it conflicts with the natural desires of others to pay less, to take fewer risks, or to expend less effort. Altruistic behavior, accordingly, is not selfish in this sense, though it may be self-interested in the very broad sense defined above. Selfishness and altruism, on this scheme, are *ways* of being self-interested.

Now although selfishness here is opposed to selflessness, it is not obvious that there is anything necessarily immoral about it; though in some forms it may indeed by vicious. In casual games, for example, players pursue their own goals in opposition to the desires or goals of opponents. If games and similar competitions are morally permissible, then selfishness may be permissible, and need not be immoral. The selfish profit motive, accordingly, may be exonerated provided we can see business activity as friendly competition or as morally permissible selfishness. Business activities and competitive games may take an immoral or vicious turn, however, and we can reserve the term *greed* for such vicious selfishness. Just as selfishness is a way of being self-interested, greed is a way of being selfish.

So long as business activity avoids vicious selfishness, then, it is morally blameless. But can business persons avoid vicious selfishness? As business is often conceived and practiced, I think, they cannot. Selfishness will be vicious when it (*a*) leads one to do wrong by violating others' legal or moral rights; or when it (*b*) precludes acting on one's moral obligations toward others, or prevents one from being virtuous. Now, however respectful of others' moral and legal rights persons may be in their selfish business activities, it is difficult to see how such activities permit fulfilling even minimal moral obligations of beneficence toward others. *Business is not charity.*

At this point in the argument it may seem reasonable to object along the following lines: Since business does not have obligations or beneficence, it cannot neglect such obligations; business selfishness is vicious, then, only to the extent that it tends toward transgressions of others' rights. This objection begins by denying business' moral obligations of beneficence. If the point of this denial is simply that *businesses* lack such obligations, then although it may be true, it is irrelevant. (We shall return to this question briefly at the end.) The issue, it will be recalled, is whether the profit motive of business *persons,* who, as persons, *do* have such obligations, is vicious selfishness; whether business selfishness precludes one's fulfilling his or her moral obligations or beneficence. Since business, as often conceived and practiced, excludes even minimal beneficence as a matter of principle, the profit motive appears to be vicious selfishness, or greed. This traditional defense of selfishness, then, cannot resolve the opposition between business and ethics unless we can find a way for business activity to provide opportunities for at least some beneficence.

II. Beneficence and Benevolence

The second type of traditional moral defense of business often employs an "end-state" moral justification of the profit motive. The idea is that the interests of morality are served best by business selfishness, even by some kinds of greed. Here we might recall Adam Smith's well-known praise of the selfish profit motive. In the view frequently attributed to him, everyone's selfish activity enables an "invisible hand" to secure public benefits. On this view, the way to be beneficent, to contribute to the good of others and the wider public good, is to be selfish. Yet this leaves us with a rather limited notion of beneficence. If our moral obligations toward others can be completely satisfied by such meager contributions to the social good as most individual business people blindly contribute through seeking profits, then business selfishness can be morally justified. Yet it is clear that in our relations with others as employees, customers, business associates, needy fellow citizens and even fellow human beings, morality requires personal commitments beyond the minimal ties that bind mere atomistic economic participants in the wider social good.

H. B. Acton, in friendly criticism of Smith on this point, attempts to show that beneficence pervades the market economy.

> It is not that each individual seeks his own interest and that some "invisible hand," to use Adam Smith's famous expression, sees to it that this results in benefits for all. . . . It is rather that the very structure or system of free exchange in a society with division of labor and limited resources is one in which what each party produces is for some others to have in return for what the producer would like to have from them. Benefiting oneself by providing what others need is the *raison d'être* of the whole affair. It is not that the good of others is a contingent by-product of selfishness, but that each party can only benefit himself by benefitting others.

In Smith's view, the way to be beneficent is to be selfish; Acton, however, suggests that in the market economy, the only way to realize selfish aims, to benefit oneself, is to benefit others directly through business activities. Instead of an "end-state" justification, we may call this a "concomitant" justification; for Acton sees the moral merit of business activity not in an "end-state" of social benefit, but in the individual actions themselves, or in their immediate beneficial consequences. In competitive markets, he writes,

> . . . individuals, whether firms or persons, provide for others in working for themselves. We might equally well say that in working for others they work for themselves. Hence, someone who was averse to helping other people would, once he understood the logic of the system, be rather disconcerted if he had to play a part in it. For business success depends on supplying people with what they want, and hence involves helping them.

Now this "market of favors," as I shall call it, is an interesting but problematic twist on the traditional consequentialist justification of the profit motive. The first problem to note lies embedded in the last sentence quoted above. Acton notes rightly that one secures profits by supplying people with what they want, but this does not necessarily involve helping them, as he claims. In fact, supplying people with what they want in certain types of profitable business activities may be quite harmful to them. Drug dealers, for example, profit by keeping their customers satisfied, though they do them great harm. It is true that the drug buyer shares guilt with the drug dealer, that the buyer shouldn't purchase and use harmful drugs; nevertheless, the concomitant of profit-motivated drug dealing, and similar activities, is quite the opposite of beneficence. Thus, while Acton suggests the profit motive requires beneficence, we see that it actually requires only satisfying others' desires.

Most people, however, generally desire what is good for them; or so it is reasonable to assume. Hence, Acton's view may be satisfactory so long as we restrict it to business activities supplying essential human goods. People desire safe, efficient, environmentally acceptable means of transportation. Automobile companies seek profit by supplying automobiles with the desired capabilities to meet this demand, and so provide what is for many people an essential human good. People also desire steady employment in safe working conditions at a fair wage; and profit-seeking automobile companies must employ thousands of workers, thereby benefitting employees.

Even here, however, automakers' providing products and jobs may not easily count as beneficence. We have seen in recent years how American auto manufacturers have resisted progress in developing safer, more fuel-efficient and pollution-free cars. The dramatic increase in government regulation of the auto industry's reluctant progress toward these goals is evidence that the automakers' profit motive is not well tuned to benefitting the car-buying public. As industry designers know well, profit does not require benefitting the consumer on an absolute scale of benefits; rather, sizable profits may be secured merely providing *relative advantages,* or selling points slightly greater than those offered by competitors. Similarly, auto workers are attracted to their jobs not through the companies' absolute beneficence, but because they find their jobs most advantageous, given their skills and the location of their homes, in comparison with other available jobs.

These considerations of relative advantage seem to tarnish the supposed beneficence of profit-seeking producers and employers. Yet insofar as relative advantages are indeed advantages and constitute goods which may be more difficult or impossible to secure in a nonprofit economy, the tarnished beneficence of producer/employers may yet secure a moral exoneration of the profit motive. Further analysis, however, seriously threatens the beneficence Acton finds pervading business activities; for his characterization of that beneficence betrays a confused, one-sided view of business activities when he writes, as quoted above, that "Benefitting oneself by providing what others need is the *raison d'être* of the whole affair . . . each party can only benefit himself by benefitting others."

Here Acton suggests that producer/employers *benefit themselves* by benefitting others; yet this is not quite an accurate description of the market of favors. Players in the market economy benefit others and *the others* benefit them. More accurately, producer/employers offer or advertise benefits to consumers and employees, but they refuse to confer those benefits until consumers and employees first benefit them. Acton, on the contrary, casts business profit as a king of "self-beneficence" following on one's beneficence to others. In so doing, he obscures the obvious strings attached to business beneficence. He hides the fact that profit usually comes from the hard-won economic resources of consumers and the hard work of employees; that business transactions are not one-sided beneficence, but, ideally, simply fair trade.

A more accurate picture of business activity shows us not that the profit motive requires genuine benefi-

cence, as Acton seems to suggest, but that it requires merely a tarnished, "strings-attached" provision of relative advantages. We may now reasonably question whether this "strings-attached beneficence" necessary for business profit can provide a moral justification for the profit motive, resolving the apparent incompatibility between business and ethics.

If it makes no moral difference how beneficence comes about, then the fact that some benefits come with strings attached should be irrelevant. Yet it is quite clear that the circumstances and motives which give rise to an act of beneficence are morally relevant. A secret revolutionary attempting a political assassination but accidentally killing instead another assassin carrying out a similar plot, may actually save the person he intended to kill. He might well be praised as a hero; that is, so long as his motives remain secret. By all appearances, he has done a good deed; yet we cannot truly say it was an act of beneficence, for whether acts are truly beneficent depends partly on their motives. In Acton's "strings-attached beneficence," therefore, it is clear that the motives of such "business benefactors" disqualify their normal business transactions from counting as genuine beneficence. Genuine, morally praiseworthy beneficence requires benevolent motives. A true benefactor, one with morally praiseworthy benevolent motives, does good to others with no strings attached.

Now Acton notes that a business person may benefit others without such strings attached by making gifts, "or what comes to the same thing in a market, by selling below what he knows to be the market price. But persistently to do this would be to opt out of the system, the very functioning of which requires service to be by exchange rather than by gift." Benevolence, we must conclude, is alien to the business system, as Acton sees it. On his view, business remains essentially incompatible with even the minimal altruistic demands of morality. Unless we can find some way to blend the profit motive and benevolence, business remains partly at odds with ethics.

Andrew Carnegie, whose name is readily associated with both business success and generous philanthropy, provides, in theory and practice, a model for coordinating the profit motive with genuine benevolence. Carnegie's view is similar to Smith's, in that he appears to offer an "end-state" justification which sees the profit motive as furthering the public good; yet rather than leave such beneficence up to an impersonal invisible hand, he places it in the highly conspicuous hands of wealthy business tycoons. In their capable hands, according to Carnegie, only the best charitable causes will be advanced; and benevolently, since philanthropists do not profit from their administration of wealth. Carnegie writes:

> This, then, is held to be the duty of the man of wealth: To set an example of modest, unostentatious living, shunning display or extravagance; to provide moderately for the legitimate wants of those dependent upon him; and, after doing to, to consider all surplus revenues which come to him simply as trust funds, which he is called upon to administer, and strictly bound as a matter of duty to administer in the manner which, in his judgment, is best calculated to produce the most beneficial results for the community—the man of wealth thus becoming the mere trustee and agent for his poorer brethren, bringing to their service his superior wisdom, experience, and ability to administer, doing for them better than they would or could do for themselves.

In Carnegie's view, though, only very few business persons are qualified for this benevolent administration of surplus wealth. These are the best business minds who, while sufficiently selfish, are distinguished chiefly by their uncommon business talent and are rewarded accordingly with great fortunes. The common run of merely competent business persons, according to Carnegie, are unfit for philanthropy both because they lack fortunes, and accordingly also because they lack the ability to administer benevolent projects to the best advantage of humanity. Consequently, on this view, business and benevolence are only rarely compatible, in persons of wealth; yet we have reason to suspect that even this rare coordination is all it appears to be.

Carnegie himself, as is evident in the above quotation, sees wealthy philanthropists as "trustees" of their surplus. This seems to imply that the great fortunes they possess and administer rightfully belong to the less fortunate, from whom, after all, they won their fortunes. Carnegie pictures philanthropists as individualistic, competitive and highly talented business persons throughout most of their lives, accumulating wealth which still belongs, in some sense, to others. Near the end of their productive years in business, when their accumulation of others' wealth amounts to a fortune beyond their capacities of enjoyment, they return the wealth they have won, with some kind of interest. This picture, however, begins to resemble Acton's picture of business beneficence. Insofar as philanthropists are merely trustees, investing others' wealth throughout their lives and returning it with interest in later years, the benefits they impart to humanity are simply their end of a lifelong

bargain. Yet if we expand our focus on the lives and practices of these philanthropists, we may be able to see how they can, in the larger picture, enter the life-long bargain with praiseworthy benevolent motives.

Instead of choosing other traditionally benevolent professions such as the clergy, medicine or social work, young, talented people benevolently wishing to benefit humanity in some way may enter business hoping to accumulate vast fortunes to be philanthropically administered. Eventual success in such a benevolent life-plan requires a long career generating wealth under the profit motive, after which such selfishness can be supplanted by the original benevolence. We need not limit these wider benevolent opportunities to only a few naturally selected business champions, as Carnegie did, but we may see such opportunities open to business people of all talents; the less talented merely administering less wealth, though no less benevolently. At last, then, it seems that business and true benevolence can be generally coordinated. Coordinated though they may be, however, they remain, as yet, incompatible.

On this model, in which original benevolence gives way to selfishness but ultimately returns, the coordination of benevolence and the profit motive is cyclical; yet the cycle preserves their opposition. Business remains, after all, a thoroughly selfish enterprise; and successful business people can atone for their selfishness, perhaps only in part, through philanthropy in their retirement years. If this cyclical coordination of business and benevolence were the best we could hope for, then we ought to celebrate it. The cycle is morally dangerous, however, and we therefore have an incentive to continue our investigation in search of a satisfactory synthesis of business and benevolence. The moral danger lurking in the cyclical coordination is this: The most ruthless and unfair business practices can seem to be justified as the means to future benevolence. On the cyclical model, because there is a time for selfishness and another time for benevolence, it can easily appear to business people that there is a time for business and another time for ethics.

III. Benevolent Business

If we are to make business and ethics fully compatible, we must find ways for business people occasionally to carry out their business activities benevolently, in fulfillment of their obligations toward others. We cannot rely on a cyclical coordination of the profit motive and benevolence which preserves their opposition; we must dissolve that opposition by introducing benevolence into business activity, by finding ways for it to co-exist in the same consciousness as the selfish profit motive. Though this appears impossible, continued reflection on selfishness and benevolence may show how they can be compatible. Selfishness, as defined above, is *giving overriding importance to satisfying one's desires and attaining one's goals when doing so conflicts with proper desires and goals of others*. It is morally objectionable, or vicious, we said, when it precludes fulfilling moral obligations toward others. Benevolence, as we have noted, is properly motivated beneficence. A benevolent act is a gesture of good will (*bene, vol*); and gestures of good will are also freely given to others, with no strings attached. How, then, can one be both selfish and benevolent?

Selfishness and benevolence, we have seen, are "other-directed" character traits or motives. Now if selfishness is giving preference to self above *all* others, and benevolence is acting with good will toward *all* others, then the two can never be compatible; it is also doubtful that anyone ever could be selfish or benevolent, on such a universal understanding of those terms. On the more limited and commonly accepted view of selfishness and benevolence, however, it is possible to deal selfishly with one person or group while dealing benevolently with another. This distinction between others with whom one deals selfishly and others with whom one is benevolent provides for the possibility of a synthesis of the profit motive and benevolence. To actualize that possibility, we need to show how one can, in the course of profit-seeking business dealings with the person or group, direct those dealings with good will in a manner beneficial to other persons or groups. In this way, gestures of good will can be carried out with selfish, profit-seeking motives.

There is no more contradiction in a gesture of good will for a selfish purpose than there is in a good-faith promise for a deceitful purpose, especially not if the promisor and the deceived are different people. If a man can borrow a new car with a good-faith promise, he may do so for the purpose of misrepresenting himself as the owner of the car to impress business associates. Similarly, one may selfishly seek profit from one person by acting benevolently toward another.

Corporate charitable contributions serving public-relations purposes are perhaps the most common and simplest form of profitable benevolence. Such donations to worthy causes are almost universally recognized as good for business. Insofar as they are truly gifts, with no strings attached, they are gestures of good will; yet as Acton failed to see, or did not fully

appreciate, one can profit in the market economy as a consequence of benevolent gifts.

In the wake of recent cutbacks in public funding of worthy causes, some corporations initially reluctant to take up the slack have discovered that the pull-out of government funds has created a marketing vacuum. The highly profitable 1984 Summer Olympics was one of the first examples of how marketing "tie-ins" to popular causes could yield generous profits. American Express, somewhat earlier, launched a successful *cause-related marketing* campaign making a small donation to the restoration of the Statue of Liberty for each credit-card charge. Similarly, MasterCard's 1987 "Choose To Make A Difference" campaign guaranteed at least $2 million in donations to several non-profit service organizations. Benevolent, cause-related marketing appears as profitable as traditional advertising gimmicks and sweepstakes prizes, perhaps more so.

Business donations to worthy causes which enhance corporate images and profits can be selfish benevolence, satisfying both the profit motive and moral obligations toward others. Unlike other forms of beneficence we have considered, such donations or good works can directly address particular individuals' or groups' immediate needs; they can be offered with no strings attached; and they are part of the business system, not alien to it.

The possibilities and potentials of business benevolence have scarcely been explored. Creative business minds are far from exhausting the many possible ways to benefit their own business enterprises and others in need at the same time. In this country's earliest example of corporate philanthropy, railroad executives financed YMCA hostels in small towns, providing inexpensive lodging for railroad employees. More recent examples include: B. Dalton Booksellers' millions of dollars in donations to fight illiteracy; McDonald's "Ronald McDonald Houses" providing support for hospitalized children and families; Southern Bell's project raising $25,000 in donations for a Florida boy needing a liver transplant by donating 50 cents from every Custom Calling feature sold in July 1985.

Among the many possible ways business can contribute to worthy causes, however, it is important to note a continuum between actions or programs which border on the merely beneficent, and those which are truly benevolent. Texaco, for example, has supported radio broadcasts of the *Metropolitan Opera* since 1940. The company behind Neiman-Marcus, Carter Hawley Hale Stores, Inc., recently shifted donations from various charities it supported to visual and performing arts programs, hoping to reach upscale consumers more effectively. While no visible strings may be attached to donations like these, a kind of subtle dragnet is thrown out with the benefits. The primary purpose of such donations is to offer benefits to potential or loyal customers. These seem sharply distinguished from benevolent contributions to identifiable groups or needy individuals from whom no return business or favors are expected. Between these two poles are questionably benevolent programs where donors oversee the management of their gifts, with some strings attached, ensuring that their own interests are served. The most praiseworthy model of business benevolence we have identified is that of gestures of good will toward some, which bring profits from others. There may be many modifications of this model which serve business interests and the interests of others, though the less they give toward good-will gestures with no strings attached, the farther they move from genuine benevolence.

Not everyone, however, sees such good works in a morally favorable light. Milton Friedman, for instance, in criticizing "business social responsibility," uses phrases such as "hypocritical window-dressing," and "tactics approaching fraud" to describe donations by a corporation attempting to "generate good will as a by-product of expenditures that are entirely justified in its own self-interest." Now Friedman here is writing about a slightly different though closely related issue, and there is therefore a danger of taking him out of context. His general point, however, is that it is deceitful to cast selfishly motivated corporate donations as fulfilling business' social responsibilities or moral obligations. Since this is exactly what we have done above, however, it seems reasonable to see Friedman's remarks as critical of the view presented here.

We may note in passing, however, that in the context of his overall view, the point Friedman expresses here is highly paradoxical. Readers familiar with Friedman's arguments on the social responsibility of business will recall that he *does* think business has a social obligation to increase profits. Thus, he must admit that selfishly motivated gestures of good will do indeed contribute toward fulfilling business' social responsibility, and therefore, they cannot be seen as hypocritical or fraudulent.

On the other hand, to be more faithful to Friedman's stated intentions, we must understand his criticism as insisting that there is a fundamental opposition between fulfilling moral obligations, "social responsibilities," and increasing profits: that actions motivated by profit cannot, not matter how beneficial the outcome, count as morally praiseworthy or virtuous. Assuming we agree with this point straightforwardly, we must concede that someone touting his selfishly motivated actions on others' behalf as morally worthy is indeed hypocritical. Friedman's point, therefore, seems quite reasonable and is potentially devastating criticism of our whole project here. If selfishly motivated actions cannot properly count as virtuous, then no matter how benevolently business people administer profitable donations, so long as their benevolence is tainted with the profit motive, moral virtue eludes them; and business remains, therefore, not fully ethical.

We can respond to this criticism, however, in a manner similar to the way we salvaged the genuine benevolence of Carnegie's philanthropists: by expanding our focus on the motives people display in entering business careers or in practicing business. Earlier we imagined how benevolent motives might lead people into careers in business, though at that point we saw no way to make business activity itself benevolent; opportunities for benevolence came only after a long career of selfishness. Having seen how business enterprises may be benevolent, though, we may now consider business persons' morally informed choices of the way they will practice business. Will they engage in purely selfish business, seeking *continually* to maximize personal and corporate profits both immediately and in the long run, or will their careers consciously include *occasional* projects of benevolent business, even if on the whole somewhat less profitable than purely selfish business?

Now the person who chooses to do business always seeking maximum profits may indeed encounter circumstances where philanthropic business activities similar to those discussed above are the most profitable use of available resources. Such a person makes good-will gestures *only when they secure maximum profits*; but this pervasively selfish attitude toward business is indeed incompatible with moral virtue. On the other hand, someone may choose to include occasional benevolent projects in her business career, or as part of the goals of her business, even if such projects are not the most profitable use of resources; and if she chooses to practice business in this manner because morality requires such beneficence, then she is a genuinely virtuous business person.

To display the complicated structure of motivation which makes room for virtuous activity in business, we may distinguish two general levels of motivation in business: the *performance* level and the *practice* level. On the *performance* level, we may examine the motivations for particular business actions or performances.

When we consider business activity as described in Acton's market of favors at this level, for example, we see business people performing such favors with a selfish motive, expecting a somewhat greater favor in return. The motives behind benevolent business actions we have illustrated above, however, cannot be displayed this simply, but require a bifurcation of motives on the *performance* level. Thus, the complex motives behind a benevolent action in business will include, on one sublevel, simply motives of good will, expecting no favors in return. On a higher sublevel, however, there is an ulterior, selfish motive: seeking profit from some as a consequence of one's good will toward others.

On the still higher level of *practice,* more general motives are operative, along with a corresponding range of ways to practice business. On one extreme, a greedy person may choose to practice business in whatever manner secures maximum profit. For such a person, laws and others' moral rights and needs are important only so far as they affect his own profit maximization. If illegal or immoral business performances promise greater profits, this person does not hesitate to seek those profits. Another person may practice business less viciously, drawing the line at breaking laws and transgressing others' moral rights, though still seeking maximum profit within only those restrictions. It is always conceivable, however, that circumstances may arise where such persons can maximize profits through beneficent business performances. Here, even the thoroughly vicious business person above, following his unrestricted motive of profit maximization, will do business beneficently. Yet because of his vicious motive on the practice level, even though his acts are good-will gestures, he is not morally praiseworthy, as Friedman would agree.

Another person, however, may practice business in a virtuous manner. This person recognizes the importance of profit in business, even of profit maximization in selected business performances. She does not, however, go to the vicious extreme of always consciously selecting only those business performances or activities which constitute the most profitable use of available resources; nor is she content with the less viciously selfish practice of profit maximization within only those limitations set by laws and others' moral rights. Sensitive to her obligations toward others, she chooses at least some business activities which allow her benevolently to contribute to others' welfare, even if these are not the most profitable alternatives. So motivated, she may seek profit in these business enterprises while acting on morally praiseworthy motives. Such a virtuous motive on the

practice level is consistent with the profit motive on a sublevel of the *performance* level, which is in turn consistent with benevolent motives, or good-will gestures on the lowest sublevel.

IV. Summary and Conclusion

With this complicated structure of motivation we see how business people, motivated by profit, can perform actions of good will toward others, without selfish strings attached, and how they can do so ultimately from morally praiseworthy motives. Selfishness, as we saw above, is not simply a matter of seeking fulfillment of one's desires, but a matter of the way one does so: in relation to the desires and goals of others. Greed, we also say, is a vicious way to be selfish: either violating rights, or, as a matter of principle, looking only after one's own best interests, never willing to sacrifice profits for the good of others. A greedy person may indeed perform beneficent business actions, freely giving to some when doing so realizes maximum profits from others; but he will do so only under those conditions. Because business can be practiced benevolently, however, there is a virtuous way to be selfish, or a virtuous way to practice business, by performing beneficent business from moral motives.

Although we have occasionally mentioned the general issue of the moral obligations or social responsibilities of businesses or corporations, our focus has been on the obligations and motives of business *persons* as moral agents. Yet these moral features of persons can have important implications for the business activities and institutions in which they participate. The central question of this discussion has been: Must virtuous people abandon benevolent motives in their business activities, with the consequence that their profit motive becomes vicious selfishness, or is there room in business for virtuous moral agents to act benevolently? If the former, then the vicious selfishness business activity requires infects business institutions and business in general. If the latter, however, then business can be fully ethical.

Having shown here how virtuous business people can practice business benevolently, we have demonstrated conditions under which business activities and institutions can be described as fully ethical, or as constituting or conducting virtuous, benevolent business. Virtuous persons practice business within the limitations set by laws and others' moral rights, but also with a conscious commitment to perform at least some benevolent business activities, even at the cost of failing to maximize profits overall. Corporations of virtuous business persons, then, should exhibit such virtuous commitments in their stated purposes and projects. Corporations lacking such commitments cannot be described as fully ethical, and virtuous persons will have a reason to favor the corporations' adoption of such commitments, or to avoid participation in such corporations altogether. We need not maintain that businesses or corporations have obligations or beneficence, but only that persons ought occasionally to be benevolent in their business activities, and ought to structure business institutions in which they participate accordingly.

Discussion and Reflection Questions

1. McCarty seeks "to harmonize the apparent opposition between business selfishness and moral benevolence." Has he succeeded?

2. In your view, to what extent should businesses attempt to be "moral"? Should morality be a part of business practices? How could you convince a businessman of your view?

3. Suppose that a businessman is faced with the choice between morally virtuous and profitable business practices, and morally questionable but very lucrative business practices: What would McCarty advise this businessman to do? What would you advise him to do?

Dennis P. McCann and Joanna Lam Kit Chun, Premodern Confucian Perspectives on Business Ethics

China is slowly but inexorably developing into a major force in the global economy. Developing business ethics in China depends on identifying and examining critically its potential foundations in traditional Chinese moral philosophy. For unless the resources of Chinese culture are fully engaged in the development of Chinese business ethics, business ethics will remain a set of abstractions, either embraced enthusiastically as another novelty from overseas, or rejected resentfully as another foreign imposition, but in either case, regarded as essentially irrelevant to Chinese business practice. In this essay, Dennis P. McCann and Joanna Lam Kit Chun examine key texts from the Confucian tradition in order to identify fundamental moral perspectives on business activities as elaborated by both Confucius and Mencius.

Reading Questions

1. According to McCann and Chun, how did Confucius and Mencius view the morality of market transactions? Did they see them as inherently immoral?

2. In the view of Confucius and Mencius, is the marketplace peripheral or central to a well-functioning social system? Why?

3. How did Confucius and Mencius view becoming a merchant, or buying and selling for a profit, as an occupation? Is it regarded as honorable or dishonorable?

4. In the views of Confucius and Mencius, is the government understood as having a moral responsibility to ensure that the outcomes of market activity are socially beneficial? If so, on what moral grounds; if not, why not?

Premodern Confucian Perspectives on Business Ethics

DENNIS P. McCANN AND JOANNA LAM KIT CHUN

Introduction

In order to advance the development of Chinese business ethics, a study of the basic moral attitudes toward business enshrined in the classics of the premodern Confucian tradition is essential. Specifically, the texts of the *Analects* (*Lun Yu*) of Confucius and the *Book of Mencius* (*Meng Zi*) need to be examined in order to identify the foundations of a business ethics suitable for China. Such an inquiry may also help to develop a critical assessment of the relative strengths and weaknesses of the Confucian tradition as a resource for business ethics in the global marketplace of the 21st century.

What, then, do the classics of the premodern Confucian tradition have to say about morality in the marketplace? More specifically, what basic moral attitudes are expressed toward the activity of market exchange, toward those who engage in such activities, and toward the role of government in relation to business? We approach each of these questions in turn.

Basic Confucian Moral Attitudes Toward the Activity of Market Exchange

Regarding the morality of market transactions, both Confucius (551–479 B.C.E.) and Mencius (c. 320 B.C.E.) have negative things to say about the desire for gain, which seems inescapably central in any account of why merchants and traders engage in market transactions professionally. Both are moral realists who recognize that people normally go into business in order to make money. At the same time, both contrast the profit motive, in sharpest terms, with the attitude proper to morality as such. Confucius, for example, famously said, "The mind of the superior man is conversant with righteousness; the mind of the mean man is conversant with gain" (*Analects*, Book 4, number 16). Similarly the *Book of Mencius* opens with the famous rebuke to King Hui of Liang, "What is the point of mentioning the word 'profit'? All that matters is that there should be benevolence and rightness" (Book 1, Part 1, number 1).

Such texts may lead some to jump to the conclusion that Confucius and Mencius consider market activity immoral as such. But a moment's reflection ought to remind us that these texts were collected and preserved in order to foster the moral education of scholars professionally engaged in government service, and that, in any case, there are other texts that seem far less negative about market activity. Confucius, for example, is quoted as recommending selling a beautiful gem provided that the price is right:

> Tsze-kung said, "There is a beautiful gem here. Should I lay it up in a case and keep it? Or should I seek for a good price and sell it?" The Master said, "Sell it! Sell it! But I would wait for one to offer the price." (*Analects*, Book 9, number 13)

Confucius here seems to regard buying and selling more favorably than hoarding, and implicitly affirms the legitimacy of self-interest. This seems to leave some small opening for a positive evaluation of the morality of market transactions. Perhaps they are not condemned as such, because Confucius could recognize that not all such transactions are motivated by greed alone, or the pursuit of gain or profit to the exclusion of all other human values.

Similarly, we find in the *Mencius* this saying, which may be exceptional for its substance as well as its brevity:

> Mencius said, "He who never misses a chance for profit cannot be killed by a bad year; he who is equipped with every virtue cannot be led astray by a wicked world." (Book 7, Part B, number 10)

This saying seems to praise profit-seeking, by comparing it favorably with the practice of virtue. Whether it actually means to do this may depend on what is meant by "a bad year" and its possible parallel or contrast with being "led astray by a wicked world." A bad year might mean a massive crop failure, in which case profit-seeking implies saving or storing resources in times of plenty to be used in times of scarcity. By extension it could also mean commodity trading under such circumstances. On

Dennis P. McCann and Joanna Lam Kit Chun, "Premodern Confucian Perspectives on Business Ethics."
Reprinted by permission of the authors.

the other hand, if "a bad year" simply contrasts with being "led astray," then it might be regarded as a matter of relatively trivial consequence. In that case, even a bad year would not justify abandoning morality in favor of profit-seeking.

The wisest—and most authentically Confucian—interpretation, we believe, will seek to balance these extremes. Confucius himself points the way toward harmony:

> The Master said, "With coarse rice to eat, with water to drink, and my bended arm for a pillow, I have still joy in the midst of these things. Riches and honors acquired by unrighteousness, are to me as a floating cloud." (*Analects*, Book 7, number 16)

Thus, wealth and rank attained through immoral means are insubstantial; the virtuous man will not be tempted by them. Note, this does not mean that poverty is to be preferred to a comfortable living. The point is simply that poverty is preferable to immorality.

Mencius makes similar points in a number of passages (for example, Book 3, Part B, number 4; Book 6, Part B, number 4). His remarks are placed within more expansive observations regarding the nature of market transactions, and their necessity in a society that encourages a division of labor on economic grounds. Mencius accepts the justice of paying wages based on performance or merit rather than need (Book 3, Part B, number 4), and specifically rejects the idea that market prices ought to be administered in such a way that every item for sale is worth the same:

> "If we follow the way of Hsu Tzu there will be only one price in the market, and dishonesty will disappear from the capital. Even if you send a mere boy to the market, no one will take advantage of him. For equal lengths of cloth or silk, for equal weights of hemp, flax or raw silk, and for equal measures of the five grains, the price will be the same; for shoes of the same size, the price will also be the same.
>
> "That things are unequal is part of their nature. Some are worth twice or five times, ten or a hundred times, even a thousand and ten thousand times, more than others. If you reduce them to the same level, it will only bring confusion to the Empire. If a roughly finished shoe sells at the same price as a finely finished one, who would make the latter? If we follow the way of Hsu Tzu, we will be showing one another the way to being dishonest. How can one govern a state in that way?" (*Mencius*, Book 3, Part A, number 4)

The full passage specifically underscores the economic advantages of a division of labor, its role in creating prosperity, the attendant need for increased market exchange, and the legitimacy of "mind work" within the division of labor, contrary to peasants' assumptions that only hard physical labor is productive. It also asserts a parallel between moral education and economic education and concludes, as we have just seen, by rejecting Hsu Tzu's attempt to equalize market prices. Mencius asserts the natural inequality of things and hence the reasonableness of price differentials reflecting that inequality.

Here Mencius seems to be defending market exchange on moral grounds and not simply for reasons of expediency or efficiency. Price differentials based on differences in quality are honest. The idealistic imposition of equalized market prices, however, will only generate immorality. Such a policy would only promote cynicism and/or dishonesty, the source of all corruption in the marketplace. Mencius clearly rates high marks for his understanding of market economics; all the more reason to take seriously his views of the priority of righteousness over profit.

Basic Moral Attitudes Toward Businessmen

Concerning the personal character of merchants and those who engage in trade as a profession, Confucius and Mencius offer a number of promising suggestions, but rarely tackle the issue head-on. Confucius' attitude generally is that while neither wealth nor poverty is to be idealized, the person who is morally exemplary in spite of wealth or poverty is clearly to be praised:

> Tsze-kung said, "What do you pronounce concerning the poor man who yet does not flatter, and the rich man who is not proud?" The Master replied, "They will do; but they are not equal to him, who, though poor, is yet cheerful, and to him, who, though rich, loves the rules of propriety." (*Analects*, Book 1, number 15)

This seems consistent with Confucius' proverbial indifference to the pursuit of wealth (*Analects*, Book 9, number 1; Ibid., Book 15, number 32).

Nevertheless, there are other passages, admittedly ambiguous in their meaning, that suggest a positive view of merchants and their personal character. One such is his remarks apparently in praise of his disciple, Zi Gong:

> The Master said, "There is Hui! He has nearly attained to perfect virtue. He is often in want.

Ts'ze does not acquiesce in the appointments of Heaven, and his goods are increased by him. Yet his judgments are often correct." (*Analects*, Book 11, number 19)

This text seems to praise Confucius' student, the famous merchant disciple, Zi Gong, here referred to as Ts'ze, precisely because he has refused to accept his lot in life (poverty) and become a successful merchant. That Zi Gong is very highly valued by Confucius is evident from *Analects*, Book 6, number 8, which praises Zi Gong as a man of understanding, which is only a step below a man of benevolence. Kuan Chung, by contrast, a successful merchant and economic adviser in the Kingdom of Qi and a founder of the school of legalism, is not praised. He is criticized, instead, as "a vessel of small capacity" (*Analects*, Book 3, number 22), and his understanding of rites is dismissed as very common. The contrast between the two merchants is not whether one makes money or not, but whether one is following propriety. Profit-seeking therefore is morally acceptable so long as it occurs within the moral boundaries established by the rites.

There are, of course, other plausible interpretations of this text. It could mean that Hui is praised for perfect virtue, with the frank recognition that perfect virtue entails poverty, and that Confucius' attitude toward Ts'ze or Zi Gong is a case of "damning with faint praise"—after all, his business calculations are merely "correct." Nevertheless, we think this interpretation unlikely in light of the other things said about Ts'ze or Zi Gong in the *Analects*. Confucius' praise of Zi Gong thus forces his disciples to admit that it is possible, however unlikely, to be both a successful merchant and a paragon of moral virtue.

Mencius, not surprisingly, echoes Confucius' principled distinction between "the good" and "the profitable" (Book 7, Part A, number 25), but his personal contribution to understanding the subtleties involved in this distinction consists in a number of passages regarding what precisely it means for anyone to follow the Confucian "Way." Here is one such passage—while not specifically directed at merchants—which recommends the self-discipline that Mencius believes is indispensable to the good life:

Mencius, speaking to Sung Kou Chien, said, "You like travelling to different courts, don't you? Let me speak with you about this kind of travelling. If you are acknowledged, just be content, and if you are not acknowledged, just be content."

Chien asked, "How do you go about 'just being content'?"

Mencius said, "If you value virtue and enjoy Righteousness, you can be content. Hence the *shih* in dire straits does not lose his sense of Righteousness, and when successful, does not lose the Path. Since he does not lose his sense of Righteousness when in dire straits, the *shih* is able to keep a grasp on himself. Since he does not lose the Path when he becomes successful, the people are not disappointed in him."

"When the ancients achieved their aims, they shared it with the people. Not attaining their aims, their self-discipline was an example to succeeding generations. In dire straits they could only develop their own goodness. Successful, they could share their goodness with the whole world." (*Mencius*, Book 7, Part A, number 9)

Self-discipline is clearly the Way to success for anyone who is seeking to serve at the courts, that is, for those scholars seeking careers as Imperial administrators. That it could also become a crucial element in the character of those virtuous merchants, like Zi Gong, whose lives bridge the gap between righteousness and profit, obviously is not Mencius' concern (cf. Book 7, Part A, number 25).

Such a possibility, however, is suggested in a number of other passages in which Mencius seeks to clarify the proper "Way" of thinking and acting with regard to gift-giving and receiving, a traditional Chinese cultural practice that, to this day, is prominent both in public administration and in private business dealings. Mencius' remarks on gift-giving and receiving show that he means to distinguish some forms of cultivating social relationships (*guanxixue*) from bribery and other forms of corruption. In one passage Mencius' own integrity seems under challenge, as he is asked to defend the consistency of his actions in two different situations. In response, Mencius articulates the proper principle:

To accept a gift without justification is tantamount to being bought. Surely a gentleman should never allow himself to be bought. (Book 2, Part B, number 3)

Further passages indicate that moral justification in such situations may rest on a number of tacit cultural assumptions.

In one intriguing example (Book 5, Part B, number 4) Mencius and his disciple, Wan Chang, are involved in an extended discussion of the propriety of receiving gifts, even in the extreme case "when the robber makes friends with one in the correct way and treats one with due ceremony." Mencius' response regarding receiving a robber's gift is an unequivocal "No!";

but when his student presses him regarding gifts received from "feudal lords" whose expropriations, in the student's view, amount to robbery, Mencius denies the parallel. But even assuming that feudal lords are not necessarily predatory in the same way that robbers are, Mencius tries to defend the propriety of receiving gifts from them, by invoking a rather odd story about Confucius.

> When Confucius took office in Lu, the people of Lu were in the habit of fighting over the catch in a hunt to use as sacrifice, and Confucius joined in the fight. If even fighting over the catch is permissible, how much more the acceptance of a gift. (Book 5, Part B, number 4)

The obscurity of Mencius' response is relieved somewhat, when one considers that both the customary fight over the catch at Lu, and the etiquette surrounding gift-giving and receiving, may both be regarded as ritually embedded actions, that themselves teach propriety. In this case, as in so many others, ritualized custom contains the key to what is acceptable and unacceptable behavior in cultivating social relationships.

Whether or not one regards Mencius' answer as anything more than a rationalization of expediency, one must admit that Mencius exhibits a fine sense of the moral ambiguity—what Western moral philosophers call "the problem of 'dirty hands'"— involved allowing the Way to form one's character as one "takes office" or exercises public responsibilities. Just like the scholar-administrators of ancient China, so today's Chinese business people must know the difference between acceptable gift-giving and receiving, on the one hand, and bribery, on the other. Conscientious and closely reasoned ethical reflection on such dilemmas as Mencius and Wan Chang puzzled over, of course, are also indispensable for contemporary business ethics, understood as the development of a professional ethic for business managers and administrators. By modeling a casuistry appropriate to the kinds of moral dilemmas faced routinely by both ancient scholars and modern business managers, Mencius, despite his principled skepticism about any positive correlation between profit and propriety, was in fact doing business ethics.

Basic Moral Attitudes about the Role of Government

Concerning the role of the government in regulating market exchanges, what Confucius and Mencius have to say on this topic is strikingly well thought out, both from an economic as well as an ethical point of view, which is perhaps not surprising, since the Confucian classics seem directed primarily to scholars hoping to exercise public responsibilities in government service.

The purpose of government, according to Confucian philosophy, is social benevolence. This means serving the people by, among other things, providing for their welfare and educating them to their responsibilities, through the exercise of exemplary moral leadership.

> Chi K'ang Tzu asked Confucius about government. Confucius answered, "To govern (cheng) is to correct (cheng). If you set an example by being correct, who would dare to remain incorrect?" (Analects, Book 12, number 17)

Mencius suggests that the quality of moral leadership exemplified in good government is but the ultimate expression of the Way that animates all aspects of life:

> Mencius said, "There is a common expression, 'The Empire, the state, the family.' The Empire has its basis in the state, the state in the family, and the family in one's own self." (Book 4, Part A, number 5)

The awesome power of the government thus is checked by the moral constraints—the self-discipline of those in positions of authority, for example—that lie at the heart of the Confucian Way. Here is Confucius' memorable saying about the proper way for the government to carry out its moral responsibilities:

> Chi K'ang Tzu asked Confucius about government, saying, "What would you think, if in order to move closer to those who possess the Way, I were to kill those who do not follow the Way?"

Confucius answered:

> In administering your government, what need is there for you to kill? Just desire the good yourself and the common people will be good. The virtue of the gentleman is like wind; the virtue of the small man is like grass. Let the wind blow over the grass and it is sure to bend. (Analects, Book 12, number 19)

If government officials follow the Way, their moral leadership will attract the people's trust and active cooperation. Under such circumstances, there is no need for legal terrorism.

What Confucius and Mencius have to say specifically about the government's responsibilities for regulating the economy helps to clarify their general approach to social benevolence. The Analects (Book

20, number 2), for example, provides a summary statement listing the five "do's" and four "don'ts" of good government:

> Tsze-chang asked Confucius, saying, "In what way should a person in authority act in order that he may conduct government properly?" The Master replied, "Let him honor the five excellent, and banish away the four bad, things; then may he conduct government properly."
>
> Tsze-chang said, "What are meant by the five excellent things?" The Master said, "(1) When the person in authority is beneficent without great expenditure; (2) when he lays tasks on the people without their repining; (3) when he pursues what he desires without being covetous; (4) when he maintains a dignified ease without being proud; (5) when he is majestic without being fierce."
>
> Tsze-chang said, "What is meant by being beneficent without great expenditure?" The Master replied, "(1) When the person in authority makes more beneficial to the people the things from which they naturally derive benefit; is not this being beneficent without great expenditure? (2) When he chooses the labors which are proper, and makes them labor on them, who will repine? (3) When his desires are set on benevolent government, and he secures it, who will accuse him of covetousness? (4) Whether he has to do with many people or few, or with things great or small, he does not dare to indicate any disrespect; is not this to maintain a dignified ease without any pride? (5) He adjusts his clothes and cap, and throws a dignity into his looks, so that, thus dignified, he is looked at with awe; is not this to be majestic without being fierce?"
>
> Tsze-chang then asked, "What are meant by the four bad things?" The Master said, "(1) To put the people to death without having instructed them; this is called cruelty. (2) To require from them, suddenly, the full tale of work, without having given them warning; this is called oppression. (3) To issue orders as if without urgency, at first, and, when the time comes, to insist on them with severity; this is called injury. And (4), generally, in the giving pay or rewards to men, to do it in a stingy way; this is called acting the part of a mere official."

Clearly, the five recommended governmental practices assume that the government has ultimate responsibility for the people's economic welfare. For example, the role of the government is to make "more beneficial to the people the things from which they naturally derive benefit." Since the people naturally derive benefit from work, the government must promote employment opportunities, and do it in as cost-effective a way as possible. In order to serve the people, the government must also maximize moral leadership, while minimizing corruption. The four repudiated governmental practices thus underscore the necessity of self-discipline on the part of government officials, who are advised to have done with personal greed, while carrying out their responsibilities. We regard this text as Confucius' definitive proposal for an administrative or managerial ethic for both government officials and business executives: the one who is the ideal ruler or, in today's world, the ideal administrator, would possess the characteristics promoted here.

The positive economic consequences of good government are also clearly taught by Confucius:

> When a country is well governed, poverty and a mean condition are things to be ashamed of. When a country is ill governed, riches and honor are things to be ashamed of. (*Analects*, Book 8, number 13)

Though good government is no guarantee of personal prosperity or business success, the presence or absence of good government does shape the personal responsibility of the individual in economic matters. If the government is managing things according to the Way, then your lack of prosperity (personal success, expression of talents) should cause you shame. On the other hand, if government is acting contrary to the Way, then your very prosperity should cause you shame. Confucius' aphorism seems to assume that if the government is thoroughly corrupt there is no way an individual person or family can become rich, without participating in and benefiting from the corruption.

A parallel may be found in *Analects*, Book 14, number 1, which gives moral advice on when and whether to accept a salaried government position:

> Hsien asked about the shameful. The Master said, "It is shameful to make salary your sole object irrespective of whether the Way prevails in the state or not."

If the Way prevails in the state, the government is fulfilling its role in promoting social benevolence. So long as one is assured of the government's social benevolence, there is nothing shameful in seeking a salaried position in the government. But if one is motivated only by considerations of economic security, and is prepared to ignore the government's departure from the Way, then one should be ashamed. Clearly, as in most other aspects of Confucian morality, here there is moral reciprocity in the relationship between the state and the scholar-administrators who serve the state. A Confucian business ethic would want to extend this pattern of moral reciprocity to the relationship between business managers and the firms that employ them.

One of Mencius' characteristic contributions to the Confucian philosophy of government is his keen understanding of the purpose and methods of government regulation of the economy. Government activity beyond enforcing the laws governing market transactions, he argues, arose from social benevolence, specifically, the necessity of protecting the people from a greedy merchant seeking to impose monopoly conditions and reap personal benefit from them:

> In antiquity, the market was for the exchange of what one had for what one lacked. The authorities merely supervised it. There was, however, a despicable fellow who always looked for a vantage point and, going up on it, gazed into the distance to the left and to the right in order to secure for himself all the profit there was in the market. The people all thought him despicable, and, as a result, they taxed him. The taxing of merchants began with this despicable fellow. (*Mencius*, Book 2, Part B, number 10)

Taxation, as a means of discouraging predatory practices in the marketplace, in later Chinese history would turn out to be only one of the weapons in the Confucian arsenal of economic regulation.

On the other hand, Mencius seems determined to promote only those forms of government intervention that will sustain rather than suppress the genuine gains in social benevolence that result from market activity. In Book 3, Part A, number 4, for example, Mencius offers some basic observations in political economy, as part of a wide-ranging discourse on good government. Crucial to his sense of what should and should not be done by the government is an insight into the relationship between the division of labor and the general level of prosperity. The encouragement of "the hundred crafts" will stimulate market activity, and Mencius sees nothing wrong in this:

> To trade grain for implements is not to inflict hardship on the potter and the blacksmith. The potter and the blacksmith, for their part, also trade their wares for grain. In doing this, surely, they are not inflicting hardship on the farmer either. . . . [I]t is necessary for each man to use the

products of all the hundred crafts. If everyone must make what he uses, the Empire will be led along the path of incessant toil. Hence, it is said, "There are those who use their minds and there are those who use their muscles. The former rule; the latter are ruled. Those who rule are supported by those who are ruled." This is a principle accepted by the whole Empire.

Later on in this passage, as we have observed already in another context, Mencius will criticize a government price control system designed to make all goods equal in value. While Mencius rejects such a scheme on ethical grounds, here he seems to add an important economic consideration. The suppression of the division of labor and free market pricing mechanisms stands rejected for reasons of efficiency: it will only result in condemning the people to incessant toil. Besides, as he observes, market transactions do not necessarily "inflict hardship" on either buyers or sellers. Indeed, their yield can be just the opposite.

Mencius, here at least, seems to hold a view of market activity that is not captive to "zero-sum" thinking. He thus is open to strategies of government regulation that will work with, rather than against, the socially benevolent dynamism of free market activity. His grasp of economics, in this area as in others relating to government regulation, seems unsurpassed in the literature of ancient moral philosophy, either Western or Chinese. Let us give him, then, the last word here:

> Mencius said, "Put in order the fields of the people, lighten their taxes, and the people can be made affluent. If one's consumption of food is confined to what is in season and one's use of other commodities is in accordance with the rites, then one's resources will be more than sufficient. The common people cannot live without water and fire, yet one never meets with a refusal when knocking on another's door in the evening to beg for water or fire. This is because they are in such abundance. In governing the Empire, the sage tries to make food as plentiful as water and fire. When that happens, how can there be any amongst his people who are not benevolent?" (Book 7, Part A, number 23)

Conclusions

In summary, there seem to be subtle differences between the two primary Confucian texts on the attitudes they reflect regarding business and business ethics. Confucius is relatively more open toward the possibility of moral business, or a just market system, than is Mencius, who, in turn, is more interested in government regulation. These differences may be a reflection of the shifting historical context: The *Analects* may reflect social conditions in the Warring States period, while the *Mencius* may already reflect the trend toward centralized government that will culminate in the establishment of the Qin and Han dynasties and the advent of the Imperial period in Chinese history. Confucius' relative openness to the possibility of moral business may be explained partially by the fact that he is active before the Imperial system was established. The *Mencius*, however, already reflects the move toward an Imperial system, and already anticipates the historic link between Confucian moral education, the scholarly elite, and government service. It is not surprising, then, that later on in Chinese history when the Imperial dynasty was more open to the social benevolence of market activity and the merchant classes, Confucian scholars, like Wang Yang Ming, were to show greater openness toward business ethics. But in those periods both before and after the Ming dynasty, when merchants were feared for their subversive potential and resented because of their wealth, Confucian scholars tended to regard business ethics with hostility and suspicion. That, at least, is one hypothesis that could be pursued in further research and reflection on the Confucian legacy in business ethics.

Discussion and Reflection Questions

1. In your view, is buying and selling for a profit, as such, morally good, bad, or indifferent? Does it depend on how much profit is at stake? What insights on these questions might be gained from Confucius and Mencius?

2. In our culture, how is going into business, becoming a merchant, or buying and selling for a profit regarded as an occupation? Is it regarded as honorable or dishonorable? How do Confucius and Mencius approach this?

3. How does choosing to become a businessperson reflect on a person's moral character? Are there certain stereotypes associated with engaging in business? How well justified are these?

4. Should the government have a moral responsibility to ensure that the outcomes of market activity are socially beneficial? If so, on what moral grounds; if not, why not? What insights have you gained from Confucius and Mencius on these questions?

Xiusheng Liu, Spirituality and Morality: An Indian Ethical View of Economics and Business

Ask any Western businessman what the goal of business activity is, and (after perhaps thinking that you are either mad or joking) he will respond that *acquiring money* is obviously the goal. The acquisition of money, in turn, is for the sake of acquiring goods, which are in turn thought to satisfy desires. This model of business is perhaps so deeply ingrained that it seems obvious, and it is hard to imagine any other model. In this essay, Xiusheng Liu associates such approaches with "hedonomics," and points out some of the problems with this approach. He contrasts it with "spirinomics," an approach to business more characteristic of the Indian tradition. If the ultimate aim of any human life is to attain spirituality, then business, too, ought to serve this end. How this is to be pursued, however, may not be immediately obvious. Liu guides the reader through the relevant parts of Indian religious and philosophical thought, and suggests how this might be done.

Reading Questions

1. What does Liu mean by "hedonomics"? Why does he think that "hedonomics" characterizes most Western business practices?
2. According to Liu, what is wrong with hedonomics?
3. What does Liu mean by "spirinomics"? Why does he think that "spirinomics ought to characterize business practices"?

Spirituality and Morality: An Indian Ethical View of Economics and Business

XIUSHENG LIU

No step could be taken in the Indian's inner or outer life without his being reminded of a spiritual existence.

SRI AUROBINDO, *THE FOUNDATIONS OF INDIAN CULTURE* (PONDICHERRY, INDIA: SRI AUROBINDO ASHRAM, 1988), P. 63.

1. Introduction

For non-Western philosophers, the most distinct feature of major Western moral theories of economics and business is that they rest on selfish considerations. For example, hedonism is the underlying main theme of all economic activities in theory or practice. Hedonism holds that pleasure or the absence of pain is the sole intrinsic good in life. It generally falls under two categories: psychological or ethical. A psychological hedonist holds that by psychological makeup we inevitably seek pleasure and avoid pain. An ethical hedonist holds that morally we should seek pleasure and avoid pain, with or without psychological hedonism's being true.

Theories such as ethical hedonism have serious normative implications, for they take self-preservation and satisfaction of desires—the secular concerns, according to Indian philosophers—as the bedrock of values. Those theories have been criticized for fostering greed and strife at all levels of social and political life. They also have been criticized for suffering deep philosophical problems. For example, Immanuel Kant claims that hedonism neglects the rational nature of human beings and degrades humanity for treating persons as merely means for pleasure. Ac-

cording to Kant, pleasure or absence of pain is not an intrinsic good. To the contrary, it is actually irrelevant to moral considerations. It is unfortunate, however, that these kinds of criticism are not being taken seriously by the hectic business world.

Non-Western philosophies often provide distinct alternatives to the mainstream of Western moral theories of economics and business. For example, ancient Indian moral philosophy denies pleasure or absence of pain as the sole intrinsic value, but for a reason different from the one raised by Kant. Indian philosophers take spirituality as the ultimate end. Pleasure, absence of pain, and satisfaction of desires are only treated in connection with the achieving of spirituality. In the following I would like to introduce Indian spiritual moral theory and explore its implications for economics and business.

2. Setting the Stage: Brahman as the Pure Spiritual Reality

The overriding Indian concern has been to live an individual life that expresses the perfect being of Brahman, the Vedantic ideal of the supreme Self. Brahman, also translated as the Absolute, is the highest spiritual reality, whose nature is eternal purity, intelligence, and freedom. Brahman is different in character from the non-intelligent, material world, but considered the basis of the world: from Brahman the origin, subsistence, and dissolution of this world proceed. The essence of Brahman is bliss; it is the cause of joy in individual existence.

Xiusheng Liu, "Spirituality and Morality: An Indian Ethical View of Economics and Business." Reprinted by permission of the author.

According to one major interpretation, the relationship between the individual and Brahman is non-difference in certain ways but difference in others. Among the common features between the two include, most importantly, spirituality and subjectivity. The differences between the two are apparent and significant. As Hajime Leggett summarizes,

> The Highest Self [Brahman] is the principle which makes possible the activity of . . . the individual self; consequently, the relationship of ruler and subject exists between the two. While Brahman has the power to create, maintain and dissolve the world, the individual self has no such powers. Brahman is the *atman* consisting of the bliss (*anandamaya*), but the individual self has no such quality. Brahman possesses the quality (*dharma*) of "transcending all evils," but the individual self has no such quality. . . . The individual self receives pain and pleasure as the consequence of his *karmic* acts [i.e., intentional actions], but the Highest Self does not experience such effects.

Since there is only one Supreme Self, one Being, one pure Consciousness, all individuals share the same Self, which is the ground-Consciousness underlying all individual conscious minds.

Brahman is transcendent in the sense that it is infinite and immortal. As the absolute, it transcends all worldly miseries and sufferings. According to Vedantic tradition, the transcendence of Brahman is taken to be intrinsic to its immanence. And the immanence does not jeopardize the transcendent perfection. Brahman is immanent in the sense that it is within all things and identifiable with some part of the universe. For example, according to one interpretation, Brahman exists in the individual soul without being influenced by it. Thus, it is said that Brahman is the light within the heart.

Brahman is the only truly free and pure Being and the only Reality. The individual self is taken in by appearance and thus lives within the oppressive chain of action and reaction, birth and rebirth, mortality and misery, and ignorance and illusion. Only the Supreme Self can elevate the suffering soul to partake in the bliss, the immortality, and the infinitude of Brahman's own transcendent Being. Thus, the only way to escape the worldly chain is to reach the highest or the pure spirituality by transcending all the misery and bondage in which the soul has become entangled. Human beings have access to the highest Reality through the existence of our consciousness; this is so because Brahman and the individual self are "not different" in fundamental ways. To achieve this

spiritual liberation, certain spiritual, moral, and physical training are necessary. Such means as meditation and (certain ways of) breathing are emphasized by almost all Vedantic schools. A liberated state manifests virtue. One point that must be noted is that spiritual liberation does not render the individual self completely identical with Brahman, because the latter alone possesses the power of creation.

3. *Economic Culture: Indian and Western*

In order to see what Indian tradition might offer to us, we need to briefly review some essential differences between Indian and Western economic cultures. Major Western theories of economics, especially neo-economics, and managerial thought have three basic philosophical presuppositions: (i) Sense-related reality is the only area of concern. (ii) Conventionally educated and trained mental-intellectual equipment can scale all heights or plumb all depths of rationality. (iii) All economic activities rest on self-preservation and other self-interests. The Indian philosopher S. K. Chakraborty has termed such an economic scheme "hedonomics," i.e., hedonism plus economics underlain by secular concerns.

The problems with Western theories of economics and managerial philosophy are many and serious. Chief among them is that hedonomics pushes the selfish, greedy, and self-centered aspect of humanity to the extreme. Community values are abandoned. Human relationships are reduced to interest calculation. International affairs are settled by economic strength and military force. What managerial/entrepreneurial ethics does is simply to create intellectual devices to resolve interest conflicts rather than to improve overall human life. Spirituality is neglected. Individual life becomes more and more complex. This is the state of "complex living, low thinking" warned by some Indian philosophers.

For an Indian philosopher, if an ethical theory takes self-preservation or self-interest as its first principle, it starts on the wrong foot. Its problematic consequences are to be expected. "Pursuit of *artha* and *kama*, i.e., economic and pleasure goals alone, with egoistic self-interest as the primary focus, culminates not in sacrifice but in misappropriation. Hence it is immoral and unspiritual. Therefore sooner or later cosmic poetic justice (*ritma*) visits mankind with a terrible backlash." The Indian tradition of spirituality contains the solution to the troubling situation. As Chakraborty says,

> Problems springing from secular pursuits cannot be resolved by inexorably pressing forward on

the secular route. . . . The answer to growing complexity is not to invite a greater or more bizarre tangle of complexity. The solutions lay in the conjunction of their opposites: the sacred and the simple.

If spiraling material greed thwarts progress, it must be subdued and contained. *Nivritti* (restraint) must guide and control *pravritti* (desires). Hence the motto "simple living, high thinking" has been worked out in its minutest detail in the course of India's long, unbroken history. This is the essence of the entire idealistic brahminical model of man.

The secular and the material must be informed and invested with the sacred and the spiritual. "India's obligation to herself and to the world is to relive this sacro-secular symbiosis for effective transformation in each epoch."

4. Wealth, Rectitude, and Spirituality

What does Brahman as pure spirituality imply? Human beings must realize that the secular life is unreal. The only reality is Brahman, pure spirituality. The improvement of the individual life cannot be measured by money and wealth (*artha*) but inner harmony and spirituality. Egoistic concern must be minimized in economic activities simply because the supreme Self is the same for each and every individual. "As humans move or transform themselves, by investing the secular with the sacred through *sadhana* (devoted spiritual practice), clashes and conflicts, dirt and poison begin to lessen because the more one progresses toward [the pure spirituality], the more one becomes all embracing, all inclusive." That insight is formulated into the four-goals system (*chaturvarga*) of human existence: *artha* (desires and needs), *kama* (money and wealth), *dharma* (rectitude and righteousness), and *moksha* (spiritual liberation and freedom from the cycle of birth and death).

Although spiritual liberation is clearly of the greatest importance, it cannot be actualized without actualizing the other three goals. In the process of spiritual cultivation, "the secular goals of *artha* and *kama* are integrated into the model *within* the bounds of *dharma* and *moksha*." *Dharma* as rectitude and righteousness signifies the proper order in the universe. It is the moral or ethical propriety. As spiritual liberation, *moksha* is the highest goal. Discussing the process of spiritual cultivation, Sri Aurobindo discerns the following sequence: Matter—Life—Mind—Spirit. In this process, as Chakraborty says,

Every act is a spiritual prayer, every step is a pilgrimage. To put it in another way, the key task of management in any secular aspect of life is to transform and elevate it into a sacred process. Otherwise, secular life is subject to entropic degeneration under cover of exterior gloss. "Simple living, high thinking" is exiled and its place usurped by "complex living, low thinking."

According to Chakraborty, Brahman as pure spirituality has the following implications for economic and secular life:

(1) A pure mind, a pure heart;
(2) A calm head, a cool brain;
(3) Smooth, deep, regulated breathing and nervous harmony;
(4) Peace, light, power, *ananda* [bliss, spiritual ecstasy];
(5) A core of luminous constancy amidst fluctuating experiences;
(6) Contacting the inner Self which is unchangeable, perfect, whole and luminous, and identical with the Self in everyone else [inner Self, the image of Brahman in each individual];
(7) A weakening of the divisive, selfish ego and strengthening the expansive, inclusive, consciousness;
(8) Greater giving and less grabbing;
(9) Diminution of pettiness and meanness, and the enhancement of dignity and nobility;
(10) Putting the faltering human intellect in contact with the infallible Supreme or Universal or Infinite Intelligence or Creative [Brahman].

5. Spirinomics, Managerial Philosophy, and Business Ethics

Vedantic spirinomics, managerial philosophy, and business ethics take distinct positions on many important issues.

(1) Intellect or reason does not decide or choose. Emotions or feelings—matters of the mind or heart, so to say—are responsible for making choices. Thus, mind-purification (*chittashuddhi*) is more important than intellect-sharpening. Murky and perverse aspects of the mind must be cleared out. "The most insistent operative principle and goal of human existence, resounding through all varieties of sacred books in India, is to aim at and strive for a 'pure mind.' . . . [For] if the primary driving power behind human actions—the mind or the heart—is not adequately groomed in wholesome ways, intellect or

reason will merely play into the hands of the murky, destructive driving force of perverse emotions."

(2) The subject is the cause, and the object the effect. In any social setting, including those related to economics and business, the collective subject—human beings as a group—has the primary responsibility for achieving any chosen goal. Systems and structures, which are created by the subject, thus belong to the object, and play only a secondary and supporting role. The quality of the subject, i.e., the purity of the mind, is of primary importance. "When turbulence or depravity is seen in the external workings of society or organizations, the root lies necessarily in the collective subjective domain concealed within these entities. In terms of management language, therefore, primary reliance on systems and structures to ameliorate organizational ill-health becomes questionable. . . . [T]he crux lay in the human, not in the systems or structural dimension." The subject must have the courage to take its responsibility.

(3) According to Vedantic spiritual tradition, personal claims to egocentric results (e.g., rewards) must not be the primary driving force for economic or business activities. This is undoubtedly a very daring claim for most Westerners. Of course, the first question is this, "Why should I work at all if not primarily propelled by the desire for some result or the other?" Or put differently, "How could one perform any intentional activity in a state of psychological vacuum?" The Vedantic answer is that the origin of all force, drive, motivation, energy and so on is in the Transcendental or Supreme Force (i.e., Brahman). "The force of ego is a pale, contaminated, and obscure shadow of this Force. So, by managing this ego, through mind-purification and work-as-worship, we can allow this . . . Universal Force to act through us." People ask the above question because they are misguided by conventional education that stresses that meaning comes to the mind from the work or from outside. The Vedantic viewpoint is that meaning flows from the mind to the work. To correct the problem in conventional education, respiritualization is necessary. A general line of argument for the Vedantic thesis of motivational force can be put in the following way:

a. The entire cosmos represents the Work of the Supreme or Cosmic Creative Consciousness. This is because there is no effect without a cause. This Master Worker is called Brahman.

b. The Master Worker works purposefully yet with a grand detachment from self-centered stimuli.

c. The result of this spontaneous capacity to work with detachment by this Master Worker is

inexhaustible creativity, coupled with perfect equanimity, i.e., *samatwa*.

d. But the universal problem with humans at work is inner turmoil or turbulence accompanying external work. This dissipates energy. Why does this happen? Because the pursuit of individual motives in work-life measures its success in terms of relative, competitive comparisons with others. Burnout symptoms thus become inevitable.

e. The very stuff of the ordinary ego is endless deficit-impulses, subtle and gross. This ego is separative and assumes that drawing everything to itself is the true mark of individuality. So the nexus of *yoga* (self-discipline) with the Universal Creative Consciousness remains barred, leading to errors and degeneration.

f. If this clogged "individual-Universal" channel for Creative Consciousness is to be restored to a state of free flow, the ego has to be cleansed. Hence the need to practice the art of working without primary concentration on fruits for the ego. This is called *nishkam karma* in Vedantic psycho-philosophy.

g. After the egocentric movement is gradually reduced, what should be replacing it as the principal energizer in human work? The rule is to cultivate the spirit of offering both the work and its fruits to the Master Worker.

h. The outer form and nature of the work then becomes a relatively less important factor.

i. This spirit of work-as-offering (or work-as-worship) is sacred and consistent with mind-purification which helps constructive and credible decision-making and choice.

j. Resolute practice of the *nishkam karma* orientation will gradually reveal to one's awareness the inner spirit-core which by definition is *poorna* or self-sufficient. It is an autonomous felicity, an independent bliss which no external transitory, relative, competitive reward can ever bring. Why should not the achievement of such felicity and bliss constitute the overarching achievement motivation for humans?

(4) Besides the spiritual general theory of "egoless" work, Vedantic tradition also offers a general moral theory for "ego-led" work. Such a theory is based on the law of cause-and-effect. A familiar way to describe the law is to cite the Biblical pronouncement: "You reap as you sow." Morally unacceptable acts will boomerang with retributive effects on their source. Vedantic thought offers this Cosmic Principle of equity (*ritam*)—the doctrine of *karma*—to rein the

wild horse of ego-led work. "An awakened internal awareness about the inescapable retributive effects of greedy, selfish, manipulative acts, sooner or later, one way or another, will serve as a salutary psychological braking device in man's slippery journey through ethico-moral traps."

(5) According to an Indian tradition, human personality comprises an outer, active, involved, and dynamic self and an inner, quiescent witness and silent self. The first part is called *prakriti*, the second *purusha*. This duality belongs to the *Samkhya* School, but *Brahman-shakti* of the Vedanta or *shiva-shakti* of the Tantra carry more or less the same import. The essence of this tradition is this: by attaining a proper understanding of what is *other* to consciousness—namely, nature—the individual conscious being finds himself and disengages from the world. Thus the individual recovers a blissful aloneness separate from nature and achieves an ecstatic transcendence *within* the world. The practice of the doctrine in human life is a crucial process for effective self-management. For example, the practice provides an effective solution to the problem we frequently encounter in anger-management. According to the doctrine, the feeling of anger does not belong to the inner self (*purusha*) but the outer self (*prakriti*). "We see that *anger always invades a person from outside*. But it is only the *prakriti* part of our personality which is subject to this external invasion. The eternally whole, imperturbable, desireless, witness *purusha* within does not quiver in the slightest. Therefore the real solution of the problem is to *step back* and summon within the awareness, the feel of this *purusha*." Being able to detach the inner self from all the worldly feelings and emotions and transcend the outer self is a necessary step toward Brahman. Even when one works in the midst of turbulent or hectic external circumstances, it is perfectly possible for one to stand back, observing in a detached equanimity.

(6) Vedantic tradition contains an exchange theory of generating the means of human sustenance and economic wealth. The theory is based on the unique relationship between the human and the cosmic that is found in the Vedantic classics. This relationship is provided by the concept of *yajnartha karma*, i.e., work done as sacrifice. "Sacrifice denotes the eternal, sacred exchange process imbedded in the human-cosmos nexus. Obviously this is a transcendent existential view where the finite and infinite meet." An example of a modern form of the exchange theory is M. K. Gandhi's idea of trusteeship in economic affairs. According to Gandhi, when an individual obtains more than his proportionate share, he becomes

a trustee of that portion for God's people. "Man's social and economic affairs should be rooted in and imbued with a comprehensive Cosmic awareness, including humble gratitude for all that is already available to him as sublime gifts from the Supreme. Greedy and arrogant appropriation of these gifts, therefore, whether in the context of man v. man or man v. Nature, are bad economics and also bad management." Gratitude and indebtedness are essential for the spiritual endeavor of any individual to realize and practice the principle of cosmic distributive justice. The systemic indebtedness includes indebtedness to supra-human powers (*deva rin*), to the sages and seers (*rishi rin*), to parents and ancestors (*pitri rin*), to humanity at large (*nri rin*), to countless members of sub-human species (*bhuta rin*). "Man's attitude towards his social existence, especially for the 'haves,' if inspired by the above indebtedness orientation, will naturally shift more towards duties, obligations, and sacrifice. Covetousness will decline, trusteeship will grow, and distributive justice will be more securely founded."

(7) How might Vedantic spiritual tradition deal with the topic of creativity and productivity? (i) Philosophers in Vedantic tradition are critical about the current culture of creativity, which can be characterized as consumerist-militarist. That culture is gradually formed in the past three centuries or so based on the near-invincible alliance of hedonomics and technology. The sad consequence of the consumerist-militarist culture, according to Vedantic tradition, is the state of "complex living, low thinking" and the neglect of spirituality. To restore the spiritual values, creativity in the future must be directed towards the "simple living, complex thinking" goal for humanity. Philosophers in Vedantic tradition believe that, although technology is a creative art, technology applied without heart produces a barren world and lifestyle. Secular decisions must be made in the light of spirituality. (ii) Philosophers in Vedantic tradition consider "spirit" the direct, intense, and original energy. A person of spirituality is an effective and wholesome "energy processor."

> It is spirit which precipitates into matter. The latter is subordinate to the former. Matter and machines made of it are only intermediaries. What they will or can yield is, therefore, a function of the strength of the directing, causal power of "spirit." Matter is undoubtedly a form of energy, "spirit" is the direct, intense, and original energy. So when by practice, a pure mind learns to concentrate within on the Self it tends to be-

come "spirit," the original, undiluted, uncontaminated energy. As this mind is then focused outwards upon any work, it is capable of an increasingly higher ratio of "output" to "input."

(8) Vedantic tradition contains important views on the issues of leadership and teamwork. (i) Along with necessary managerial skills, the credibility of a leader is of the greatest importance. According to Vedantic tradition, the credibility of a leader rests ultimately on the attribute of "impersonal love" springing from the Supreme Self. This is a spiritual and transcendental quality. The Supreme Self is universal for all individuals. The attribute of impersonal love goes beyond petty likes and dislikes, narrow preferences and abhorrence. (ii) Contemporary moral and political philosophy emphasizes self-centered individuality. This, according to Vedantic tradition, is responsible for the unfortunate features in our society such as arrogance and separateness. Healthy cooperation and teamwork thus suffer greatly. In Vedantic tradition it is the consciousness of unity rather than the awareness of individuality that is of primary importance to spiritual life. R. Tagore says, "consciousness of personality begins with the feeling of separateness from all, but has its culmination in the feeling of unity with all . . . the life in which the consciousness of unity is the primary and separateness the secondary factor, and therefore the personality is large and bright in truth—this is the soul of life." Consciousness or oneness is the very ground for cooperation and teamwork.

6. Concluding Observations

In concluding this essay, I make the following observations.

(1) "Man is primarily a spiritual entity which must realize unity with the Infinite, the Universal. So all his activities, [including those of economics and business,] must subserve this spiritual consummation."

(2) According to Aristotelian tradition, (active) virtues are constitutive of the human good. Vedantic tradition does not view virtues in the same way. Nonetheless, it claims that a liberated state of existence manifests virtues. A list of major business virtues in Vedantic tradition includes the following: spirituality, impersonal Love, simplicity, cooperativeness, indebtedness, humility, gratitude, straightforwardness, self-restraint, integrity, trustworthiness, cool-headedness.

(3) It is obvious that most Vedantic claims about economics and business run against the current accepted values. It is natural to raise the question: Is Vedantic heritage anti-productive? Some Indian philosophers insist that the answer is "No." For, otherwise, we would not be able to explain the "splendour of wealth, commercial prosperity, material appointment, social organization" India had reached before modern times.

Discussion and Reflection Questions

1. Liu contrasts the typically Western emphasis on "satisfaction of desire" with India's emphasis on the "attainment of spirituality." To what extent do you think this characterization is accurate?

2. According to the Indian tradition Liu discusses, the "secular and the material must be informed and invested with the sacred and the spiritual." What does he mean by this? How might this be implemented in business practices? What might be the effects of such an implementation?

3. How does Liu respond to the challenge that embracing Indian values would be counterproductive for business? Does he convince you?

Suggestions for Further Reading

Good places to continue exploring business ethics from various Eastern philosophical perspectives include: Stephen J. Gould, "The Buddhist Perspective on Business Ethics: Experiential Exercises for Exploration and Practice," *Journal of Business Ethics* 14 (1995): 63–70; Gregory K. Ornatowski, "Confucian Values, Japanese Economic Development, and the Creation of a Modern Japanese Business Ethic," in *International Business Ethics: Challenges and Approaches*, edited by Georges Enderle (Notre Dame, Ind.: University of Notre Dame Press, 1999); Daryl Koehn, "What Can Eastern Philosophy Teach Us About Business Ethics?" *Journal of Business Ethics* 19 (1999): 71–79; and Blaine McCormick, "Make Money, Not War: A Brief Critique of Sun Tzu's 'The Art of War'," *Journal of Business Ethics* 29 (2001): 285–286. Aristotelian perspectives on business ethics are articulated in Elaine Sternberg's *Just Business: Business Ethics in Action* (New York: Oxford University Press, 2000); Sherwin Klein, "An Aristotelian View of Theory and Practice in Business Ethics," *International Journal of Applied Philosophy* 12 (1998): 203–222; Mary Catherine Sommers, "Useful Friendships: A Foundation for Business Ethics," *Journal of Business Ethics* 16 (1997): 1453–1458. Manuel Velasquez and Neil Brady discuss a Natural Law perspective on business ethics in "Natural Law and Business Ethics," *Business Ethics Quarterly* 7 (1997): 83–107. William B. Carlin and Kelly C. Strong explicate classical Greek, Kantian, and utilitarian orientations to business ethics in "A Critique of Western Philosophical Ethics: Multidisciplinary Alternatives for Framing Ethical Dilemmas," *Journal of Business Ethics* 14 (1995): 387–396. For further work on Kantian ethical concepts in business ethics, see *Business Ethics: A Philosophical Reader*, edited by Thomas I. White (New York: Macmillan Publishers, 1993); Norman Bowie, *Business Ethics: A Kantian Perspective* (Malden, Mass: Blackwell Publishers, 1999); and Robert M. Martin, "The Inadequacy of a Deontological Analysis of Peer Relations in Organizations," *Journal of Business Ethics* 10 (1991): 133–139.

InfoTrac

business ethics, corporate social responsibility, "business intelligence, moral and ethical aspects", egotism, "diversity and business"

Chapter 16

The Environment

Introduction: The Value of Nature

By now nearly everyone is aware that we face a serious environmental problem of unprecedented immensity. Ozone depletion, deforestation, desertification, pollution, and the destruction of species are issues that are constantly in the news. Most reflective people feel some degree of concern about the fate of the natural world, at least insofar as its integrity affects human beings. But it is often difficult to know what we, as individuals, can do about it. It is also difficult to know what we *should* do about it. Before we can respond to the environmental crisis in the right way, we need to have some sense of what *is* the right way. Although virtually everyone agrees that we should do something about it, just what this something is is a matter of intense controversy and debate, a debate that often centers on recognizably ethical issues. What sort of value does nature have? Do natural entities deserve respect? Do natural entities have rights? How are we to balance concern for the integrity of the environment with legitimate human needs and desires?

The growing recognition of the ethical dimensions to the environmental crisis has spawned a new field of inquiry: environmental ethics. Environmental ethics addresses all the questions posed above and more. It is concerned more broadly with our relationship to nature, which may include aesthetic, religious, scientific, economic, and political issues as well. Given the diversity of issues involved, it is not surprising that there has been a great deal of disagreement over the right way to answer the questions posed above, and even whether these are the right questions to ask.

Besides having strong ethical and interdisciplinary dimensions, the environmental crisis and attempts to create an acceptable environmental ethic are by their very nature global in scope. Given the interconnectedness of the systems constituting the earth's air, land, and water, practices in one part of the world affect everyone on earth.

Given the global nature of the problem and its importance for the fate of the earth and humanity, it would be surprising if different cultures did not have something valuable to contribute to the solution of these problems. The reading selections that follow represent a variety of different perspectives on the ethics of the environment from different ethical traditions, West and East, as well as different points of view within each tradition. Some of the positions represented point in opposite directions. It would be hard to imagine two positions more different than those of Paul W. Taylor (defending a Kantian-like argument) and William Baxter (using a more utilitarian approach). On the other hand, the views of Lily de Silva (a Buddhist perspective) and Mary Evelyn Tucker (a Taoist perspective), coming from distinct moral traditions, are nonetheless remarkably congruent.

It would be a mistake to assume that each moral tradition provides exactly one unambiguous perspective on environmental issues. For some moral traditions it can only be conjectured what position would be adopted concerning a particular environmental issue. For example, as we saw in Part III, Confucianism is, above all else, an ethics of humanity. The nonhuman world possesses no special dignity that must be vouchsafed. This emphasis would lead Confucians to take a more human-centered perspective on environmental problems. On the other hand, a concern for the future welfare of humanity (the ultimate realization of the Confucian ideal of heaven) might make resolving the environmental crisis a top priority. Moral traditions are typically rich enough to permit several different perspectives to be justifiably grounded in them. This is not, of course, to say that all perspectives are equally plausible. You will need to decide for yourself which positions you find most persuasive, and how these positions relate to the moral traditions from which they take their point of departure.

Paul W. Taylor, The Ethics of Respect for Nature

Paul W. Taylor argues for the position that we should not think of human beings as inherently superior to other living things. Rather, we should view each organism as a "teleological center of life" engaged in the pursuit of its own good. Out of this fundamental "biocentric" perspective, he develops a distinctive view of the duties humans have toward nature and the basic principles that ought to govern our interactions with nature. The result is a shift of emphasis from what is good for human beings to a concern for equitable dealings between human beings and the rest of the natural world. Taylor challenges us to rethink our natural bias toward human beings, and in the process to reconsider our obligations to the rest of the natural world.

Reading Questions

1. Taylor contrasts a "life-centered" with an "anthropocentric" view of environmental ethics. What is this distinction? Why is it important for his argument?

2. Taylor explicitly compares his ethical theory to that of Kant. In what ways is Taylor's view like that of Kant? In what important respect is it different?

3. Taylor proposes what he calls an "attitude of respect for nature." What are the essential components of this attitude?

4. Taylor launches an extended attack on the notion of human superiority. Why is doing so essential to his project?

The Ethics of Respect for Nature

PAUL W. TAYLOR

I. Human-Centered and Life-Centered Systems of Environmental Ethics

In this paper I show how the taking of a certain ultimate moral attitude toward nature, which I call "respect for nature," has a central place in the foundations of a life-centered system of environmental ethics. I hold that a set of moral norms (both standards of character and rules of conduct) governing human treatment of the natural world is a rationally grounded set if and only if, first, commitment to those norms is a practical entailment of adopting the attitude of respect for nature as an ultimate moral attitude, and second, the adopting of that attitude on the part of all rational agents can itself be justified. When the basic characteristics of the attitude of respect for nature are made clear, it will be seen that a life-centered system of environmental ethics need not be holistic or organic in its conception of the kinds of entities that are deemed the appropriate objects of moral concern and consideration. Nor does such a system require that the concepts of ecological homeostasis, equilibrium, and integrity provide us with normative principles from which could be derived (with the addition of factual knowledge) our obligations with regard to natural ecosystems. The "balance of nature" is not itself a moral norm, however important may be the role it plays in our general outlook on the natural world that underlies the attitude of respect for nature. I argue that finally it is the good (well-being, welfare) of individual organisms, considered as entities having inherent worth, that determines our moral relations with the Earth's wild communities of life.

In designating the theory to be set forth as life-centered, I intend to contrast it with all anthropocentric views. According to the latter, human actions affecting the natural environment and its nonhuman inhabitants are right (or wrong) by either of two criteria: they have consequences which are favorable (or unfavorable) to human well-being, or they are consistent (or inconsistent) with the system of norms that protect and implement human rights. From this human-centered standpoint it is to humans and only to humans that all duties are ultimately owed. We may have responsibilities *with regard to* the natural ecosystems and biotic communities of our planet, but these responsibilities are in every case based on the contingent fact that our treatment of those ecosystems and communities of life can further the realization of human values and/or human rights. We have no obligation to promote or protect the good of nonhuman living things, independently of this contingent fact.

A life-centered system of environmental ethics is opposed to human-centered ones precisely on this point. From the perspective of a life-centered theory, we have prima facie moral obligations that are owed to wild plants and animals themselves as members of the Earth's biotic community. We are morally bound (other things being equal) to protect or promote their good for *their* sake. Our duties to respect the integrity of natural ecosystems, to preserve endangered species, and to avoid environmental pollution stem from the fact that these are ways in which we can help make it possible for wild species populations to achieve and maintain a healthy existence in a natural state. Such obligations are due those living things out of recognition of their inherent worth. They are entirely additional to and independent of the obligations we owe to our fellow humans. Although many of the actions that fulfill one set of obligations will also fulfill the other, two different grounds of obligation are involved. Their well-being, as well as human well-being, is something to be realized as an end in itself.

If we were to accept a life-centered theory of environmental ethics, a profound reordering of our moral universe would take place. We would begin to look at the whole of the Earth's biosphere in a new light. Our duties with respect to the "world" of nature would be seen as making prima facie claims upon us to be balanced against our duties with respect to the "world" of human civilization. We could no longer simply

Paul W. Taylor, "The Ethics of Respect for Nature," Environmental Ethics, vol. 3, no. 3 (Fall 1981), pp. 197–218. Reprinted by permission of the author and Environmental Ethics.

take the human point of view and consider the effects of our actions exclusively from the perspective of our own good.

II. The Good of a Being and the Concept of Inherent Worth

What would justify acceptance of a life-centered system of ethical principles? In order to answer this it is first necessary to make clear the fundamental moral attitude that underlies and makes intelligible the commitment to live by such a system. It is then necessary to examine the considerations that would justify any rational agent's adopting that moral attitude.

Two concepts are essential to the taking of a moral attitude of the sort in question. A being which does not "have" these concepts, that is, which is unable to grasp their meaning and conditions of applicability, cannot be said to have the attitude as part of its moral outlook. These concepts are, first, that of the good (well-being, welfare) of a living thing, and second, the idea of an entity possessing inherent worth. I examine each concept in turn.

(1) Every organism, species population, and community of life has a good of its own which moral agents can intentionally further or damage by their actions. To say that an entity has a good of its own is simply to say that, without reference to any *other* entity, it can be benefited or harmed. One can act in its overall interest or contrary to its overall interest, and environmental conditions can be good for it (advantageous to it) or bad for it (disadvantageous to it). What is good for an entity is what "does it good" in the sense of enhancing or preserving its life and well-being. What is bad for an entity is something that is detrimental to its life and well-being.

We can think of the good of an individual nonhuman organism as consisting in the full development of its biological powers. Its good is realized to the extent that it is strong and healthy. It possesses whatever capacities it needs for successfully coping with its environment and so preserving its existence throughout the various stages of the normal life cycle of its species. The good of a population or community of such individuals consists in the population or community maintaining itself from generation to generation as a coherent system of genetically and ecologically related organisms whose average good is at an optimum level for the given environment. (Here *average good* means that the degree of realization of the good of *individual organisms* in the population or community is, on average, greater than would be the case under any other ecologically functioning order

of interrelations among those species populations in the given ecosystem.)

The idea of a being having a good of its own, as I understand it, does not entail that the being must have interests or take an interest in what affects its life for better or for worse. We can act in a being's interest or contrary to its interest without its being interested in what we are doing to it in the sense of wanting or not wanting us to do it. It may, indeed, be wholly unaware that favorable and unfavorable events are taking place in its life. I take it that trees, for example, have no knowledge or desires or feelings. Yet it is undoubtedly the case that trees can be harmed or benefited by our actions. We can crush their roots by running a bulldozer too close to them. We can see to it that they get adequate nourishment and moisture by fertilizing and watering the soil around them. Thus we can help or hinder them in the realization of their good. It is the good of trees themselves that is thereby affected. We can similarly act so as to further the good of an entire tree population of a certain species (say, all the redwood trees in a California valley) or the good of a whole community of plant life in a given wilderness area, just as we can do harm to such a population or community. . . .

(2) The second concept essential to the moral attitude of respect for nature is the idea of inherent worth. We take that attitude toward wild living things (individuals, species populations, or whole biotic communities) when and only when we regard them as entities possessing inherent worth. Indeed, it is only because they are conceived in this way that moral agents can think of themselves as having validly binding duties, obligations, and responsibilities that are *owed* to them as their *due*. I am not at this juncture arguing why they *should* be so regarded; I consider it at length below. But so regarding them is a presupposition of our taking the attitude of respect toward them and accordingly understanding ourselves as bearing certain moral relations to them. This can be shown as follows:

What does it mean to regard an entity that has a good of its own as possessing inherent worth? Two general principles are involved: the principle of moral consideration and the principle of intrinsic value.

According to the principle of moral consideration, wild living things are deserving of the concern and consideration of all moral agents simply in virtue of their being members of the Earth's community of life. From the moral point of view their good must be taken into account whenever it is affected for better or worse by the conduct of rational agents. This holds no matter what species the creature belongs to. The good of each is to be accorded some value and so acknowledged as having some weight in the deliberations of all rational agents. Of course, it may be necessary for such agents to act in ways contrary to the good of this or that particular organism or group of organisms in order to further the good of others, including the good of humans. But the principle of moral consideration prescribes that, with respect to each being an entity having its own good, every individual is deserving of consideration.

The principle of intrinsic value states that, regardless of what kind of entity it is in other respects, if it is a member of the Earth's community of life, the realization of its good is something *intrinsically* valuable. This means that its good is prima facie worthy of being preserved or promoted as an end in itself and for the sake of the entity whose good it is. Insofar as we regard any organism, species population, or life community as an entity having inherent worth, we believe that it must never be treated as if it were a mere object or thing whose entire value lies in being instrumental to the good of some other entity. The well-being of each is judged to have value in and of itself.

Combining these two principles, we can now define what it means for a living thing or group of living things to possess inherent worth. To say that it possesses inherent worth is to say that its good is deserving of the concern and consideration of all moral agents, and that the realization of its good has intrinsic value, to be pursued as an end in itself and for the sake of the entity whose good it is.

The duties owed to wild organisms, species populations, and communities of life in the Earth's natural ecosystems are grounded on their inherent worth. When rational, autonomous agents regard such entities as possessing inherent worth, they place intrinsic value on the realization of their good and so hold themselves responsible for performing actions that will have this effect and for refraining from actions having the contrary effect.

III. The Attitude of Respect for Nature

Why should moral agents regard wild living things in the natural world as possessing inherent worth? To answer this question we must first take into account the fact that, when rational, autonomous agents subscribe to the principles of moral consideration and intrinsic value and so conceive of wild living things as having that kind of worth, such agents are *adopting a certain ultimate moral attitude toward the natural world.* This is the attitude I call "respect for nature." It paral-

lels the attitude of respect for persons in human ethics. When we adopt the attitude of respect for persons as the proper (fitting, appropriate) attitude to take toward all persons as persons, we consider the fulfillment of the basic interests of each individual to have intrinsic value. We thereby make a moral commitment to live a certain kind of life in relation to other persons. We place ourselves under the direction of a system of standards and rules that we consider validly binding on all moral agents as such.

Similarly, when we adopt the attitude of respect for nature as an ultimate moral attitude we make a commitment to live by certain normative principles. These principles constitute the rules of conduct and standards of character that are to govern our treatment of the natural world. This is, first, an *ultimate* commitment because it is not derived from any higher norm. The attitude of respect for nature is not grounded on some other, more general, or more fundamental attitude. It sets the total framework for our responsibilities toward the natural world. It can be justified, as I show below, but its justification cannot consist in referring to a more general attitude or a more basic normative principle.

Second, the commitment is a *moral* one because it is understood to be a disinterested matter of principle. It is this feature that distinguishes the attitude of respect for nature from the set of feelings and dispositions that comprise the love of nature. The latter stems from one's personal interest in and response to the natural world. Like the affectionate feelings we have toward certain individual human beings, one's love of nature is nothing more than the particular way one feels about the natural environment and its wild inhabitants. And just as our love for an individual person differs from our respect for all persons as such (whether we happen to love them or not), so love of nature differs from respect for nature. Respect for nature is an attitude we believe all moral agents ought to have simply as moral agents, regardless of whether or not they also love nature. Indeed, we have not truly taken the attitude of respect for nature ourselves unless we believe this. To put it in a Kantian way, to adopt the attitude of respect for nature is to take a stance that one wills it to be a universal law for all rational beings. It is to hold that stance categorically, as being validly applicable to every moral agent without exception, irrespective of whatever personal feelings toward nature such an agent might have or might lack.

Although the attitude of respect for nature is in this sense a disinterested and universalizable attitude, anyone who does adopt it has certain steady, more or less permanent dispositions. These dispositions, which are themselves to be considered disinterested and universalizable, comprise three interlocking sets: dispositions to seek certain ends, dispositions to carry on one's practical reasoning and deliberation in a certain way, and dispositions to have certain feelings. We may accordingly analyze the attitude of respect for nature into the following components. (a) The disposition to aim at, and to take steps to bring about, as final and disinterested ends, the promoting and protecting of the good of organisms, species populations, and life communities in natural ecosystems. (These ends are "final" in not being pursued as means to further ends. They are "disinterested" in being independent of the self-interest of the agent.) (b) The disposition to consider actions that tend to realize those ends to be prima facie obligatory *because* they have that tendency. (c) The disposition to experience positive and negative feelings toward states of affairs in the world *because* they are favorable or unfavorable to the good of organisms, species populations, and life communities in natural ecosystems.

The logical connection between the attitude of respect for nature and the duties of a life-centered system of environmental ethics can now be made clear. Insofar as one sincerely takes that attitude and so has the three sets of dispositions, one will at the same time be disposed to comply with certain rules of duty (such as nonmaleficence and noninterference) and with standards of character (such as fairness and benevolence) that determine the obligations and virtues of moral agents with regard to the Earth's wild living things. We can say that the actions one performs and the character traits one develops in fulfilling these moral requirements are the way one *expresses* or *embodies* the attitude in one's conduct and character. In his famous essay, "Justice as Fairness," John Rawls describes the rules of the duties of human morality (such as fidelity, gratitude, honesty, and justice) as "forms of conduct in which recognition of others as persons is manifested." I hold that the rules of duty governing our treatment of the natural world and its inhabitants are forms of conduct in which the attitude of respect for nature is manifested.

IV. The Justifiability of the Attitude of Respect for Nature

I return to the question posed earlier, which has not yet been answered: why *should* moral agents regard wild living things as possessing inherent worth? I now argue that the only way we can answer this question is by showing how adopting the attitude of respect for nature is justified for all moral agents. Let us suppose that we were able to establish that there are good reasons for adopting the attitude, reasons which are intersubjectively valid for every rational agent. If there are such reasons, they would justify anyone's having the three sets of dispositions mentioned above as constituting what it means to have the attitude. Since these include the disposition to promote or protect the good of wild living things as a disinterested and ultimate end, as well as the disposition to perform actions for the reason that they tend to realize that end, we see that such dispositions commit a person to the principles of moral consideration and intrinsic value. To be disposed to further, as an end in itself, the good of any entity in nature just because it is that kind of entity, is to be disposed to give consideration to *every* such entity and to place intrinsic value on the realization of its good. Insofar as we subscribe to these two principles we regard living things as possessing inherent worth. Subscribing to the principles is what it *means* to so regard them. To justify the attitude of respect for nature, then, is to justify commitment to these principles and thereby to justify regarding wild creatures as possessing inherent worth.

We must keep in mind that inherent worth is not some mysterious sort of objective property belonging to living things that can be discovered by empirical observation or scientific investigation. To ascribe inherent worth to an entity is not to describe it by citing some feature discernible by sense perception or inferable by inductive reasoning. Nor is there a logically necessary connection between the concept of a being having a good of its own and the concept of inherent worth. We do not contradict ourselves by asserting that an entity that has a good of its own lacks inherent worth. In order to show that such an entity "has" inherent worth we must give good reasons for ascribing that kind of value to it (placing that kind of value upon it, conceiving of it to be valuable in that way). Although it is humans (persons, valuers) who must do the valuing, for the ethics of respect for nature, the value so ascribed is not a human value. That is to say, it is not a value derived from considerations regarding human well-being or human rights. It is a value that is ascribed to nonhuman animals and plants themselves, independently of their relationship to what humans judge to be conducive to their own good.

Whatever reasons, then, justify our taking the attitude of respect for nature as defined above are also reasons that show why we *should* regard the living things of the natural world as possessing inherent worth. We saw earlier that, since the attitude is an ultimate one, it cannot be derived from a more fundamental attitude nor shown to be a special case of a more general one. On what sort of grounds, then, can it be established?

The attitude we take toward living things in the natural world depends on the way we look at them, on what kind of beings we conceive them to be, and on how we understand the relations we bear to them. Underlying and supporting our attitude is a certain *belief system* that constitutes a particular worldview or outlook on nature and the place of human life in it. To give good reasons for adopting the attitude of respect for nature, then, we must first articulate the belief system which underlies and supports that attitude. If it appears that the belief system is internally coherent and well-ordered, and if, as far as we can now tell, it is consistent with all known scientific truths relevant to our knowledge of the object of the attitude (which in this case includes the whole set of the Earth's natural ecosystems and their communities of life), then there remains the task of indicating why scientifically informed and rational thinkers with a developed capacity of reality awareness can find it acceptable as a way of conceiving of the natural world and our place in it. To the extent we can do this we provide at least a reasonable argument for accepting the belief system and the ultimate moral attitude it supports.

I do not hold that such a belief system can be *proven* to be true, either inductively or deductively. As we shall see, not all of its components can be stated in the form of empirically verifiable propositions. Nor is its internal order governed by purely logical relationships. But the system as a whole, I contend, constitutes a coherent, unified, and rationally acceptable "picture" or "map" of a total world. By examining each of its main components and seeing how they fit together, we obtain a scientifically informed and well-ordered conception of nature and the place of humans in it.

This belief system underlying the attitude of respect for nature I call (for want of a better name) "the biocentric outlook on nature." Since it is not wholly analyzable into empirically confirmable assertions, it should not be thought of as simply a compendium of the biological sciences concerning our planet's ecosystem. It might best be described as a philosophical worldview, to distinguish it from a scientific theory or explanatory system. However, one of its major tenets is the great lesson we have learned from the science of ecology: the interdependence of all living things in an organically unified order whose balance and stability are necessary conditions for the realization of the good of its constituent biotic communities....

V. The Biocentric Outlook on Nature

The biocentric outlook on nature has four main components. (1) Humans are thought of as members of the Earth's community of life, holding that membership on the same terms as apply to all the nonhuman members. (2) The Earth's natural ecosystems as a totality are seen as a complex web of interconnected elements, with the sound biological functioning of each being dependent on the sound biological functioning of the others. (This is the component referred to above as the great lesson that the science of ecology has taught us.) (3) Each individual organism is conceived of as a teleological center of life pursuing its own good in its own way. (4) Whether we are concerned with standards of merit or with the concept of inherent worth, the claim that humans by their very nature are superior to other species is a groundless claim and, in the light of elements (1), (2), and (3) above, must be rejected as nothing more than an irrational bias in our own favor.

The conjunction of these four ideas constitutes the biocentric outlook on nature. In the remainder of this paper I give a brief account of the first three components, followed by a more detailed analysis of the fourth. I then conclude by indicating how this outlook provides a way of justifying the attitude of respect for nature.

VI. Humans as Members of the Earth's Community of Life

We share with other species a common relationship to the Earth. In accepting the biocentric outlook we take the fact of our being an animal species to be a fundamental feature of our existence. We consider it an essential aspect of "the human condition." We do not deny the differences between ourselves and other species, but we keep in the forefront of our consciousness the fact that in relation to our planet's natural ecosystems we are but one species population among many. Thus we acknowledge our origin in the very same evolutionary process that gave rise to all other species and we recognize ourselves to be confronted with similar environmental challenges to those that confront them. The laws of genetics, of natural selection, and of adaptation apply equally to all of us as biological creatures. In this light we consider ourselves as one with them, not set apart from them. We, as well as they, must face certain basic conditions of existence that impose requirements on us for our survival and well-being. Each animal and plant is like us in having a good of its own. Although our human good (what is of true value in human life, including the exercise of individual autonomy in choosing our own particular value systems) is not like the good of a nonhuman animal or plant; it can no more be realized than their good can without the biological necessities for survival and physical health. . . .

VII. The Natural World as an Organic System

To accept the biocentric outlook and regard ourselves and our place in the world from its perspective is to see the whole natural order of the Earth's biosphere as a complex but unified web of interconnected organisms, objects, and events. The ecological relationships between any community of living things and their environment form an organic whole of functionally interdependent parts. Each ecosystem is a small universe itself in which the interactions of its various species populations comprise an intricately woven network of cause-effect relations. Such dynamic but at the same time relatively stable structures as food chains, predator-prey relations, and plant succession in a forest are self-regulating, energy-recycling mechanisms that preserve the equilibrium of the whole.

As far as the well-being of wild animals and plants is concerned, this ecological equilibrium must not be destroyed. The same holds true of the well-being of humans. When one views the realm of nature from the perspective of the biocentric outlook, one never forgets that in the long run the integrity of the entire biosphere of our planet is essential to the realization of the good of its constituent communities of life, both human and nonhuman. . . .

VIII. Individual Organisms as Teleological Centers of Life

As our knowledge of living things increases, as we come to a deeper understanding of their life cycles, their interactions with other organisms, and the manifold ways in which they adjust to the environment, we become more fully aware of how each of them is carrying out its biological functions according to the laws of its species-specific nature. But besides this, our increasing knowledge and understanding also develop in us a sharpened awareness of the uniqueness of each individual organism. Scientists who have made careful studies of particular plants and animals, whether in the field or in laboratories, have often acquired a knowledge of their subjects as identifiable individuals. Close observation over extended periods of time has led them to an appreciation of the unique "personalities" of their subjects. Sometimes a scientist may come to take a special interest in a particular animal or plant, all the while remaining strictly objective in the gathering and recording of data. Nonscientists may likewise experience this development of interest when, as amateur naturalists, they make accurate observations over sustained periods of close acquaintance with an individual organism. As one becomes more and more familiar with the organism and its behavior, one becomes fully sensitive to the particular way it is living out its life cycle. One may become fascinated by it and even experience some involvement with its good and bad fortunes (that is, with the occurrence of environmental conditions favorable or unfavorable to the realization of its good). The organism comes to mean something to one as a unique, irreplaceable individual. The final culmination of this process is the achievement of a genuine understanding of its point of view and, with that understanding, an ability to "take" that point of view. *Conceiving of it as a center of life, one is able to look at the world from its perspective.*

This development from objective knowledge to the recognition of individuality, and from the recognition of individuality to full awareness of an organism's standpoint, is a process of heightening our consciousness of what it means to be an individual living thing. We grasp the particularity of the organism as a teleological center of life, striving to preserve itself and to realize its own good in its own unique way. . . .

When considered from an ethical point of view, a teleological center of life is an entity whose "world" can be viewed from the perspective of *its* life. In looking at the world from that perspective we recognize objects and events occurring in its life as being beneficent, maleficent, or indifferent. The first are occurrences which increase its powers to preserve its existence and realize its good. The second decrease or destroy those powers. The third have neither of these effects on the entity. With regard to our human role as moral agents, we can conceive of a teleological center of life as a being whose standpoint we can take in making judgments about what events in the world are good or evil, desirable or undesirable. In making those judgments it is what promotes or protects the being's own good, not what benefits moral agents themselves, that sets the standard of evaluation. Such judgments can be made about anything that happens to the entity which is favorable or unfavorable in relation to its good. As was pointed out earlier, the entity itself need not have any (conscious) *interest* in what is happening to it for such judgments to be meaningful and true.

It is precisely judgments of this sort that we are disposed to make when we take the attitude of respect for nature. In adopting that attitude those judgments are given weight as reasons for action in our practical deliberation. They become morally relevant facts in the guidance of our conduct.

IX. The Denial of Human Superiority

This fourth component of the biocentric outlook on nature is the single most important idea in establishing the justifiability of the attitude of respect for nature. Its central role is due to the special relationship it bears to the first three components of the outlook. This relationship will be brought out after the concept of human superiority is examined and analyzed.

In what sense are humans alleged to be superior to other animals? We are different from them in having certain capacities that they lack. But why should these capacities be a mark of superiority? From what point of view are they judged to be signs of superiority and what sense of superiority is meant? After all, various nonhuman species have capacities that humans lack. There is the speed of a cheetah, the vision of an eagle, the agility of a monkey. Why should not these be taken as signs of *their* superiority over humans?

One answer that comes immediately to mind is that these capacities are not as *valuable* as the human capacities that are claimed to make us superior. Such uniquely human characteristics as rational thought, aesthetic creativity, autonomy and self-determination, and moral freedom, it might be held, have a higher value than the capacities found in other species. Yet we must ask: valuable to whom, and on what grounds?

The human characteristics mentioned are all valuable to humans. They are essential to the preservation and enrichment of our civilization and culture. Clearly it is from the human standpoint that they are being judged to be desirable and good. It is not difficult here to recognize a begging of the question. Humans are claiming human superiority from a strictly human point of view, that is, from a point of view in which the good of humans is taken as the standard of judgment. All we need to do is to look at the capacities of nonhuman animals (or plants, for that matter) from the standpoint of *their* good to find a contrary judgment of superiority. The speed of the cheetah, for example, is a sign of its superiority to humans when considered from the standpoint of the good of its species. If it were as slow a runner as a human, it would not be able to survive. And so for all the other abilities of nonhumans which further their good but which are lacking in humans. In each case the claim to human superiority would be rejected from a nonhuman standpoint. . . .

The question that naturally arises at this juncture is: why should standards that are based on human values be assumed to be the only valid criteria of merit and hence the only true signs of superiority? This question is especially pressing when humans are being judged superior in merit to nonhumans. It is true that a human being may be a better mathematician than a monkey, but the monkey may be a better tree climber than a human being. If we humans value mathematics more than tree climbing, that is because our conception of civilized life makes the development of mathematical ability more desirable than the ability to climb trees. But is it not unreasonable to judge nonhumans by the values of human civilization, rather than by values connected with what it is for a member of *that* species to live a good life? If all living things have a good of their own, it at least makes sense to judge the merits of nonhumans by standards derived from *their* good. To use only standards based on human values is already to commit oneself to holding that humans are superior to nonhumans, which is the point in question. . . .

Up to this point I have been interpreting the claim that humans are superior to other living things as a grading or ranking judgment regarding their comparative merits. There is, however, another way of understanding the idea of human superiority. According to this interpretation, humans are superior to nonhumans not as regards their merits but as regards their inherent worth. Thus the claim of human superiority is to be understood as asserting that all humans, simply in virtue of their humanity, have *a greater inherent worth* than other living things. . . .

That the claim is nothing more than a deep-seated prejudice is brought home to us when we look at our relation to other species in the light of the first three elements of the biocentric outlook. Those elements taken conjointly give us a certain overall view of the natural world and of the place of humans in it. When we take this view we come to understand other living things, their environmental conditions, and their ecological relationships in such a way as to awake in us a deep sense of our kinship with them as fellow members of the Earth's community of life. Humans and nonhumans alike are viewed together as integral parts of one unified whole in which all living things are functionally interrelated. Finally, when our awareness focuses on the individual lives of plants and animals, each is seen to share with us the characteristic of being a teleological center of life striving to realize its own good in its own unique way.

As this entire belief system becomes part of the conceptual framework through which we understand and perceive the world, we come to see ourselves as bearing a certain moral relation to nonhuman forms of life. Our ethical role in nature takes on a new significance. We begin to look at other species as we look at ourselves, seeing them as beings which have a good they are striving to realize just as we have a good we are striving to realize. We accordingly develop the disposition to view the world from the standpoint of their good as well as from the standpoint of our own good. Now if the groundlessness of the claim that humans are inherently superior to other species were brought clearly before our minds, we would not remain intellectually neutral toward that claim but would reject it as being fundamentally at variance with our total world outlook. In the absence of any good reasons for holding it, the assertion of human superiority would then appear simply as the expression of an irrational and self-serving prejudice that favors one particular species over several million others.

Rejecting the notion of human superiority entails its positive counterpart: the doctrine of species impartiality. One who accepts that doctrine regards all living things as possessing inherent worth—the *same* inherent worth, since no one species has been shown to be either "higher" or "lower" than any other. Now we saw earlier that, insofar as one thinks of a living thing as possessing inherent worth, one considers it

to be the appropriate object of the attitude of respect and believes that attitude to be the only fitting or suitable one for all moral agents to take toward it.

Here, then, is the key to understanding how the attitude of respect is rooted in the biocentric outlook on nature. The basic connection is made through the denial of human superiority. Once we reject the claim that humans are superior either in merit or in worth to other living things, we are ready to adopt the attitude of respect. The denial of human superiority is itself the result of taking the perspective on nature built into the first three elements of the biocentric outlook.

Now the first three elements of the biocentric outlook, it seems clear, would be found acceptable to any rational and scientifically informed thinker who is fully "open" to the reality of the lives of nonhuman organisms. Without denying our distinctively human characteristics, such a thinker can acknowledge the fundamental respects in which we are members of the Earth's community of life and in which the biological conditions necessary for the realization of our human values are inextricably linked with the whole system of nature. In addition, the conception of individual living things as teleological centers of life simply articulates how a scientifically informed thinker comes to understand them as the result of increasingly careful and detailed observations. Thus, the biocentric outlook recommends itself as an acceptable system of concepts and beliefs to anyone who is clear-minded, unbiased, and factually enlightened, and who has a developed capacity of reality awareness with regard to the lives of individual organisms. This, I submit, is as good a reason for making the moral commitment involved in adopting the attitude of respect for nature as any theory of environmental ethics could possibly have. . . .

Discussion and Reflection Questions

1. What sort of difference would it make if we adopted Taylor's "biocentric outlook on nature"? How would our thinking about, and our actions toward, nature have to change? What might be some of the obstacles to this transformation of outlook? Assuming that we should try, how could they be overcome?

2. Taylor speaks of "respect for nature" as an attitude that we should adopt. What reasons has he given for adopting this attitude? What sorts of reasons can one give for adopting a particular attitude?

3. Taylor writes that "the claim that humans by their very nature are superior to other species is a groundless claim and . . . must be rejected as nothing more than an irrational bias in our own favor." How does this thesis help to support his life-centered ethics of the environment? Do you think that this is a defensible claim?

4. Suppose that a terrorist kidnapped Taylor's daughter and informed him that he intended to kill her but would be willing to kill a cockroach instead if Taylor could con-

vince him, consistent with his (i.e., Taylor's) own principles, to spare his daughter and kill the cockroach. Could Taylor, consistent with his stated principles, prevent the terrorist from killing his daughter? How does this question bear on the acceptability of Taylor's view?

William F. Baxter, A "Good" Environment: Just One of the Set of Human Objectives

In the following reading, taken from his book *People or Penguins: The Case for Optimal Pollution*, William F. Baxter defends a position just the opposite of that advanced by Taylor in the previous selection. Baxter endorses the anthropocentric viewpoint that Taylor wanted to reject and consequently draws conclusions quite different from those Taylor arrived at. He proposes four criteria by which we can judge proposals for dealing with pollution. These criteria are, as he says, "oriented to people, not penguins." Penguins, and other natural entities, are valuable only insofar as people value them and hence have no "inherent value" that must be taken into consideration. Baxter's position is likely to upset many environmentalists. The challenge, however, is to adequately address the claims and arguments he develops.

Reading Questions

1. Baxter explicitly makes human interests the center of his environmental viewpoint. Why? In what sense are each of his four criteria "human-centered"?

2. According to Baxter, "Questions of *ought* are unique to the human mind and world—they are meaningless as applied to a nonhuman situation." What does he mean by this? Why is this claim important for defending his position?

3. In what sense is Baxter proposing a kind of economic environmental ethic? How do economic concerns inform his proposal? How does the strategy of cost-benefit analysis figure in his account?

4. Baxter is willing to admit frankly that his human-centered point of view is "selfish." Why is he unconcerned with this feature of his view?

A "Good" Environment: Just One of the Set of Human Objectives

WILLIAM F. BAXTER

I START WITH the modest proposition that, in dealing with pollution, or indeed with any problem, it is helpful to know what one is attempting to accomplish. Agreement on how and whether to pursue a particular objective, such as pollution control, is not possible unless some more general objective has been identified and stated with reasonable precision. We talk loosely of having clean air and clean water, of

William F. Baxter, "A 'Good' Environment: Just One of the Set of Human Objectives," in People or Penguins: The Case for Optimal Pollution *(New York: Columbia University Press, 1974), pp. 1–13. Reprinted by permission of the publisher.*

preserving our wilderness areas, and so forth. But none of these is a sufficiently general objective: each is more accurately viewed as a means rather than as an end.

With regard to clean air, for example, one may ask, "how clean?" and "what does clean mean?" It is even reasonable to ask, "why have clean air?" Each of these questions is an implicit demand that a more general community goal be stated—a goal sufficiently general in its scope and enjoying sufficiently general assent among the community of actors that such "why" questions no longer seem admissible with respect to that goal.

If, for example, one states as a goal the proposition that "every person should be free to do whatever he wishes in contexts where his actions do not interfere with the interests of other human beings," the speaker is unlikely to be met with a response of "why." The goal may be criticized as uncertain in its implications or difficult to implement, but it is so basic a tenet of our civilization—it reflects a cultural value so broadly shared, at least in the abstract—that the question of "why" is seen as impertinent or imponderable or both.

I do not mean to suggest that everyone would agree with the "spheres of freedom" objective just stated. Still less do I mean to suggest that a society could subscribe to four or five such general objectives that would be adequate in their coverage to serve as testing criteria by which all other disagreements might be measured. One difficulty in the attempt to construct such a list is that each new goal added will conflict, in certain applications, with each prior goal listed; and thus each goal serves as a limited qualification on prior goals.

Without any expectation of obtaining unanimous consent to them, let me set forth four goals that I generally use as ultimate testing criteria in attempting to frame solutions to problems of human organization. My position regarding pollution stems from these four criteria. If the criteria appeal to you and any part of what appears hereafter does not, our disagreement will have a helpful focus; which of us is correct, analytically, in supposing that his position on pollution would better serve these general goals. If the criteria do not seem acceptable to you, then it is to be expected that our more particular judgments will differ, and the task will then be yours to identify the basic set of criteria upon which your particular judgments rest.

My criteria are as follows:

1. The spheres of freedom criterion stated above.
2. Waste is a bad thing. The dominant feature of

human existence is scarcity—our available resources, our aggregate labors, and our skill in employing both have always been, and will continue for some time to be, inadequate to yield to every man all the tangible and intangible satisfactions he would like to have. Hence, none of those resources, or labors, or skills, should be wasted—that is, employed so as to yield less than they might yield in human satisfactions.

3. Every human being should be regarded as an end rather than as a means to be used for the betterment of another. Each should be afforded dignity and regarded as having an absolute claim to an evenhanded application of such rules as the community may adopt for its governance.

4. Both the incentive and the opportunity to improve his share of satisfactions should be preserved to every individual. Preservation of incentive is dictated by the "no-waste" criterion and enjoins against the continuous, totally egalitarian redistribution of satisfactions, or wealth; but subject to that constraint, everyone should receive, by continuous redistribution if necessary, some minimal share of aggregate wealth so as to avoid a level of privation from which the opportunity to improve his situation becomes illusory.

The relationship of these highly general goals to the more specific environmental issues at hand may not be readily apparent, and I am not yet ready to demonstrate their pervasive implications. But let me give one indication of their implications. Recently scientists have informed us that use of DDT in food production is causing damage to the penguin population. For the present purposes let us accept that assertion as an indisputable scientific fact. The scientific fact is often asserted as if the correct implication—that we must stop agricultural use of DDT—followed from the mere statement of the fact of penguin damage. But plainly it does not follow if my criteria are employed.

My criteria are oriented to people, not penguins. Damage to penguins, or sugar pines, or geological marvels is, without more, simply irrelevant. One must go further, by my criteria, and say: Penguins are important because people enjoy seeing them walk about rocks; and furthermore, the well-being of people would be less impaired by halting use of DDT than by giving up penguins. In short, my observations about environmental problems will be people-oriented, as are my criteria. I have no interest in preserving penguins for their own sake.

It may be said by way of objection to this position that it is very selfish of people to act as if each person represented one unit of importance and nothing else was of any importance. It is undeniably selfish. Nevertheless I think it is the only tenable starting place for analysis for several reasons. First, no other position corresponds to the way most people really think and act—i.e., corresponds to reality.

Second, this attitude does not portend any massive destruction of nonhuman flora and fauna, for people depend on them in many obvious ways, and they will be preserved because and to the degree that humans do depend on them.

Third, what is good for humans is, in many respects, good for penguins and pine trees—clean air for example. So that humans are, in these respects, surrogates for plant and animal life.

Fourth, I do not know how we could administer any other system. Our decisions are either private or collective. Insofar as Mr. Jones is free to act privately, he may give such preferences as he wishes to other forms of life: he may feed birds in winter and do with less himself, and he may even decline to resist an advancing polar bear on the ground that the bear's appetite is more important than those portions of himself that the bear may choose to eat. In short my basic premise does not rule out private altruism to competing life-forms. It does rule out, however, Mr. Jones's inclination to feed Mr. Smith to the bear, however hungry the bear, however despicable Mr. Smith.

Insofar as we act collectively, on the other hand, only humans can be afforded an opportunity to participate in the collective decisions. Penguins cannot vote now and are unlikely subjects for the franchise—pine trees more unlikely still. Again each individual is free to cast his vote so as to benefit sugar pines if that is his inclination. But many of the more extreme assertions that one hears from some conservationists amount to tacit assertions that they are specially appointed representatives of sugar pines, and hence that their preferences should be weighted more heavily than the preferences of other humans who do not enjoy equal rapport with "nature." The simplistic assertion that agricultural use of DDT must stop at once because it is harmful to penguins is of that type.

Fifth, if polar bears or pine trees or penguins, like men, are to be regarded as ends rather than means, if they are to count in our calculus of social organization, someone must tell me how much each one counts, and someone must tell me how these life-forms are to be permitted to express their preferences, for I do not know either answer. If the answer is that certain people are to hold their proxies, then I want to

know how those proxy-holders are to be selected: self-appointment does not seem workable to me.

Sixth, and by way of summary of all the foregoing, let me point out that the set of environmental issues under discussion—although they raise very complex technical questions of how to achieve any objective—ultimately raise a normative question: what *ought* we to do. Questions of *ought* are unique to the human mind and world—they are meaningless as applied to a nonhuman situation.

I reject the proposition that we *ought* to respect the "balance of nature" or to "preserve the environment" unless the reason for doing so, expressed or implied, is the benefit of man.

I reject the idea that there is a "right" or "morally correct" state of nature to which we should return. The word "nature" has no normative connotation. Was it "right" or "wrong" for the earth's crust to heave in contortion and create mountains and seas? Was it "right" for the first amphibian to crawl up out of the primordial ooze? Was it "wrong" for plants to reproduce themselves and alter the atmospheric composition in favor of oxygen? For animals to alter the atmosphere in favor of carbon dioxide both by breathing oxygen and eating plants? No answers can be given to these questions because they are meaningless questions.

All this may seem obvious to the point of being tedious, but much of the present controversy over environment and pollution rests on tacit normative assumptions about just such nonnormative phenomena: that it is "wrong" to impair penguins with DDT, but not to slaughter cattle for prime rib roasts. That it is wrong to kill stands of sugar pines with industrial fumes, but not to cut sugar pines and build housing for the poor. Every man is entitled to his own preferred definition of Walden Pond, but there is no definition that has any moral superiority over another, except by reference to the selfish needs of the human race.

From the fact that there is no normative definition of the natural state, it follows that there is no normative definition of clean air or pure water—hence no definition of polluted air—or of pollution—except by reference to the needs of man. The "right" composition of the atmosphere is one which has some dust in it and some lead in it and some hydrogen sulfide in it—just those amounts that attend a sensibly organized society thoughtfully and knowledgeably pursuing the greatest possible satisfaction for its human members.

The first and most fundamental step toward solution of our environmental problems is a clear recognition that our objective is not pure air or water but rather some optimal state of pollution. That step immediately suggests the question: How do we define and attain the level of pollution that will yield the maximum possible amount of human satisfaction?

Low levels of pollution contribute to human satisfaction but so do food and shelter and education and music. To attain ever lower levels of pollution, we must pay the cost of having less of these other things. I contrast that view of the cost of pollution control with the more popular statement that pollution control will "cost" very large numbers of dollars. The popular statement is true in some senses, false in others; sorting out the true and false senses is of some importance. The first step in that sorting process is to achieve a clear understanding of the difference between dollars and resources. Resources are the wealth of our nation; dollars are merely claim checks upon those resources. Resources are of vital importance; dollars are comparatively trivial.

Four categories of resources are sufficient for our purposes: at any given time a nation, or a planet if you prefer, has a stock of labor, of technological skill, of capital goods, and of natural resources (such as mineral deposits, timber, water, land, etc.). These resources can be used in various combinations to yield goods and services of all kinds—in some limited quantity. The quantity will be larger if they are combined efficiently, smaller if combined inefficiently. But in either event the resource stock is limited, the goods and services that they can be made to yield are limited; even the most efficient use of them will yield less than our population, in the aggregate, would like to have.

If one considers building a new dam, it is appropriate to say that it will be costly in the sense that it will require x hours of labor, y tons of steel and concrete, and z amount of capital goods. If these resources are devoted to the dam, then they cannot be used to build hospitals, fishing rods, schools, or electric can openers. That is the meaningful sense in which the dam is costly.

Quite apart from the very important question of how wisely we can combine our resources to produce goods and services is the very different question of how they get distributed—who gets how many goods? Dollars constitute the claim checks which are distributed among people and which control their share of national output. Dollars are nearly valueless pieces of paper except to the extent that they do represent claim checks to some fraction of the output of goods and services. Viewed as claim checks, all the dollars outstanding during any period of time are worth, in the aggregate, the goods and services that are available to be claimed with them during that period—neither more nor less.

It is far easier to increase the supply of dollars than to increase the production of goods and services—printing dollars is easy. But printing more dollars doesn't help because each dollar then simply becomes a claim to fewer goods, i.e., becomes worth less.

The point is this: many people fall into error upon hearing the statement that the decision to build a dam, or to clean up a river, will cost $X million. It is regrettably easy to say: "It's only money. This is a wealthy country, and we have lots of money." But you cannot build a dam or clean a river with $X million—unless you also have a match, you can't even make a fire. One builds a dam or cleans a river by diverting labor and steel and trucks and factories from making one kind of goods to making another. The cost in dollars is merely a shorthand way of describing the extent of the diversion necessary. If we build a dam for $X million, then we must recognize that we will have $X million less housing and food and medical care and electric can openers as a result.

Similarly, the costs of controlling pollution are best expressed in terms of the other goods we will have to give up to do the job. This is not to say the job should not be done. Badly as we need more housing, more medical care, and more can openers, and more symphony orchestras, we could do with somewhat less of them, in my judgment at least, in exchange for somewhat cleaner air and rivers. But that is the nature of the trade-off, and analysis of the problem is advanced if that unpleasant reality is kept in mind. Once the trade-off relationship is clearly perceived, it is possible to state in a very general way what the optimal level of pollution is. I would state it as follows:

People enjoy watching penguins. They enjoy relatively clean air and smog-free vistas. Their health is improved by relatively clean water and air. Each of these benefits is a type of good or service. As a society we would be well advised to give up one washing machine if the resources that would have gone into that washing machine can yield greater human satisfaction when diverted into pollution control. We should give up one hospital if the resources thereby freed would yield more human satisfaction when devoted to elimination of noise in our cities. And so on, trade-off by trade-off, we should divert our productive capacities from the production of existing goods and services to the production of a cleaner, quieter, more pastoral nation up to—and no further than—the point at which we value more highly the next washing machine or hospital that we would have to do without than we value the next unit of environmental improvement that the diverted resources would create.

Now this proposition seems to me unassailable but so general and abstract as to be unhelpful—at least unadministerable in the form stated. It assumes we can measure in some way the incremental units of human satisfaction yielded by very different types of goods. The proposition must remain a pious abstraction until I can explain how this measurement process can occur. . . . But I insist that the proposition stated describes the result for which we should be striving—and again, that it is always useful to know what your target is even if your weapons are too crude to score a bull's eye.

Discussion and Reflection Questions

1. Is a completely human-centered environmental ethic acceptable? What sorts of objections could there be to such a perspective?

2. Baxter holds that nature is not normative. That is, we cannot validly derive moral responsibilities from facts about nature. Is this true? Are there any facts about nature that entail moral responsibilities on our part?

3. What sort of role should economic considerations play in our actions toward the environment? Should ethics be based on economics, or economics upon ethics, or is there a more complicated relationship between the two?

4. Baxter embraces a human-centered environmental ethic, because the individuals constructing the ethic are human beings. How might Baxter deal with the following situation: Suppose that intelligent, but utterly selfish, extraterrestrial beings arrived on earth and decided to turn it into their playground, torturing, killing, and eating people as the urge struck them. Is there anything Baxter could say to them, consistent with his own principles, to dissuade them from continuing to treat humanity in this way? If he could not, would he consider this an objection to his view?

Lily de Silva, The Buddhist Attitude Toward Nature

In the following article Lily de Silva describes her interpretation of the Buddhist attitude toward the natural world. Although Buddhism is primarily concerned with human suffering and the means to its transcendence, its practices also show how human beings can live more harmoniously with nature. Buddhist solutions to the environmental crisis would focus less on passing legislation of a certain kind (although this is not ruled out) and more on effecting an inner spiritual transformation such that one cultivates virtues that lead to a nonexploitative relationship with the natural world. The ultimate aim of developing this relationship, she argues, is to achieve harmonious existence within nature.

Reading Questions

1. What sort of connection do Buddhists see between the moral state of humanity and the quality of the environment? What does this imply about the essential interdependence of human beings and nature?

2. What sorts of virtues does Buddhism advocate? How does the cultivation of these virtues bear on our treatment of the environment?

3. What is the Buddhist attitude toward plant and animal life? How is this attitude manifested in daily life? How does the example of the bee illustrate this basic attitude?

4. How does the saint's appreciation of nature differ from that of the poet? How does this difference bear on the author's view of the correct attitude toward nature?

The Buddhist Attitude Toward Nature

LILY DE SILVA

MODERN MAN in his search for pleasure and affluence has exploited nature without any moral restraint to such an extent that nature has been rendered almost incapable of sustaining healthy life. Invaluable gifts of nature, such as air and water, have been polluted with severely disastrous consequences. Man is now searching for ways and means of overcoming the pollution problem as his health too is alarmingly threatened. He also feels that it is irresponsible and morally wrong on his part to commit the future generations to a polluted planet. If man is to act with a sense of responsibility to the natural world, to his fellow human beings and to unborn future generations, he has to find an appropriate environmental ethic today to prevent further aggravation of the present pollution problem. Hence his search for wisdom and attitudes in a hitherto neglected area of knowledge, namely, religion.

Buddhism strictly limits itself to the delineation of a way of life designed to eradicate human suffering. The Buddha refused to answer questions which did not directly or indirectly bear on the central problem of human suffering and its ending. Furthermore, environmental pollution is a problem of the modern age, unheard of and unsuspected during the time of the Buddha. Therefore it is difficult to find any specific discourse which deals with the topic we are interested in here. Nevertheless, as Buddhism is a full-fledged philosophy of life reflecting all aspects of experience, it is possible to find enough material in the Pali Canon to delineate the Buddhist attitude toward nature. . . .

Nature as Dynamic

According to Buddhism changeability is one of the perennial principles of nature. Everything changes in nature and nothing remains static. This concept is expressed by the Pali term *anicca*. Everything formed is in a constant process of change. The world is therefore defined as that which disintegrates; the world is so called because it is dynamic and kinetic, it is constantly in a process of undergoing change. In nature there are no static and stable "things"; there are only ever-changing, ever-moving processes. Rain is a good example to illustrate this point. Though we use a noun called "rain" which appears to denote a "thing," rain is nothing but the process of drops of water falling from the skies. Apart from this process, the activity of raining, there is not rain as such which could be expressed by a seemingly static nominal concept. The very elements of solidity, liquidity, heat and mobility, recognized as the building material of nature, are all ever-changing phenomena. Even the most solid-looking mountains and the very earth that supports everything on it are not beyond this inexorable law of change. One sutta explains how the massive king of mountains—Mount Sineru, which is rooted in the great ocean to a depth of 84,000 leagues and which rises above sea level another great height of 84,000 leagues and which is the very classical symbol of stability and steadfastness—also gets destroyed by heat, without leaving even ashes, with the appearance of multiple suns. Thus change is the very essence of nature.

Lily de Silva, "The Buddhist Attitude Toward Nature," in Buddhist Perspectives on the Ecocrisis, *K. Sandell, ed. (Kandy, Sri Lanka: Buddhist Publication Society, 1987), pp. 9–29. Reprinted by permission of the Buddhist Publication Society.*

Morality and Nature

The world passes through alternative cycles of evolution and dissolution, each of which endures for a long period of time. Though change is inherent in nature, Buddhism believes that natural processes are affected by the morals of man.

According to the *Aggañña Sutta*, which relates the Buddhist legend regarding the evolution of the world, the appearance of greed in the primordial beings who at that time were self-luminous, subsisting on joy and traversing in the skies, caused the gradual loss of their radiance, the ability to subsist on joy and move about in the sky. The moral degradation had effects on the external environment too. At that time the entire earth was covered over by a very flavorsome fragrant substance similar to butter. When beings started partaking of this substance with more and more greed, on the one hand their subtle bodies became coarser and coarser. On the other hand the flavorsome substance itself started gradually diminishing. With the solidification of bodies differences of form appeared; some were beautiful while others were homely. Thereupon conceit manifested itself in those beings, and the beautiful ones started looking down upon the others. As a result of these moral blemishes the delicious edible earth-substance completely disappeared. In its place there appeared edible mushrooms and later another kind of edible creeper. In the beings who subsisted on them successively sex differentiation became manifest and the former method of spontaneous birth was replaced by sexual reproduction.

Self-growing rice appeared on earth and through laziness to collect each meal man grew accustomed to hoarding food. As a result of this hoarding habit, the growth rate of food could not keep pace with the rate of demand. Therefore land had to be divided among families. After private ownership of land became the order of the day, those who were of a more greedy disposition started robbing from others' plots of land. When they were detected they denied that they had stolen. Thus through greed vices such as stealing and lying became manifest in society. To curb the wrongdoers and punish them a king was elected by the people and thus the original simple society became much more complex and complicated. It is said that this moral degeneration of man had adverse effects on nature. The richness of the earth diminished and self-growing rice disappeared. Man had to till the land and cultivate rice for food. This rice grain was enveloped in chaff; it needed cleaning before consumption.

The point I wish to emphasize by citing this evolutionary legend is that Buddhism believes that though change is a factor inherent in nature, man's moral deterioration accelerates the process of change and brings about changes which are adverse to human well-being and happiness.

The *Cakkavattisīhanāda Sutta* of the Dīgha Nikāya predicts the future course of events when human morals undergo further degeneration. Gradually man's health will deteriorate so much that life expectancy will diminish until at last the average human life-span is reduced to ten years and marriageable age to five years. At that time all delicacies such as ghee, butter, honey, etc. will have disappeared from the earth; what is considered the poorest coarse food today will become a delicacy of that day. Thus Buddhism maintains that there is a close link between man's morals and the natural resources available to him.

According to a discourse in the Anguttara Nikāya, when profligate lust, wanton greed and wrong values grip the heart of man and immorality becomes widespread in society, timely rain does not fall. When timely rain does not fall crops get adversely affected with various kinds of pests and plant diseases. Through lack of nourishing food the human mortality rate rises.

Thus several suttas from the Pali Canon show that early Buddhism believes there to be a close relationship between human morality and the natural environment. This idea has been systematized in the theory of the five natural laws. . . . According to this theory, in the cosmos there are five natural laws or forces at work. . . . They can be translated as physical laws, biological laws, psychological laws, moral laws and causal laws, respectively. While the first four laws operate within their respective spheres, the last-mentioned law of causality operates *within* each of them as well as *among* them.

This means that the physical environment of any given area conditions the growth and development of its biological component, i.e., flora and fauna. These in turn influence the thought pattern of the people interacting with them. Modes of thinking determine moral standards. The opposite process of interaction is also possible. The morals of man influence not only the psychological make-up of the people but the biological and physical environment of the area as well. Thus the five laws demonstrate that man and nature are bound together in a reciprocal causal relationship with changes in one necessarily bringing about changes in the other.

The commentary on the *Cakkavattisīhanāda Sutta* goes on to explain the pattern of mutual interaction further. When mankind is demoralized through greed, famine is the natural outcome; when moral degeneration is due to ignorance, epidemic is the inevitable result; when hatred is the demoralizing force, widespread violence is the ultimate outcome. If and when mankind realizes that large-scale devastation has taken place as a result of his moral degeneration, a change of heart takes place among the few surviving human beings. With gradual moral regeneration conditions improve through a long period of cause and effect and mankind again starts to enjoy gradually increasing prosperity and longer life. The world, including nature and mankind, stands or falls with the type of moral force at work. If immorality grips society, man and nature deteriorate; if morality reigns, the quality of human life and nature improves. Thus greed, hatred and delusion produce pollution within and without. Generosity, compassion and wisdom produce purity within and without. This is one reason the Buddha has pronounced that the world is led by the mind, *cittena niyati loko*. Thus man and nature, according to the ideas expressed in early Buddhism, are interdependent.

Human Use of Natural Resources

For survival mankind has to depend on nature for his food, clothing, shelter, medicine and other requisites. For optimum benefits man has to understand nature so that he can utilize natural resources and live harmoniously with nature. By understanding the working of nature—for example, the seasonal rainfall pattern, methods of conserving water by irrigation, the soil types, the physical conditions required for growth of various food crops, etc.—man can learn to get better returns from his agricultural pursuits. But his learning has to be accompanied by moral restraint if he is to enjoy the benefits of natural resources for a long time. Man must learn to satisfy his needs and not feed his greeds. The resources of the world are not unlimited whereas man's greed knows neither limit nor satiation. Modern man in his unbridled voracious greed for pleasure and acquisition of wealth has exploited nature to the point of near impoverishment.

Ostentatious consumerism is accepted as the order of the day. One writer says that within forty years Americans alone have consumed natural resources to the quantity of what all mankind has consumed for the last 4000 years. The vast nonreplenishable resources of fossil fuels which took millions of years to form have been consumed within a couple of centuries to the point of near exhaustion. This consumerism has given rise to an energy crisis

on the one hand and a pollution problem on the other. Man's unrestrained exploitation of nature to gratify his insatiate greed reminds one of the traditional parable of the goose that laid the golden eggs.

Buddhism tirelessly advocates the virtues of nongreed, nonhatred and nondelusion in all human pursuits. Greed breeds sorrow and unhealthy consequences. Contentment is a much praised virtue in Buddhism. The man leading a simple life with few wants easily satisfied is upheld and appreciated as an exemplary character. Miserliness and wastefulness are equally deplored in Buddhism as two degenerate extremes. Wealth has only instrumental value; it is to be utilized for the satisfaction of man's needs. Hoarding is a senseless antisocial habit comparable to the attitude of the dog in the manger. The vast hoarding of wealth in some countries and the methodical destruction of large quantities of agricultural produce to keep the market prices from falling, while half the world is dying of hunger and starvation, is really a sad paradox of the present affluent age.

Buddhism commends frugality as a virtue in its own right. Once Ānanda explained to King Udena the thrifty economic use of robes by the monks in the following order. When new robes are received the old robes are used as coverlets, the old coverlets as mattress covers, the old mattress covers as rugs, the old rugs as dusters, and the old tattered dusters are kneaded with clay and used to repair cracked floors and walls. Thus nothing usable is wasted. Those who waste are derided as "wood-apple eaters." A man shakes the branch of a wood-apple tree and all the fruits, ripe as well as unripe, fall. The man would collect only what he wants and walk away leaving the rest to rot. Such a wasteful attitude is certainly deplored in Buddhism as not only antisocial but criminal. The excessive exploitation of nature as is done today would certainly be condemned by Buddhism in the strongest possible terms.

Buddhism advocates a gentle nonaggressive attitude toward nature. According to the *Sigālovāda Sutta* a householder should accumulate wealth as a bee collects pollen from a flower. The bee harms neither the fragrance nor the beauty of the flower, but gathers pollen to turn it into sweet honey. Similarly, man is expected to make legitimate use of nature so that he can rise above nature and realize his innate spiritual potential.

Attitude Toward Animal and Plant Life

The well-known Five Precepts form the minimum code of ethics that every lay Buddhist is expected to adhere to. Its first precept involves abstention from injury to life. It is explained as the casting aside of all forms of weapons, being conscientious about depriving a living being of life. In its positive sense it means the cultivation of compassion and sympathy for all living beings. The Buddhist layman is expected to abstain from trading in meat too.

The Buddhist monk has to abide by an even stricter code of ethics than the layman. He has to abstain from practices which would involve even unintentional injury to living creatures. For instance, the Buddha promulgated the rule against going on a journey during the rainy season because of possible injury to worms and insects that come to the surface in wet weather. The same concern for nonviolence prevents a monk from digging the ground. Once a monk who was a potter prior to ordination built for himself a clay hut and set it on fire to give it a fine finish. The Buddha strongly objected to this as so many living creatures would have been burnt in the process. The hut was broken down on the Buddha's instructions to prevent it from creating a bad precedent for later generations. The scrupulous nonviolent attitude toward even the smallest living creatures prevents the monks from drinking unstrained water. It is no doubt a sound hygienic habit, but what is noteworthy is the reason which prompts the practice, namely, sympathy for living creatures.

Buddhism also prescribes the practice of . . . "loving-kindness" toward all creatures of all quarters without restriction. The *Karaṇīyamettā Sutta* enjoins the cultivation of loving-kindness toward all creatures, timid and steady, long and short, big and small, minute and great, visible and invisible, near and far, born and awaiting birth. All quarters are to be suffused with this loving attitude. Just as one's own life is precious to oneself, so is the life of the other precious to himself. Therefore a reverential attitude must be cultivated toward all forms of life.

The *Nandivisāla Jātaka* illustrates how kindness should be shown to animals domesticated for human service. Even a wild animal can be tamed with kind words. Pārileyya was a wild elephant who attended on the Buddha when he spent time in the forest away from the monks. The infuriated elephant Nālāgiri was tamed by the Buddha with no other miraculous power than the power of loving-kindness. Man and beast can live and let live without fear of one another if only man cultivates sympathy and regards all life with compassion.

The understanding of karma and rebirth, too, prepares the Buddhist to adopt a sympathetic attitude toward animals. According to this belief it is possible for human beings to be reborn in subhuman states among the animals. The *Kukkuravatika Sutta* can be cited as a canonical reference which substantiates this view. The *Jātakas* provide ample testimony to this view from commentarial literature. It is possible that our own close relatives have been reborn as animals. Therefore it is only right that we should treat animals with kindness and sympathy. The Buddhist notion of merit also engenders a gentle nonviolent attitude toward living creatures. It is said that if one throws dish-washing water into a pool where there are insects and living creatures, intending that they feed on the tiny particles of food thus washed away, one accumulates merit even by such trivial generosity. According to the *Macchuddāna Jātaka* the Bodhisatta threw his leftover food into a river in order to feed the fish, and by the power of that merit he was saved from an impending disaster. Thus kindness to animals, be they big or small, is a source of merit—merit needed for human beings to improve their lot in the cycle of rebirths and to approach the final goal of Nibbāna.

Buddhism expresses a gentle nonviolent attitude toward the vegetable kingdom as well. It is said that one should not even break the branch of a tree that has given one shelter. Plants are so helpful to us in providing us with all necessities of life that we are expected not to adopt a callous attitude toward them. The more strict monastic rules prevent monks from injuring plant life.

Prior to the rise of Buddhism people regarded natural phenomena such as mountains, forests, groves and trees with a sense of awe and reverence. They considered them as the abode of powerful nonhuman beings who could assist human beings at times of need. . . . Therefore among the Buddhists there is a reverential attitude toward specially long-standing gigantic trees. They are called *vanaspati* in Pali, meaning "lords of the forests." As huge trees such as the ironwood, the sāla and the fig are also recognized as the Bodhi trees of former Buddhas, the deferential attitude toward trees is further strengthened. It is well known that the *ficus religiosa* is held as an object of great veneration in the Buddhist world today as the tree under which the Buddha attained Enlightenment.

The construction of parks and pleasure groves for public use is considered a great meritorious deed. Sakka the lord of gods is said to have reached this status as a result of social services such as the construction of parks, pleasure groves, ponds, wells and roads.

The open air, natural habits and forest trees have a special fascination for the Eastern mind as symbols of

CHAPTER 16: THE ENVIRONMENT

spiritual freedom. The home life is regarded as a fetter that keeps man in bondage and misery. Renunciation is like the open air, nature unhampered by man's activity. The chief events in the life of the Buddha too took place in the open air. He was born in a park at the foot of a tree in Kapilavatthu; he attained Enlightenment in the open air at the foot of the Bodhi tree in Bodhgayā; he inaugurated his missionary activity in the open air in the sāla grove of the Mallas in Pāvā. The Buddha's constant advice to his disciples also was to resort to natural habitats such as forest groves and glades. There, undisturbed by human activity, they could zealously engage themselves in meditation.

Attitude Toward Pollution

Environmental pollution has assumed such vast proportions today that man has been forced to recognize the presence of an ecological crisis. He can no longer turn a blind eye to the situation as he is already threatened with new pollution-related diseases. Pollution to this extent was unheard of during the time of the Buddha. But there is sufficient evidence in the Pali Canon to give us insight into the Buddhist attitude toward the pollution problem. Several Vinaya rules prohibit monks from polluting green grass and water with saliva, urine and feces. These were the common agents of pollution known during the Buddha's day and rules were promulgated against causing such pollution. Cleanliness was highly commended by the Buddhist both in the person and in the environment. They were much concerned about keeping water clean, be it in the river, pond or well. These sources of water were for public use and each individual had to use them with proper public-spirited caution so that others after him could use them with the same degree of cleanliness. Rules regarding the cleanliness of green grass were prompted by ethical and aesthetic considerations. Moreover, grass is food for most animals and it is man's duty to refrain from polluting it by his activities.

Noise is today recognized as a serious personal and environmental pollutant troubling everyone to some extent. It causes deafness, stress and irritation, breeds resentment, saps energy and inevitably lowers efficiency. The Buddha's attitude to noise is very clear from the Pali Canon. He was critical of noise and did not hesitate to voice his stern disapproval whenever occasion arose. Once he ordered a group of monks to leave the monastery for noisy behavior. He enjoyed solitude and silence immensely and spoke in praise of silence as it is most appropriate for mental

culture. Noise is described as a thorn to one engaged in the first step of meditation, but thereafter noise ceases to be a disturbance as the meditator passes beyond the possibility of being disturbed by sound.

The Buddha and his disciples reveled in the silent solitary natural habitats unencumbered by human activity. Even in the choice of monasteries the presence of undisturbed silence was an important quality they looked for. Silence invigorates those who are pure at heart and raises their efficiency for meditation. But silence overawes those who are impure with ignoble impulses of greed, hatred and delusion. The *Bhayabherava Sutta* beautifully illustrates how even the rustle of leaves by a falling twig in the forest sends tremors through an impure heart. This may perhaps account for the present craze for constant auditory stimulation with transistors and cassettes. The moral impurity caused by greed, avarice, acquisitive instincts and aggression has rendered man so timid that he cannot bear silence which lays bare the reality of self-awareness. He therefore prefers to drown himself in loud music. Unlike classical music which tends to soothe nerves and induce relaxation, rock music excites the senses. Constant exposure to it actually renders man incapable of relaxation and sound sleep without tranquilizers.

As to the question of the Buddhist attitude to music, it is recorded that the Buddha has spoken quite appreciatively of music on one occasion. When Pañcasikha the divine musician sang a song while playing the lute in front of the Buddha, the Buddha praised his musical ability saying that the instrumental music blended well with his song. Again, the remark of an Arahat that the joy of seeing the real nature of things is far more exquisite than orchestral music shows the recognition that music affords a certain amount of pleasure even if it is inferior to higher kinds of pleasure. But it is stressed that the ear is a powerful sensory channel through which man gets addicted to sense pleasures. Therefore, to dissuade monks from getting addicted to melodious sounds, the monastic discipline describes music as a lament.

The psychological training of the monks is so advanced that they are expected to cultivate a taste not only for external silence, but for inner silence of speech, desire and thought as well. The subvocal speech, the inner chatter that goes on constantly within us in our waking life, is expected to be silenced through meditation. The sage who succeeds in quelling this inner speech completely is described as a *muni*, a silent one. His inner silence is maintained even when he speaks!

It is not inappropriate to pay passing notice to the Buddhist attitude to speech as well. Moderation in speech is considered a virtue, as one can avoid four unwholesome vocal activities thereby, namely, falsehood, slander, harsh speech and frivolous talk. In its positive aspect moderation in speech paves the path to self-awareness. Buddhism commends speaking at the appropriate time, speaking the truth, speaking gently, speaking what is useful, and speaking out of loving-kindness; the opposite modes of speech are condemned. The Buddha's general advice to the monks regarding speech is to be engaged in discussing the Dharma or maintain noble silence. The silence that reigned in vast congregations of monks during the Buddha's day was indeed a surprise even to the kings of the time. Silence is serene and noble as it is conducive to the spiritual progress of those who are pure at heart. . . .

Nature as Beautiful

The Buddha and his disciples regarded natural beauty as a source of great joy and aesthetic satisfaction. The saints who purged themselves of sensuous worldly pleasures responded to natural beauty with a detached sense of appreciation. The average poet looks at nature and derives inspiration mostly by the sentiments it evokes in his own heart; he becomes emotionally involved with nature. For instance, he may compare the sun's rays passing over the mountain tops to the blush on a sensitive face, he may see a tear in a dew drop, the lips of his beloved in a rose petal, etc. But the appreciation of the saint is quite different. He appreciates nature's beauty for its own sake and derives joy unsullied by sensuous associations and self-projected ideas. The simple spontaneous appreciation of nature's exquisite beauty is expressed by the Elder Mahākassapa in the following words:

Those upland glades delightful to the soul,
Where the Kaveri spreads its wildering wreaths,
Where sound the trumpet-calls of elephants:
Those are the hills where my soul delights.

Those rocky heights with hue of dark blue clouds
Where lies embossed many a shining lake
Of crystal-clear, cool waters, and whose slopes
The "herds of Indra" cover and bedeck:
Those are the hills wherein my soul delights.

Fair uplands rain-refreshed, and resonant
With crested creatures' cries antiphonal,
Lone heights where silent Rishis oft resort:
These are the hills wherein my soul delights.

Again the poem of Kāludāyi inviting the Buddha to visit Kapilavatthu, contains a beautiful description of spring:

Now crimson glow the trees, dear Lord, and cast
Their ancient foliage in quest of fruit,
Like crests of flame they shine irradiant
And rich in hope, great Hero, is the hour.

Verdure and blossom-time in every tree
Wherever we look delightful to the eye,
And every quarter breathing fragrant airs,
While petals falling, yearning comes fruit:
It is time, O Hero, that we set out hence.

The long poem of Tālaputa is a fascinating soliloquy. His religious aspirations are beautifully blended with a profound knowledge of the teachings of the Buddha against the background of a sylvan resort. Many more poems could be cited for saintly appreciation of nature, but it is not necessary to burden the essay with any more quotations. Suffice it to know that the saints, too, were sensitive to the beauties and harmony of nature and that their appreciation is colored by spontaneity, simplicity and a nonsensuous spirituality.

Conclusion

In the modern age man has become alienated from himself and nature. When science started opening new vistas of knowledge revealing the secrets of nature one by one, man gradually lost faith in theistic religions. Consequently, he developed scanty respect for moral and spiritual values as well. With the advent of the Industrial Revolution and the acquisition of wealth by mechanical exploitation of natural resources, man has become more and more materialistic in his attitudes and values. The pursuit of sense pleasures and the acquisition of possessions have become ends in themselves. Man's sense faculties dominate him to an unrelenting degree and man has become a slave to his insatiable passions. (Incidentally the sense faculties are called in Pali *indriyas* or lords, because they control man unless he is sufficiently vigilant to become their master.) Thus man has become alienated from himself as he abandoned himself to the influence of sense pleasures and acquisitive instincts.

In his greed for more and more possessions he has adopted a violent and aggressive attitude toward nature. Forgetting that he is a part and parcel of nature, he exploits it with unrestrained greed, thus alienating himself from nature as well. The net result is the deterioration of man's physical and mental health on the one hand, and the rapid depletion of nonreplenishable natural resources and environmental pollution on the other. These results remind us of the Buddhist teachings in the suttas discussed above, which maintain that the moral degeneration of man leads to the decrease of his lifespan and the depletion of natural resources.

Moral degeneration is a double-edged weapon; it exercises adverse effects of man's psycho-physical well-being as well as on nature. Already killer diseases such as heart ailments, cancer, diabetes, AIDS, etc., are claiming victims on an unprecedented scale. In the final analysis these can all be traced to man's moral deterioration. Depletion of vast resources of fossil fuels and forests have given rise to a very severe energy crisis. It cannot be emphasized too strongly that such rapid depletion of nonrenewable natural resources within less than two centuries, an infinitesimal fraction of the millions of years taken for them to form, is due to modern man's inordinate greed and acquisitiveness. A number of simple ancient societies had advanced technological skills, as is evident by their vast sophisticated irrigation schemes designed to feed the fundamental needs of several millions. Yet they survived in some countries over 2000 years without such problems as environmental pollution and depletion of natural resources. This was no doubt due to the validity of the philosophy which inspired and formed the basis of these civilizations.

In the present ecocrisis man has to look for radical solutions. "Pollution cannot be dealt with in the long term on a remedial or cosmetic basis or by tackling symptoms: all measures should deal with basic causes. These are determined largely by our values, priorities and choices." Man must reappraise his value system. The materialism that has guided his lifestyle has landed him in very severe problems. Buddhism teaches that mind is the forerunner of all things, mind is supreme. If one acts with an impure mind, i.e., a mind sullied with greed, hatred and delusion, suffering is the inevitable result. If one acts with a pure mind, i.e., with the opposite qualities of contentment, compassion and wisdom, happiness will follow like a shadow. Man has to understand that pollution in the environment has been caused because there has been psychological pollution within himself. If he wants a clean environment he has to adopt a lifestyle that springs from a moral and spiritual dimension.

Buddhism offers man a simple moderate lifestyle eschewing both extremes of self-deprivation and self-indulgence. Satisfaction of basic human necessities, reduction of wants to the minimum, frugality and contentment are its important characteristics. Each man has to order his life on normal principles, exercise self-control in the enjoyment of the senses, discharge his duties in his various social roles, and conduct himself with wisdom and self-awareness in all activities. It is only when each man adopts a simple moderate lifestyle that mankind as a whole will stop polluting the environment. This seems to be the only way of overcoming the present ecocrisis and the problem of alienation. With such a lifestyle, man will adopt a nonexploitative, nonaggressive, gentle attitude toward nature. He can then live in harmony with nature, utilizing its resources for the satisfaction of his basic needs. The Buddhist admonition is to utilize nature in the same way as a bee collects pollen from the flower, neither polluting its beauty nor depleting its fragrance. Just as the bee manufactures honey out of pollen, so man should be able to find happiness and fulfillment in life without harming the natural world in which he lives.

Discussion and Reflection Questions

1. A problem for Western approaches to environmental ethics is to see how human values can be related to the natural world. Is this an equally acute problem for Buddhism? According to Buddhism, is humanity apart from, or a part of, the natural world? Do you think that this way of looking at things makes some difference?

2. Do you think that there are specifically environmental virtues, whose cultivation would lead to a more harmonious relationship with the natural world? How could such virtues be promoted in the world? What role could education play?

3. Is there a spiritual, as well as an ethical, dimension to the solution of the environmental crisis? How might one argue that there is?

4. Do you think that one has to be a Buddhist in order to gain insights from the Buddhist attitude toward nature? What insights have you gleaned from this reading?

Mary Evelyn Tucker, Ecological Themes in Taoism and Confucianism

In this reading, Mary Evelyn Tucker examines some of the key texts of Taoism and Confucianism in order to uncover the ecological worldviews of these traditions. Both share a worldview that is organic, vitalistic, and holistic, and both see the universe as a dynamic, ongoing process of transformation, characterized by both creativity and unity. Yet each develops these themes in different ways which may, Tucker suggests, complement one another. Whereas the principal concern in Taoism is to achieve harmony with the Tao, the nameless Way which is the source of all existence, in Confucianism the emphasis is placed on how humans can live together and create a just society with a benevolent government. Since clearly any solution to the world's environmental problems requires that we learn harmonious ways of interacting with nature and with one another, Taoist and Confucian perspectives on the environment promise to offer us valuable insights.

Reading Questions

1. According to Tucker, in what sense do Confucianism and Taoism present an "organic, vitalistic worldview which has special relevance for developing a contemporary ecological perspective"?

2. In what sense does Confucianism tend toward an "active" role for humans in relation to nature, whereas Taoism tends toward a more "passive" approach?

3. According to Tucker, what are the implications of a Taoist perspective for environmental ethics? What are the implications of a Confucian perspective for environmental ethics?

4. How does the theme of "interrelatedness" inform both Confucian and Taoist perspectives on the human and natural worlds? Why might this theme be important?

Ecological Themes in Taoism and Confucianism

MARY EVELYN TUCKER

Humans do not oppose Earth and therefore can comfort all things, for their standard is the Earth. Earth does not oppose Heaven and therefore can sustain all things, for its standard is Heaven. Heaven does not oppose Tao and therefore can cover all things, for its standard is Tao. Tao does not oppose Nature and therefore it attains its character of being.

(A TAOIST COMMENTARY FROM WANG PI, 226–249 c.e.)[1]

[1]*Commentary on the Lao Tzu,* trans. Wing-tsit Chan, in *A Source Book in Chinese Philosophy* (Princeton: Princeton University Press, 1963), 321.

Mencius answered [King Hui], "If your majesty can practice a humane government to the people, reduce punishments and fines, lower taxes and levies, make it possible for the fields to be plowed deep and the weeding well done, men of strong body, in their days of leisure may cultivate their filial piety, brotherly respect, loyalty, and faithfulness, thereby serving their fathers and elder brothers at home and their elders and superiors abroad."

(A CONFUCIAN TEXT FROM MENCIUS, 372–289 b.c.e.)[2]

[2]*Mencius* 1A:5, trans. Wing-tsit Chan, *A Source Book in Chinese Philosophy,* 61.

Mary Evelyn Tucker, "Ecological Themes in Taoism and Confucianism," in World Views and Ecology, *edited by Mary Evelyn Tucker and John A. Grim (Orbis Books), pp. 151–159. Reprinted by permission of Associate University Presses.*

NEARLY TWO DECADES AGO Thomas Berry called for "creating a new consciousness of the multiform religious traditions of humankind" as a means toward renewal of the human spirit in addressing the urgent problems of contemporary society.[3] More recently Tu Wei-ming has written of the need to go "beyond the Enlightenment mentality" in exploring the spiritual resources of the global community to meet the challenge of the ecological crisis.[4]

In drawing upon the great religious traditions of the past for a new ecological orientation in the present, it is clear that the traditions of East Asia have much to offer. My method in this essay is to examine some of the principal texts of Taoism and Confucianism for a phenomenological description of ecological worldviews embedded in these traditions. I risk the inevitable distortions of reducing complex teachings from 2500-year-old traditions to generalizations that need qualification and development. I am also relying primarily on the philosophical and religious ideas of these traditions as evident in their texts and am not discussing their varied religious practices which arose in different periods of Chinese history. Nor am I making claims for a historical consciousness in China of the issues of ecology as we are beginning to understand them in the late twentieth century. Furthermore, I am aware of the ever-present gap between theoretical positions and practical applications in dealing with the environment throughout history.[5] I am also conscious of the dark side of each religious tradition as it developed in particular historical contexts. Nonetheless, in seeking guidance from the past it is becoming increasingly important to examine the perspectives of earlier civilizations and

their attitudes toward nature as we seek new and more comprehensive worldviews and environmental ethics in the present.[6] There is not sufficient time or space to work out all of these methodological issues here. However, I would suggest that this project is an important step in creating a new ecumenism of the multiform religious traditions of the human community in dialogue with pressing contemporary problems such as the environment and social justice.[7]

General Comments on Taoism and Confucianism

The two indigenous traditions of China, Taoism and Confucianism, arose in the so-called Axial Age in the first millennium before the birth of Christ. As Karl Jaspers noted, this was approximately the same time as the philosophers in Greece, the prophets in Israel, Zoroaster in Persia, and Buddha in India.[8] In China this period in the Chou dynasty was a time of great intellectual creativity known as the age of the 100 philosophers.

Although there are many historical uncertainties and ongoing scholarly debates about the life and the writings of Lao Tzu and Confucius, it is indisputable that these two figures are of primary importance in Chinese religion and philosophy. Indeed, some writers on Chinese thought see these traditions as complementary to each other and in a kind of creative tension. While Taoism and Confucianism are quite different in their specific teachings, they share a worldview that might be described as organic, vitalistic, and holistic. They see the universe as a dynamic, ongoing process of continual transformation.[9] The creativity and unity of the cosmos are constant themes which appear in the Taoist and Confucian texts. The

---

[3] Thomas Berry wrote: "The religious traditions must not only become acclimated to the new scientific and technological environment, they must undergo a breathtaking expansion of their own horizons as they become universalized, mutually present to each other, and begin creation of the multiform global religious tradition of humankind, a tradition that is already further advanced in the realities of human history than in the books we write." From "Future Forms of Religious Experience," in Berry's Riverdale Papers (an unpublished collection of essays).

[4] Tu Wei-ming, "Beyond the Enlightenment Mentality: An Exploration of Spiritual Resources in the Global Community," a paper presented at the Fourth Conference on World Spirituality, East-West Center, Honolulu, June 15–19, 1992, and adapted for publication in the Bucknell Review.

[5] The Chinese have not had a strong environmental record in the modern period as demonstrated by Vaclay Smil, The Bad Earth (Armonk, N.Y.: Sharpe, 1984) and Lester Ross, Environmental Policy in China (Bloomington: Indiana University Press, 1988).

[6] Charlene Spretnak has attempted such an examination in her comprehensive book States of Grace (San Francisco: Harper San Francisco, 1991). Another significant contribution is J. Baird Callicott and Roger T. Ames, eds., Nature in Asian Traditions of Thought (Albany: State University of New York Press, 1989).

[7] This was also one of the aims of the Parliament of World Religions held in Chicago in September 1993.

[8] Karl Jaspers describes the Axial period in his book The Origin and Goal of History (New Haven: Yale University Press, 1953).

[9] For a more detailed account of this see Frederick Mote, Intellectual Foundations of China (New York: Knopf, 1971), Chap. 2, and Tu Wei-mings essays in Confucian Thought: Selfhood as Creative Transformation (Albany: State University of New York Press, 1985), esp. "The Continuity of Being: Chinese Visions of Nature," 35–50.

human has a special role in this vitalistic universe. This is viewed in a more passive manner by the Taoists and a more active mode by the Confucians.

It is, however, this organic, vitalistic worldview which has special relevance for developing a contemporary ecological perspective. Indeed, it can be said that within this holistic view Taoist and Confucian thought might provide an important balance of passive and active models for ecological theory and practice.[10] Like a yin-yang circle of complementary opposites, Taoist and Confucian thinkers have evoked important considerations from each other and may still do the same for us today.

In very general terms we can compare and contrast these two traditions as follows. Taoism emphasizes primary causality as resting in the Tao, while Confucianism stresses the importance of secondary causality in the activities of human beings. Thus the principal concern in Taoism is for harmony with the Tao, the nameless Way which is the source of all existence. In Confucianism the stress is on how humans can live together and create a just society with a benevolent government. For both the Taoists and the Confucians harmony with nature is important. The Taoists emphasize the primacy of unmediated closeness to nature to encourage simplicity and spontaneity in individuals and in human relations. For the Taoists, developing techniques of meditation is critical. The Confucians, especially the Neo-Confucians, stress harmonizing with the changing patterns in nature so as to adapt human action and human society appropriately to nature's deeper rhythms. For them the *Book of Changes* is an important means of establishing balance with nature and with other humans.

For the Taoists, in order to be in consonance with the Tao in nature one must withdraw from active involvement in social and political affairs and learn how to preserve and nourish nature and human life. For the Confucians, social and political commitment was an indispensable part of human responsibility to create an orderly society in harmony with nature. Indeed, for the Confucians cultivating oneself morally and intellectually was a means of establishing a peaceful and productive society. The ideal for the Taoist, then, was the hermit in a mountain retreat, while for the Confucian it was the sage, the teacher,

and the civil servant in the midst of affairs of government and education. Taoism did provide a model of an ideal ruler: one who led without overt involvement but rather by subtle indirection and detachment. The Confucians, on the other hand, called for a moral ruler who would be like a pole star for the people, practicing humane government for the benefit of all. The Taoists stressed the principle of non-egocentric action (*wu wei*) in harmony with nature for both ruler and followers. The Confucians, on the other hand, underscored the importance of human action for the betterment of society by the ruler, ministers, teachers, and ordinary citizens. A pristine innocence and spontaneity was valued by the Taoists, while the Confucians continually emphasized humanistic education and ethical practice for the improvement of individuals and society as a whole.

It is perhaps some combination of these two perspectives which may be fruitful for our own thinking today. In order to understand and respect natural processes, we need a greater Taoist attention to the subtle unfolding of the principles and processes of nature. As the deep ecologists constantly remind us, without this fine attunement to the complexities of nature and to ourselves as one species among many others, we may continue to contribute unwittingly to destructive environmental practices. Yet without the Confucian understanding of the importance of moral leadership, an emphasis on education, and a sense of human responsibility to a larger community of life, we may lose the opportunity to change the current pattern of assault on the natural world. Taoism challenges us to radically reexamine human-earth relations, while Confucianism calls us to rethink the profound interconnection of individual-society-nature. Let us turn to examine the worldview of each of these traditions and their potential contributions to a newly emerging environmental ethics.

Taoism and Ecology: Cosmology and Ethics

The principal text of Taoism is the *Tao te Ching* (*The Way and Its Power*), also known by the title *Lao Tzu*, its author. There have been numerous translations of this text into many languages and perhaps no other Chinese work compares to it in terms of international popularity.[11] The *Tao te Ching* contains a cosmology

[10]Indeed, just as Rene Dubos noted the need for both a "passive" Franciscan model of reverence for nature along with the more "active" model of Benedictine stewardship in the West, so too can Taoism and Confucianism provide this complementary model. See Rene Dubos, "Franciscan Conservation versus Benedictine Stewardship" in *A God Within* (New York: Scribners, 1972).

[11]There are many editions of this text in English, including the James Legge translation (first published in 1891 and reissued by Dover in 1962), the Witter Bynner translation (published by Capricorn in 1944), the D. C. Lau translation (published by Penguin in 1963). See also Wing-tsit Chan's translation in *A Source Book in Chinese Philosophy*.

and an ethics which may have some relevance in our contemporary discussions on ecology.

In terms of cosmology the Tao refers to the unmanifest source of all life which is eternal and ineffable yet fecund and creative. "The Nameless [the Tao] is the origin of Heaven and Earth; / The named is the mother of all things."[12] The Tao, then, is the self-existent source of all things, namely, a primary cause. It is both a power which generates and a process which sustains. It is the unity behind the multiplicity of the manifest world. It is beyond distinction or name and can only be approached through image, paradox, or intuition. In its manifest form in the phenomenal world it is said to have no particular characteristics and thus be empty. As such it is full of potentiality. Indeed, the "Tao is empty (like a bowl), / It may be used but its capacity is never exhausted" (4). It can be described, however, with images such as valley, womb, and vessel, suggestive of receptivity and productivity.

The implications of this holistic cosmology for an environmental ethic should be somewhat self-evident. There is a distinct emphasis in Taoist thought on valuing nature for its own sake, not for utilitarian ends. The natural world is not a resource to exploit but a complex of dynamic life processes to appreciate and respect. Harmony with nature rather than control is the ultimate Taoist goal. This tradition has certain affinities with contemporary movements in deep ecology which decry an overly anthropocentric position of human dominance over nature.[13] Indeed, the Taoists, like the deep ecologists, would say that manipulation of nature will only lead to counterproductive results.[14]

To achieve harmony with nature the Taoists value simplicity and spontaneity. They distrust education and the imposition of moral standards as interfering with true naturalness. Intuitive knowledge and a pristine innocence are highly regarded.[15] A direct, unmediated encounter with nature is far better than book knowledge or hypocritical morality. As Lao Tzu urges, one should: "Abandon sageliness and discard wisdom; Then the people will benefit a hundredfold. . . . Manifest plainness, embrace simplicity, reduce selfishness, have few desires" (19).

Moreover, in terms of human action that which is understated, not forceful or directive, is considered optimal. Excess, extravagance, and arrogance are to be avoided. Nonegocentric action (wu wei), which is free from desire and attachments, is essential.[16] In short, "By acting without action, all things will be in order" (3). In light of this, the Tao te Ching celebrates the paradox that yielding brings strength, passivity creates power, death creates new life.

These ideas are illustrated in the text with feminine images of fecundity and strength springing from openness and receptivity such as in motherhood, in an empty vessel, or in a valley. They also underlie images such as water wearing away at solid rock or the idea of an uncarved block waiting to reveal its form at the hands of a skilled sculptor. These demonstrate the potentiality and generative power which exist in unexpected and hidden places.[17]

> He who knows the male (active force) and keeps
>   to the female (the passive force or receptive
>   element)
> Becomes the ravine of the world.
> . . .
> He will never part from eternal virtue.
> He who knows glory but keeps to humility,
> Becomes the valley of the world.
> . . .
> He will be proficient in eternal virtue,
> And returns to the state of simplicity (uncarved
>   wood). (28)

In short, the Tao te Ching demonstrates the ultimate paradox of the coincidence of opposites, namely, that yielding is a form of strength. (This is clearly illustrated in the martial art of judo, which means the "way of yielding.") Indeed, the lesson of Taoism is that reversal is the movement of the Tao, for things easily turn into their opposites. "Reversion is the action of Tao. Weakness is the function of Tao. All things in the world come from being. And being comes from non-being" (40).

Thus both personally and politically Taoism calls for noninterfering action. A Taoist government would

[12]The Tao te Ching, Chap. 1. Unless otherwise noted, the translations here are Wing-tsit Chan's; subsequent references will be cited by chapter number in the text.
[13]The term "deep ecology" implies that the human is deeply embedded in nature and not set apart from it. This term was coined by Arne Naess and is developed by Bill Devall and George Sessions in their book Deep Ecology (Salt Lake City, Utah: Peregrine Smith, 1985). Also, see the article in this volume by George Sessions on deep ecology.
[14]Witter Bynner translates the opening of Chapter 29 of the Tao te Ching: "Those who would take over the earth / and shape it to their will / Never, I notice, succeed." (Chan and Lau translate "earth" as "empire.")
[15]See the Tao te Ching, Chaps. 18, 19, 20, and 38 for examples of this.

[16]See the Tao te Ching, Chaps. 29, 37, 43, 48, 63, and 64.
[17]See the Tao te Ching, Chaps. 6, 10, 20, 25, 28, 32, 52, 55, 59, 78.

be one of conscious detachment and the ideal leader would be one who governs least. While this seems antithetical to the Confucian notion of active political involvement, the wisdom of the Taoist ideal of noninterference was not lost in the highest quarters of Chinese Confucian government. Over one of the thrones in the imperial palace in Beijing are the characters for *wu wei* (nonegocentric action), perhaps serving as a reminder of the importance of a detached attitude in political affairs.

All of this has enormous implications for our interactions with nature, namely that humans cannot arrogantly or blindly force nature into our mold.[18] To cooperate with nature in a Taoist manner requires a better understanding of and appreciation for nature's processes. While an extreme Taoist position might advocate complete noninterference with nature, a more moderate Taoist approach would call for interaction with nature in a far less exploitive manner. Such cooperation with nature would sanction the use of appropriate or intermediate technology when necessary and would favor the use of organic fertilizers and natural farming methods. In terms of economic policy it would foster limited growth within a steady state economy that could support sustainable not exploitive development. Clearly, a Taoist ecological position is one with significant potential in the contemporary world.

Confucianism and Ecology: Cosmology and Ethics

Let us turn to the early classical texts of the *Analects* and the *Mencius* to explore the ecological dimensions of Confucian thought.[19] These works have had an enormous impact on Chinese society, education, and government for over two millennia. Along with two shorter texts, the *Great Learning* and the *Doctrine of the Mean*, these became known as the Four Books and were the basis of the civil service examination system from the fourteenth century until the twentieth.

Cosmologically, early Confucianism, like Taoism, understood the world to be part of a changing, dynamic, and unfolding universe.[20] The ongoing and unfolding process of nature was affirmed by the Confucians and seasonal harmony was highly valued. There is no common creation myth per se for the Confucians or Taoists.[21] Rather, the universe is seen as self-generating, guided by the unfolding of the Tao, a term the Confucians shared with the Taoists although with variations on its meaning in different contexts and periods. There is no personification of evil; instead, there is a balance of opposite forces in the concept of the yin and the yang.

Indeed, there is no radical split between transcendence and immanence such as occurs in the Western religions. In fact, it has become widely accepted that the sense of immanence rather than transcendence dominates both Taoist and Confucian thought. Although this needs qualification, it is true that the notion of "the secular as the sacred" was critical in Chinese philosophy and religion.[22] The significance of this view is that a balance of the natural and the human worlds was essential in both Taoist and Confucian thought. While the Taoists emphasized harmony with nature and downplayed human action, the Confucians stressed the importance of human action and the critical role of social and political institutions.

Within this cosmology certain ethical patterns emerged in Confucianism which are distinct from Taoism. Examining these patterns may be helpful for our understanding of the ecological dimensions of Confucian thought. While Taoism can be characterized as a naturalistic ecology having certain affinities with contemporary deep ecology, Confucianism might be seen as a form of social ecology having some similarities with the contemporary movement of the same name.[23] Taoism is clearly nature centered, while Confucianism tends to be more human centered. Neither tradition, however, succumbs to the problem of egocentric anthropocentrism or radical

[18] The degree of our contemporary hubris toward nature is revealed in an editorial essay in *Time*, 17 June 1991: "Nature is our ward. It is not our master. It is to be respected and even cultivated. But it is man's world. And when man has to choose between his well-being and that of nature, nature will have to accommodate."

[19] See Arthur Waley's translation of the *Analects* (New York: Vintage Books, 1938) and D. C. Lau's translation of *Mencius* (Harmondsworth: Penguin Books, 1970).

[20] See Tu Wei-ming's essays in *Confucian Thought*, esp. "The Continuity of Being"; also see Mote, *Intellectual Foundations of China*, Chap. 2.

[21] See Mote, *Intellectual Foundations of China*, 17–18.

[22] See Herbert Fingarette, *Confucius—The Secular as Sacred* (New York: Harper Torchbooks, 1972).

[23] Social ecology has been developed by such theorists as Murray Bookchin. See his book *The Ecology of Freedom: The Emergence and Dissolution of Hierarchy* (Palo Alto, Calif.: Chesire Books, 1982). However, in contrast to Bookchin's position, which chooses to ignore the spiritual dimensions of ecology in the interest of establishing social justice in the human order, Confucianism tends to see the individual as embedded in a spiritual universe infused with *ch'i* (matter-energy). Harmonizing with the *ch'i* in the universe is essential for humans in a Confucian framework.

individualism such as has been characteristic of certain movements in the modern West. Both have a profound sense of the importance of nature as primary. For the Taoists nature is the basis of nourishing individual life and for the Confucians it is indispensable for sustaining communal life.

A Confucian ethic might be described as a form of social ecology because a key component is relationality in the human order against the background of the natural order. A profound sense of the interconnectedness of the human with one another and with nature is central to Confucian thinking. The individual is never seen as an isolated entity but always as a person in relation to another and to the cosmos. A useful image for describing the Confucian ethical system is a series of concentric circles with the person in the center. In the circle closest to the individual is one's family, then one's teachers, one's friends, the government, and in the outer circle is the universe itself. In the Confucian system relationality extends from the individual in the family outward to the cosmos. This worldview has been described as an anthropocosmic one, embracing heaven, earth, and human as an interactive whole.[24] In Confucianism from the time of the early classical text of the *Book of History*, heaven and earth have been called the great parents who have provided life and sustenance.[25] Just as parents in the family deserve filial respect, so do heaven and earth.[26] Indeed, we are told they should not be exploited wantonly by humans.

In Confucianism, then, the individual is both supported by and supportive of those in the other circles which surround him or her. The exchange of mutual obligations and responsibilities between the individual, others in these circles, and the cosmos itself constitute the relational basis of Confucian societies. Like a social glue, the give and take of these relationships help to give shape and character to these societies. Many of these patterns of social and cosmological exchanges become embedded in rituals which constitute the means of expressing reciprocal relations between people and with nature. Thus the value of mutual reciprocity and of belonging to a series of groups

is fostered in Confucian societies. In all of this, education was critical. As the *Great Learning (Ta Hsueh)* so clearly demonstrates, to establish peace under heaven we must begin with the cultivation of the mind-and-heart of the person.[27] Education for the Confucians embraced the moral and intellectual dimensions of a person and was intended to prepare them to be a fully contributing citizen to the larger society.

In addition to these ethical patterns of social ecology for the individual in relation to others and to the cosmos itself, Confucianism developed an elaborate theory of government which might be described as a political ecology. Taking the same model of the individual embedded in a series of concentric circles, the Confucians situated the emperor at the center and suggested that his moral example would have a rippling effect outward like a pebble dropped into a pond. The influence of this morality would be felt by all the people and humane government would be possible when the emperor had compassion on the people and established appropriate economic, social, and ecological policies.

Thus while both Confucianism and Taoism are relational in their overall orientation, Confucianism is clearly more activist, especially with regard to moral leadership and practical policies. Many of the principles of humane government such as those advocated by Mencius and other Confucians include policies such as an ecological sensitivity to land and other resources, equitable distribution of goods and services, fair taxation, and allowing the people to enjoy nature and cultivate human relations.[28] The recognition that humane government rests on sustainable agriculture and maintaining a balance with nature is key to all Confucian political thought.

Thus both in terms of individuals and society as a whole there was a concern for larger relationships that would lead toward harmony of people with one another and with nature, which supported them. This social and political ecology within an anthropocosmic worldview has something to offer in our own period of rampant individualism, self-interested government, and exploitation of natural resources. The continuation of cooperative group effort to achieve common goals that are for the benefit of the whole society is an important model for a new form of social ecology. At the same time the ideal of humane

[24]See Tu Wei-ming's use of this term in *Centrality and Commonality* (Albany: State University of New York Press, 1989) and in *Confucian Thought*.

[25]See *Book of Chou, The Great Declaration* in *The Chinese Classics*, vol. 3, *Book of History*,
trans. James Legge (Oxford: Clarendon Press, 1865), 283.

[26]See Kaibara Ekken's *Yamato Zokkun*, translated in my book *Moral and Spiritual Cultivation in Japanese Neo-Confucianism* (Albany: State University of New York Press, 1989) 54–55, 136–142.

[27]See the *Great Learning*, trans. Wing-tsit Chan, *Source Book in Chinese Philosophy*, 84–94.

[28]See examples of humane government in Book 1 of *Mencius*.

government which develops and distributes resources equitably is central to a political ecology so much needed at the present.

Conclusion

This essay only begins to suggest some of the rich resources available in the traditions of Taoism and Confucianism for formulating an ecological cosmology and an environmental ethics in our time. As we seek a new balance in human-earth relations, it is clear that the perspectives from other religious and philosophical traditions may be instrumental in formulating new ways of thinking and acting more appropriate to both the vast rhythms and the inevitable limitations of nature. As our worldview in relation to nature is more clearly defined, we can hope that our actions will reflect both a Taoist appreciation for natural ecology and a Confucian commitment to social and political ecology.

Discussion and Reflection Questions

1. In what sense could Confucianism be described as a form of "social ecology"? How might this feature of Confucianism be applied to understanding and dealing with environmental issues?

2. Given the different emphases of Confucian and Taoist thought identified by Tucker, how might the two be *combined* to create a more comprehensive ethical perspective on ecological problems?

3. In your view, what are the chief advantages and strengths of approaching environmental issues from Confucian and/or Taoist perspectives? Are they any weaknesses associated with these perspectives?

4. Do you think that Confucian and Taoist perspectives on the environment would always be in agreement? What areas of disagreement might arise? How would you resolve such differences?

Suggestions for Further Reading

There are a number of good anthologies available dealing with environmental ethics. Among them are: *People, Penguins, and Plastic Trees: Basic Issues in Environmental Ethics*, edited by Donald Van DeVeer and Christine Pierce (Belmont, Calif.: Wadsworth Publishing Co., 1986); *Environmental Ethics: Divergence and Convergence*, edited by Susan J. Armstrong and Richard G. Botzler (New York: McGraw-Hill, 1993); T. Regan, ed., *Earthbound: New Introductory Essays in Environmental Ethics* (New York: Random House, 1984); *Environmental Philosophy: From Animal Rights to Radical Ecology*, edited by Michael E. Zimmerman et al. (Englewood Cliffs, N.J.: Prentice-Hall, 1993); *A Companion to Environmental Philosophy*, edited by Dale Jamieson (Oxford: Blackwell Companions to Philosophy, 2000). For a good, brief overview of some of the perspectives relevant to environmental ethics, see Robert Elliott, "Environmental Ethics," in *A Companion to Ethics*, edited by Peter Singer (Oxford: Blackwell, 1991), pp. 284–293. Studies defending particular positions in environmental ethics include R. Attfield, *The Ethics of Environmental Concern* (Oxford: Blackwell, 1983); B. Norton, *Why Preserve Natural Variety?* (Princeton: Princeton University Press, 1988); Holmes Rolston III, *Environmental Ethics: Duties to and Values in the Natural World* (Philadelphia: Temple University Press, 1988); and Paul Taylor, *Respect for Nature* (Princeton: Princeton University Press, 1986). The issue of the environment is one moral issue where there has been an extensive contribution from Eastern perspectives. For a sampling, see: J. Baird Callicott, "Conceptual Resources for Environmental Ethics in Asian Traditions of Thought: A Propaedeutic," *Philosophy East and West*, vol. 37 (1987), pp. 115–130; J. Baird Callicott and Roger T. Ames, eds., *Nature in Asian Traditions of Thought: Essays in Environ-*

mental Philosophy (Albany: State University of New York Press, 1989); Chung-ying Cheng, "On the Environmental Ethics of the *Tao* and the *Ch'i*," *Environmental Ethics*, vol. 8 (1986), pp. 351–370; O. P. Dwivedi and B. N. Tiwari, *Environmental Crisis and Hindu Religion* (New Delhi: Gitanjali Publishing House, 1987); Eugene C. Hargrove, ed., *Religion and Environmental Crisis* (Athens, Ga.: University of Georgia Press, 1986); R. P. Peerenboom, "Beyond Naturalism: A Reconstruction of Daoist Environmental Ethics," *Environmental Ethics*, vol. 13 (1991), pp. 3–22; Holmes Rolston III, "Can the East Help the West to Value Nature?" *Philosophy East and West*, vol. 37 (1987), pp. 172–190; Holmes Rolston III, "Respect for Life: Can Zen Buddhism Help in Forming an Environmental Ethic?" in *Zen Buddhism Today, Annual Report of the Kyoto Zen Symposium No. 7* (Kyoto, Japan: Kyoto Seminar for Religious Philosophy, 1989); David Edward Shaner and R. Shannon Duval, "Conservation Ethics and the Japanese Intellectual Tradition," *Environmental Ethics*, vol. 11 (1989), pp. 197–214. For further exploration of Buddhist perspectives on environmental ethics see *Buddhism and Ecology: The Interconnection of Dharma and Deeds*, edited by Mary Evelyn Tucker and Duncan Ryuken Williams (Cambridge, Mass.: Harvard University Press, 1997) and Padmasiri de Silva's *Environmental Philosophy and Ethics in Buddhism* (New York: St. Martin's Press, 1998). *Purifying the Earthly Body of God: Religion and Ecology in Hindu India*, edited by Lance E. Nelson (New York: State University of New York Press, 1998), is a solid survey of environmental ethics from a Hindu perspective. For more on Confucianism and the environment, see *Confucianism and Ecology: the Interrelation of Heaven, Earth, and Humans*, edited by Mary Evelyn Tucker and John Berthrong (Cambridge, Mass: Distributed by Harvard University Press for the Harvard University Center for the Study of World Religions, 1998). Peter P. Cvek develops a thorough account of the implications of Natural Law for environmental ethics in "Thomas Aquinas, Natural Law, and Environmental Ethics," in *Vera-Lex* 1 (2000): 5-18. For an egalitarian/utilitarian debate on pollution read Constantine Hadjilambrinos' "An Egalitarian Response to Utilitarian Analysis of Long-Lived Pollution: The Case of High-Level Radioactive Waste," in *Environmental Ethics* 22 (2001): 43-62.

InfoTrac

human ecology, environmental protection, environmental policy, "nature and destruction"

CPSIA information can be obtained
at www.ICGtesting.com
Printed in the USA
BVHW092030220720
584381BV00006B/48

9 780534 505998